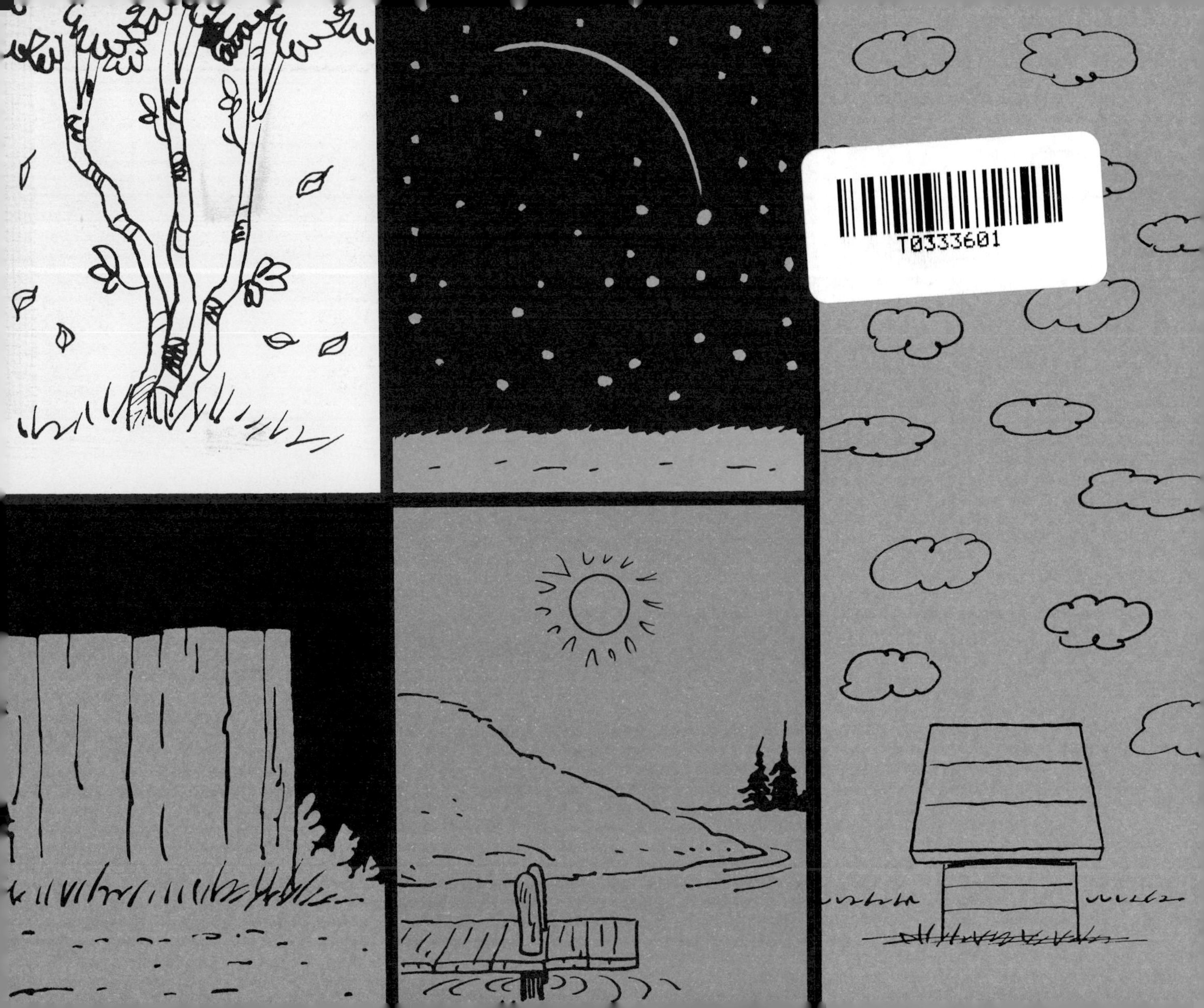

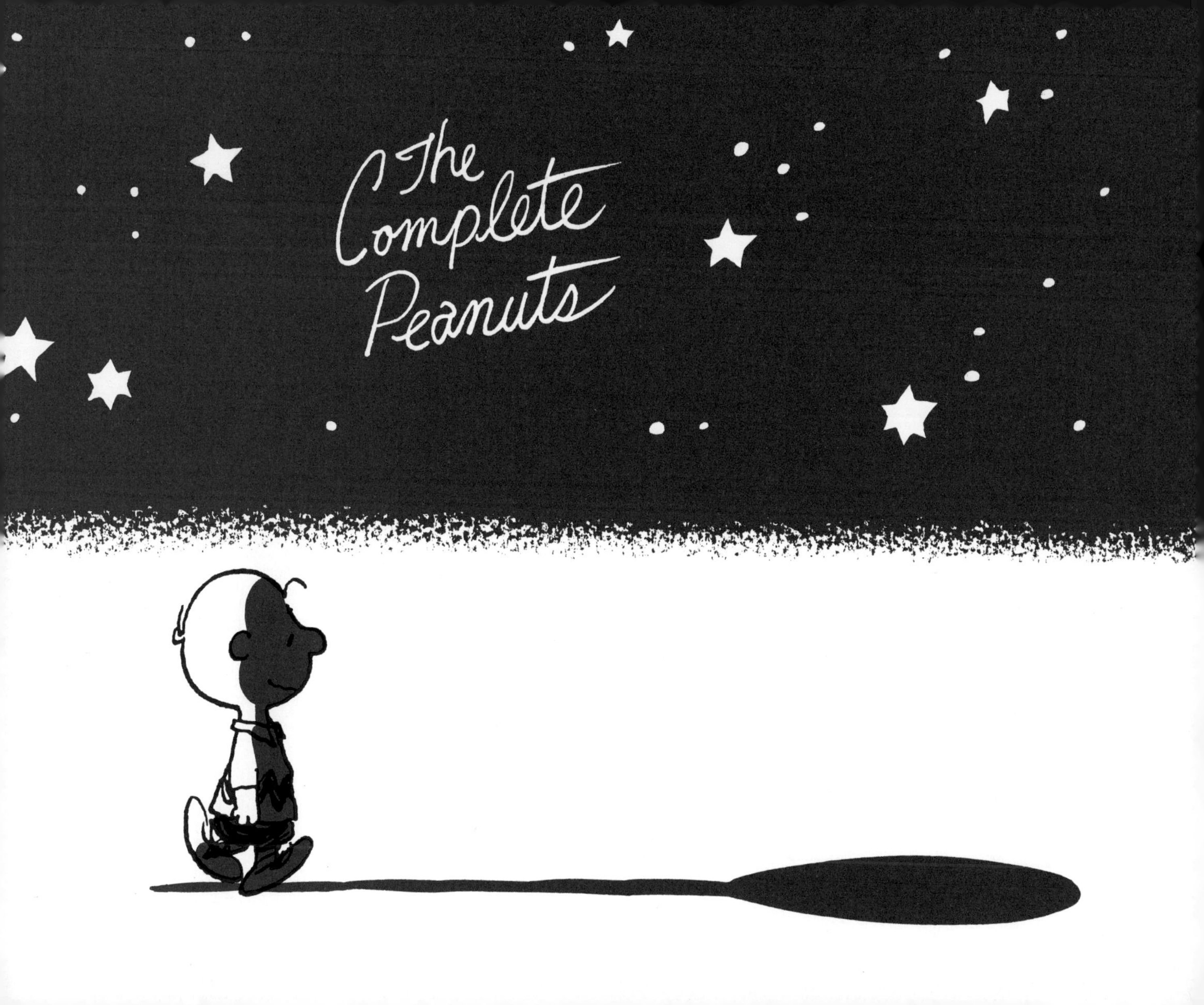
The Complete Peanuts

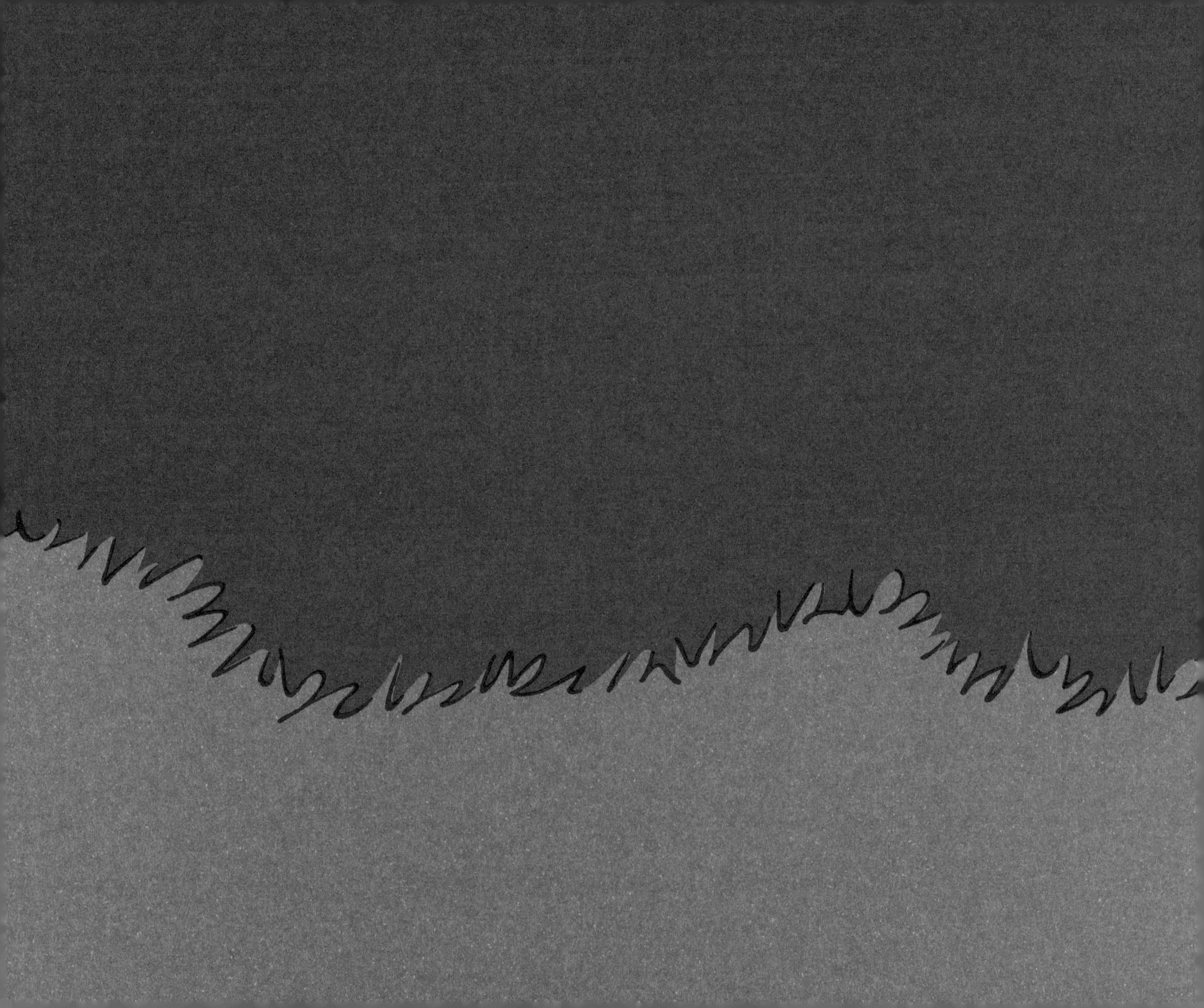

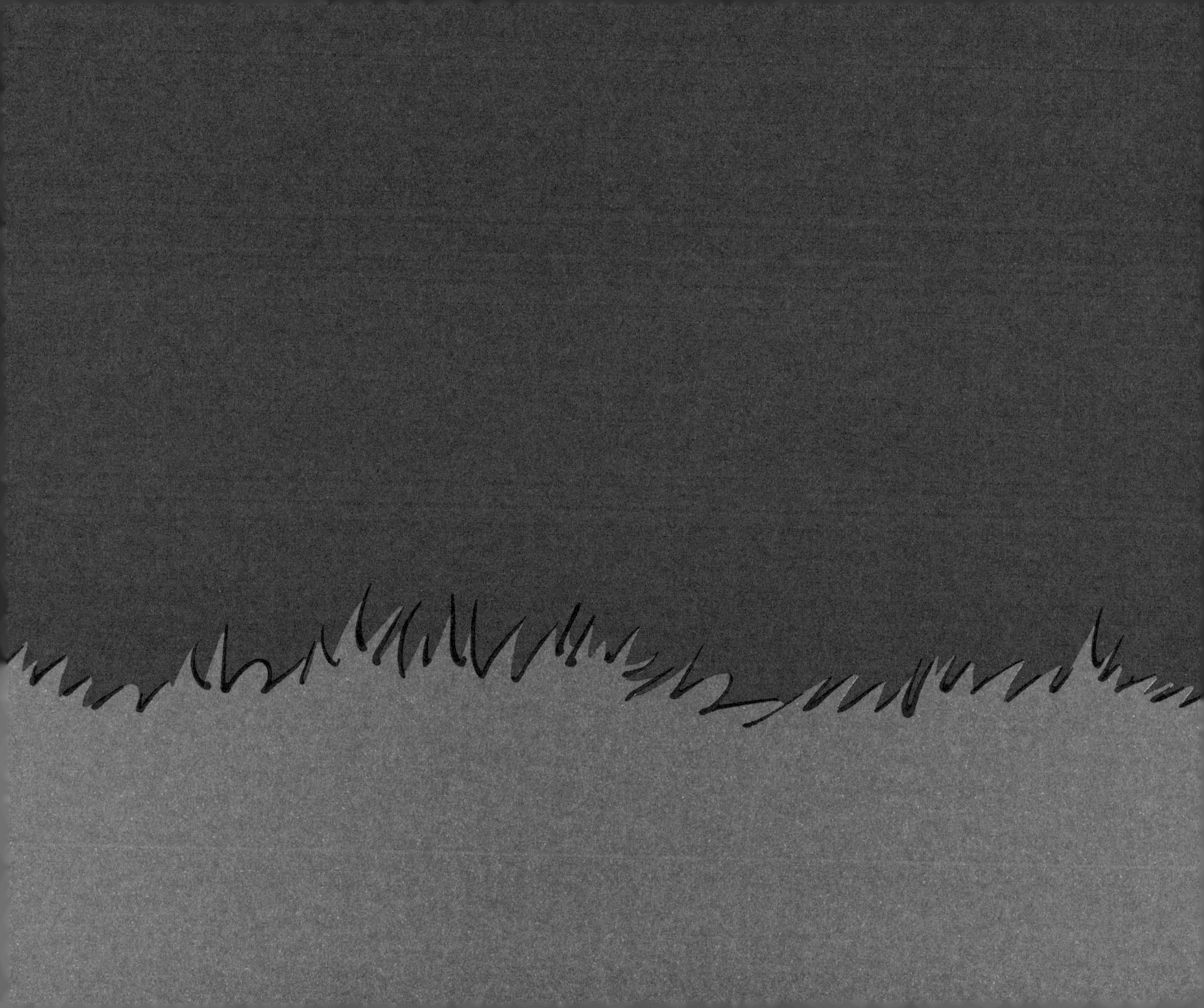

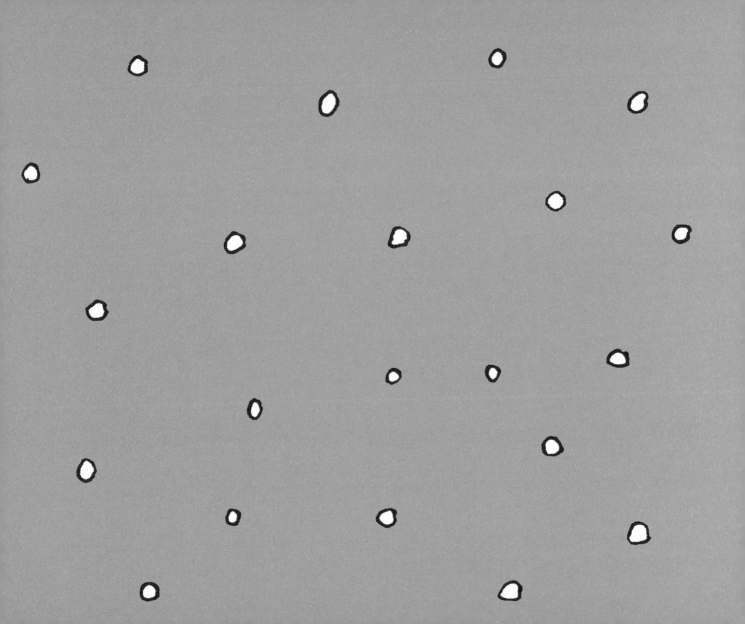

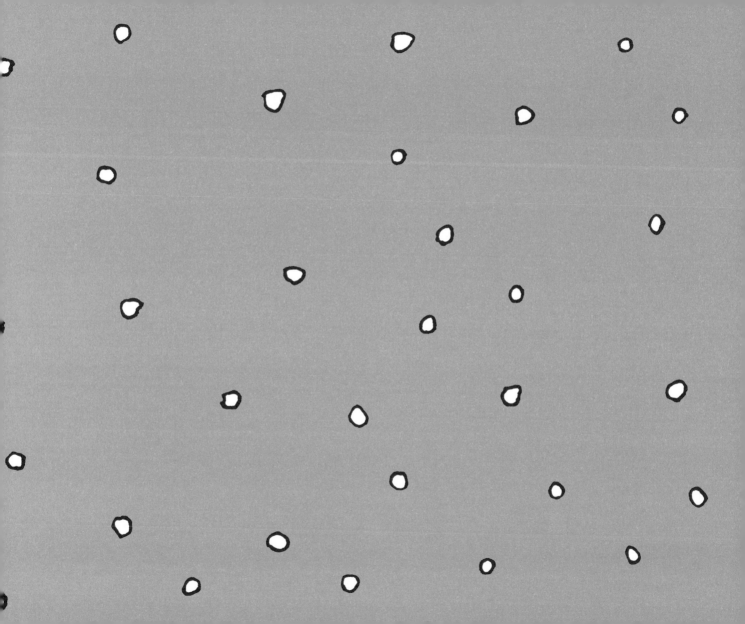

THE COMPLETE PEANUTS
by Charles M. Schulz

Editor: Gary Groth
Designer: Seth
Production Manager: Kim Thompson
Production, assembly and restoration: Paul Baresh
Archival assistance: Marcie Lee
Index compiled by Melissa Gray, Jamie Hibdon, Michael Litven, Christine Texeira
Associate Publisher: Eric Reynolds
Publishers: Gary Groth & Kim Thompson

Special thanks to Jeannie Schulz, without whom
this project would not have come to fruition.
Thanks also to John R. Troy and the
Charles M. Schulz Creative Associates,
especially Paige Braddock and Kim Towner.
Thanks for special support from Peanuts International, LLC.

First published in America in 2011 by Fantagraphics Books,
7563 Lake City Way, Seattle, WA 98115, USA

First published in Great Britain in 2014 by Canongate Books Ltd,
14 High Street, Edinburgh, EH1 1TE

3

British Library Cataloguing-in-Publication Data
A catalogue record for this book is available on request from the British Library.

ISBN 978 1 78211 101 6
Printed in Malaysia
canongate.co.uk

CHARLES M. SCHULZ

THE COMPLETE PEANUTS

1979 to 1980

" YOU KNOW WHAT WOULD
TASTE GOOD RIGHT NOW?
A BIG PIECE OF
ANGEL FOOD CAKE!"

CANONGATE BOOKS

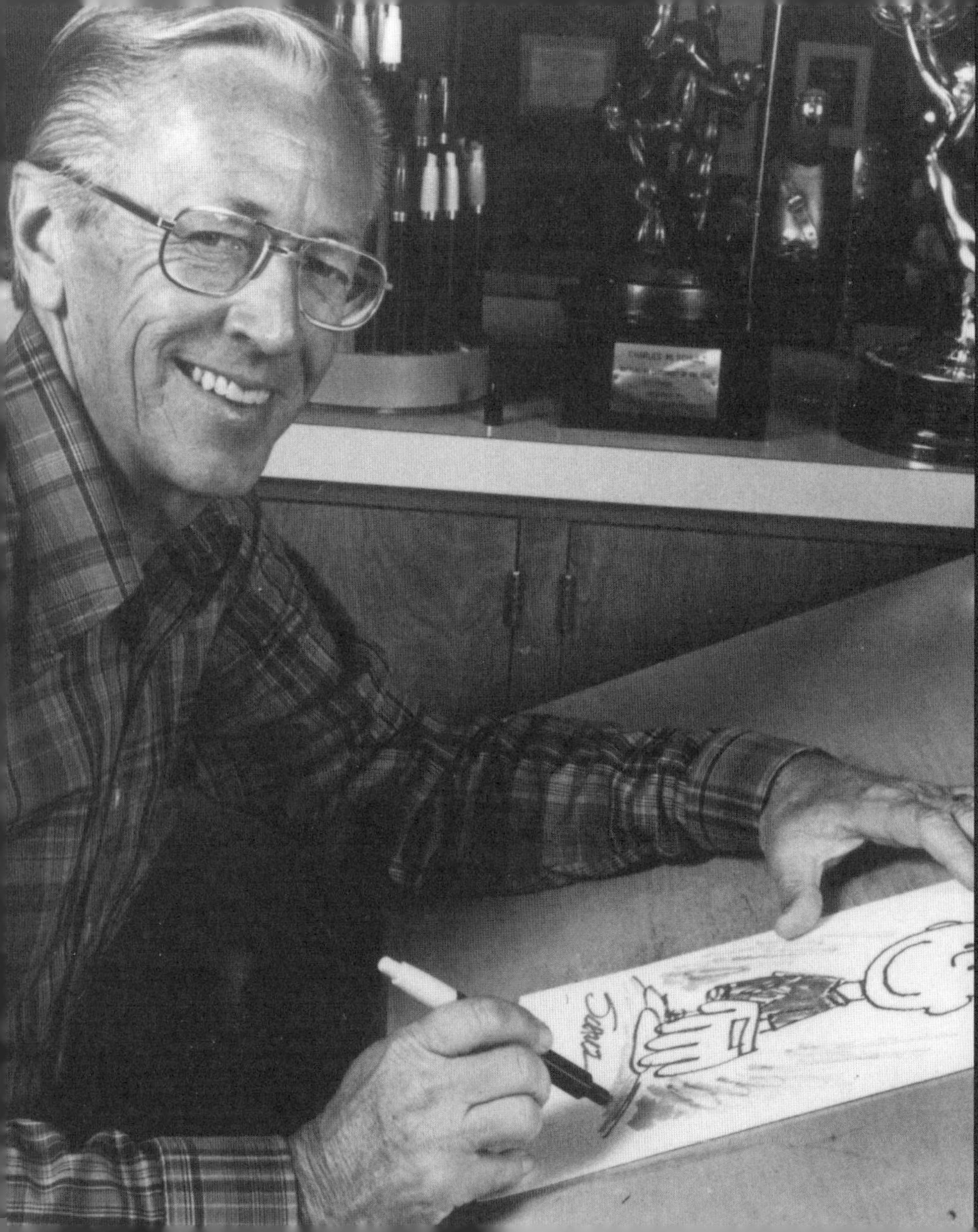

Charles M. Schulz at his drawing board at 1 Snoopy Place, circa 1975. Courtesy of the Schulz Family.

FOREWORD by AL ROKER

It was March of 1963. I was seven years old. We had moved from the Rockaway projects in Brooklyn to a small development in St. Albans, Queens.

My folks had scrimped and saved to buy a home in this working class neighborhood — a neighborhood in "transition": whites were moving out and African-Americans were moving in. In other words, Archie Bunker was running away, George Jefferson was moving in.

We were families searching for the American dream of home ownership. Black teachers, postal workers, state and city workers all looking for a decent place to live, good schools, and a well manicured lawn to call their own. A Black bus driver, Al Roker, Sr., and his growing brood of six found that plot of land.

One of the first things my mother, Isabel Roker, did after we moved in was to subscribe to the local paper, *The Long Island Press*. That was the first time I read *Peanuts*. (My dad used to bring home the *Daily News*, but *Peanuts* was not part of the arsenal of comics they used to flatten their rival, the *NY Post*.) No, it wasn't until the *Long Island Press* that I became close personal friends with Linus, Lucy, Snoopy, and of course good ol' Charlie Brown.

I loved comics. I dreamed of becoming a comic strip artist, or better still, an animator. I drew comics constantly in my spare time, and practiced signing my name so that it would look good. How good could the signature of a seven-year-old look? But to my untrained eye, it was right up there with Walt Disney's.

To a seven-year-old, a lot of the comic strips were either too silly (*Nancy*) or too old (*Mary Worth*, *Brenda Starr*). Some seemed too weird (*Dick Tracy*, *Gasoline Alley*). But *Peanuts* somehow transcended them all.

Even then, I was attracted to the simple yet sophisticated message that *Peanuts* imparted every day. Here were these big-headed children (though in time, their bodies caught up with their overly-inflated noggins), saying things wise beyond their years yet understandable to kids my age.

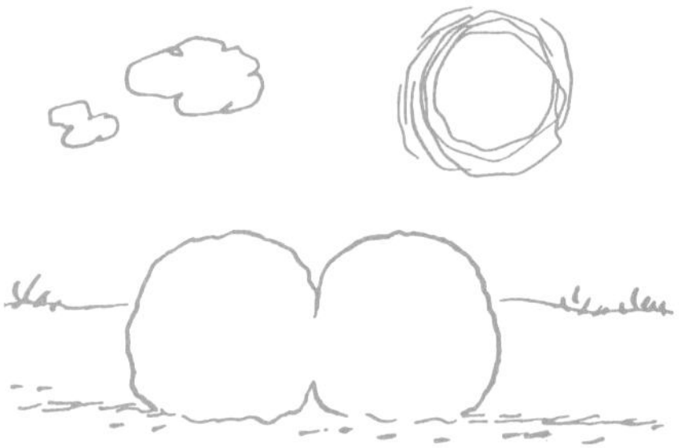

Like any great comedy — say, Warner Bros. cartoons, or the *Soupy Sales Show* — the humor played to two audiences: kids and their parents. And if you were a kid whose sense of humor skewed upward toward adult, it was like getting let into a secret club. You understood stuff your friends didn't.

It wasn't long before I started clipping each day's *Peanuts* strip from the paper and carefully scotch-taping it to a piece of loose leaf paper. I would put five strips on a single page, then the Saturday strip and Sunday full-color strip on their own page.

I saved the weekly strips in a binder and added two pages to it every week. I thought that some day these would be valuable. A collection of *Peanuts* comic strips in order! Who would ever think of doing such a thing? I was so ahead of my time.

I remember in the summer of 1964 walking into the St. Albans Public Library and there in the Children's section a Fawcett-Crest collection of *Peanuts* comic strips, Charlie Brown and Snoopy. Somebody stole my idea! But wait, there were other collections. These Fawcett people were geniuses... like me. Now I could stop clipping the strips out of newspapers and instead devote my energy to other more worthwhile endeavors — like figuring out who was faster, Superman or the Flash.

In 1968, a young African-American could search high and low through the daily comic strips and you would never find anyone who looked like you. Sure, there was Punjab in *Little Orphan Annie*, but what was he? Black, Indian, Italian with a really bad tan? Who knew. No, no one who looked like me lived in the pages of the funny papers.

And then, Franklin showed up. July 1968. My devotion to *Peanuts* had only grown, but this was a momentous occasion for me — and cemented my adoration of Charles Schulz. Franklin helped Charlie Brown build a sand castle at the beach. Charlie invited Franklin to visit him later and Franklin took him up on it. Eventually, as we move into the '70s, Franklin is seen in school with Marcie and Peppermint Patty.

For a voracious reader of the daily comics, this was a big deal. Blacks were on TV, in the movies, and on the radio with hit records. But we weren't in the comics. And then, suddenly, we were.

Others would follow Schulz's lead. *Beetle Bailey*'s Mort Walker introduced Lt. Jackson Flap, with his afro and cool demeanor, in 1970 — but it was Franklin who blazed a trail.

I had an opportunity to interview Schulz for the 50th anniversary of *Peanuts*. I asked him about Franklin. He said at the time he wasn't making a statement about race relations or felt any pressure to introduce a black kid to Charlie and the gang. It just happened. When I told him how much it had meant to a small black kid growing up, he smiled and said he was glad it did. He talked about how surprised he was at the reaction of Franklin; how some newspapers in the South threatened to pull *Peanuts* from their papers, while others hailed him as a proponent of race relations.

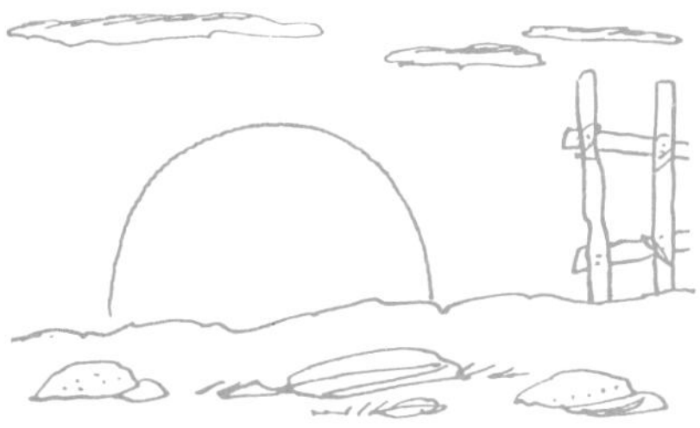

Sparky insisted Franklin was just a character whose time had come. I couldn't agree more. Yet the strip itself is truly timeless. The fact that *Peanuts* still runs in today's newspapers in reprints, eleven years after its creator's death, and seems as fresh as when those strips first ran, is a testament to the genius of Charles Schulz.

I remember vividly hearing about Sparky's cancer and the profound sadness I felt. Then a week later getting a call from his wife, Jeannie, saying Sparky wanted to give one more interview before his passing and would I come out to Santa Rosa to do it?

It was one of the hardest interviews I had to do. Speaking to a man whose life work had brought so much joy, yet I was speaking to him as he was about to die.

There was a certain peace about the man, as we talked only a few feet away from a battered and well-used drawing table where these iconic characters lived and played. So many people took so much away from the daily doings of these "li'l folks," as Sparky originally titled the strip. I was one of them. And I watch as my children discover what I did almost 50 years ago: That you're a good man, Charlie Brown. And all your pals are pretty good, too, day in and day out.

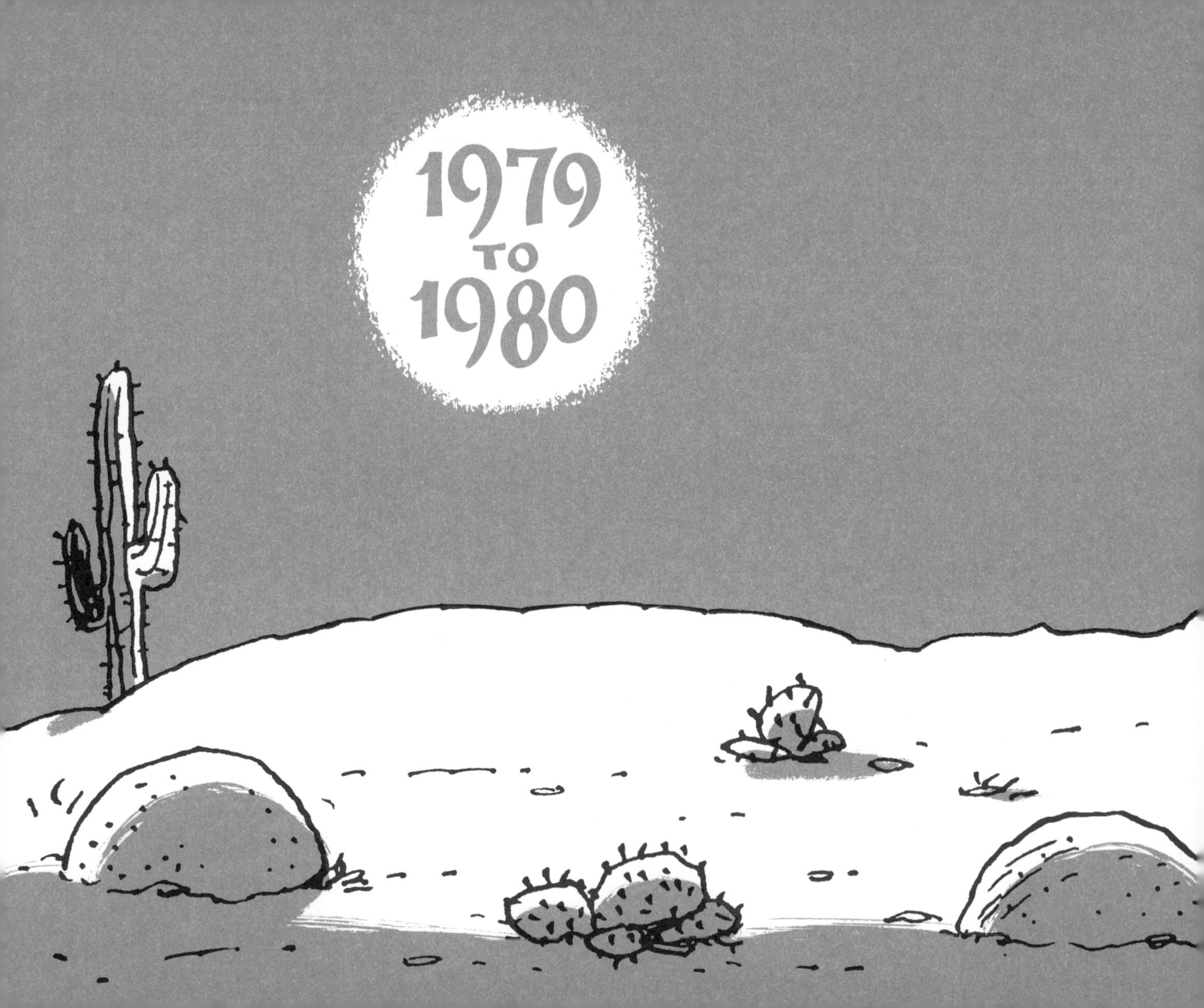
1979
TO
1980

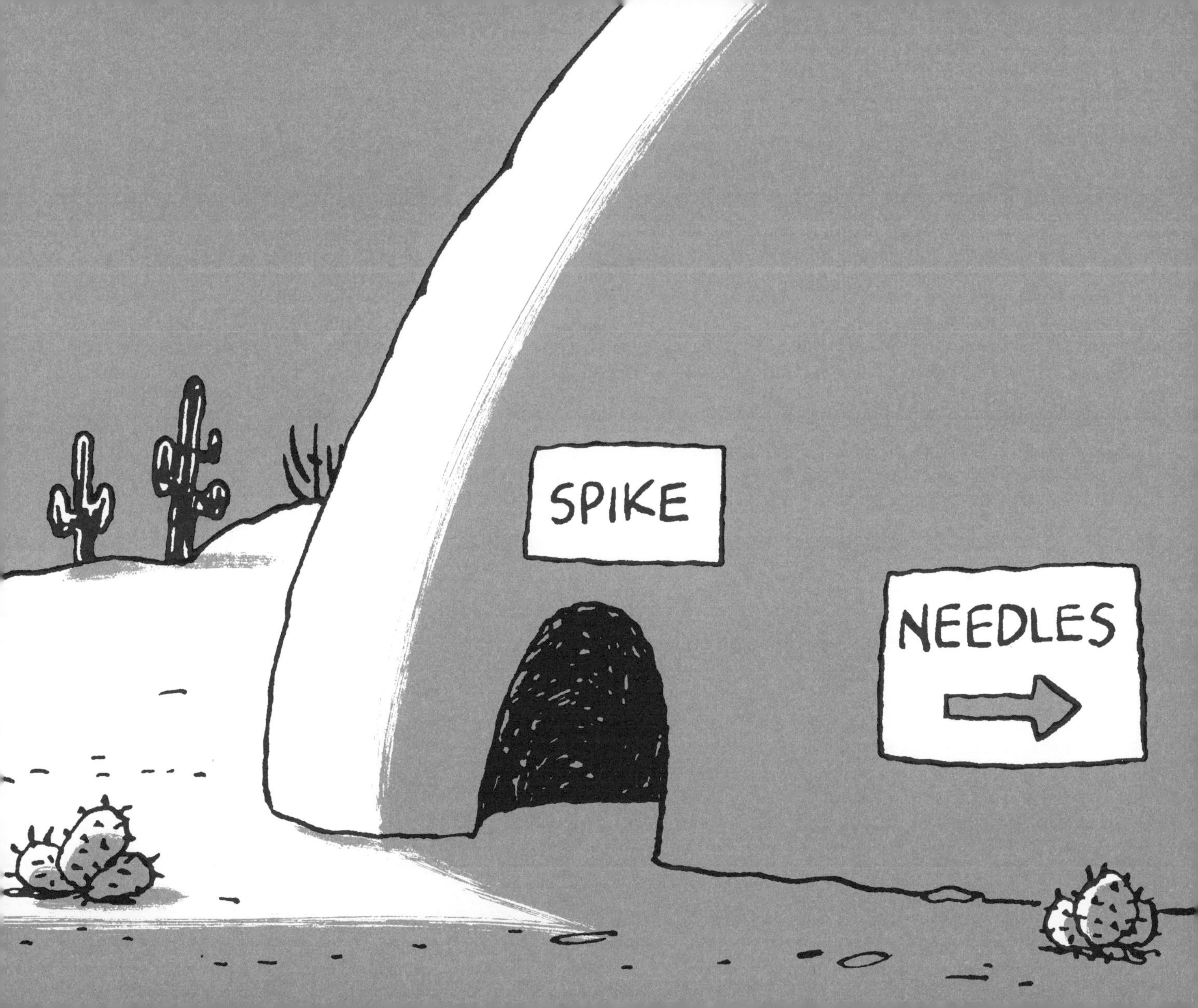
SPIKE
NEEDLES

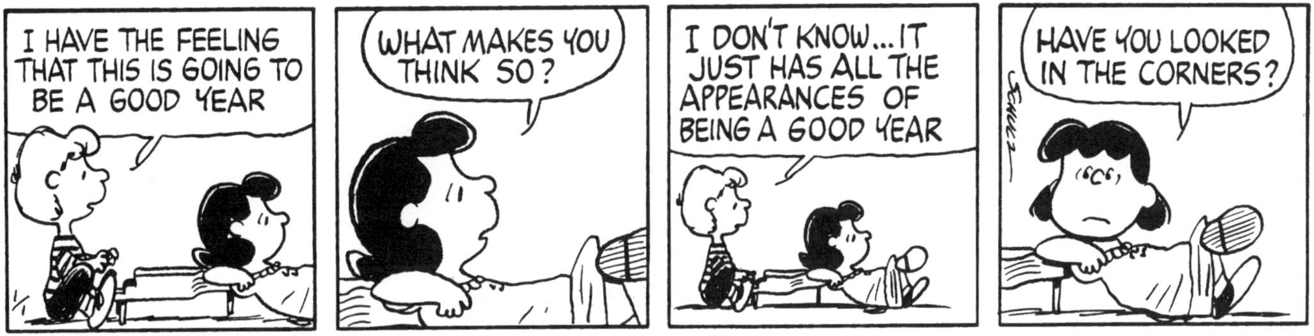
I HAVE THE FEELING THAT THIS IS GOING TO BE A GOOD YEAR
WHAT MAKES YOU THINK SO?
I DON'T KNOW... IT JUST HAS ALL THE APPEARANCES OF BEING A GOOD YEAR
HAVE YOU LOOKED IN THE CORNERS?

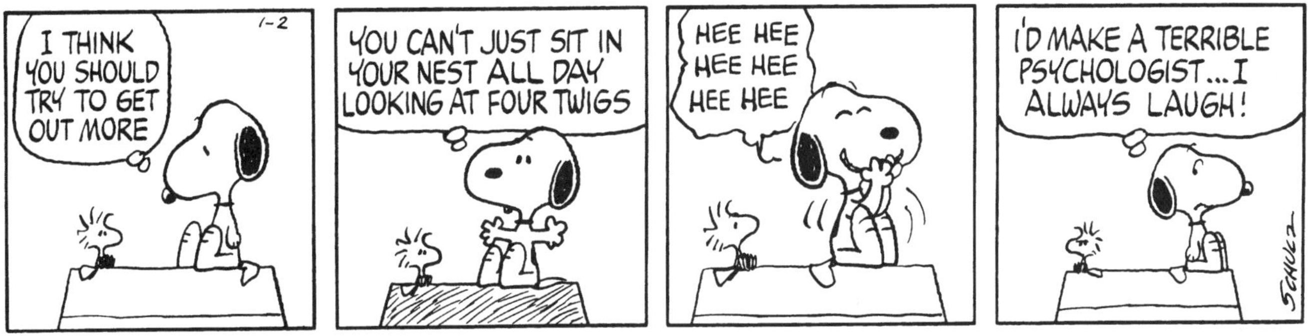
1-2
I THINK YOU SHOULD TRY TO GET OUT MORE
YOU CAN'T JUST SIT IN YOUR NEST ALL DAY LOOKING AT FOUR TWIGS
HEE HEE HEE HEE HEE HEE
I'D MAKE A TERRIBLE PSYCHOLOGIST... I ALWAYS LAUGH!

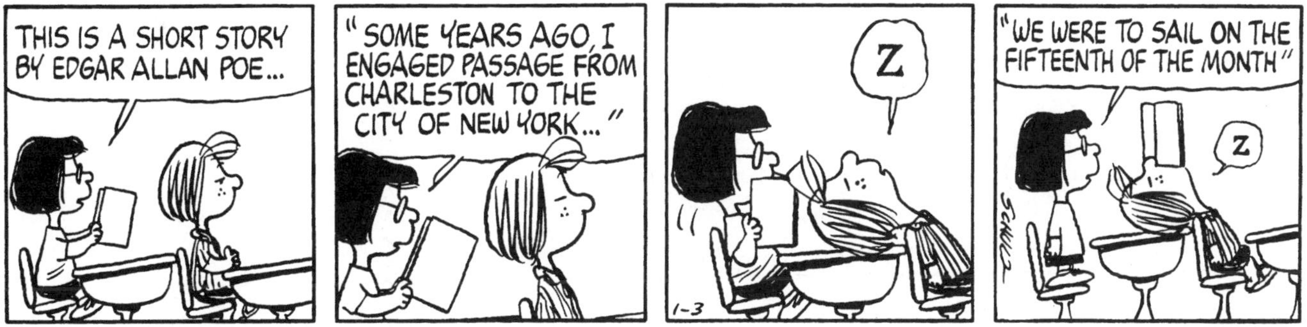
THIS IS A SHORT STORY BY EDGAR ALLAN POE...
"SOME YEARS AGO, I ENGAGED PASSAGE FROM CHARLESTON TO THE CITY OF NEW YORK..."
Z
1-3
"WE WERE TO SAIL ON THE FIFTEENTH OF THE MONTH"
Z

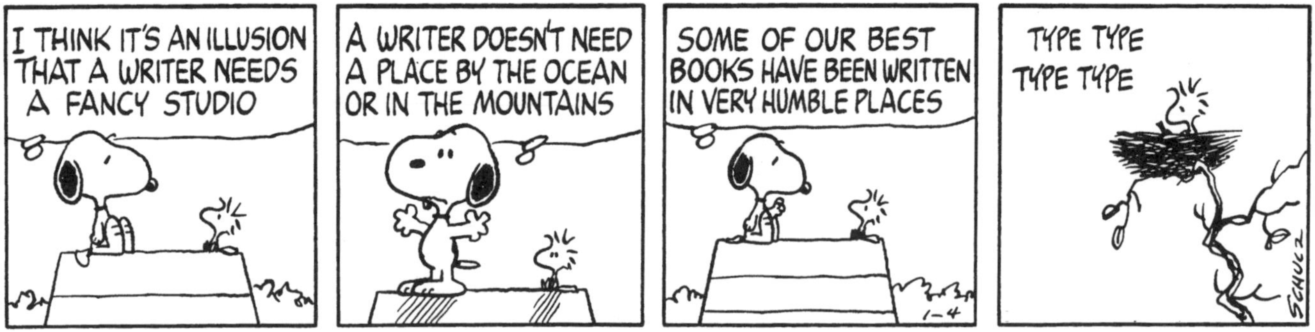
I THINK IT'S AN ILLUSION THAT A WRITER NEEDS A FANCY STUDIO
A WRITER DOESN'T NEED A PLACE BY THE OCEAN OR IN THE MOUNTAINS
SOME OF OUR BEST BOOKS HAVE BEEN WRITTEN IN VERY HUMBLE PLACES
1-4
TYPE TYPE TYPE TYPE
SCHULZ

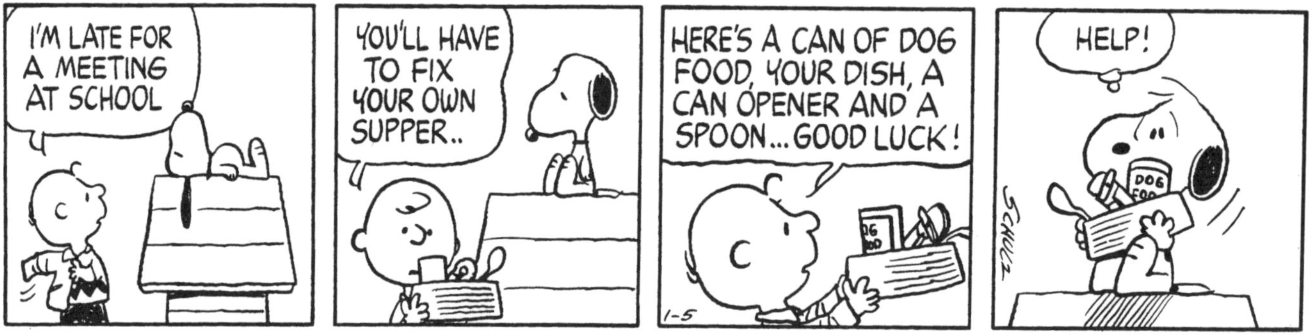
I'M LATE FOR A MEETING AT SCHOOL
YOU'LL HAVE TO FIX YOUR OWN SUPPER..
HERE'S A CAN OF DOG FOOD, YOUR DISH, A CAN OPENER AND A SPOON...GOOD LUCK!
1-5
HELP!
SCHULZ
DOG FOOD

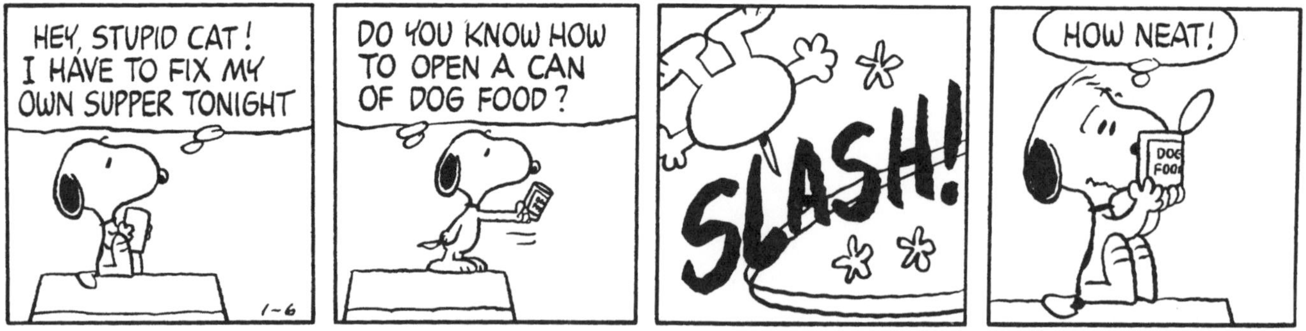
HEY, STUPID CAT! I HAVE TO FIX MY OWN SUPPER TONIGHT
1-6
DO YOU KNOW HOW TO OPEN A CAN OF DOG FOOD?
SLASH!
HOW NEAT!
DOG FOOD

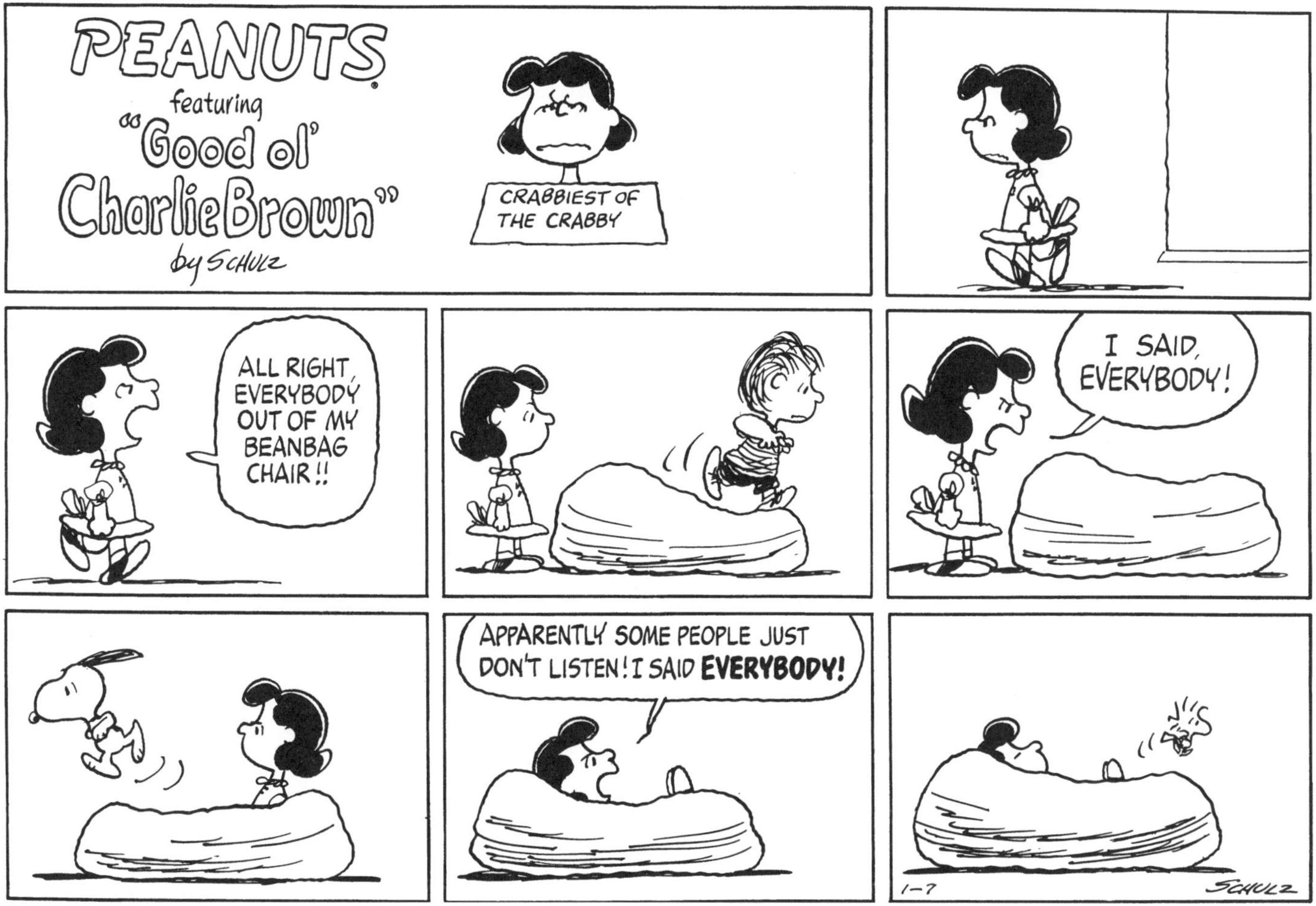
PEANUTS
featuring
"Good ol' CharlieBrown"
by SCHULZ
CRABBIEST OF THE CRABBY
ALL RIGHT, EVERYBODY OUT OF MY BEANBAG CHAIR!!
I SAID, EVERYBODY!
APPARENTLY SOME PEOPLE JUST DON'T LISTEN! I SAID EVERYBODY!
1-7
SCHULZ

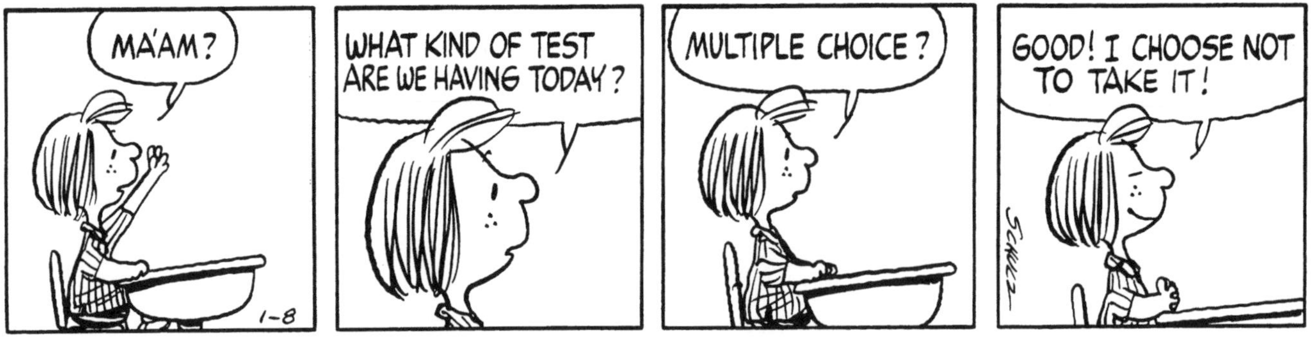
MA'AM?
WHAT KIND OF TEST ARE WE HAVING TODAY?
MULTIPLE CHOICE?
GOOD! I CHOOSE NOT TO TAKE IT!

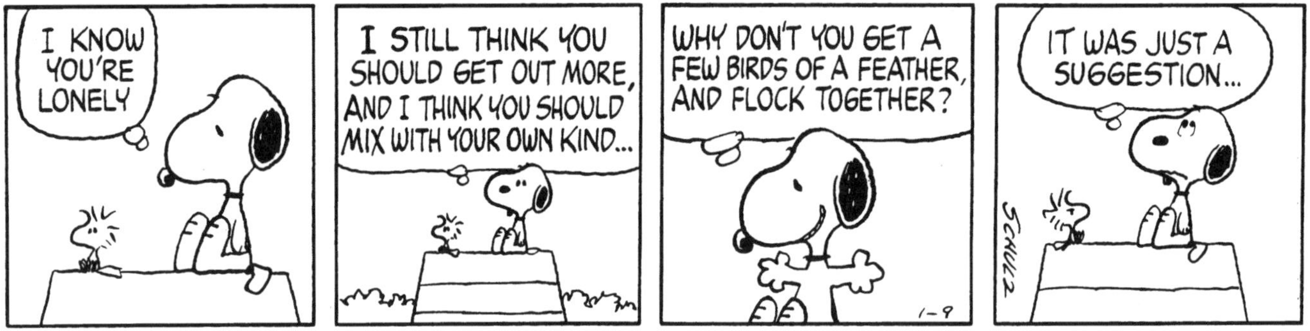
I KNOW YOU'RE LONELY
I STILL THINK YOU SHOULD GET OUT MORE, AND I THINK YOU SHOULD MIX WITH YOUR OWN KIND...
WHY DON'T YOU GET A FEW BIRDS OF A FEATHER, AND FLOCK TOGETHER?
IT WAS JUST A SUGGESTION...

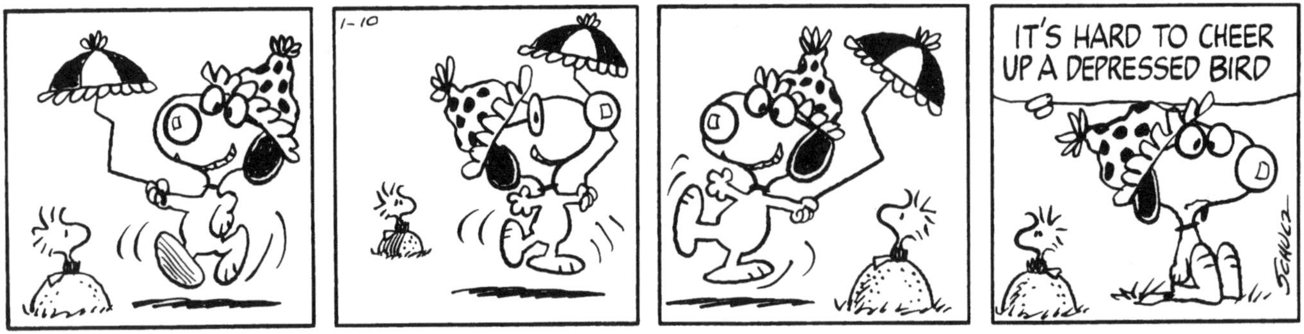
IT'S HARD TO CHEER UP A DEPRESSED BIRD

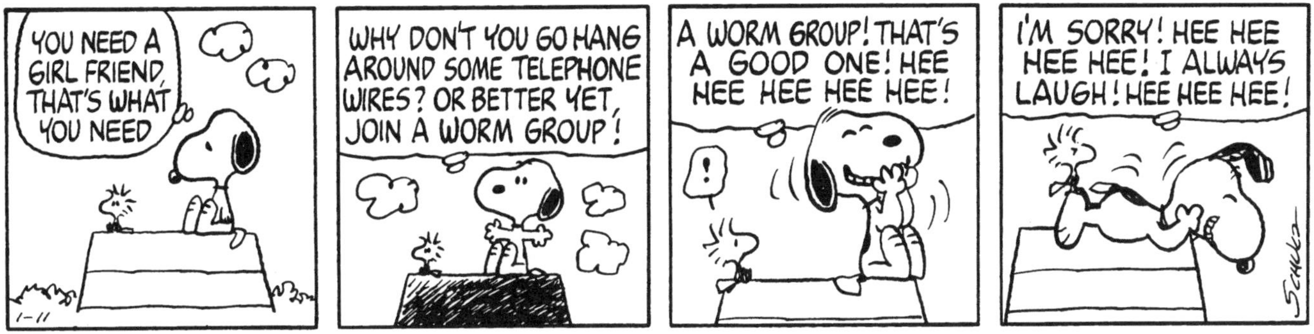
YOU NEED A GIRL FRIEND, THAT'S WHAT YOU NEED
1-11
WHY DON'T YOU GO HANG AROUND SOME TELEPHONE WIRES? OR BETTER YET, JOIN A WORM GROUP!
A WORM GROUP! THAT'S A GOOD ONE! HEE HEE HEE HEE HEE!
!
I'M SORRY! HEE HEE HEE HEE! I ALWAYS LAUGH! HEE HEE HEE!
SCHULZ

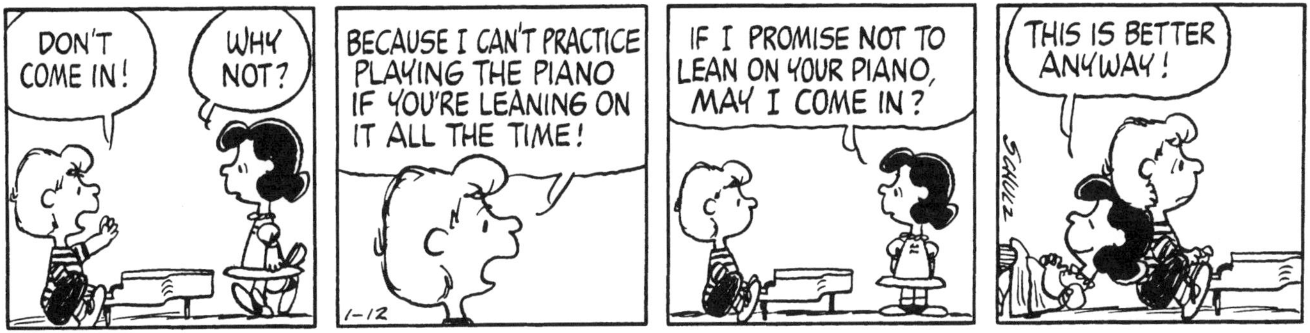
DON'T COME IN!
WHY NOT?
BECAUSE I CAN'T PRACTICE PLAYING THE PIANO IF YOU'RE LEANING ON IT ALL THE TIME!
1-12
IF I PROMISE NOT TO LEAN ON YOUR PIANO, MAY I COME IN?
SCHULZ
THIS IS BETTER ANYWAY!

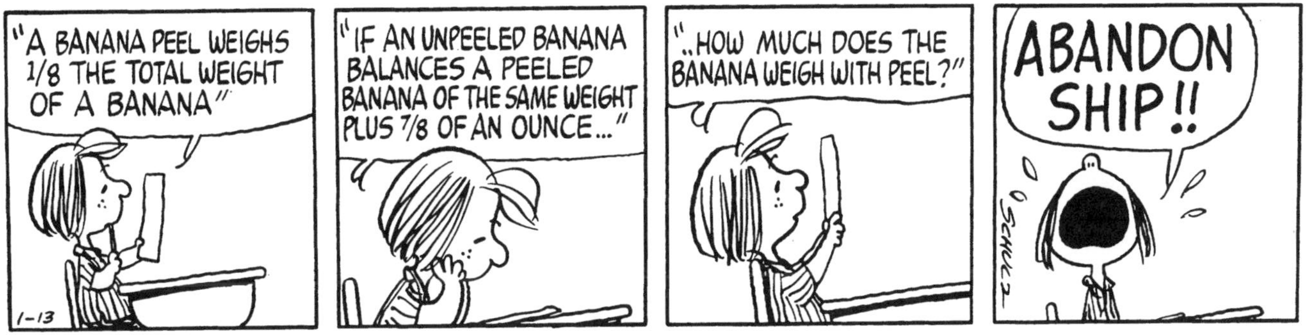
"A BANANA PEEL WEIGHS 1/8 THE TOTAL WEIGHT OF A BANANA"
1-13
"IF AN UNPEELED BANANA BALANCES A PEELED BANANA OF THE SAME WEIGHT PLUS 7/8 OF AN OUNCE..."
"..HOW MUCH DOES THE BANANA WEIGH WITH PEEL?"
SCHULZ
ABANDON SHIP!!

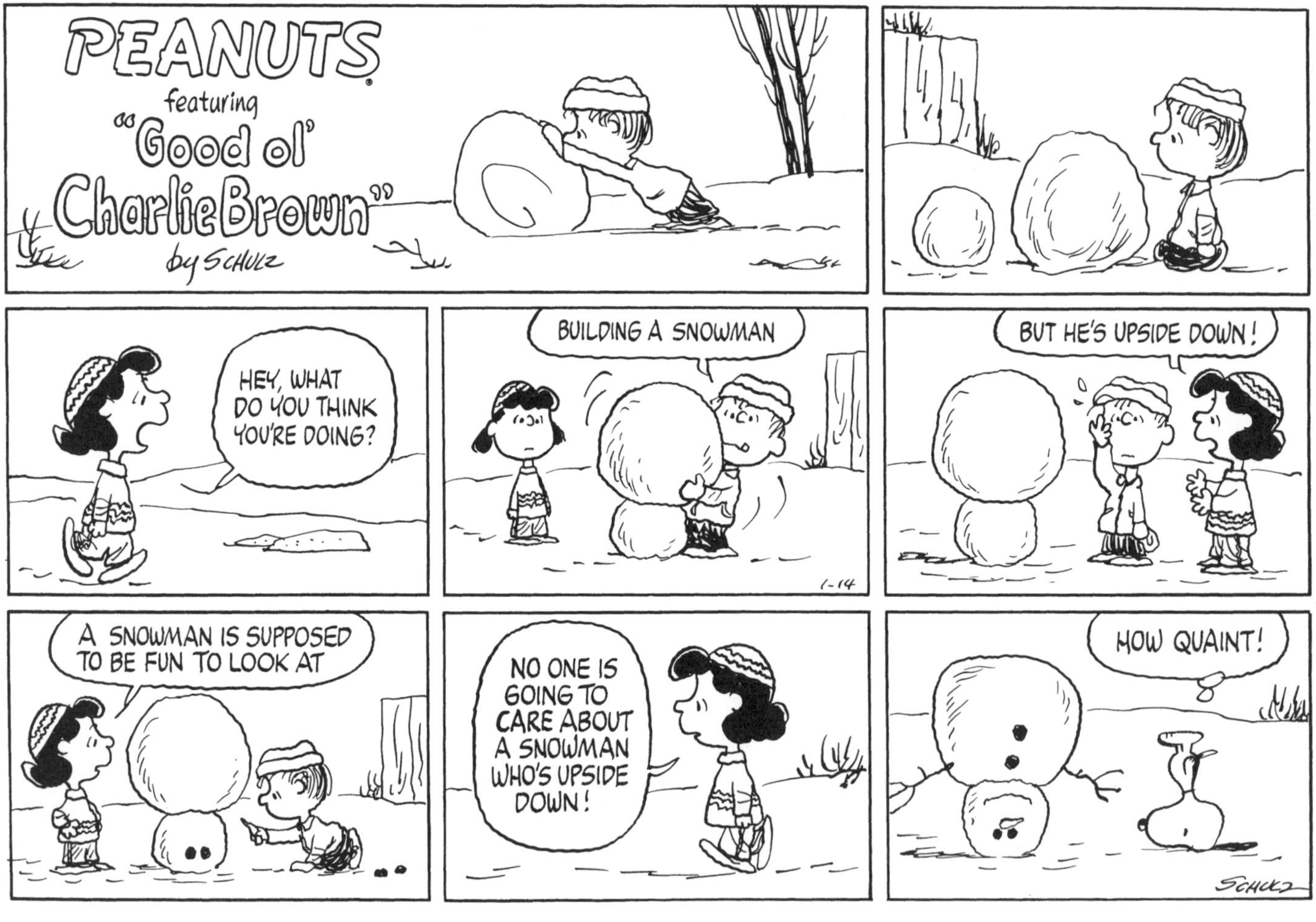
PEANUTS
featuring
"Good ol' Charlie Brown"
by SCHULZ
HEY, WHAT DO YOU THINK YOU'RE DOING?
BUILDING A SNOWMAN
1-14
BUT HE'S UPSIDE DOWN!
A SNOWMAN IS SUPPOSED TO BE FUN TO LOOK AT
NO ONE IS GOING TO CARE ABOUT A SNOWMAN WHO'S UPSIDE DOWN!
HOW QUAINT!
SCHULZ

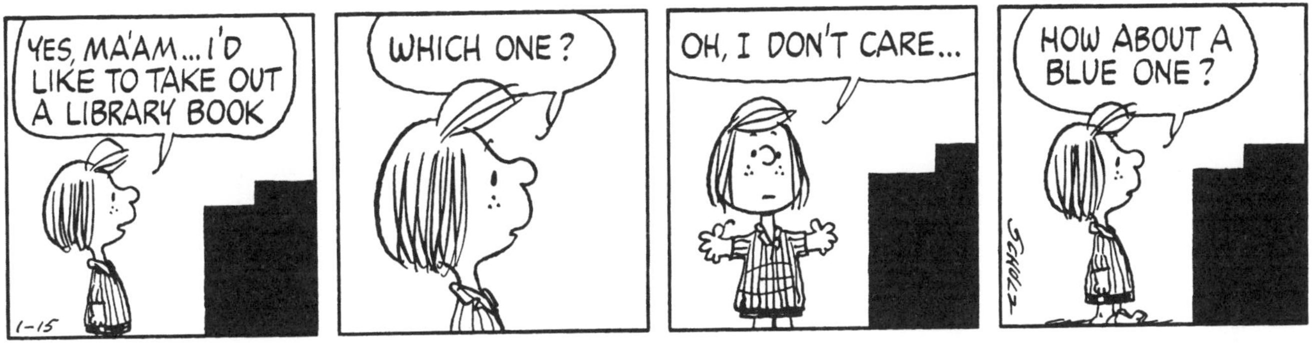
YES, MA'AM...I'D LIKE TO TAKE OUT A LIBRARY BOOK
WHICH ONE?
OH, I DON'T CARE...
HOW ABOUT A BLUE ONE?

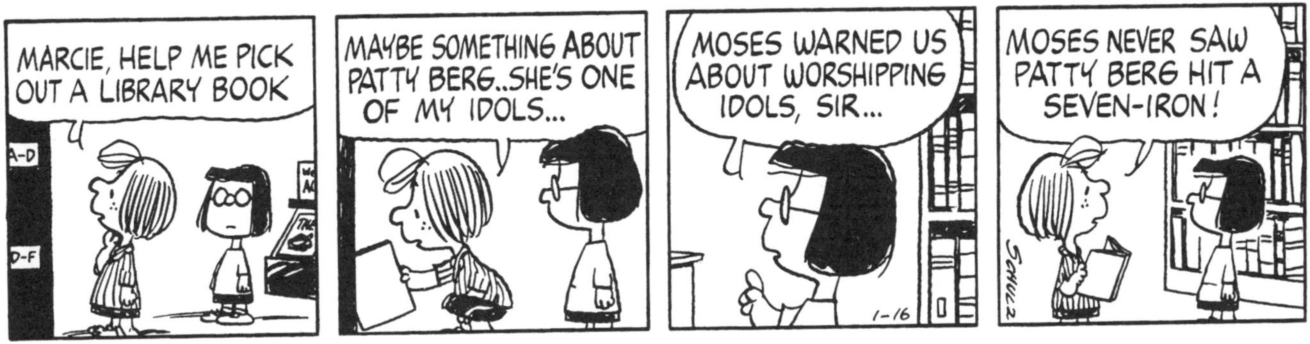
MARCIE, HELP ME PICK OUT A LIBRARY BOOK
MAYBE SOMETHING ABOUT PATTY BERG..SHE'S ONE OF MY IDOLS...
MOSES WARNED US ABOUT WORSHIPPING IDOLS, SIR...
MOSES NEVER SAW PATTY BERG HIT A SEVEN-IRON!

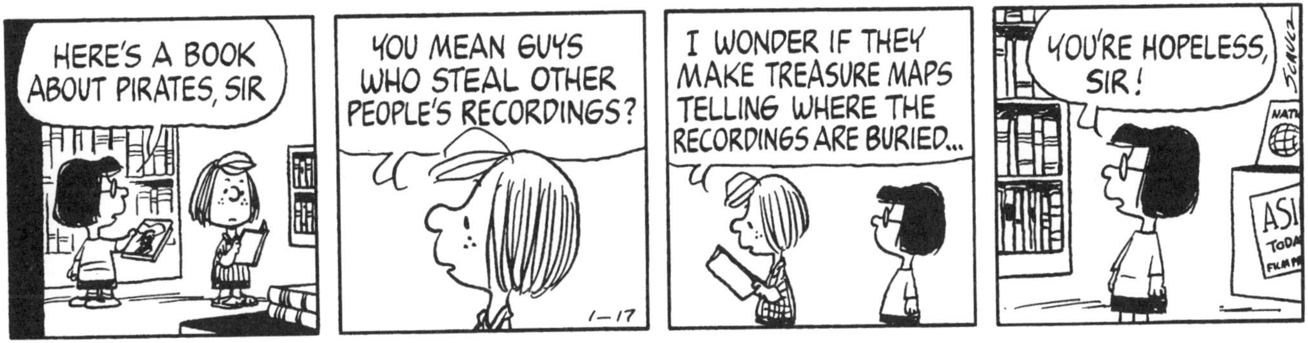
HERE'S A BOOK ABOUT PIRATES, SIR
YOU MEAN GUYS WHO STEAL OTHER PEOPLE'S RECORDINGS?
I WONDER IF THEY MAKE TREASURE MAPS TELLING WHERE THE RECORDINGS ARE BURIED...
YOU'RE HOPELESS, SIR!

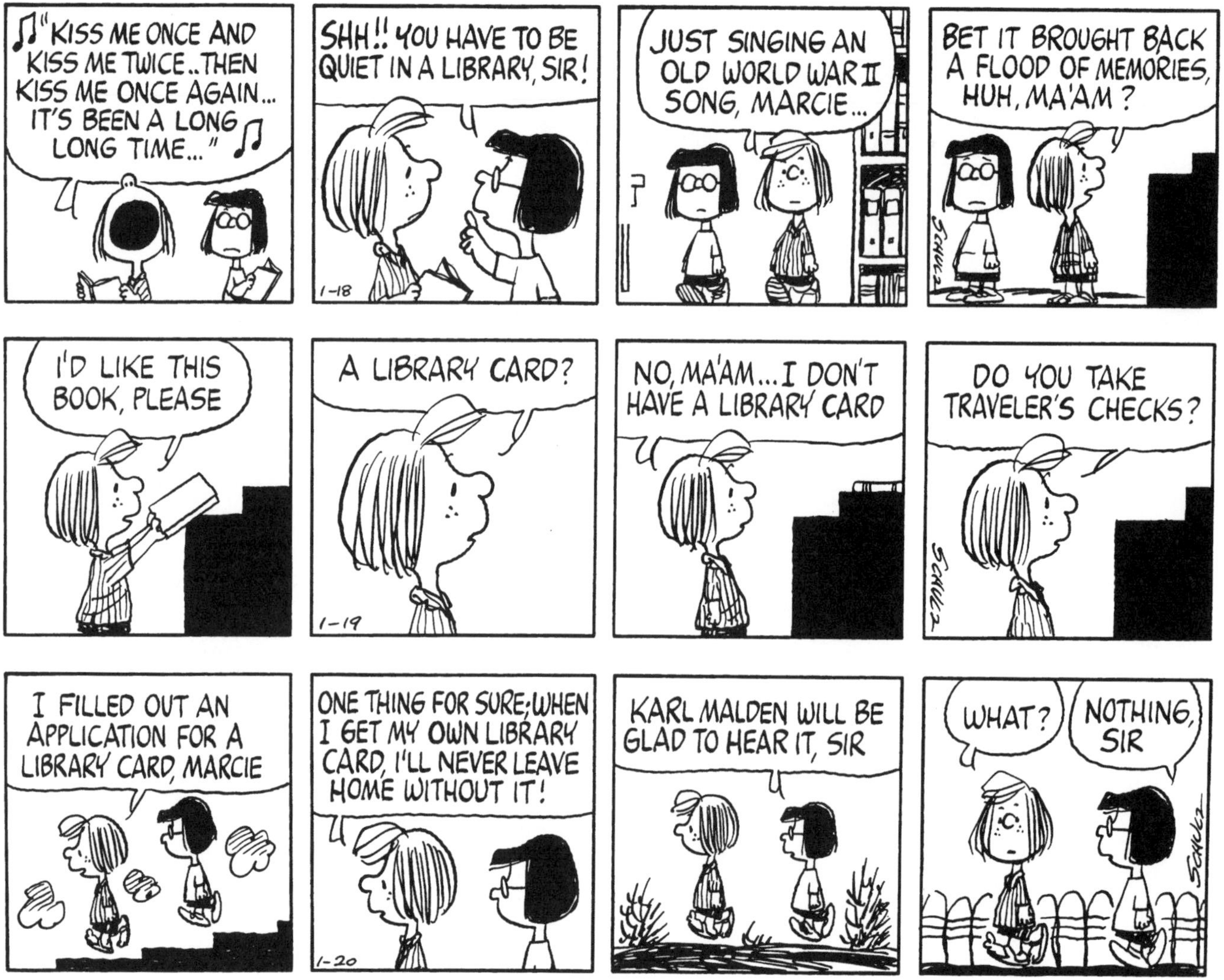
♫ "KISS ME ONCE AND KISS ME TWICE..THEN KISS ME ONCE AGAIN... IT'S BEEN A LONG LONG TIME..." ♫
SHH!! YOU HAVE TO BE QUIET IN A LIBRARY, SIR!
1-18
JUST SINGING AN OLD WORLD WAR II SONG, MARCIE...
BET IT BROUGHT BACK A FLOOD OF MEMORIES, HUH, MA'AM?
SCHULZ
I'D LIKE THIS BOOK, PLEASE
A LIBRARY CARD?
1-19
NO, MA'AM...I DON'T HAVE A LIBRARY CARD
DO YOU TAKE TRAVELER'S CHECKS?
SCHULZ
I FILLED OUT AN APPLICATION FOR A LIBRARY CARD, MARCIE
ONE THING FOR SURE; WHEN I GET MY OWN LIBRARY CARD, I'LL NEVER LEAVE HOME WITHOUT IT!
1-20
KARL MALDEN WILL BE GLAD TO HEAR IT, SIR
WHAT?
NOTHING, SIR
SCHULZ

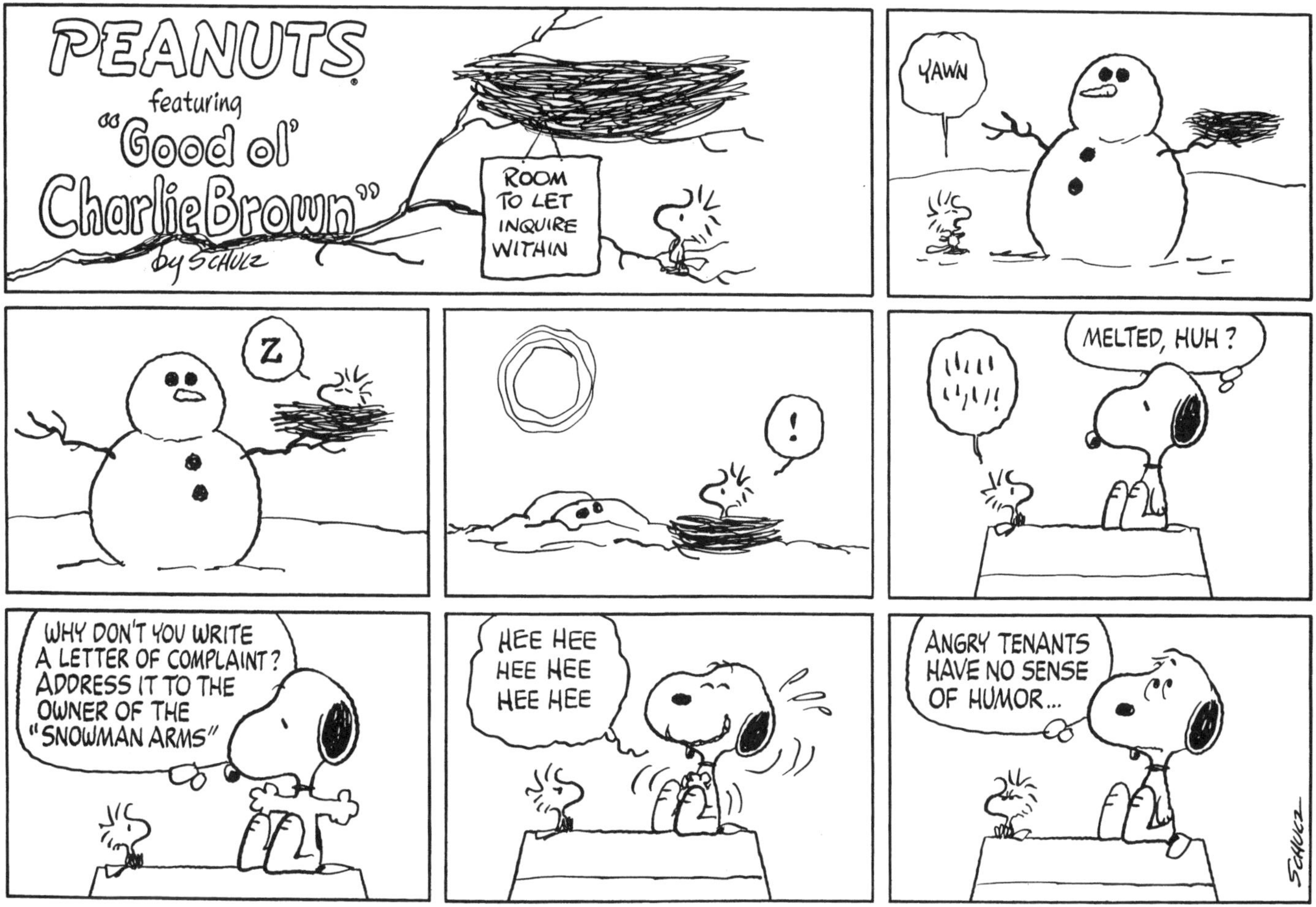
PEANUTS
featuring
"Good ol' Charlie Brown"
by SCHULZ
ROOM TO LET INQUIRE WITHIN
YAWN
Z
!
MELTED, HUH ?
WHY DON'T YOU WRITE A LETTER OF COMPLAINT? ADDRESS IT TO THE OWNER OF THE "SNOWMAN ARMS"
HEE HEE HEE HEE HEE HEE
ANGRY TENANTS HAVE NO SENSE OF HUMOR...
SCHULZ

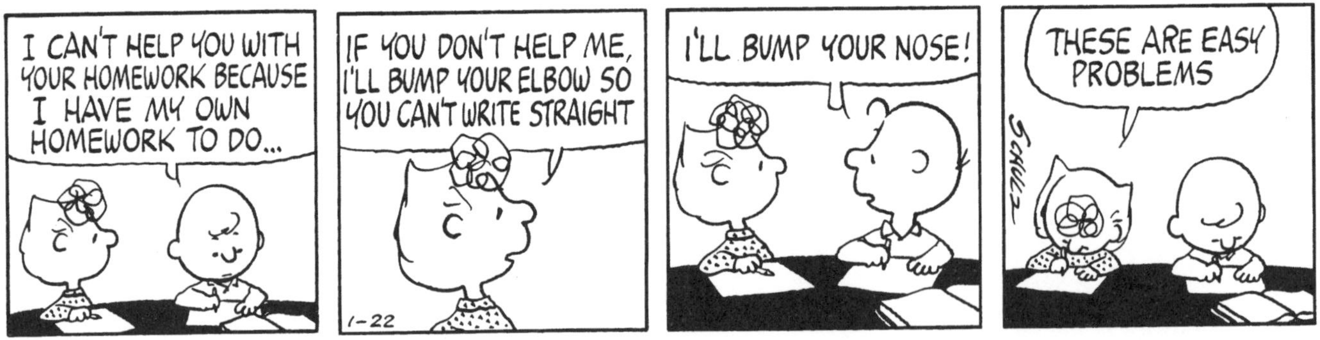
I CAN'T HELP YOU WITH YOUR HOMEWORK BECAUSE I HAVE MY OWN HOMEWORK TO DO...
IF YOU DON'T HELP ME, I'LL BUMP YOUR ELBOW SO YOU CAN'T WRITE STRAIGHT
1-22
I'LL BUMP YOUR NOSE!
THESE ARE EASY PROBLEMS

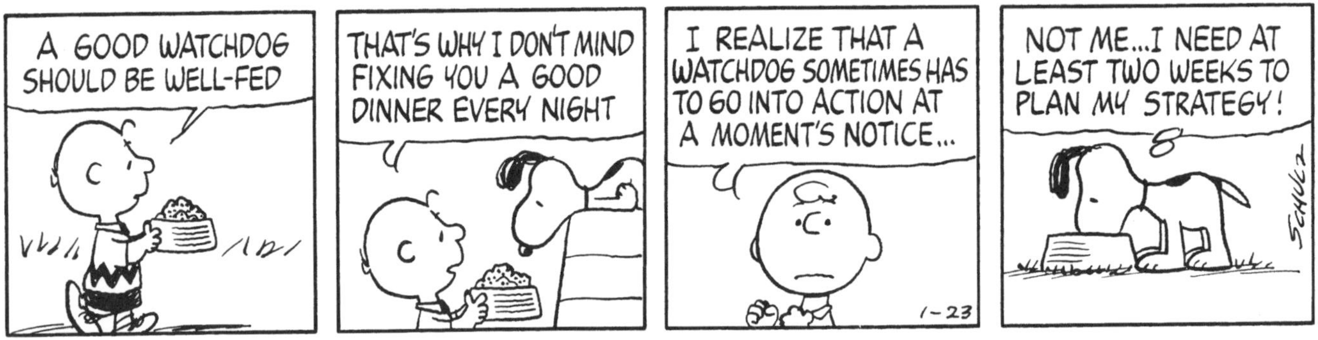
A GOOD WATCHDOG SHOULD BE WELL-FED
THAT'S WHY I DON'T MIND FIXING YOU A GOOD DINNER EVERY NIGHT
I REALIZE THAT A WATCHDOG SOMETIMES HAS TO GO INTO ACTION AT A MOMENT'S NOTICE...
1-23
NOT ME...I NEED AT LEAST TWO WEEKS TO PLAN MY STRATEGY!

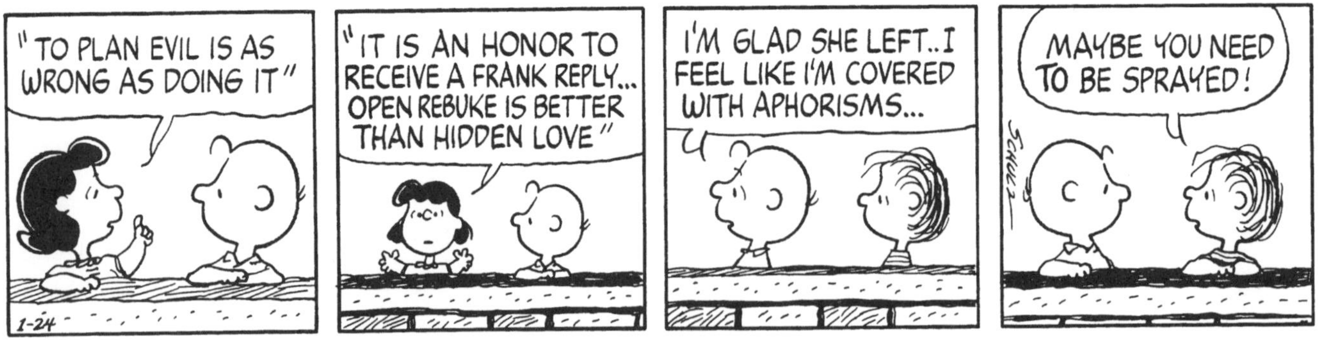
"TO PLAN EVIL IS AS WRONG AS DOING IT"
1-24
"IT IS AN HONOR TO RECEIVE A FRANK REPLY... OPEN REBUKE IS BETTER THAN HIDDEN LOVE"
I'M GLAD SHE LEFT..I FEEL LIKE I'M COVERED WITH APHORISMS...
MAYBE YOU NEED TO BE SPRAYED!

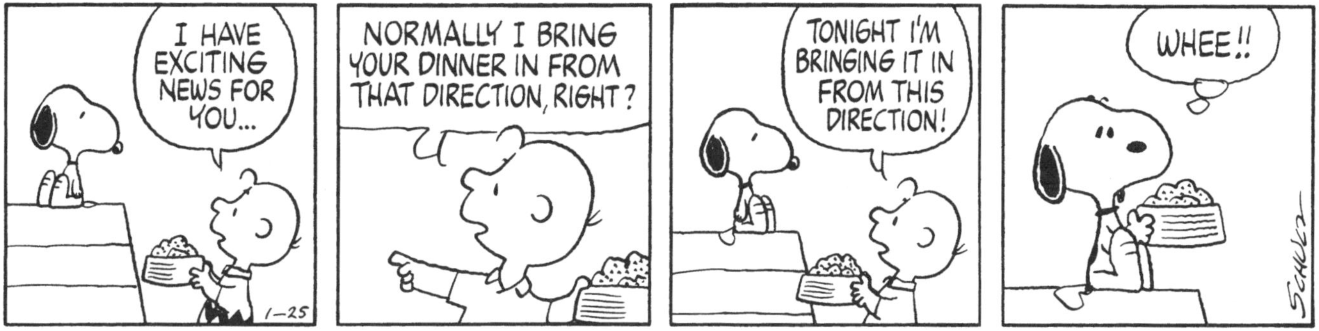
I HAVE EXCITING NEWS FOR YOU...
NORMALLY I BRING YOUR DINNER IN FROM THAT DIRECTION, RIGHT?
TONIGHT I'M BRINGING IT IN FROM THIS DIRECTION!
WHEE!!

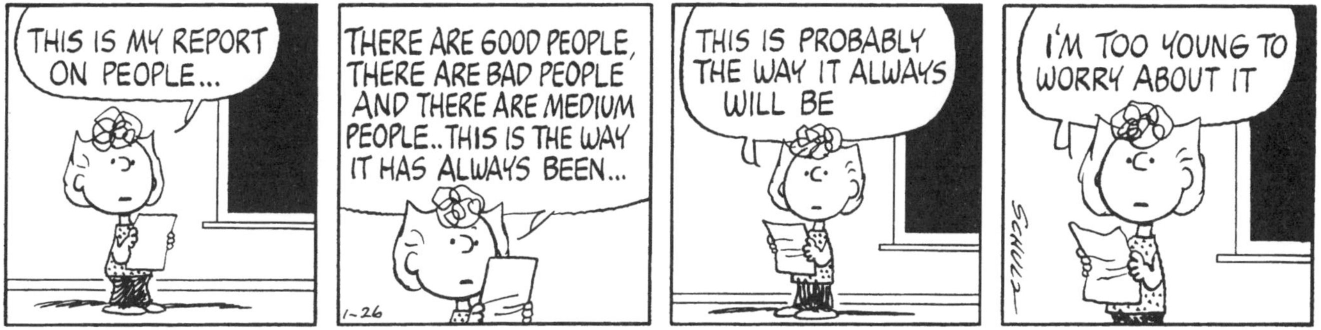
THIS IS MY REPORT ON PEOPLE...
THERE ARE GOOD PEOPLE, THERE ARE BAD PEOPLE AND THERE ARE MEDIUM PEOPLE.. THIS IS THE WAY IT HAS ALWAYS BEEN...
THIS IS PROBABLY THE WAY IT ALWAYS WILL BE
I'M TOO YOUNG TO WORRY ABOUT IT

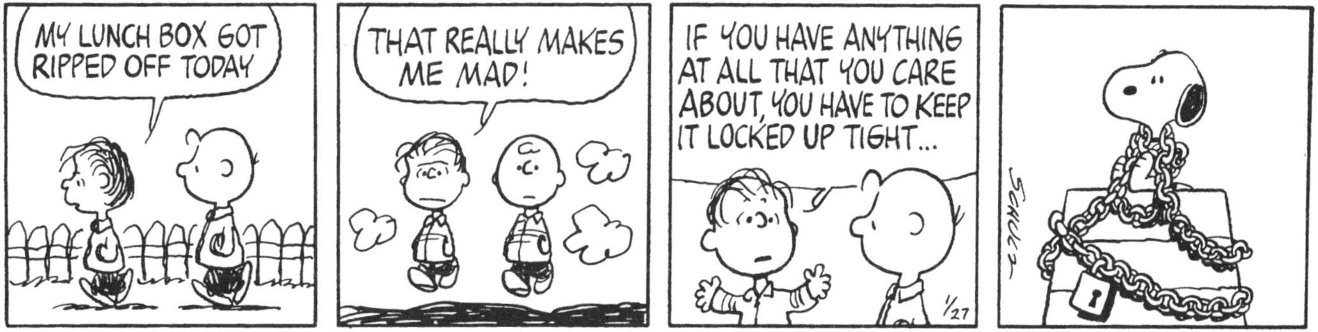
MY LUNCH BOX GOT RIPPED OFF TODAY
THAT REALLY MAKES ME MAD!
IF YOU HAVE ANYTHING AT ALL THAT YOU CARE ABOUT, YOU HAVE TO KEEP IT LOCKED UP TIGHT...

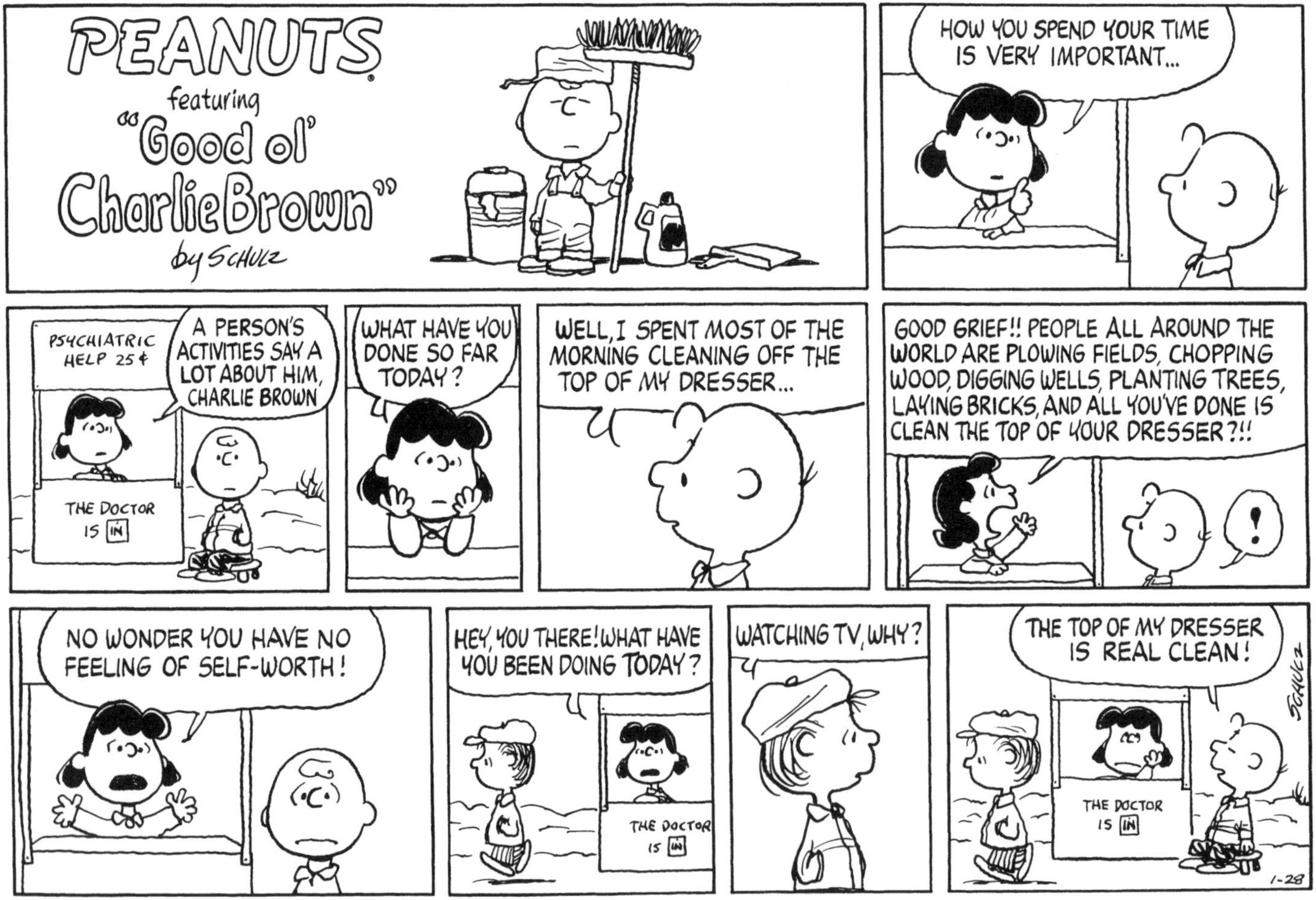
PEANUTS
featuring
"Good ol' CharlieBrown"
by SCHULZ
HOW YOU SPEND YOUR TIME IS VERY IMPORTANT...
PSYCHIATRIC HELP 25¢
A PERSON'S ACTIVITIES SAY A LOT ABOUT HIM, CHARLIE BROWN
THE DOCTOR IS IN
WHAT HAVE YOU DONE SO FAR TODAY?
WELL, I SPENT MOST OF THE MORNING CLEANING OFF THE TOP OF MY DRESSER...
GOOD GRIEF!! PEOPLE ALL AROUND THE WORLD ARE PLOWING FIELDS, CHOPPING WOOD, DIGGING WELLS, PLANTING TREES, LAYING BRICKS, AND ALL YOU'VE DONE IS CLEAN THE TOP OF YOUR DRESSER?!!
!
NO WONDER YOU HAVE NO FEELING OF SELF-WORTH!
HEY, YOU THERE! WHAT HAVE YOU BEEN DOING TODAY?
THE DOCTOR IS IN
WATCHING TV, WHY?
THE TOP OF MY DRESSER IS REAL CLEAN!
THE DOCTOR IS IN
SCHULZ
1-28

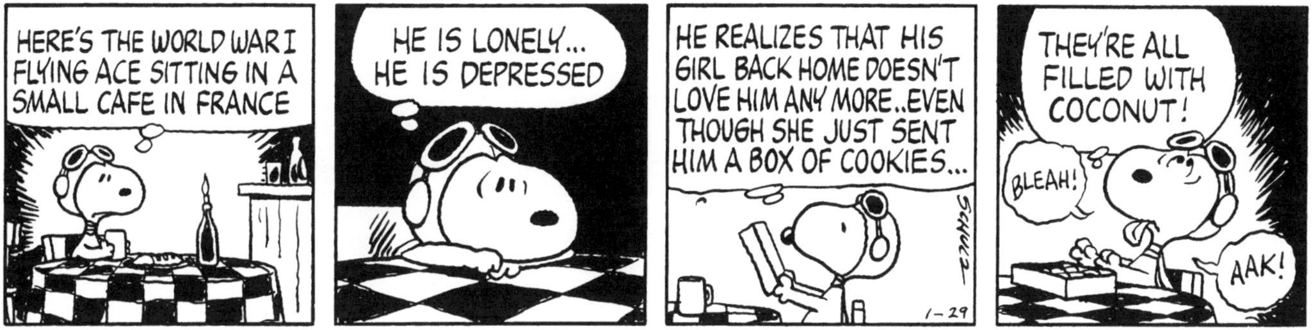
HERE'S THE WORLD WAR I FLYING ACE SITTING IN A SMALL CAFE IN FRANCE
HE IS LONELY... HE IS DEPRESSED
HE REALIZES THAT HIS GIRL BACK HOME DOESN'T LOVE HIM ANY MORE..EVEN THOUGH SHE JUST SENT HIM A BOX OF COOKIES...
SCHULZ
1-29
THEY'RE ALL FILLED WITH COCONUT!
BLEAH!
AAK!

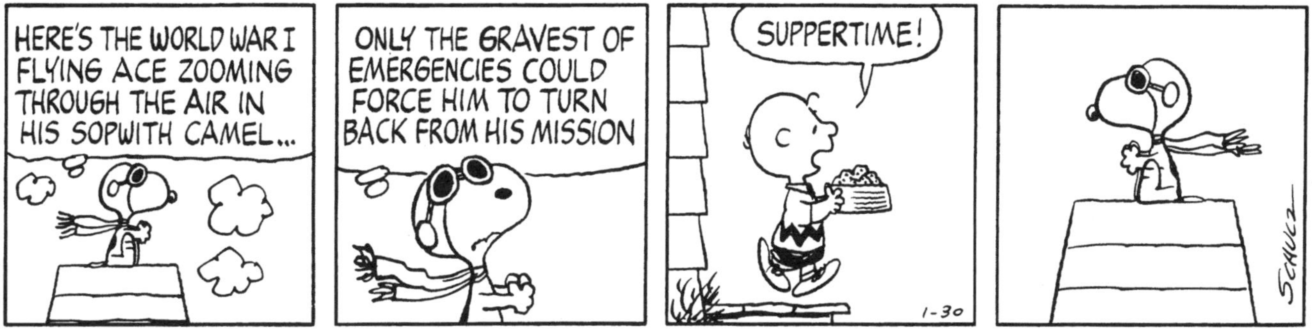
HERE'S THE WORLD WAR I FLYING ACE ZOOMING THROUGH THE AIR IN HIS SOPWITH CAMEL...
ONLY THE GRAVEST OF EMERGENCIES COULD FORCE HIM TO TURN BACK FROM HIS MISSION
SUPPERTIME!
1-30
SCHULZ

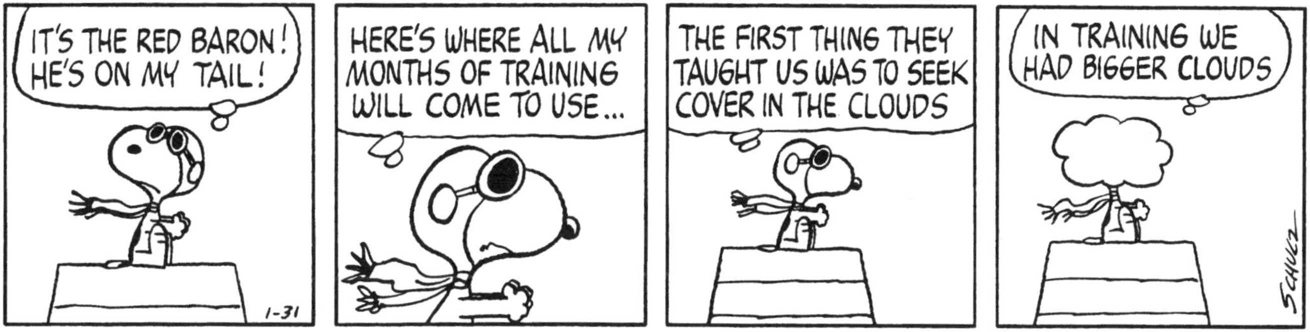
IT'S THE RED BARON! HE'S ON MY TAIL!
1-31
HERE'S WHERE ALL MY MONTHS OF TRAINING WILL COME TO USE...
THE FIRST THING THEY TAUGHT US WAS TO SEEK COVER IN THE CLOUDS
IN TRAINING WE HAD BIGGER CLOUDS
SCHULZ

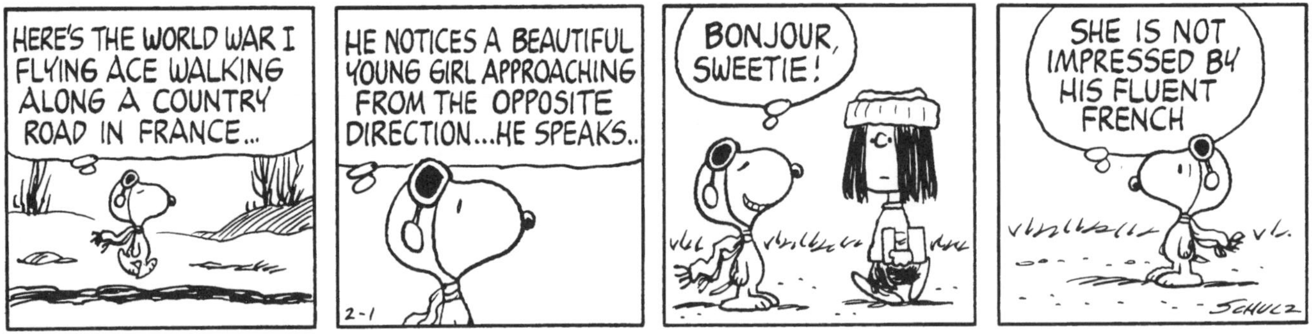
HERE'S THE WORLD WAR I FLYING ACE WALKING ALONG A COUNTRY ROAD IN FRANCE...
HE NOTICES A BEAUTIFUL YOUNG GIRL APPROACHING FROM THE OPPOSITE DIRECTION...HE SPEAKS..
2-1
BONJOUR, SWEETIE!
SHE IS NOT IMPRESSED BY HIS FLUENT FRENCH
SCHULZ

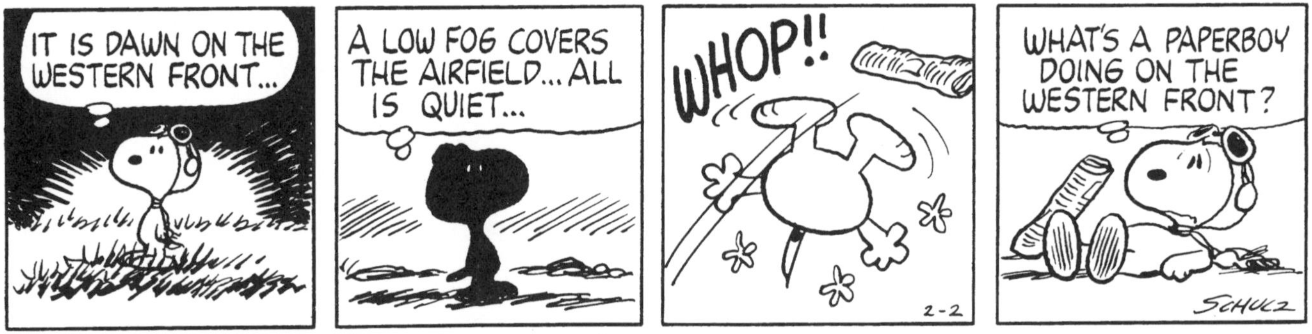
IT IS DAWN ON THE WESTERN FRONT...
A LOW FOG COVERS THE AIRFIELD...ALL IS QUIET...
WHOP!!
2-2
WHAT'S A PAPERBOY DOING ON THE WESTERN FRONT?
SCHULZ

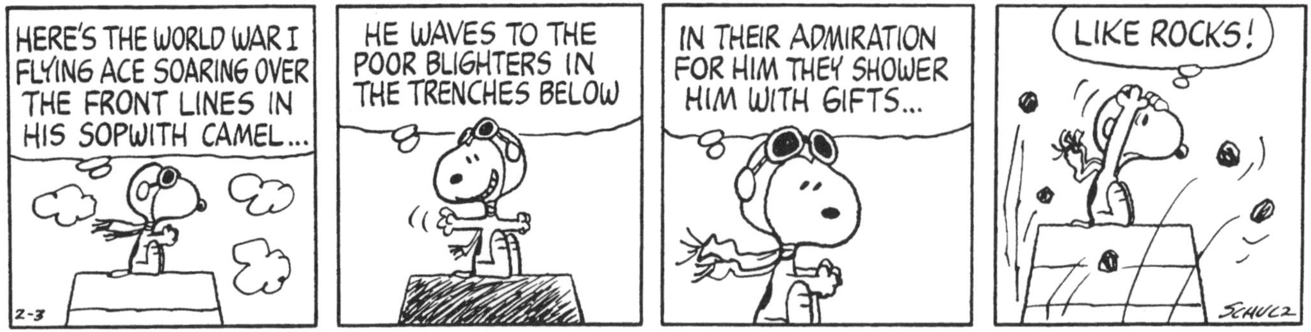
HERE'S THE WORLD WAR I FLYING ACE SOARING OVER THE FRONT LINES IN HIS SOPWITH CAMEL...
2-3
HE WAVES TO THE POOR BLIGHTERS IN THE TRENCHES BELOW
IN THEIR ADMIRATION FOR HIM THEY SHOWER HIM WITH GIFTS...
LIKE ROCKS!
SCHULZ

PEANUTS featuring "Good ol' Charlie Brown" by Schulz

$$x^2 + \div \begin{matrix} 5 \end{matrix} \begin{matrix} (z-2)^2 \\ y \end{matrix} + \text{forget it!}$$

$=$

FIFTEEN TIMES SEVEN? HMM...

2-4

PSST! WHAT DID YOU PUT DOWN FOR THE THIRD QUESTION, SIR?

I PUT DOWN "GREEN"

GREEN?!

BUT THE QUESTION WAS, "HOW MUCH IS FIFTEEN TIMES SEVEN?"

I THOUGHT MAYBE IT WAS A TRICK QUESTION!

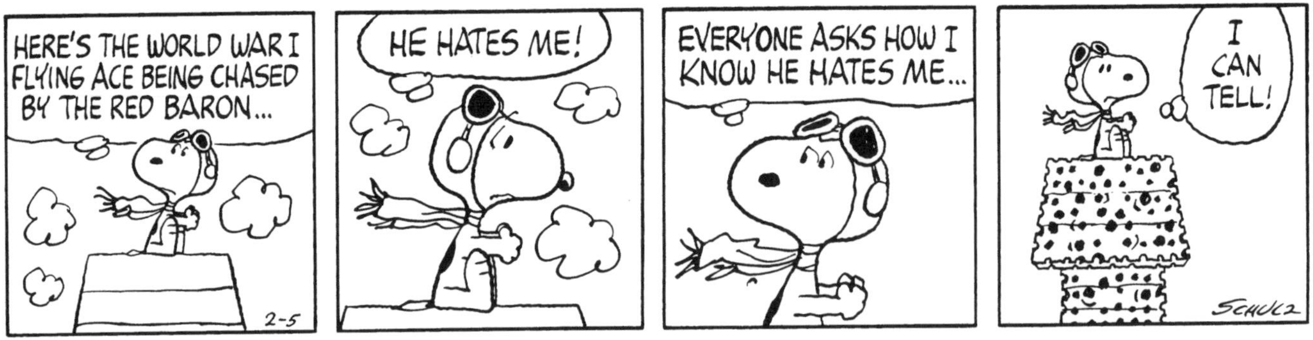
HERE'S THE WORLD WAR I FLYING ACE BEING CHASED BY THE RED BARON...
2-5
HE HATES ME!
EVERYONE ASKS HOW I KNOW HE HATES ME...
I CAN TELL!
SCHULZ

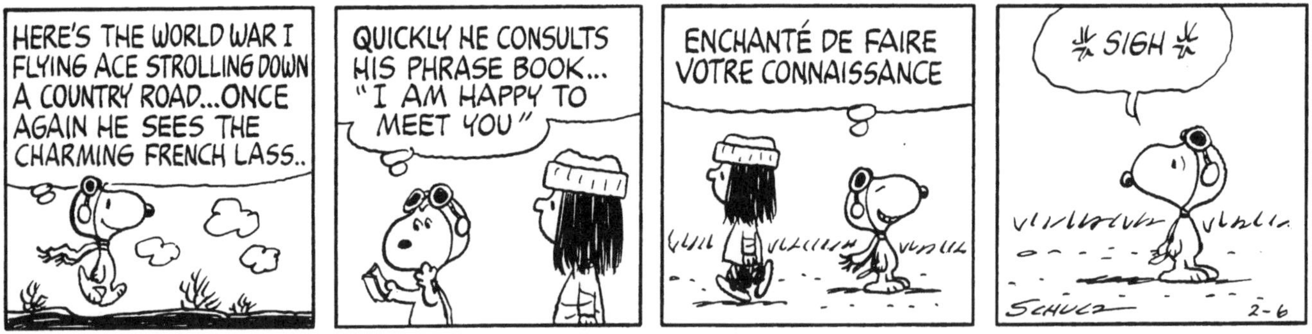
HERE'S THE WORLD WAR I FLYING ACE STROLLING DOWN A COUNTRY ROAD...ONCE AGAIN HE SEES THE CHARMING FRENCH LASS..
QUICKLY HE CONSULTS HIS PHRASE BOOK... "I AM HAPPY TO MEET YOU"
ENCHANTÉ DE FAIRE VOTRE CONNAISSANCE
SIGH
SCHULZ
2-6

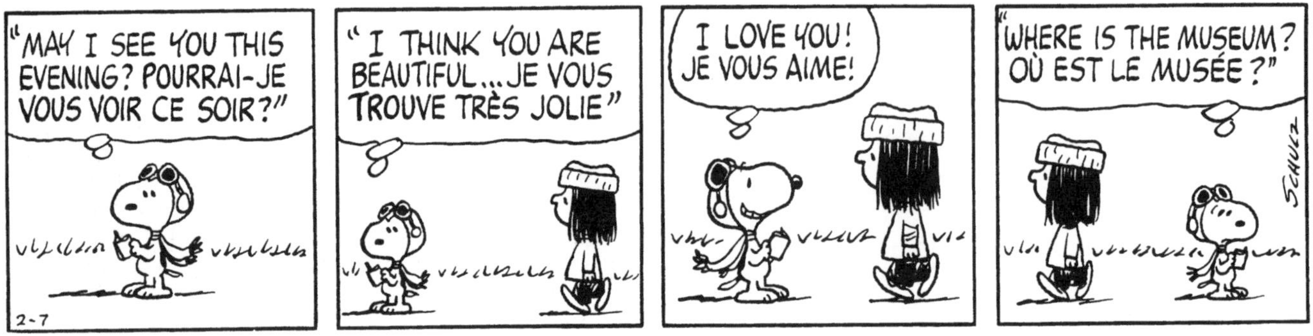
"MAY I SEE YOU THIS EVENING? POURRAI-JE VOUS VOIR CE SOIR?"
2-7
"I THINK YOU ARE BEAUTIFUL...JE VOUS TROUVE TRÈS JOLIE"
I LOVE YOU! JE VOUS AIME!
"WHERE IS THE MUSEUM? OÙ EST LE MUSÉE?"
SCHULZ

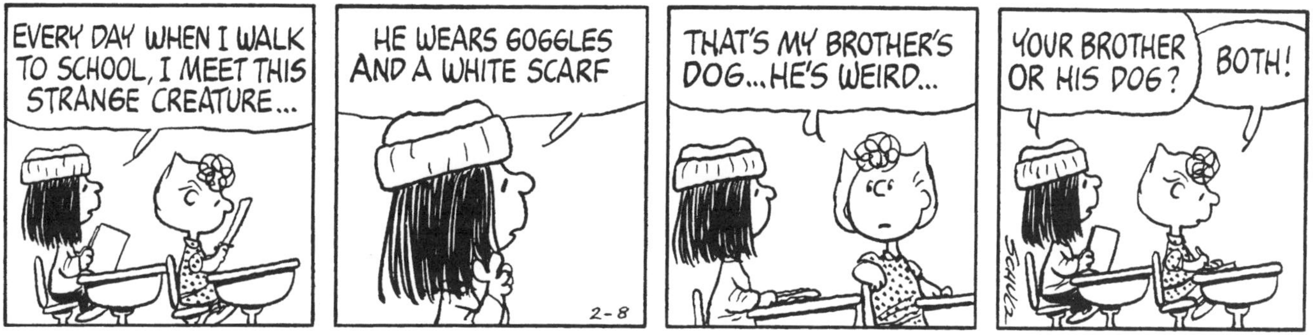
EVERY DAY WHEN I WALK TO SCHOOL, I MEET THIS STRANGE CREATURE...
HE WEARS GOGGLES AND A WHITE SCARF
THAT'S MY BROTHER'S DOG...HE'S WEIRD...
YOUR BROTHER OR HIS DOG?
BOTH!

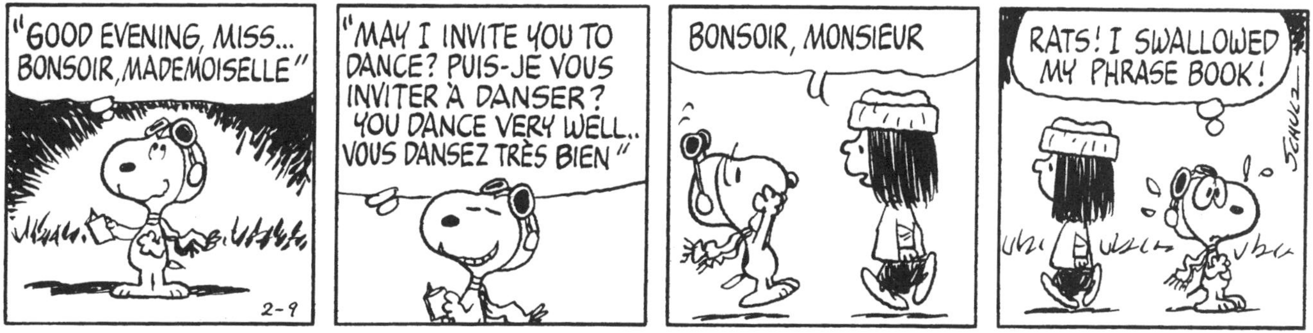
"GOOD EVENING, MISS... BONSOIR, MADEMOISELLE"
"MAY I INVITE YOU TO DANCE? PUIS-JE VOUS INVITER À DANSER? YOU DANCE VERY WELL.. VOUS DANSEZ TRÈS BIEN"
BONSOIR, MONSIEUR
RATS! I SWALLOWED MY PHRASE BOOK!

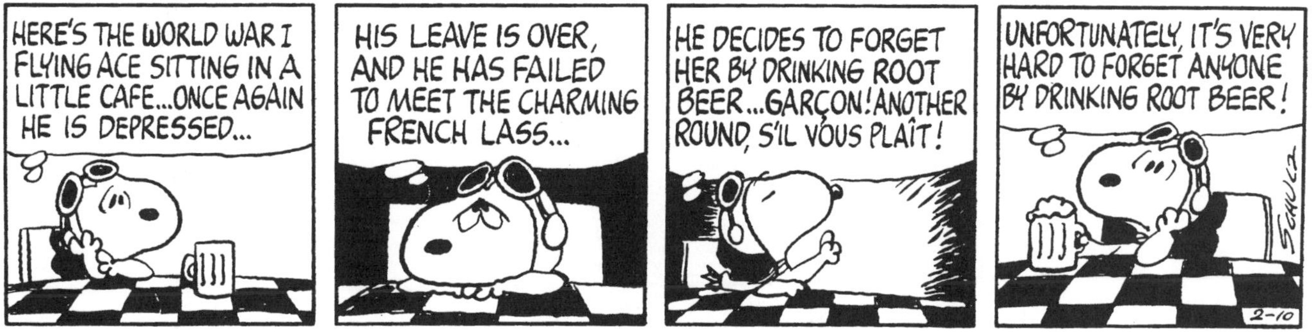
HERE'S THE WORLD WAR I FLYING ACE SITTING IN A LITTLE CAFE...ONCE AGAIN HE IS DEPRESSED...
HIS LEAVE IS OVER, AND HE HAS FAILED TO MEET THE CHARMING FRENCH LASS...
HE DECIDES TO FORGET HER BY DRINKING ROOT BEER...GARÇON! ANOTHER ROUND, S'IL VOUS PLAÎT!
UNFORTUNATELY, IT'S VERY HARD TO FORGET ANYONE BY DRINKING ROOT BEER!

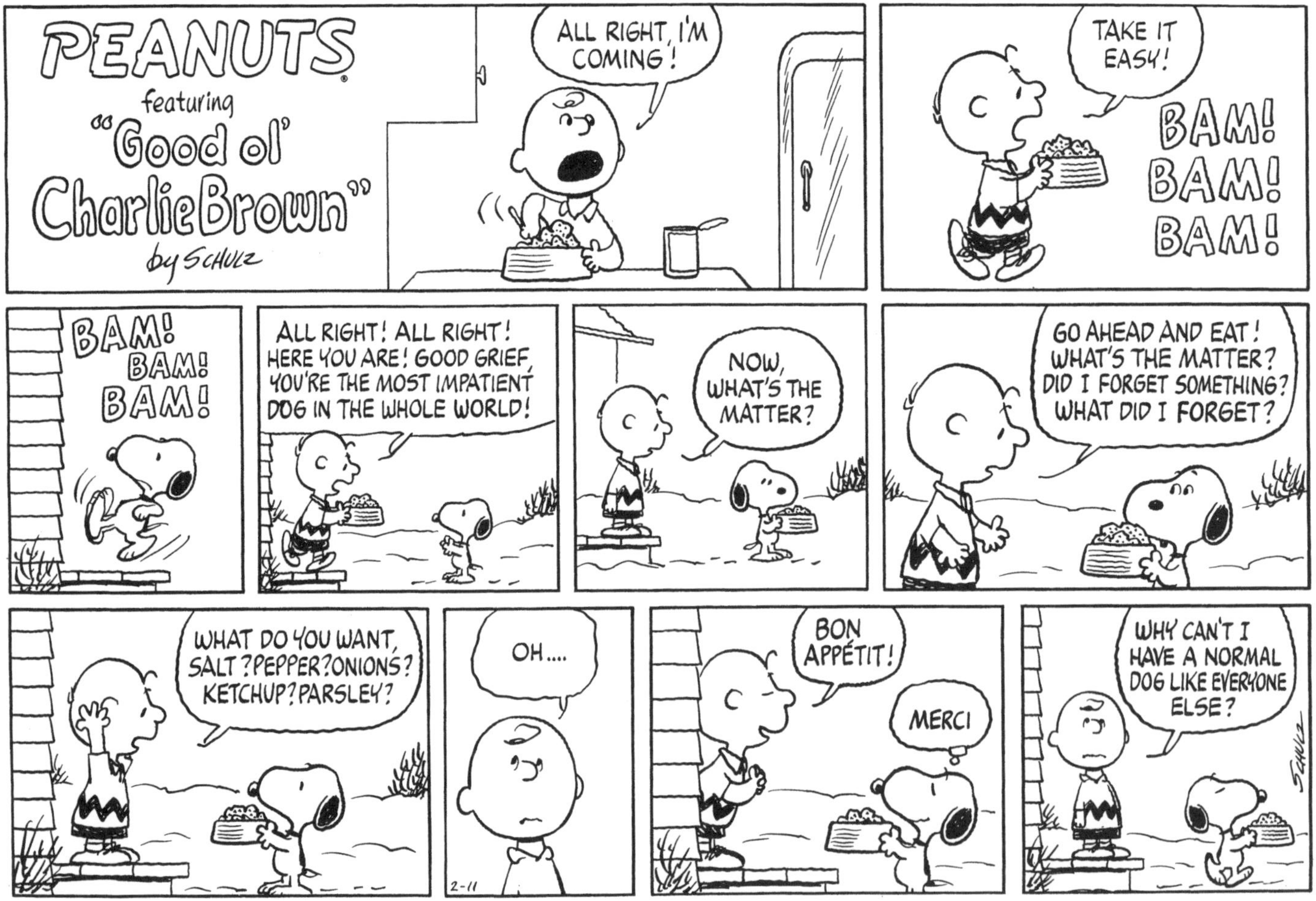
PEANUTS
featuring
"Good ol' CharlieBrown"
by SCHULZ
ALL RIGHT, I'M COMING!
TAKE IT EASY!
BAM! BAM! BAM!
BAM! BAM! BAM!
ALL RIGHT! ALL RIGHT! HERE YOU ARE! GOOD GRIEF, YOU'RE THE MOST IMPATIENT DOG IN THE WHOLE WORLD!
NOW, WHAT'S THE MATTER?
GO AHEAD AND EAT! WHAT'S THE MATTER? DID I FORGET SOMETHING? WHAT DID I FORGET?
WHAT DO YOU WANT, SALT? PEPPER? ONIONS? KETCHUP? PARSLEY?
OH....
2-11
BON APPÉTIT!
MERCI
WHY CAN'T I HAVE A NORMAL DOG LIKE EVERYONE ELSE?
SCHULZ

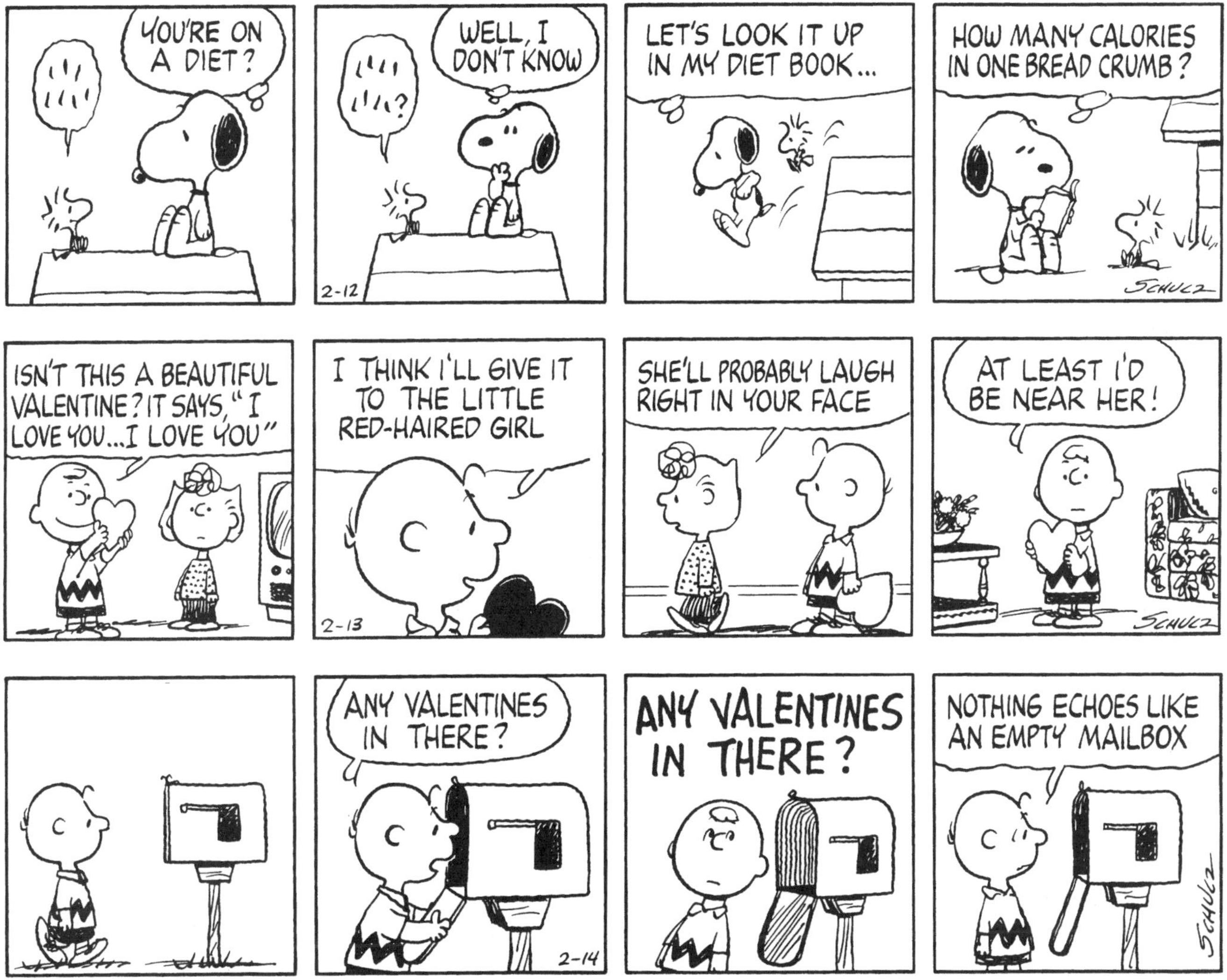
YOU'RE ON A DIET?
WELL, I DON'T KNOW
2-12
LET'S LOOK IT UP IN MY DIET BOOK...
HOW MANY CALORIES IN ONE BREAD CRUMB?
SCHULZ
ISN'T THIS A BEAUTIFUL VALENTINE? IT SAYS, "I LOVE YOU...I LOVE YOU"
I THINK I'LL GIVE IT TO THE LITTLE RED-HAIRED GIRL
2-13
SHE'LL PROBABLY LAUGH RIGHT IN YOUR FACE
AT LEAST I'D BE NEAR HER!
SCHULZ
ANY VALENTINES IN THERE?
2-14
ANY VALENTINES IN THERE?
NOTHING ECHOES LIKE AN EMPTY MAILBOX
SCHULZ

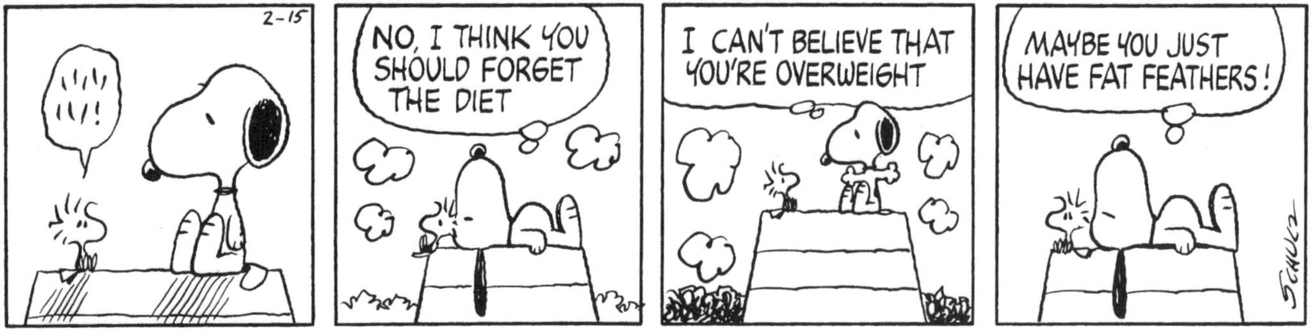
2-15
NO, I THINK YOU SHOULD FORGET THE DIET
I CAN'T BELIEVE THAT YOU'RE OVERWEIGHT
MAYBE YOU JUST HAVE FAT FEATHERS!
SCHULZ

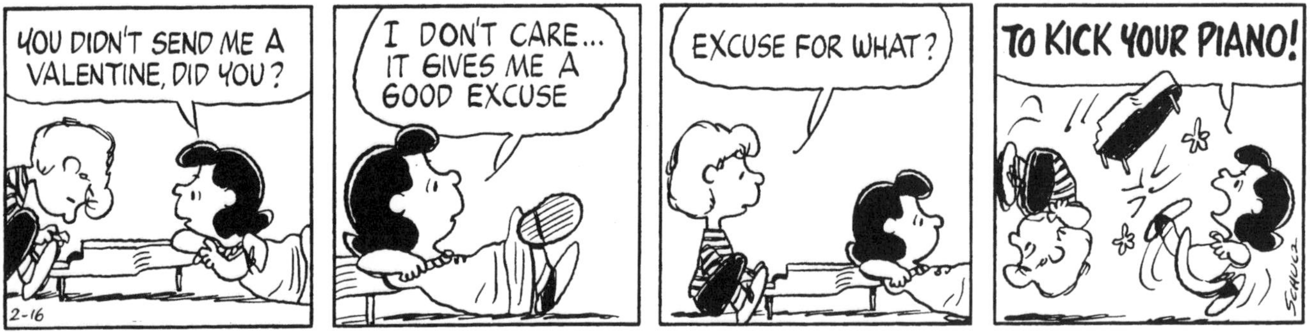
YOU DIDN'T SEND ME A VALENTINE, DID YOU?
2-16
I DON'T CARE... IT GIVES ME A GOOD EXCUSE
EXCUSE FOR WHAT?
TO KICK YOUR PIANO!
SCHULZ

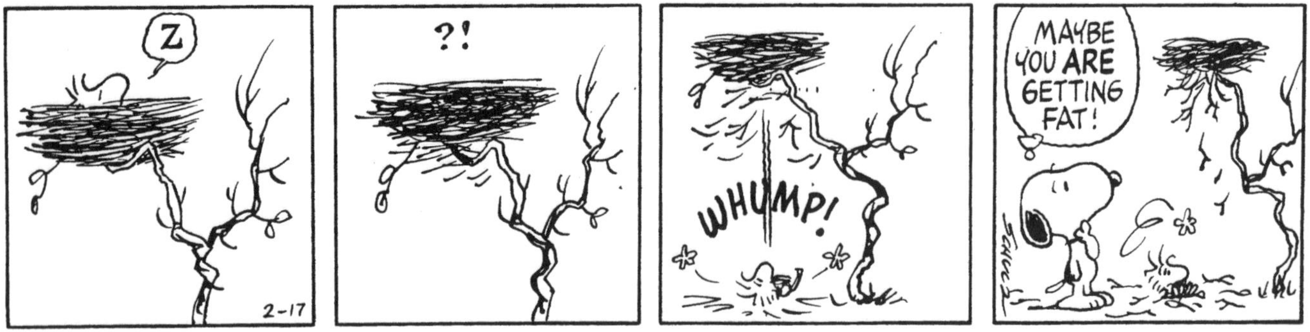
Z
2-17
?!
WHUMP!
MAYBE YOU ARE GETTING FAT!
SCHULZ

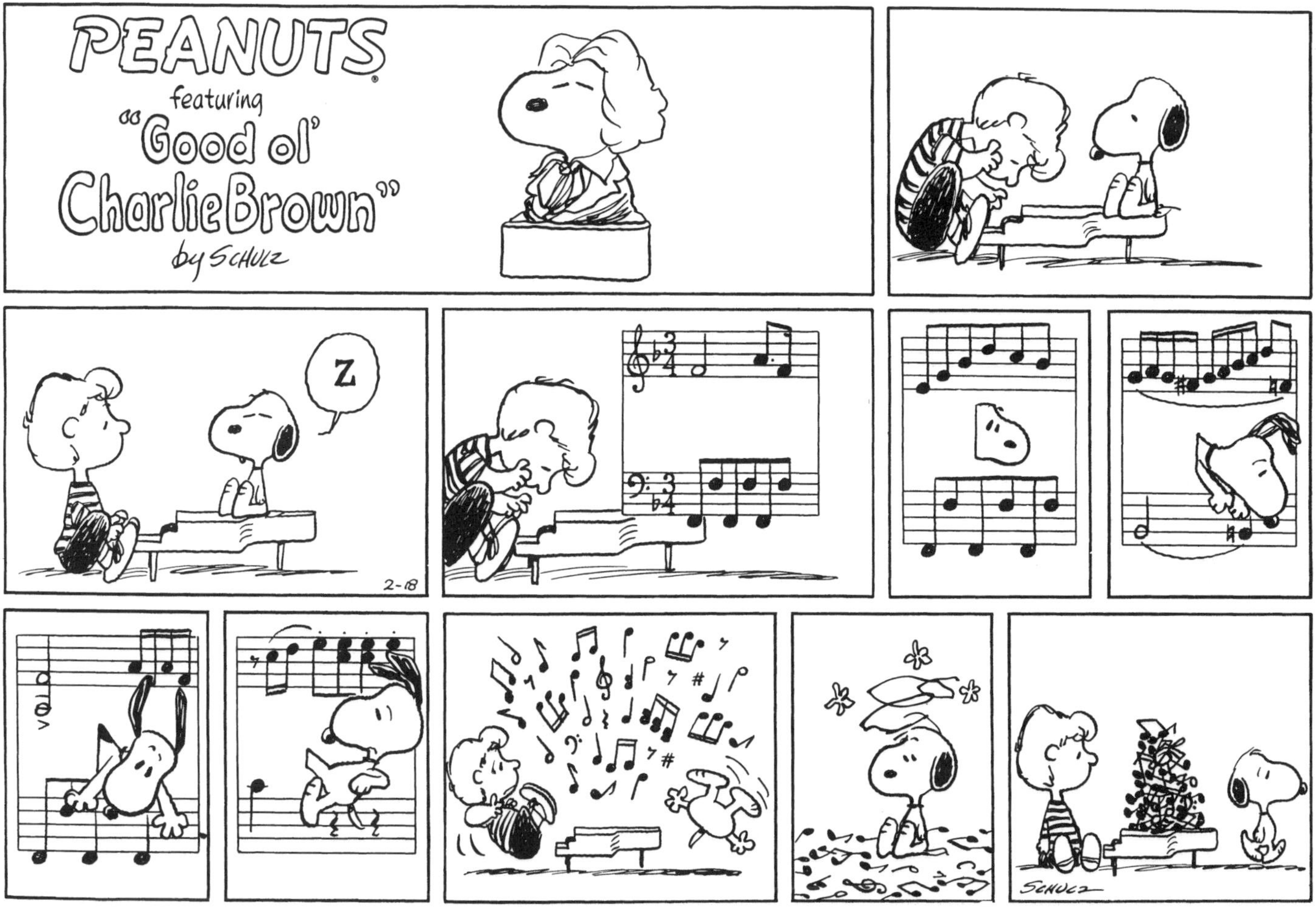
PEANUTS
featuring
"Good ol' Charlie Brown"
by SCHULZ
Z
2-18
SCHULZ

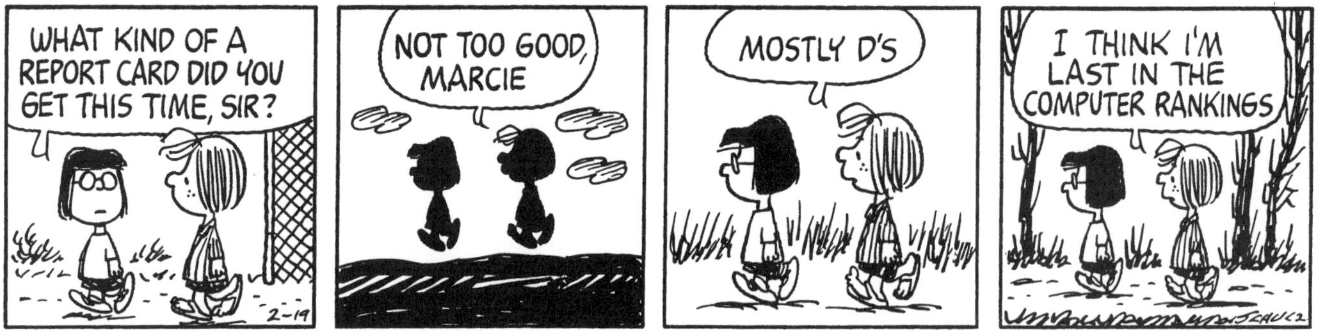
WHAT KIND OF A REPORT CARD DID YOU GET THIS TIME, SIR?
2-19
NOT TOO GOOD, MARCIE
MOSTLY D'S
I THINK I'M LAST IN THE COMPUTER RANKINGS
SCHULZ

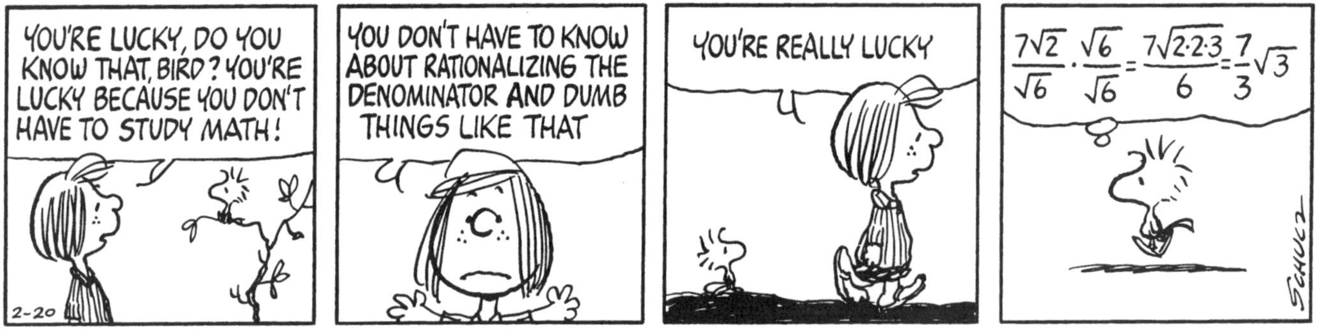
YOU'RE LUCKY, DO YOU KNOW THAT, BIRD? YOU'RE LUCKY BECAUSE YOU DON'T HAVE TO STUDY MATH!
2-20
YOU DON'T HAVE TO KNOW ABOUT RATIONALIZING THE DENOMINATOR AND DUMB THINGS LIKE THAT
YOU'RE REALLY LUCKY
$\frac{7\sqrt{2}}{\sqrt{6}} \cdot \frac{\sqrt{6}}{\sqrt{6}} = \frac{7\sqrt{2 \cdot 2 \cdot 3}}{6} = \frac{7}{3}\sqrt{3}$
SCHULZ

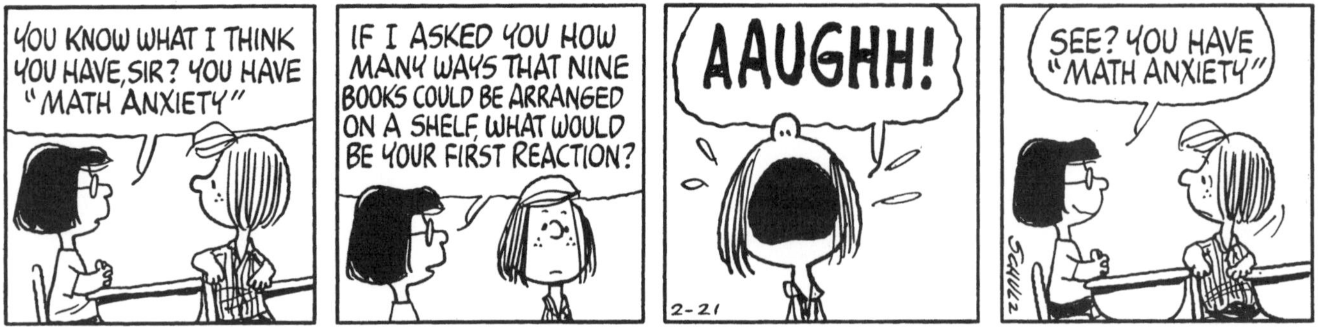
YOU KNOW WHAT I THINK YOU HAVE, SIR? YOU HAVE "MATH ANXIETY"
IF I ASKED YOU HOW MANY WAYS THAT NINE BOOKS COULD BE ARRANGED ON A SHELF, WHAT WOULD BE YOUR FIRST REACTION?
AAUGHH!
2-21
SEE? YOU HAVE "MATH ANXIETY"
SCHULZ

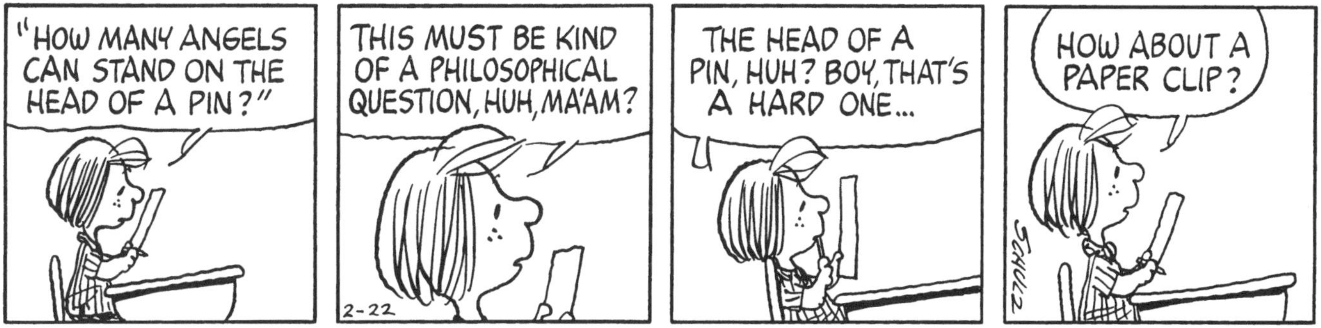
"HOW MANY ANGELS CAN STAND ON THE HEAD OF A PIN?"
THIS MUST BE KIND OF A PHILOSOPHICAL QUESTION, HUH, MA'AM?
THE HEAD OF A PIN, HUH? BOY, THAT'S A HARD ONE...
HOW ABOUT A PAPER CLIP?
2-22
SCHULZ

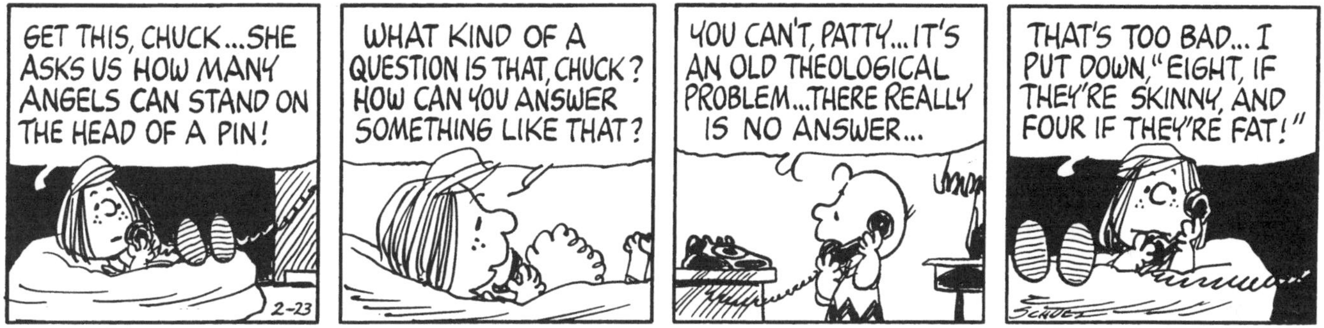
GET THIS, CHUCK...SHE ASKS US HOW MANY ANGELS CAN STAND ON THE HEAD OF A PIN!
WHAT KIND OF A QUESTION IS THAT, CHUCK? HOW CAN YOU ANSWER SOMETHING LIKE THAT?
YOU CAN'T, PATTY...IT'S AN OLD THEOLOGICAL PROBLEM...THERE REALLY IS NO ANSWER...
THAT'S TOO BAD... I PUT DOWN, "EIGHT, IF THEY'RE SKINNY, AND FOUR IF THEY'RE FAT!"
2-23
SCHULZ

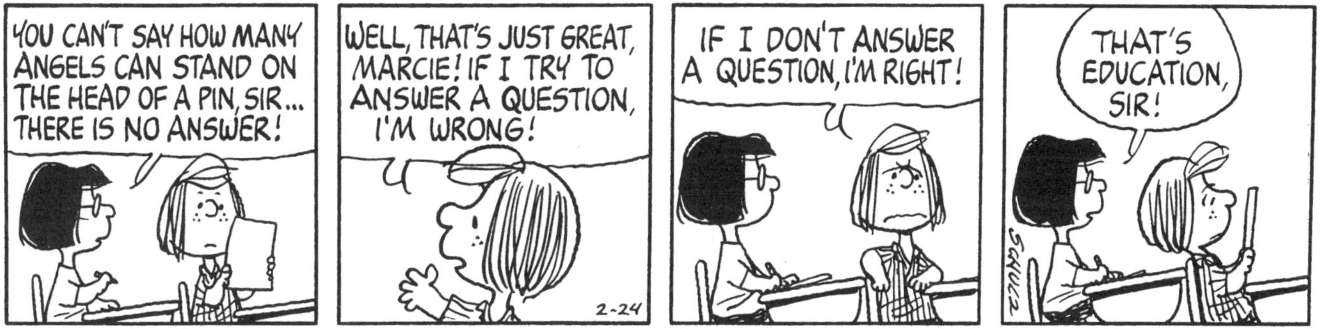
YOU CAN'T SAY HOW MANY ANGELS CAN STAND ON THE HEAD OF A PIN, SIR... THERE IS NO ANSWER!
WELL, THAT'S JUST GREAT, MARCIE! IF I TRY TO ANSWER A QUESTION, I'M WRONG!
IF I DON'T ANSWER A QUESTION, I'M RIGHT!
THAT'S EDUCATION, SIR!
2-24
SCHULZ

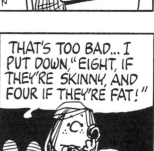

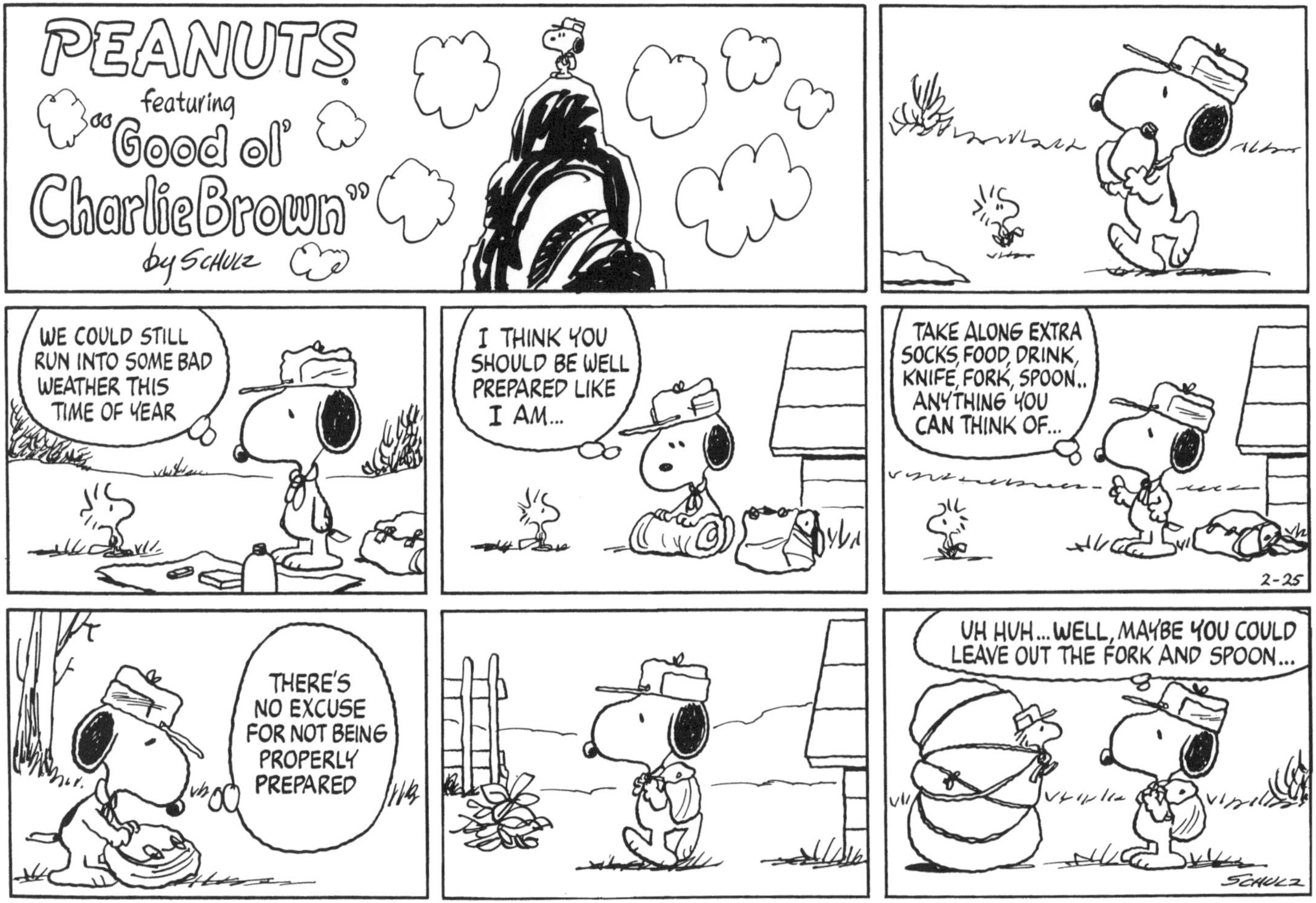
PEANUTS
featuring
"Good ol' CharlieBrown"
by SCHULZ
WE COULD STILL RUN INTO SOME BAD WEATHER THIS TIME OF YEAR
I THINK YOU SHOULD BE WELL PREPARED LIKE I AM...
TAKE ALONG EXTRA SOCKS, FOOD, DRINK, KNIFE, FORK, SPOON.. ANYTHING YOU CAN THINK OF...
2-25
THERE'S NO EXCUSE FOR NOT BEING PROPERLY PREPARED
UH HUH... WELL, MAYBE YOU COULD LEAVE OUT THE FORK AND SPOON...
SCHULZ

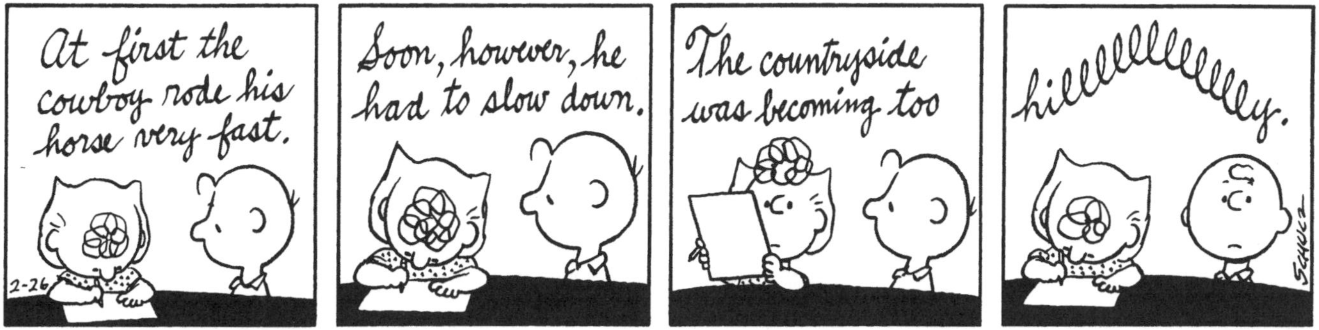
At first the cowboy rode his horse very fast.
Soon, however, he had to slow down.
The countryside was becoming too
hillllllllllly.
2-26
SCHULZ

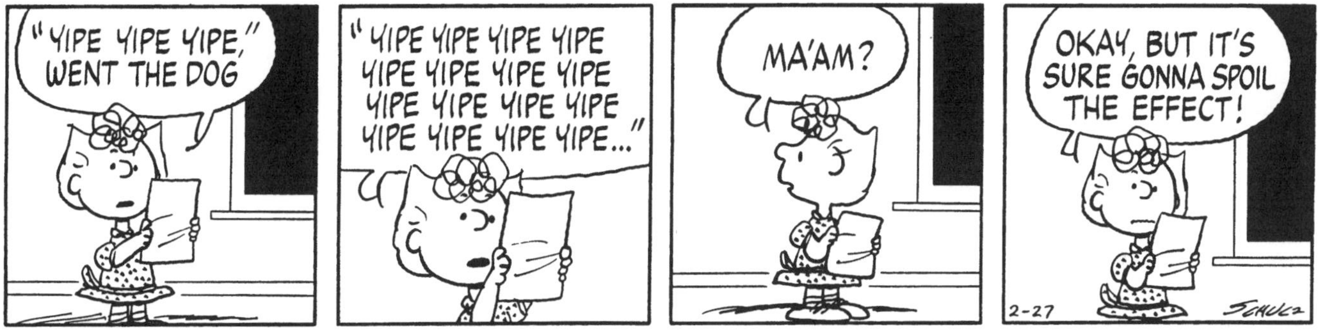
"YIPE YIPE YIPE," WENT THE DOG
"YIPE YIPE YIPE YIPE YIPE YIPE YIPE YIPE YIPE YIPE YIPE YIPE YIPE YIPE YIPE YIPE..."
MA'AM?
OKAY, BUT IT'S SURE GONNA SPOIL THE EFFECT!
2-27
SCHULZ

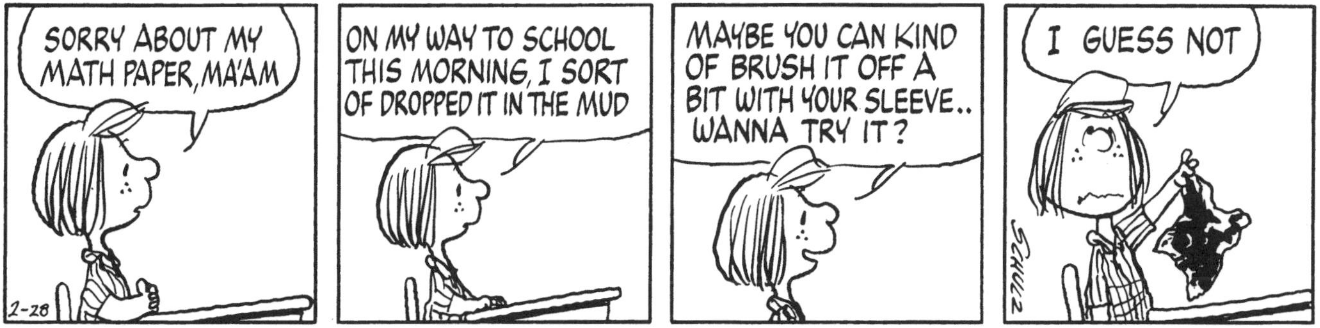
SORRY ABOUT MY MATH PAPER, MA'AM
ON MY WAY TO SCHOOL THIS MORNING, I SORT OF DROPPED IT IN THE MUD
MAYBE YOU CAN KIND OF BRUSH IT OFF A BIT WITH YOUR SLEEVE.. WANNA TRY IT?
I GUESS NOT
2-28
SCHULZ

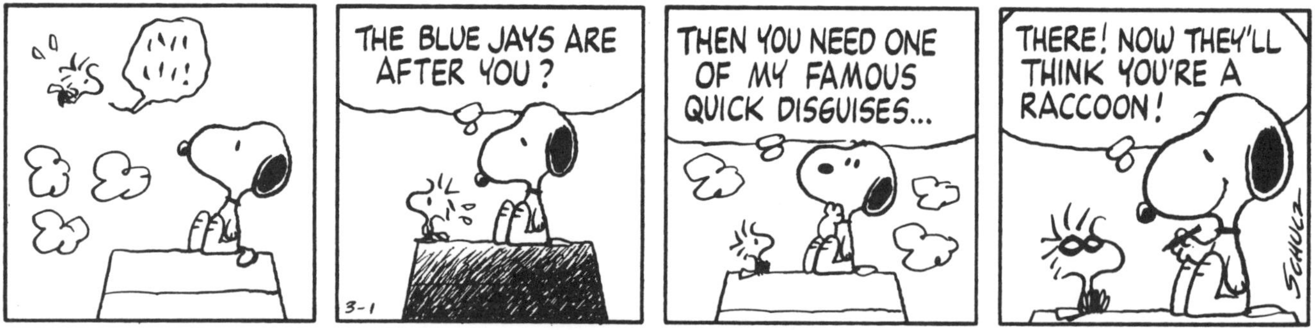
THE BLUE JAYS ARE AFTER YOU ?
3-1
THEN YOU NEED ONE OF MY FAMOUS QUICK DISGUISES...
THERE! NOW THEY'LL THINK YOU'RE A RACCOON!
SCHULZ

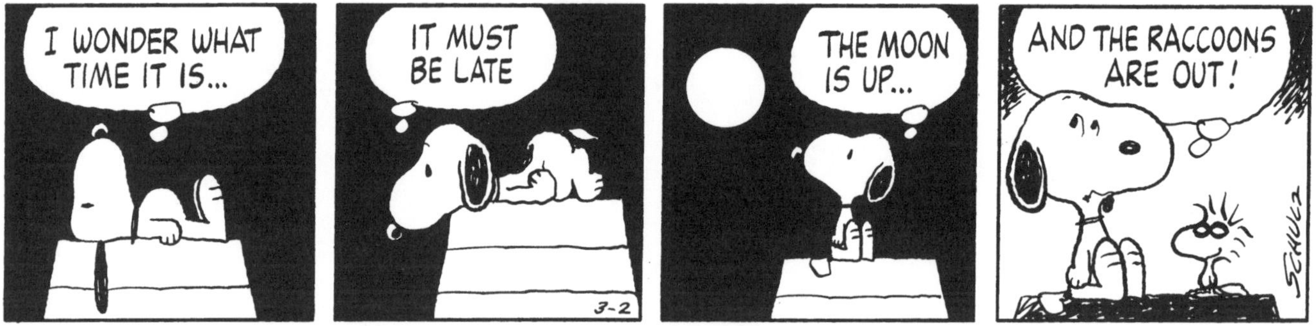
I WONDER WHAT TIME IT IS...
IT MUST BE LATE
3-2
THE MOON IS UP...
AND THE RACCOONS ARE OUT!
SCHULZ

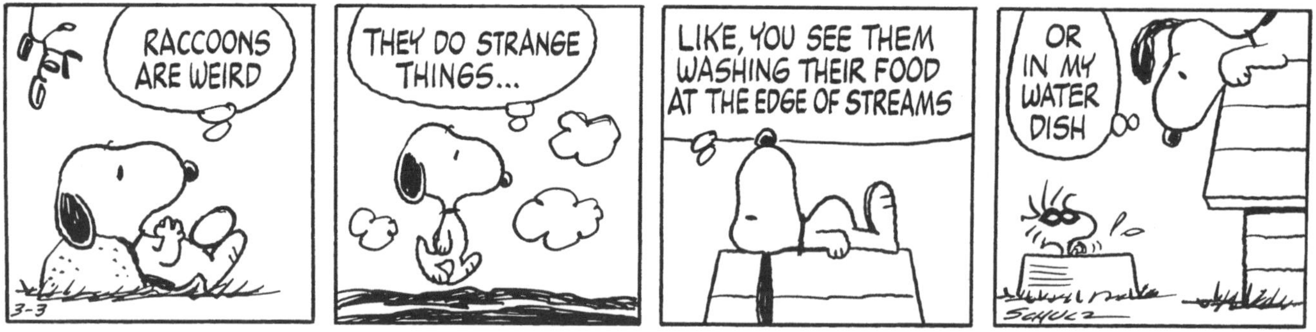
RACCOONS ARE WEIRD
3-3
THEY DO STRANGE THINGS...
LIKE, YOU SEE THEM WASHING THEIR FOOD AT THE EDGE OF STREAMS
OR IN MY WATER DISH
SCHULZ

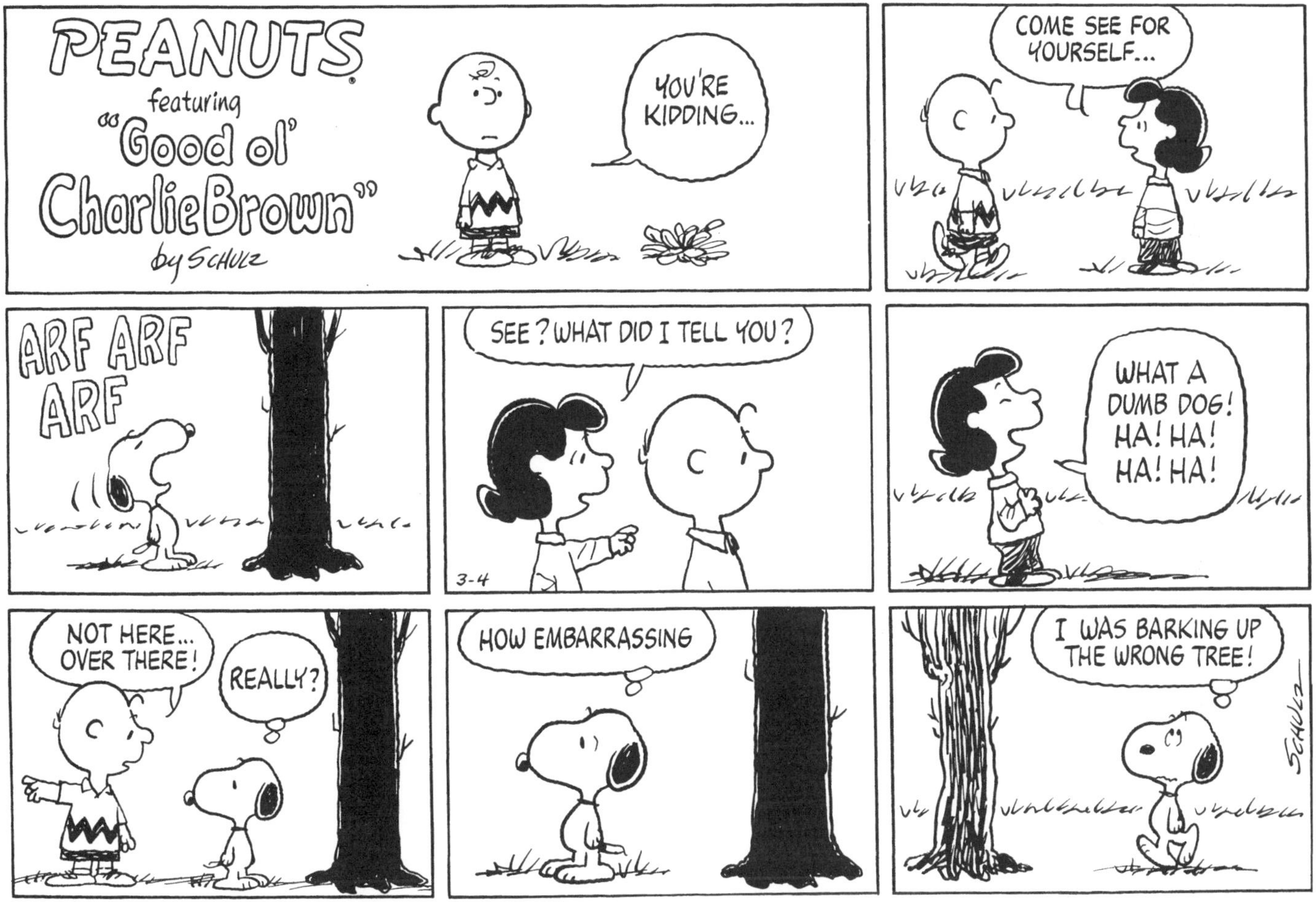
PEANUTS
featuring
"Good ol' CharlieBrown"
by SCHULZ
YOU'RE KIDDING...
COME SEE FOR YOURSELF...
ARF ARF ARF
SEE? WHAT DID I TELL YOU?
3-4
WHAT A DUMB DOG! HA! HA! HA! HA!
NOT HERE... OVER THERE!
REALLY?
HOW EMBARRASSING
I WAS BARKING UP THE WRONG TREE!
SCHULZ

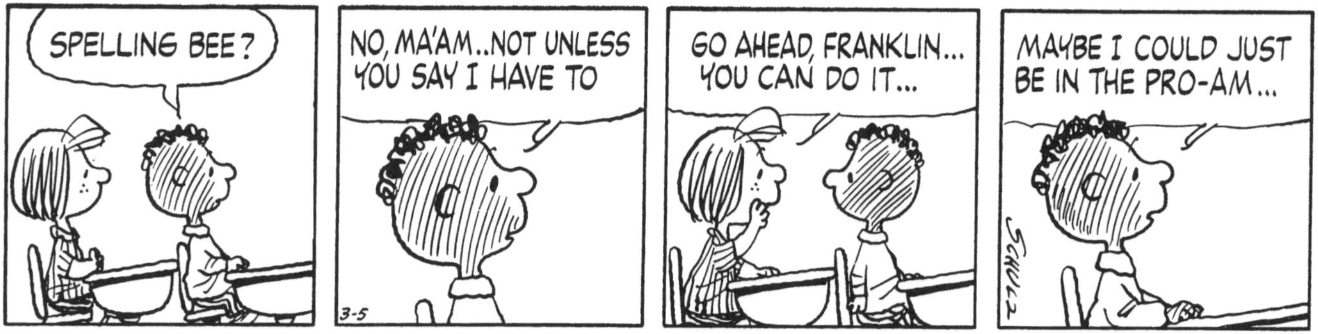
SPELLING BEE?
NO, MA'AM..NOT UNLESS YOU SAY I HAVE TO
3-5
GO AHEAD, FRANKLIN... YOU CAN DO IT...
MAYBE I COULD JUST BE IN THE PRO-AM...

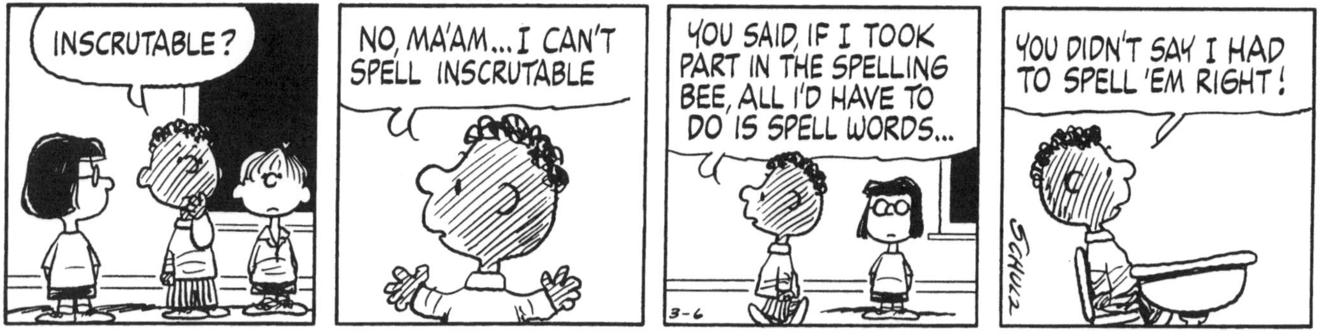
INSCRUTABLE?
NO, MA'AM... I CAN'T SPELL INSCRUTABLE
YOU SAID, IF I TOOK PART IN THE SPELLING BEE, ALL I'D HAVE TO DO IS SPELL WORDS...
3-6
YOU DIDN'T SAY I HAD TO SPELL 'EM RIGHT!

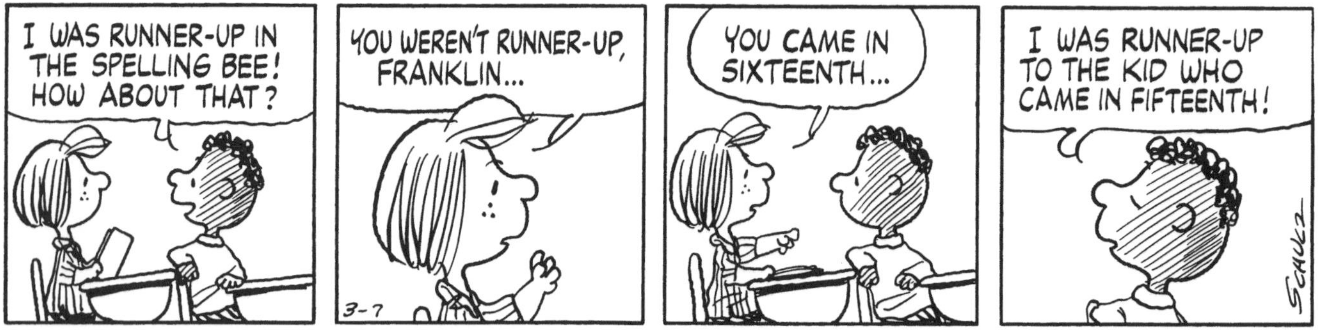
I WAS RUNNER-UP IN THE SPELLING BEE! HOW ABOUT THAT?
YOU WEREN'T RUNNER-UP, FRANKLIN...
3-7
YOU CAME IN SIXTEENTH...
I WAS RUNNER-UP TO THE KID WHO CAME IN FIFTEENTH!

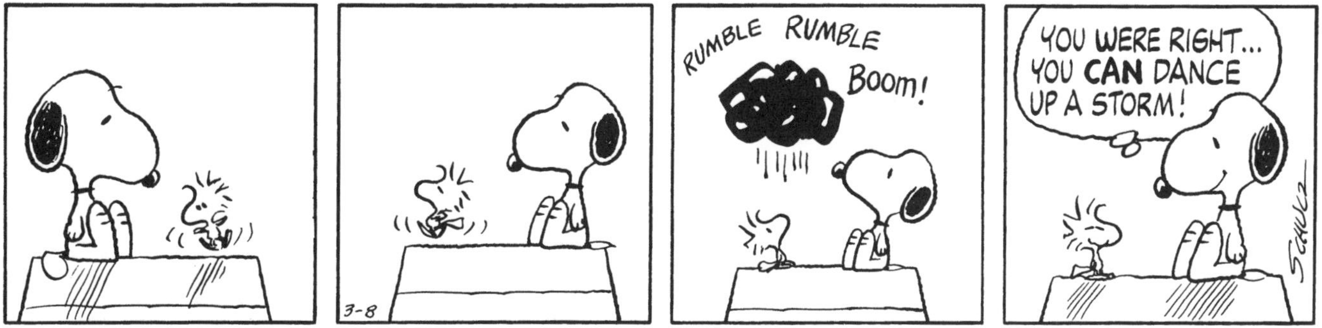
RUMBLE RUMBLE
Boom!
YOU WERE RIGHT... YOU **CAN** DANCE UP A STORM!

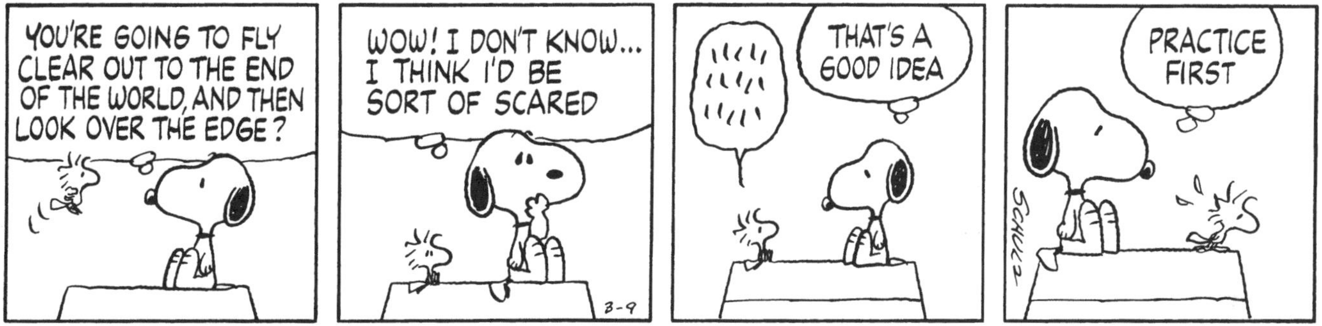
YOU'RE GOING TO FLY CLEAR OUT TO THE END OF THE WORLD, AND THEN LOOK OVER THE EDGE?
WOW! I DON'T KNOW... I THINK I'D BE SORT OF SCARED
THAT'S A GOOD IDEA
PRACTICE FIRST

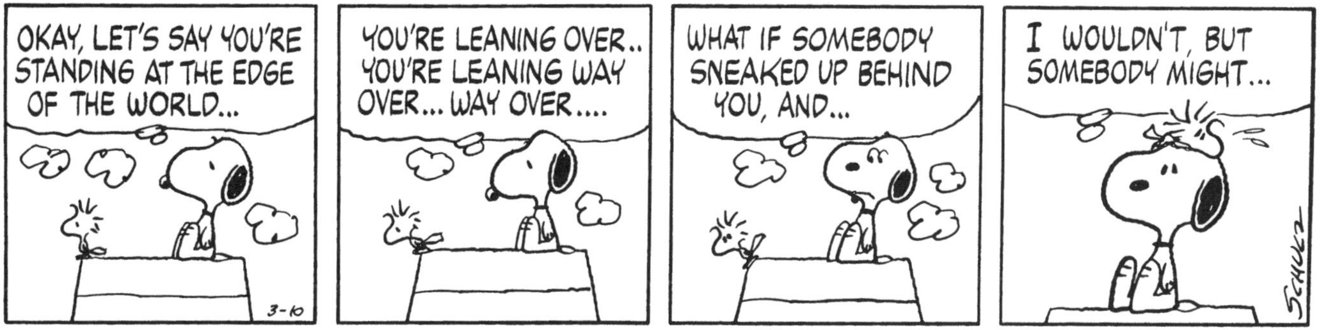
OKAY, LET'S SAY YOU'RE STANDING AT THE EDGE OF THE WORLD...
YOU'RE LEANING OVER.. YOU'RE LEANING WAY OVER... WAY OVER....
WHAT IF SOMEBODY SNEAKED UP BEHIND YOU, AND...
I WOULDN'T, BUT SOMEBODY MIGHT...

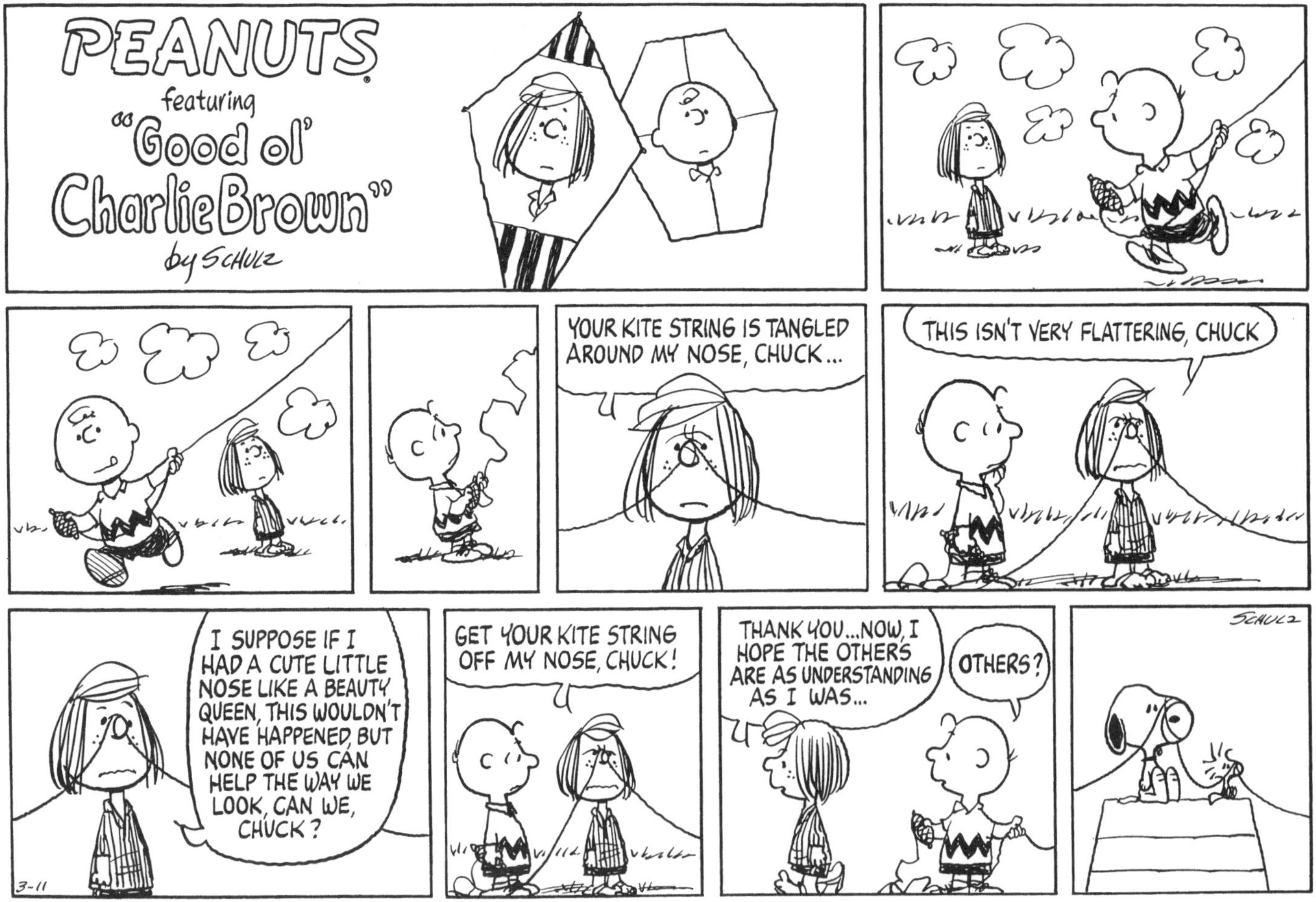
PEANUTS
featuring
"Good ol' Charlie Brown"
by SCHULZ
YOUR KITE STRING IS TANGLED AROUND MY NOSE, CHUCK...
THIS ISN'T VERY FLATTERING, CHUCK
I SUPPOSE IF I HAD A CUTE LITTLE NOSE LIKE A BEAUTY QUEEN, THIS WOULDN'T HAVE HAPPENED, BUT NONE OF US CAN HELP THE WAY WE LOOK, CAN WE, CHUCK?
3-11
GET YOUR KITE STRING OFF MY NOSE, CHUCK!
THANK YOU...NOW, I HOPE THE OTHERS ARE AS UNDERSTANDING AS I WAS...
OTHERS?
SCHULZ

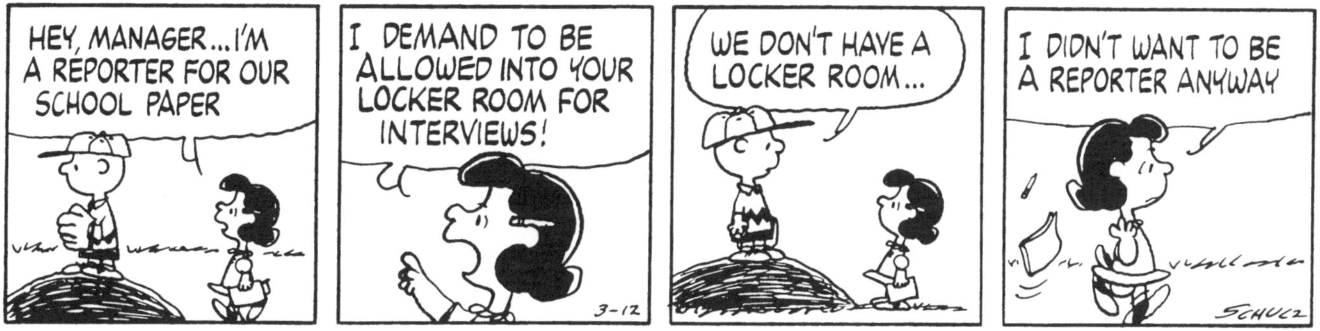
HEY, MANAGER...I'M A REPORTER FOR OUR SCHOOL PAPER
I DEMAND TO BE ALLOWED INTO YOUR LOCKER ROOM FOR INTERVIEWS!
3-12
WE DON'T HAVE A LOCKER ROOM...
I DIDN'T WANT TO BE A REPORTER ANYWAY
SCHULZ

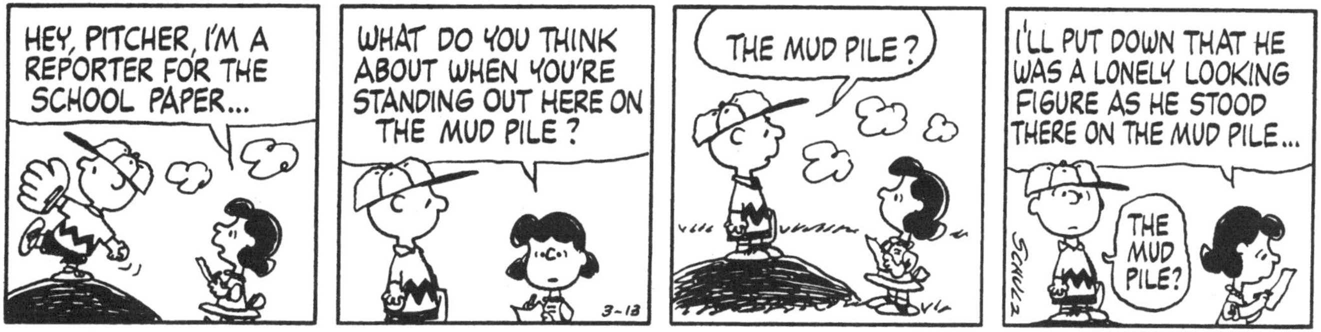
HEY, PITCHER, I'M A REPORTER FOR THE SCHOOL PAPER...
WHAT DO YOU THINK ABOUT WHEN YOU'RE STANDING OUT HERE ON THE MUD PILE?
3-13
THE MUD PILE?
I'LL PUT DOWN THAT HE WAS A LONELY LOOKING FIGURE AS HE STOOD THERE ON THE MUD PILE...
THE MUD PILE?
SCHULZ

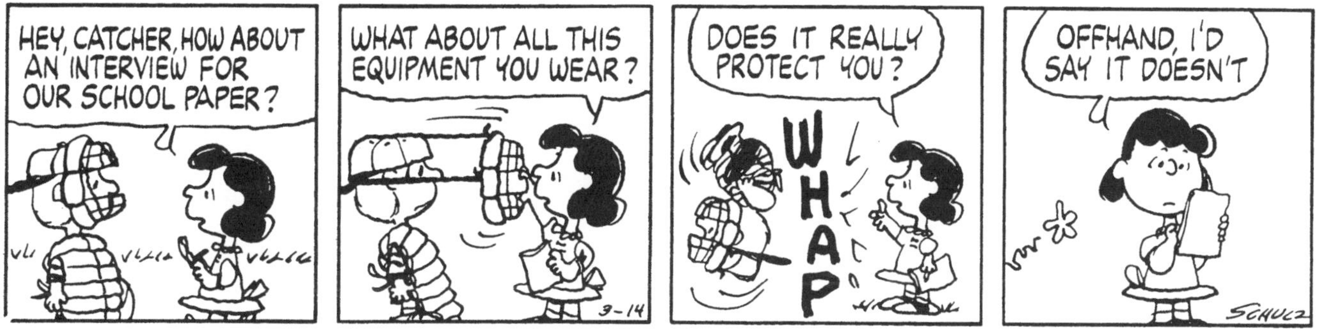
HEY, CATCHER, HOW ABOUT AN INTERVIEW FOR OUR SCHOOL PAPER?
WHAT ABOUT ALL THIS EQUIPMENT YOU WEAR?
3-14
DOES IT REALLY PROTECT YOU?
WHAP
OFFHAND, I'D SAY IT DOESN'T
SCHULZ

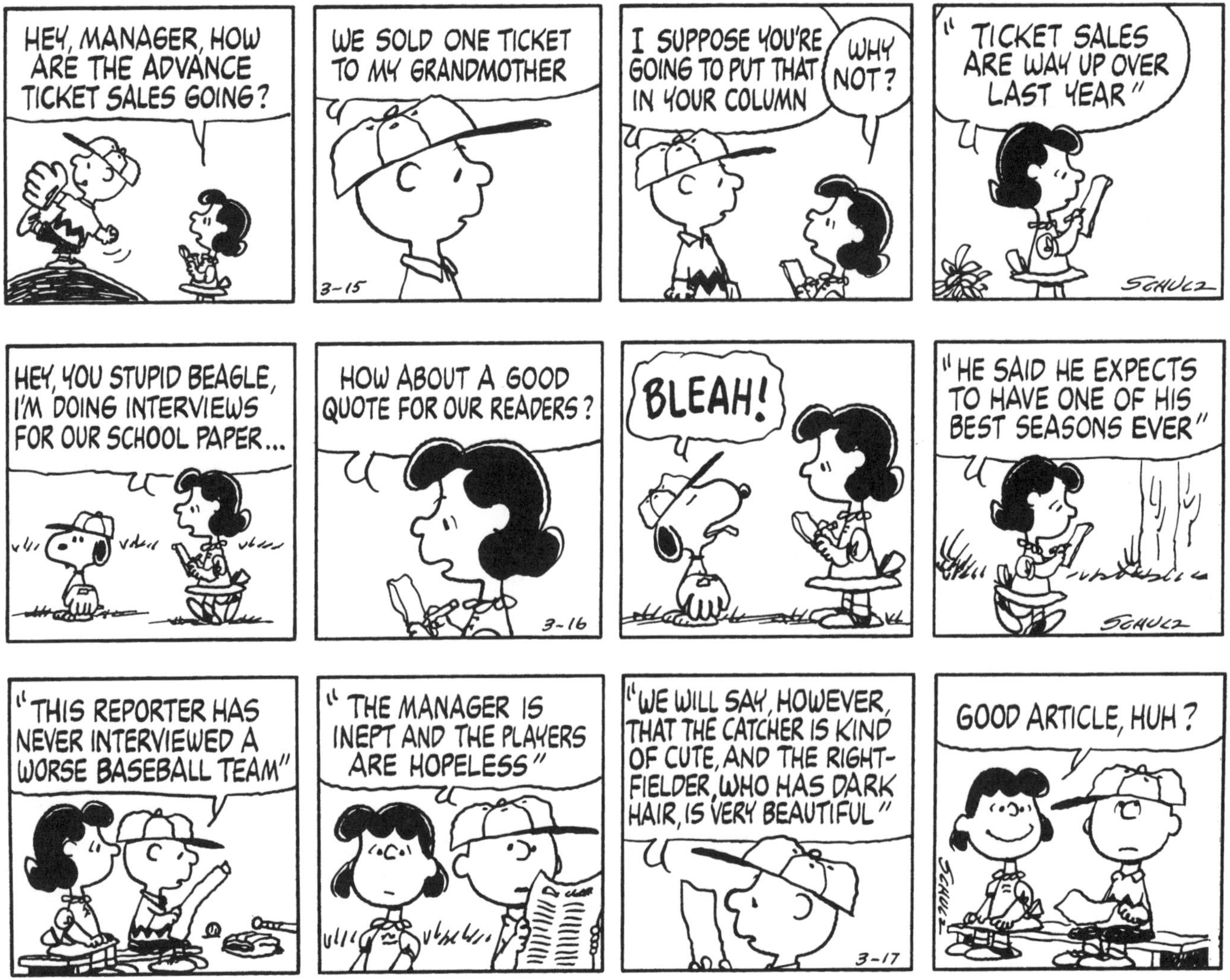
HEY, MANAGER, HOW ARE THE ADVANCE TICKET SALES GOING?
WE SOLD ONE TICKET TO MY GRANDMOTHER
I SUPPOSE YOU'RE GOING TO PUT THAT IN YOUR COLUMN
WHY NOT?
"TICKET SALES ARE WAY UP OVER LAST YEAR"
3-15
SCHULZ
HEY, YOU STUPID BEAGLE, I'M DOING INTERVIEWS FOR OUR SCHOOL PAPER...
HOW ABOUT A GOOD QUOTE FOR OUR READERS?
BLEAH!
"HE SAID HE EXPECTS TO HAVE ONE OF HIS BEST SEASONS EVER"
3-16
SCHULZ
"THIS REPORTER HAS NEVER INTERVIEWED A WORSE BASEBALL TEAM"
"THE MANAGER IS INEPT AND THE PLAYERS ARE HOPELESS"
"WE WILL SAY, HOWEVER, THAT THE CATCHER IS KIND OF CUTE, AND THE RIGHT-FIELDER, WHO HAS DARK HAIR, IS VERY BEAUTIFUL"
GOOD ARTICLE, HUH?
3-17
SCHULZ

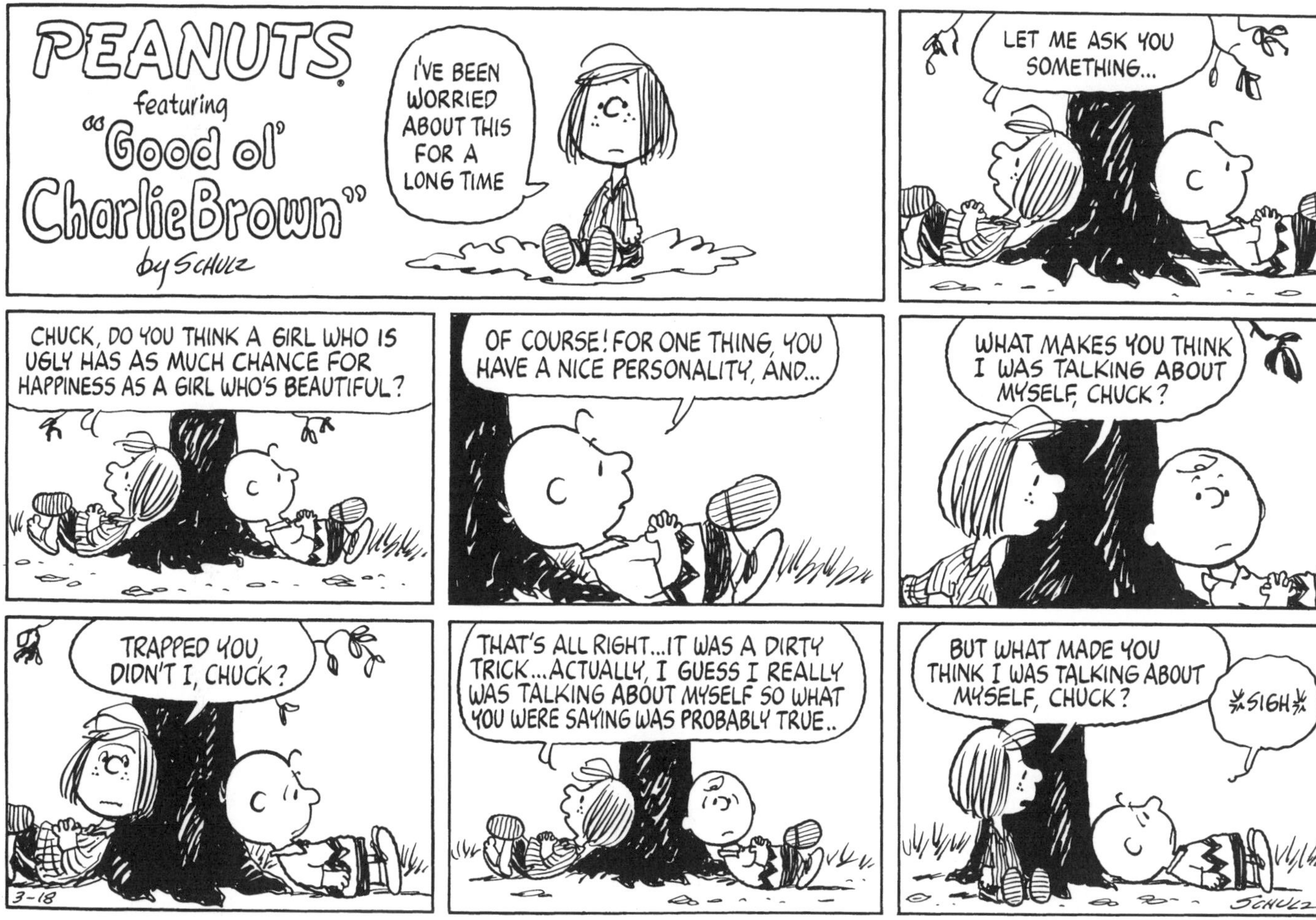
PEANUTS
featuring
"Good ol' CharlieBrown"
by SCHULZ
I'VE BEEN WORRIED ABOUT THIS FOR A LONG TIME
LET ME ASK YOU SOMETHING...
CHUCK, DO YOU THINK A GIRL WHO IS UGLY HAS AS MUCH CHANCE FOR HAPPINESS AS A GIRL WHO'S BEAUTIFUL?
OF COURSE! FOR ONE THING, YOU HAVE A NICE PERSONALITY, AND...
WHAT MAKES YOU THINK I WAS TALKING ABOUT MYSELF, CHUCK?
TRAPPED YOU, DIDN'T I, CHUCK?
3-18
THAT'S ALL RIGHT...IT WAS A DIRTY TRICK...ACTUALLY, I GUESS I REALLY WAS TALKING ABOUT MYSELF SO WHAT YOU WERE SAYING WAS PROBABLY TRUE..
BUT WHAT MADE YOU THINK I WAS TALKING ABOUT MYSELF, CHUCK?
SIGH
SCHULZ

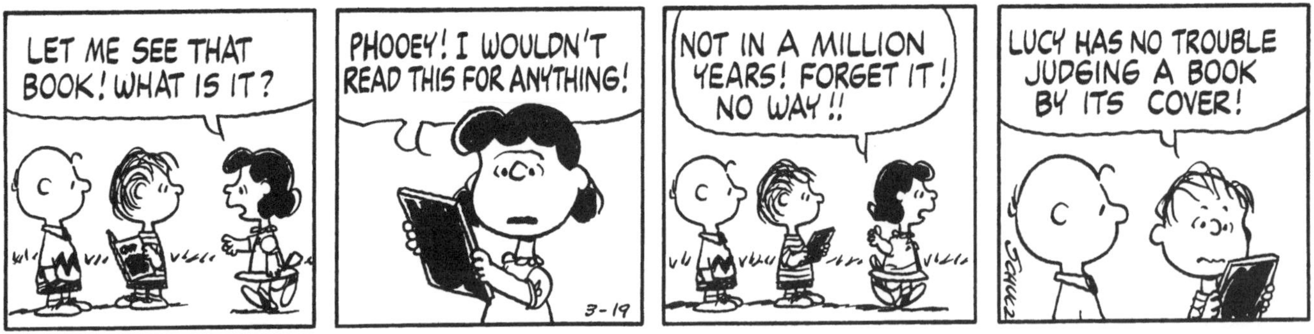
LET ME SEE THAT BOOK! WHAT IS IT?
PHOOEY! I WOULDN'T READ THIS FOR ANYTHING!
3-19
NOT IN A MILLION YEARS! FORGET IT! NO WAY!!
LUCY HAS NO TROUBLE JUDGING A BOOK BY ITS COVER!
SCHULZ

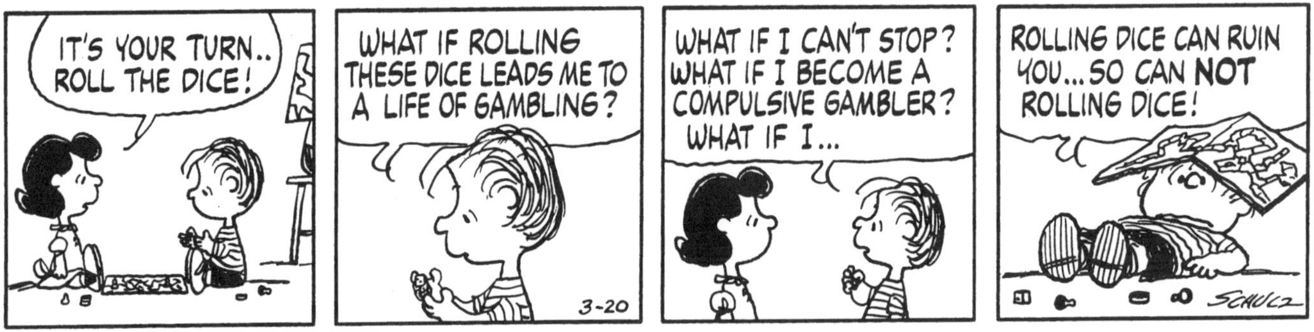
IT'S YOUR TURN.. ROLL THE DICE!
WHAT IF ROLLING THESE DICE LEADS ME TO A LIFE OF GAMBLING?
3-20
WHAT IF I CAN'T STOP? WHAT IF I BECOME A COMPULSIVE GAMBLER? WHAT IF I...
ROLLING DICE CAN RUIN YOU...SO CAN **NOT** ROLLING DICE!
SCHULZ

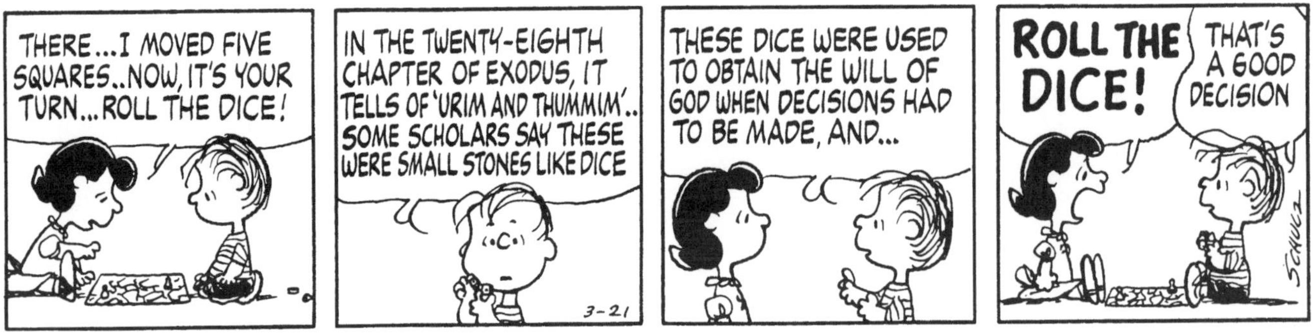
THERE...I MOVED FIVE SQUARES..NOW, IT'S YOUR TURN...ROLL THE DICE!
IN THE TWENTY-EIGHTH CHAPTER OF EXODUS, IT TELLS OF 'URIM AND THUMMIM'.. SOME SCHOLARS SAY THESE WERE SMALL STONES LIKE DICE
3-21
THESE DICE WERE USED TO OBTAIN THE WILL OF GOD WHEN DECISIONS HAD TO BE MADE, AND...
ROLL THE DICE!
THAT'S A GOOD DECISION
SCHULZ

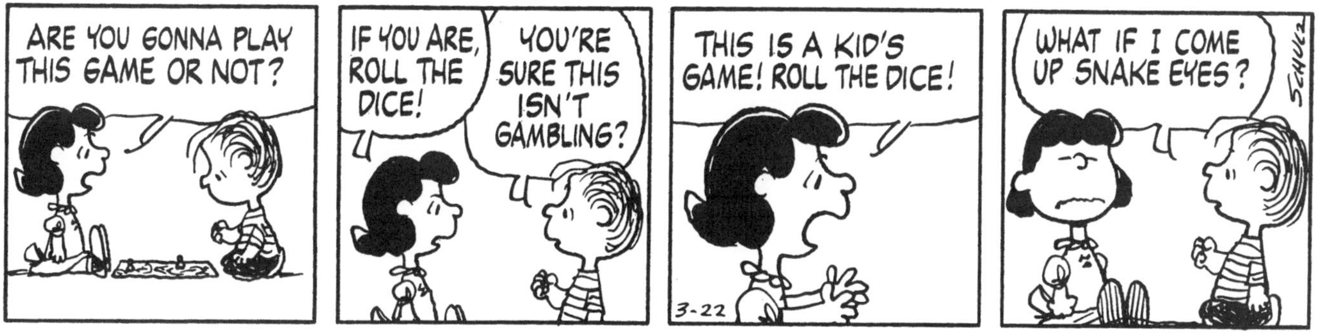
ARE YOU GONNA PLAY THIS GAME OR NOT?
IF YOU ARE, ROLL THE DICE!
YOU'RE SURE THIS ISN'T GAMBLING?
THIS IS A KID'S GAME! ROLL THE DICE!
3-22
WHAT IF I COME UP SNAKE EYES?
SCHULZ

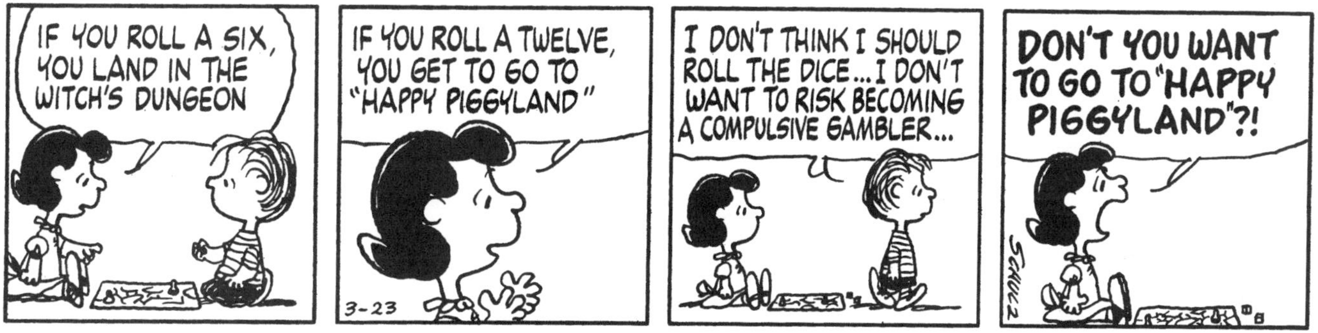
IF YOU ROLL A SIX, YOU LAND IN THE WITCH'S DUNGEON
IF YOU ROLL A TWELVE, YOU GET TO GO TO "HAPPY PIGGYLAND"
3-23
I DON'T THINK I SHOULD ROLL THE DICE... I DON'T WANT TO RISK BECOMING A COMPULSIVE GAMBLER...
DON'T YOU WANT TO GO TO "HAPPY PIGGYLAND"?!
SCHULZ

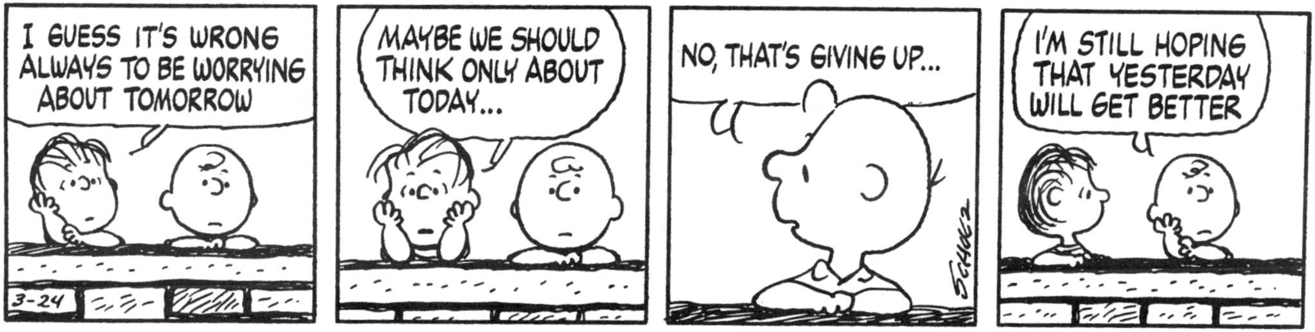
I GUESS IT'S WRONG ALWAYS TO BE WORRYING ABOUT TOMORROW
3-24
MAYBE WE SHOULD THINK ONLY ABOUT TODAY...
NO, THAT'S GIVING UP...
SCHULZ
I'M STILL HOPING THAT YESTERDAY WILL GET BETTER

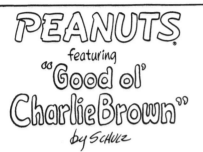

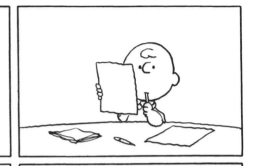

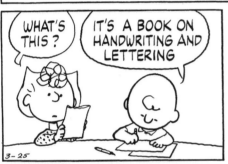

PEANUTS
featuring
"Good ol' Charlie Brown"
by SCHULZ
a c d g a c a g
e e e m n h n
r k r k f j s x x
WHAT'S THIS ?
IT'S A BOOK ON HANDWRITING AND LETTERING
3-25
" AFTER PRACTICING THE CORRECT HAND MOVEMENTS WITH A PENCIL, YOU ARE NOW READY FOR PEN AND INK "
" AS AN AID TO SPEED, YOU WILL NOTE THAT SOME LETTERS ARE JOINED OR LINKED TOGETHER "
" DURING PRACTICE, HOWEVER, IT IS BEST NOT TO TRY TO LINK UP CERTAIN LETTERS..."
I THINK YOU LINKED THEM UP!
SCHULZ

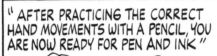

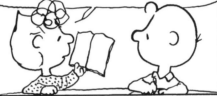

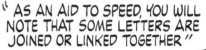

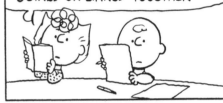

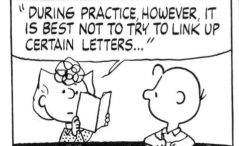

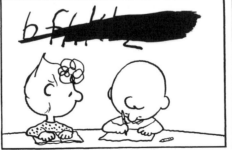

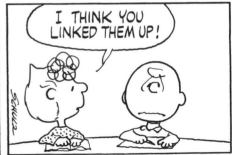

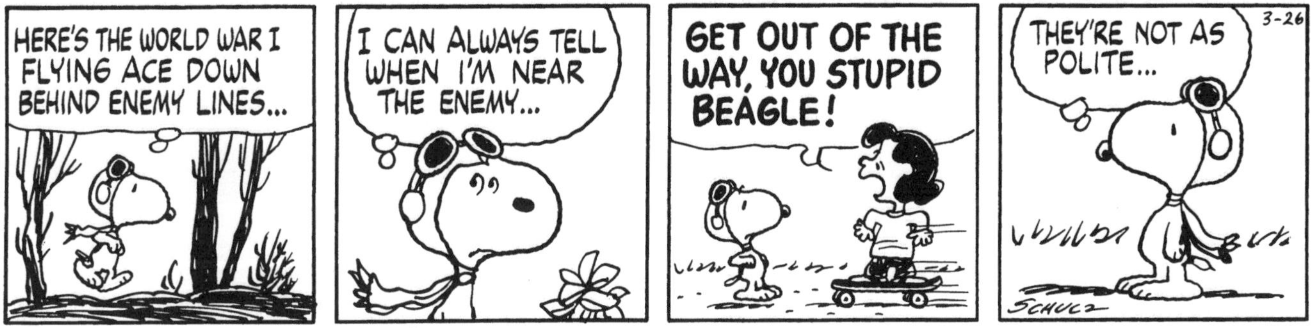
HERE'S THE WORLD WAR I FLYING ACE DOWN BEHIND ENEMY LINES...
I CAN ALWAYS TELL WHEN I'M NEAR THE ENEMY...
GET OUT OF THE WAY, YOU STUPID BEAGLE!
THEY'RE NOT AS POLITE...
3-26
SCHULZ

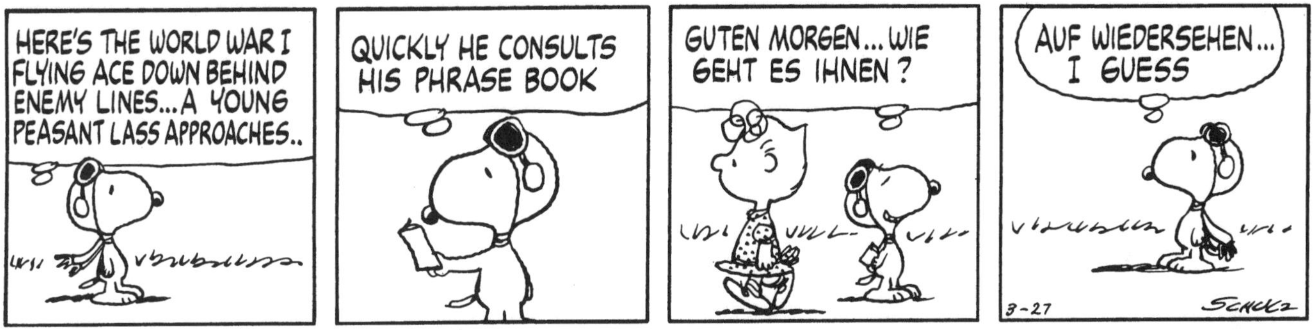
HERE'S THE WORLD WAR I FLYING ACE DOWN BEHIND ENEMY LINES...A YOUNG PEASANT LASS APPROACHES..
QUICKLY HE CONSULTS HIS PHRASE BOOK
GUTEN MORGEN...WIE GEHT ES IHNEN?
AUF WIEDERSEHEN... I GUESS
3-27
SCHULZ

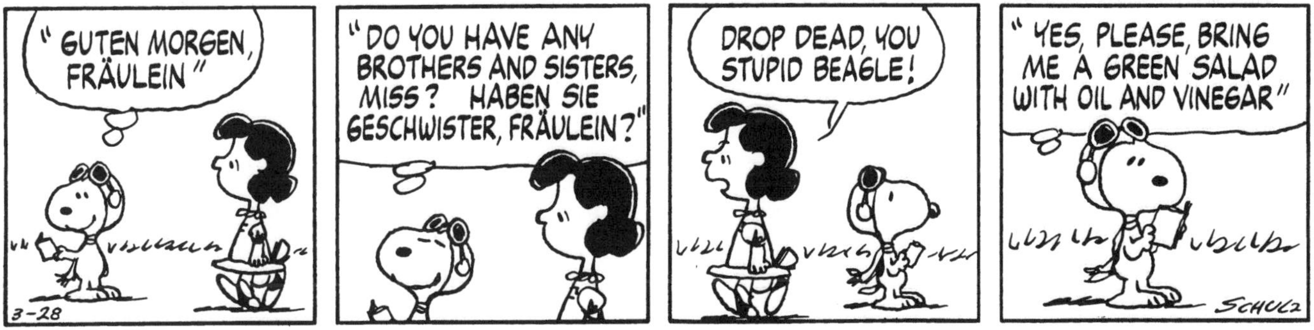
"GUTEN MORGEN, FRÄULEIN"
"DO YOU HAVE ANY BROTHERS AND SISTERS, MISS? HABEN SIE GESCHWISTER, FRÄULEIN?"
DROP DEAD, YOU STUPID BEAGLE!
"YES, PLEASE, BRING ME A GREEN SALAD WITH OIL AND VINEGAR"
3-28
SCHULZ

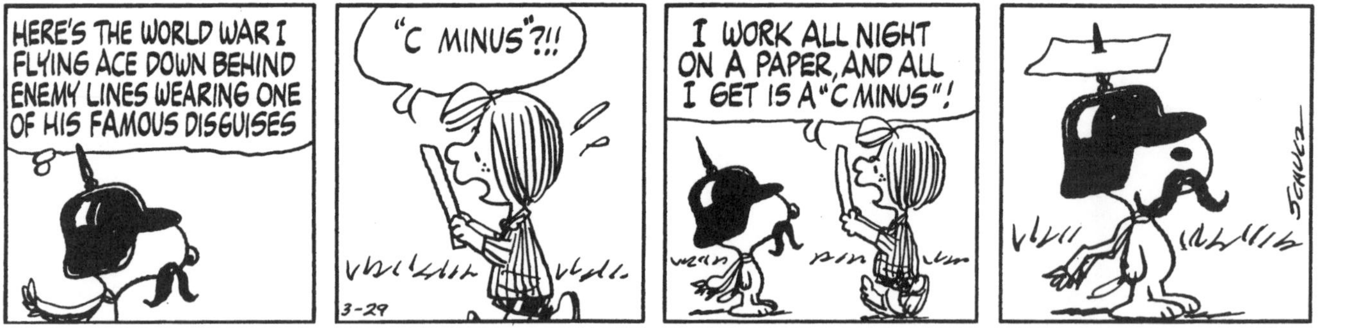
HERE'S THE WORLD WAR I FLYING ACE DOWN BEHIND ENEMY LINES WEARING ONE OF HIS FAMOUS DISGUISES
"C MINUS"?!!
3-29
I WORK ALL NIGHT ON A PAPER, AND ALL I GET IS A "C MINUS"!
SCHULZ

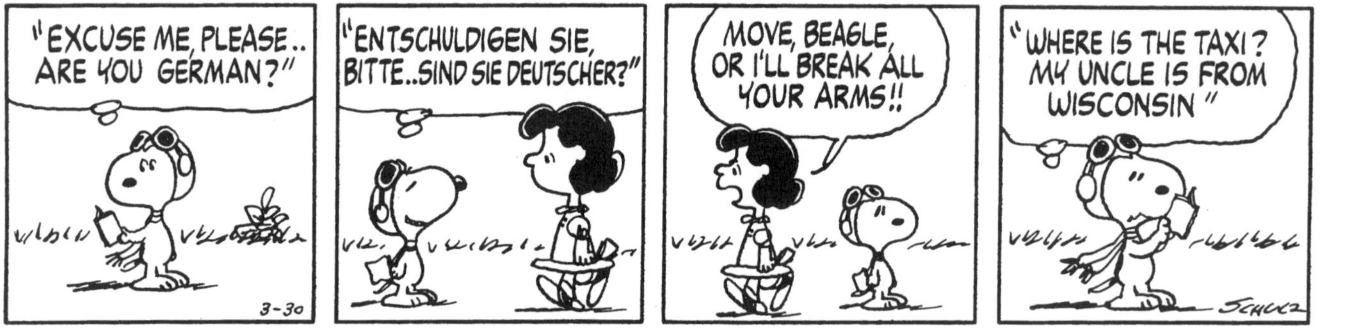
"EXCUSE ME, PLEASE.. ARE YOU GERMAN?"
3-30
"ENTSCHULDIGEN SIE, BITTE..SIND SIE DEUTSCHER?"
MOVE, BEAGLE, OR I'LL BREAK ALL YOUR ARMS!!
"WHERE IS THE TAXI? MY UNCLE IS FROM WISCONSIN"
SCHULZ

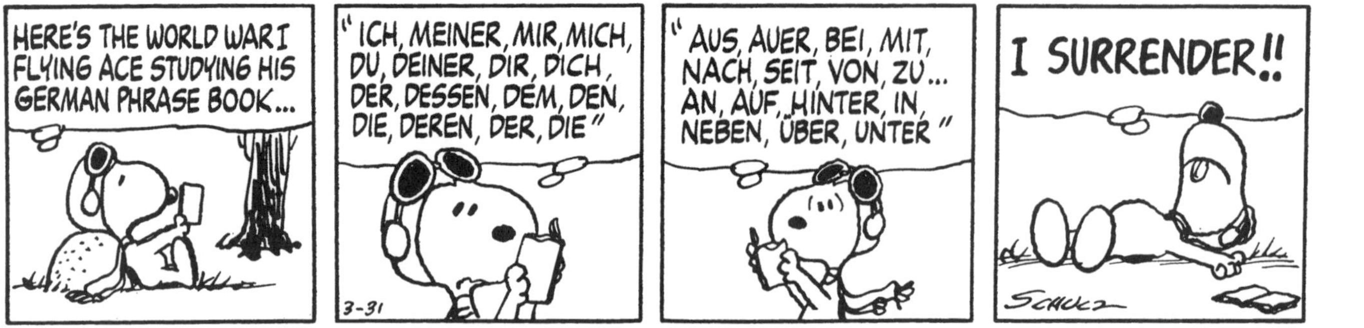
HERE'S THE WORLD WAR I FLYING ACE STUDYING HIS GERMAN PHRASE BOOK...
"ICH, MEINER, MIR, MICH, DU, DEINER, DIR, DICH, DER, DESSEN, DEM, DEN, DIE, DEREN, DER, DIE"
3-31
"AUS, AUER, BEI, MIT, NACH, SEIT, VON, ZU... AN, AUF, HINTER, IN, NEBEN, ÜBER, UNTER"
I SURRENDER!!
SCHULZ

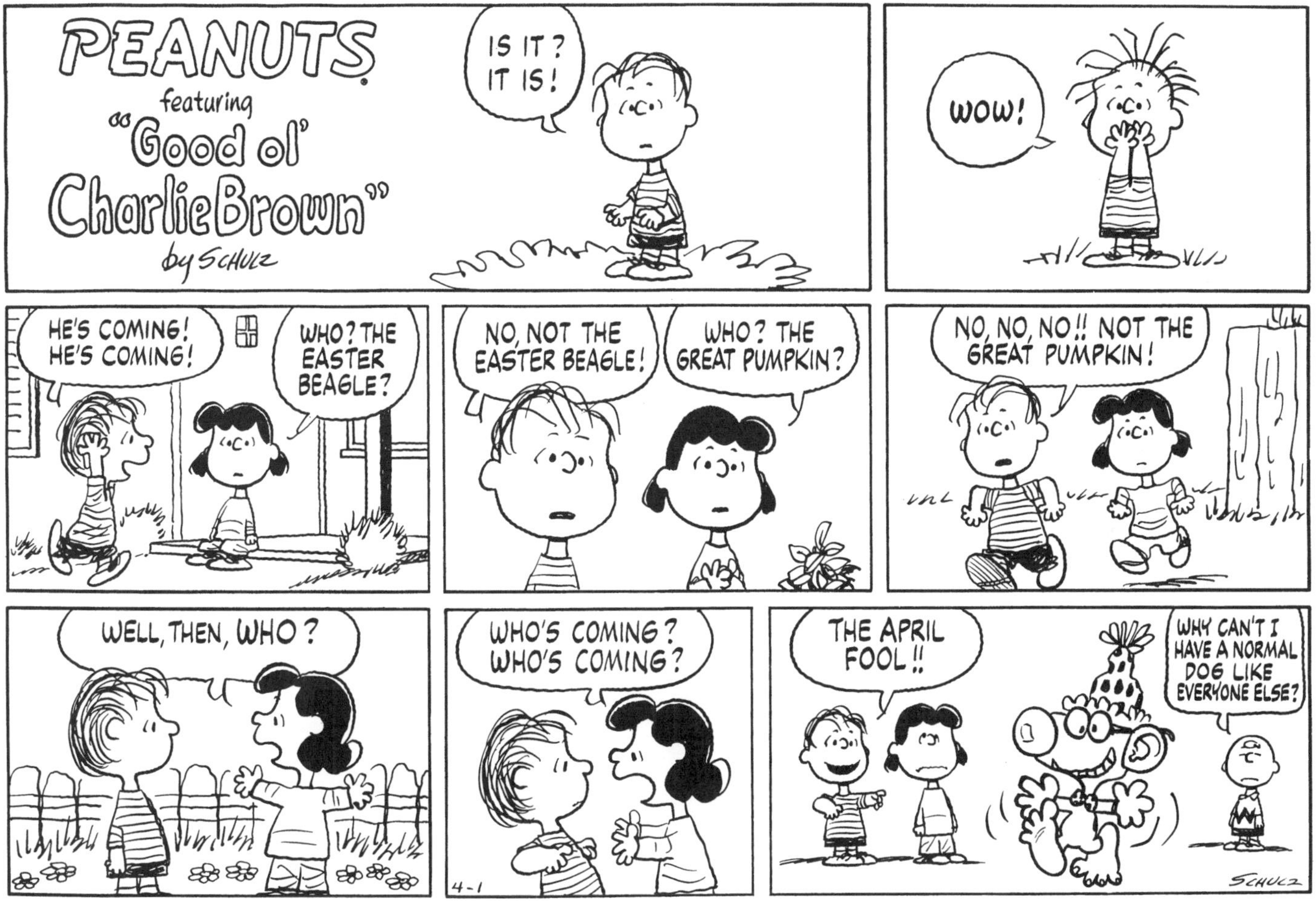
PEANUTS
featuring "Good ol' Charlie Brown"
by SCHULZ
IS IT? IT IS!
WOW!
HE'S COMING! HE'S COMING!
WHO? THE EASTER BEAGLE?
NO, NOT THE EASTER BEAGLE!
WHO? THE GREAT PUMPKIN?
NO, NO, NO!! NOT THE GREAT PUMPKIN!
WELL, THEN, WHO?
WHO'S COMING? WHO'S COMING?
4-1
THE APRIL FOOL!!
WHY CAN'T I HAVE A NORMAL DOG LIKE EVERYONE ELSE?
SCHULZ

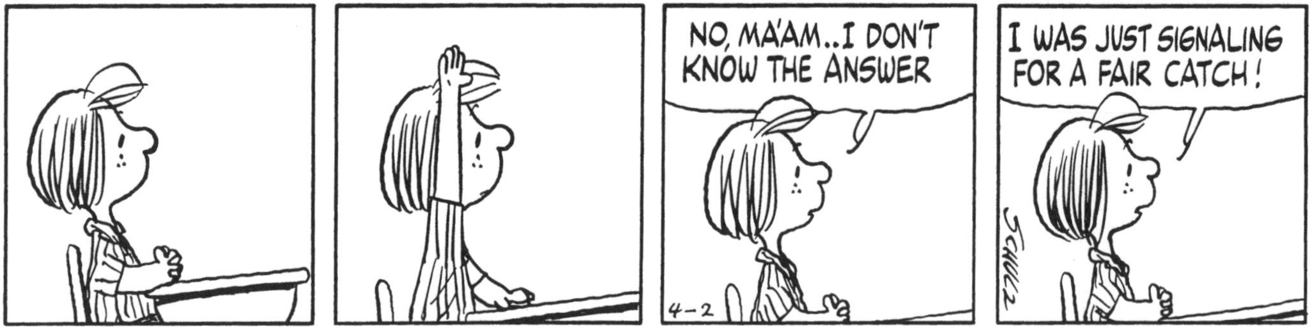
NO, MA'AM..I DON'T KNOW THE ANSWER
I WAS JUST SIGNALING FOR A FAIR CATCH!

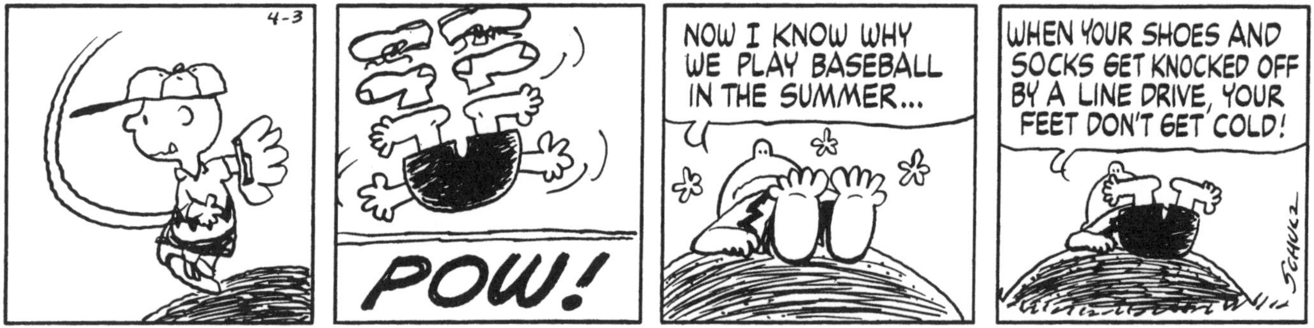
POW!
NOW I KNOW WHY WE PLAY BASEBALL IN THE SUMMER...
WHEN YOUR SHOES AND SOCKS GET KNOCKED OFF BY A LINE DRIVE, YOUR FEET DON'T GET COLD!

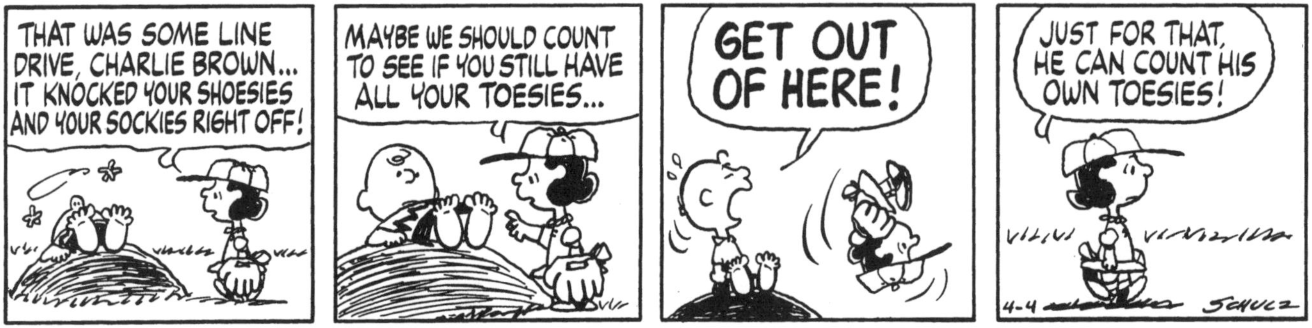
THAT WAS SOME LINE DRIVE, CHARLIE BROWN... IT KNOCKED YOUR SHOESIES AND YOUR SOCKIES RIGHT OFF!
MAYBE WE SHOULD COUNT TO SEE IF YOU STILL HAVE ALL YOUR TOESIES...
GET OUT OF HERE!
JUST FOR THAT, HE CAN COUNT HIS OWN TOESIES!

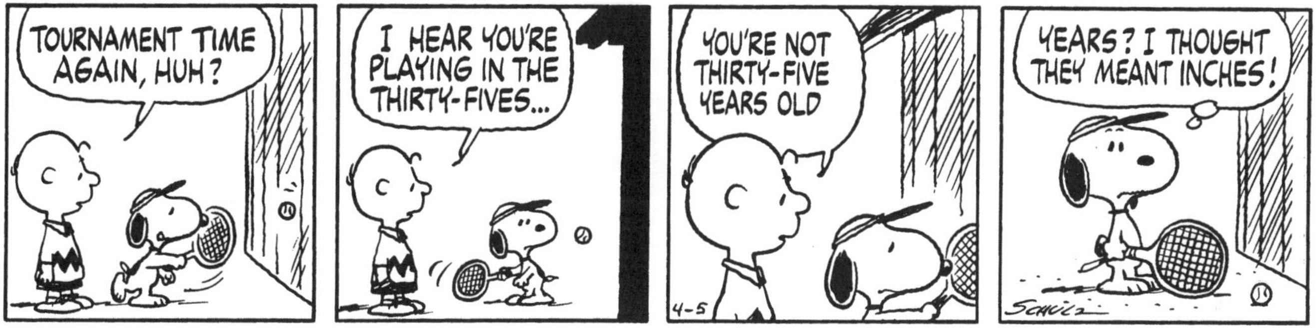
TOURNAMENT TIME AGAIN, HUH?
I HEAR YOU'RE PLAYING IN THE THIRTY-FIVES...
YOU'RE NOT THIRTY-FIVE YEARS OLD
YEARS? I THOUGHT THEY MEANT INCHES!
4-5

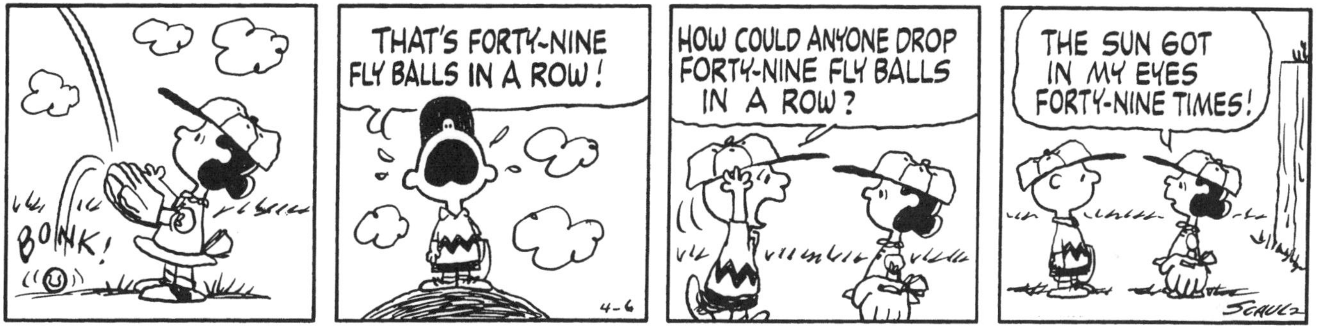
BONK!
THAT'S FORTY-NINE FLY BALLS IN A ROW!
4-6
HOW COULD ANYONE DROP FORTY-NINE FLY BALLS IN A ROW?
THE SUN GOT IN MY EYES FORTY-NINE TIMES!

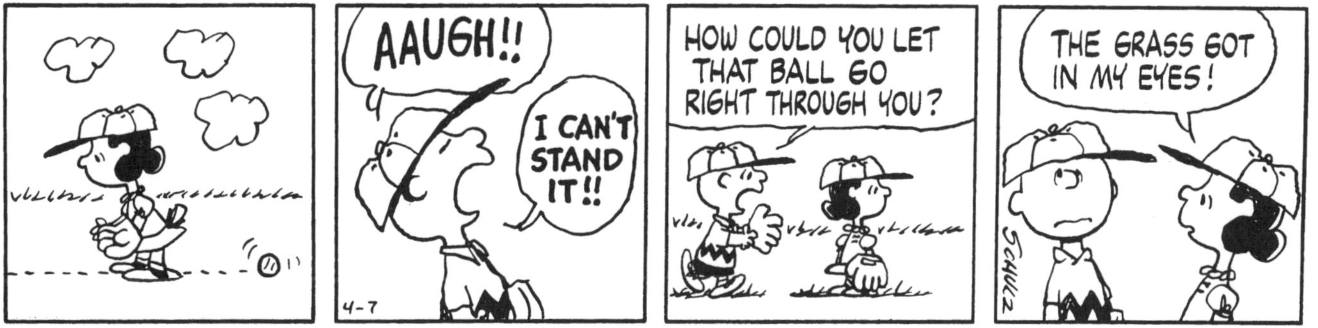
AAUGH!!
I CAN'T STAND IT!!
4-7
HOW COULD YOU LET THAT BALL GO RIGHT THROUGH YOU?
THE GRASS GOT IN MY EYES!

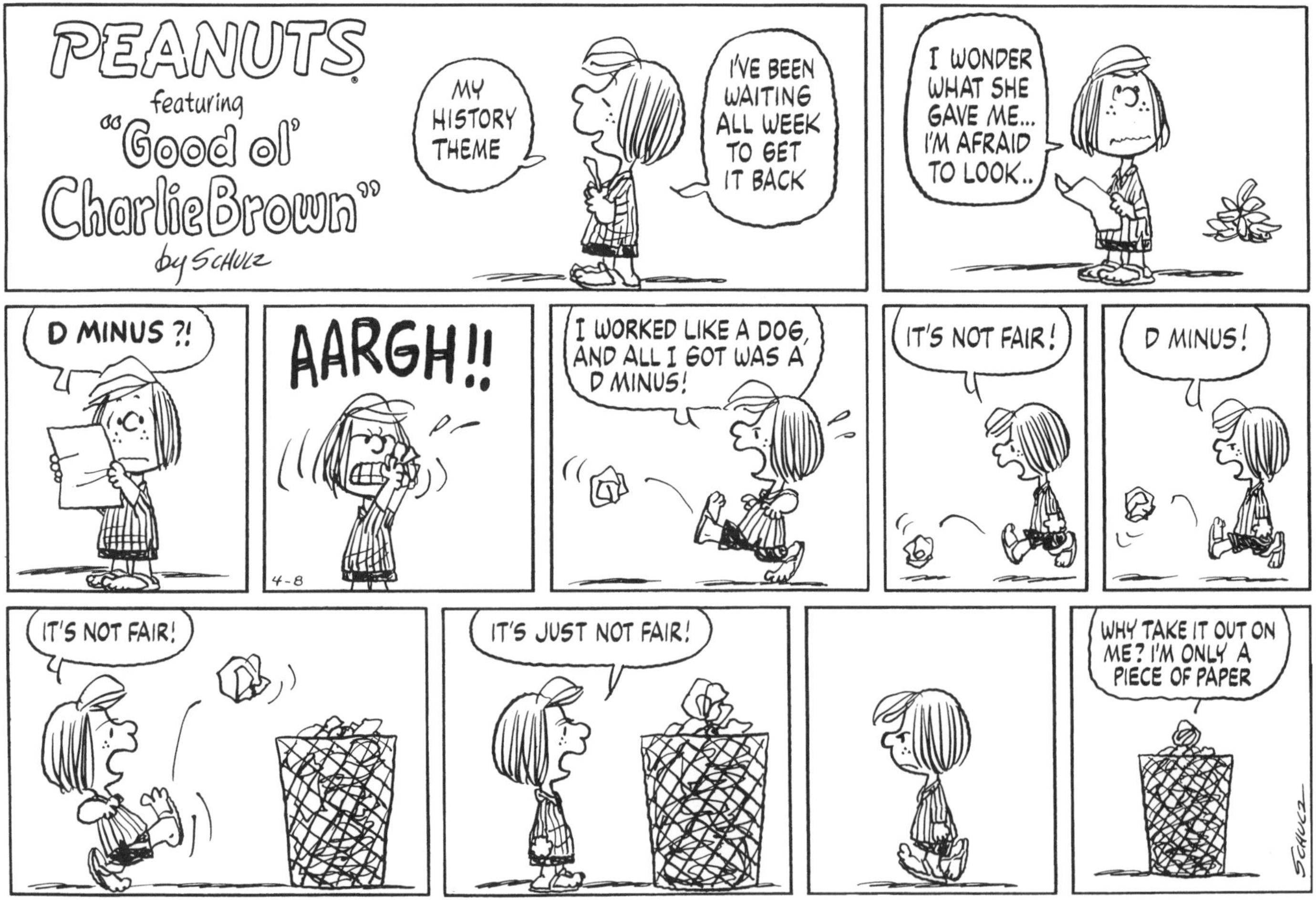
PEANUTS
featuring "Good ol' Charlie Brown"
by SCHULZ
MY HISTORY THEME
I'VE BEEN WAITING ALL WEEK TO GET IT BACK
I WONDER WHAT SHE GAVE ME... I'M AFRAID TO LOOK..
D MINUS ?!
AARGH!!
4-8
I WORKED LIKE A DOG, AND ALL I GOT WAS A D MINUS!
IT'S NOT FAIR!
D MINUS!
IT'S NOT FAIR!
IT'S JUST NOT FAIR!
WHY TAKE IT OUT ON ME? I'M ONLY A PIECE OF PAPER
SCHULZ

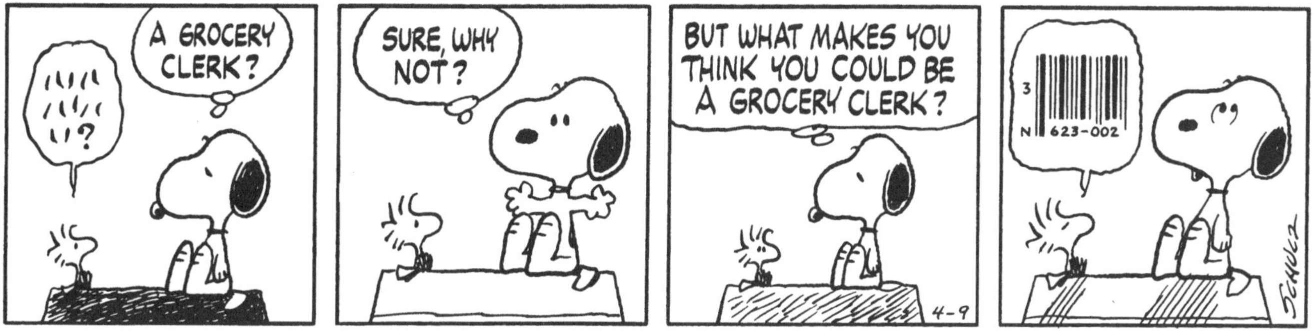
A GROCERY CLERK?
SURE, WHY NOT?
BUT WHAT MAKES YOU THINK YOU COULD BE A GROCERY CLERK?
3
N 623-002
4-9
SCHULZ

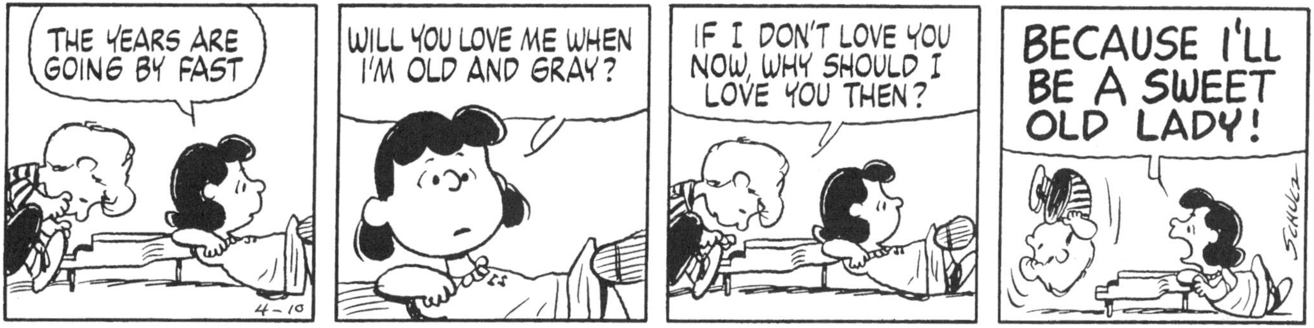
THE YEARS ARE GOING BY FAST
4-10
WILL YOU LOVE ME WHEN I'M OLD AND GRAY?
IF I DON'T LOVE YOU NOW, WHY SHOULD I LOVE YOU THEN?
BECAUSE I'LL BE A SWEET OLD LADY!
SCHULZ

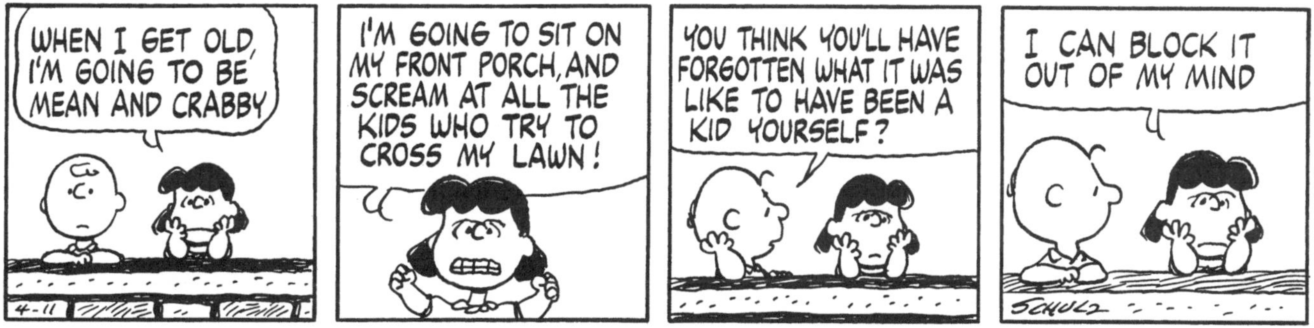
WHEN I GET OLD, I'M GOING TO BE MEAN AND CRABBY
4-11
I'M GOING TO SIT ON MY FRONT PORCH, AND SCREAM AT ALL THE KIDS WHO TRY TO CROSS MY LAWN!
YOU THINK YOU'LL HAVE FORGOTTEN WHAT IT WAS LIKE TO HAVE BEEN A KID YOURSELF?
I CAN BLOCK IT OUT OF MY MIND
SCHULZ

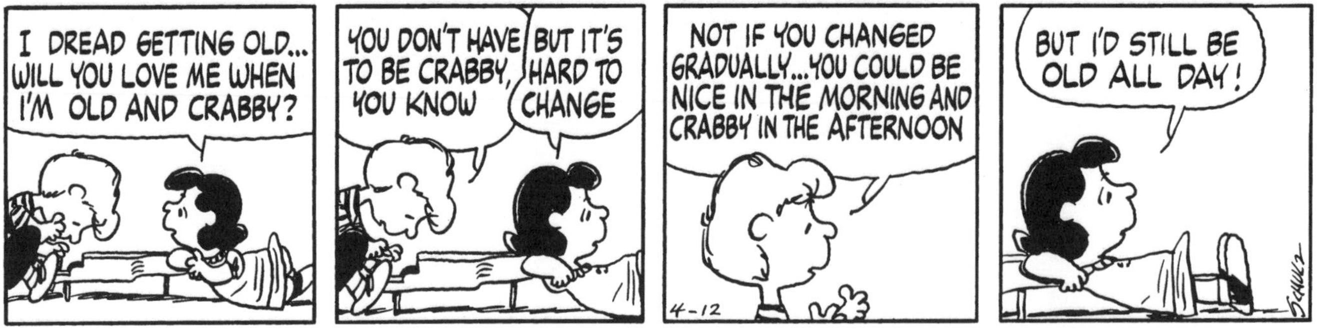
I DREAD GETTING OLD... WILL YOU LOVE ME WHEN I'M OLD AND CRABBY?
YOU DON'T HAVE TO BE CRABBY, YOU KNOW
BUT IT'S HARD TO CHANGE
NOT IF YOU CHANGED GRADUALLY...YOU COULD BE NICE IN THE MORNING AND CRABBY IN THE AFTERNOON
4-12
BUT I'D STILL BE OLD ALL DAY!

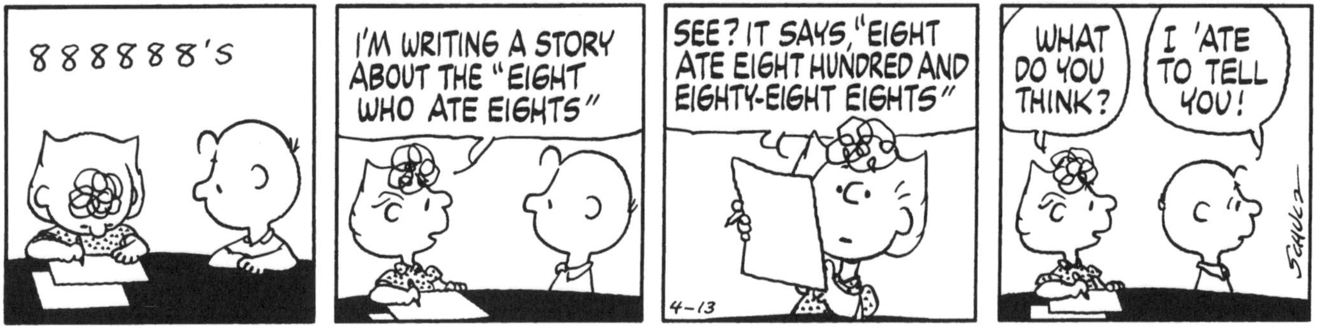
888888'S
I'M WRITING A STORY ABOUT THE "EIGHT WHO ATE EIGHTS"
SEE? IT SAYS, "EIGHT ATE EIGHT HUNDRED AND EIGHTY-EIGHT EIGHTS"
4-13
WHAT DO YOU THINK?
I 'ATE TO TELL YOU!

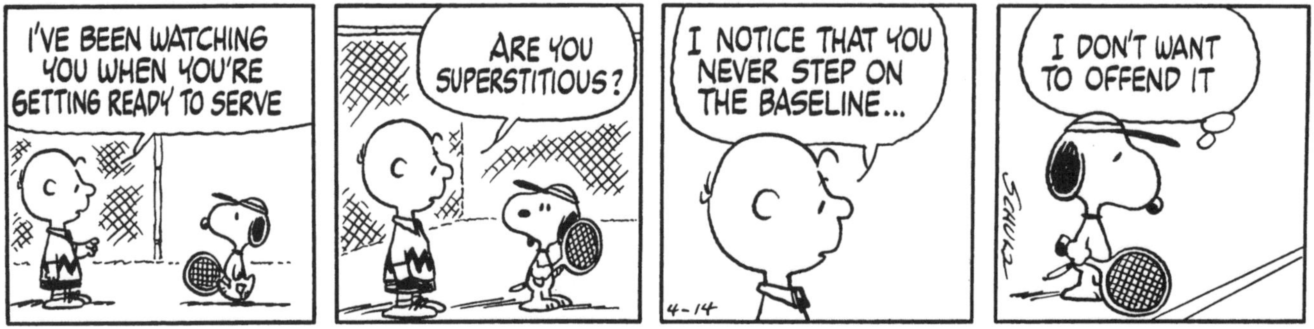
I'VE BEEN WATCHING YOU WHEN YOU'RE GETTING READY TO SERVE
ARE YOU SUPERSTITIOUS?
I NOTICE THAT YOU NEVER STEP ON THE BASELINE...
4-14
I DON'T WANT TO OFFEND IT

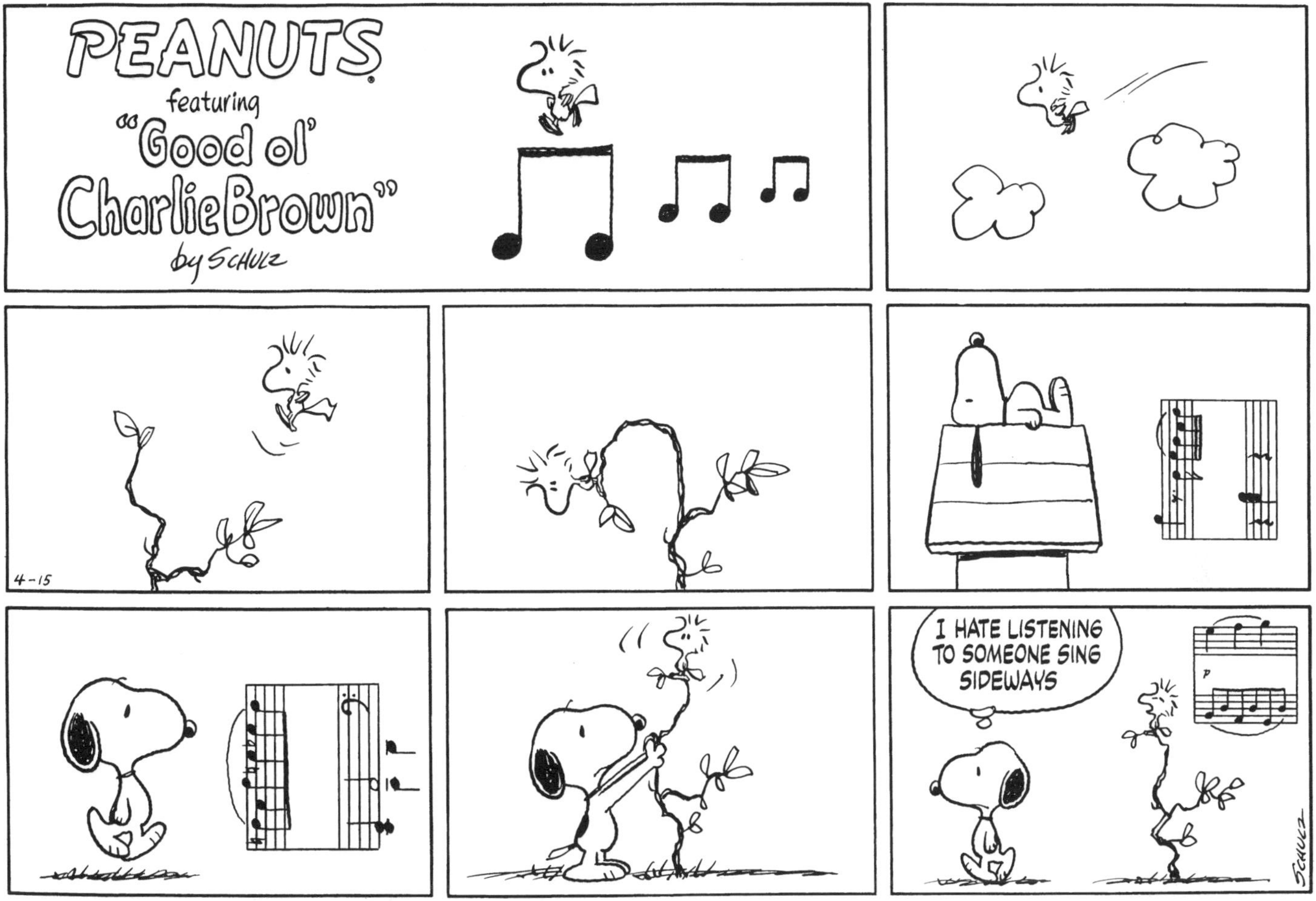
PEANUTS
featuring
"Good ol' Charlie Brown"
by SCHULZ
4-15
I HATE LISTENING TO SOMEONE SING SIDEWAYS
SCHULZ

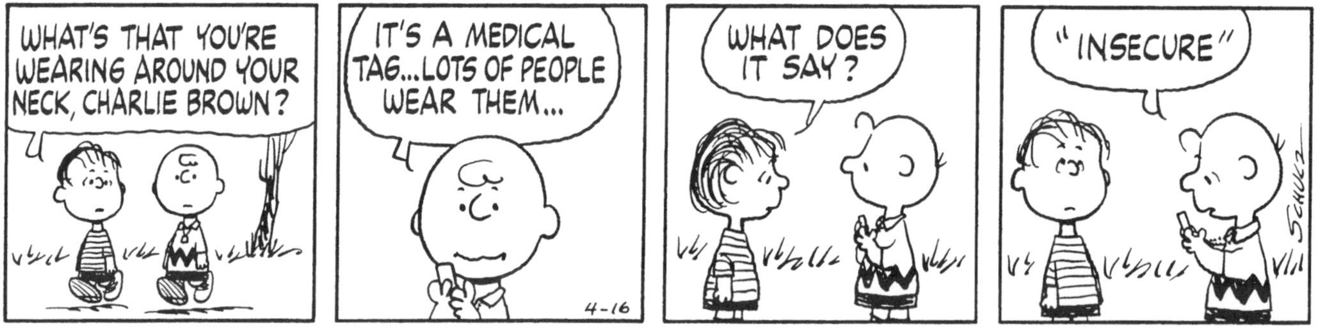
WHAT'S THAT YOU'RE WEARING AROUND YOUR NECK, CHARLIE BROWN?
IT'S A MEDICAL TAG...LOTS OF PEOPLE WEAR THEM...
4-16
WHAT DOES IT SAY?
"INSECURE"
SCHULZ

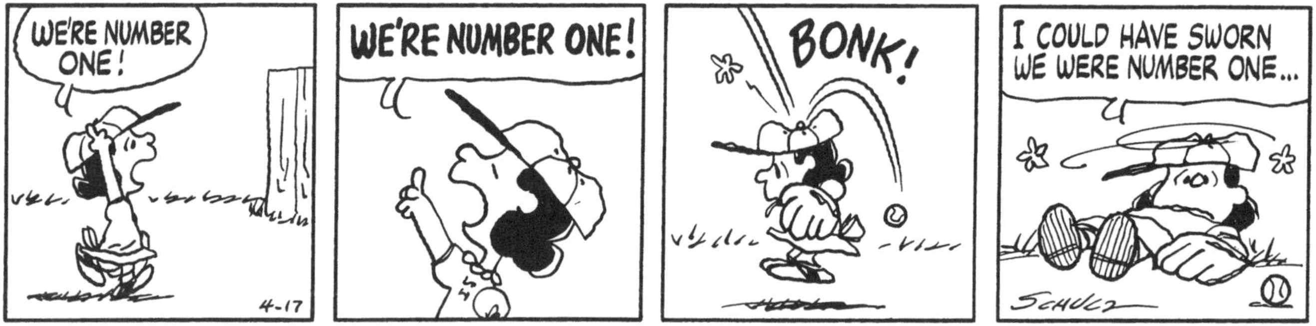
WE'RE NUMBER ONE!
4-17
WE'RE NUMBER ONE!
BONK!
I COULD HAVE SWORN WE WERE NUMBER ONE...
SCHULZ

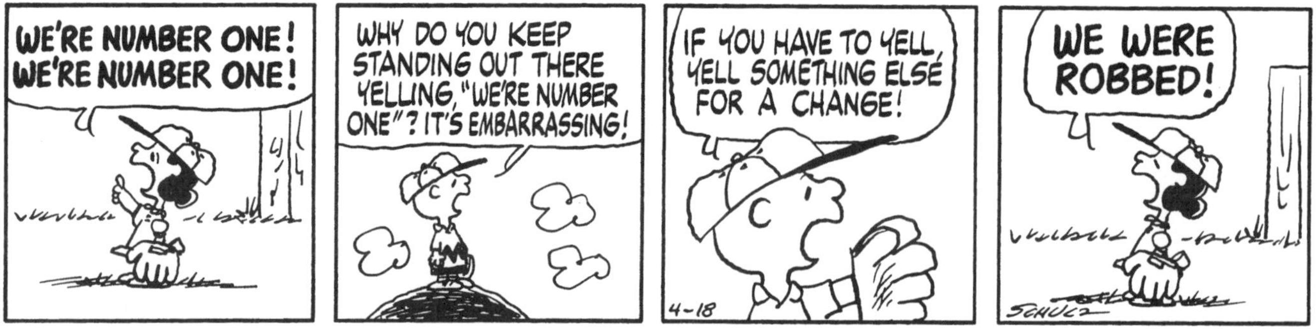
WE'RE NUMBER ONE! WE'RE NUMBER ONE!
WHY DO YOU KEEP STANDING OUT THERE YELLING, "WE'RE NUMBER ONE"? IT'S EMBARRASSING!
IF YOU HAVE TO YELL, YELL SOMETHING ELSE FOR A CHANGE!
4-18
WE WERE ROBBED!
SCHULZ

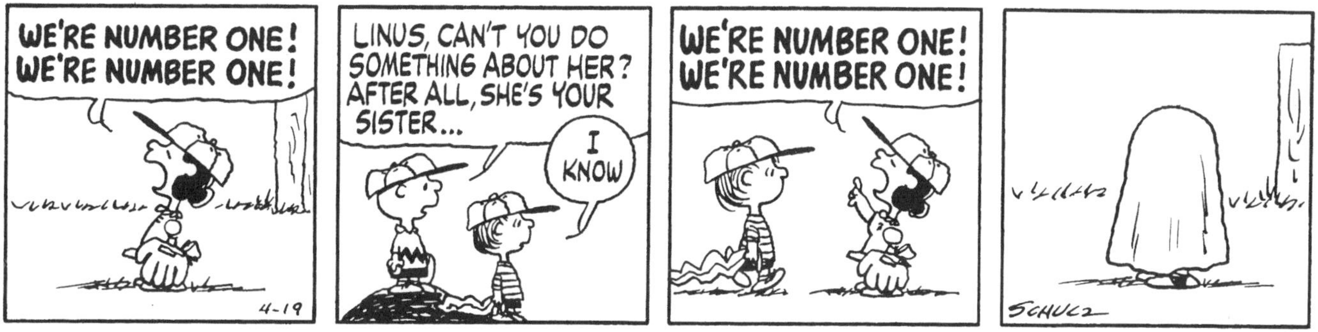
WE'RE NUMBER ONE! WE'RE NUMBER ONE!
4-19
LINUS, CAN'T YOU DO SOMETHING ABOUT HER? AFTER ALL, SHE'S YOUR SISTER...
I KNOW
WE'RE NUMBER ONE! WE'RE NUMBER ONE!
SCHULZ

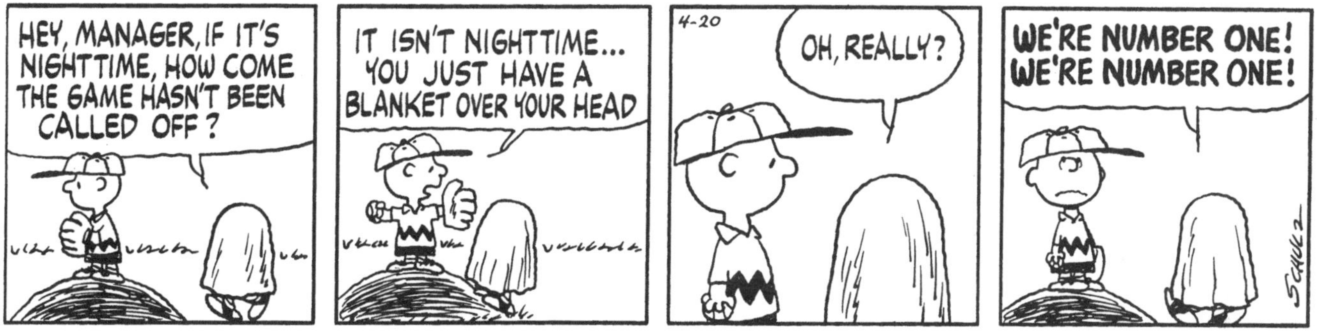
HEY, MANAGER, IF IT'S NIGHTTIME, HOW COME THE GAME HASN'T BEEN CALLED OFF?
IT ISN'T NIGHTTIME... YOU JUST HAVE A BLANKET OVER YOUR HEAD
4-20
OH, REALLY?
WE'RE NUMBER ONE! WE'RE NUMBER ONE!
SCHULZ

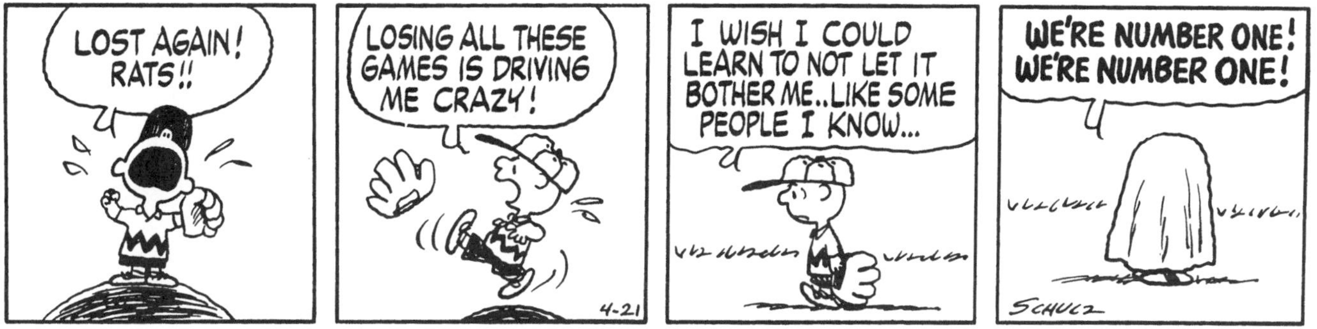
LOST AGAIN! RATS!!
LOSING ALL THESE GAMES IS DRIVING ME CRAZY!
4-21
I WISH I COULD LEARN TO NOT LET IT BOTHER ME..LIKE SOME PEOPLE I KNOW...
WE'RE NUMBER ONE! WE'RE NUMBER ONE!
SCHULZ

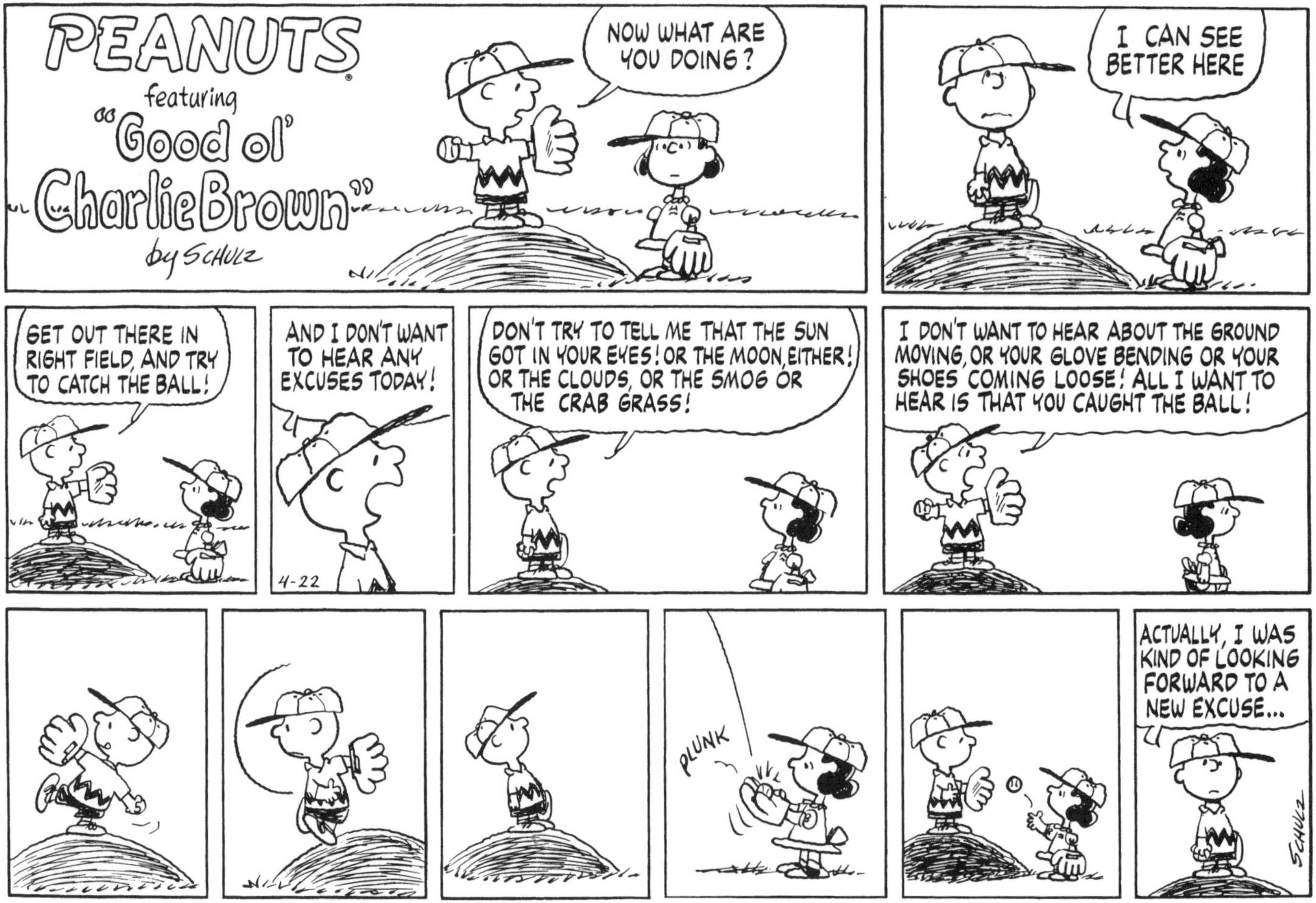
PEANUTS
featuring "Good ol' Charlie Brown"
by SCHULZ
NOW WHAT ARE YOU DOING?
I CAN SEE BETTER HERE
GET OUT THERE IN RIGHT FIELD, AND TRY TO CATCH THE BALL!
AND I DON'T WANT TO HEAR ANY EXCUSES TODAY!
4-22
DON'T TRY TO TELL ME THAT THE SUN GOT IN YOUR EYES! OR THE MOON, EITHER! OR THE CLOUDS, OR THE SMOG OR THE CRAB GRASS!
I DON'T WANT TO HEAR ABOUT THE GROUND MOVING, OR YOUR GLOVE BENDING OR YOUR SHOES COMING LOOSE! ALL I WANT TO HEAR IS THAT YOU CAUGHT THE BALL!
PLUNK
ACTUALLY, I WAS KIND OF LOOKING FORWARD TO A NEW EXCUSE...
SCHULZ

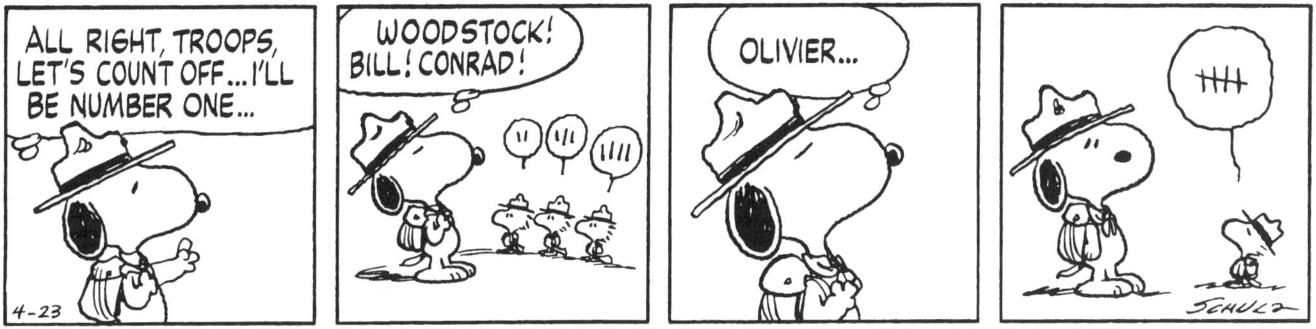
ALL RIGHT, TROOPS, LET'S COUNT OFF... I'LL BE NUMBER ONE...
4-23
WOODSTOCK! BILL! CONRAD!
OLIVIER...
SCHULZ

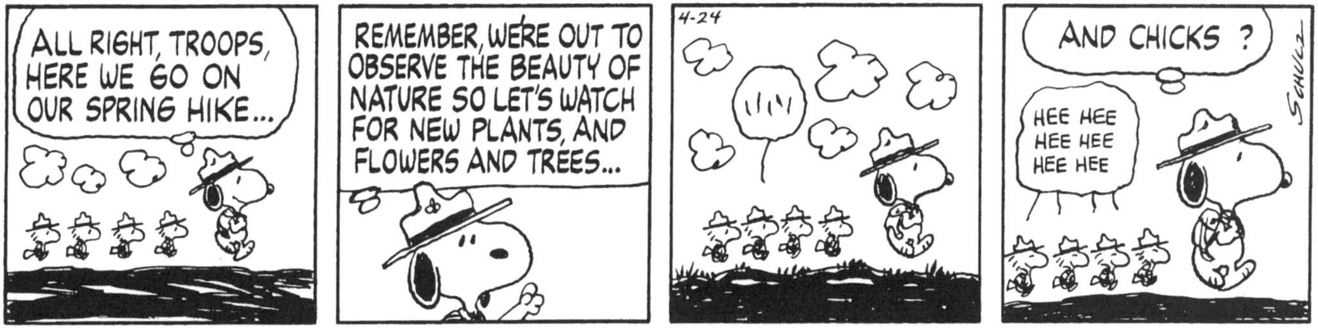
ALL RIGHT, TROOPS, HERE WE GO ON OUR SPRING HIKE...
REMEMBER, WE'RE OUT TO OBSERVE THE BEAUTY OF NATURE SO LET'S WATCH FOR NEW PLANTS, AND FLOWERS AND TREES...
4-24
AND CHICKS ?
HEE HEE HEE HEE HEE HEE
SCHULZ

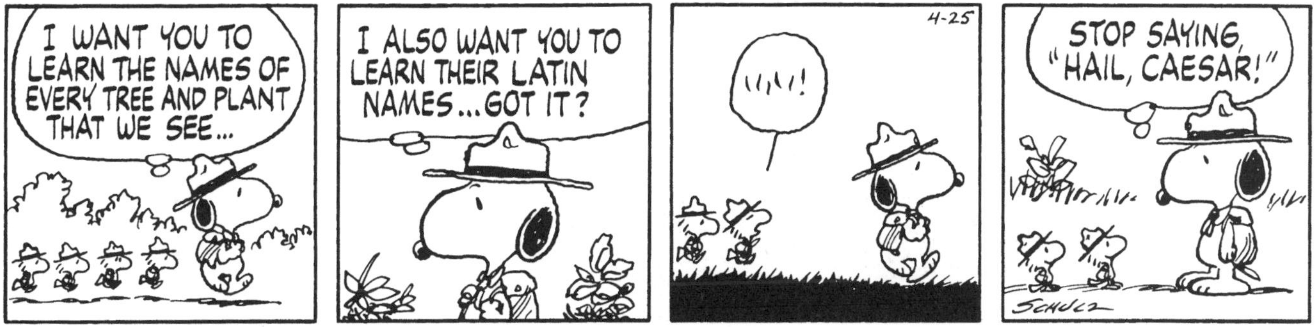
I WANT YOU TO LEARN THE NAMES OF EVERY TREE AND PLANT THAT WE SEE...
I ALSO WANT YOU TO LEARN THEIR LATIN NAMES... GOT IT?
4-25
STOP SAYING, "HAIL, CAESAR!"
SCHULZ

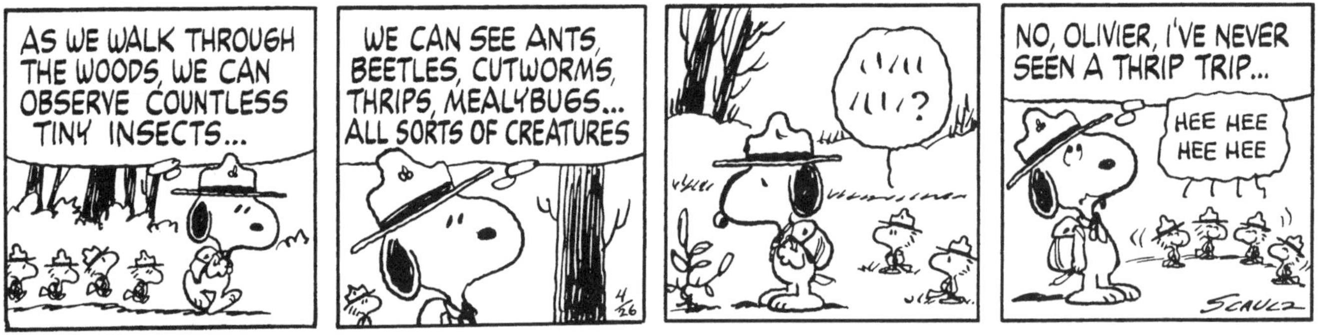
AS WE WALK THROUGH THE WOODS, WE CAN OBSERVE COUNTLESS TINY INSECTS...
WE CAN SEE ANTS, BEETLES, CUTWORMS, THRIPS, MEALYBUGS... ALL SORTS OF CREATURES
4/26
?
NO, OLIVIER, I'VE NEVER SEEN A THRIP TRIP...
HEE HEE HEE HEE
SCHULZ

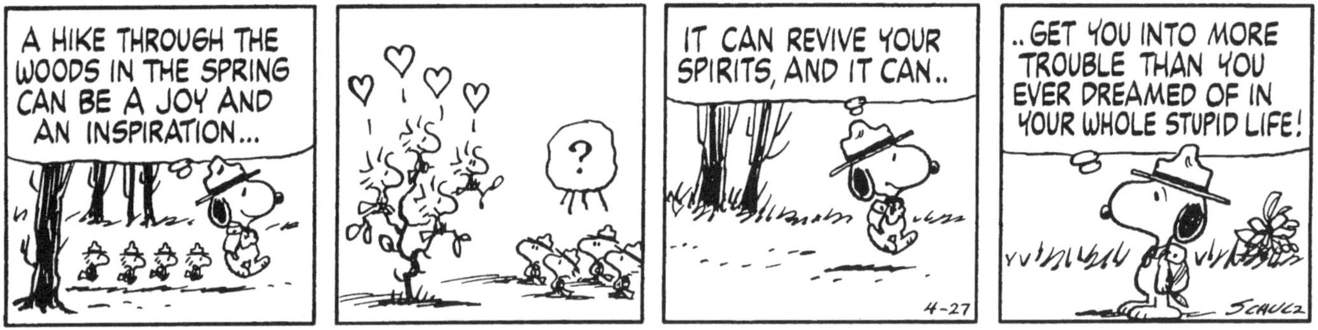
A HIKE THROUGH THE WOODS IN THE SPRING CAN BE A JOY AND AN INSPIRATION...
?
IT CAN REVIVE YOUR SPIRITS, AND IT CAN..
4-27
..GET YOU INTO MORE TROUBLE THAN YOU EVER DREAMED OF IN YOUR WHOLE STUPID LIFE!
SCHULZ

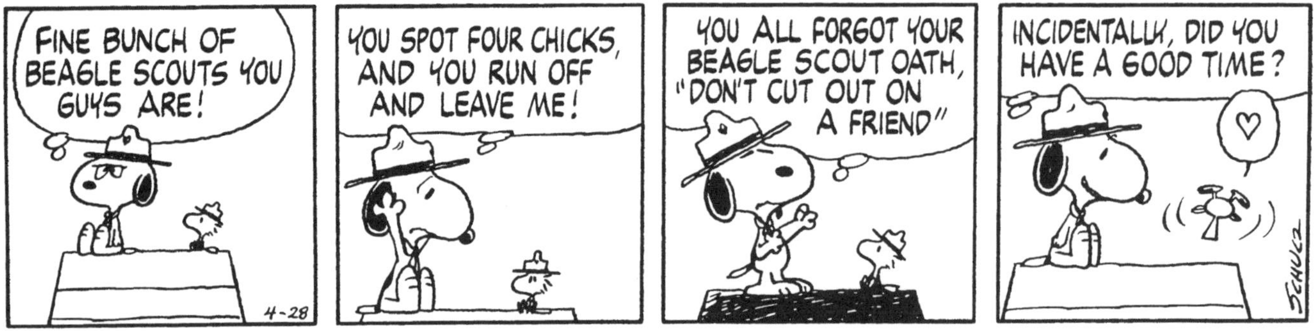
FINE BUNCH OF BEAGLE SCOUTS YOU GUYS ARE!
4-28
YOU SPOT FOUR CHICKS, AND YOU RUN OFF AND LEAVE ME!
YOU ALL FORGOT YOUR BEAGLE SCOUT OATH, "DON'T CUT OUT ON A FRIEND"
INCIDENTALLY, DID YOU HAVE A GOOD TIME?
SCHULZ

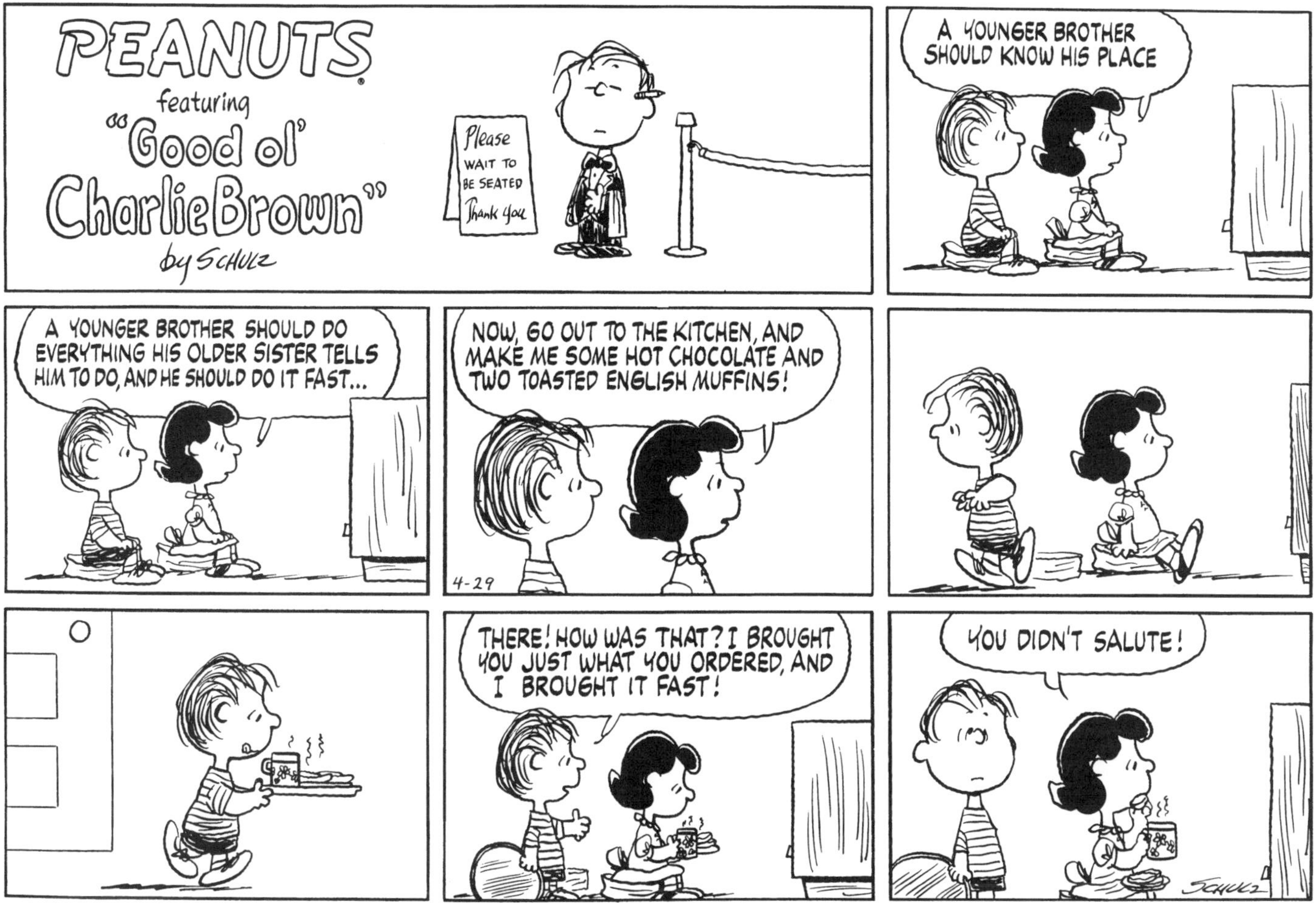
PEANUTS
featuring
"Good ol' CharlieBrown"
by SCHULZ
Please WAIT TO BE SEATED Thank You
A YOUNGER BROTHER SHOULD KNOW HIS PLACE
A YOUNGER BROTHER SHOULD DO EVERYTHING HIS OLDER SISTER TELLS HIM TO DO, AND HE SHOULD DO IT FAST...
NOW, GO OUT TO THE KITCHEN, AND MAKE ME SOME HOT CHOCOLATE AND TWO TOASTED ENGLISH MUFFINS!
4-29
THERE! HOW WAS THAT? I BROUGHT YOU JUST WHAT YOU ORDERED, AND I BROUGHT IT FAST!
YOU DIDN'T SALUTE!
SCHULZ

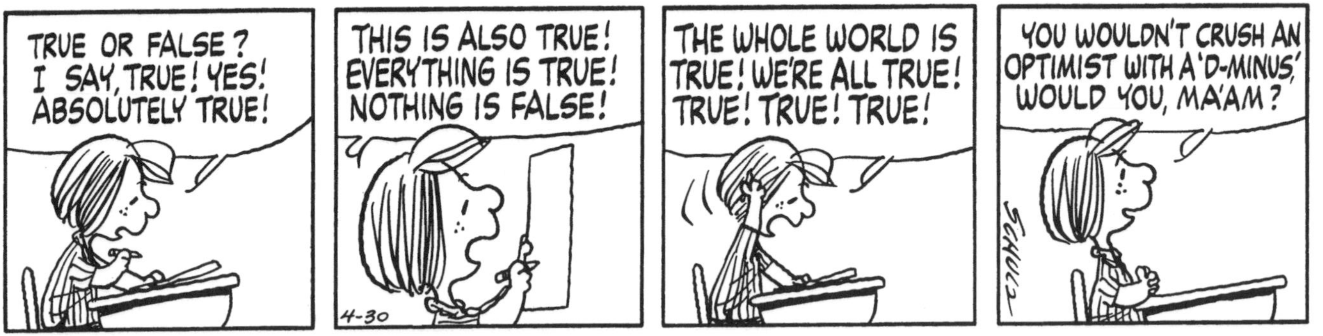
TRUE OR FALSE ? I SAY, TRUE! YES! ABSOLUTELY TRUE!
THIS IS ALSO TRUE! EVERYTHING IS TRUE! NOTHING IS FALSE!
4-30
THE WHOLE WORLD IS TRUE! WE'RE ALL TRUE! TRUE! TRUE! TRUE!
YOU WOULDN'T CRUSH AN OPTIMIST WITH A 'D-MINUS,' WOULD YOU, MA'AM ?
SCHULZ

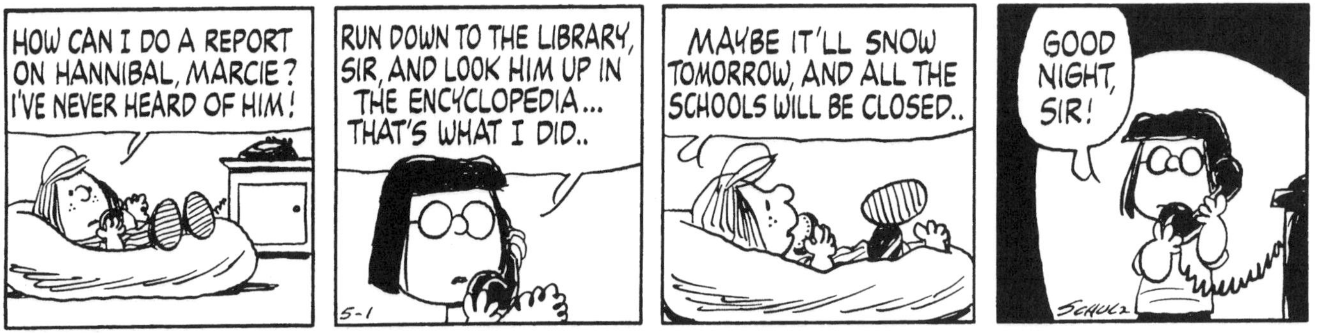
HOW CAN I DO A REPORT ON HANNIBAL, MARCIE? I'VE NEVER HEARD OF HIM!
RUN DOWN TO THE LIBRARY, SIR, AND LOOK HIM UP IN THE ENCYCLOPEDIA... THAT'S WHAT I DID..
5-1
MAYBE IT'LL SNOW TOMORROW, AND ALL THE SCHOOLS WILL BE CLOSED..
GOOD NIGHT, SIR!
SCHULZ

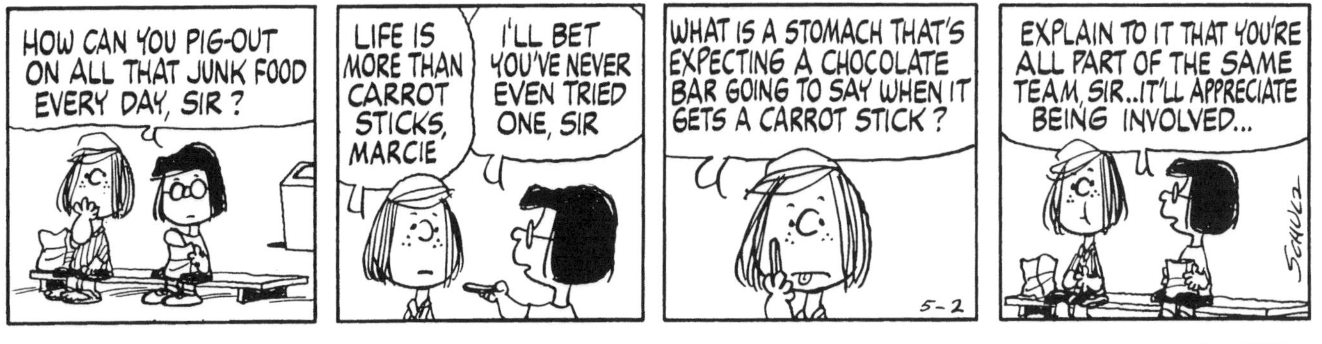
HOW CAN YOU PIG-OUT ON ALL THAT JUNK FOOD EVERY DAY, SIR ?
LIFE IS MORE THAN CARROT STICKS, MARCIE
I'LL BET YOU'VE NEVER EVEN TRIED ONE, SIR
WHAT IS A STOMACH THAT'S EXPECTING A CHOCOLATE BAR GOING TO SAY WHEN IT GETS A CARROT STICK ?
5-2
EXPLAIN TO IT THAT YOU'RE ALL PART OF THE SAME TEAM, SIR..IT'LL APPRECIATE BEING INVOLVED...
SCHULZ

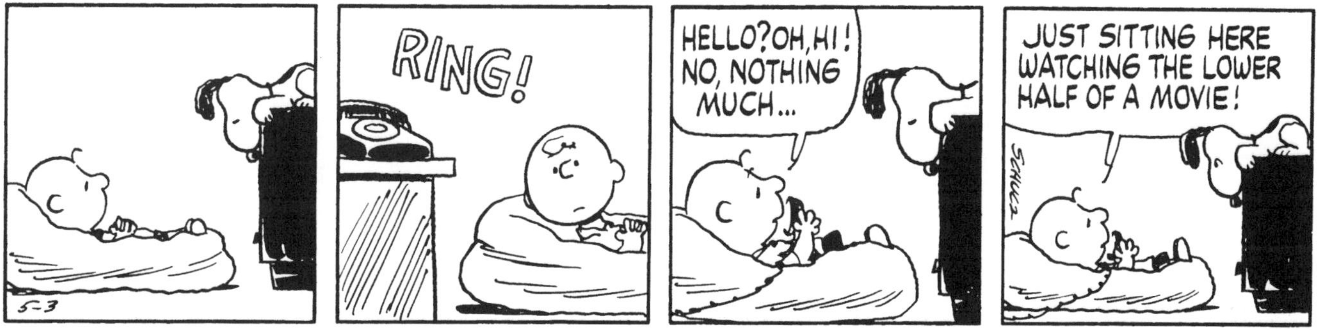
5-3
RING!
HELLO? OH, HI! NO, NOTHING MUCH...
JUST SITTING HERE WATCHING THE LOWER HALF OF A MOVIE!
SCHULZ

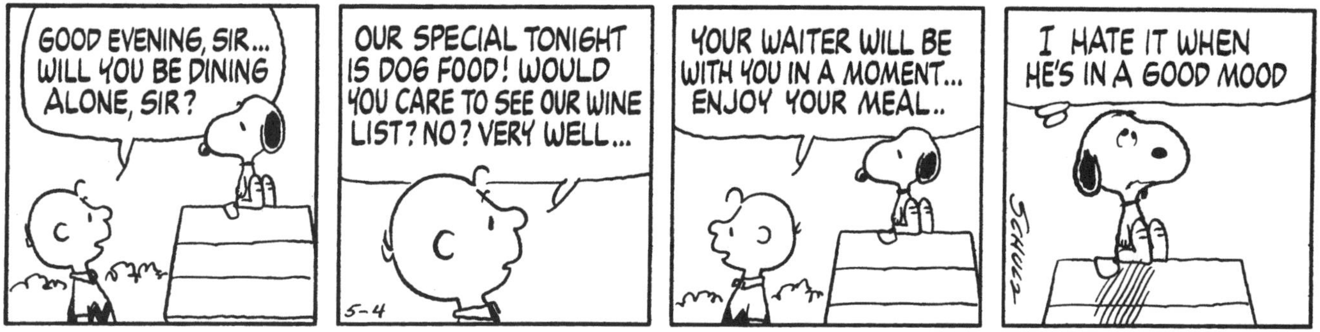
GOOD EVENING, SIR... WILL YOU BE DINING ALONE, SIR?
OUR SPECIAL TONIGHT IS DOG FOOD! WOULD YOU CARE TO SEE OUR WINE LIST? NO? VERY WELL...
5-4
YOUR WAITER WILL BE WITH YOU IN A MOMENT... ENJOY YOUR MEAL..
I HATE IT WHEN HE'S IN A GOOD MOOD
SCHULZ

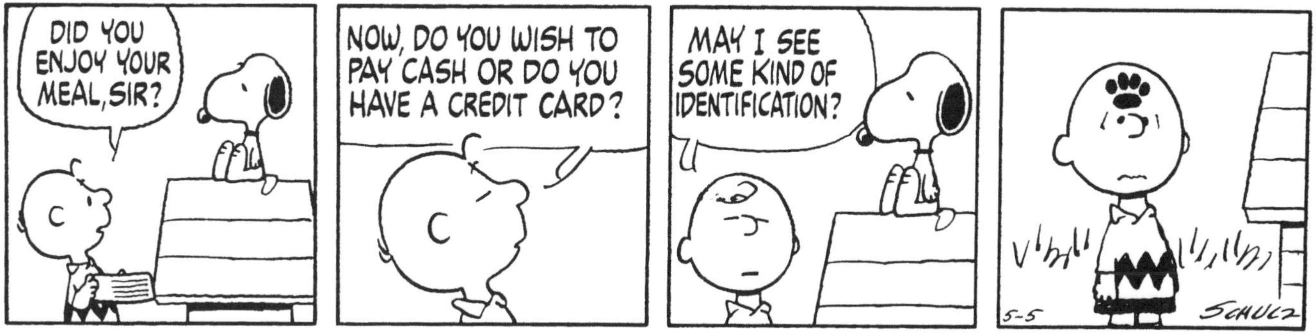
DID YOU ENJOY YOUR MEAL, SIR?
NOW, DO YOU WISH TO PAY CASH OR DO YOU HAVE A CREDIT CARD?
MAY I SEE SOME KIND OF IDENTIFICATION?
5-5
SCHULZ

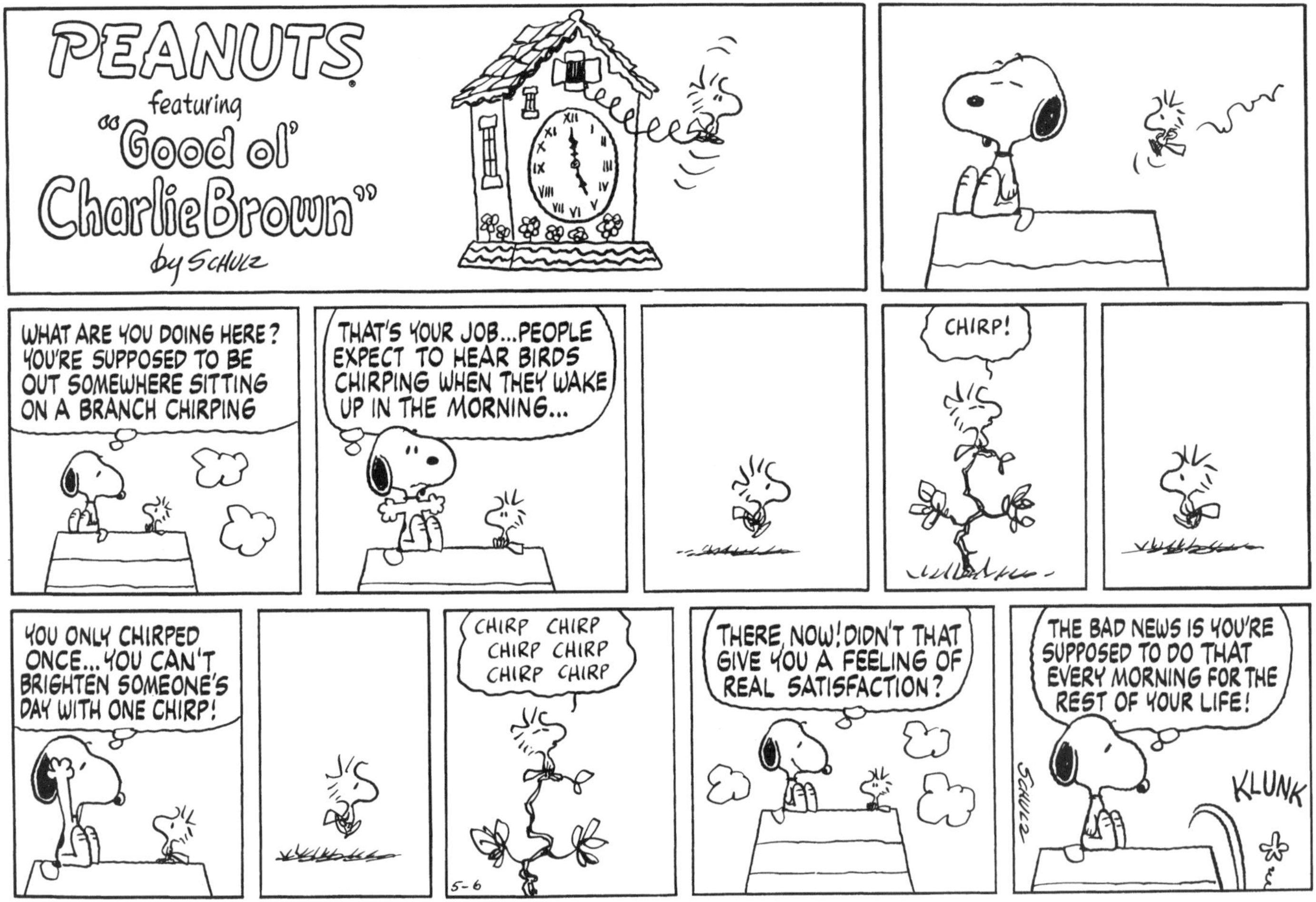
PEANUTS
featuring
"Good ol' Charlie Brown"
by SCHULZ
WHAT ARE YOU DOING HERE? YOU'RE SUPPOSED TO BE OUT SOMEWHERE SITTING ON A BRANCH CHIRPING
THAT'S YOUR JOB...PEOPLE EXPECT TO HEAR BIRDS CHIRPING WHEN THEY WAKE UP IN THE MORNING...
CHIRP!
YOU ONLY CHIRPED ONCE...YOU CAN'T BRIGHTEN SOMEONE'S DAY WITH ONE CHIRP!
CHIRP CHIRP CHIRP CHIRP CHIRP CHIRP
5-6
THERE, NOW! DIDN'T THAT GIVE YOU A FEELING OF REAL SATISFACTION?
THE BAD NEWS IS YOU'RE SUPPOSED TO DO THAT EVERY MORNING FOR THE REST OF YOUR LIFE!
SCHULZ
KLUNK

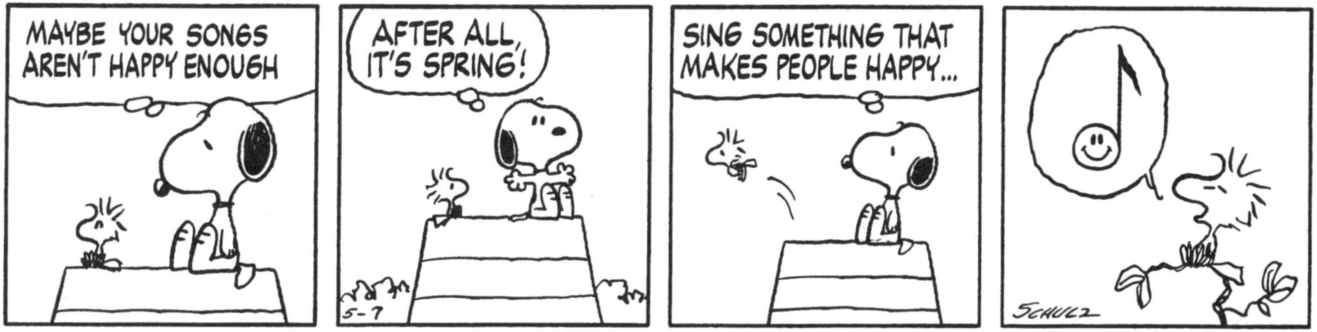
MAYBE YOUR SONGS AREN'T HAPPY ENOUGH
AFTER ALL, IT'S SPRING!
5-7
SING SOMETHING THAT MAKES PEOPLE HAPPY...
SCHULZ

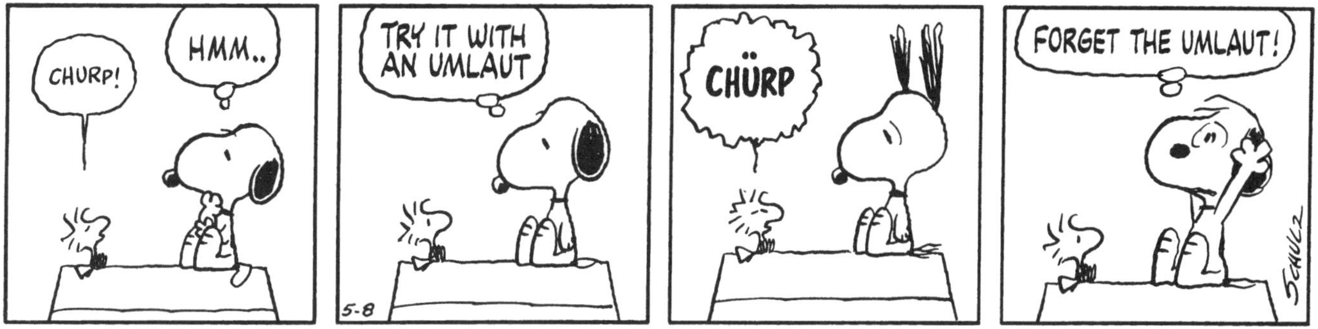
CHURP!
HMM..
TRY IT WITH AN UMLAUT
5-8
CHÜRP
FORGET THE UMLAUT!
SCHULZ

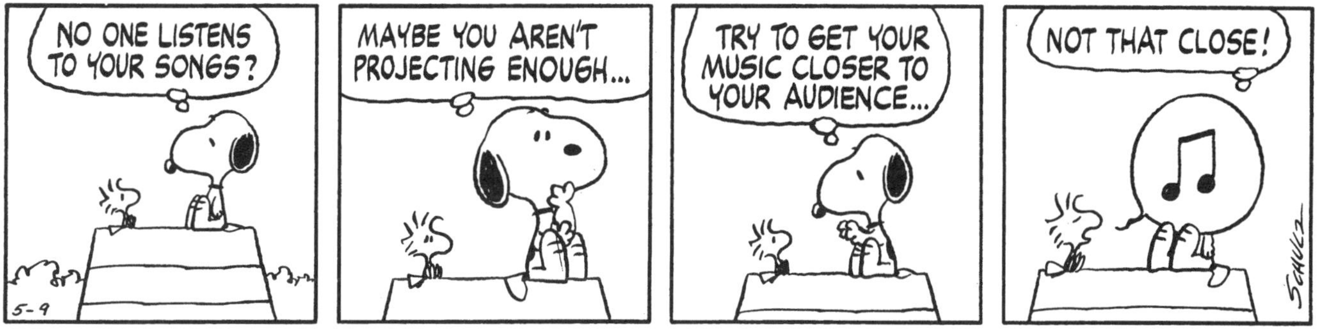
NO ONE LISTENS TO YOUR SONGS?
5-9
MAYBE YOU AREN'T PROJECTING ENOUGH...
TRY TO GET YOUR MUSIC CLOSER TO YOUR AUDIENCE...
NOT THAT CLOSE!
SCHULZ

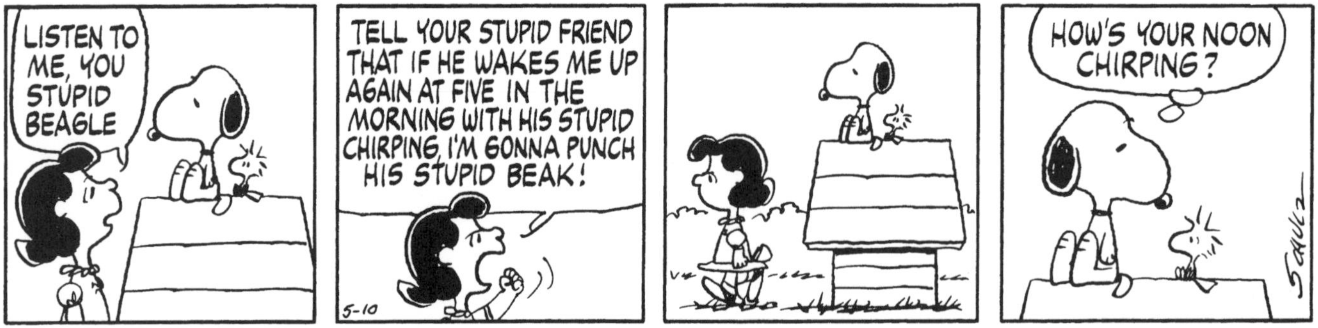
LISTEN TO ME, YOU STUPID BEAGLE
TELL YOUR STUPID FRIEND THAT IF HE WAKES ME UP AGAIN AT FIVE IN THE MORNING WITH HIS STUPID CHIRPING, I'M GONNA PUNCH HIS STUPID BEAK!
5-10
HOW'S YOUR NOON CHIRPING?
SCHULZ

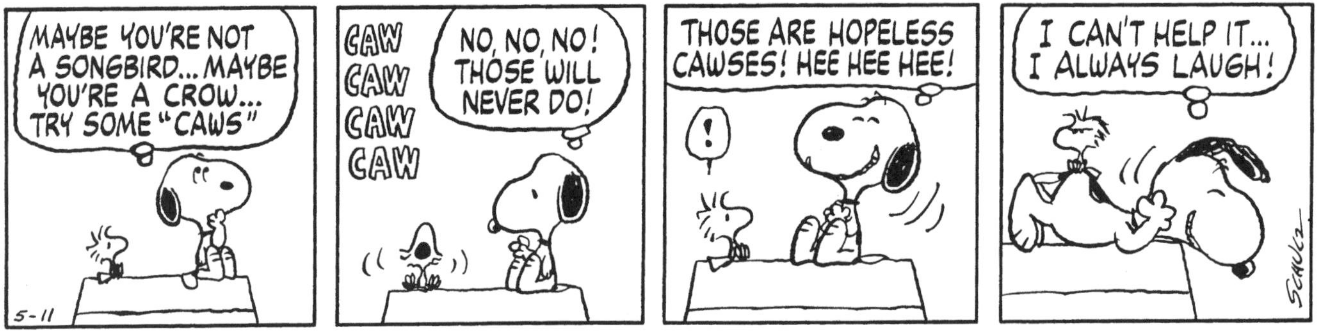
MAYBE YOU'RE NOT A SONGBIRD... MAYBE YOU'RE A CROW... TRY SOME "CAWS"
5-11
CAW
CAW
CAW
CAW
NO, NO, NO! THOSE WILL NEVER DO!
THOSE ARE HOPELESS CAWSES! HEE HEE HEE!
!
I CAN'T HELP IT... I ALWAYS LAUGH!
SCHULZ

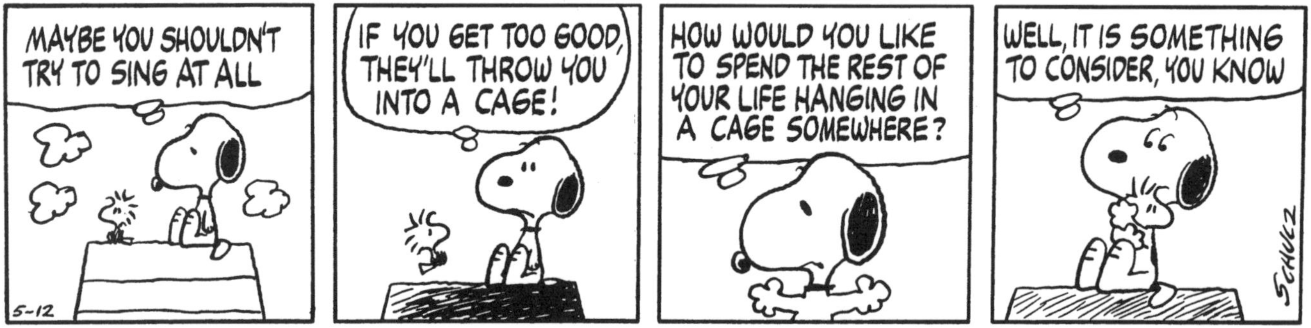
MAYBE YOU SHOULDN'T TRY TO SING AT ALL
5-12
IF YOU GET TOO GOOD, THEY'LL THROW YOU INTO A CAGE!
HOW WOULD YOU LIKE TO SPEND THE REST OF YOUR LIFE HANGING IN A CAGE SOMEWHERE?
WELL, IT IS SOMETHING TO CONSIDER, YOU KNOW
SCHULZ

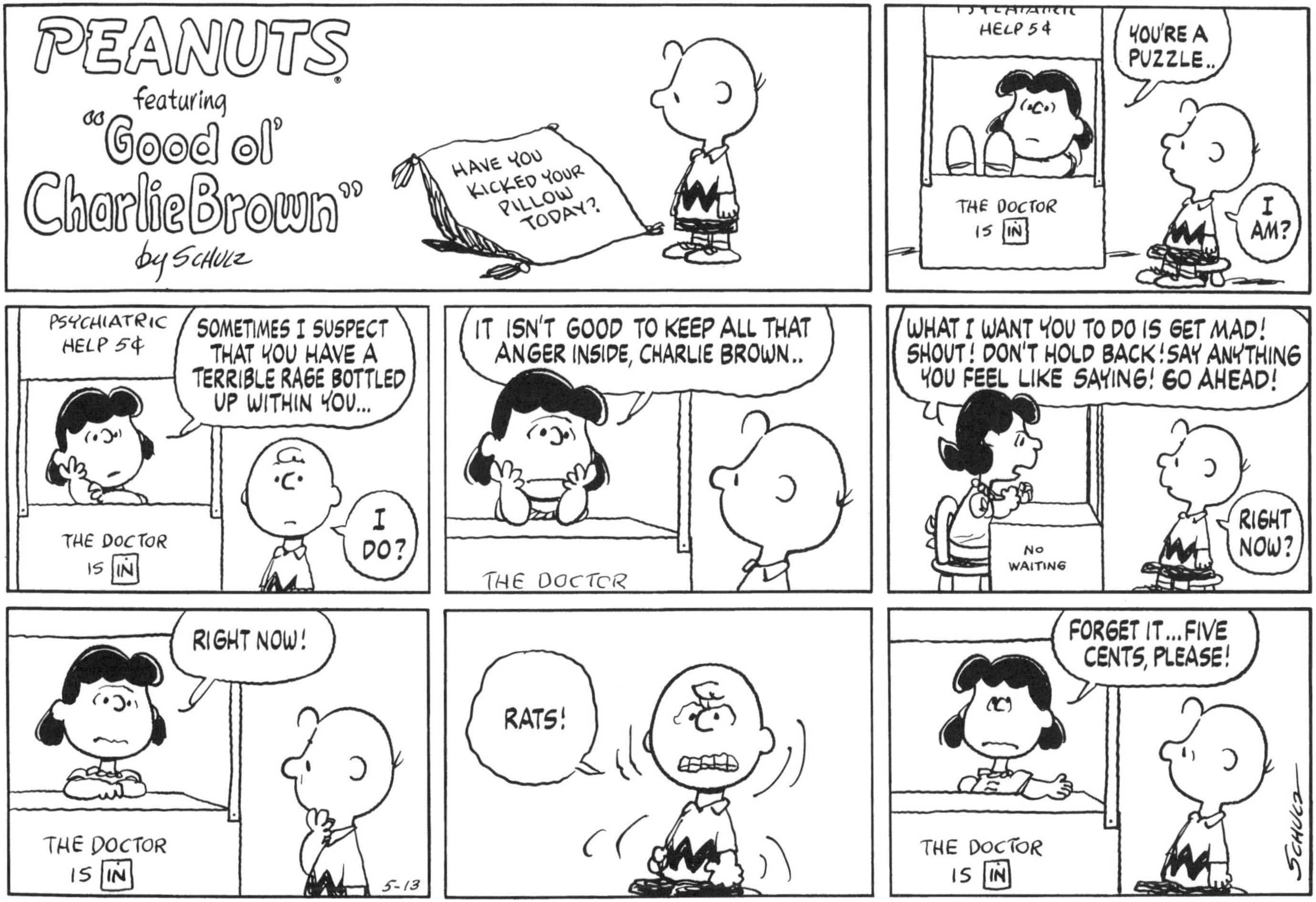
PEANUTS
featuring
"Good ol' Charlie Brown"
by SCHULZ
HAVE YOU KICKED YOUR PILLOW TODAY?
HELP 5¢
THE DOCTOR IS IN
YOU'RE A PUZZLE..
I AM?
PSYCHIATRIC HELP 5¢
THE DOCTOR IS IN
SOMETIMES I SUSPECT THAT YOU HAVE A TERRIBLE RAGE BOTTLED UP WITHIN YOU...
I DO?
IT ISN'T GOOD TO KEEP ALL THAT ANGER INSIDE, CHARLIE BROWN..
THE DOCTOR
WHAT I WANT YOU TO DO IS GET MAD! SHOUT! DON'T HOLD BACK! SAY ANYTHING YOU FEEL LIKE SAYING! GO AHEAD!
NO WAITING
RIGHT NOW?
RIGHT NOW!
THE DOCTOR IS IN
5-13
RATS!
FORGET IT...FIVE CENTS, PLEASE!
THE DOCTOR IS IN
SCHULZ

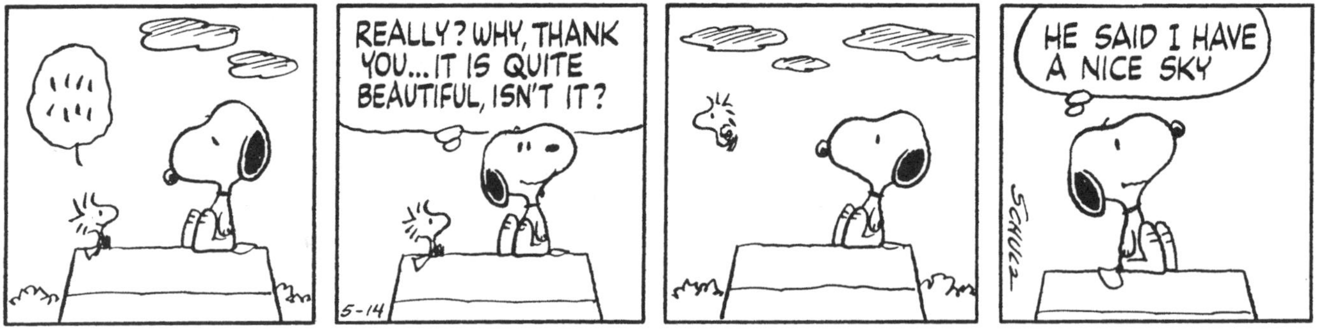
5-14
REALLY? WHY, THANK YOU... IT IS QUITE BEAUTIFUL, ISN'T IT?
HE SAID I HAVE A NICE SKY

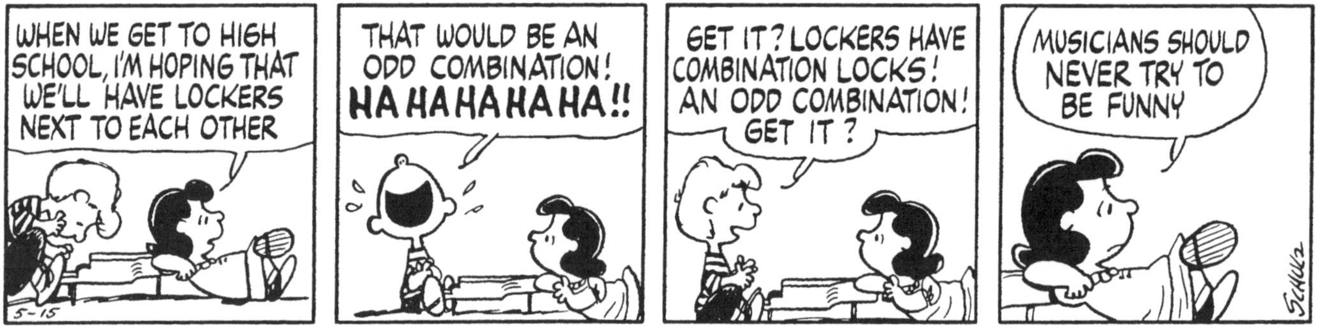
5-15
WHEN WE GET TO HIGH SCHOOL, I'M HOPING THAT WE'LL HAVE LOCKERS NEXT TO EACH OTHER
THAT WOULD BE AN ODD COMBINATION! HA HA HA HA HA!!
GET IT? LOCKERS HAVE COMBINATION LOCKS! AN ODD COMBINATION! GET IT?
MUSICIANS SHOULD NEVER TRY TO BE FUNNY

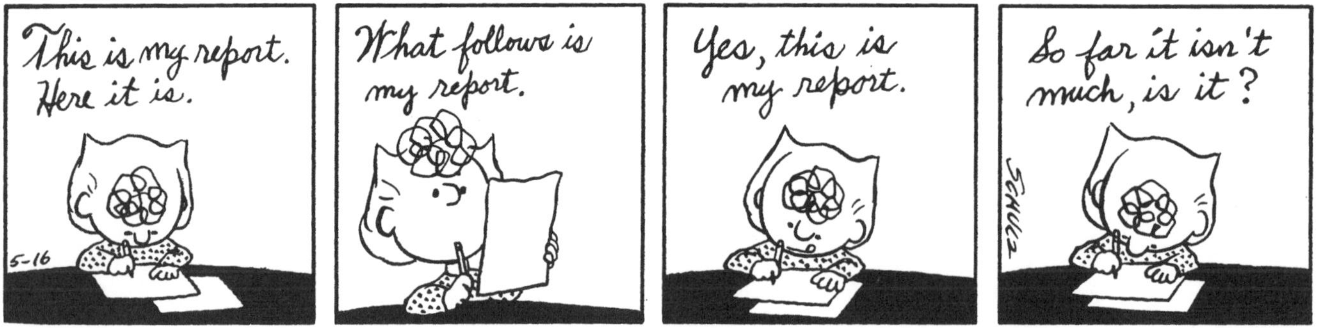
5-16
This is my report. Here it is.
What follows is my report.
Yes, this is my report.
So far it isn't much, is it?

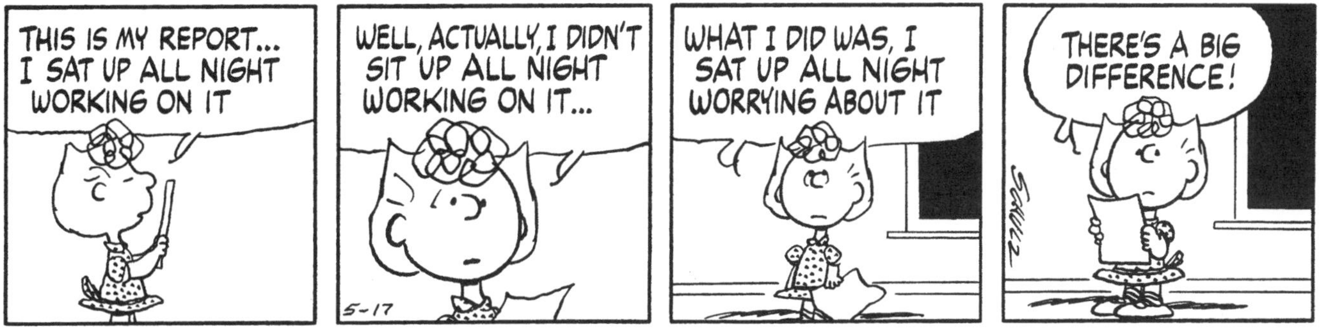
THIS IS MY REPORT... I SAT UP ALL NIGHT WORKING ON IT
WELL, ACTUALLY, I DIDN'T SIT UP ALL NIGHT WORKING ON IT...
5-17
WHAT I DID WAS, I SAT UP ALL NIGHT WORRYING ABOUT IT
THERE'S A BIG DIFFERENCE!
SCHULZ

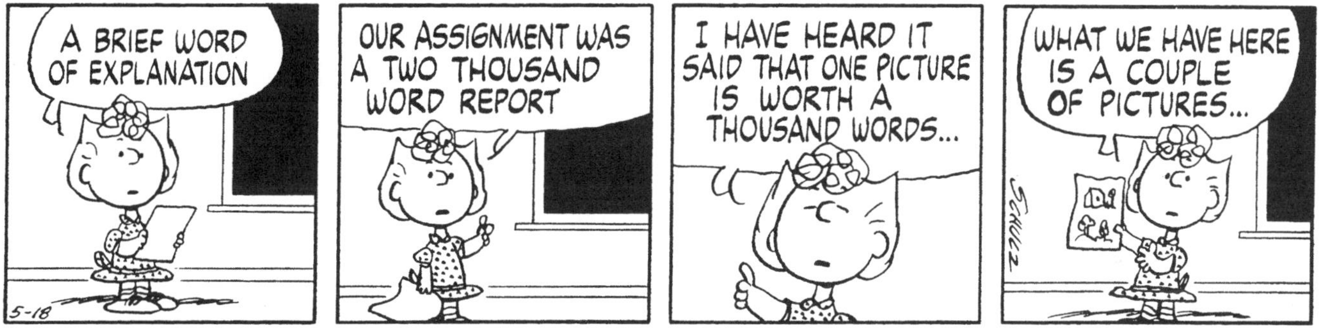
A BRIEF WORD OF EXPLANATION
5-18
OUR ASSIGNMENT WAS A TWO THOUSAND WORD REPORT
I HAVE HEARD IT SAID THAT ONE PICTURE IS WORTH A THOUSAND WORDS...
WHAT WE HAVE HERE IS A COUPLE OF PICTURES...
SCHULZ

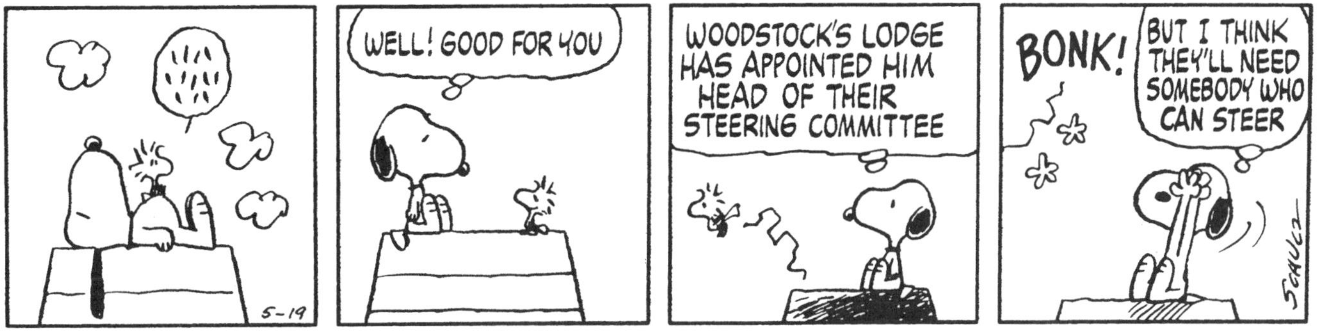
5-19
WELL! GOOD FOR YOU
WOODSTOCK'S LODGE HAS APPOINTED HIM HEAD OF THEIR STEERING COMMITTEE
BONK!
BUT I THINK THEY'LL NEED SOMEBODY WHO CAN STEER
SCHULZ

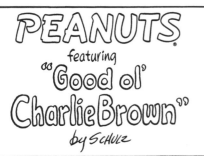

PEANUTS
featuring
"Good ol' CharlieBrown"
by SCHULZ

LOOK!

A JELLY DOUGHNUT!

5-20

THERE'S NOTHING IN THE WORLD BETTER THAN A BIG FAT JELLY DOUGHNUT

THERE'S ONLY ONE PROBLEM..

YOU HAVE TO BE CAREFUL WHEN YOU EAT ONE

SOMETIMES WHEN YOU BITE INTO A JELLY DOUGHNUT, THE JELLY..

..SQUIRTS OUT THE SIDE!

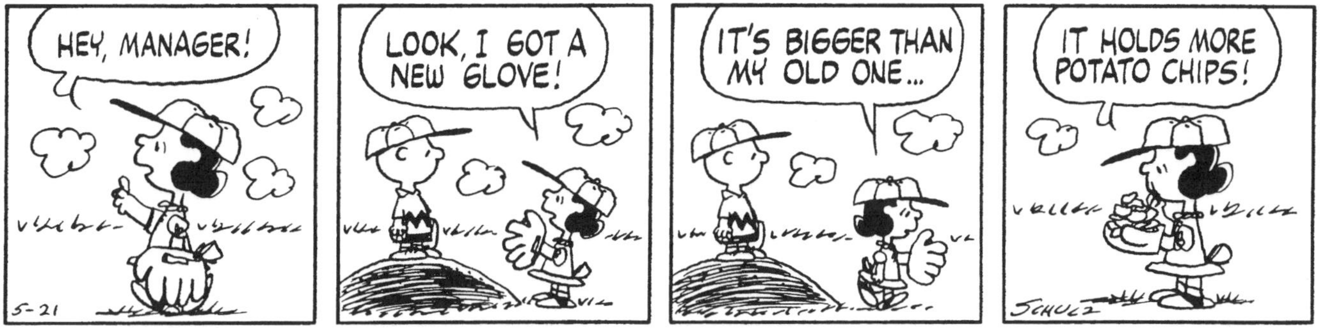
HEY, MANAGER!
LOOK, I GOT A NEW GLOVE!
IT'S BIGGER THAN MY OLD ONE...
IT HOLDS MORE POTATO CHIPS!
5-21

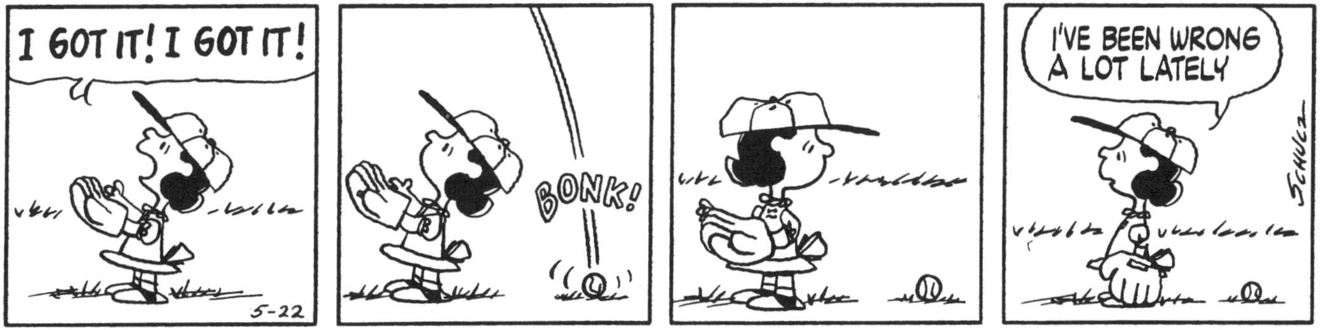
I GOT IT! I GOT IT!
BONK!
I'VE BEEN WRONG A LOT LATELY
5-22

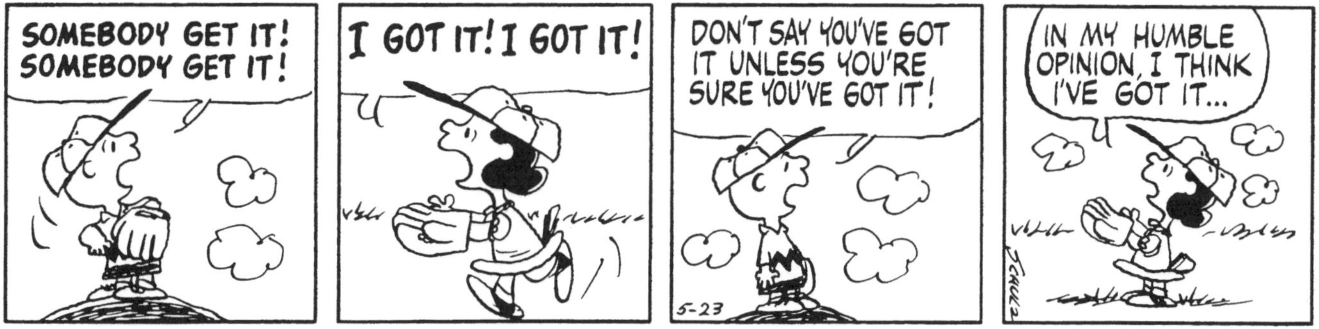
SOMEBODY GET IT! SOMEBODY GET IT!
I GOT IT! I GOT IT!
DON'T SAY YOU'VE GOT IT UNLESS YOU'RE SURE YOU'VE GOT IT!
IN MY HUMBLE OPINION, I THINK I'VE GOT IT...
5-23

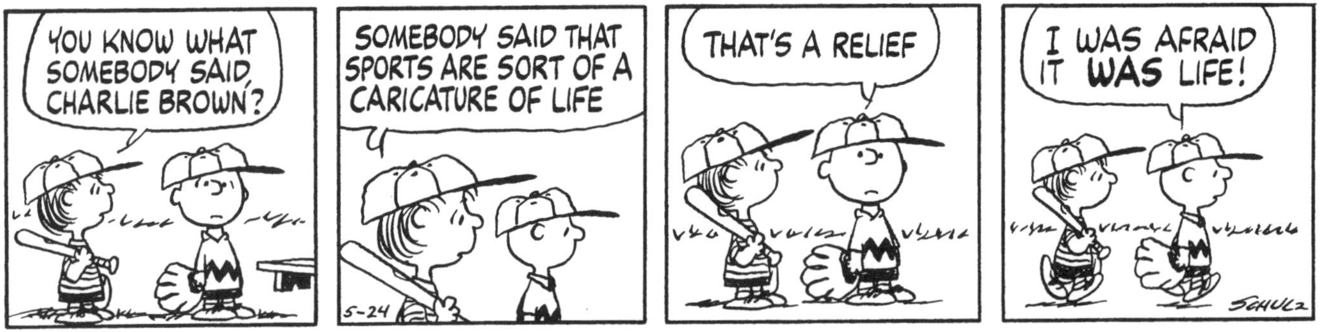
YOU KNOW WHAT SOMEBODY SAID, CHARLIE BROWN?
SOMEBODY SAID THAT SPORTS ARE SORT OF A CARICATURE OF LIFE
THAT'S A RELIEF
I WAS AFRAID IT **WAS** LIFE!

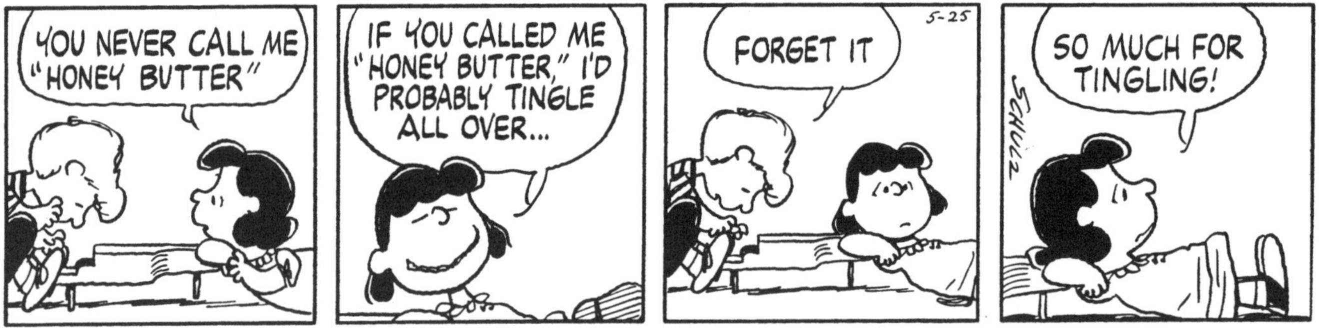
YOU NEVER CALL ME "HONEY BUTTER"
IF YOU CALLED ME "HONEY BUTTER," I'D PROBABLY TINGLE ALL OVER...
FORGET IT
SO MUCH FOR TINGLING!

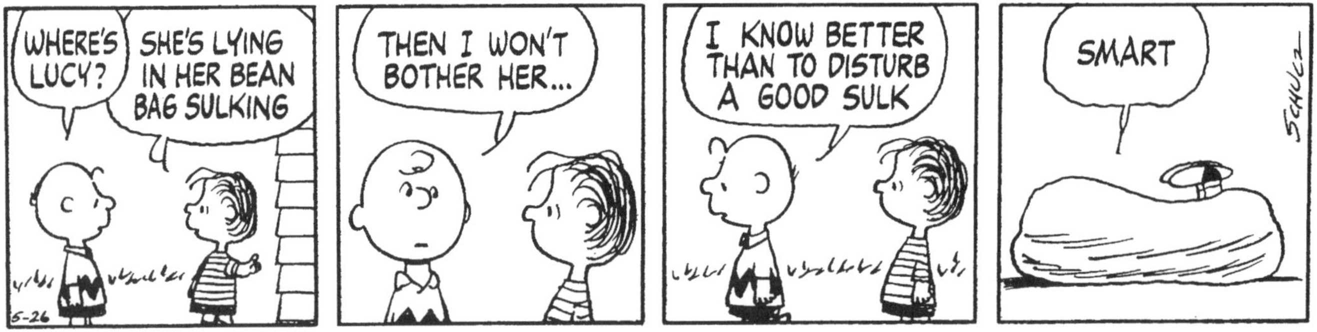
WHERE'S LUCY?
SHE'S LYING IN HER BEAN BAG SULKING
THEN I WON'T BOTHER HER...
I KNOW BETTER THAN TO DISTURB A GOOD SULK
SMART

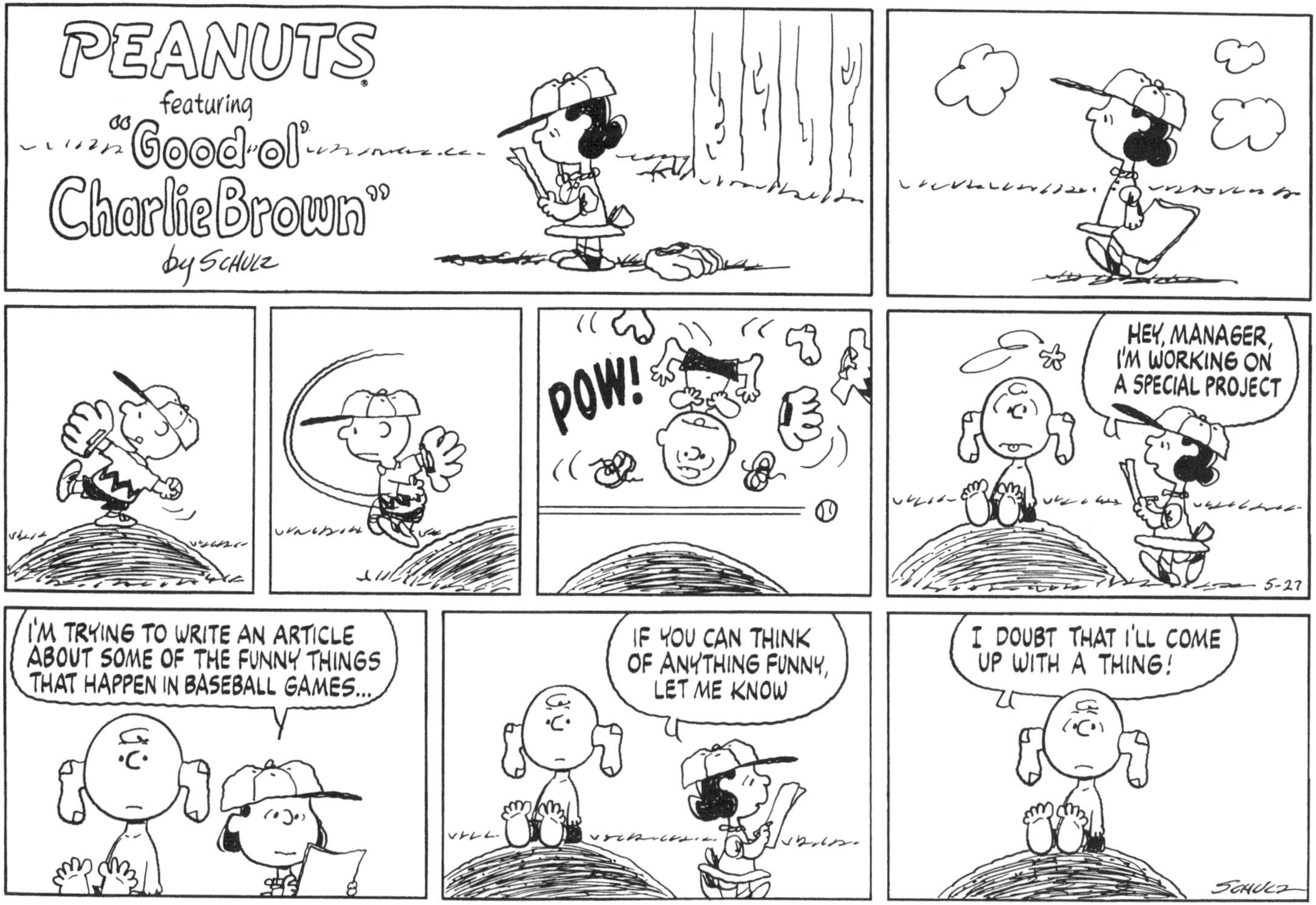
PEANUTS
featuring
"Good ol' Charlie Brown"
by SCHULZ
POW!
HEY, MANAGER, I'M WORKING ON A SPECIAL PROJECT
5-27
I'M TRYING TO WRITE AN ARTICLE ABOUT SOME OF THE FUNNY THINGS THAT HAPPEN IN BASEBALL GAMES...
IF YOU CAN THINK OF ANYTHING FUNNY, LET ME KNOW
I DOUBT THAT I'LL COME UP WITH A THING!
SCHULZ

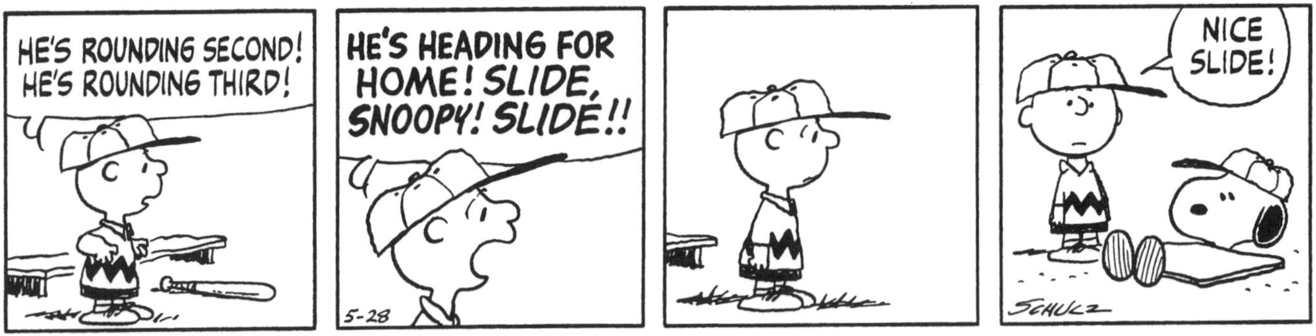
HE'S ROUNDING SECOND! HE'S ROUNDING THIRD!
HE'S HEADING FOR HOME! SLIDE, SNOOPY! SLIDE!!
5-28
NICE SLIDE!
SCHULZ

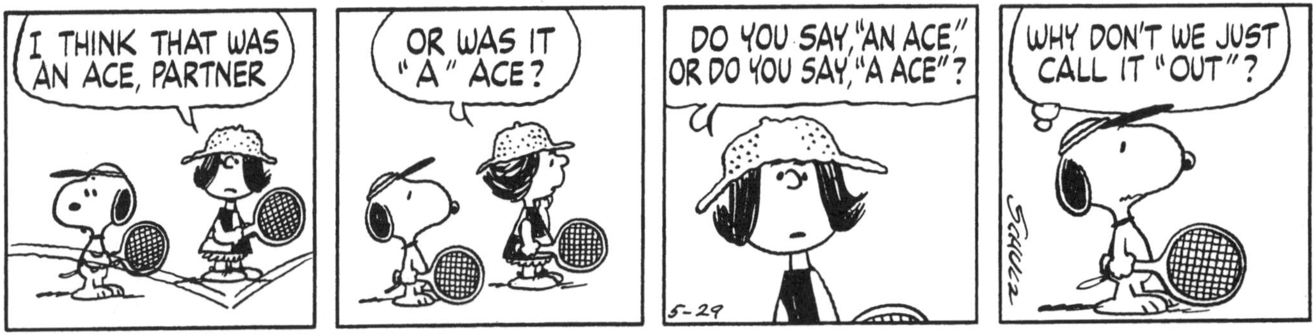
I THINK THAT WAS AN ACE, PARTNER
OR WAS IT "A" ACE?
DO YOU SAY, "AN ACE," OR DO YOU SAY, "A ACE"?
5-29
WHY DON'T WE JUST CALL IT "OUT"?
SCHULZ

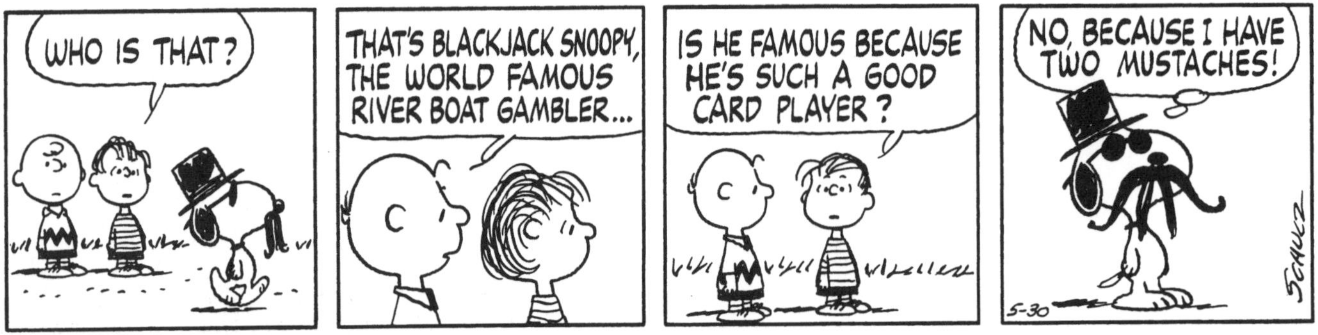
WHO IS THAT?
THAT'S BLACKJACK SNOOPY, THE WORLD FAMOUS RIVER BOAT GAMBLER...
IS HE FAMOUS BECAUSE HE'S SUCH A GOOD CARD PLAYER?
NO, BECAUSE I HAVE TWO MUSTACHES!
5-30
SCHULZ

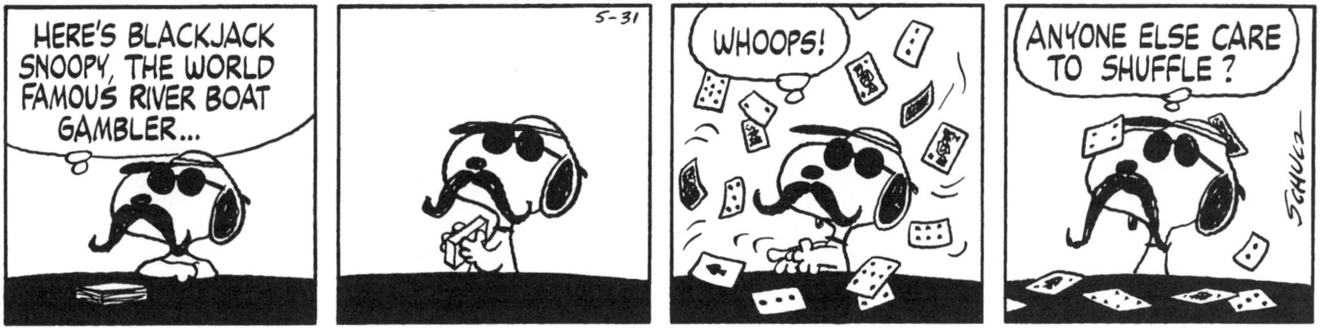
HERE'S BLACKJACK SNOOPY, THE WORLD FAMOUS RIVER BOAT GAMBLER...
5-31
WHOOPS!
ANYONE ELSE CARE TO SHUFFLE ?

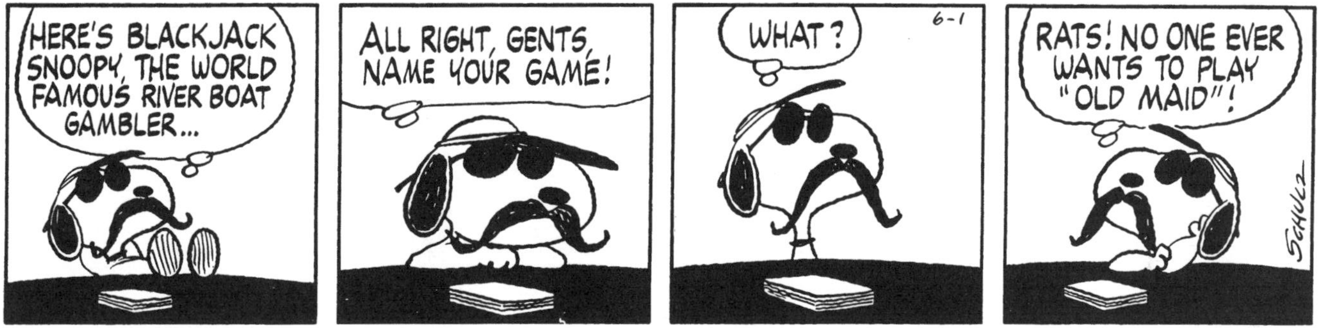
HERE'S BLACKJACK SNOOPY, THE WORLD FAMOUS RIVER BOAT GAMBLER...
ALL RIGHT, GENTS, NAME YOUR GAME!
WHAT ?
6-1
RATS! NO ONE EVER WANTS TO PLAY "OLD MAID"!

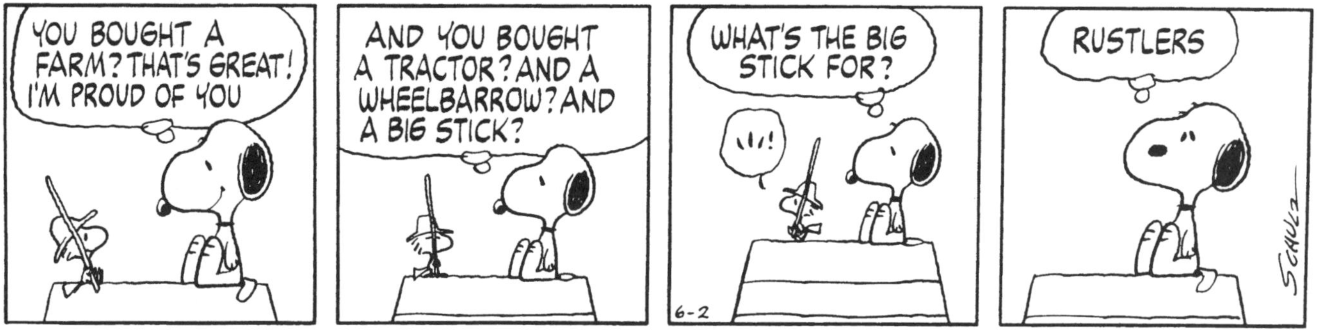
YOU BOUGHT A FARM? THAT'S GREAT! I'M PROUD OF YOU
AND YOU BOUGHT A TRACTOR? AND A WHEELBARROW? AND A BIG STICK?
WHAT'S THE BIG STICK FOR?
6-2
RUSTLERS

PEANUTS
featuring
"Good ol'
Charlie Brown"
by SCHULZ

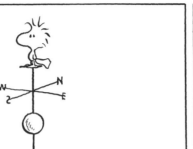

YOU LOOK EXHAUSTED! RUNNING A FARM IS HARD WORK

6-3

WELL, OKAY...

I DON'T MIND HELPING OUT ON A FRIEND'S FARM ONCE IN A WHILE...

BUT I HATE BEING THE SCARECROW!

June

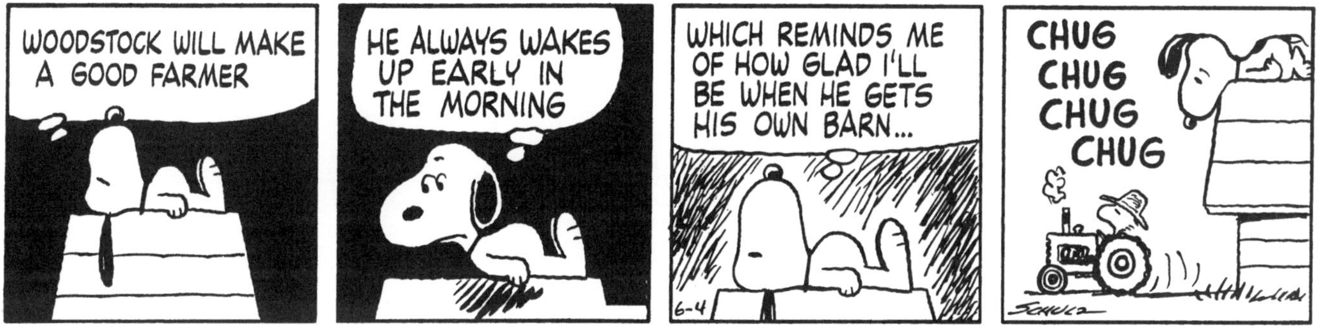
WOODSTOCK WILL MAKE A GOOD FARMER
HE ALWAYS WAKES UP EARLY IN THE MORNING
WHICH REMINDS ME OF HOW GLAD I'LL BE WHEN HE GETS HIS OWN BARN...
6-4
CHUG CHUG CHUG CHUG
SCHULZ

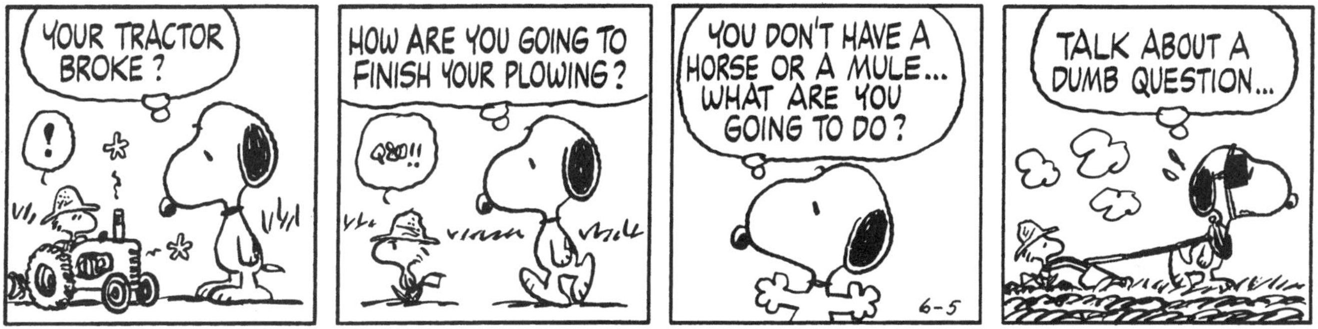
YOUR TRACTOR BROKE ?
!
HOW ARE YOU GOING TO FINISH YOUR PLOWING ?
YOU DON'T HAVE A HORSE OR A MULE... WHAT ARE YOU GOING TO DO ?
6-5
TALK ABOUT A DUMB QUESTION...

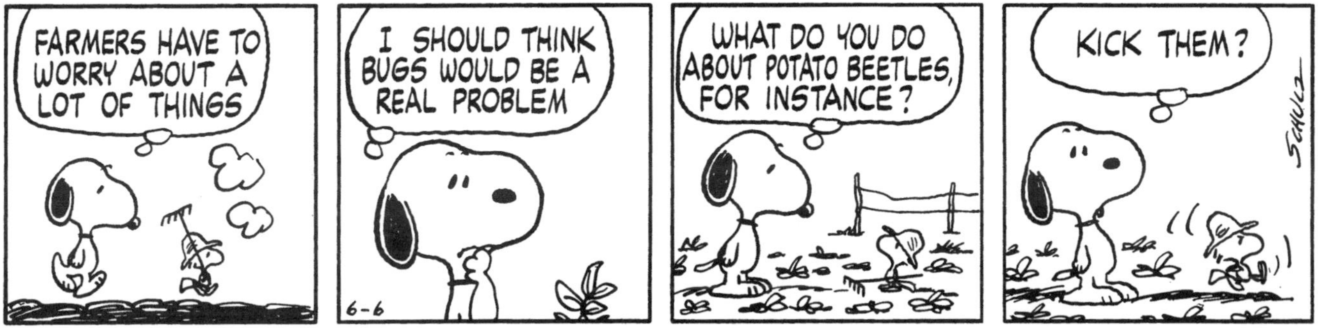
FARMERS HAVE TO WORRY ABOUT A LOT OF THINGS
I SHOULD THINK BUGS WOULD BE A REAL PROBLEM
6-6
WHAT DO YOU DO ABOUT POTATO BEETLES, FOR INSTANCE ?
KICK THEM ?
SCHULZ

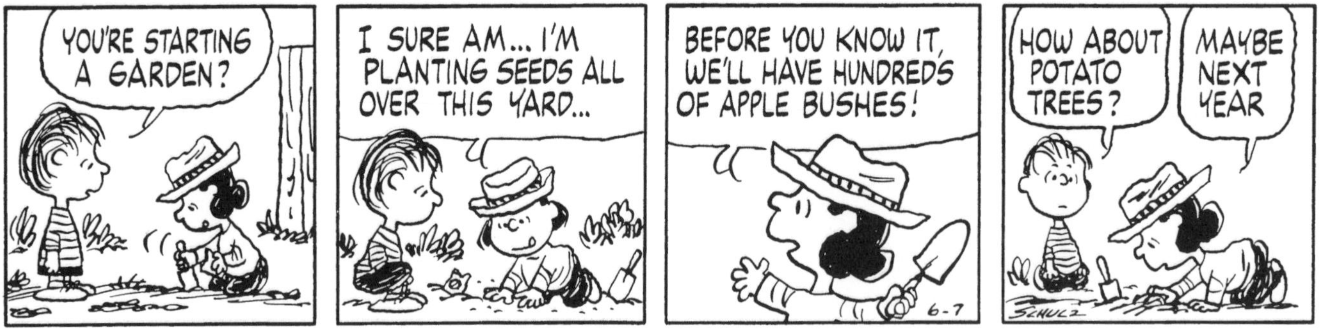
YOU'RE STARTING A GARDEN?
I SURE AM... I'M PLANTING SEEDS ALL OVER THIS YARD...
BEFORE YOU KNOW IT, WE'LL HAVE HUNDREDS OF APPLE BUSHES!
HOW ABOUT POTATO TREES?
MAYBE NEXT YEAR

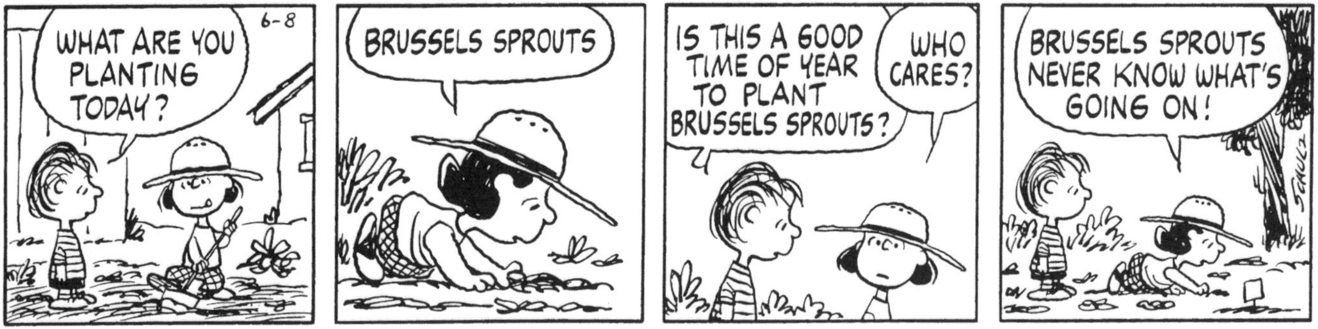
WHAT ARE YOU PLANTING TODAY?
BRUSSELS SPROUTS
IS THIS A GOOD TIME OF YEAR TO PLANT BRUSSELS SPROUTS?
WHO CARES?
BRUSSELS SPROUTS NEVER KNOW WHAT'S GOING ON!

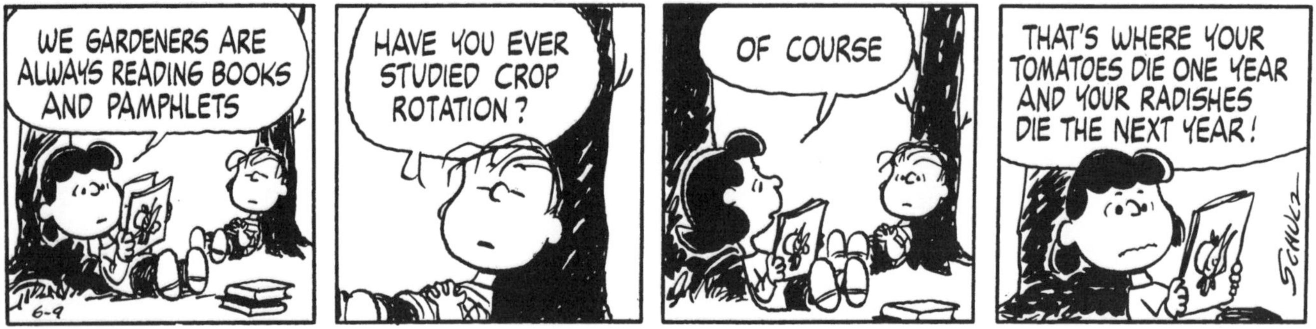
WE GARDENERS ARE ALWAYS READING BOOKS AND PAMPHLETS
HAVE YOU EVER STUDIED CROP ROTATION?
OF COURSE
THAT'S WHERE YOUR TOMATOES DIE ONE YEAR AND YOUR RADISHES DIE THE NEXT YEAR!

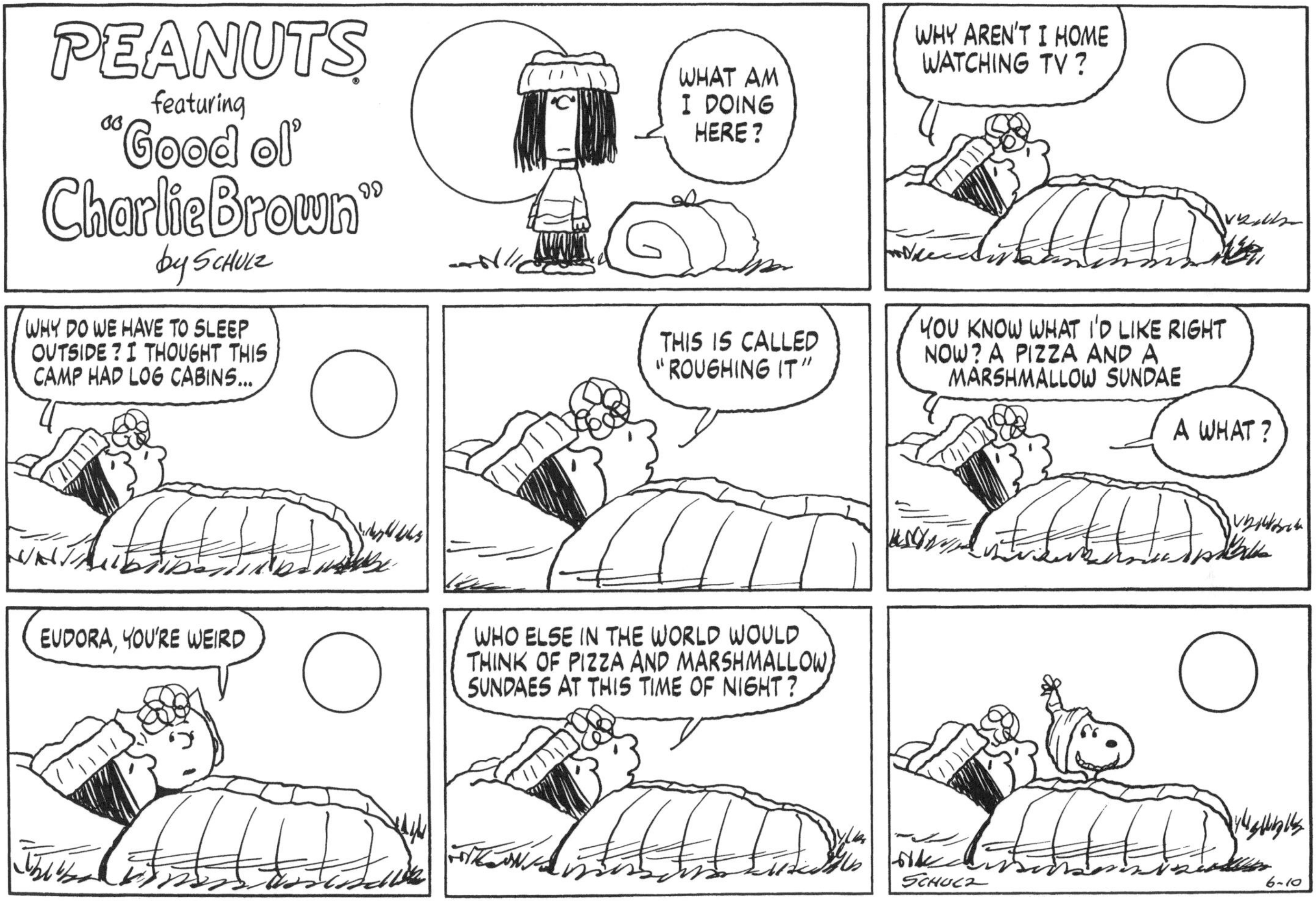
PEANUTS
featuring
"Good ol' CharlieBrown"
by SCHULZ
WHAT AM I DOING HERE?
WHY AREN'T I HOME WATCHING TV?
WHY DO WE HAVE TO SLEEP OUTSIDE? I THOUGHT THIS CAMP HAD LOG CABINS...
THIS IS CALLED "ROUGHING IT"
YOU KNOW WHAT I'D LIKE RIGHT NOW? A PIZZA AND A MARSHMALLOW SUNDAE
A WHAT?
EUDORA, YOU'RE WEIRD
WHO ELSE IN THE WORLD WOULD THINK OF PIZZA AND MARSHMALLOW SUNDAES AT THIS TIME OF NIGHT?
SCHULZ
6-10

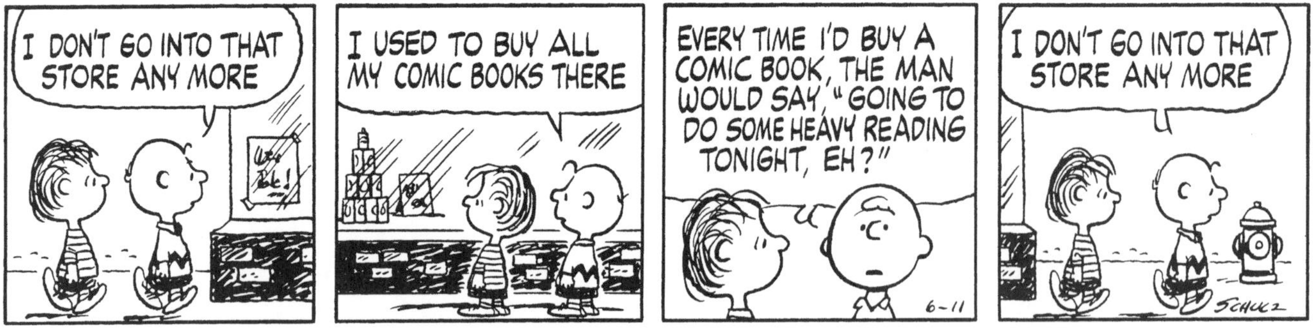
I DON'T GO INTO THAT STORE ANY MORE
I USED TO BUY ALL MY COMIC BOOKS THERE
EVERY TIME I'D BUY A COMIC BOOK, THE MAN WOULD SAY, "GOING TO DO SOME HEAVY READING TONIGHT, EH?"
6-11
I DON'T GO INTO THAT STORE ANY MORE
SCHULZ

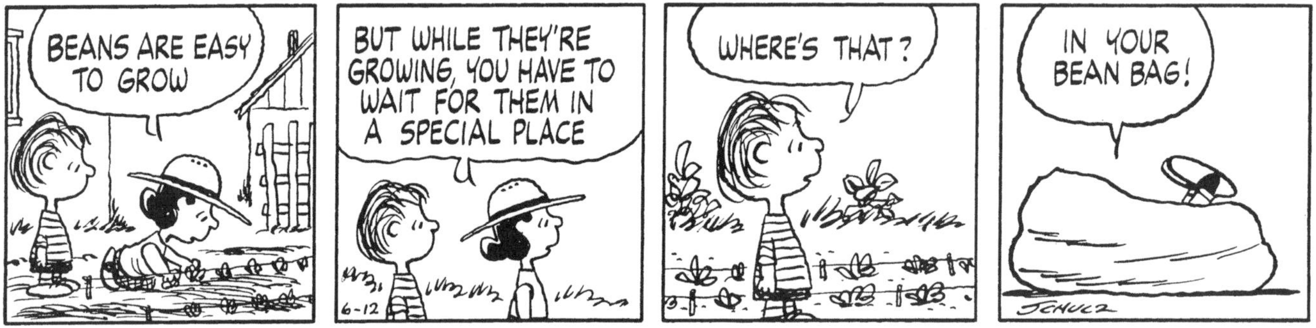
BEANS ARE EASY TO GROW
BUT WHILE THEY'RE GROWING, YOU HAVE TO WAIT FOR THEM IN A SPECIAL PLACE
6-12
WHERE'S THAT?
IN YOUR BEAN BAG!
SCHULZ

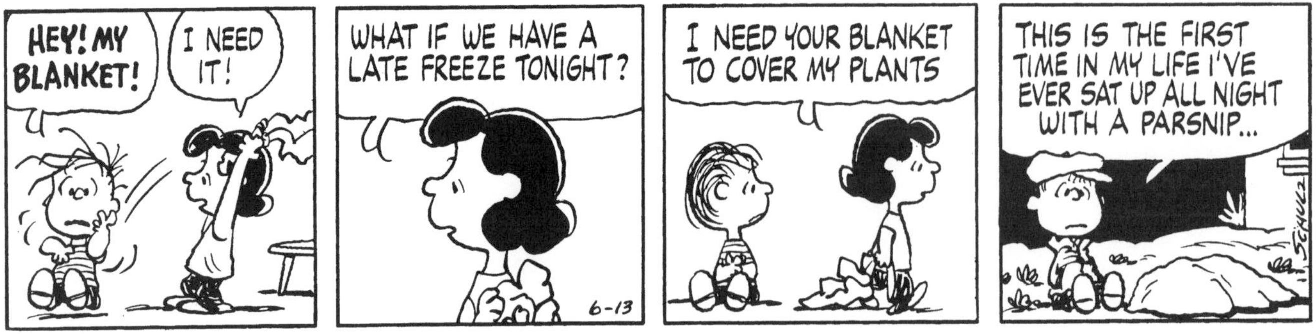
HEY! MY BLANKET!
I NEED IT!
WHAT IF WE HAVE A LATE FREEZE TONIGHT?
6-13
I NEED YOUR BLANKET TO COVER MY PLANTS
THIS IS THE FIRST TIME IN MY LIFE I'VE EVER SAT UP ALL NIGHT WITH A PARSNIP...
SCHULZ

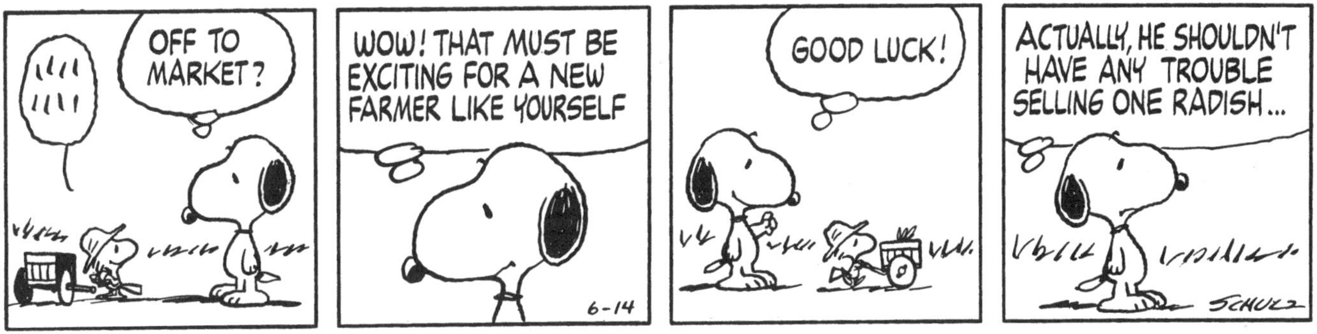
OFF TO MARKET?
WOW! THAT MUST BE EXCITING FOR A NEW FARMER LIKE YOURSELF
6-14
GOOD LUCK!
ACTUALLY, HE SHOULDN'T HAVE ANY TROUBLE SELLING ONE RADISH...
SCHULZ

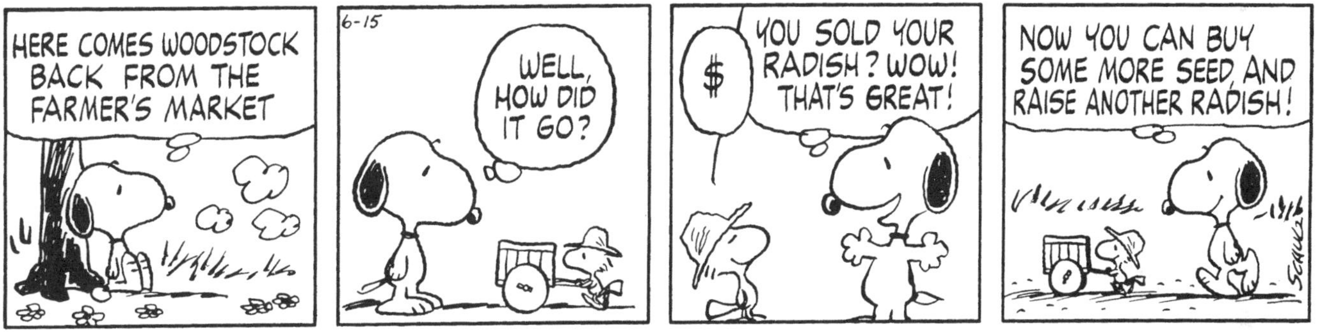
HERE COMES WOODSTOCK BACK FROM THE FARMER'S MARKET
6-15
WELL, HOW DID IT GO?
$
YOU SOLD YOUR RADISH? WOW! THAT'S GREAT!
NOW YOU CAN BUY SOME MORE SEED AND RAISE ANOTHER RADISH!
SCHULZ

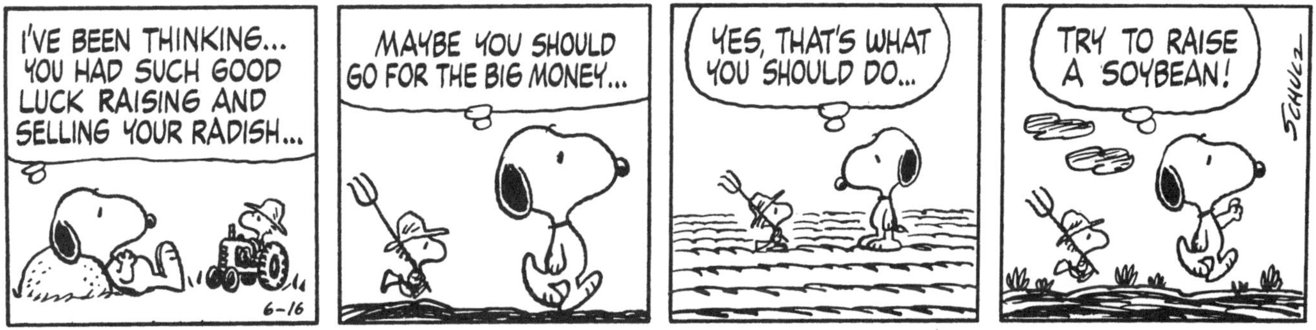
I'VE BEEN THINKING... YOU HAD SUCH GOOD LUCK RAISING AND SELLING YOUR RADISH...
6-16
MAYBE YOU SHOULD GO FOR THE BIG MONEY...
YES, THAT'S WHAT YOU SHOULD DO...
TRY TO RAISE A SOYBEAN!
SCHULZ

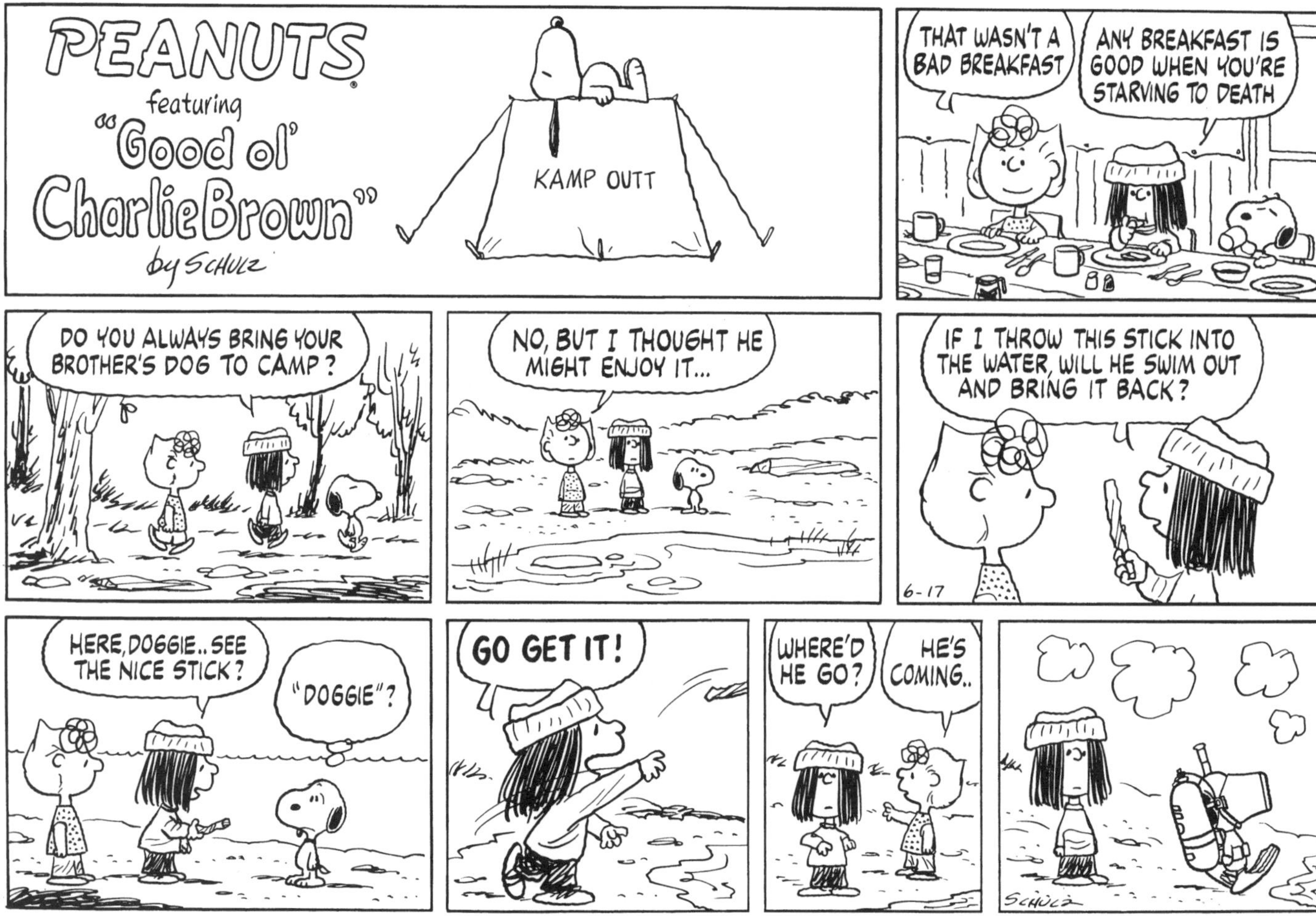
PEANUTS
featuring
"Good ol' Charlie Brown"
by SCHULZ
KAMP OUTT
THAT WASN'T A BAD BREAKFAST
ANY BREAKFAST IS GOOD WHEN YOU'RE STARVING TO DEATH
DO YOU ALWAYS BRING YOUR BROTHER'S DOG TO CAMP?
NO, BUT I THOUGHT HE MIGHT ENJOY IT...
IF I THROW THIS STICK INTO THE WATER, WILL HE SWIM OUT AND BRING IT BACK?
6-17
HERE, DOGGIE.. SEE THE NICE STICK?
"DOGGIE"?
GO GET IT!
WHERE'D HE GO?
HE'S COMING..
SCHULZ

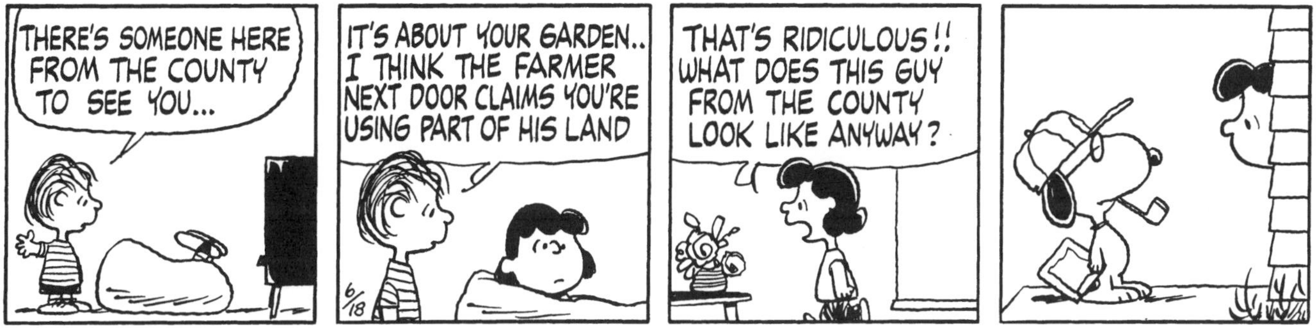
THERE'S SOMEONE HERE FROM THE COUNTY TO SEE YOU...
IT'S ABOUT YOUR GARDEN.. I THINK THE FARMER NEXT DOOR CLAIMS YOU'RE USING PART OF HIS LAND
6/18
THAT'S RIDICULOUS!! WHAT DOES THIS GUY FROM THE COUNTY LOOK LIKE ANYWAY?

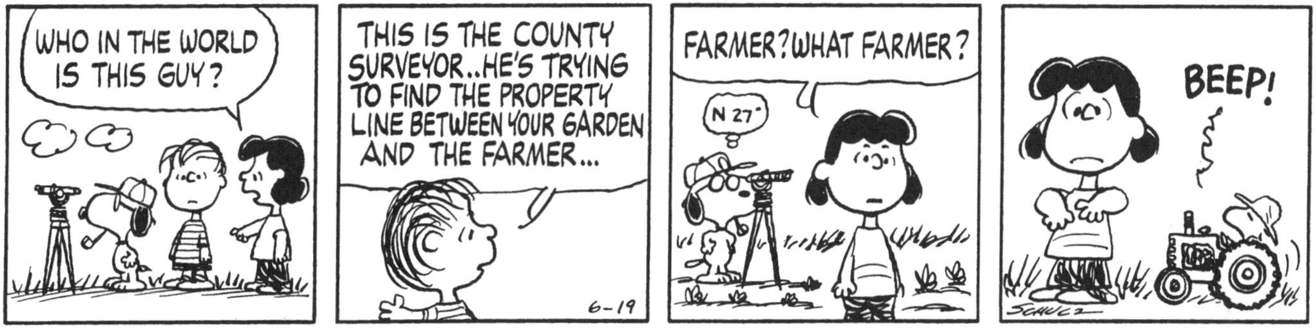
WHO IN THE WORLD IS THIS GUY?
THIS IS THE COUNTY SURVEYOR..HE'S TRYING TO FIND THE PROPERTY LINE BETWEEN YOUR GARDEN AND THE FARMER...
6-19
FARMER? WHAT FARMER?
N 27°
BEEP!
SCHULZ

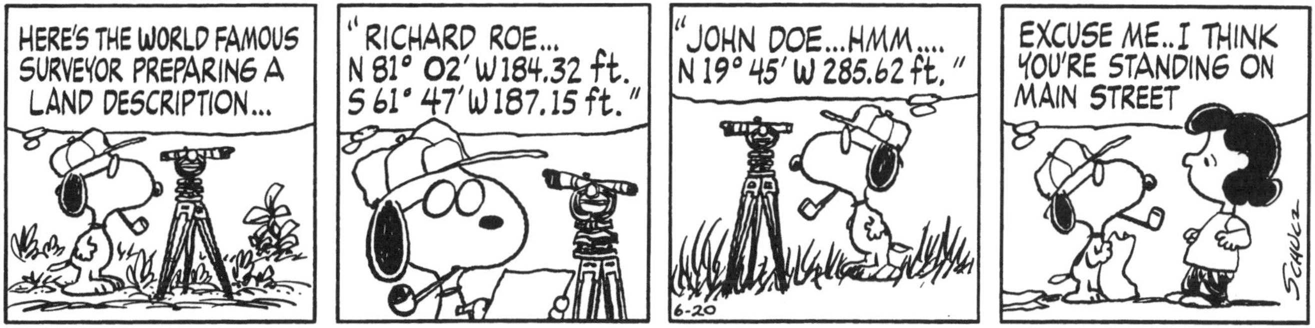
HERE'S THE WORLD FAMOUS SURVEYOR PREPARING A LAND DESCRIPTION...
"RICHARD ROE... N 81° 02' W 184.32 ft. S 61° 47' W 187.15 ft."
"JOHN DOE...HMM.... N 19° 45' W 285.62 ft."
6-20
EXCUSE ME..I THINK YOU'RE STANDING ON MAIN STREET
SCHULZ

Panel 1: I DON'T CARE ABOUT ANY COUNTY SURVEYOR!

Panel 2: THIS IS **MY** GARDEN! I PLANTED THESE TOMATOES! I PLANTED THESE BEANS!

Panel 3: NOBODY'S GONNA MOVE ME OFF **MY** LAND!!

6-21

Panel 4: BEEP!

Panel 5: HERE'S THE REPORT ON YOUR PROPERTY.. ACCORDING TO THE SURVEYOR, YOU'RE BOTH WRONG...

N91° W161

Panel 6: HE SAYS YOUR GARDEN BELONGS TO JOHN DOE, AND THE FARMER'S LAND BELONGS TO RICHARD ROE

6-22

Panel 7: **WHERE IS THAT SURVEYOR? I'LL BREAK HIS BONES!**

Panel 8: NOBODY HERE BUT US SCARECROWS

Panel 9: IF I CAME BACK FROM A LONG JOURNEY, WOULD YOU SMOTHER ME WITH KISSES?

NOPE!

6-23

Panel 10: IF I STAYED BY YOUR SIDE FOR THE REST OF YOUR LIFE, WOULD YOU SMOTHER ME WITH KISSES?

Panel 11: I DOUBT IT

Panel 12: EITHER WAY, I DON'T GET SMOTHERED WITH KISSES...

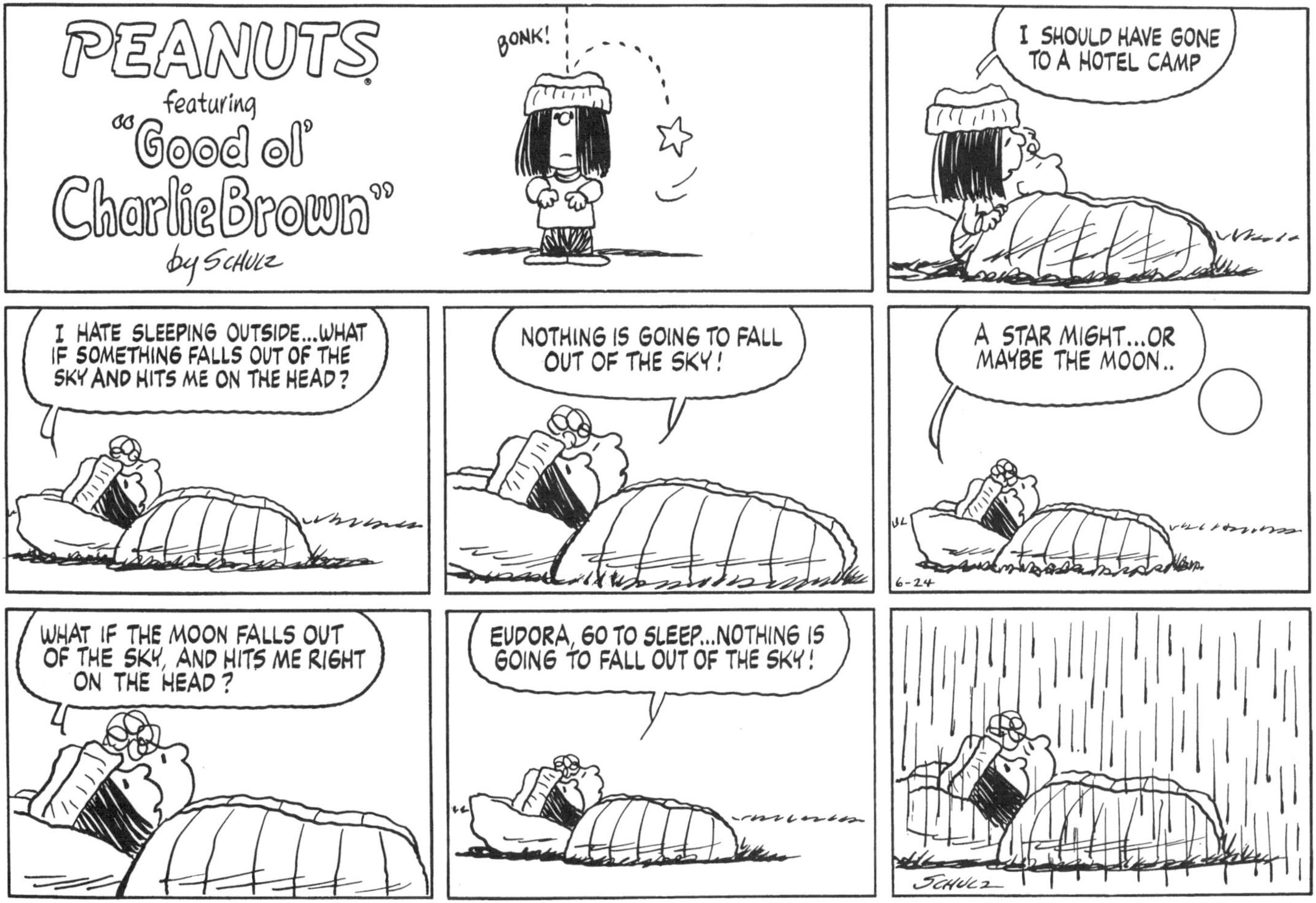
PEANUTS
featuring
"Good ol' Charlie Brown"
by SCHULZ
BONK!
I SHOULD HAVE GONE TO A HOTEL CAMP
I HATE SLEEPING OUTSIDE...WHAT IF SOMETHING FALLS OUT OF THE SKY AND HITS ME ON THE HEAD?
NOTHING IS GOING TO FALL OUT OF THE SKY!
A STAR MIGHT...OR MAYBE THE MOON..
6-24
WHAT IF THE MOON FALLS OUT OF THE SKY, AND HITS ME RIGHT ON THE HEAD?
EUDORA, GO TO SLEEP...NOTHING IS GOING TO FALL OUT OF THE SKY!
SCHULZ

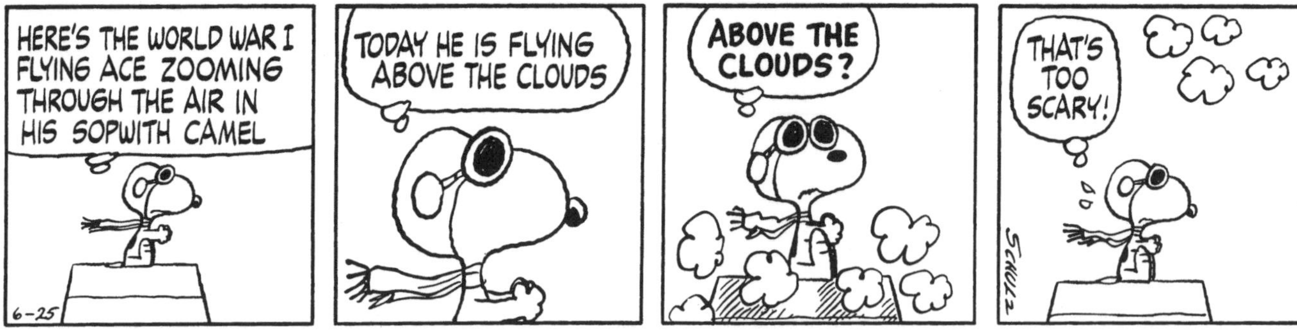
HERE'S THE WORLD WAR I FLYING ACE ZOOMING THROUGH THE AIR IN HIS SOPWITH CAMEL
6-25
TODAY HE IS FLYING ABOVE THE CLOUDS
ABOVE THE CLOUDS?
THAT'S TOO SCARY!
SCHULZ

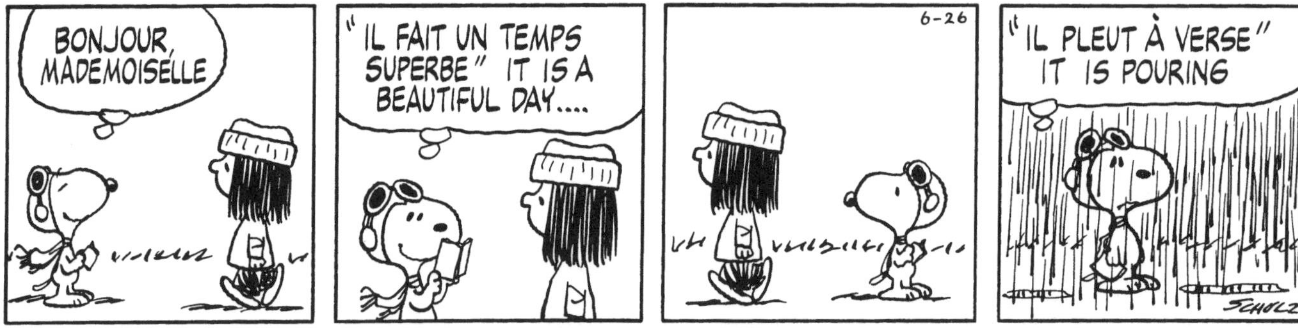
BONJOUR, MADEMOISELLE
"IL FAIT UN TEMPS SUPERBE" IT IS A BEAUTIFUL DAY....
6-26
"IL PLEUT À VERSE" IT IS POURING
SCHULZ

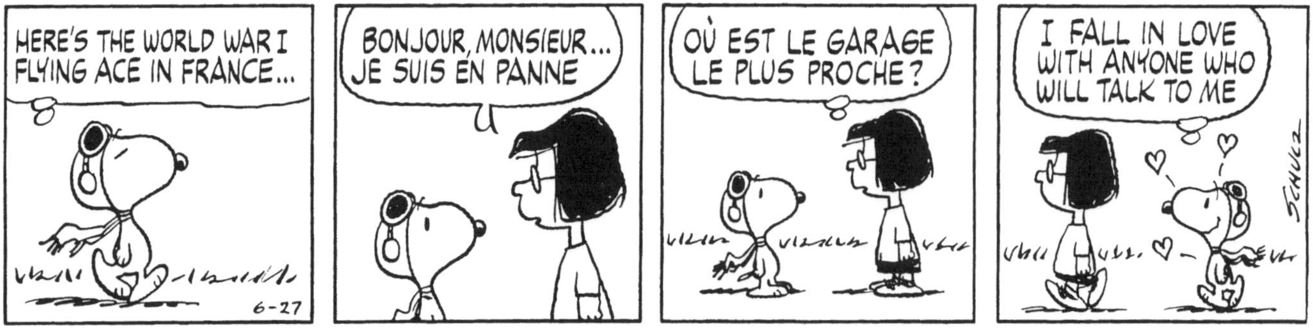
HERE'S THE WORLD WAR I FLYING ACE IN FRANCE...
6-27
BONJOUR, MONSIEUR... JE SUIS EN PANNE
OÙ EST LE GARAGE LE PLUS PROCHE?
I FALL IN LOVE WITH ANYONE WHO WILL TALK TO ME
SCHULZ

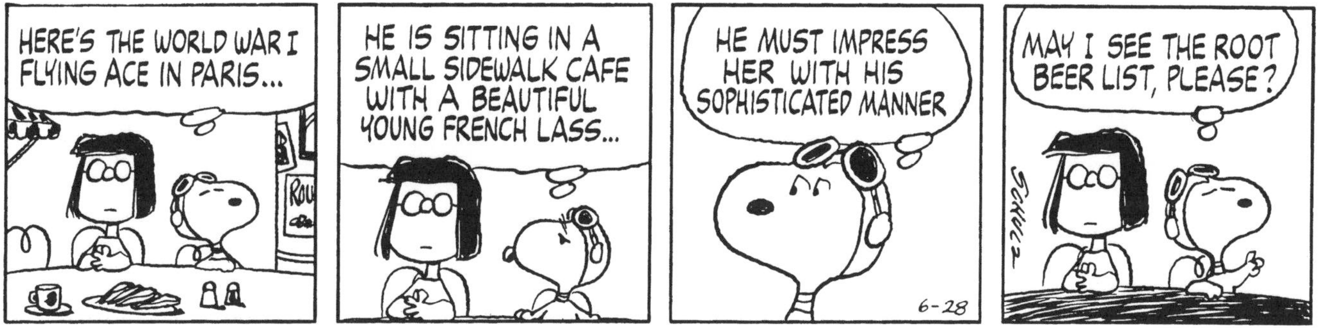
HERE'S THE WORLD WAR I FLYING ACE IN PARIS...
HE IS SITTING IN A SMALL SIDEWALK CAFE WITH A BEAUTIFUL YOUNG FRENCH LASS...
HE MUST IMPRESS HER WITH HIS SOPHISTICATED MANNER
6-28
MAY I SEE THE ROOT BEER LIST, PLEASE?
SCHULZ

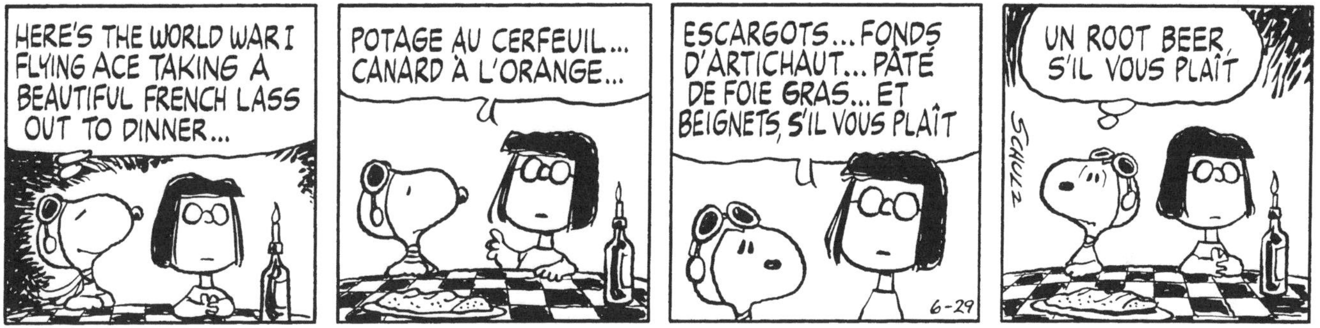
HERE'S THE WORLD WAR I FLYING ACE TAKING A BEAUTIFUL FRENCH LASS OUT TO DINNER...
POTAGE AU CERFEUIL... CANARD À L'ORANGE...
ESCARGOTS... FONDS D'ARTICHAUT... PÂTÉ DE FOIE GRAS... ET BEIGNETS, S'IL VOUS PLAÎT
6-29
UN ROOT BEER, S'IL VOUS PLAÎT
SCHULZ

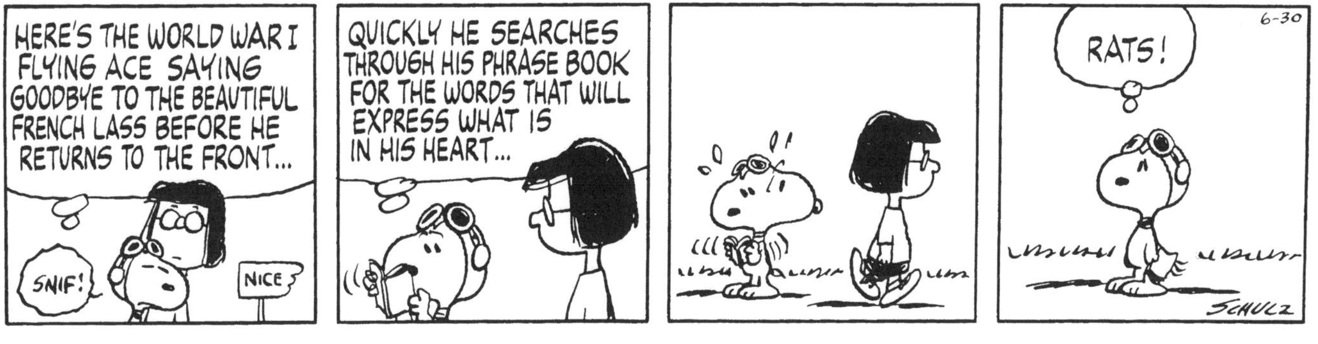
HERE'S THE WORLD WAR I FLYING ACE SAYING GOODBYE TO THE BEAUTIFUL FRENCH LASS BEFORE HE RETURNS TO THE FRONT...
SNIF!
NICE
QUICKLY HE SEARCHES THROUGH HIS PHRASE BOOK FOR THE WORDS THAT WILL EXPRESS WHAT IS IN HIS HEART...
6-30
RATS!
SCHULZ

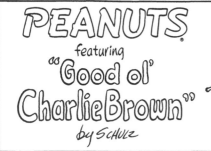

PEANUTS
featuring
"Good ol' CharlieBrown"
by SCHULZ

COME IN! COME IN! SIT ANYWHERE!

GOOD EVENING, SIR.. WELCOME TO THE FANCIEST RESTAURANT IN TOWN!

7-1

OUR SPECIAL TONIGHT IS DOG FOOD...IT IS SCOOPED CAREFULLY FROM THE CAN, PLOPPED LIGHTLY INTO THE DISH AND STIRRED VIGOROUSLY INTO AN APPETIZING DELIGHT...

YOU'LL HAVE THE SPECIAL THEN, SIR? GOOD! YOU'LL NOT BE SORRY!

WOULD YOU CARE FOR A DRINK BEFORE DINNER? A BOWL OF WATER PERHAPS? FINE!

YOUR WAITER WILL BE WITH YOU IN A MOMENT...

IF THIS IS SUCH A FANCY PLACE, WHY THE PAPER NAPKIN?

SCHULZ

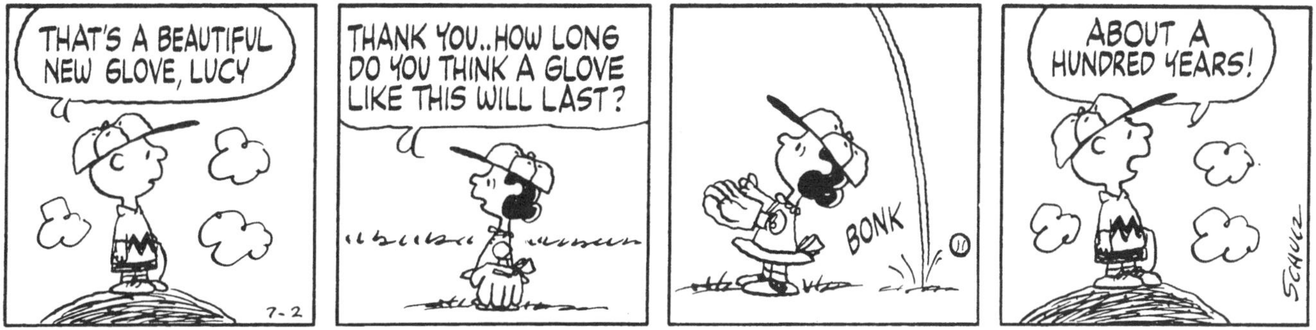
THAT'S A BEAUTIFUL NEW GLOVE, LUCY
7-2
THANK YOU..HOW LONG DO YOU THINK A GLOVE LIKE THIS WILL LAST?
BONK
ABOUT A HUNDRED YEARS!
SCHULZ

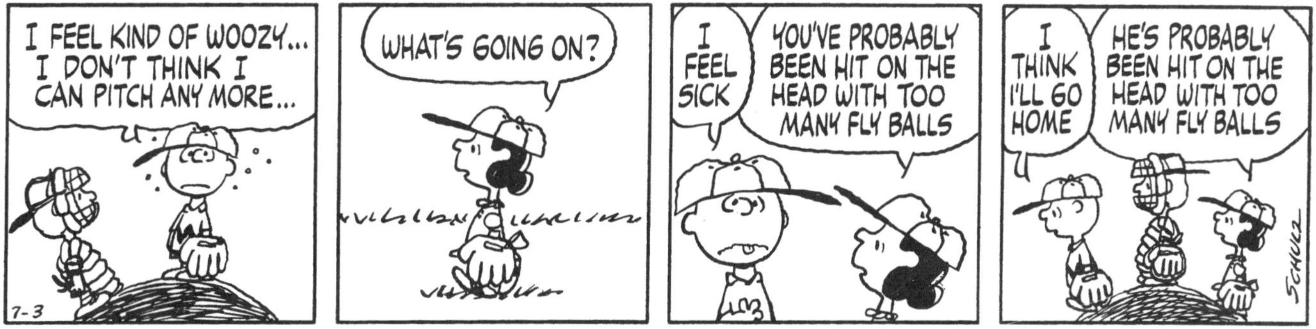
I FEEL KIND OF WOOZY... I DON'T THINK I CAN PITCH ANY MORE...
7-3
WHAT'S GOING ON?
I FEEL SICK
YOU'VE PROBABLY BEEN HIT ON THE HEAD WITH TOO MANY FLY BALLS
I THINK I'LL GO HOME
HE'S PROBABLY BEEN HIT ON THE HEAD WITH TOO MANY FLY BALLS
SCHULZ

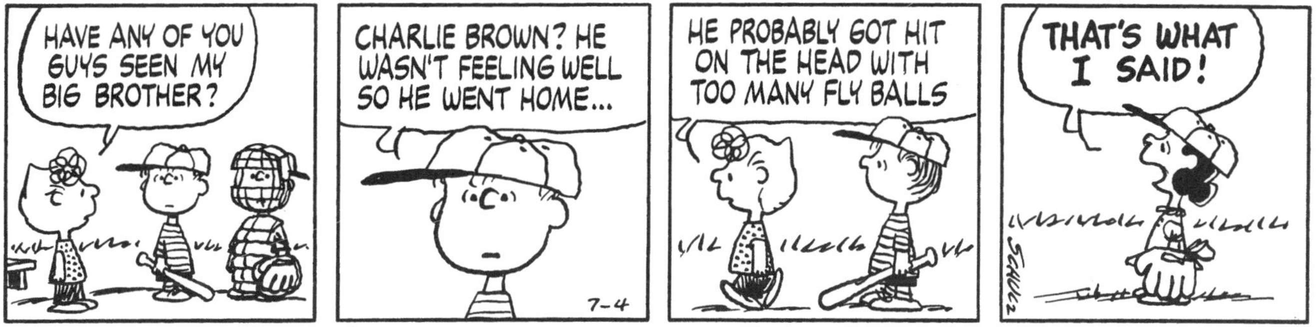
HAVE ANY OF YOU GUYS SEEN MY BIG BROTHER?
CHARLIE BROWN? HE WASN'T FEELING WELL SO HE WENT HOME...
7-4
HE PROBABLY GOT HIT ON THE HEAD WITH TOO MANY FLY BALLS
THAT'S WHAT I SAID!
SCHULZ

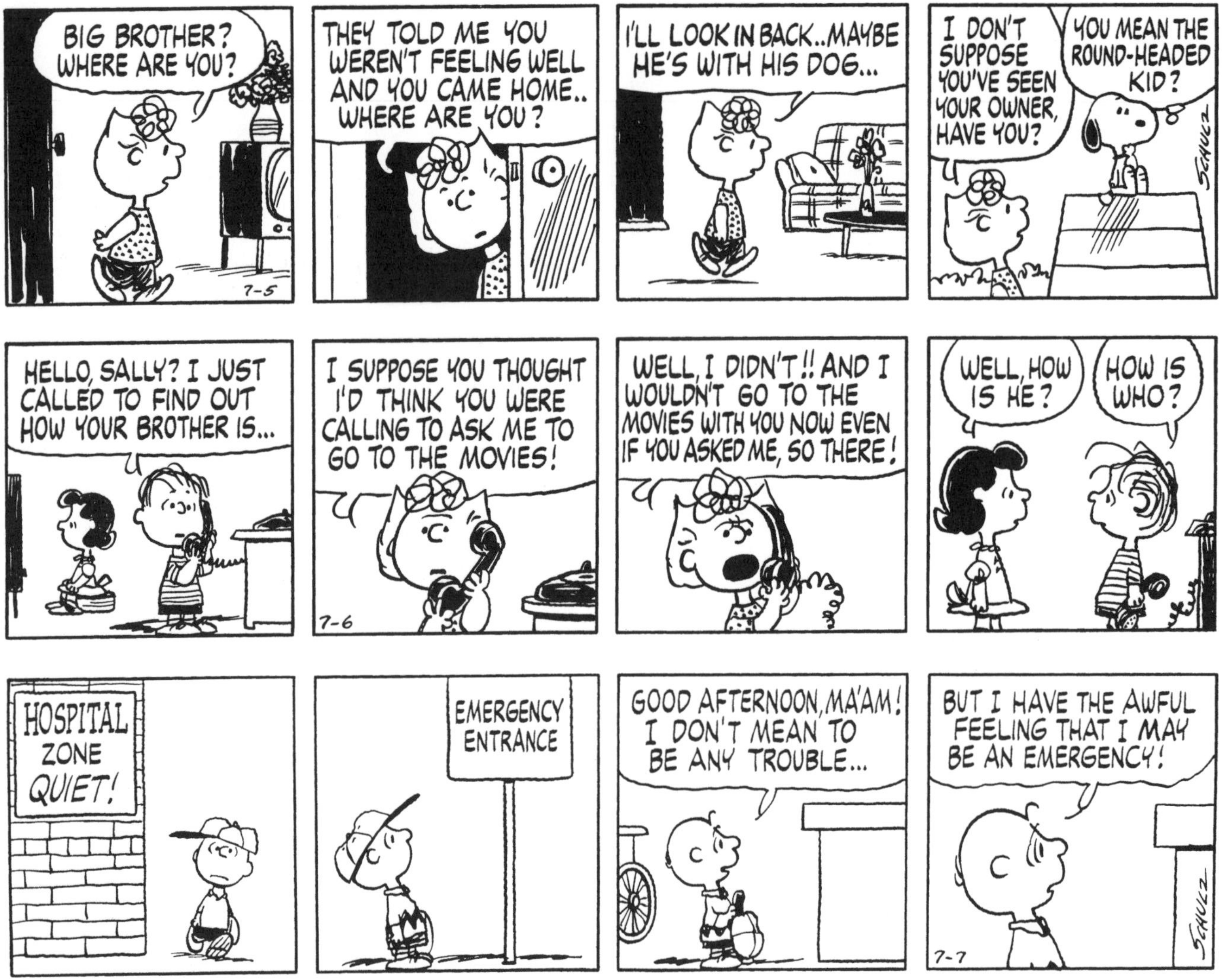
BIG BROTHER? WHERE ARE YOU?
7-5
THEY TOLD ME YOU WEREN'T FEELING WELL AND YOU CAME HOME.. WHERE ARE YOU?
I'LL LOOK IN BACK..MAYBE HE'S WITH HIS DOG...
I DON'T SUPPOSE YOU'VE SEEN YOUR OWNER, HAVE YOU?
YOU MEAN THE ROUND-HEADED KID?
SCHULZ
HELLO, SALLY? I JUST CALLED TO FIND OUT HOW YOUR BROTHER IS...
I SUPPOSE YOU THOUGHT I'D THINK YOU WERE CALLING TO ASK ME TO GO TO THE MOVIES!
7-6
WELL, I DIDN'T!! AND I WOULDN'T GO TO THE MOVIES WITH YOU NOW EVEN IF YOU ASKED ME, SO THERE!
WELL, HOW IS HE?
HOW IS WHO?
HOSPITAL ZONE QUIET!
EMERGENCY ENTRANCE
GOOD AFTERNOON, MA'AM! I DON'T MEAN TO BE ANY TROUBLE...
BUT I HAVE THE AWFUL FEELING THAT I MAY BE AN EMERGENCY!
7-7
SCHULZ

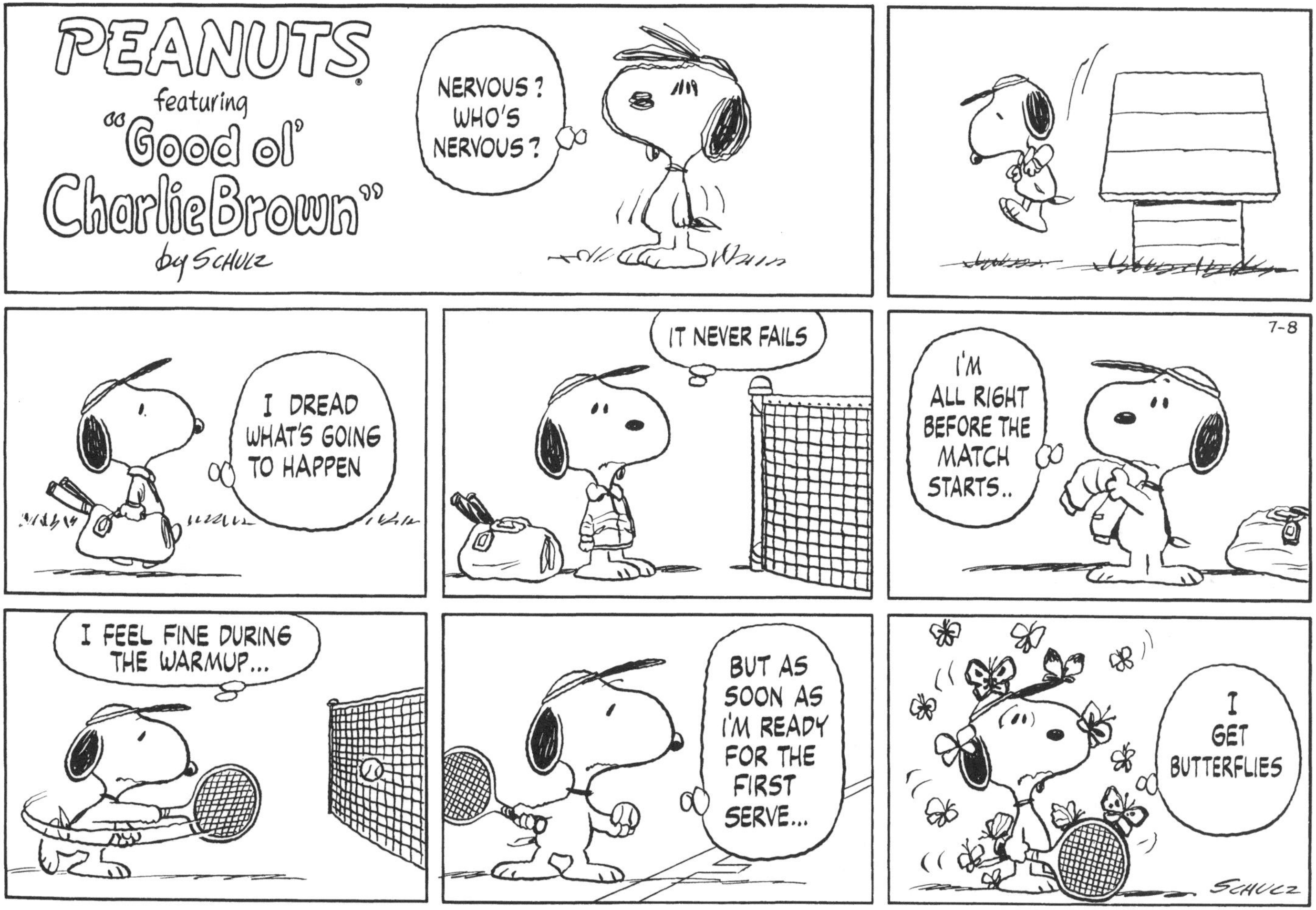
PEANUTS
featuring
"Good ol' Charlie Brown"
by SCHULZ
NERVOUS? WHO'S NERVOUS?
I DREAD WHAT'S GOING TO HAPPEN
IT NEVER FAILS
7-8
I'M ALL RIGHT BEFORE THE MATCH STARTS..
I FEEL FINE DURING THE WARMUP...
BUT AS SOON AS I'M READY FOR THE FIRST SERVE...
I GET BUTTERFLIES
SCHULZ

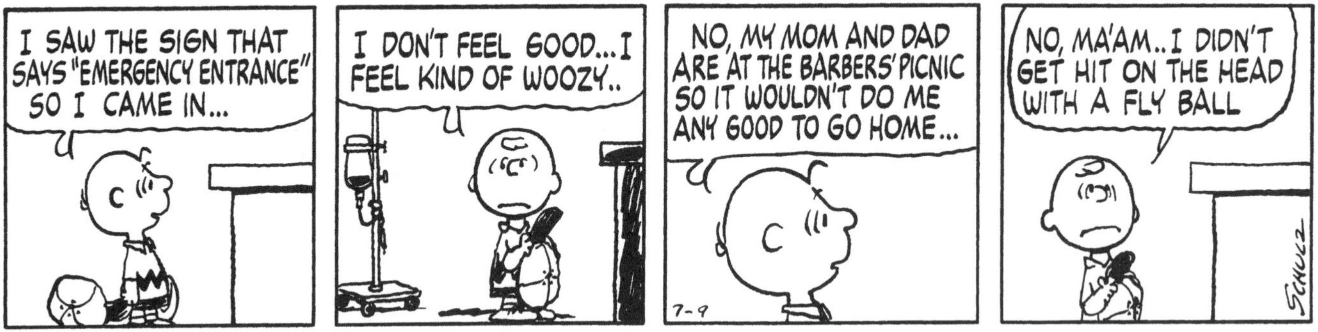
I SAW THE SIGN THAT SAYS "EMERGENCY ENTRANCE" SO I CAME IN...
I DON'T FEEL GOOD...I FEEL KIND OF WOOZY..
NO, MY MOM AND DAD ARE AT THE BARBERS' PICNIC SO IT WOULDN'T DO ME ANY GOOD TO GO HOME...
NO, MA'AM..I DIDN'T GET HIT ON THE HEAD WITH A FLY BALL

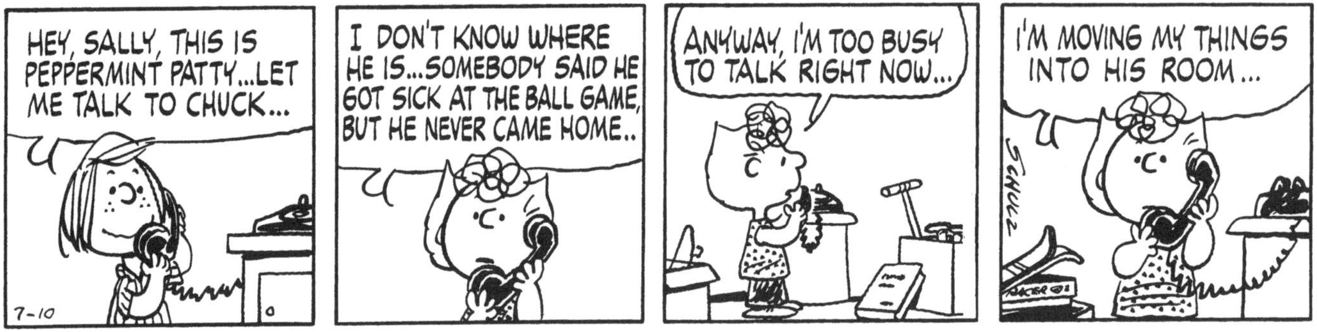
HEY, SALLY, THIS IS PEPPERMINT PATTY...LET ME TALK TO CHUCK...
I DON'T KNOW WHERE HE IS...SOMEBODY SAID HE GOT SICK AT THE BALL GAME, BUT HE NEVER CAME HOME..
ANYWAY, I'M TOO BUSY TO TALK RIGHT NOW...
I'M MOVING MY THINGS INTO HIS ROOM...

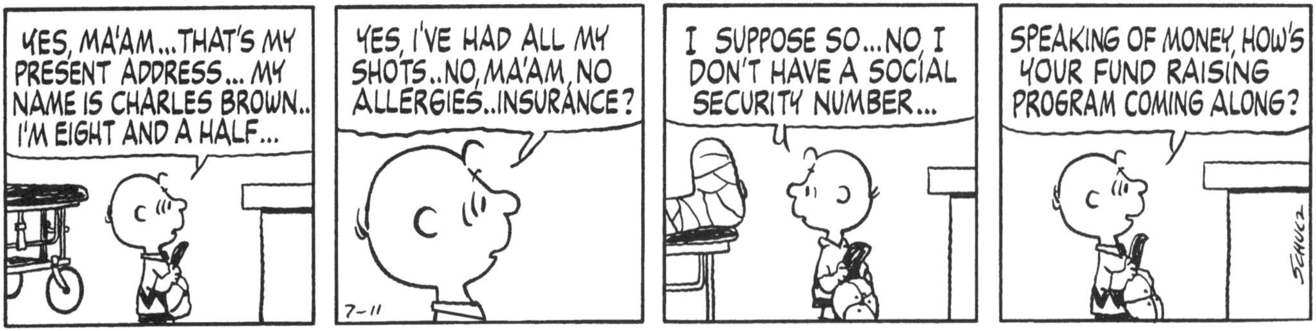
YES, MA'AM...THAT'S MY PRESENT ADDRESS... MY NAME IS CHARLES BROWN.. I'M EIGHT AND A HALF...
YES, I'VE HAD ALL MY SHOTS..NO, MA'AM, NO ALLERGIES..INSURANCE?
I SUPPOSE SO...NO, I DON'T HAVE A SOCIAL SECURITY NUMBER...
SPEAKING OF MONEY, HOW'S YOUR FUND RAISING PROGRAM COMING ALONG?

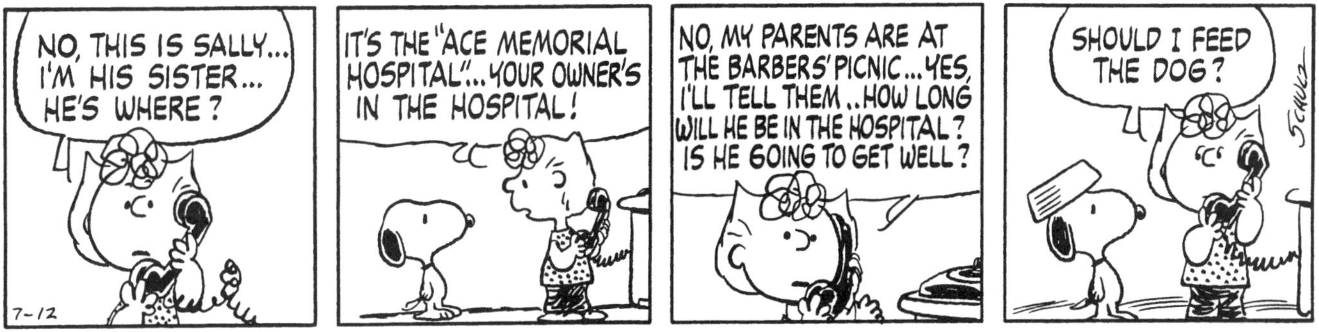
NO, THIS IS SALLY... I'M HIS SISTER... HE'S WHERE ?
7-12
IT'S THE "ACE MEMORIAL HOSPITAL"... YOUR OWNER'S IN THE HOSPITAL!
NO, MY PARENTS ARE AT THE BARBERS' PICNIC... YES, I'LL TELL THEM.. HOW LONG WILL HE BE IN THE HOSPITAL? IS HE GOING TO GET WELL?
SHOULD I FEED THE DOG?
SCHULZ

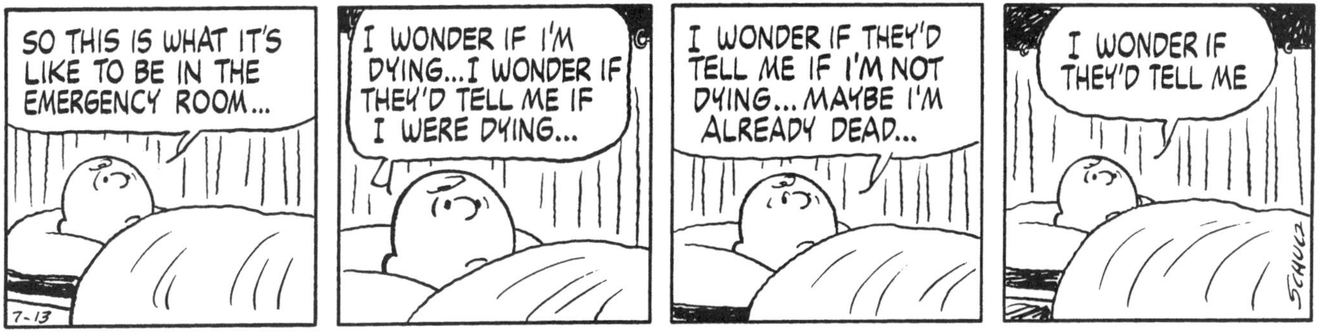
SO THIS IS WHAT IT'S LIKE TO BE IN THE EMERGENCY ROOM...
7-13
I WONDER IF I'M DYING... I WONDER IF THEY'D TELL ME IF I WERE DYING...
I WONDER IF THEY'D TELL ME IF I'M NOT DYING... MAYBE I'M ALREADY DEAD...
I WONDER IF THEY'D TELL ME
SCHULZ

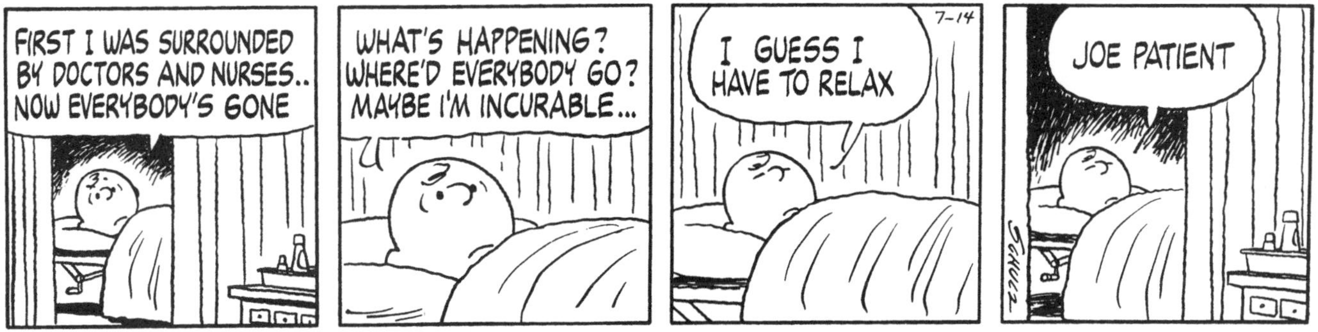
FIRST I WAS SURROUNDED BY DOCTORS AND NURSES.. NOW EVERYBODY'S GONE
WHAT'S HAPPENING? WHERE'D EVERYBODY GO? MAYBE I'M INCURABLE...
7-14
I GUESS I HAVE TO RELAX
SCHULZ
JOE PATIENT

PEANUTS featuring **"Good ol' Charlie Brown"** by SCHULZ

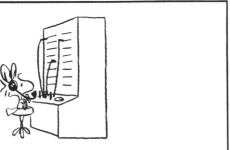

RING!

HELLO?

YES, UH HUH.. ALL RIGHT... GOODBYE

7-15

SOME PEOPLE GET SO UPSET IF THEY HAVE TO CALL YOU TO THE PHONE!

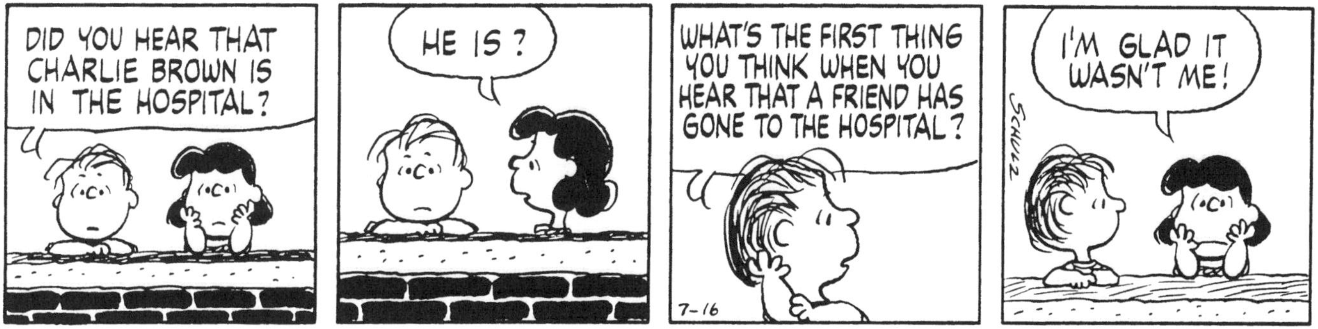
DID YOU HEAR THAT CHARLIE BROWN IS IN THE HOSPITAL?
HE IS?
WHAT'S THE FIRST THING YOU THINK WHEN YOU HEAR THAT A FRIEND HAS GONE TO THE HOSPITAL?
7-16
I'M GLAD IT WASN'T ME!

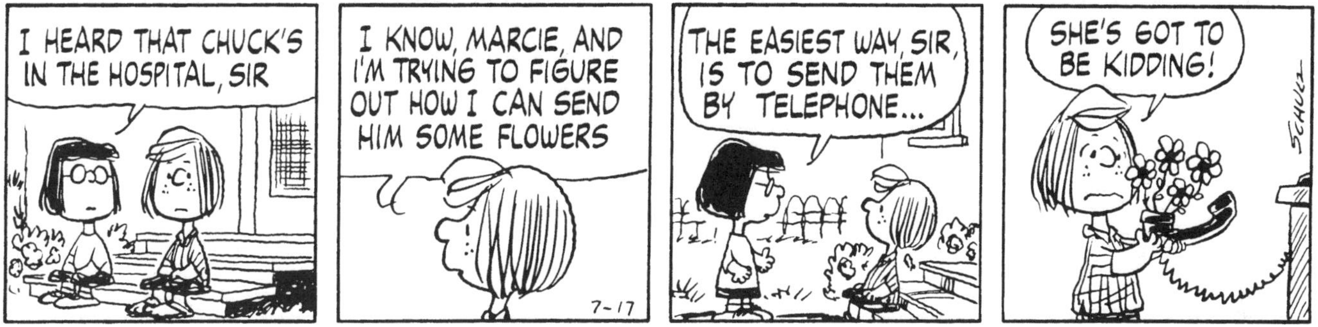
I HEARD THAT CHUCK'S IN THE HOSPITAL, SIR
I KNOW, MARCIE, AND I'M TRYING TO FIGURE OUT HOW I CAN SEND HIM SOME FLOWERS
7-17
THE EASIEST WAY, SIR, IS TO SEND THEM BY TELEPHONE...
SHE'S GOT TO BE KIDDING!

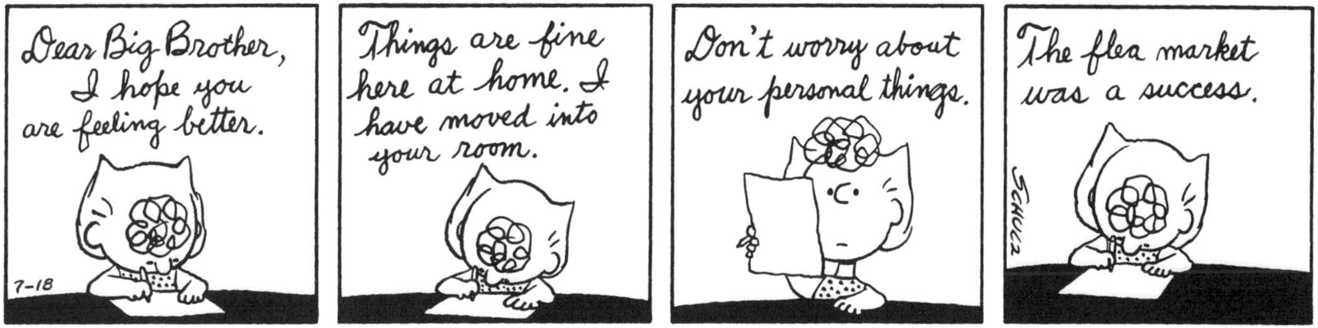
Dear Big Brother, I hope you are feeling better.
7-18
Things are fine here at home. I have moved into your room.
Don't worry about your personal things.
The flea market was a success.

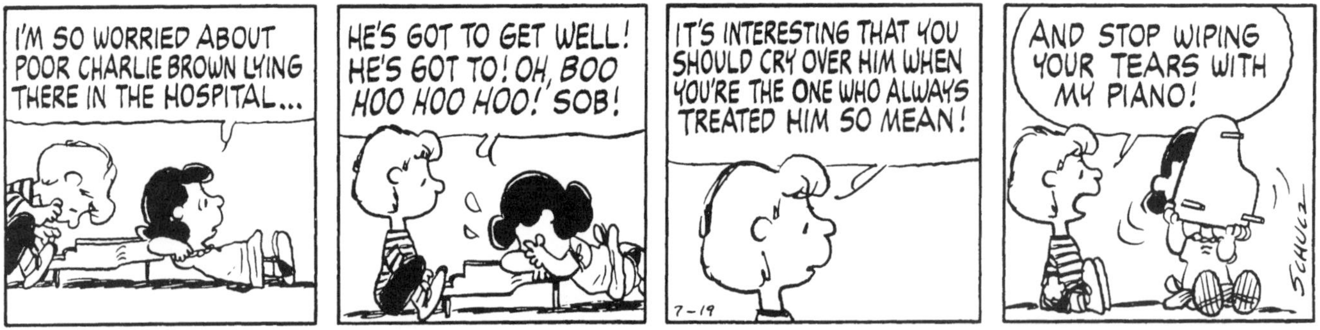
I'M SO WORRIED ABOUT POOR CHARLIE BROWN LYING THERE IN THE HOSPITAL...
HE'S GOT TO GET WELL! HE'S GOT TO! OH, BOO HOO HOO HOO! SOB!
IT'S INTERESTING THAT YOU SHOULD CRY OVER HIM WHEN YOU'RE THE ONE WHO ALWAYS TREATED HIM SO MEAN!
7-19
AND STOP WIPING YOUR TEARS WITH MY PIANO!
SCHULZ

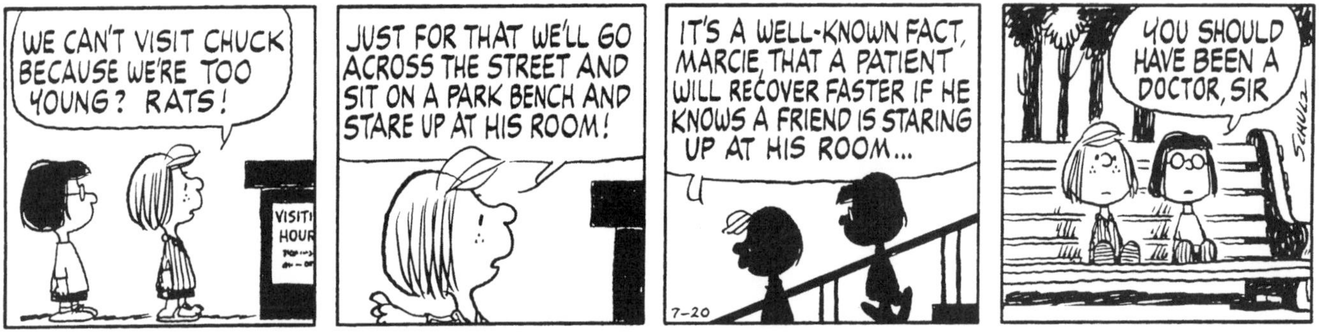
WE CAN'T VISIT CHUCK BECAUSE WE'RE TOO YOUNG? RATS!
VISITI
HOUR
JUST FOR THAT WE'LL GO ACROSS THE STREET AND SIT ON A PARK BENCH AND STARE UP AT HIS ROOM!
IT'S A WELL-KNOWN FACT, MARCIE, THAT A PATIENT WILL RECOVER FASTER IF HE KNOWS A FRIEND IS STARING UP AT HIS ROOM...
7-20
YOU SHOULD HAVE BEEN A DOCTOR, SIR
SCHULZ

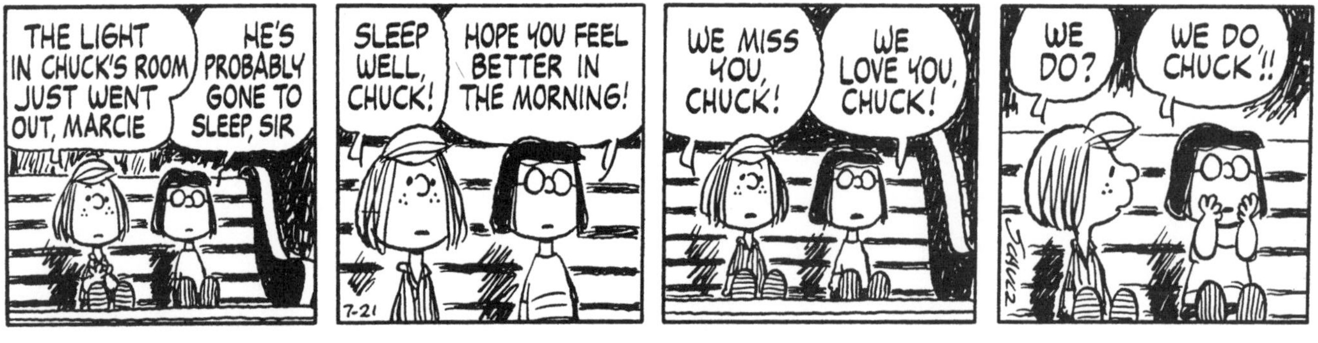
THE LIGHT IN CHUCK'S ROOM JUST WENT OUT, MARCIE
HE'S PROBABLY GONE TO SLEEP, SIR
SLEEP WELL, CHUCK!
HOPE YOU FEEL BETTER IN THE MORNING!
7-21
WE MISS YOU, CHUCK!
WE LOVE YOU, CHUCK!
WE DO?
WE DO, CHUCK!!
SCHULZ

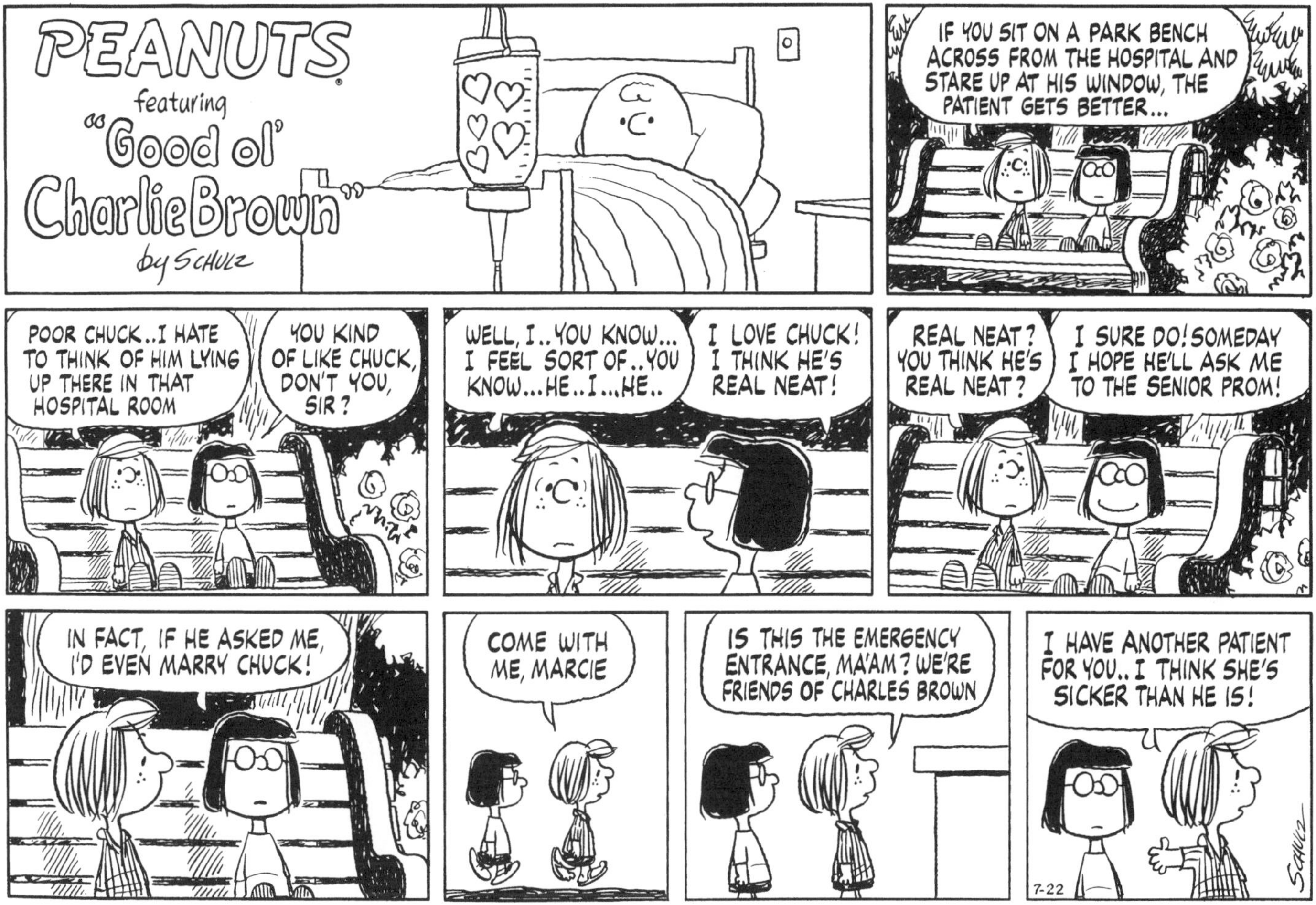
PEANUTS
featuring "Good ol' Charlie Brown"
by SCHULZ
IF YOU SIT ON A PARK BENCH ACROSS FROM THE HOSPITAL AND STARE UP AT HIS WINDOW, THE PATIENT GETS BETTER...
POOR CHUCK..I HATE TO THINK OF HIM LYING UP THERE IN THAT HOSPITAL ROOM
YOU KIND OF LIKE CHUCK, DON'T YOU, SIR?
WELL, I..YOU KNOW... I FEEL SORT OF..YOU KNOW...HE..I...HE..
I LOVE CHUCK! I THINK HE'S REAL NEAT!
REAL NEAT? YOU THINK HE'S REAL NEAT?
I SURE DO! SOMEDAY I HOPE HE'LL ASK ME TO THE SENIOR PROM!
IN FACT, IF HE ASKED ME, I'D EVEN MARRY CHUCK!
COME WITH ME, MARCIE
IS THIS THE EMERGENCY ENTRANCE, MA'AM? WE'RE FRIENDS OF CHARLES BROWN
I HAVE ANOTHER PATIENT FOR YOU.. I THINK SHE'S SICKER THAN HE IS!
7-22
SCHULZ

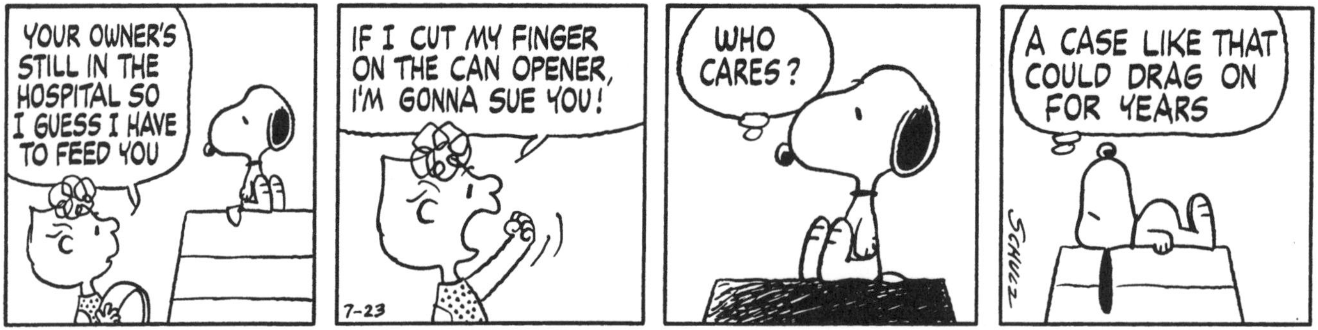
YOUR OWNER'S STILL IN THE HOSPITAL SO I GUESS I HAVE TO FEED YOU
IF I CUT MY FINGER ON THE CAN OPENER, I'M GONNA SUE YOU!
7-23
WHO CARES?
A CASE LIKE THAT COULD DRAG ON FOR YEARS
SCHULZ

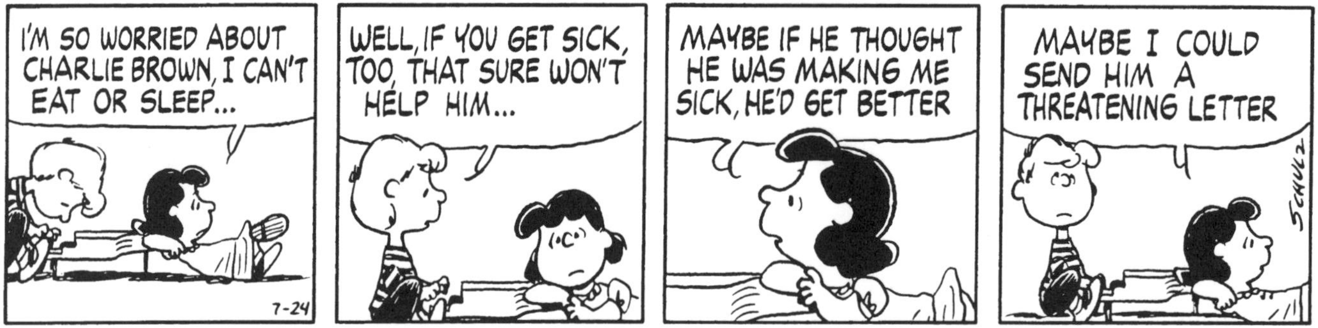
I'M SO WORRIED ABOUT CHARLIE BROWN, I CAN'T EAT OR SLEEP...
7-24
WELL, IF YOU GET SICK, TOO, THAT SURE WON'T HELP HIM...
MAYBE IF HE THOUGHT HE WAS MAKING ME SICK, HE'D GET BETTER
MAYBE I COULD SEND HIM A THREATENING LETTER
SCHULZ

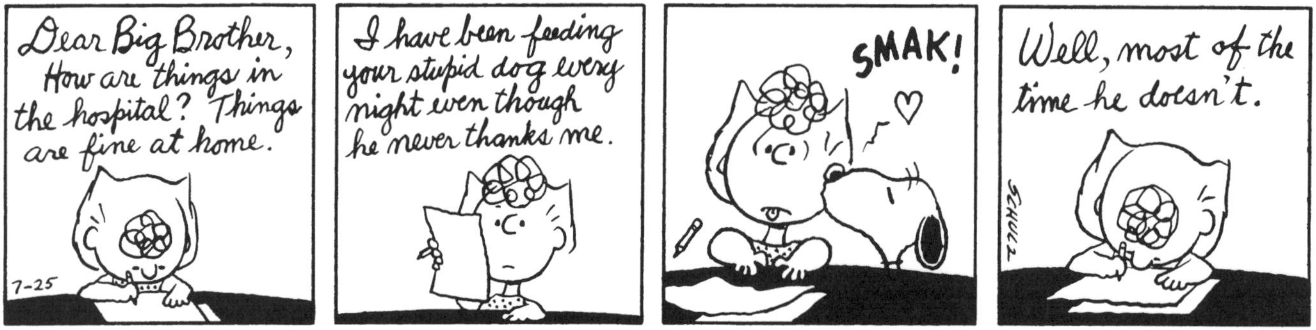
Dear Big Brother,
How are things in the hospital? Things are fine at home.
7-25
I have been feeding your stupid dog every night even though he never thanks me.
SMAK!
SCHULZ
Well, most of the time he doesn't.

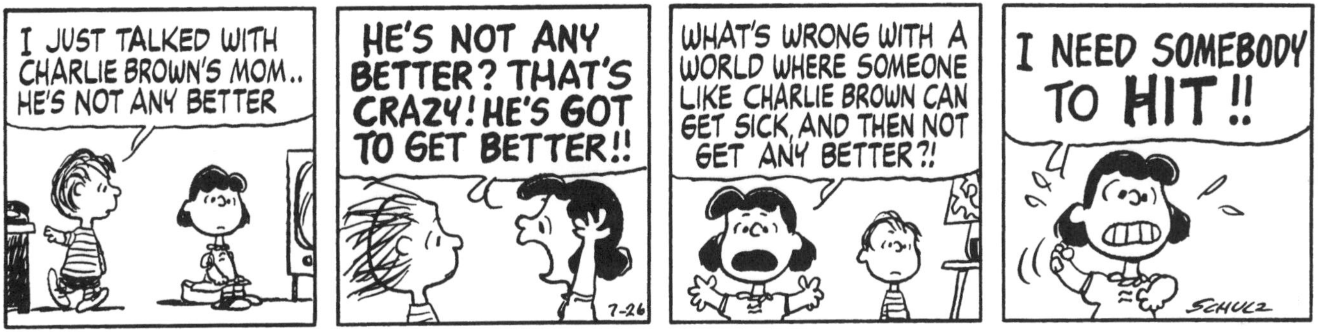
I JUST TALKED WITH CHARLIE BROWN'S MOM.. HE'S NOT ANY BETTER
HE'S NOT ANY BETTER? THAT'S CRAZY! HE'S GOT TO GET BETTER!!
WHAT'S WRONG WITH A WORLD WHERE SOMEONE LIKE CHARLIE BROWN CAN GET SICK, AND THEN NOT GET ANY BETTER?!
I NEED SOMEBODY TO HIT!!

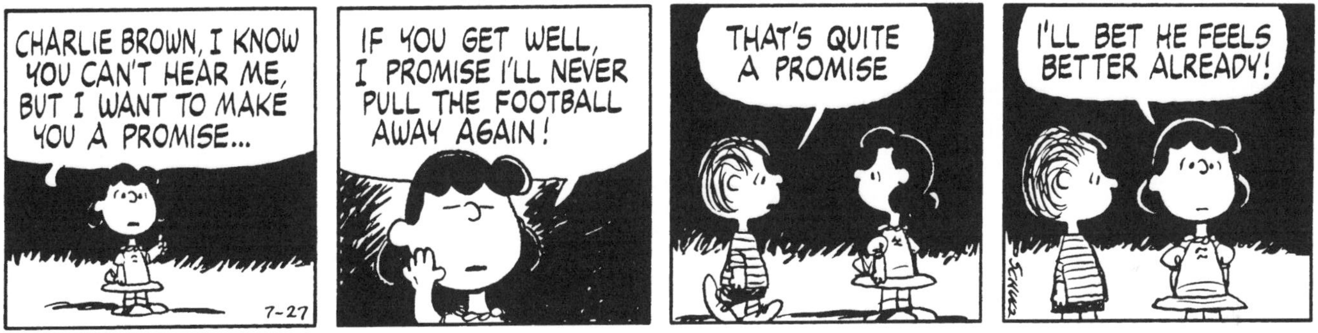
CHARLIE BROWN, I KNOW YOU CAN'T HEAR ME, BUT I WANT TO MAKE YOU A PROMISE...
IF YOU GET WELL, I PROMISE I'LL NEVER PULL THE FOOTBALL AWAY AGAIN!
THAT'S QUITE A PROMISE
I'LL BET HE FEELS BETTER ALREADY!

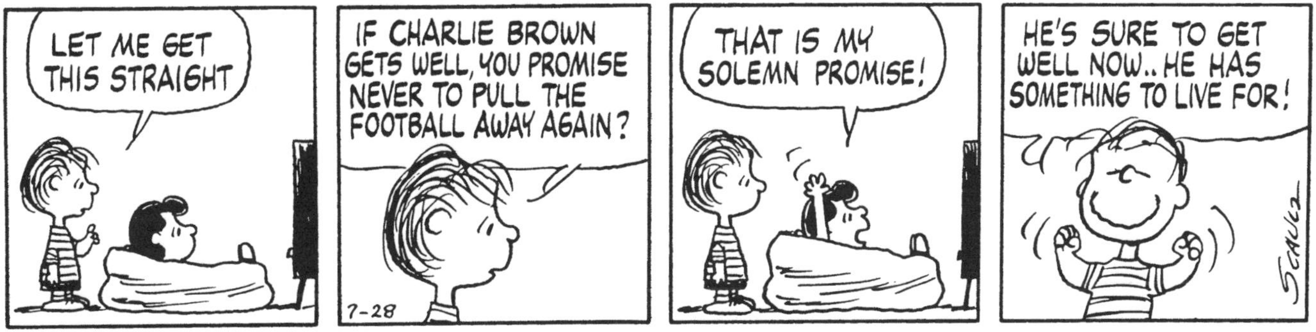
LET ME GET THIS STRAIGHT
IF CHARLIE BROWN GETS WELL, YOU PROMISE NEVER TO PULL THE FOOTBALL AWAY AGAIN?
THAT IS MY SOLEMN PROMISE!
HE'S SURE TO GET WELL NOW.. HE HAS SOMETHING TO LIVE FOR!

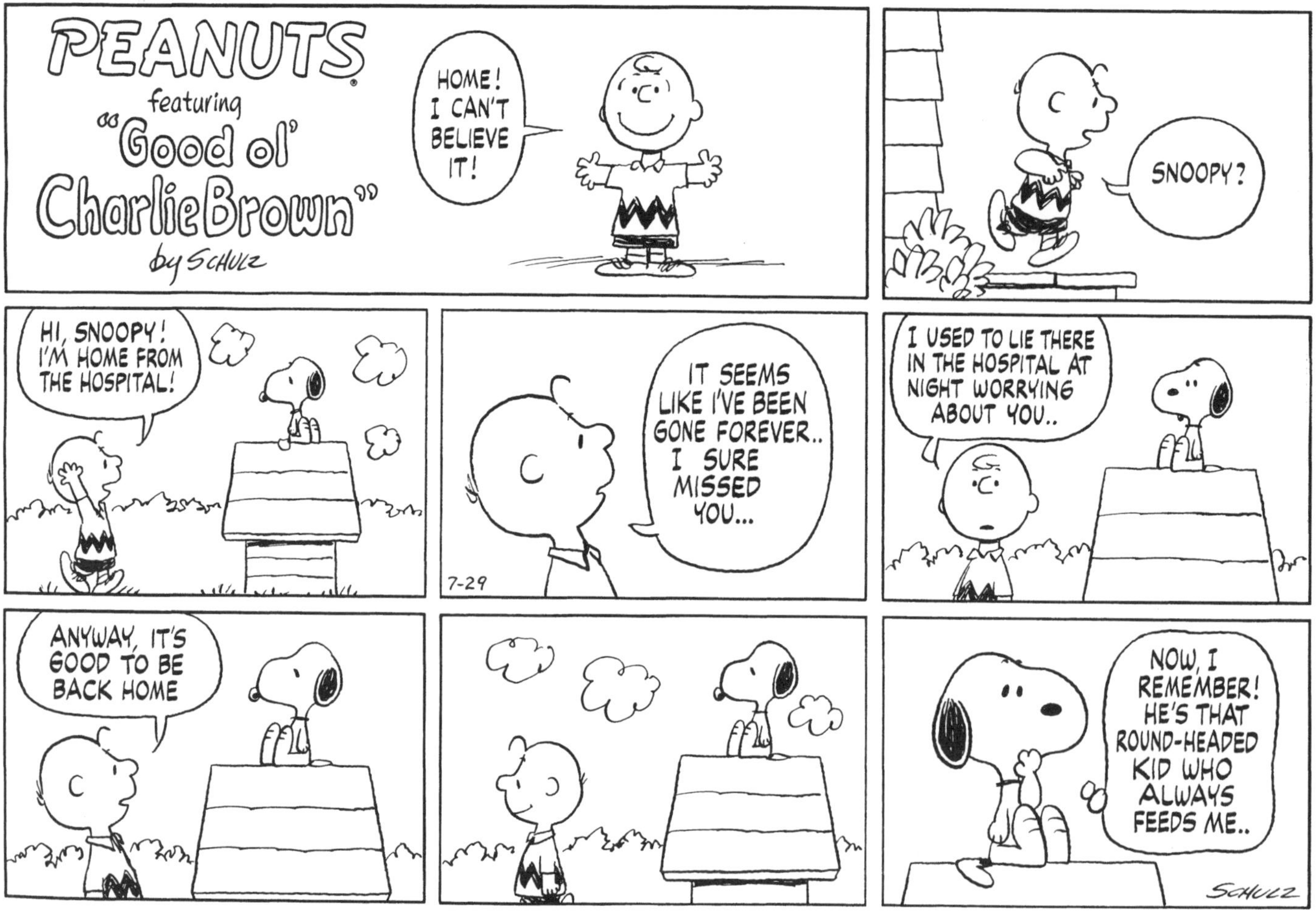
PEANUTS
featuring
"Good ol' Charlie Brown"
by SCHULZ
HOME! I CAN'T BELIEVE IT!
SNOOPY?
HI, SNOOPY! I'M HOME FROM THE HOSPITAL!
IT SEEMS LIKE I'VE BEEN GONE FOREVER.. I SURE MISSED YOU...
7-29
I USED TO LIE THERE IN THE HOSPITAL AT NIGHT WORRYING ABOUT YOU..
ANYWAY, IT'S GOOD TO BE BACK HOME
NOW, I REMEMBER! HE'S THAT ROUND-HEADED KID WHO ALWAYS FEEDS ME..
SCHULZ

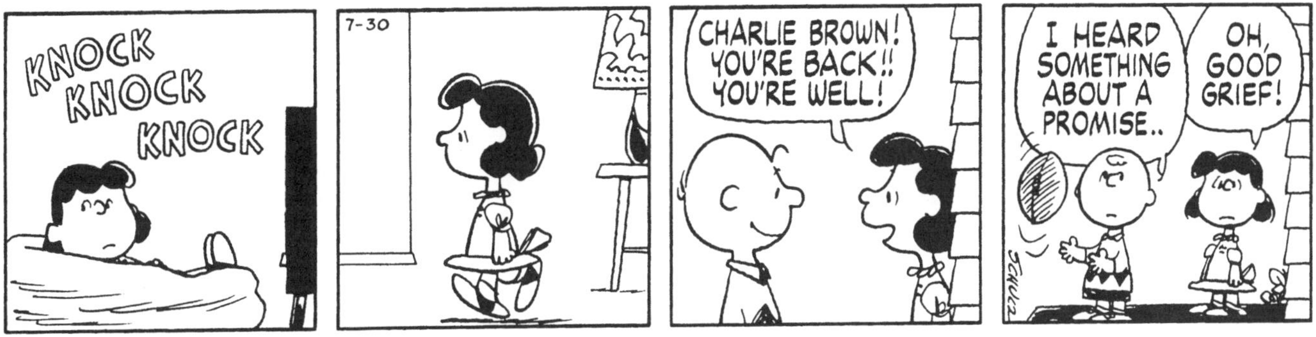
KNOCK KNOCK KNOCK
7-30
CHARLIE BROWN! YOU'RE BACK!! YOU'RE WELL!
I HEARD SOMETHING ABOUT A PROMISE..
OH, GOOD GRIEF!
SCHULZ

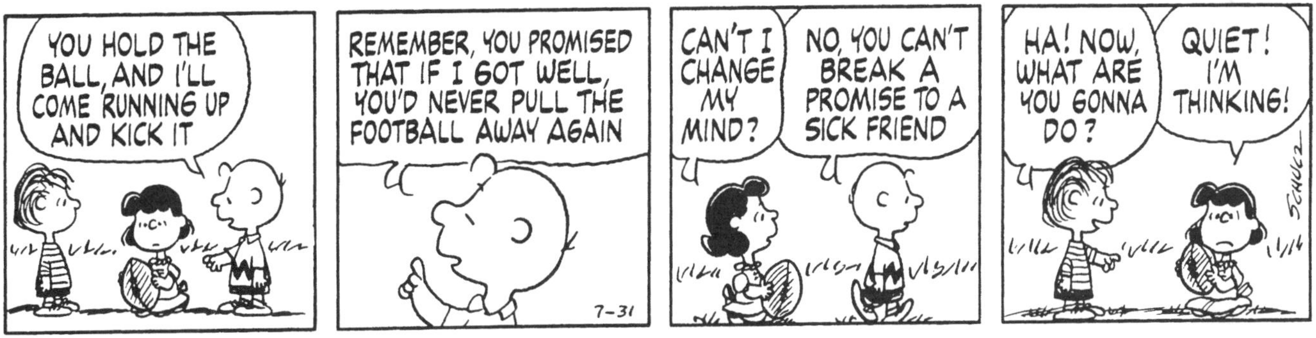
YOU HOLD THE BALL, AND I'LL COME RUNNING UP AND KICK IT
REMEMBER, YOU PROMISED THAT IF I GOT WELL, YOU'D NEVER PULL THE FOOTBALL AWAY AGAIN
7-31
CAN'T I CHANGE MY MIND?
NO, YOU CAN'T BREAK A PROMISE TO A SICK FRIEND
HA! NOW, WHAT ARE YOU GONNA DO?
QUIET! I'M THINKING!
SCHULZ

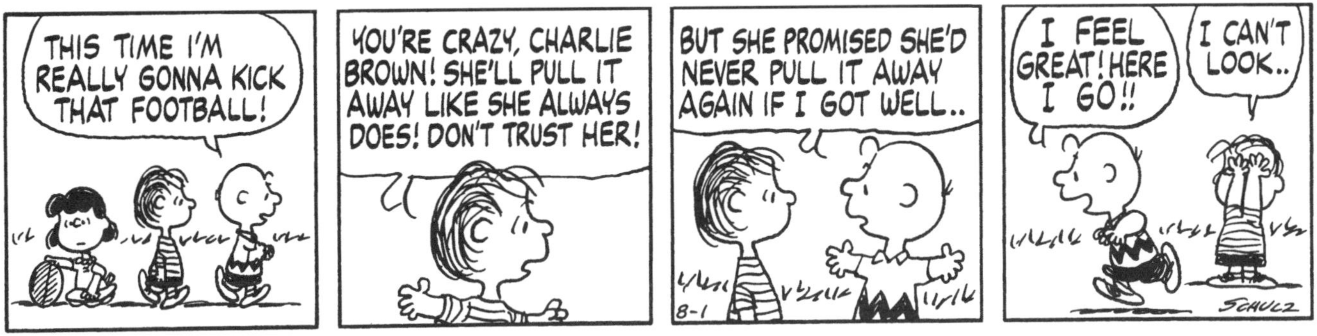
THIS TIME I'M REALLY GONNA KICK THAT FOOTBALL!
YOU'RE CRAZY, CHARLIE BROWN! SHE'LL PULL IT AWAY LIKE SHE ALWAYS DOES! DON'T TRUST HER!
BUT SHE PROMISED SHE'D NEVER PULL IT AWAY AGAIN IF I GOT WELL..
8-1
I FEEL GREAT! HERE I GO!!
I CAN'T LOOK..
SCHULZ

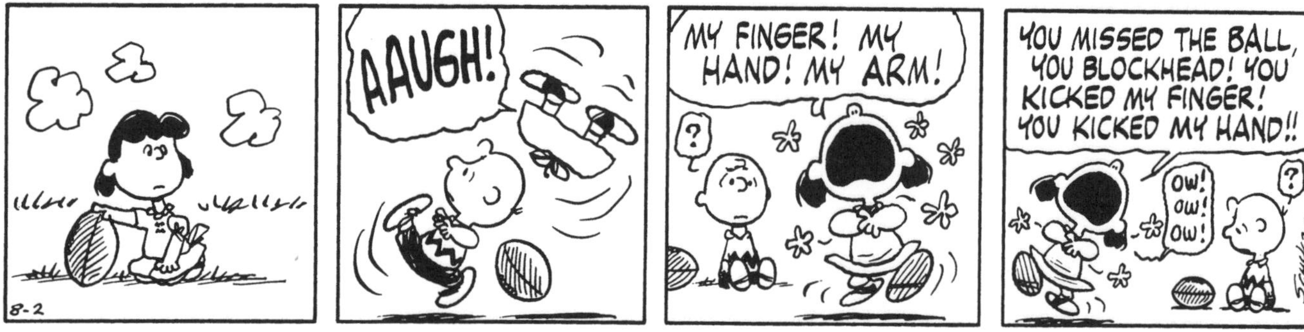
8-2
AAUGH!
MY FINGER! MY HAND! MY ARM!
?
YOU MISSED THE BALL, YOU BLOCKHEAD! YOU KICKED MY FINGER! YOU KICKED MY HAND!!
OW! OW! OW!
?
SCHULZ

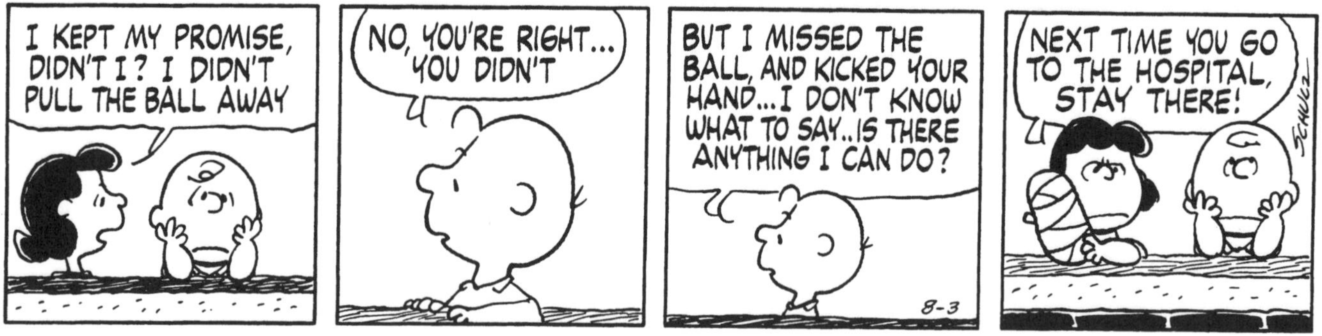
I KEPT MY PROMISE, DIDN'T I? I DIDN'T PULL THE BALL AWAY
NO, YOU'RE RIGHT... YOU DIDN'T
BUT I MISSED THE BALL, AND KICKED YOUR HAND...I DON'T KNOW WHAT TO SAY..IS THERE ANYTHING I CAN DO?
8-3
NEXT TIME YOU GO TO THE HOSPITAL, STAY THERE!
SCHULZ

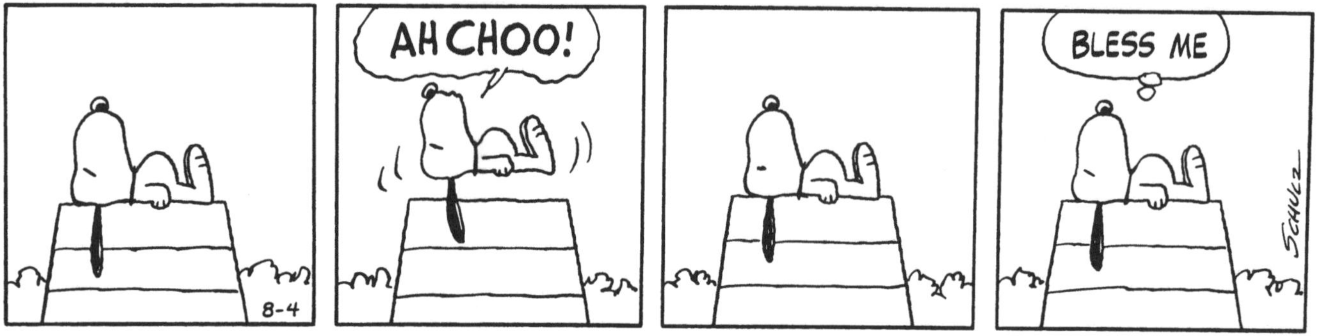
8-4
AH CHOO!
BLESS ME
SCHULZ

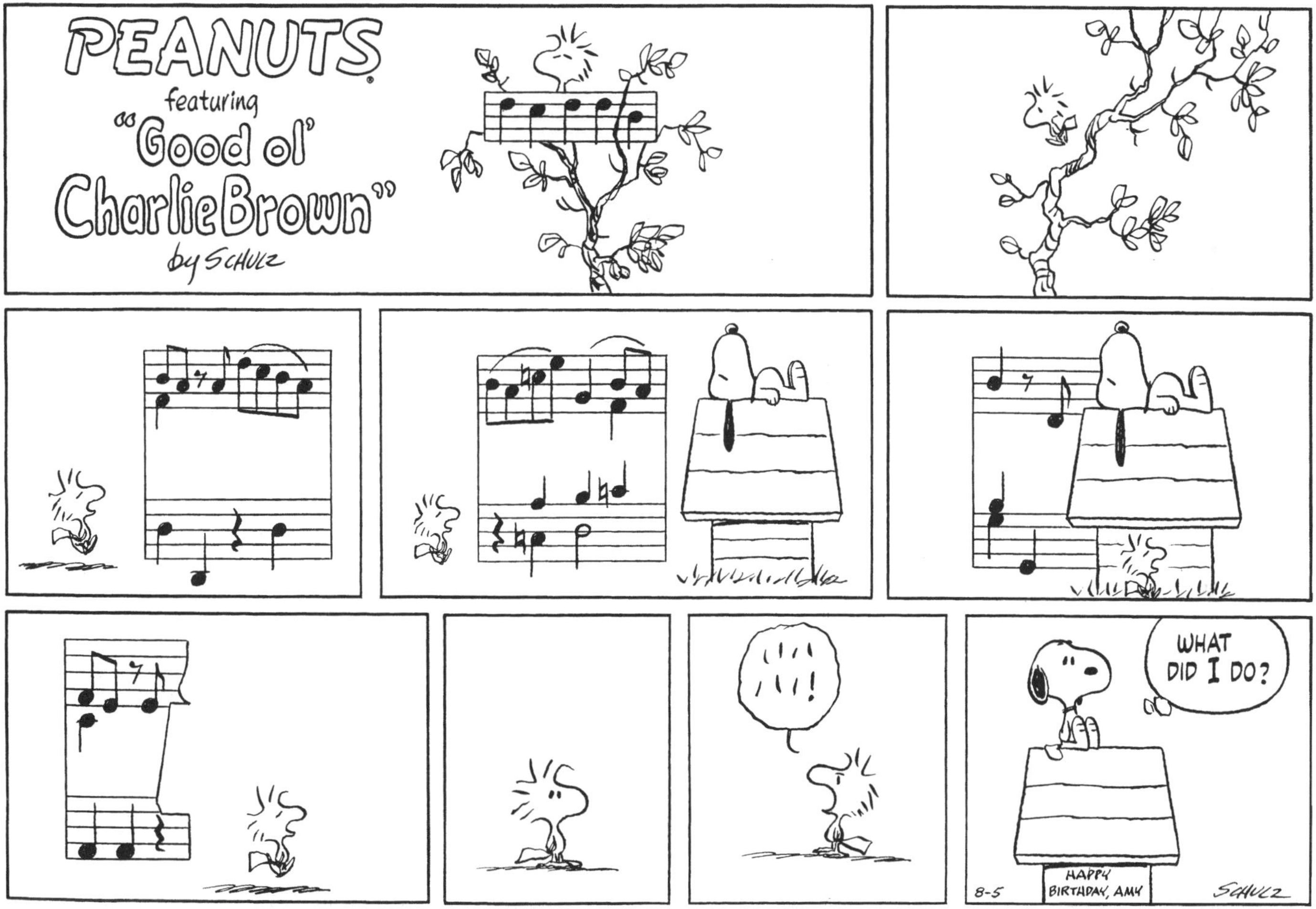
PEANUTS
featuring
"Good ol' Charlie Brown"
by SCHULZ
WHAT DID I DO?
8-5
HAPPY BIRTHDAY, AMY
SCHULZ

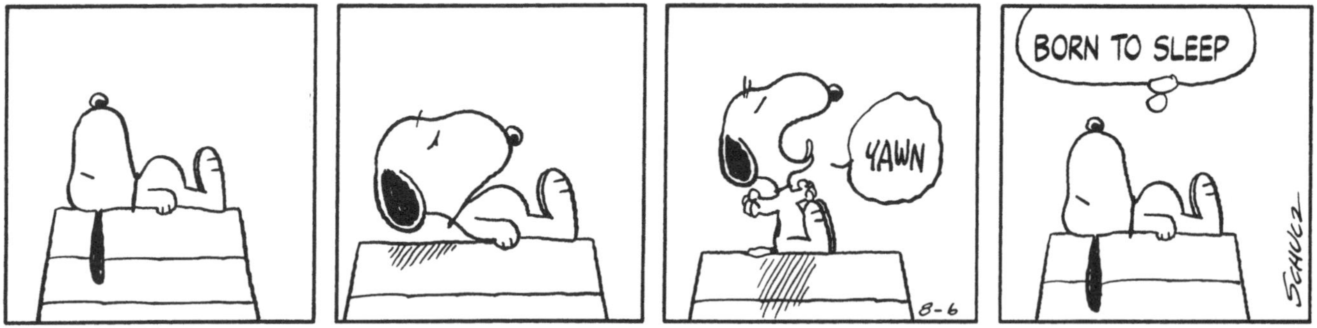
YAWN
BORN TO SLEEP

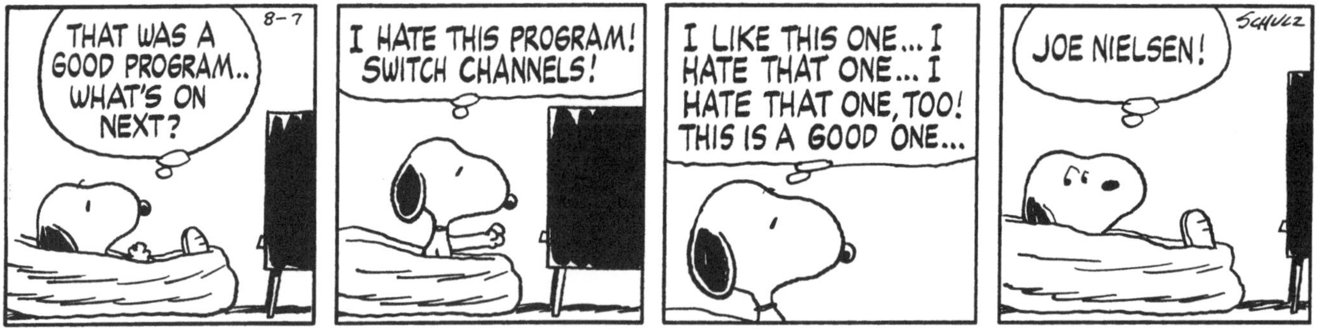
THAT WAS A GOOD PROGRAM.. WHAT'S ON NEXT?
I HATE THIS PROGRAM! SWITCH CHANNELS!
I LIKE THIS ONE... I HATE THAT ONE... I HATE THAT ONE, TOO! THIS IS A GOOD ONE...
JOE NIELSEN!

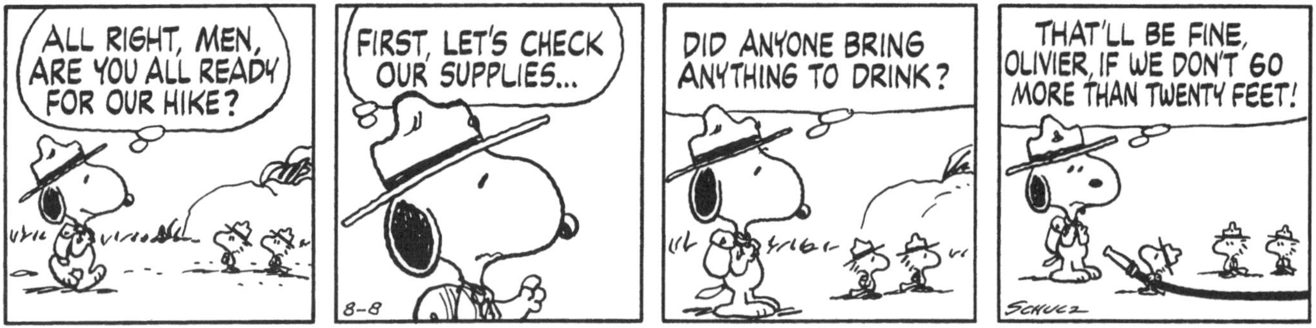
ALL RIGHT, MEN, ARE YOU ALL READY FOR OUR HIKE?
FIRST, LET'S CHECK OUR SUPPLIES...
DID ANYONE BRING ANYTHING TO DRINK?
THAT'LL BE FINE, OLIVIER, IF WE DON'T GO MORE THAN TWENTY FEET!

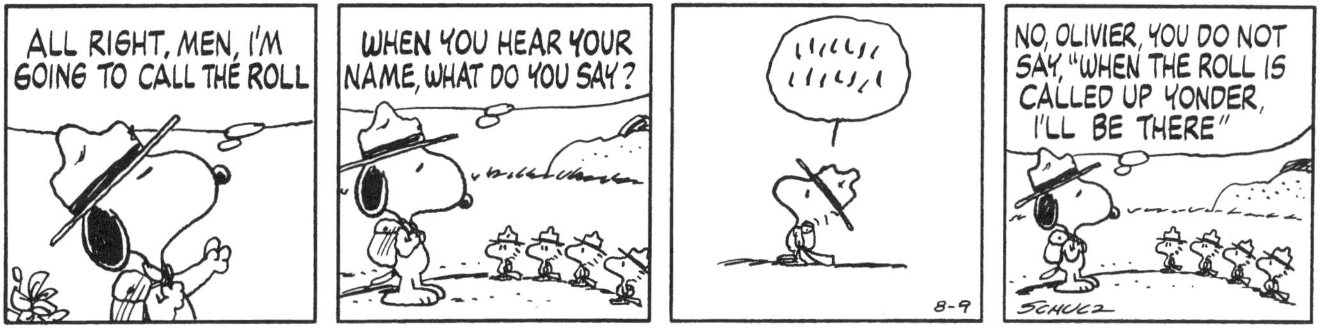
ALL RIGHT, MEN, I'M GOING TO CALL THE ROLL
WHEN YOU HEAR YOUR NAME, WHAT DO YOU SAY?
NO, OLIVIER, YOU DO NOT SAY, "WHEN THE ROLL IS CALLED UP YONDER, I'LL BE THERE"
8-9
SCHULZ

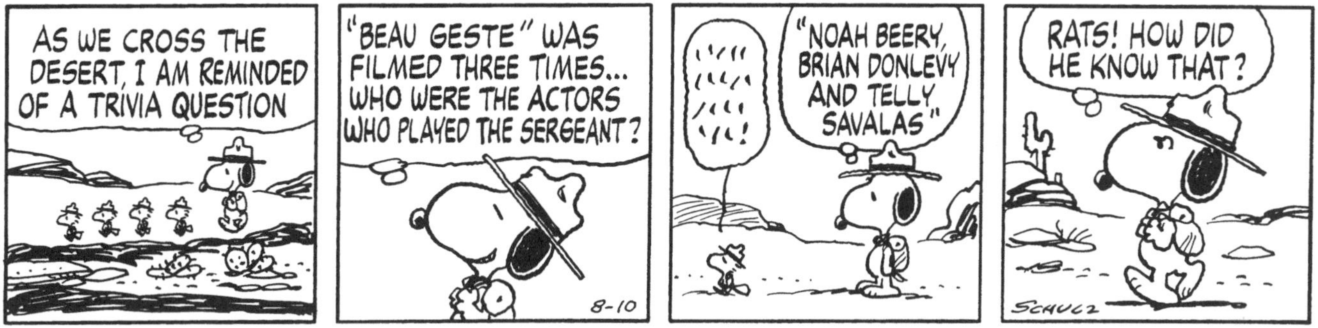
AS WE CROSS THE DESERT, I AM REMINDED OF A TRIVIA QUESTION
"BEAU GESTE" WAS FILMED THREE TIMES... WHO WERE THE ACTORS WHO PLAYED THE SERGEANT?
"NOAH BEERY, BRIAN DONLEVY AND TELLY SAVALAS"
RATS! HOW DID HE KNOW THAT?
8-10
SCHULZ

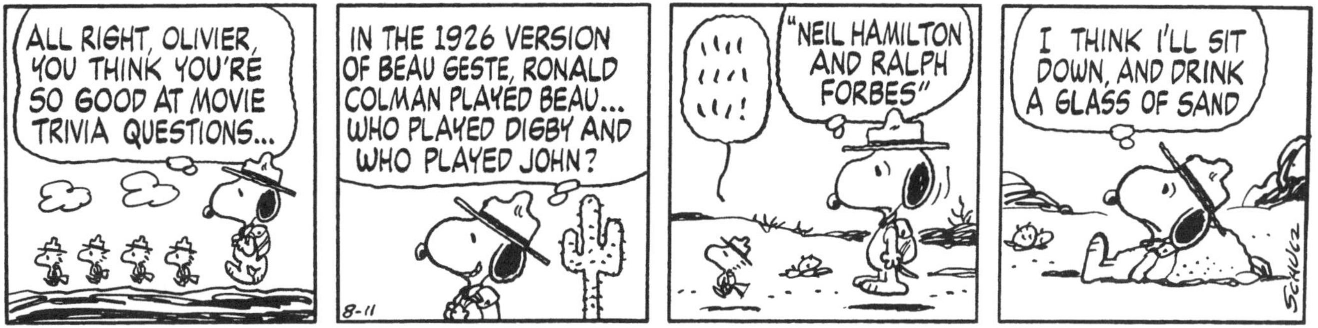
ALL RIGHT, OLIVIER, YOU THINK YOU'RE SO GOOD AT MOVIE TRIVIA QUESTIONS...
IN THE 1926 VERSION OF BEAU GESTE, RONALD COLMAN PLAYED BEAU... WHO PLAYED DIGBY AND WHO PLAYED JOHN?
"NEIL HAMILTON AND RALPH FORBES"
I THINK I'LL SIT DOWN, AND DRINK A GLASS OF SAND
8-11
SCHULZ

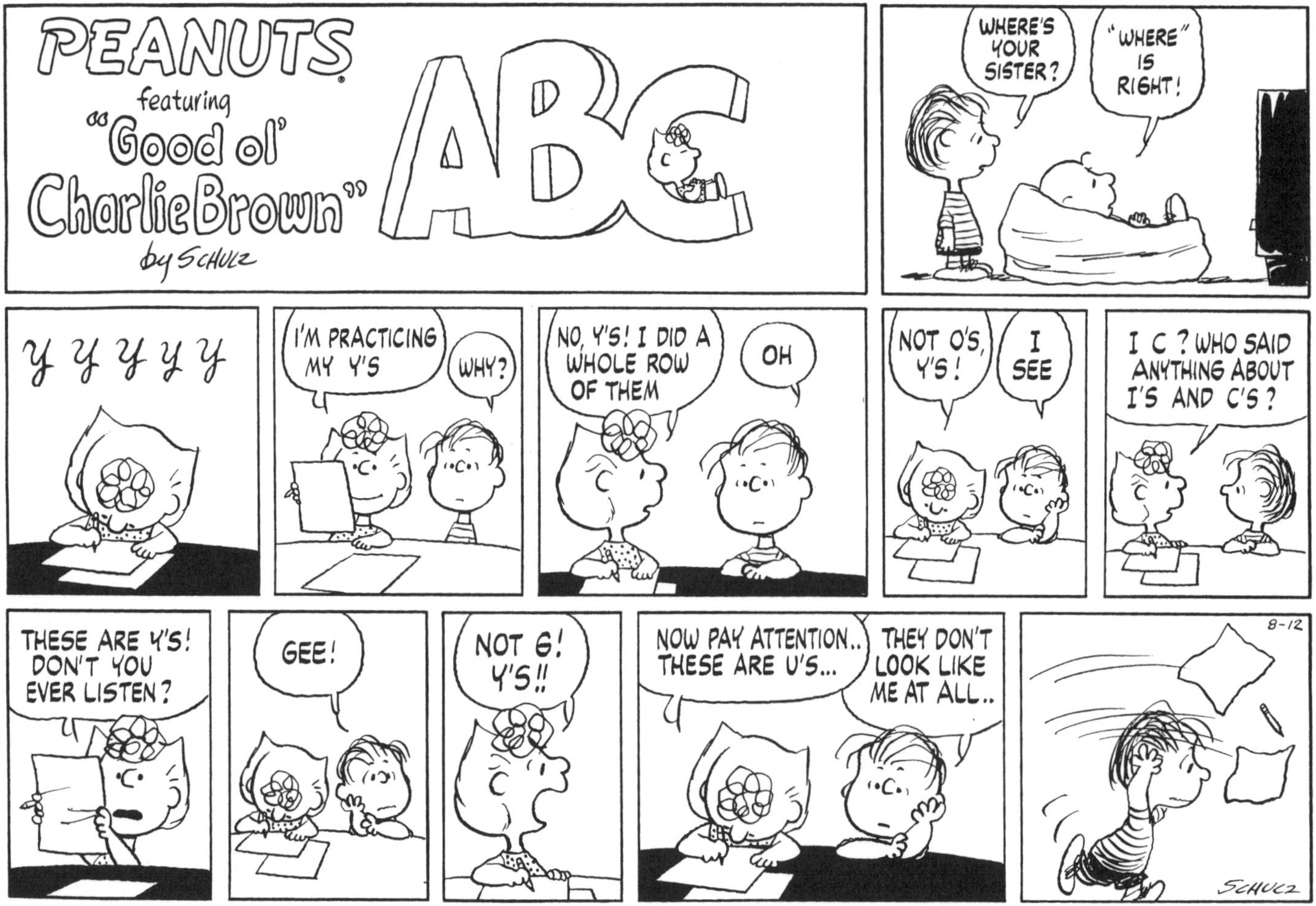
PEANUTS
featuring "Good ol' Charlie Brown"
by SCHULZ
ABC
WHERE'S YOUR SISTER?
"WHERE" IS RIGHT!
I'M PRACTICING MY Y'S
WHY?
NO, Y'S! I DID A WHOLE ROW OF THEM
OH
NOT O'S, Y'S!
I SEE
I C ? WHO SAID ANYTHING ABOUT I'S AND C'S?
THESE ARE Y'S! DON'T YOU EVER LISTEN?
GEE!
NOT G! Y'S!!
NOW PAY ATTENTION.. THESE ARE U'S...
THEY DON'T LOOK LIKE ME AT ALL..
8-12
SCHULZ

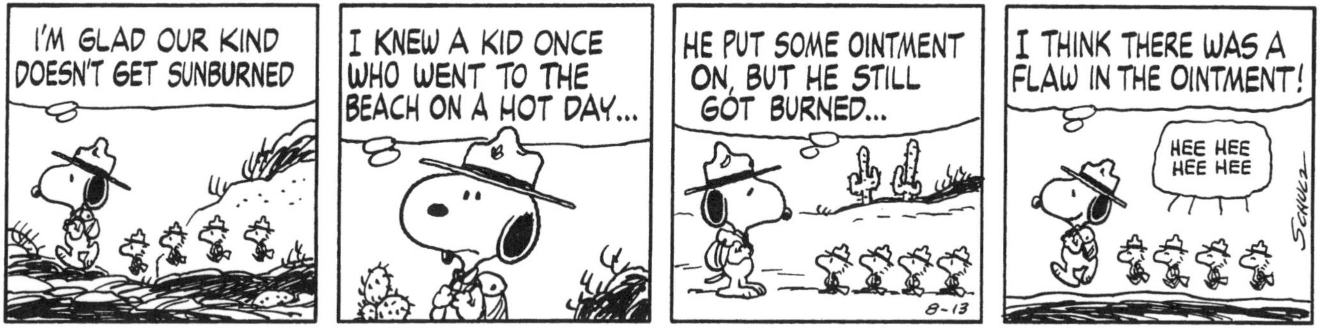
I'M GLAD OUR KIND DOESN'T GET SUNBURNED
I KNEW A KID ONCE WHO WENT TO THE BEACH ON A HOT DAY...
HE PUT SOME OINTMENT ON, BUT HE STILL GOT BURNED...
8-13
I THINK THERE WAS A FLAW IN THE OINTMENT!
HEE HEE HEE HEE
SCHULZ

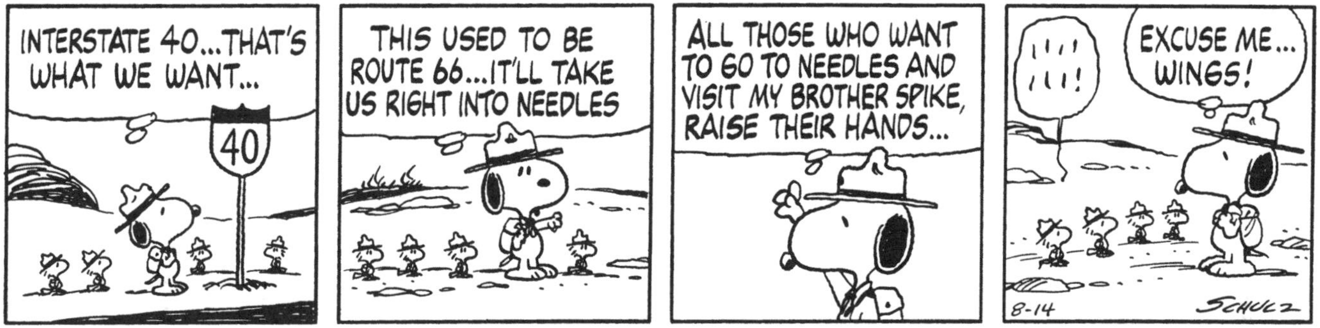
INTERSTATE 40...THAT'S WHAT WE WANT...
40
THIS USED TO BE ROUTE 66...IT'LL TAKE US RIGHT INTO NEEDLES
ALL THOSE WHO WANT TO GO TO NEEDLES AND VISIT MY BROTHER SPIKE, RAISE THEIR HANDS...
EXCUSE ME... WINGS!
8-14
SCHULZ

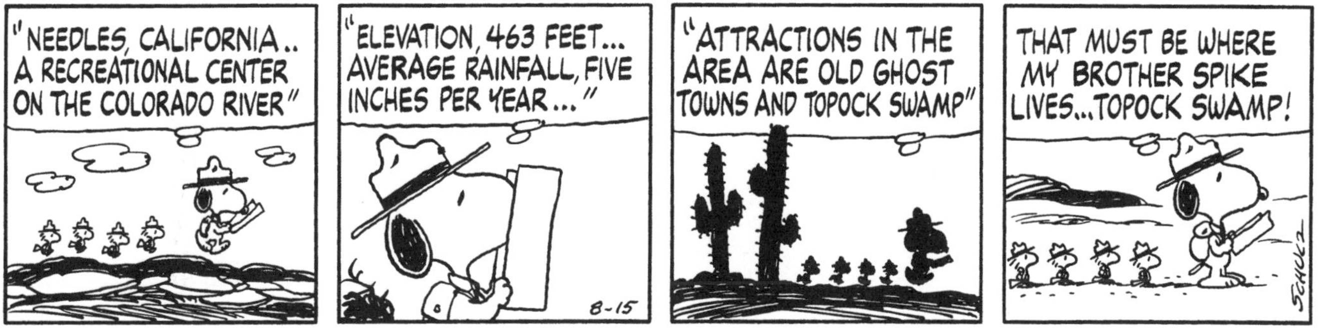
"NEEDLES, CALIFORNIA.. A RECREATIONAL CENTER ON THE COLORADO RIVER"
"ELEVATION, 463 FEET... AVERAGE RAINFALL, FIVE INCHES PER YEAR..."
8-15
"ATTRACTIONS IN THE AREA ARE OLD GHOST TOWNS AND TOPOCK SWAMP"
THAT MUST BE WHERE MY BROTHER SPIKE LIVES...TOPOCK SWAMP!
SCHULZ

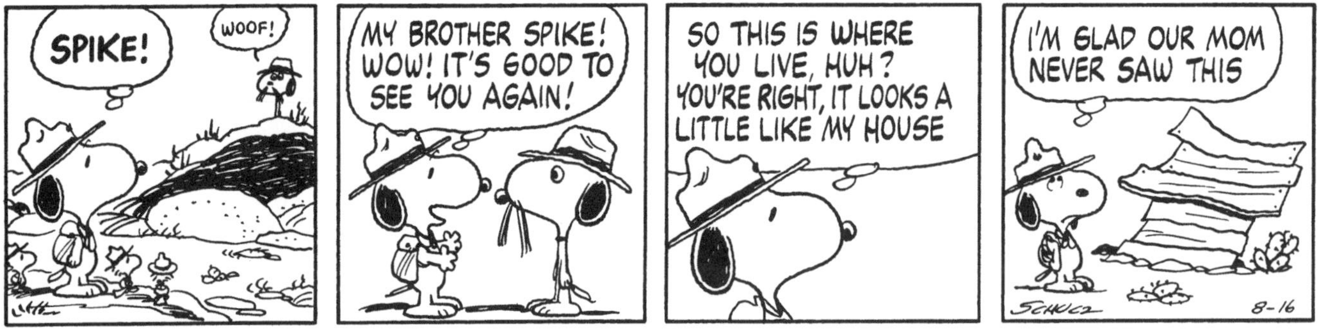
SPIKE!
WOOF!
MY BROTHER SPIKE! WOW! IT'S GOOD TO SEE YOU AGAIN!
SO THIS IS WHERE YOU LIVE, HUH? YOU'RE RIGHT, IT LOOKS A LITTLE LIKE MY HOUSE
I'M GLAD OUR MOM NEVER SAW THIS
SCHULZ
8-16

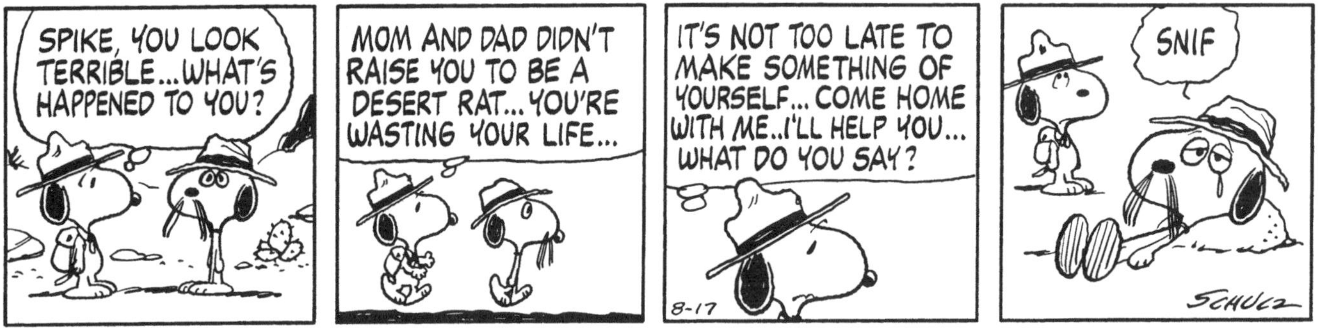
SPIKE, YOU LOOK TERRIBLE...WHAT'S HAPPENED TO YOU?
MOM AND DAD DIDN'T RAISE YOU TO BE A DESERT RAT...YOU'RE WASTING YOUR LIFE...
IT'S NOT TOO LATE TO MAKE SOMETHING OF YOURSELF... COME HOME WITH ME..I'LL HELP YOU... WHAT DO YOU SAY?
8-17
SNIF
SCHULZ

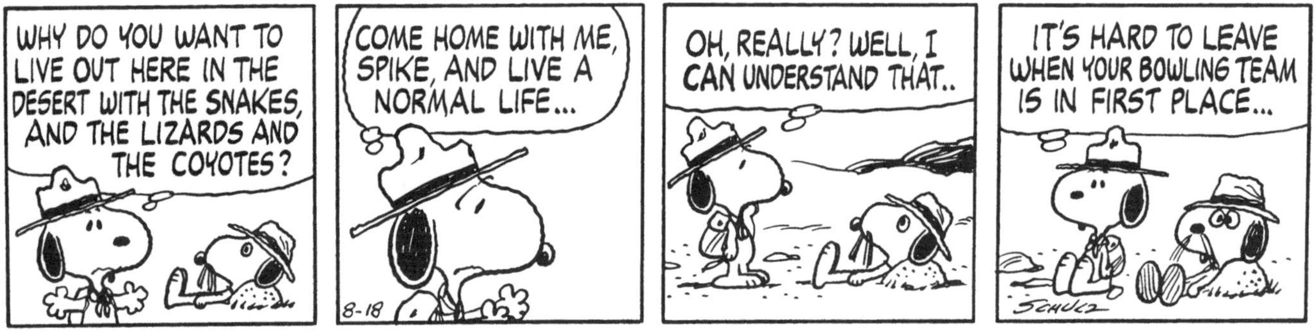
WHY DO YOU WANT TO LIVE OUT HERE IN THE DESERT WITH THE SNAKES, AND THE LIZARDS AND THE COYOTES?
COME HOME WITH ME, SPIKE, AND LIVE A NORMAL LIFE...
8-18
OH, REALLY? WELL, I CAN UNDERSTAND THAT..
IT'S HARD TO LEAVE WHEN YOUR BOWLING TEAM IS IN FIRST PLACE...
SCHULZ

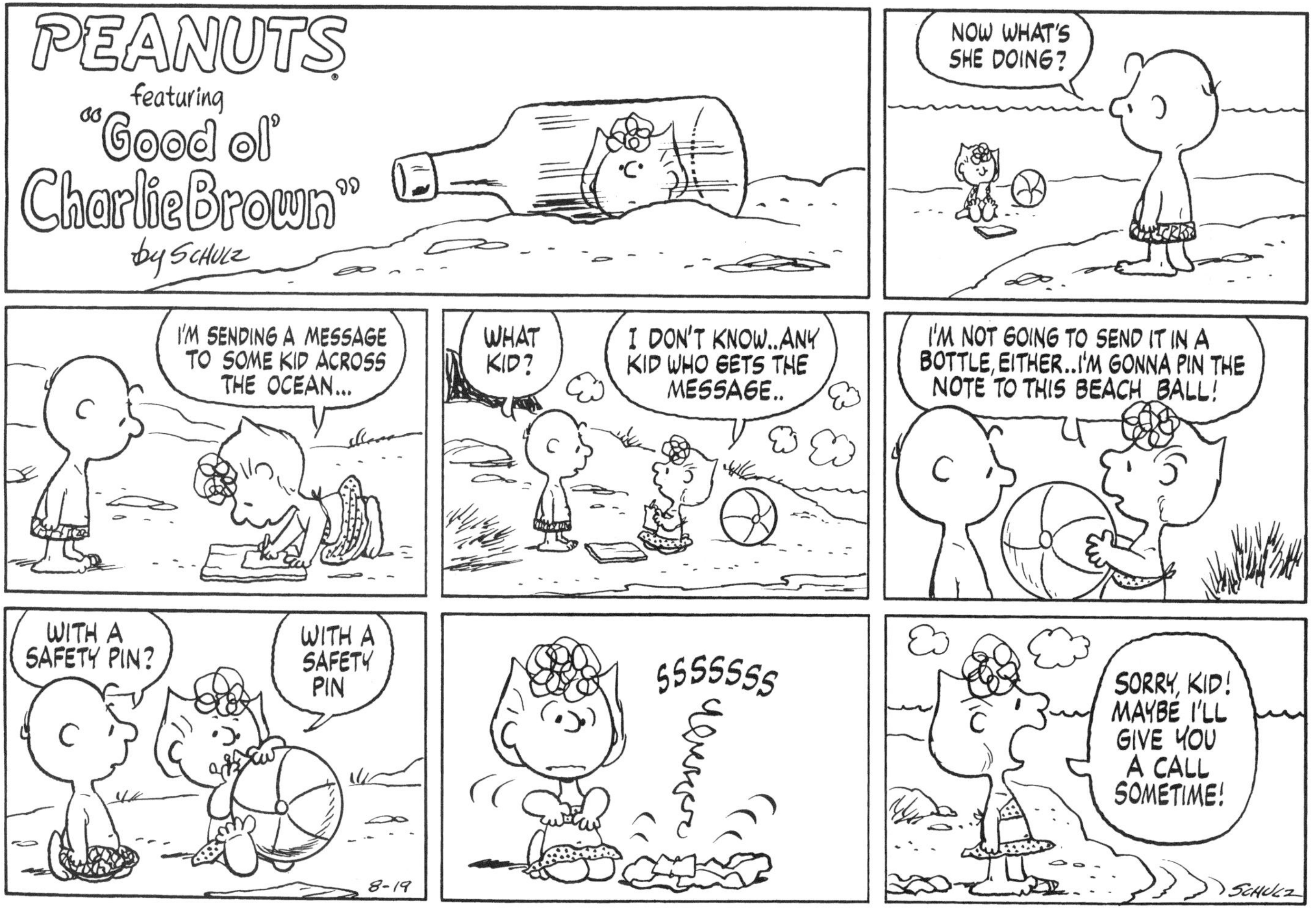
PEANUTS
featuring "Good ol' CharlieBrown"
by SCHULZ
NOW WHAT'S SHE DOING?
I'M SENDING A MESSAGE TO SOME KID ACROSS THE OCEAN...
WHAT KID?
I DON'T KNOW..ANY KID WHO GETS THE MESSAGE..
I'M NOT GOING TO SEND IT IN A BOTTLE, EITHER..I'M GONNA PIN THE NOTE TO THIS BEACH BALL!
WITH A SAFETY PIN?
WITH A SAFETY PIN
8-19
SSSSSSS
SORRY, KID! MAYBE I'LL GIVE YOU A CALL SOMETIME!
SCHULZ

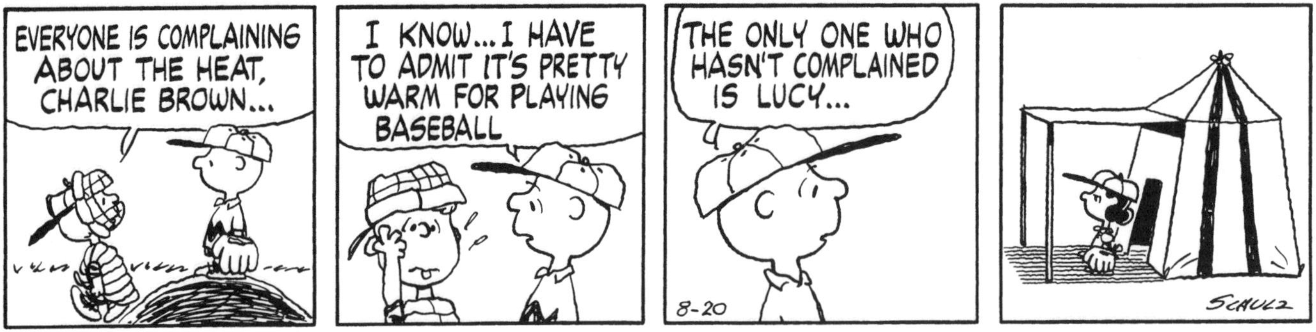
EVERYONE IS COMPLAINING ABOUT THE HEAT, CHARLIE BROWN...
I KNOW...I HAVE TO ADMIT IT'S PRETTY WARM FOR PLAYING BASEBALL
THE ONLY ONE WHO HASN'T COMPLAINED IS LUCY...
8-20
SCHULZ

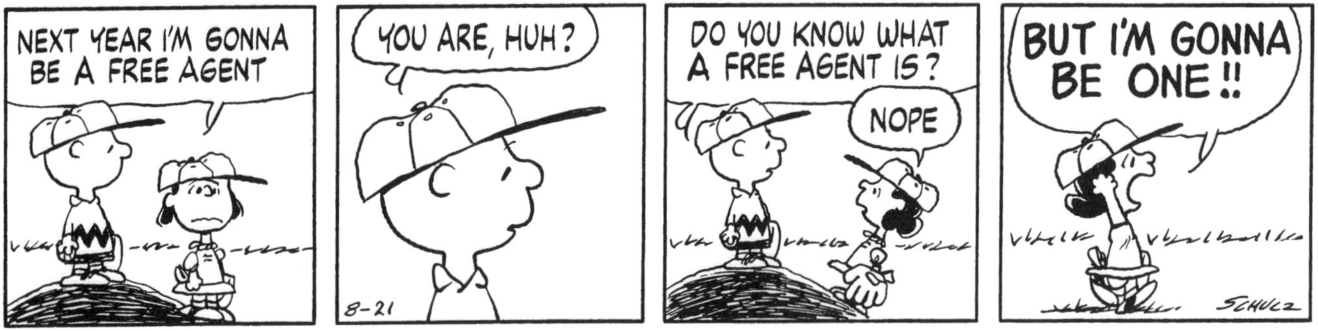
NEXT YEAR I'M GONNA BE A FREE AGENT
YOU ARE, HUH?
8-21
DO YOU KNOW WHAT A FREE AGENT IS?
NOPE
BUT I'M GONNA BE ONE!!
SCHULZ

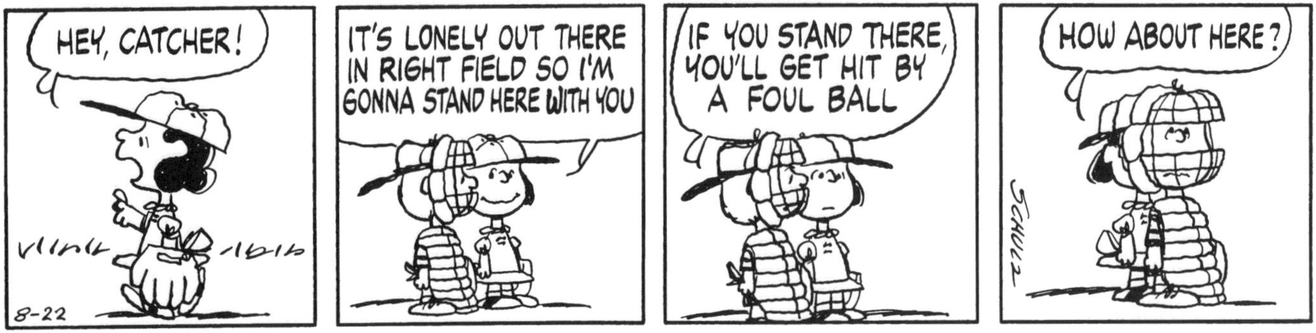
HEY, CATCHER!
8-22
IT'S LONELY OUT THERE IN RIGHT FIELD SO I'M GONNA STAND HERE WITH YOU
IF YOU STAND THERE, YOU'LL GET HIT BY A FOUL BALL
HOW ABOUT HERE?
SCHULZ

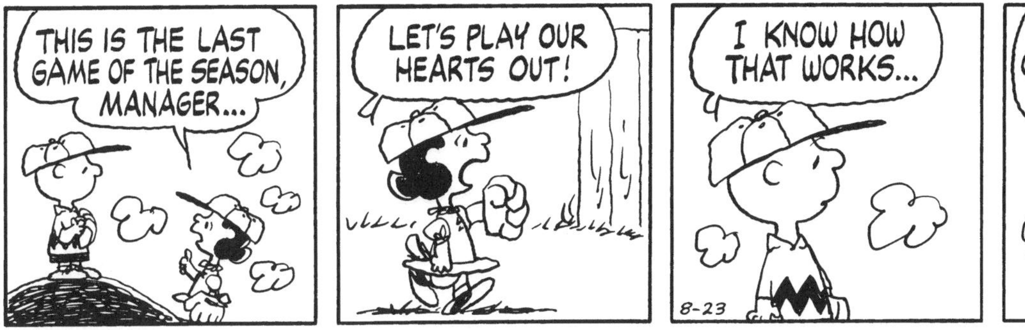
THIS IS THE LAST GAME OF THE SEASON, MANAGER...
LET'S PLAY OUR HEARTS OUT!
I KNOW HOW THAT WORKS...
8-23
YOU PLAY YOUR HEART OUT, AND YOU GET A STOMACHACHE!
SCHULZ

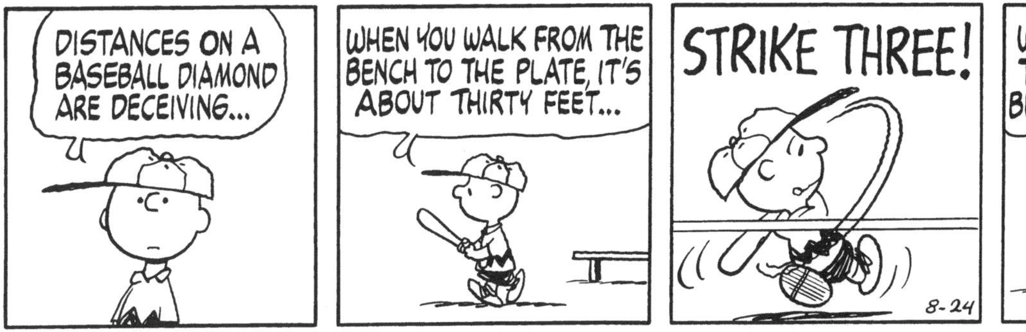
DISTANCES ON A BASEBALL DIAMOND ARE DECEIVING...
WHEN YOU WALK FROM THE BENCH TO THE PLATE, IT'S ABOUT THIRTY FEET...
STRIKE THREE!
8-24
WHEN YOU WALK FROM THE PLATE TO THE BENCH, IT'S FOUR MILES!
SCHULZ

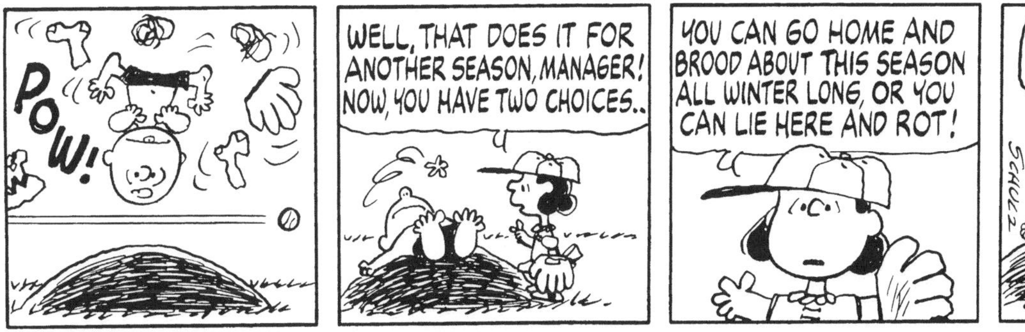
POW!
WELL, THAT DOES IT FOR ANOTHER SEASON, MANAGER! NOW, YOU HAVE TWO CHOICES..
YOU CAN GO HOME AND BROOD ABOUT THIS SEASON ALL WINTER LONG, OR YOU CAN LIE HERE AND ROT!
SCHULZ
8-25
THOSE ARE GREAT CHOICES

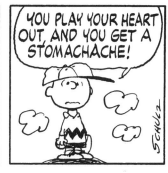

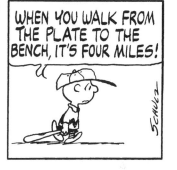

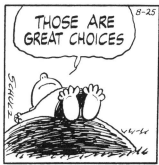

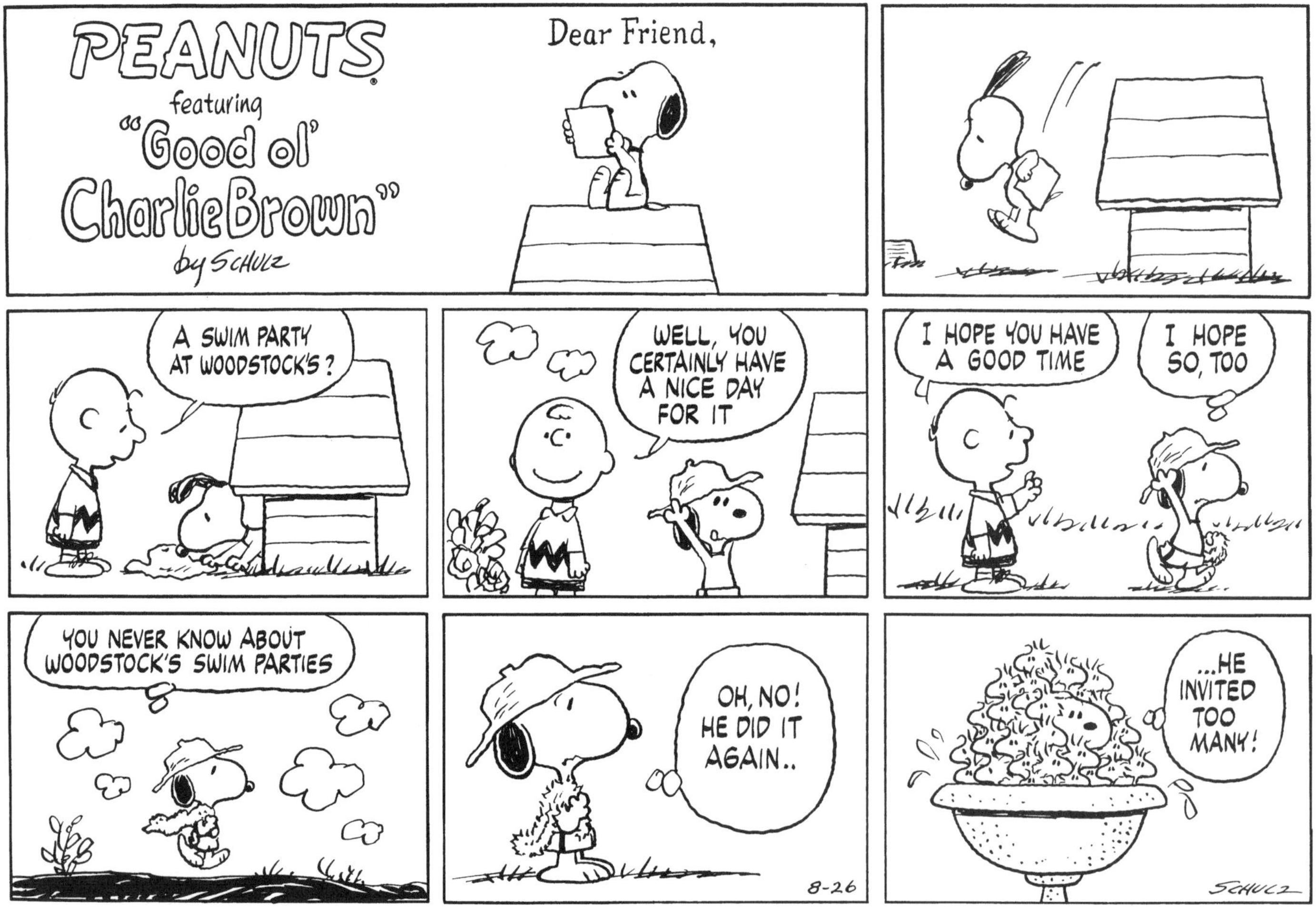
PEANUTS
featuring
"Good ol' Charlie Brown"
by SCHULZ
Dear Friend,
A SWIM PARTY AT WOODSTOCK'S ?
WELL, YOU CERTAINLY HAVE A NICE DAY FOR IT
I HOPE YOU HAVE A GOOD TIME
I HOPE SO, TOO
YOU NEVER KNOW ABOUT WOODSTOCK'S SWIM PARTIES
OH, NO! HE DID IT AGAIN..
8-26
...HE INVITED TOO MANY!
SCHULZ

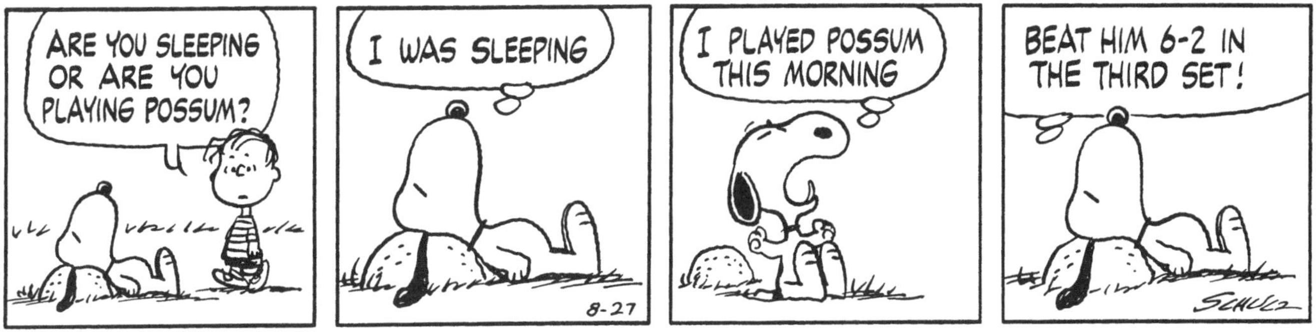
ARE YOU SLEEPING OR ARE YOU PLAYING POSSUM?
I WAS SLEEPING
8-27
I PLAYED POSSUM THIS MORNING
BEAT HIM 6-2 IN THE THIRD SET!
SCHULZ

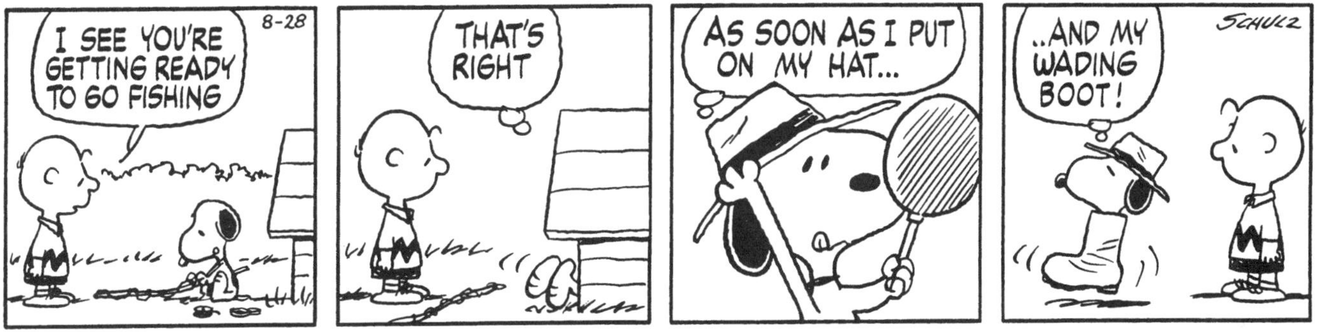
I SEE YOU'RE GETTING READY TO GO FISHING
8-28
THAT'S RIGHT
AS SOON AS I PUT ON MY HAT...
..AND MY WADING BOOT!
SCHULZ

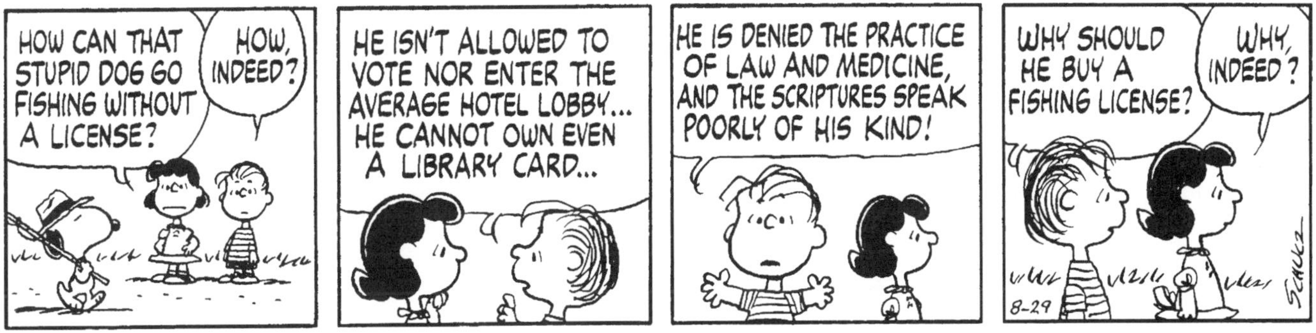
HOW CAN THAT STUPID DOG GO FISHING WITHOUT A LICENSE?
HOW, INDEED?
HE ISN'T ALLOWED TO VOTE NOR ENTER THE AVERAGE HOTEL LOBBY... HE CANNOT OWN EVEN A LIBRARY CARD...
HE IS DENIED THE PRACTICE OF LAW AND MEDICINE, AND THE SCRIPTURES SPEAK POORLY OF HIS KIND!
WHY SHOULD HE BUY A FISHING LICENSE?
WHY, INDEED?
8-29
SCHULZ

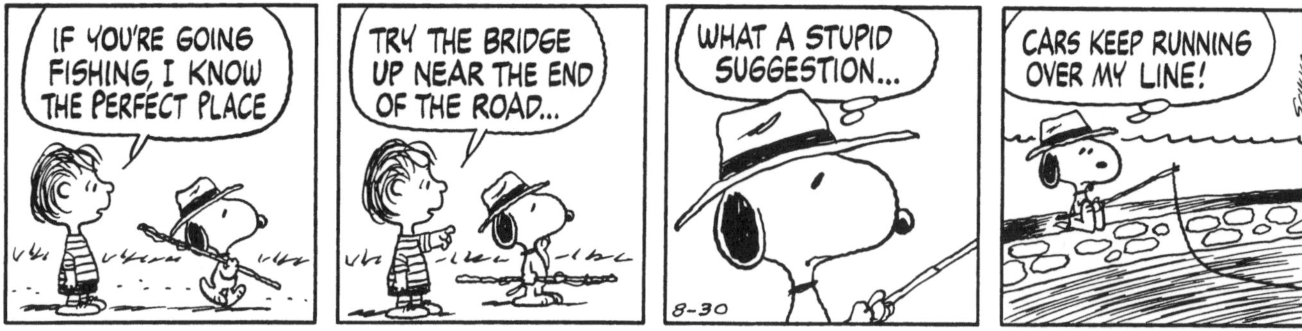
IF YOU'RE GOING FISHING, I KNOW THE PERFECT PLACE
TRY THE BRIDGE UP NEAR THE END OF THE ROAD...
WHAT A STUPID SUGGESTION...
8-30
CARS KEEP RUNNING OVER MY LINE!
SCHULZ

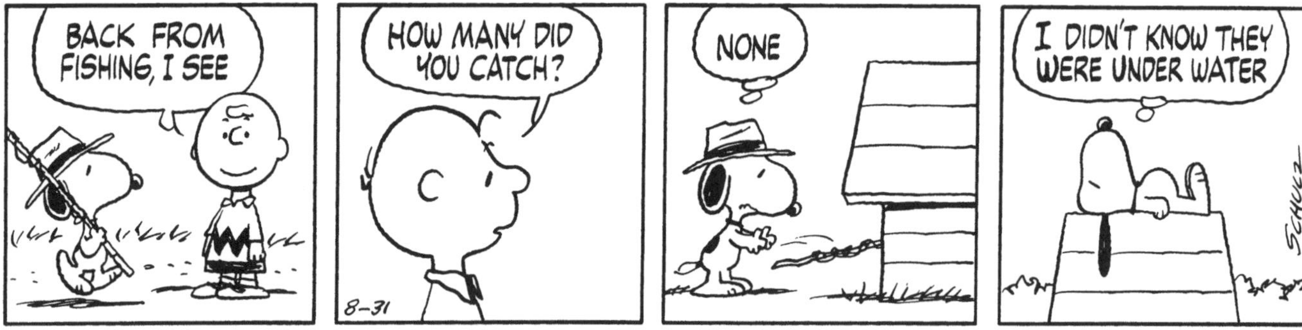
BACK FROM FISHING, I SEE
HOW MANY DID YOU CATCH?
8-31
NONE
I DIDN'T KNOW THEY WERE UNDER WATER
SCHULZ

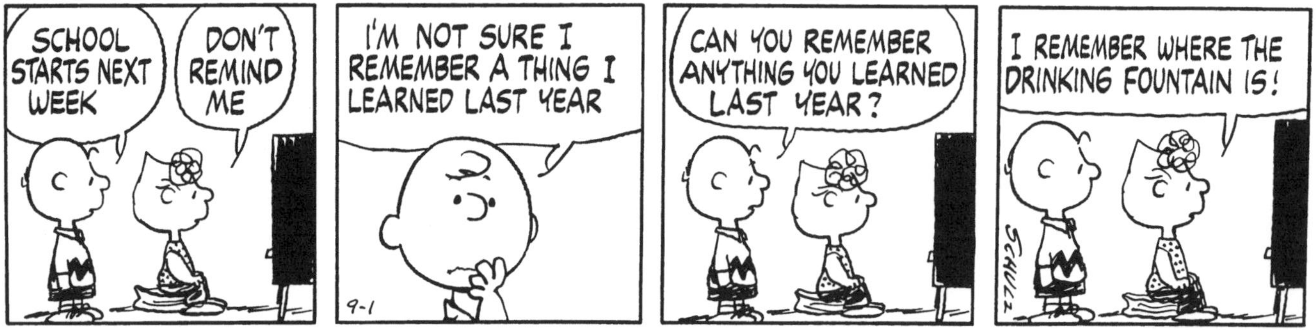
SCHOOL STARTS NEXT WEEK
DON'T REMIND ME
I'M NOT SURE I REMEMBER A THING I LEARNED LAST YEAR
9-1
CAN YOU REMEMBER ANYTHING YOU LEARNED LAST YEAR?
SCHULZ
I REMEMBER WHERE THE DRINKING FOUNTAIN IS!

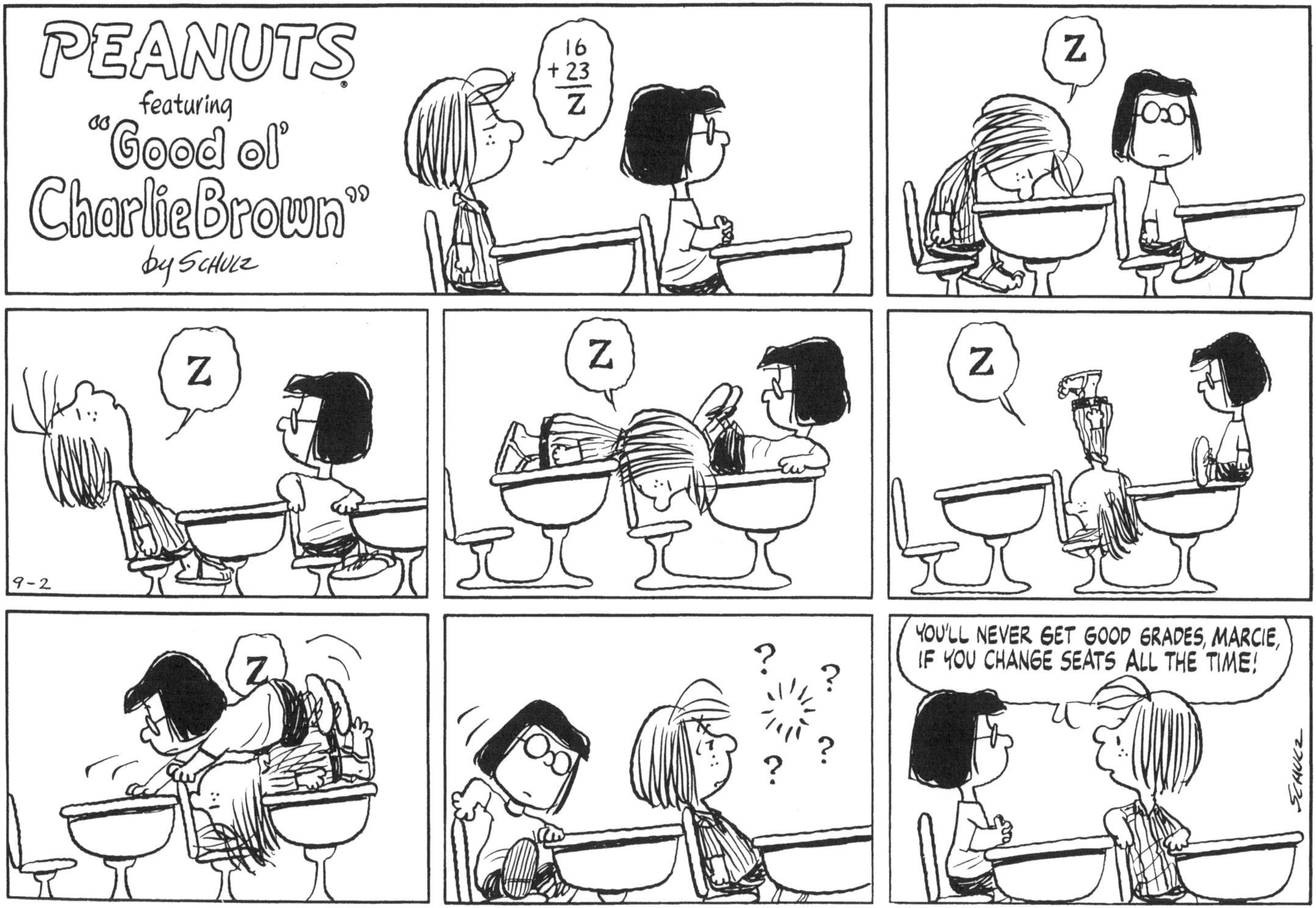
PEANUTS
featuring
"Good ol' CharlieBrown"
by SCHULZ
16
+ 23
Z
Z
9-2
Z
Z
Z
Z
? ? ? ?
YOU'LL NEVER GET GOOD GRADES, MARCIE, IF YOU CHANGE SEATS ALL THE TIME!
SCHULZ

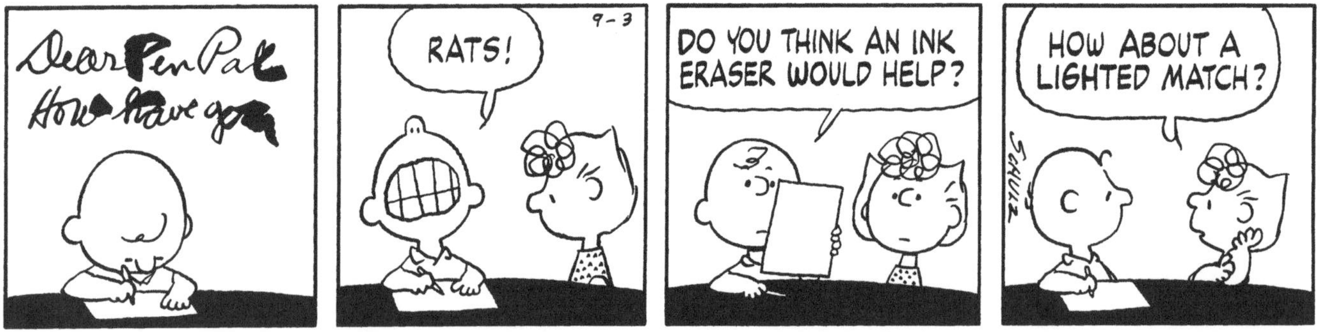
RATS!
DO YOU THINK AN INK ERASER WOULD HELP?
HOW ABOUT A LIGHTED MATCH?

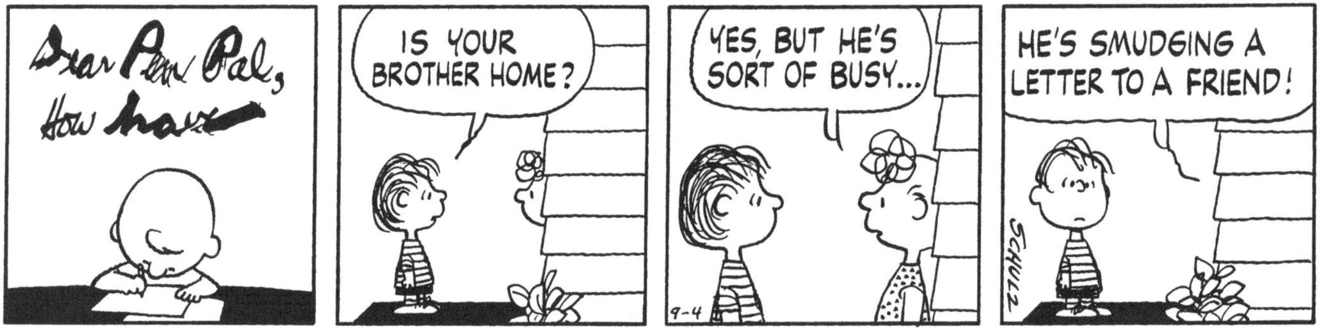
IS YOUR BROTHER HOME?
YES, BUT HE'S SORT OF BUSY...
HE'S SMUDGING A LETTER TO A FRIEND!

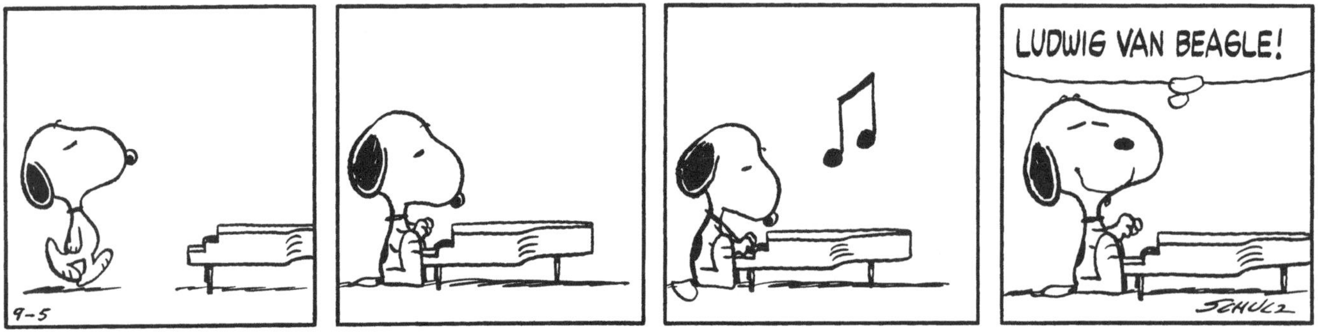
LUDWIG VAN BEAGLE!

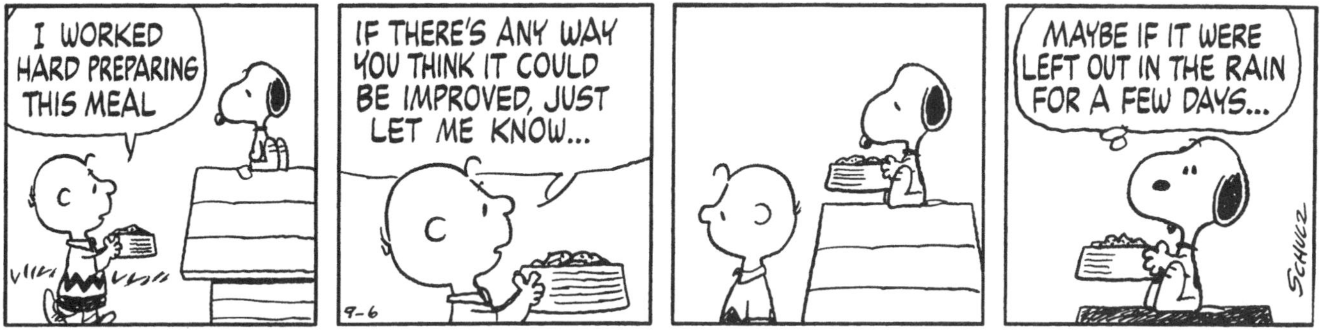
I WORKED HARD PREPARING THIS MEAL
IF THERE'S ANY WAY YOU THINK IT COULD BE IMPROVED, JUST LET ME KNOW...
9-6
MAYBE IF IT WERE LEFT OUT IN THE RAIN FOR A FEW DAYS...
SCHULZ

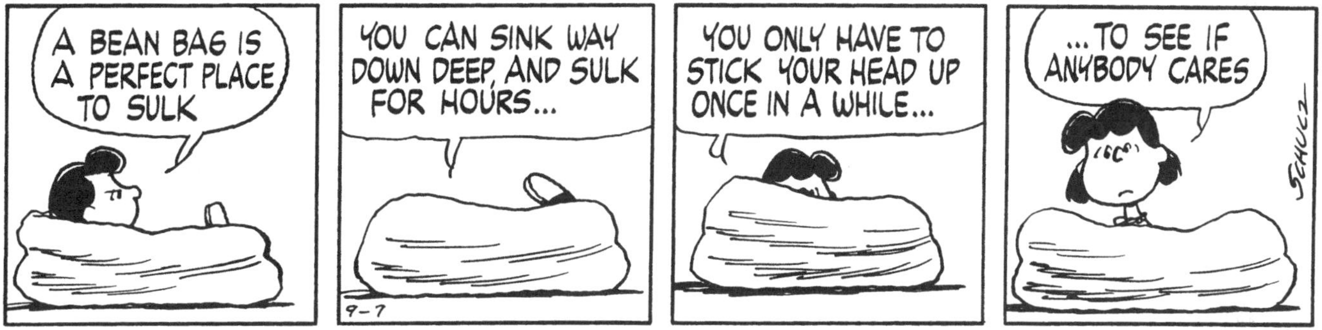
A BEAN BAG IS A PERFECT PLACE TO SULK
YOU CAN SINK WAY DOWN DEEP, AND SULK FOR HOURS...
9-7
YOU ONLY HAVE TO STICK YOUR HEAD UP ONCE IN A WHILE...
...TO SEE IF ANYBODY CARES
SCHULZ

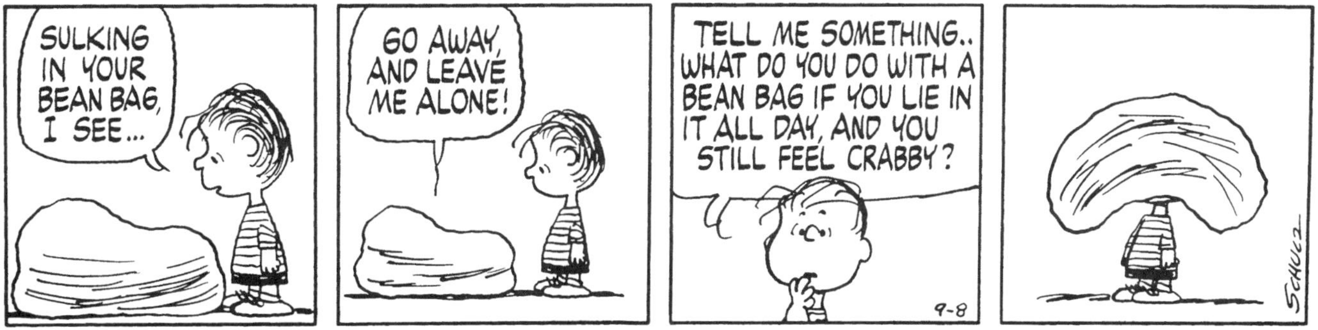
SULKING IN YOUR BEAN BAG, I SEE...
GO AWAY, AND LEAVE ME ALONE!
TELL ME SOMETHING.. WHAT DO YOU DO WITH A BEAN BAG IF YOU LIE IN IT ALL DAY, AND YOU STILL FEEL CRABBY?
9-8
SCHULZ

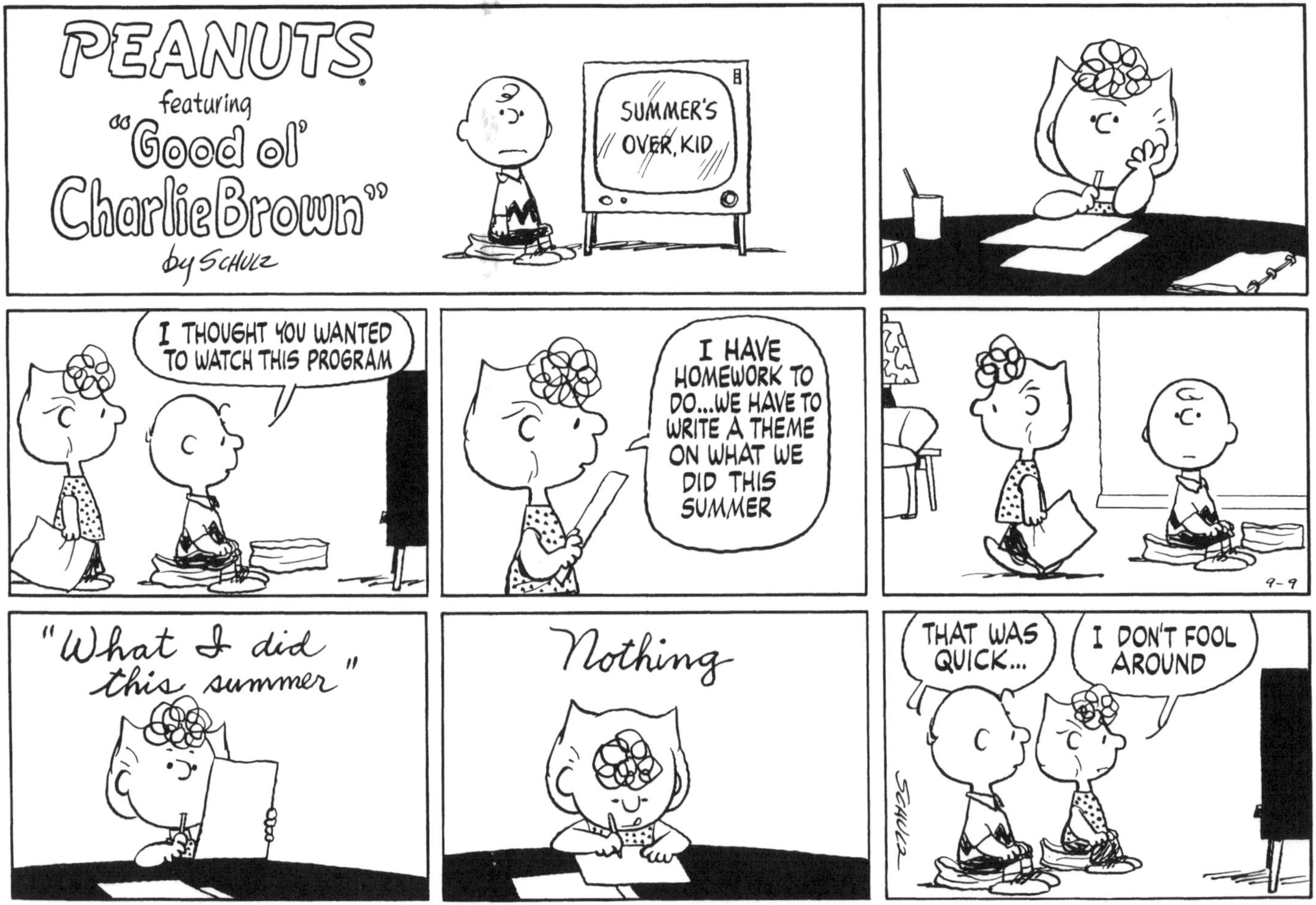
PEANUTS
featuring
"Good ol' Charlie Brown"
by SCHULZ
SUMMER'S OVER, KID
I THOUGHT YOU WANTED TO WATCH THIS PROGRAM
I HAVE HOMEWORK TO DO...WE HAVE TO WRITE A THEME ON WHAT WE DID THIS SUMMER
9-9
"What I did this summer"
Nothing
THAT WAS QUICK...
I DON'T FOOL AROUND
SCHULZ

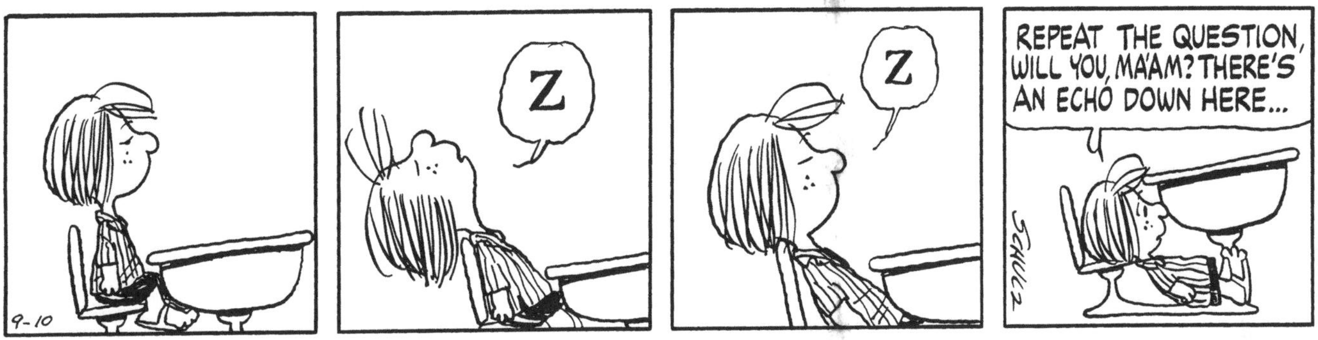
9-10
Z
Z
REPEAT THE QUESTION, WILL YOU, MA'AM? THERE'S AN ECHO DOWN HERE...
SCHULZ

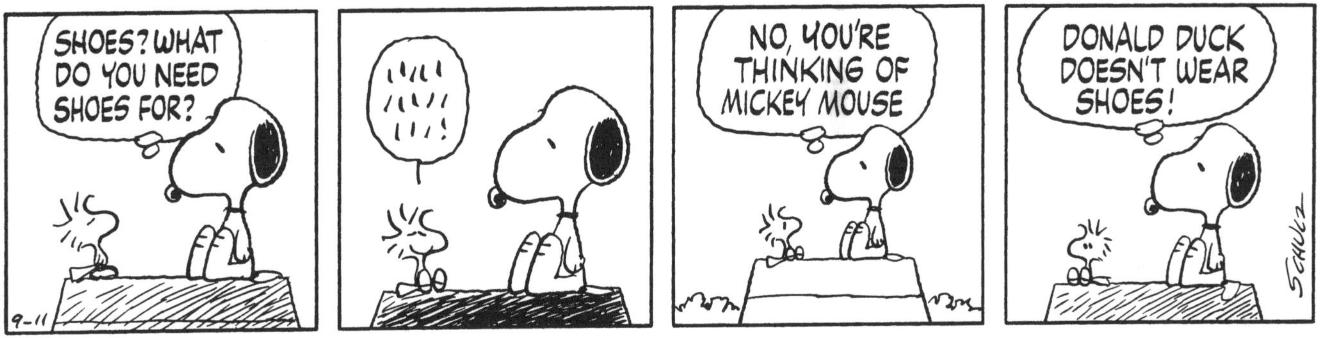
9-11
SHOES? WHAT DO YOU NEED SHOES FOR?
NO, YOU'RE THINKING OF MICKEY MOUSE
DONALD DUCK DOESN'T WEAR SHOES!
SCHULZ

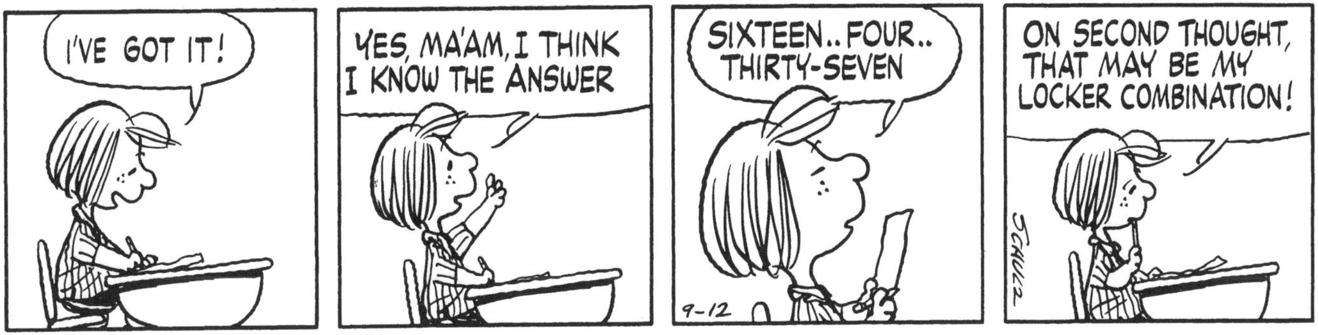
I'VE GOT IT!
YES, MA'AM, I THINK I KNOW THE ANSWER
SIXTEEN.. FOUR.. THIRTY-SEVEN
9-12
ON SECOND THOUGHT, THAT MAY BE MY LOCKER COMBINATION!
SCHULZ

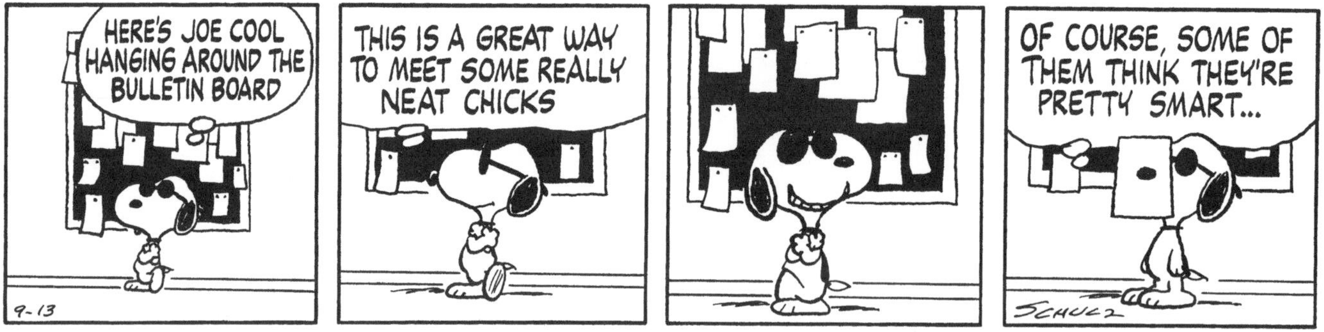
HERE'S JOE COOL HANGING AROUND THE BULLETIN BOARD
9-13
THIS IS A GREAT WAY TO MEET SOME REALLY NEAT CHICKS
OF COURSE, SOME OF THEM THINK THEY'RE PRETTY SMART...
SCHULZ

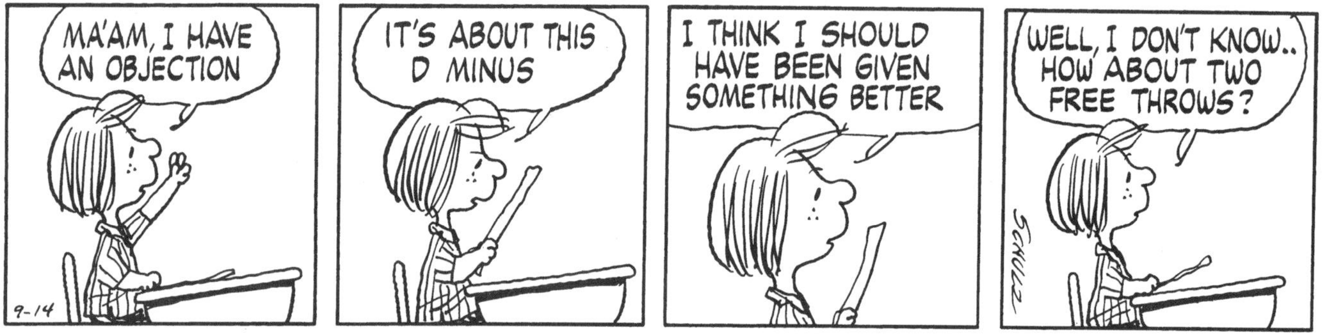
MA'AM, I HAVE AN OBJECTION
9-14
IT'S ABOUT THIS D MINUS
I THINK I SHOULD HAVE BEEN GIVEN SOMETHING BETTER
WELL, I DON'T KNOW.. HOW ABOUT TWO FREE THROWS?
SCHULZ

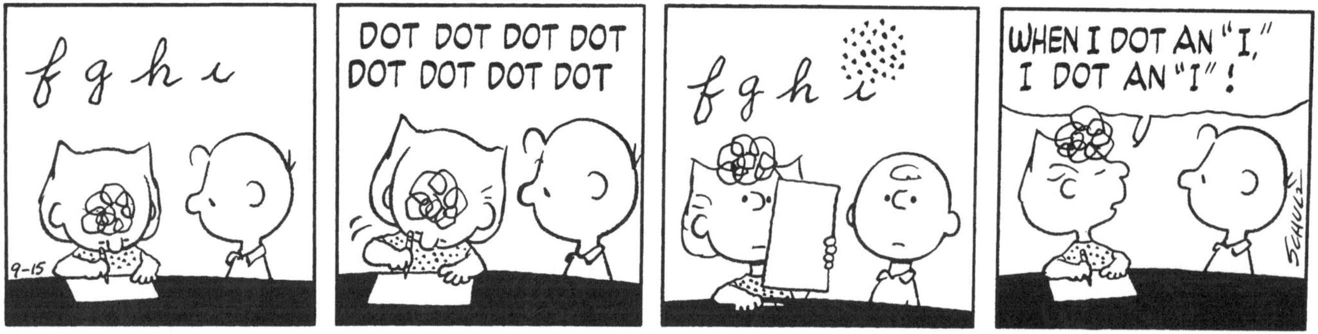
f g h i
9-15
DOT DOT DOT DOT DOT DOT DOT DOT
f g h i
WHEN I DOT AN "I," I DOT AN "I"!
SCHULZ

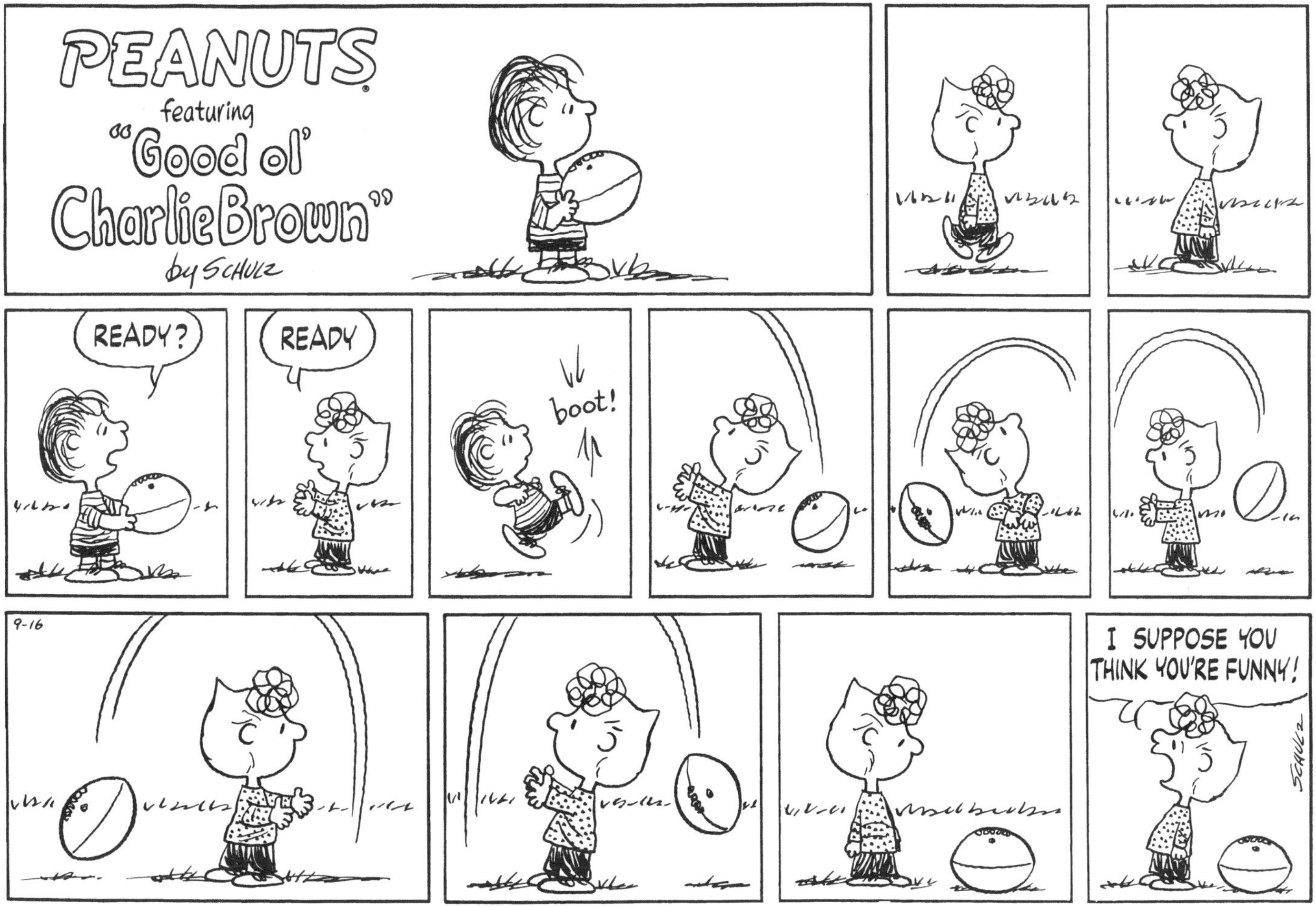
PEANUTS
featuring
"Good ol' Charlie Brown"
by SCHULZ
READY?
READY
boot!
9-16
I SUPPOSE YOU THINK YOU'RE FUNNY!
SCHULZ

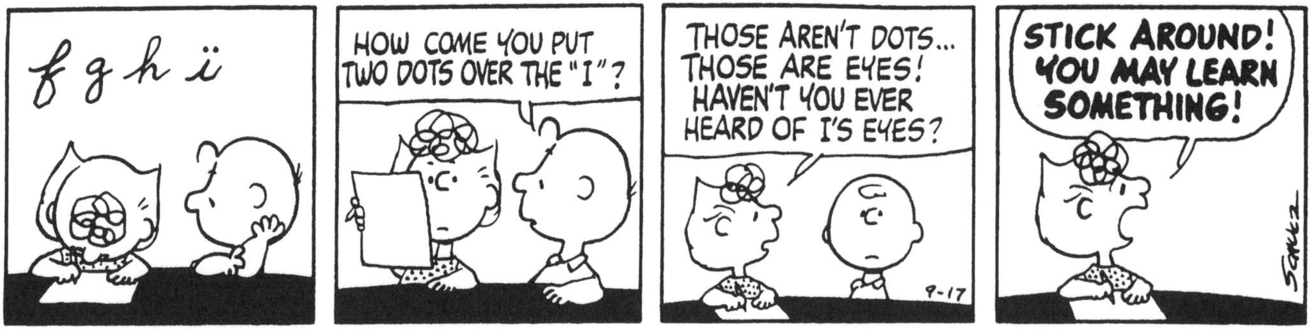
f g h ï
HOW COME YOU PUT TWO DOTS OVER THE "I"?
THOSE AREN'T DOTS... THOSE ARE EYES! HAVEN'T YOU EVER HEARD OF I'S EYES?
9-17
STICK AROUND! YOU MAY LEARN SOMETHING!
SCHULZ

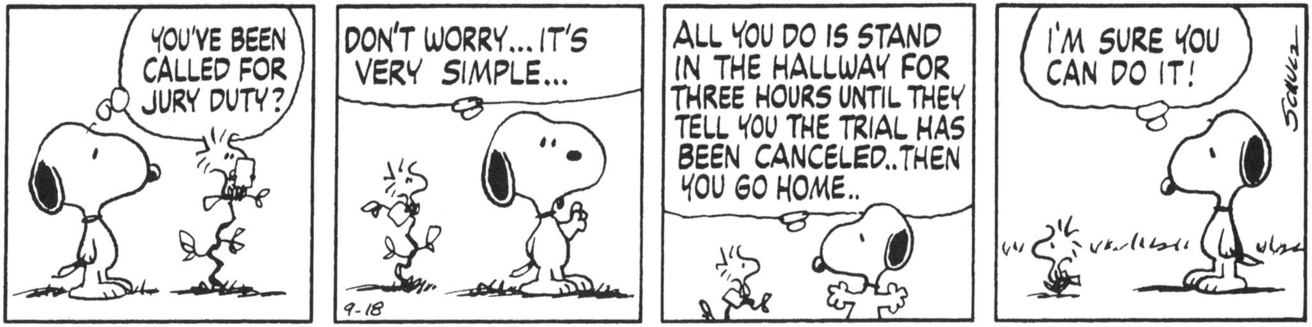
YOU'VE BEEN CALLED FOR JURY DUTY?
DON'T WORRY... IT'S VERY SIMPLE...
9-18
ALL YOU DO IS STAND IN THE HALLWAY FOR THREE HOURS UNTIL THEY TELL YOU THE TRIAL HAS BEEN CANCELED..THEN YOU GO HOME..
I'M SURE YOU CAN DO IT!
SCHULZ

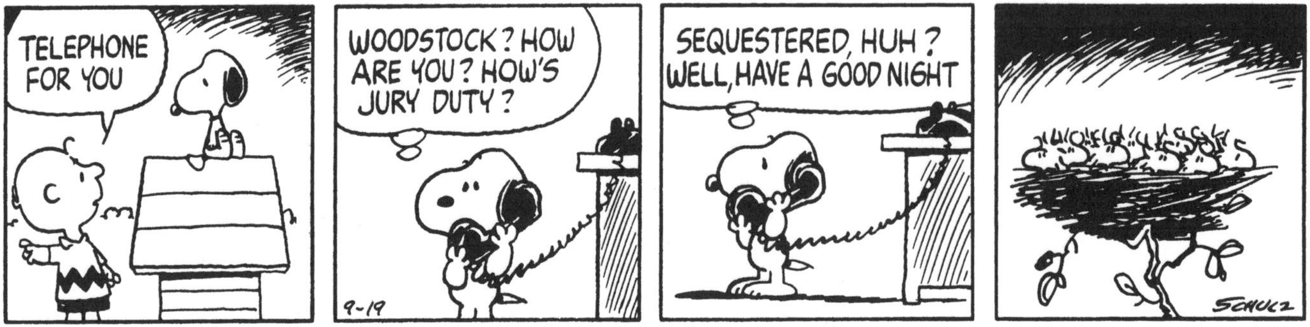
TELEPHONE FOR YOU
WOODSTOCK? HOW ARE YOU? HOW'S JURY DUTY?
9-19
SEQUESTERED, HUH? WELL, HAVE A GOOD NIGHT
SCHULZ

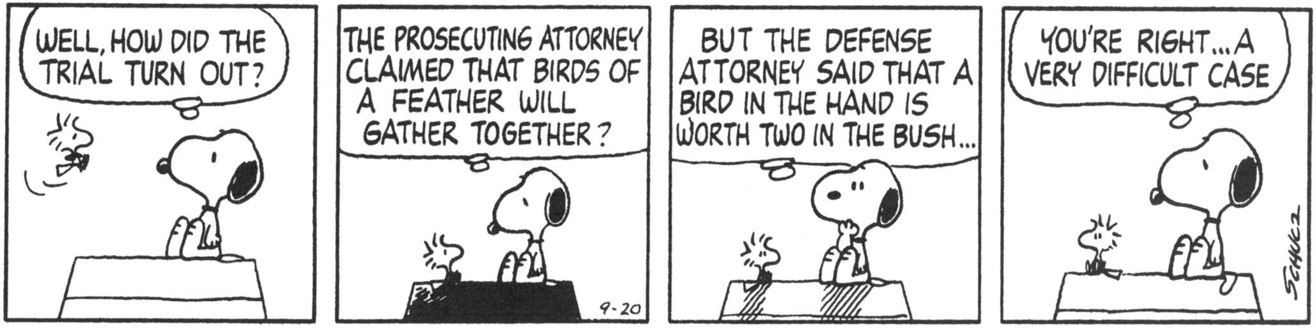
WELL, HOW DID THE TRIAL TURN OUT?
THE PROSECUTING ATTORNEY CLAIMED THAT BIRDS OF A FEATHER WILL GATHER TOGETHER?
9-20
BUT THE DEFENSE ATTORNEY SAID THAT A BIRD IN THE HAND IS WORTH TWO IN THE BUSH...
YOU'RE RIGHT... A VERY DIFFICULT CASE
SCHULZ

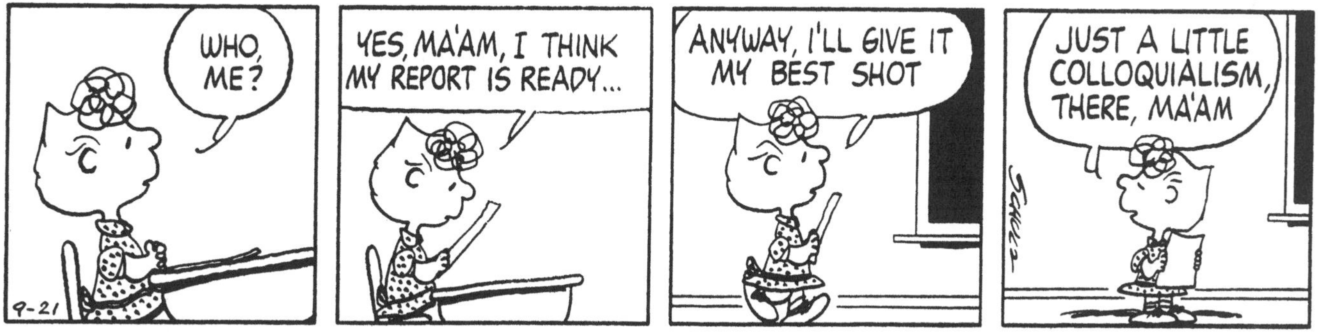
WHO, ME?
9-21
YES, MA'AM, I THINK MY REPORT IS READY...
ANYWAY, I'LL GIVE IT MY BEST SHOT
JUST A LITTLE COLLOQUIALISM, THERE, MA'AM
SCHULZ

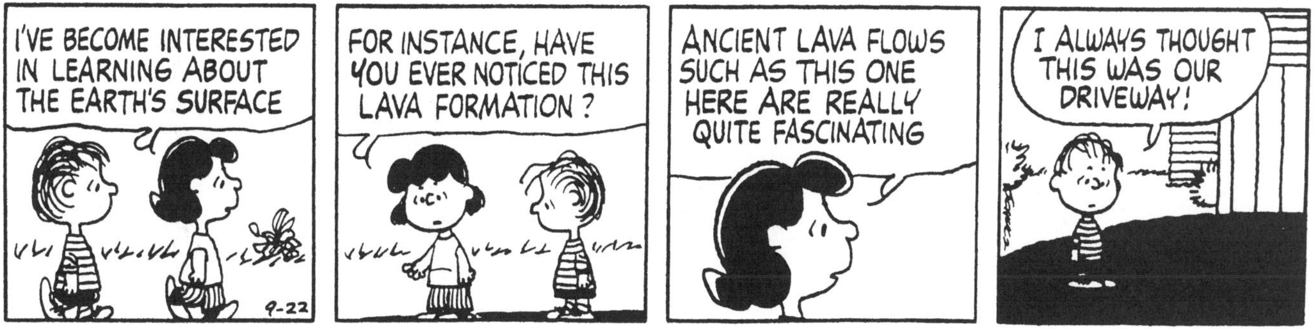
I'VE BECOME INTERESTED IN LEARNING ABOUT THE EARTH'S SURFACE
9-22
FOR INSTANCE, HAVE YOU EVER NOTICED THIS LAVA FORMATION?
ANCIENT LAVA FLOWS SUCH AS THIS ONE HERE ARE REALLY QUITE FASCINATING
I ALWAYS THOUGHT THIS WAS OUR DRIVEWAY!

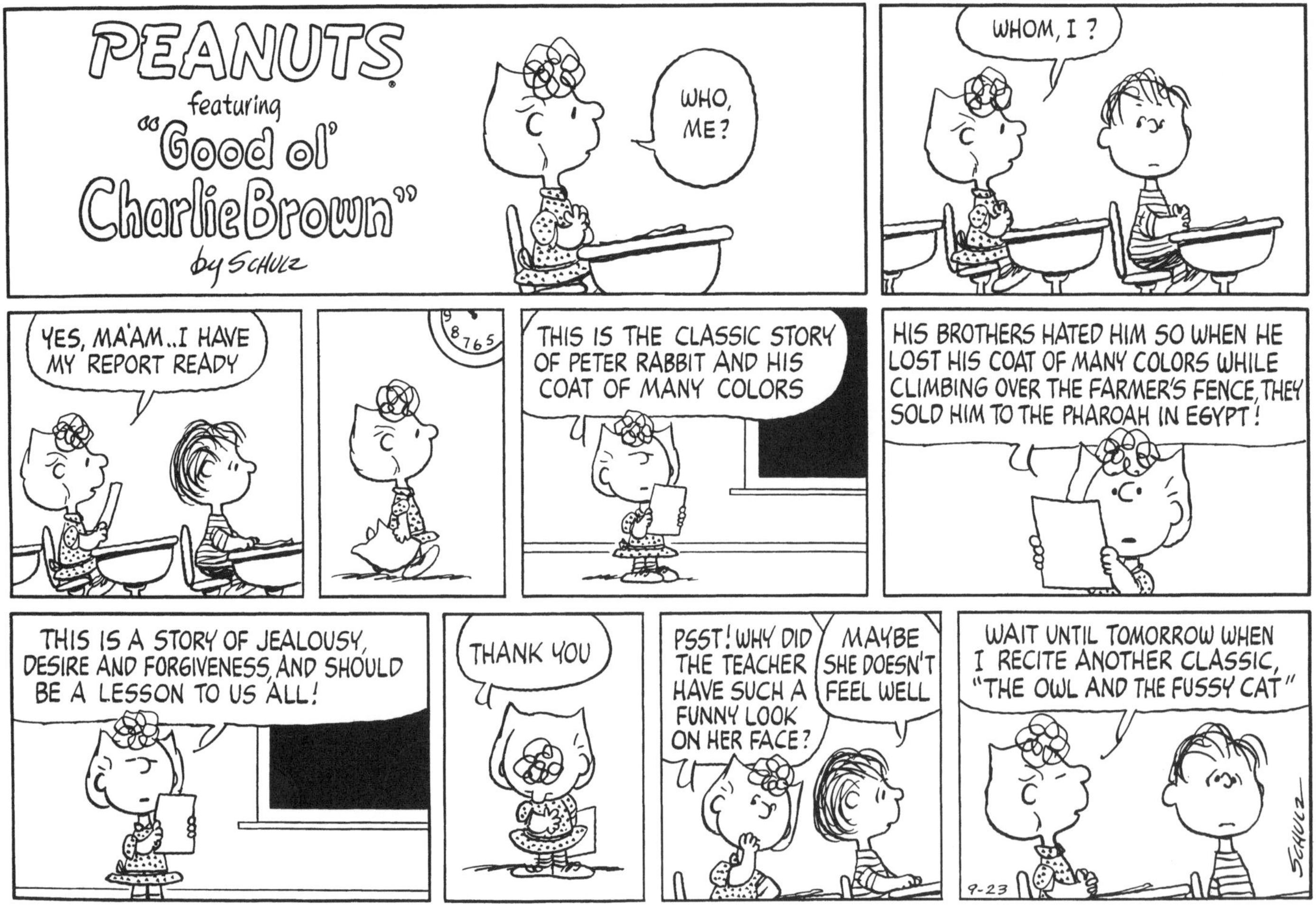
PEANUTS
featuring
"Good ol' Charlie Brown"
by SCHULZ
WHO, ME?
WHOM, I ?
YES, MA'AM..I HAVE MY REPORT READY
THIS IS THE CLASSIC STORY OF PETER RABBIT AND HIS COAT OF MANY COLORS
HIS BROTHERS HATED HIM SO WHEN HE LOST HIS COAT OF MANY COLORS WHILE CLIMBING OVER THE FARMER'S FENCE, THEY SOLD HIM TO THE PHAROAH IN EGYPT!
THIS IS A STORY OF JEALOUSY, DESIRE AND FORGIVENESS, AND SHOULD BE A LESSON TO US ALL!
THANK YOU
PSST! WHY DID THE TEACHER HAVE SUCH A FUNNY LOOK ON HER FACE?
MAYBE SHE DOESN'T FEEL WELL
WAIT UNTIL TOMORROW WHEN I RECITE ANOTHER CLASSIC, "THE OWL AND THE FUSSY CAT"
9-23
SCHULZ

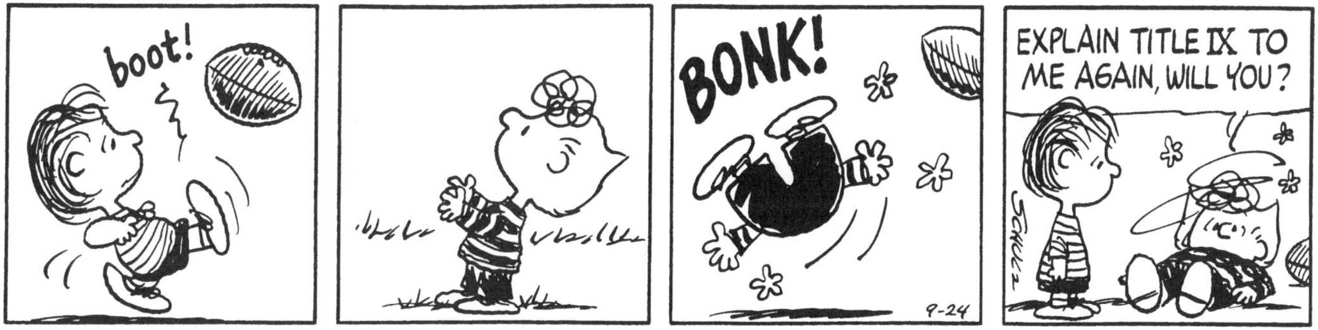
boot!
BONK!
9-24
EXPLAIN TITLE IX TO ME AGAIN, WILL YOU?

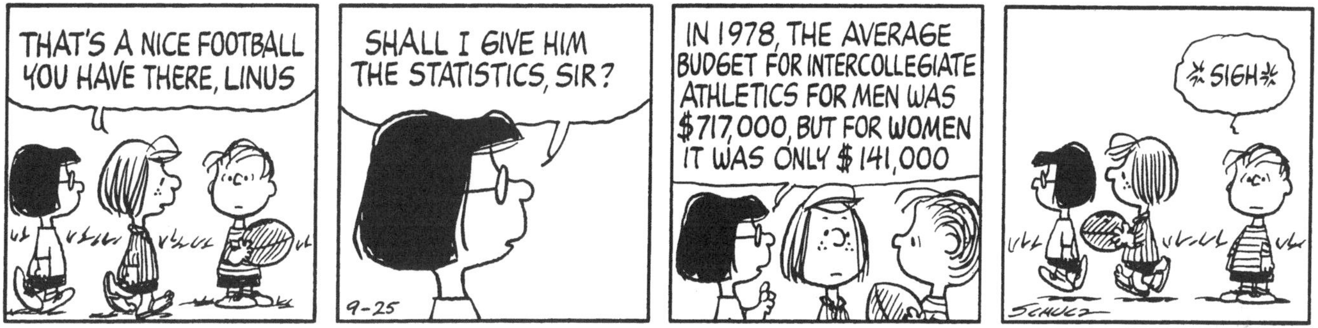
THAT'S A NICE FOOTBALL YOU HAVE THERE, LINUS
SHALL I GIVE HIM THE STATISTICS, SIR?
9-25
IN 1978, THE AVERAGE BUDGET FOR INTERCOLLEGIATE ATHLETICS FOR MEN WAS $717,000, BUT FOR WOMEN IT WAS ONLY $141,000
SIGH

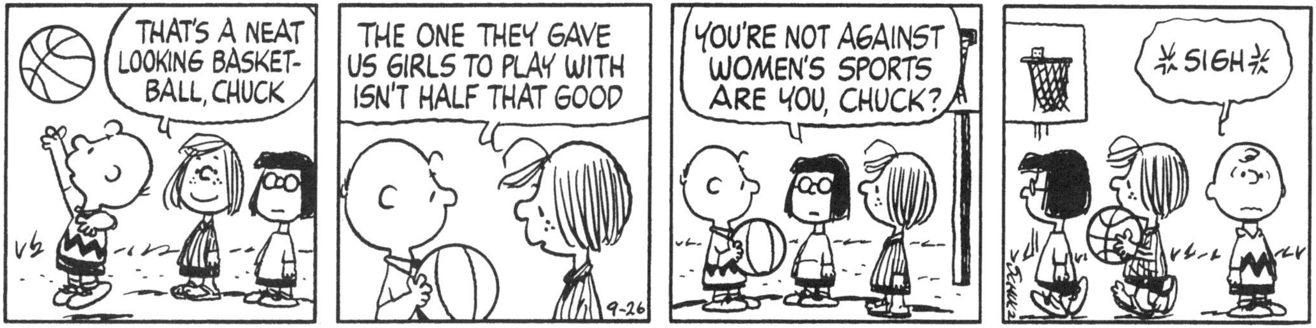
THAT'S A NEAT LOOKING BASKET-BALL, CHUCK
THE ONE THEY GAVE US GIRLS TO PLAY WITH ISN'T HALF THAT GOOD
9-26
YOU'RE NOT AGAINST WOMEN'S SPORTS ARE YOU, CHUCK?
SIGH

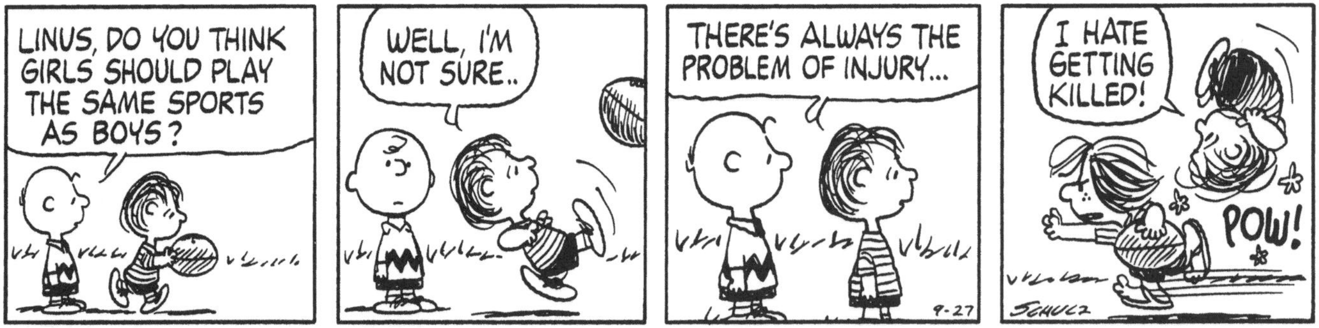
LINUS, DO YOU THINK GIRLS SHOULD PLAY THE SAME SPORTS AS BOYS?
WELL, I'M NOT SURE..
THERE'S ALWAYS THE PROBLEM OF INJURY...
I HATE GETTING KILLED!
POW!
9-27
SCHULZ

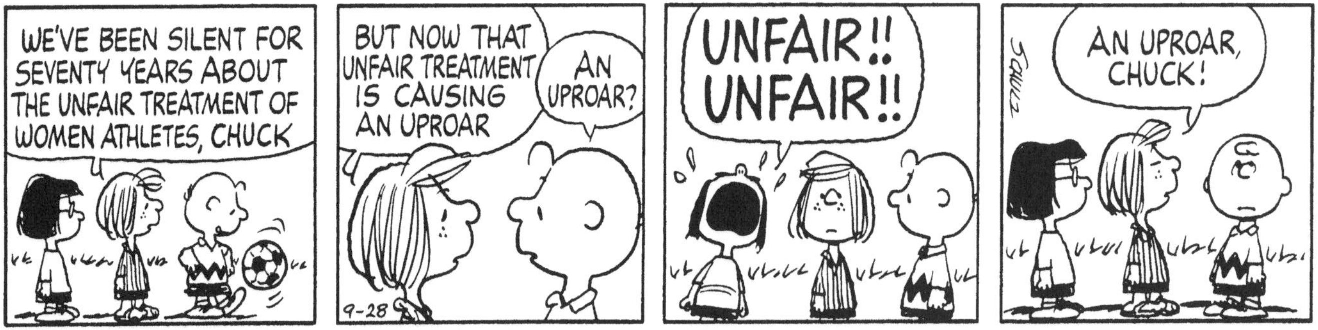
WE'VE BEEN SILENT FOR SEVENTY YEARS ABOUT THE UNFAIR TREATMENT OF WOMEN ATHLETES, CHUCK
BUT NOW THAT UNFAIR TREATMENT IS CAUSING AN UPROAR
AN UPROAR?
9-28
UNFAIR!! UNFAIR!!
AN UPROAR, CHUCK!
SCHULZ

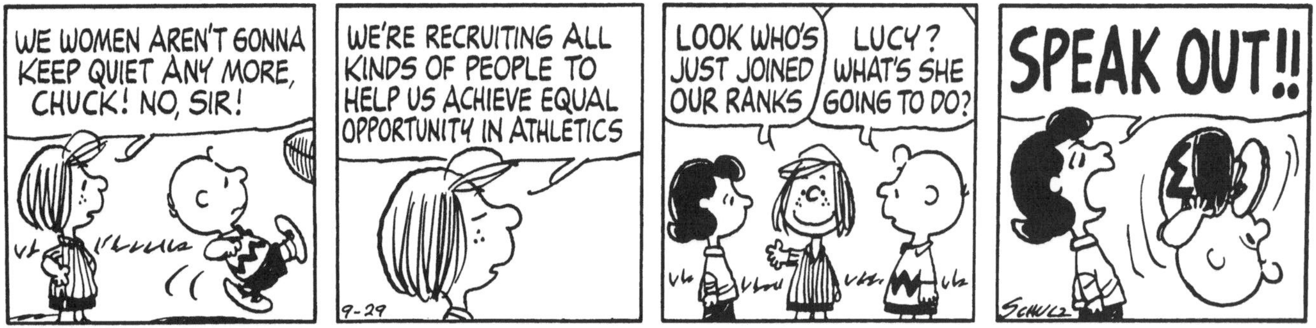
WE WOMEN AREN'T GONNA KEEP QUIET ANY MORE, CHUCK! NO, SIR!
WE'RE RECRUITING ALL KINDS OF PEOPLE TO HELP US ACHIEVE EQUAL OPPORTUNITY IN ATHLETICS
9-29
LOOK WHO'S JUST JOINED OUR RANKS
LUCY? WHAT'S SHE GOING TO DO?
SPEAK OUT!!
SCHULZ

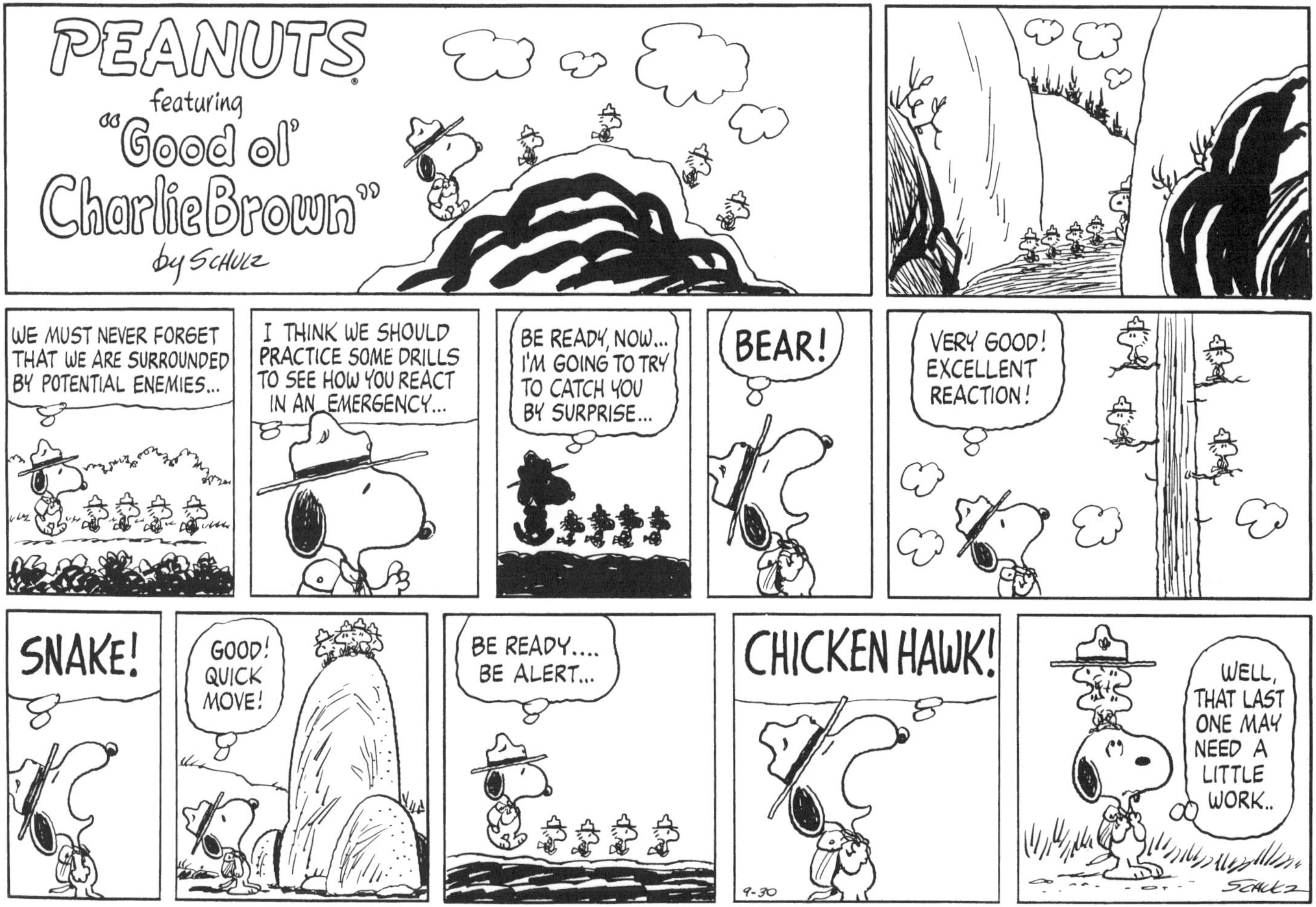
PEANUTS
featuring
"Good ol' Charlie Brown"
by SCHULZ
WE MUST NEVER FORGET THAT WE ARE SURROUNDED BY POTENTIAL ENEMIES...
I THINK WE SHOULD PRACTICE SOME DRILLS TO SEE HOW YOU REACT IN AN EMERGENCY...
BE READY, NOW... I'M GOING TO TRY TO CATCH YOU BY SURPRISE...
BEAR!
VERY GOOD! EXCELLENT REACTION!
SNAKE!
GOOD! QUICK MOVE!
BE READY.... BE ALERT...
CHICKEN HAWK!
9-30
WELL, THAT LAST ONE MAY NEED A LITTLE WORK..
SCHULZ

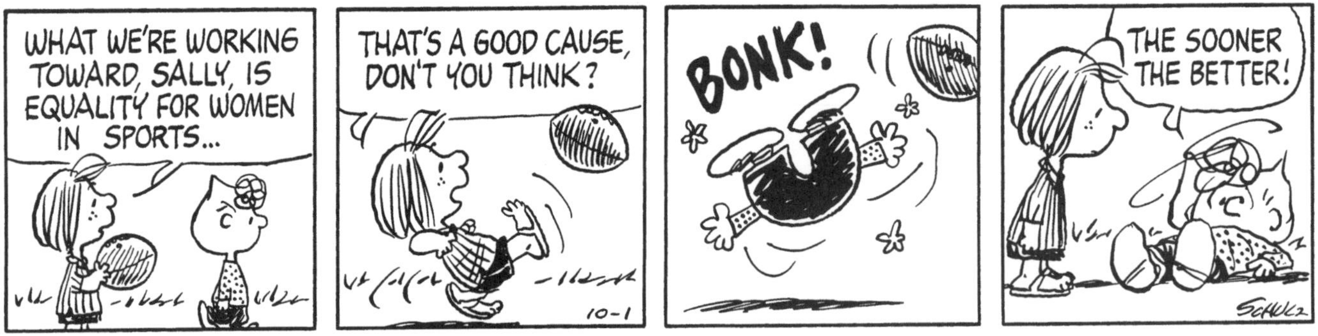
WHAT WE'RE WORKING TOWARD, SALLY, IS EQUALITY FOR WOMEN IN SPORTS...
THAT'S A GOOD CAUSE, DON'T YOU THINK?
10-1
BONK!
THE SOONER THE BETTER!
SCHULZ

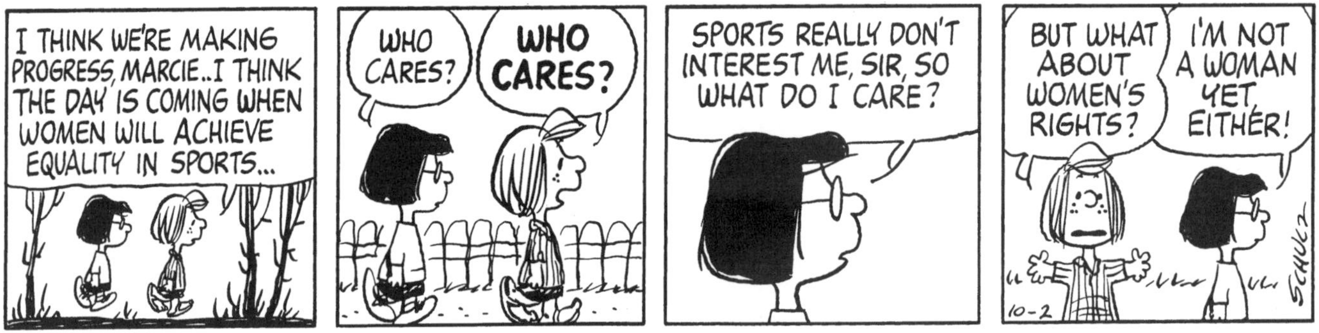
I THINK WE'RE MAKING PROGRESS, MARCIE..I THINK THE DAY IS COMING WHEN WOMEN WILL ACHIEVE EQUALITY IN SPORTS...
WHO CARES?
WHO CARES?
SPORTS REALLY DON'T INTEREST ME, SIR, SO WHAT DO I CARE?
BUT WHAT ABOUT WOMEN'S RIGHTS?
I'M NOT A WOMAN YET, EITHER!
10-2
SCHULZ

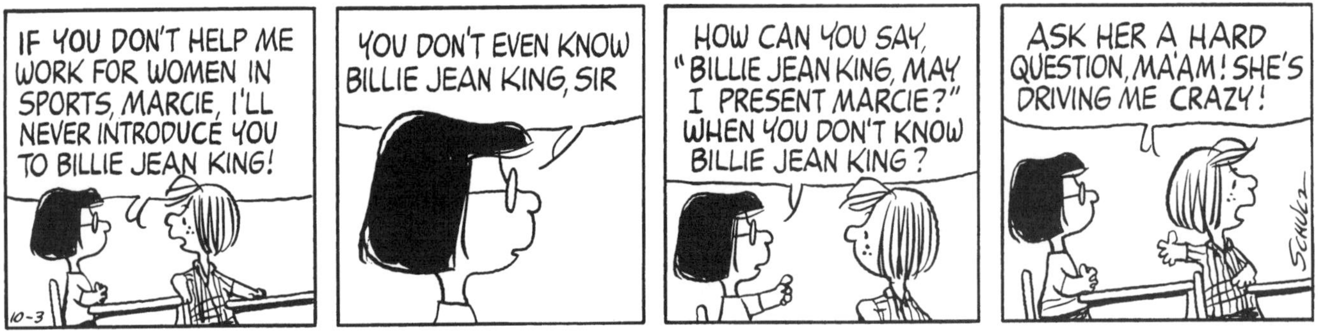
IF YOU DON'T HELP ME WORK FOR WOMEN IN SPORTS, MARCIE, I'LL NEVER INTRODUCE YOU TO BILLIE JEAN KING!
10-3
YOU DON'T EVEN KNOW BILLIE JEAN KING, SIR
HOW CAN YOU SAY, "BILLIE JEAN KING, MAY I PRESENT MARCIE?" WHEN YOU DON'T KNOW BILLIE JEAN KING?
ASK HER A HARD QUESTION, MA'AM! SHE'S DRIVING ME CRAZY!
SCHULZ

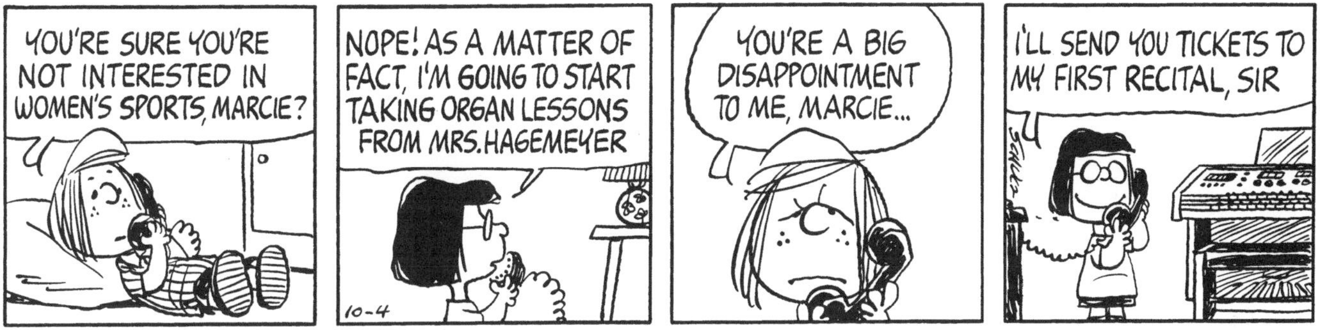
YOU'RE SURE YOU'RE NOT INTERESTED IN WOMEN'S SPORTS, MARCIE?
NOPE! AS A MATTER OF FACT, I'M GOING TO START TAKING ORGAN LESSONS FROM MRS. HAGEMEYER
10-4
YOU'RE A BIG DISAPPOINTMENT TO ME, MARCIE...
I'LL SEND YOU TICKETS TO MY FIRST RECITAL, SIR
SCHULZ

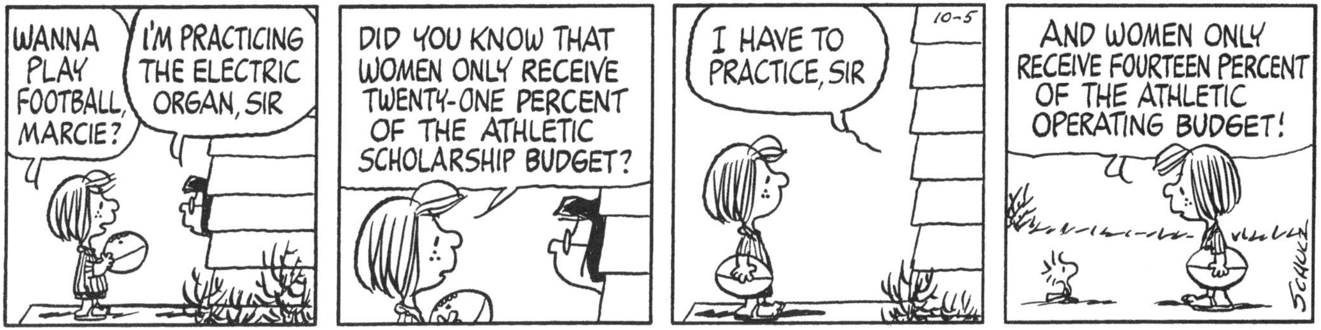
WANNA PLAY FOOTBALL, MARCIE?
I'M PRACTICING THE ELECTRIC ORGAN, SIR
DID YOU KNOW THAT WOMEN ONLY RECEIVE TWENTY-ONE PERCENT OF THE ATHLETIC SCHOLARSHIP BUDGET?
10-5
I HAVE TO PRACTICE, SIR
AND WOMEN ONLY RECEIVE FOURTEEN PERCENT OF THE ATHLETIC OPERATING BUDGET!
SCHULZ

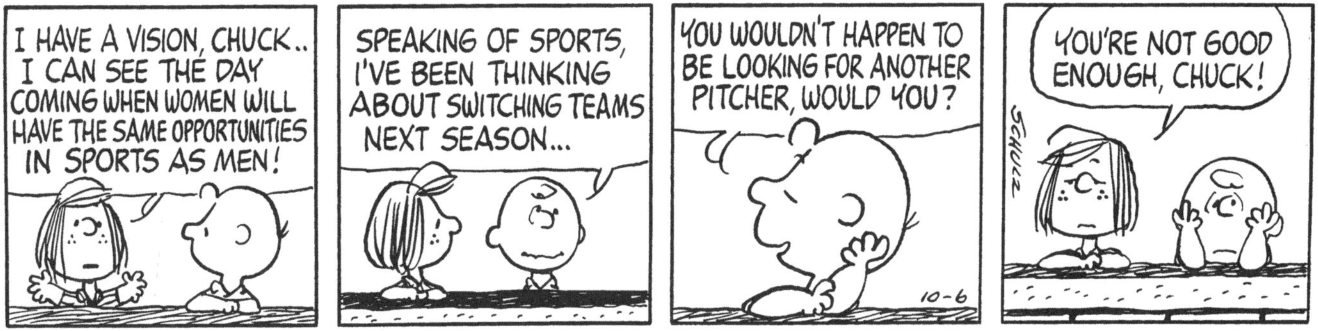
I HAVE A VISION, CHUCK.. I CAN SEE THE DAY COMING WHEN WOMEN WILL HAVE THE SAME OPPORTUNITIES IN SPORTS AS MEN!
SPEAKING OF SPORTS, I'VE BEEN THINKING ABOUT SWITCHING TEAMS NEXT SEASON...
YOU WOULDN'T HAPPEN TO BE LOOKING FOR ANOTHER PITCHER, WOULD YOU?
10-6
YOU'RE NOT GOOD ENOUGH, CHUCK!
SCHULZ

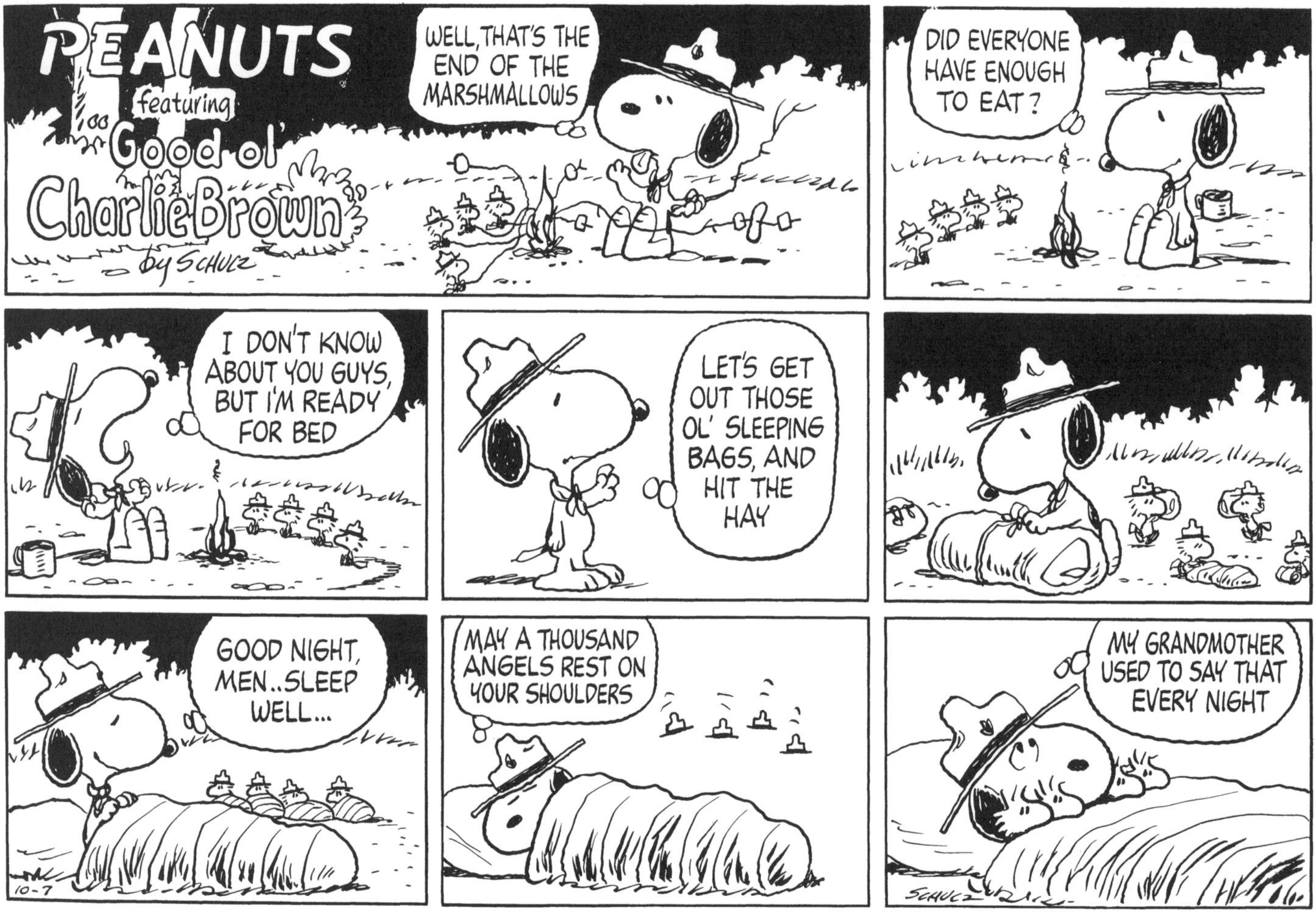
PEANUTS
featuring
Good ol' Charlie Brown
by SCHULZ
WELL, THAT'S THE END OF THE MARSHMALLOWS
DID EVERYONE HAVE ENOUGH TO EAT?
I DON'T KNOW ABOUT YOU GUYS, BUT I'M READY FOR BED
LET'S GET OUT THOSE OL' SLEEPING BAGS, AND HIT THE HAY
GOOD NIGHT, MEN..SLEEP WELL...
10-7
MAY A THOUSAND ANGELS REST ON YOUR SHOULDERS
MY GRANDMOTHER USED TO SAY THAT EVERY NIGHT
SCHULZ

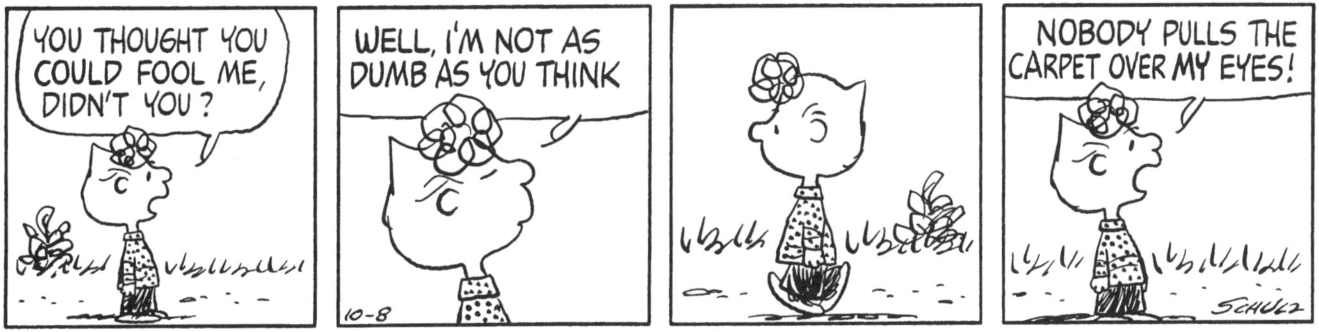
YOU THOUGHT YOU COULD FOOL ME, DIDN'T YOU ?
WELL, I'M NOT AS DUMB AS YOU THINK
10-8
NOBODY PULLS THE CARPET OVER MY EYES!
SCHULZ

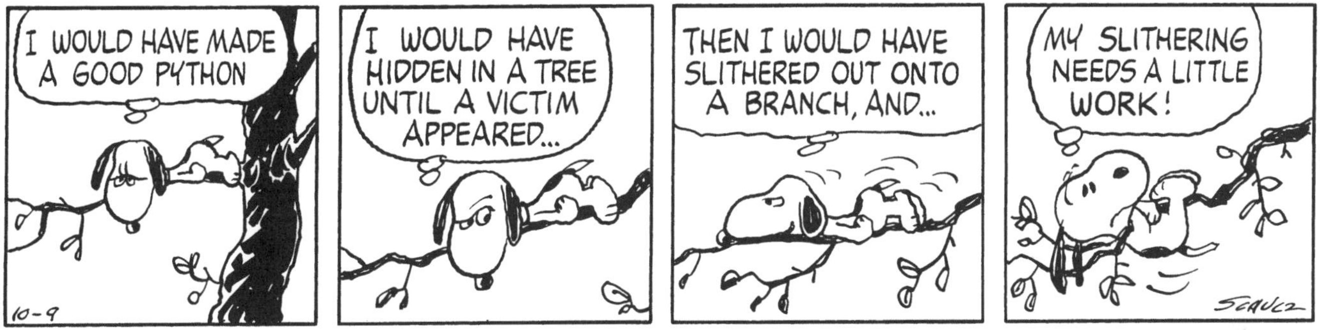
I WOULD HAVE MADE A GOOD PYTHON
10-9
I WOULD HAVE HIDDEN IN A TREE UNTIL A VICTIM APPEARED...
THEN I WOULD HAVE SLITHERED OUT ONTO A BRANCH, AND...
MY SLITHERING NEEDS A LITTLE WORK!
SCHULZ

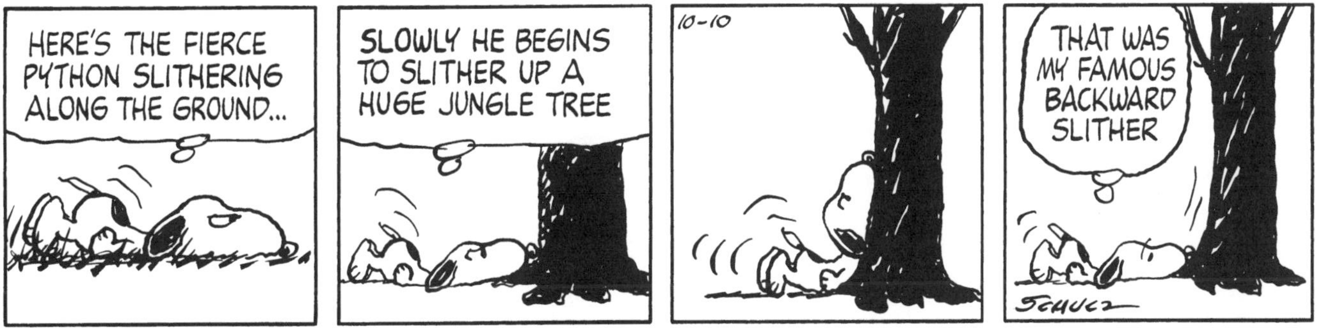
HERE'S THE FIERCE PYTHON SLITHERING ALONG THE GROUND...
SLOWLY HE BEGINS TO SLITHER UP A HUGE JUNGLE TREE
10-10
THAT WAS MY FAMOUS BACKWARD SLITHER
SCHULZ

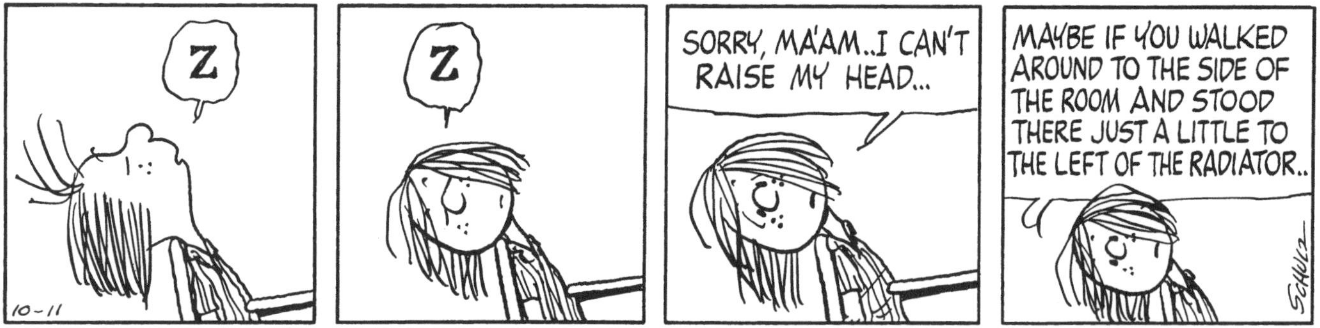
10-11
Z
Z
SORRY, MA'AM..I CAN'T RAISE MY HEAD...
MAYBE IF YOU WALKED AROUND TO THE SIDE OF THE ROOM AND STOOD THERE JUST A LITTLE TO THE LEFT OF THE RADIATOR..
SCHULZ

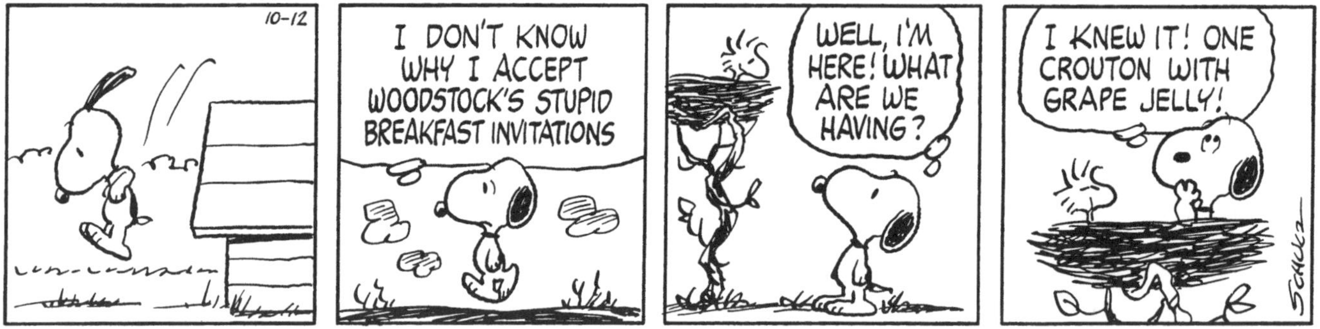
10-12
I DON'T KNOW WHY I ACCEPT WOODSTOCK'S STUPID BREAKFAST INVITATIONS
WELL, I'M HERE! WHAT ARE WE HAVING?
I KNEW IT! ONE CROUTON WITH GRAPE JELLY!
SCHULZ

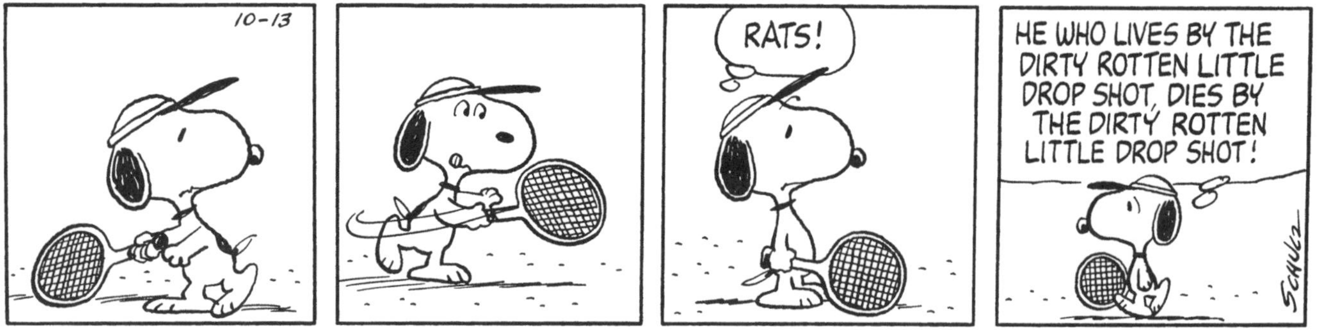
10-13
RATS!
HE WHO LIVES BY THE DIRTY ROTTEN LITTLE DROP SHOT, DIES BY THE DIRTY ROTTEN LITTLE DROP SHOT!
SCHULZ

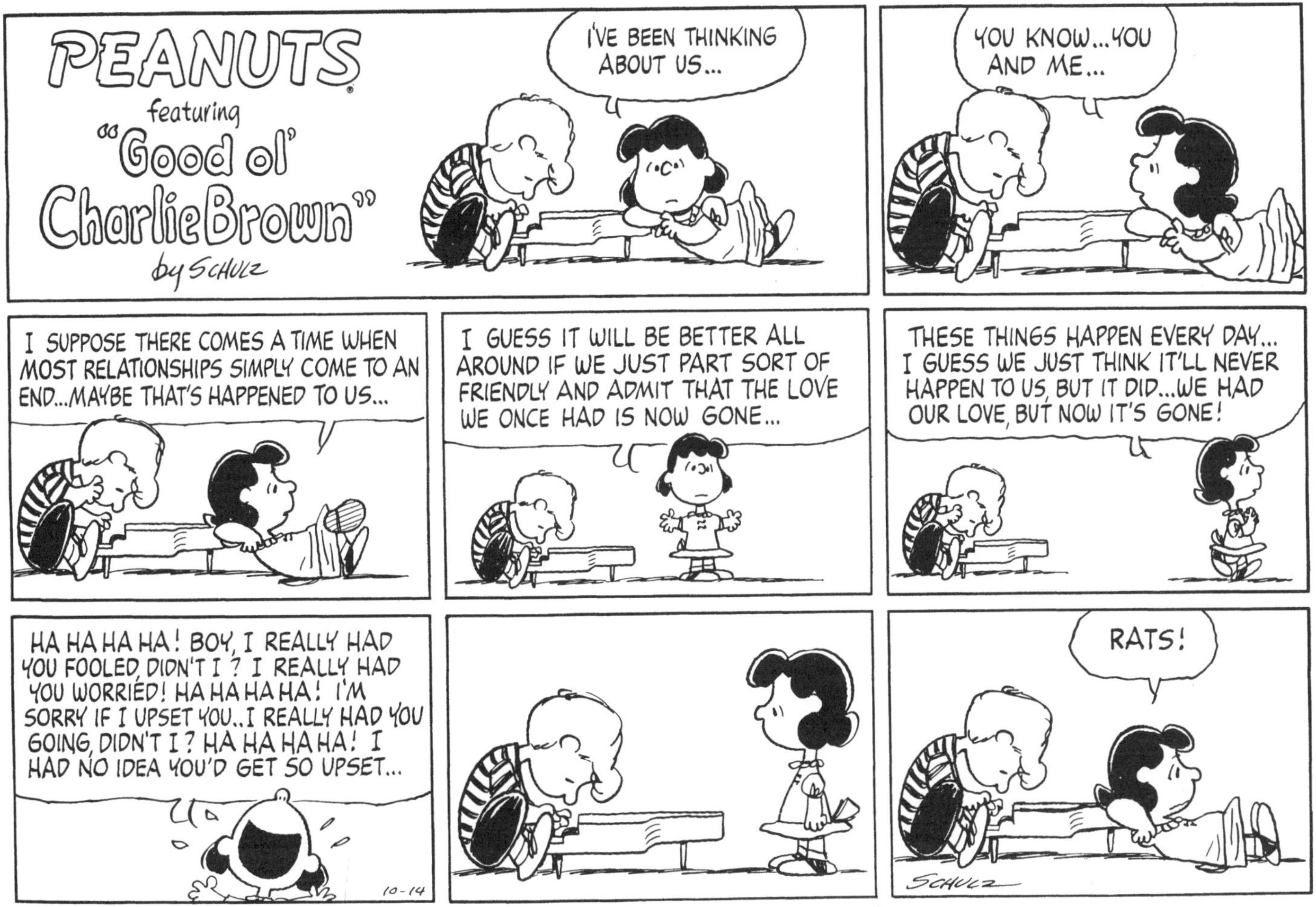
PEANUTS
featuring "Good ol' CharlieBrown"
by SCHULZ
I'VE BEEN THINKING ABOUT US...
YOU KNOW...YOU AND ME...
I SUPPOSE THERE COMES A TIME WHEN MOST RELATIONSHIPS SIMPLY COME TO AN END...MAYBE THAT'S HAPPENED TO US...
I GUESS IT WILL BE BETTER ALL AROUND IF WE JUST PART SORT OF FRIENDLY AND ADMIT THAT THE LOVE WE ONCE HAD IS NOW GONE...
THESE THINGS HAPPEN EVERY DAY... I GUESS WE JUST THINK IT'LL NEVER HAPPEN TO US, BUT IT DID...WE HAD OUR LOVE, BUT NOW IT'S GONE!
HA HA HA HA! BOY, I REALLY HAD YOU FOOLED, DIDN'T I? I REALLY HAD YOU WORRIED! HA HA HA HA! I'M SORRY IF I UPSET YOU..I REALLY HAD YOU GOING, DIDN'T I? HA HA HA HA! I HAD NO IDEA YOU'D GET SO UPSET...
10-14
RATS!
SCHULZ

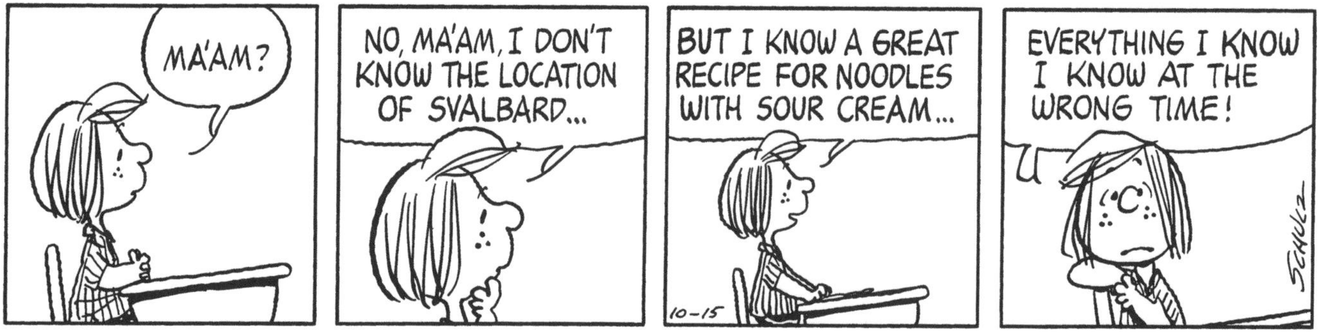
MA'AM?
NO, MA'AM, I DON'T KNOW THE LOCATION OF SVALBARD...
BUT I KNOW A GREAT RECIPE FOR NOODLES WITH SOUR CREAM...
10-15
EVERYTHING I KNOW I KNOW AT THE WRONG TIME!
SCHULZ

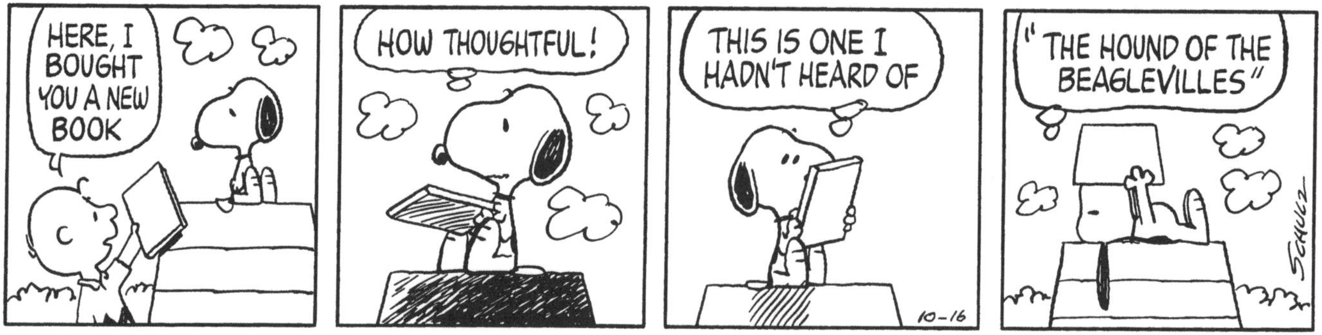
HERE, I BOUGHT YOU A NEW BOOK
HOW THOUGHTFUL!
THIS IS ONE I HADN'T HEARD OF
10-16
"THE HOUND OF THE BEAGLEVILLES"
SCHULZ

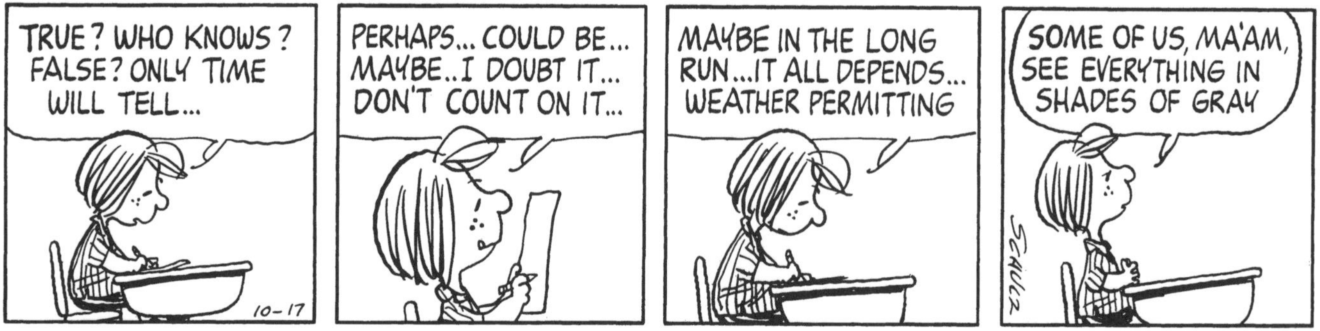
TRUE? WHO KNOWS? FALSE? ONLY TIME WILL TELL...
10-17
PERHAPS... COULD BE... MAYBE..I DOUBT IT... DON'T COUNT ON IT...
MAYBE IN THE LONG RUN...IT ALL DEPENDS... WEATHER PERMITTING
SCHULZ
SOME OF US, MA'AM, SEE EVERYTHING IN SHADES OF GRAY

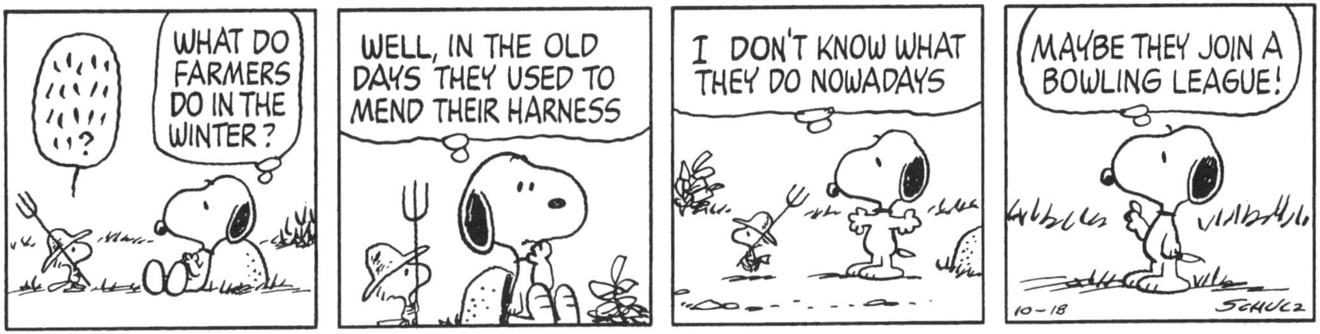
?
WHAT DO FARMERS DO IN THE WINTER?
WELL, IN THE OLD DAYS THEY USED TO MEND THEIR HARNESS
I DON'T KNOW WHAT THEY DO NOWADAYS
MAYBE THEY JOIN A BOWLING LEAGUE!
10-18
SCHULZ

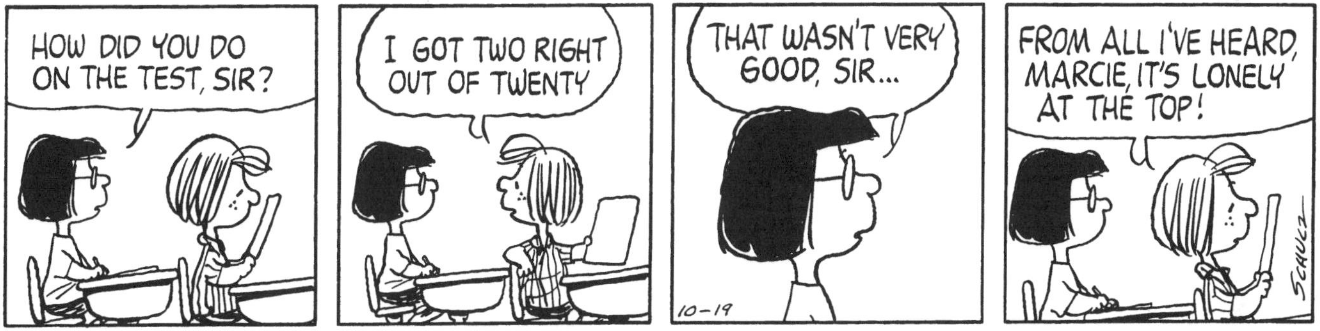
HOW DID YOU DO ON THE TEST, SIR?
I GOT TWO RIGHT OUT OF TWENTY
THAT WASN'T VERY GOOD, SIR...
10-19
FROM ALL I'VE HEARD, MARCIE, IT'S LONELY AT THE TOP!
SCHULZ

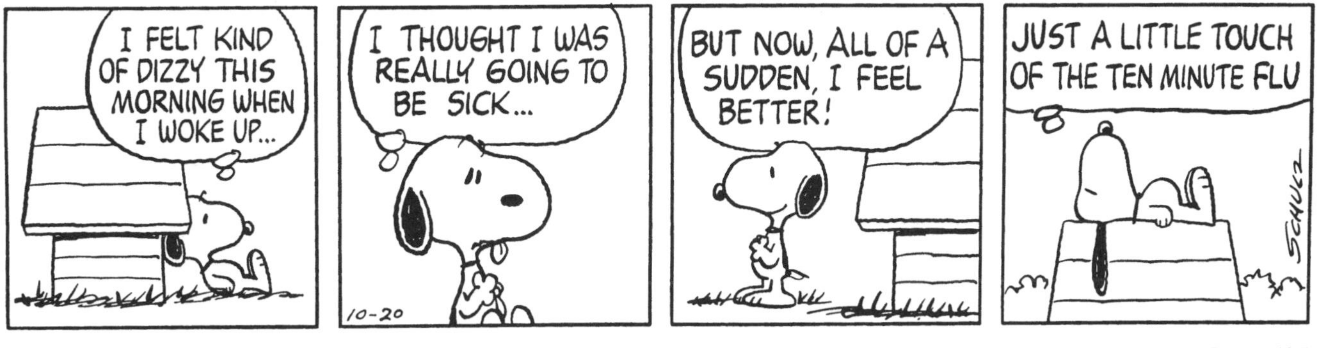
I FELT KIND OF DIZZY THIS MORNING WHEN I WOKE UP...
I THOUGHT I WAS REALLY GOING TO BE SICK...
10-20
BUT NOW, ALL OF A SUDDEN, I FEEL BETTER!
JUST A LITTLE TOUCH OF THE TEN MINUTE FLU
SCHULZ

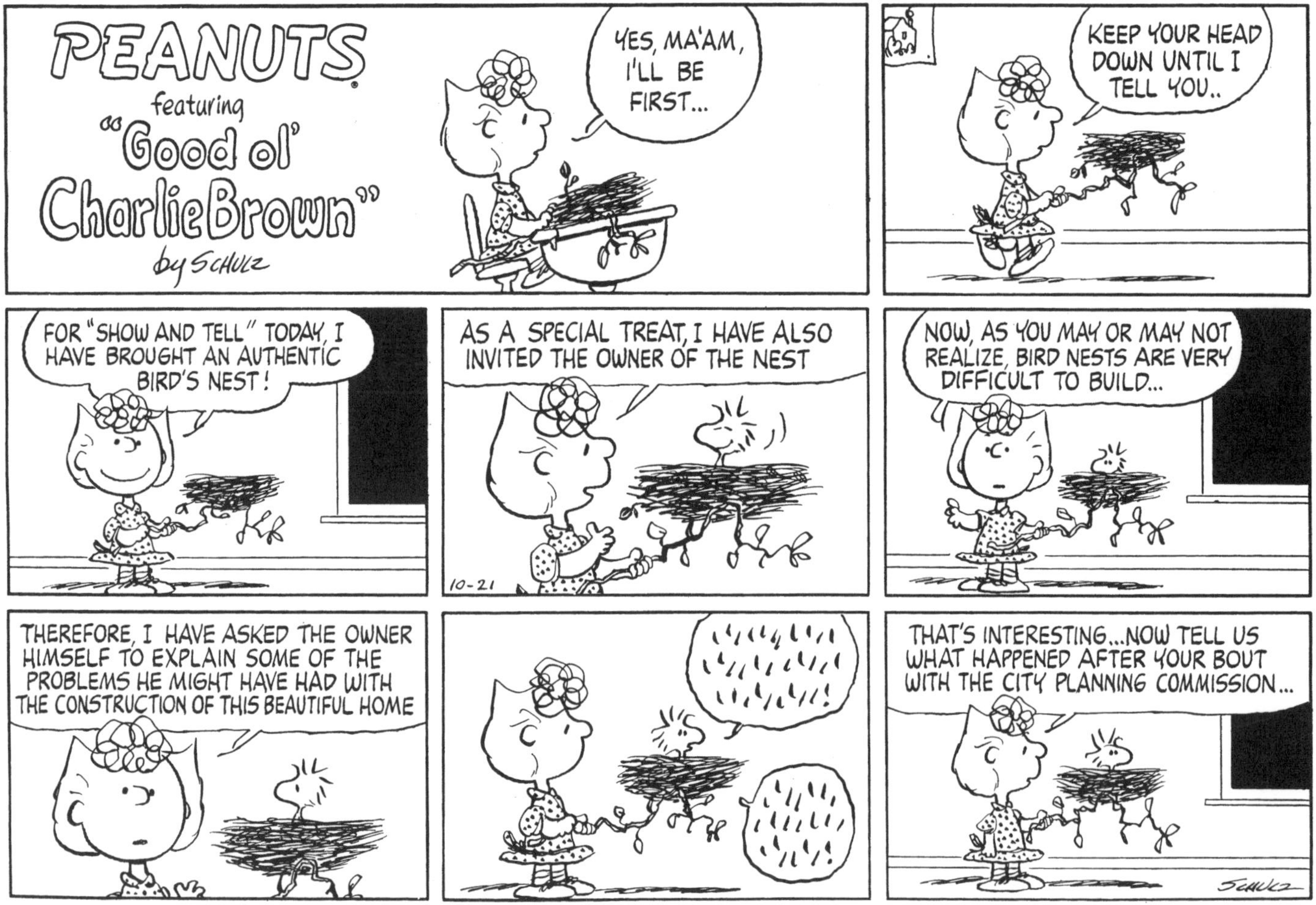
PEANUTS
featuring
"Good ol' CharlieBrown"
by SCHULZ
YES, MA'AM, I'LL BE FIRST...
KEEP YOUR HEAD DOWN UNTIL I TELL YOU..
FOR "SHOW AND TELL" TODAY, I HAVE BROUGHT AN AUTHENTIC BIRD'S NEST!
AS A SPECIAL TREAT, I HAVE ALSO INVITED THE OWNER OF THE NEST
10-21
NOW, AS YOU MAY OR MAY NOT REALIZE, BIRD NESTS ARE VERY DIFFICULT TO BUILD...
THEREFORE, I HAVE ASKED THE OWNER HIMSELF TO EXPLAIN SOME OF THE PROBLEMS HE MIGHT HAVE HAD WITH THE CONSTRUCTION OF THIS BEAUTIFUL HOME
THAT'S INTERESTING...NOW TELL US WHAT HAPPENED AFTER YOUR BOUT WITH THE CITY PLANNING COMMISSION...
SCHULZ

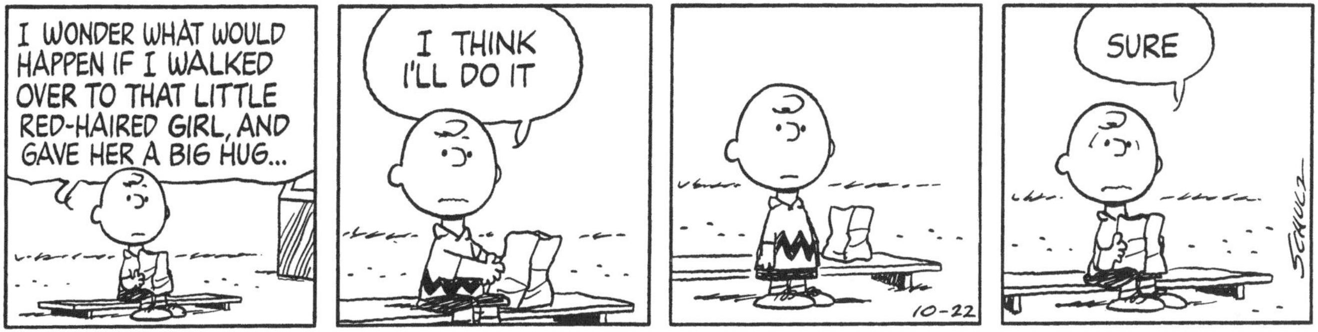
I WONDER WHAT WOULD HAPPEN IF I WALKED OVER TO THAT LITTLE RED-HAIRED GIRL, AND GAVE HER A BIG HUG...
I THINK I'LL DO IT
10-22
SURE
SCHULZ

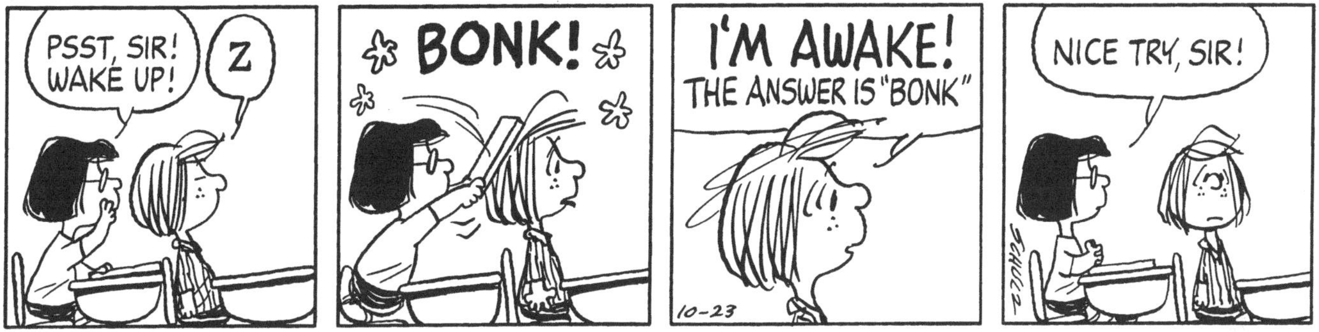
PSST, SIR! WAKE UP!
Z
BONK!
I'M AWAKE! THE ANSWER IS "BONK"
10-23
SCHULZ
NICE TRY, SIR!

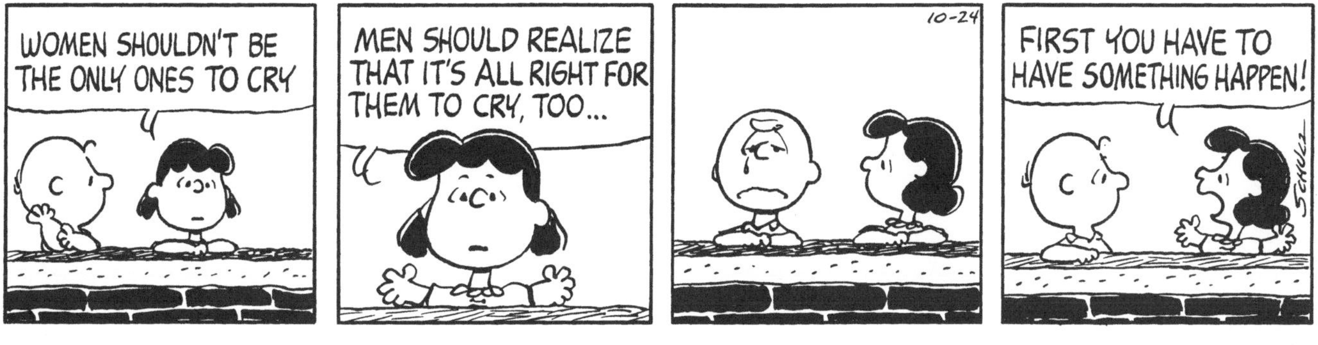
WOMEN SHOULDN'T BE THE ONLY ONES TO CRY
MEN SHOULD REALIZE THAT IT'S ALL RIGHT FOR THEM TO CRY, TOO...
10-24
FIRST YOU HAVE TO HAVE SOMETHING HAPPEN!
SCHULZ

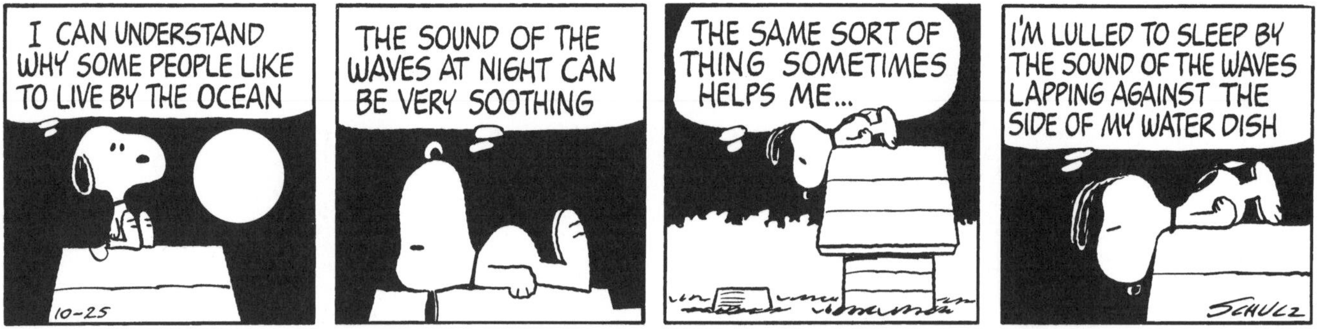
I CAN UNDERSTAND WHY SOME PEOPLE LIKE TO LIVE BY THE OCEAN
10-25
THE SOUND OF THE WAVES AT NIGHT CAN BE VERY SOOTHING
THE SAME SORT OF THING SOMETIMES HELPS ME...
I'M LULLED TO SLEEP BY THE SOUND OF THE WAVES LAPPING AGAINST THE SIDE OF MY WATER DISH
SCHULZ

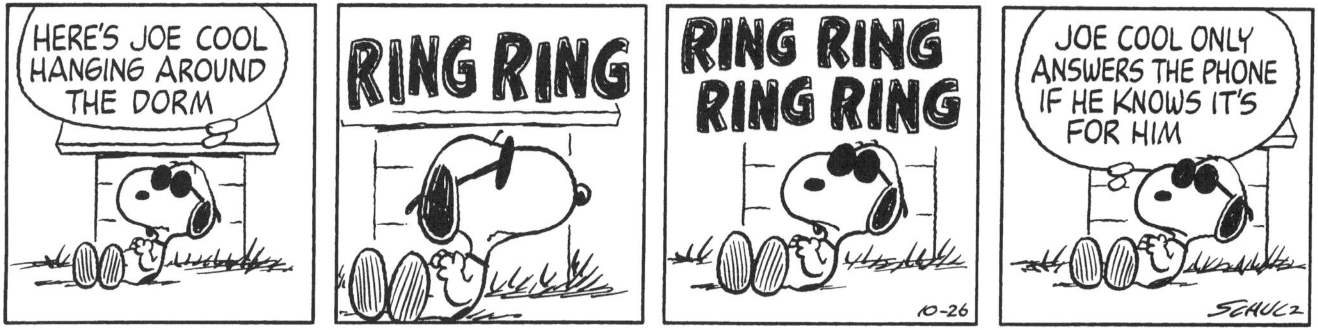
HERE'S JOE COOL HANGING AROUND THE DORM
RING RING
RING RING RING RING
10-26
JOE COOL ONLY ANSWERS THE PHONE IF HE KNOWS IT'S FOR HIM
SCHULZ

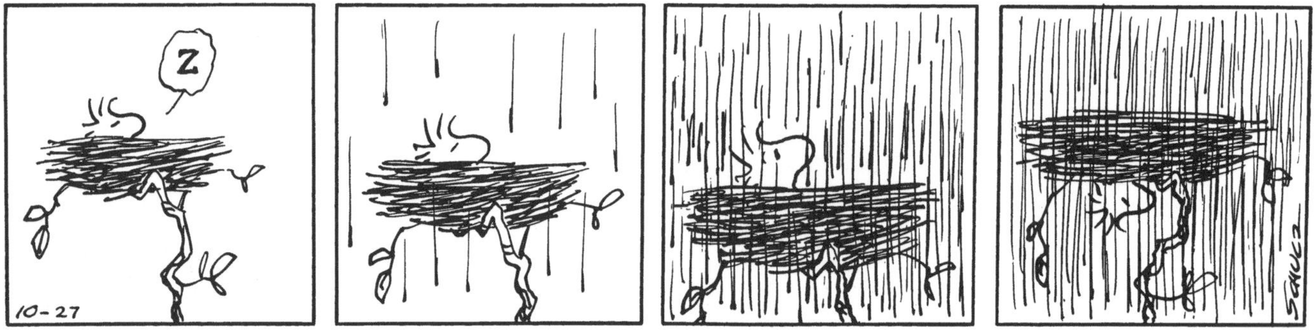
Z
10-27
SCHULZ

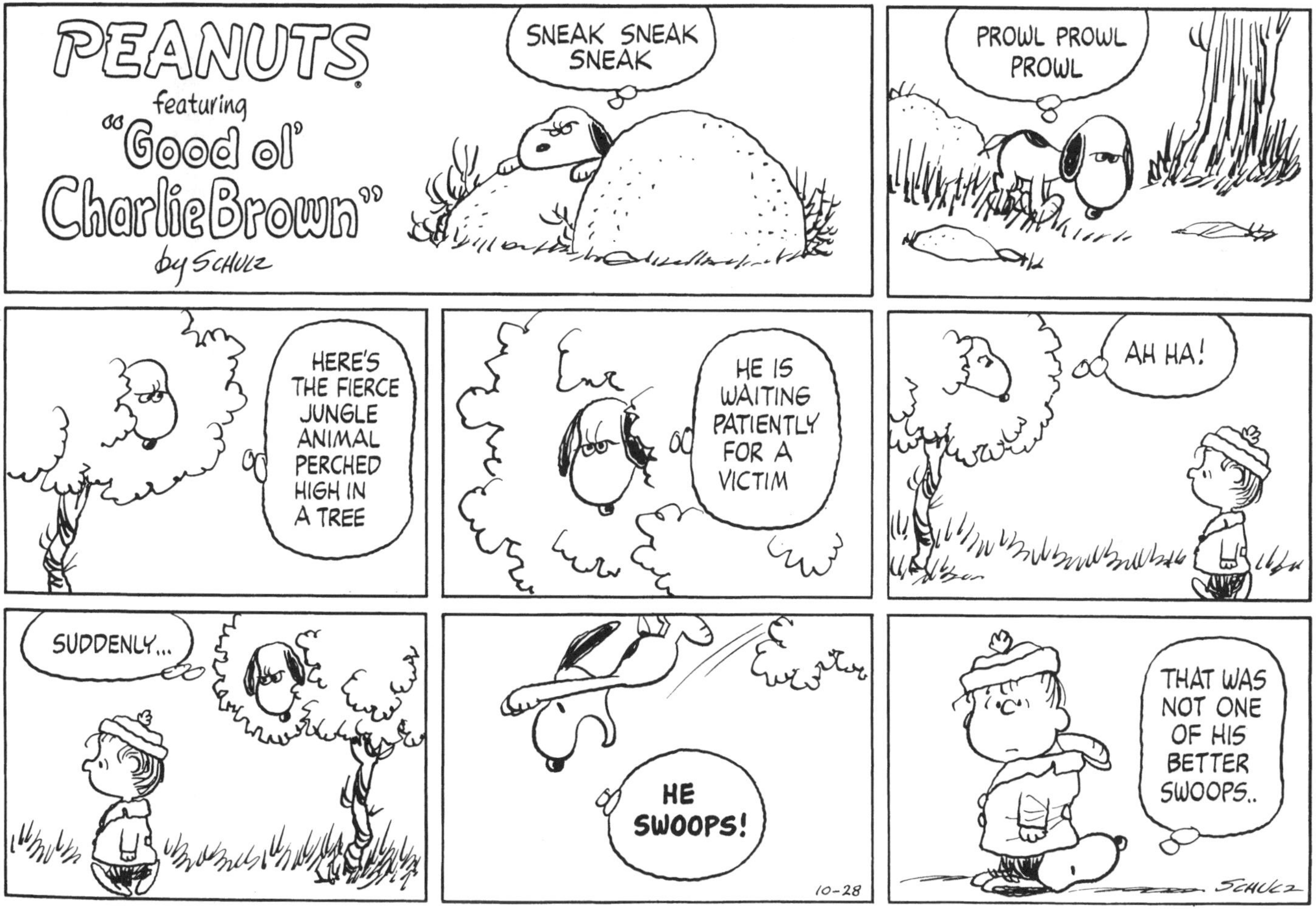
PEANUTS
featuring "Good ol' Charlie Brown"
by SCHULZ
SNEAK SNEAK SNEAK
PROWL PROWL PROWL
HERE'S THE FIERCE JUNGLE ANIMAL PERCHED HIGH IN A TREE
HE IS WAITING PATIENTLY FOR A VICTIM
AH HA!
SUDDENLY...
HE SWOOPS!
10-28
THAT WAS NOT ONE OF HIS BETTER SWOOPS..
SCHULZ

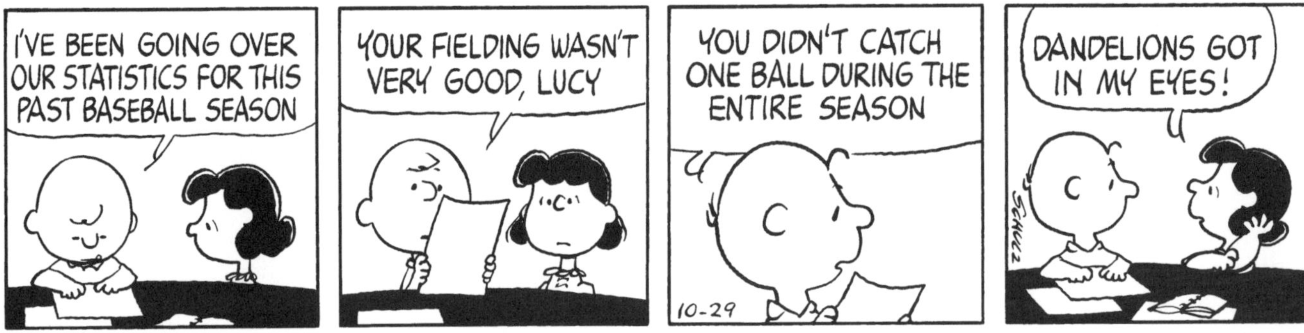
I'VE BEEN GOING OVER OUR STATISTICS FOR THIS PAST BASEBALL SEASON
YOUR FIELDING WASN'T VERY GOOD, LUCY
YOU DIDN'T CATCH ONE BALL DURING THE ENTIRE SEASON
10-29
DANDELIONS GOT IN MY EYES!

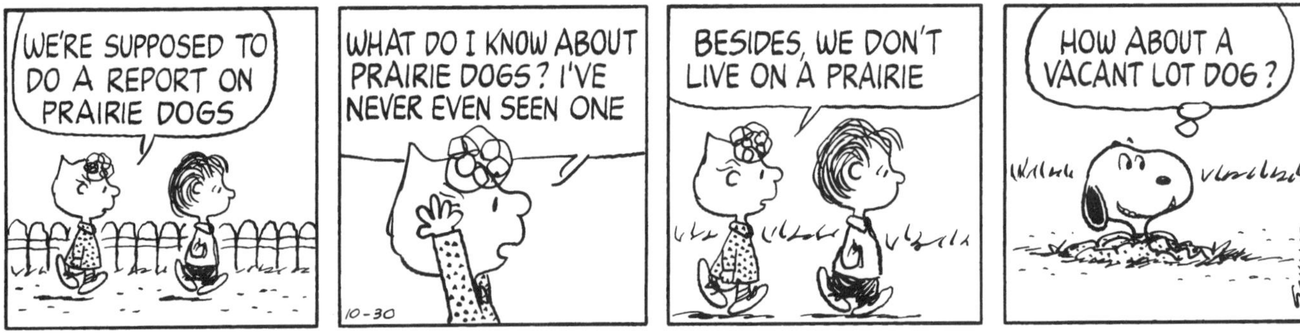
WE'RE SUPPOSED TO DO A REPORT ON PRAIRIE DOGS
WHAT DO I KNOW ABOUT PRAIRIE DOGS? I'VE NEVER EVEN SEEN ONE
10-30
BESIDES, WE DON'T LIVE ON A PRAIRIE
HOW ABOUT A VACANT LOT DOG?

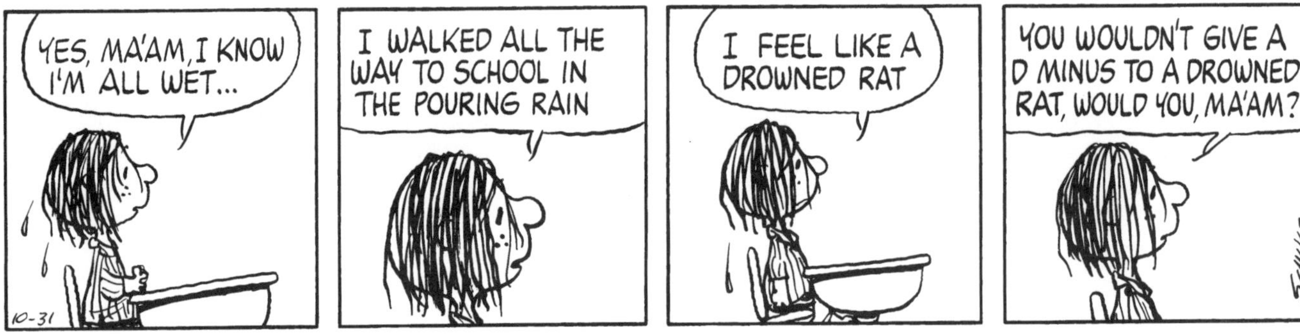
YES, MA'AM, I KNOW I'M ALL WET...
10-31
I WALKED ALL THE WAY TO SCHOOL IN THE POURING RAIN
I FEEL LIKE A DROWNED RAT
YOU WOULDN'T GIVE A D MINUS TO A DROWNED RAT, WOULD YOU, MA'AM?

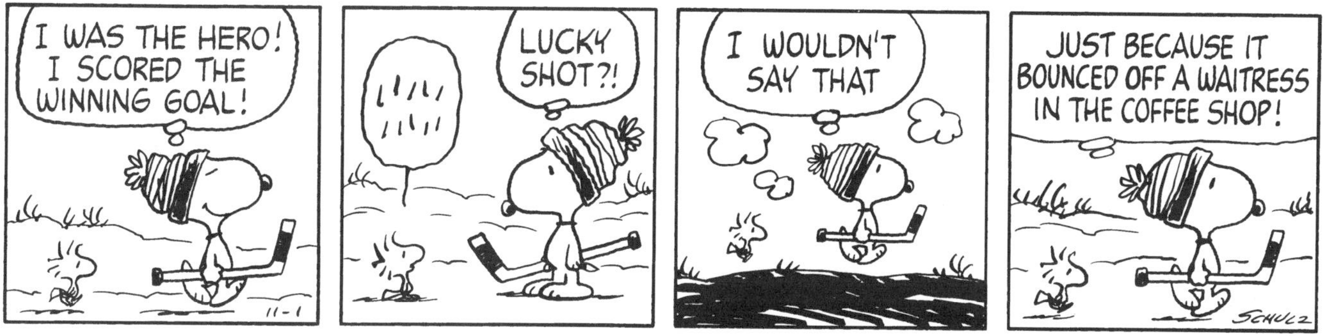
I WAS THE HERO! I SCORED THE WINNING GOAL!
LUCKY SHOT?!
I WOULDN'T SAY THAT
JUST BECAUSE IT BOUNCED OFF A WAITRESS IN THE COFFEE SHOP!

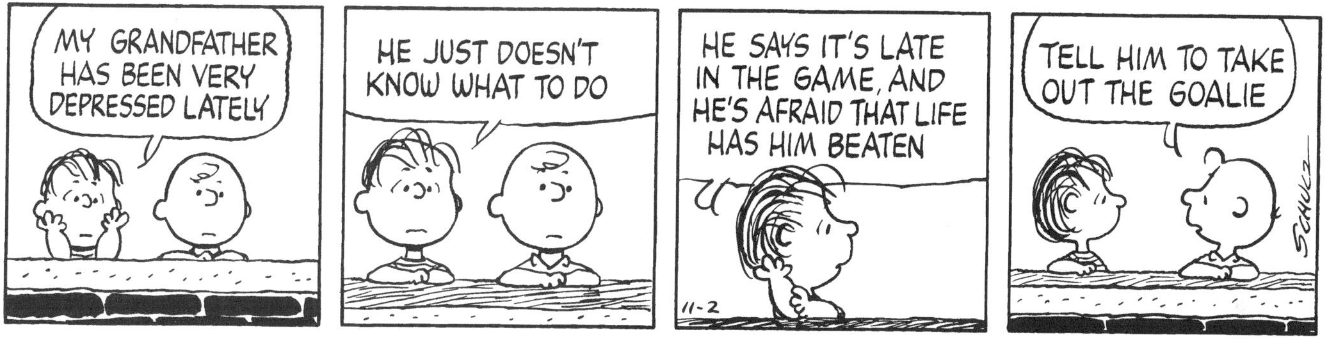
MY GRANDFATHER HAS BEEN VERY DEPRESSED LATELY
HE JUST DOESN'T KNOW WHAT TO DO
HE SAYS IT'S LATE IN THE GAME, AND HE'S AFRAID THAT LIFE HAS HIM BEATEN
TELL HIM TO TAKE OUT THE GOALIE

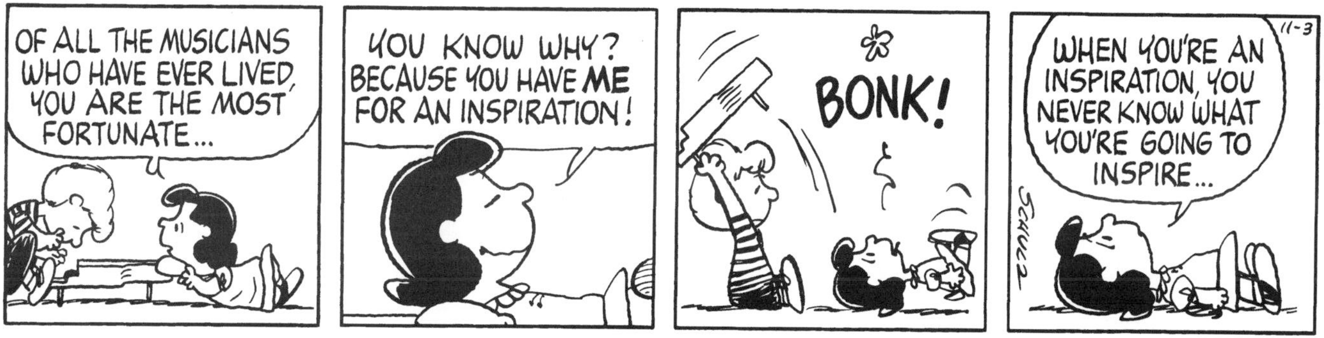
OF ALL THE MUSICIANS WHO HAVE EVER LIVED, YOU ARE THE MOST FORTUNATE...
YOU KNOW WHY? BECAUSE YOU HAVE ME FOR AN INSPIRATION!
BONK!
WHEN YOU'RE AN INSPIRATION, YOU NEVER KNOW WHAT YOU'RE GOING TO INSPIRE...

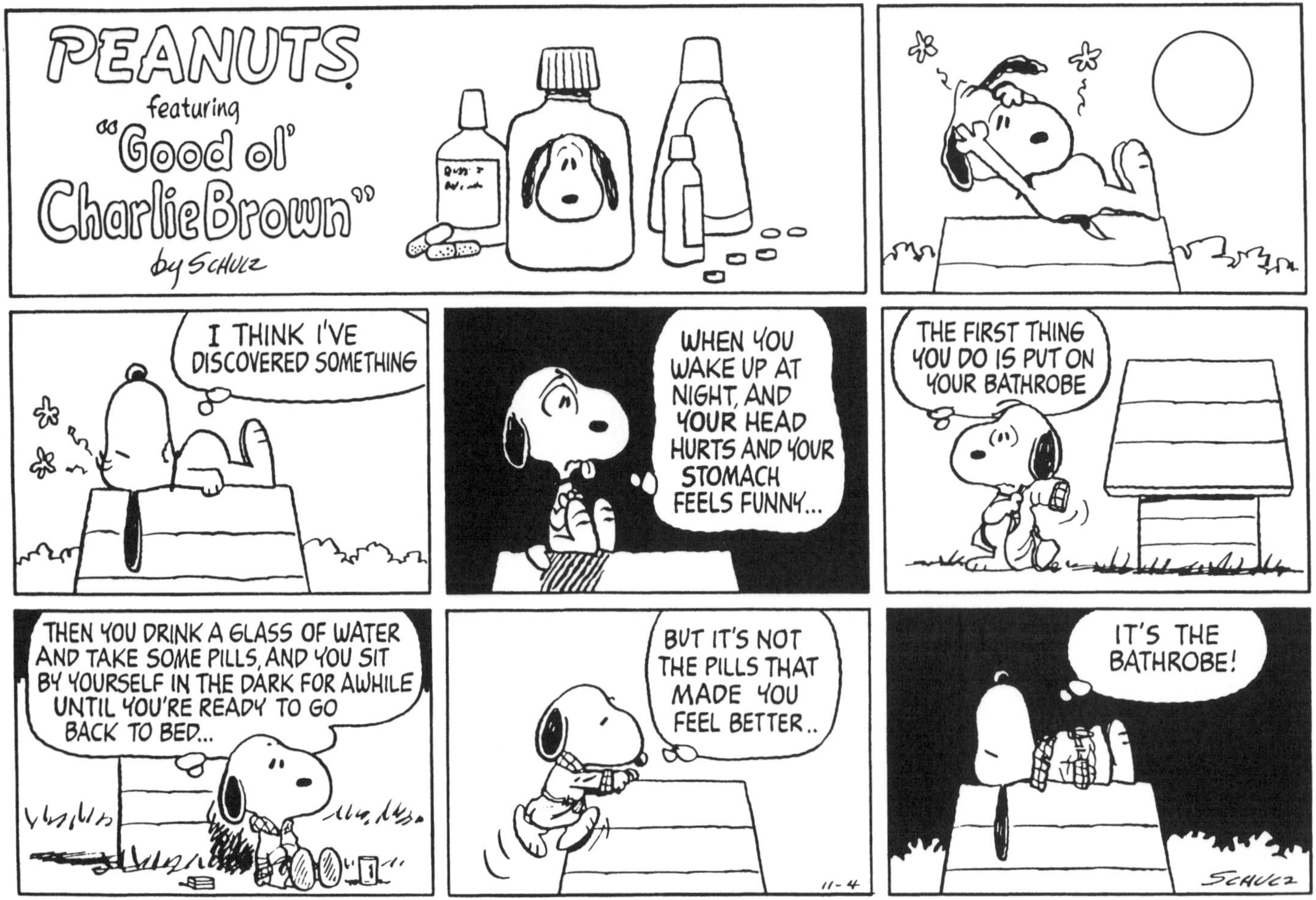
PEANUTS
featuring
"Good ol' Charlie Brown"
by SCHULZ
I THINK I'VE DISCOVERED SOMETHING
WHEN YOU WAKE UP AT NIGHT, AND YOUR HEAD HURTS AND YOUR STOMACH FEELS FUNNY...
THE FIRST THING YOU DO IS PUT ON YOUR BATHROBE
THEN YOU DRINK A GLASS OF WATER AND TAKE SOME PILLS, AND YOU SIT BY YOURSELF IN THE DARK FOR AWHILE UNTIL YOU'RE READY TO GO BACK TO BED...
BUT IT'S NOT THE PILLS THAT MADE YOU FEEL BETTER..
IT'S THE BATHROBE!
SCHULZ

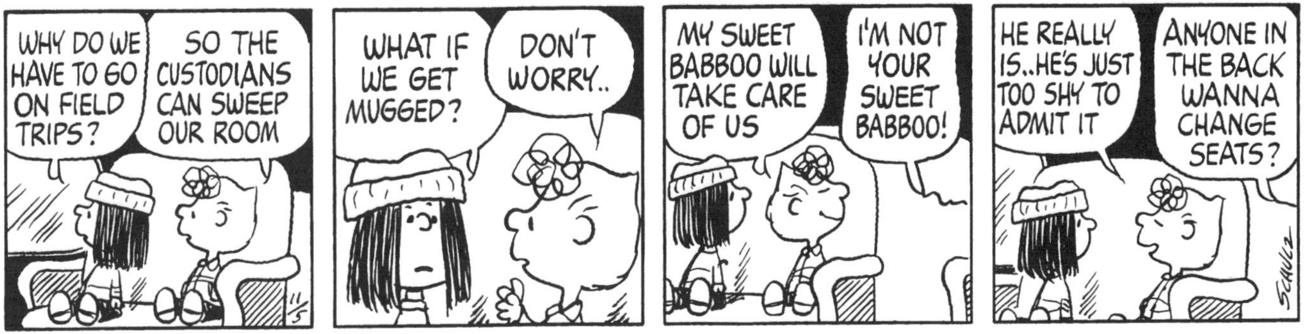
WHY DO WE HAVE TO GO ON FIELD TRIPS?
SO THE CUSTODIANS CAN SWEEP OUR ROOM
11/5
WHAT IF WE GET MUGGED?
DON'T WORRY..
MY SWEET BABBOO WILL TAKE CARE OF US
I'M NOT YOUR SWEET BABBOO!
HE REALLY IS..HE'S JUST TOO SHY TO ADMIT IT
ANYONE IN THE BACK WANNA CHANGE SEATS?
SCHULZ

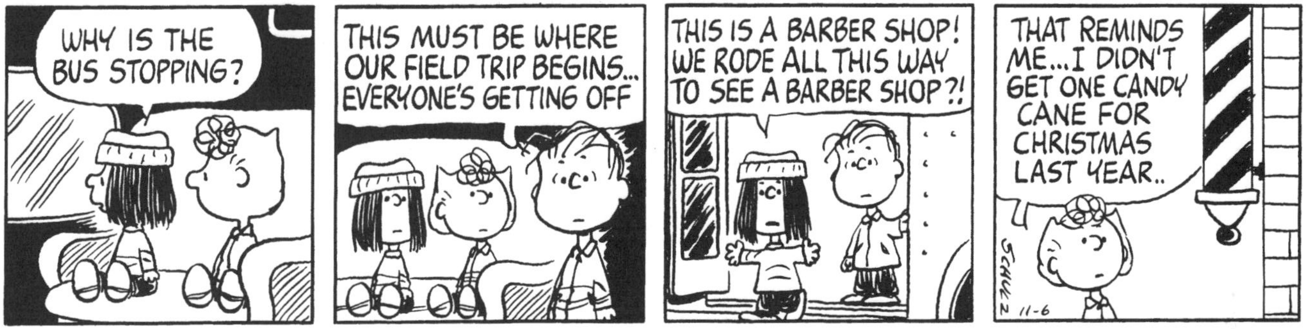
WHY IS THE BUS STOPPING?
THIS MUST BE WHERE OUR FIELD TRIP BEGINS... EVERYONE'S GETTING OFF
THIS IS A BARBER SHOP! WE RODE ALL THIS WAY TO SEE A BARBER SHOP?!
THAT REMINDS ME...I DIDN'T GET ONE CANDY CANE FOR CHRISTMAS LAST YEAR..
SCHULZ
11-6

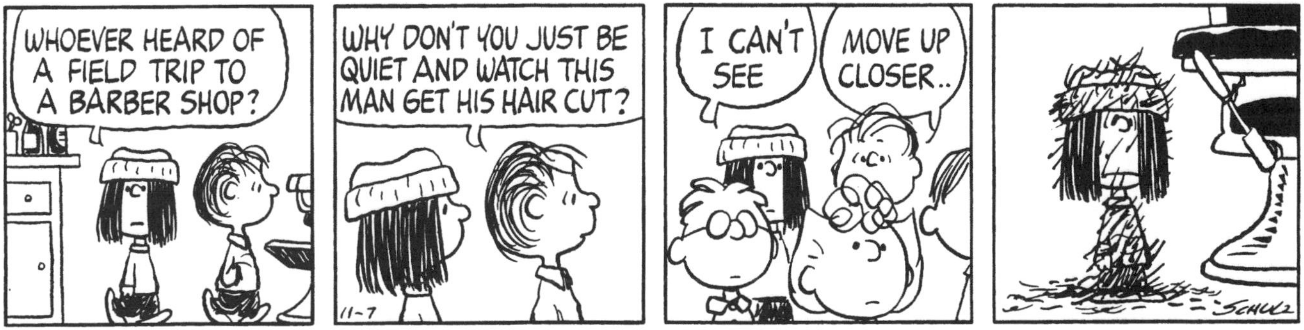
WHOEVER HEARD OF A FIELD TRIP TO A BARBER SHOP?
WHY DON'T YOU JUST BE QUIET AND WATCH THIS MAN GET HIS HAIR CUT?
11-7
I CAN'T SEE
MOVE UP CLOSER..
SCHULZ

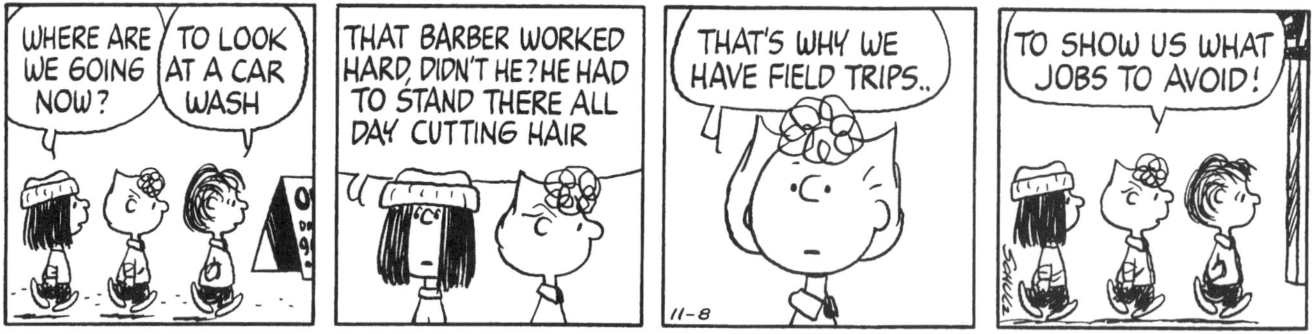
WHERE ARE WE GOING NOW?
TO LOOK AT A CAR WASH
THAT BARBER WORKED HARD, DIDN'T HE? HE HAD TO STAND THERE ALL DAY CUTTING HAIR
THAT'S WHY WE HAVE FIELD TRIPS..
11-8
TO SHOW US WHAT JOBS TO AVOID!
SCHULZ

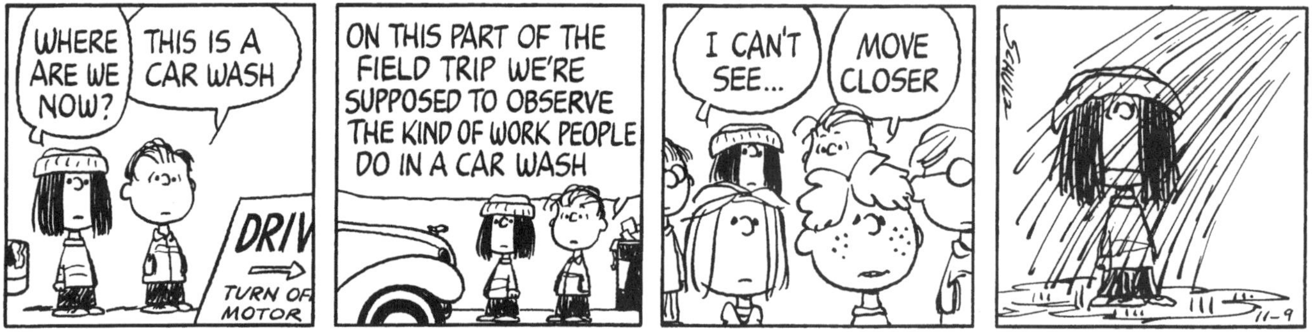
WHERE ARE WE NOW?
THIS IS A CAR WASH
DRIV
TURN OF
MOTOR
ON THIS PART OF THE FIELD TRIP WE'RE SUPPOSED TO OBSERVE THE KIND OF WORK PEOPLE DO IN A CAR WASH
I CAN'T SEE...
MOVE CLOSER
SCHULZ
11-9

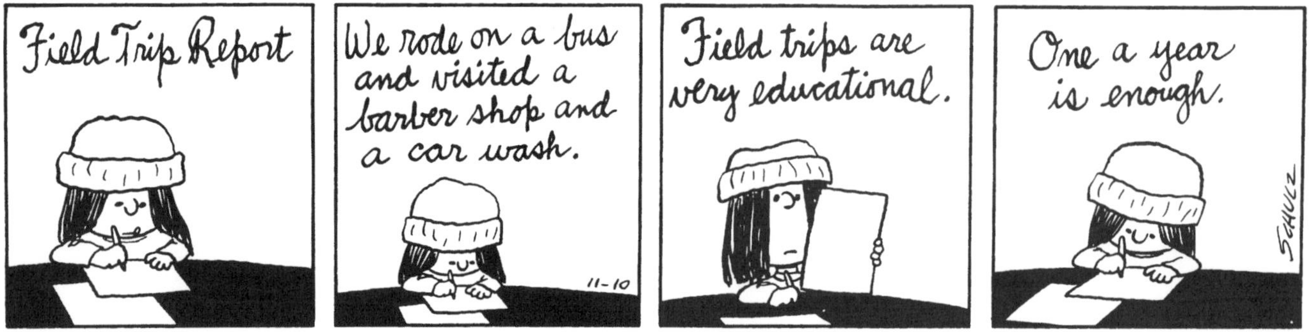
Field Trip Report
We rode on a bus and visited a barber shop and a car wash.
11-10
Field trips are very educational.
One a year is enough.
SCHULZ

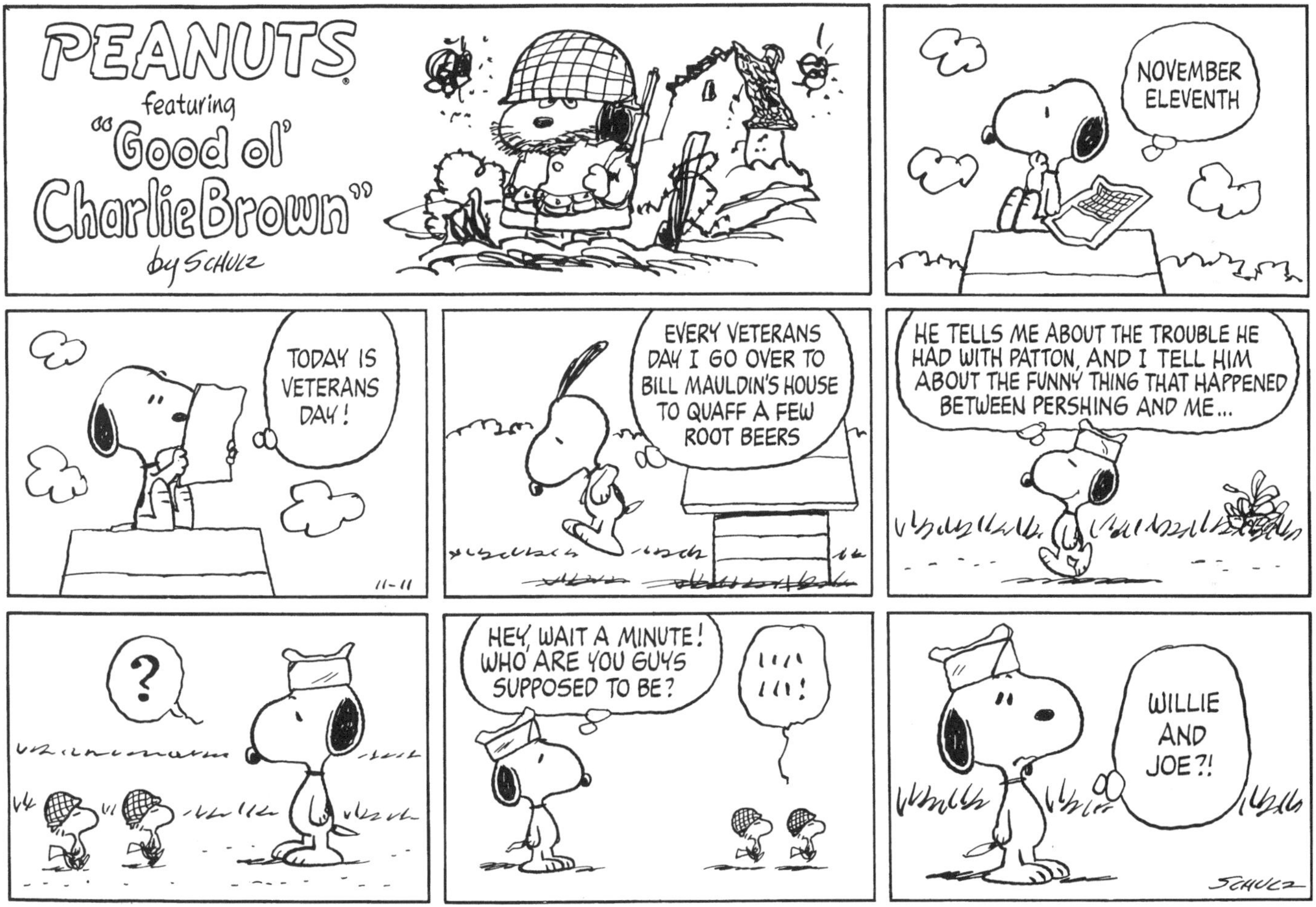
PEANUTS
featuring "Good ol' CharlieBrown"
by SCHULZ
NOVEMBER ELEVENTH
TODAY IS VETERANS DAY!
11-11
EVERY VETERANS DAY I GO OVER TO BILL MAULDIN'S HOUSE TO QUAFF A FEW ROOT BEERS
HE TELLS ME ABOUT THE TROUBLE HE HAD WITH PATTON, AND I TELL HIM ABOUT THE FUNNY THING THAT HAPPENED BETWEEN PERSHING AND ME...
?
HEY, WAIT A MINUTE! WHO ARE YOU GUYS SUPPOSED TO BE?
WILLIE AND JOE?!
SCHULZ

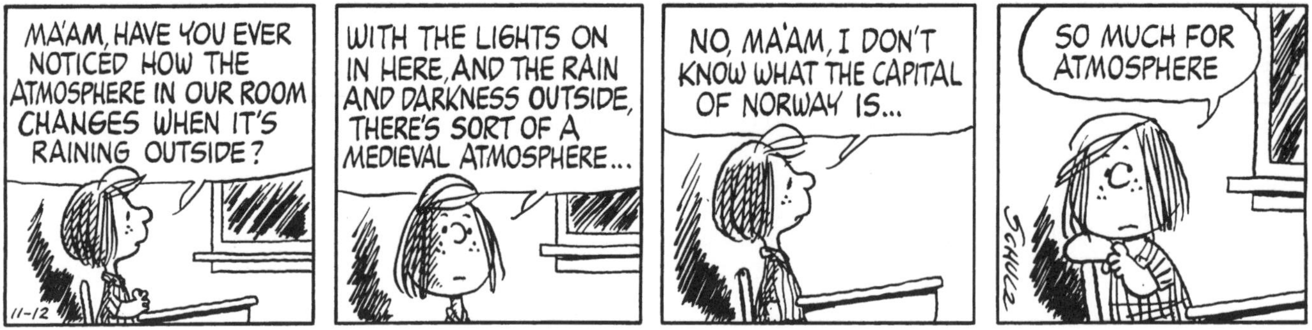
MA'AM, HAVE YOU EVER NOTICED HOW THE ATMOSPHERE IN OUR ROOM CHANGES WHEN IT'S RAINING OUTSIDE?
11-12
WITH THE LIGHTS ON IN HERE, AND THE RAIN AND DARKNESS OUTSIDE, THERE'S SORT OF A MEDIEVAL ATMOSPHERE...
NO, MA'AM, I DON'T KNOW WHAT THE CAPITAL OF NORWAY IS...
SO MUCH FOR ATMOSPHERE
SCHULZ

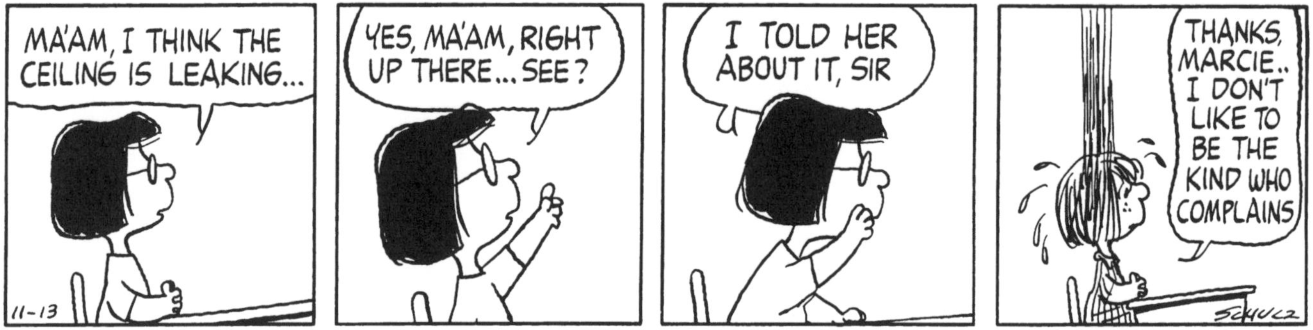
MA'AM, I THINK THE CEILING IS LEAKING...
11-13
YES, MA'AM, RIGHT UP THERE... SEE?
I TOLD HER ABOUT IT, SIR
THANKS, MARCIE.. I DON'T LIKE TO BE THE KIND WHO COMPLAINS
SCHULZ

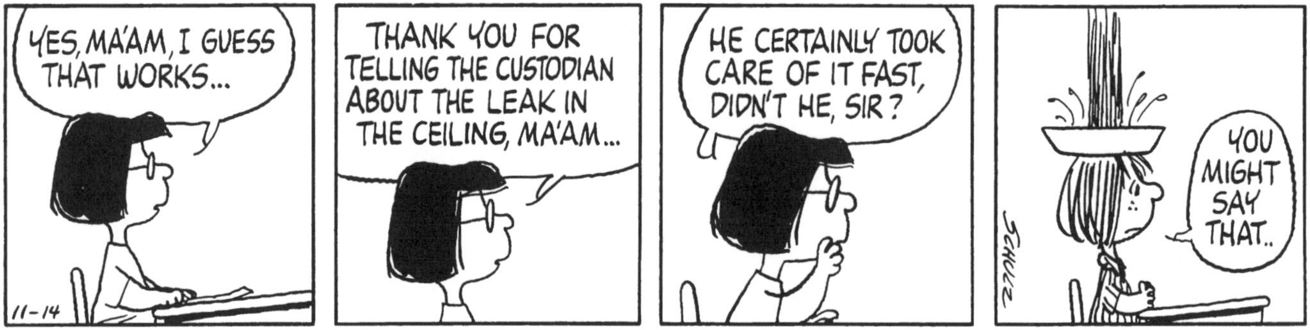
YES, MA'AM, I GUESS THAT WORKS...
11-14
THANK YOU FOR TELLING THE CUSTODIAN ABOUT THE LEAK IN THE CEILING, MA'AM...
HE CERTAINLY TOOK CARE OF IT FAST, DIDN'T HE, SIR?
YOU MIGHT SAY THAT..
SCHULZ

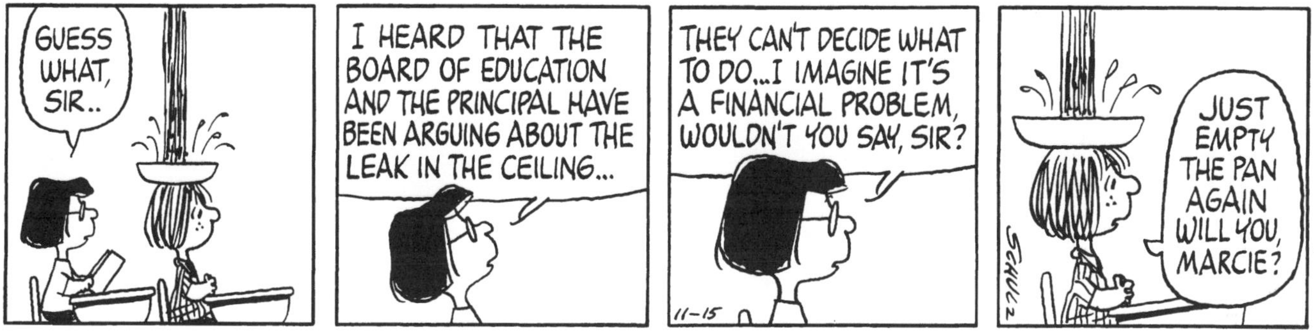
GUESS WHAT, SIR..
I HEARD THAT THE BOARD OF EDUCATION AND THE PRINCIPAL HAVE BEEN ARGUING ABOUT THE LEAK IN THE CEILING...
THEY CAN'T DECIDE WHAT TO DO...I IMAGINE IT'S A FINANCIAL PROBLEM, WOULDN'T YOU SAY, SIR?
JUST EMPTY THE PAN AGAIN WILL YOU, MARCIE?
11-15
SCHULZ

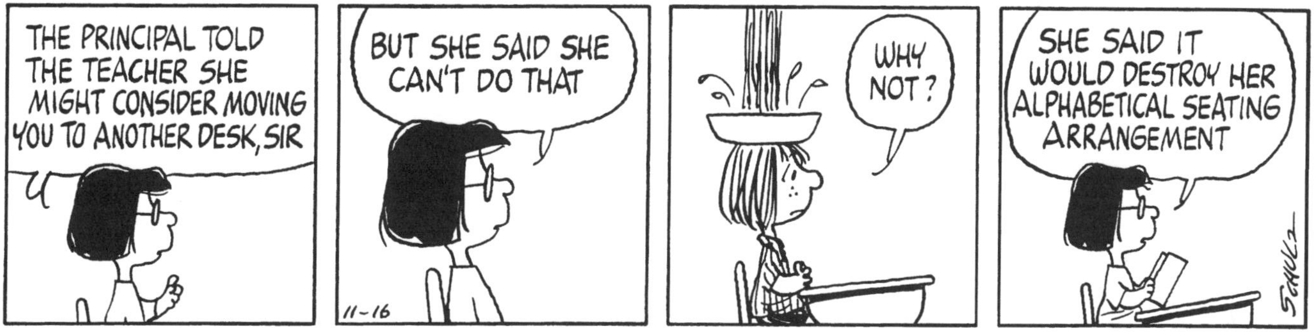
THE PRINCIPAL TOLD THE TEACHER SHE MIGHT CONSIDER MOVING YOU TO ANOTHER DESK, SIR
BUT SHE SAID SHE CAN'T DO THAT
WHY NOT?
SHE SAID IT WOULD DESTROY HER ALPHABETICAL SEATING ARRANGEMENT
11-16
SCHULZ

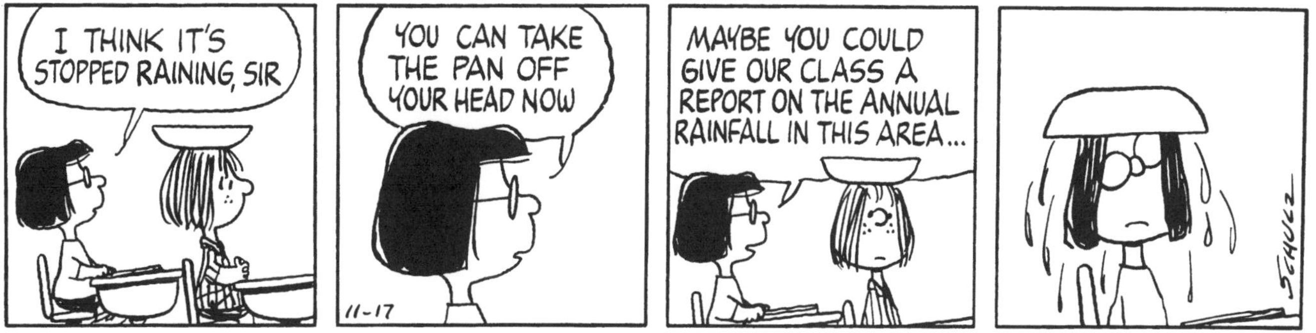
I THINK IT'S STOPPED RAINING, SIR
YOU CAN TAKE THE PAN OFF YOUR HEAD NOW
MAYBE YOU COULD GIVE OUR CLASS A REPORT ON THE ANNUAL RAINFALL IN THIS AREA...
11-17
SCHULZ

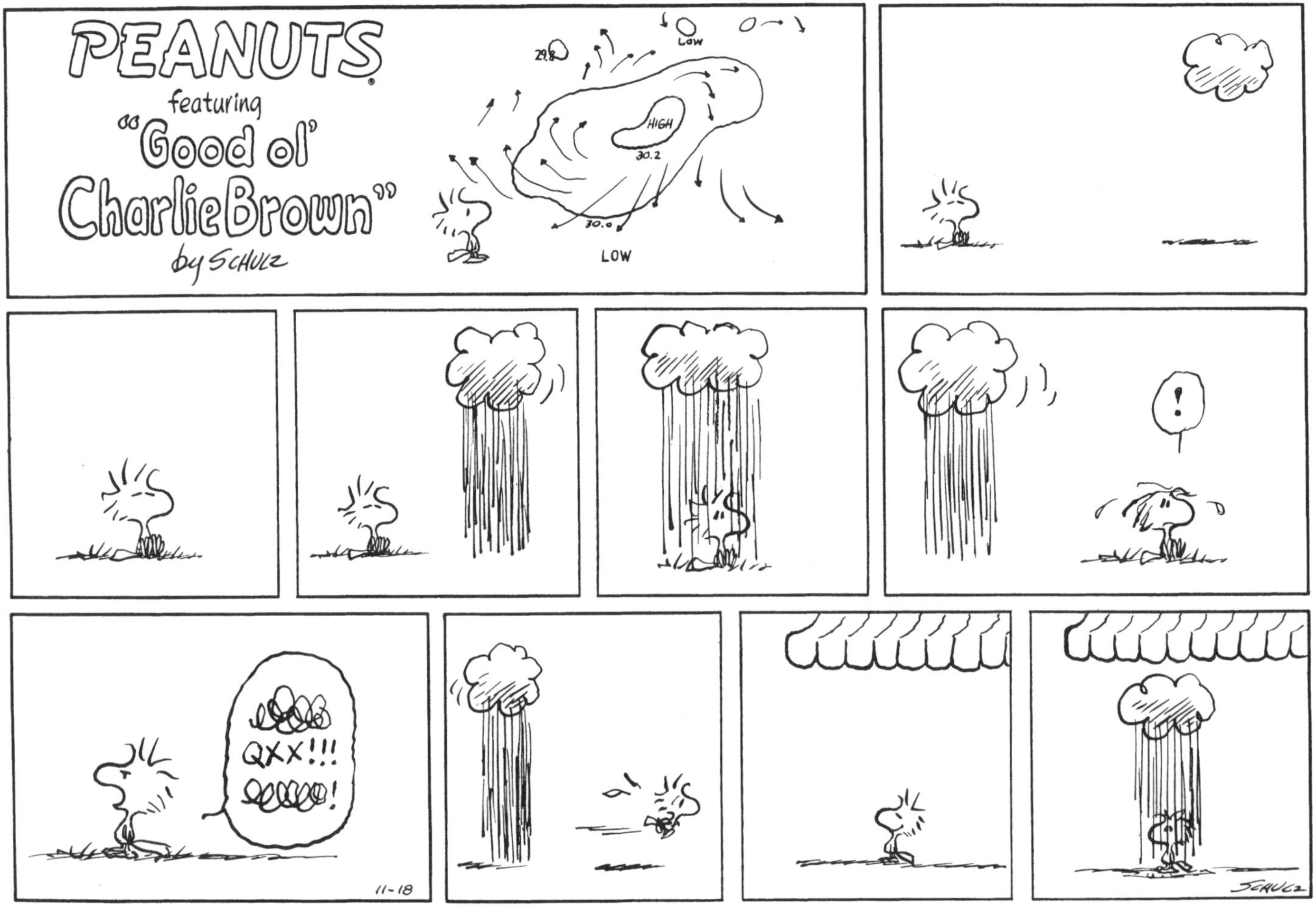
PEANUTS
featuring
"Good ol' Charlie Brown"
by SCHULZ
29.8
LOW
HIGH
30.2
30.0
LOW
!
QXX!!!
11-18
SCHULZ

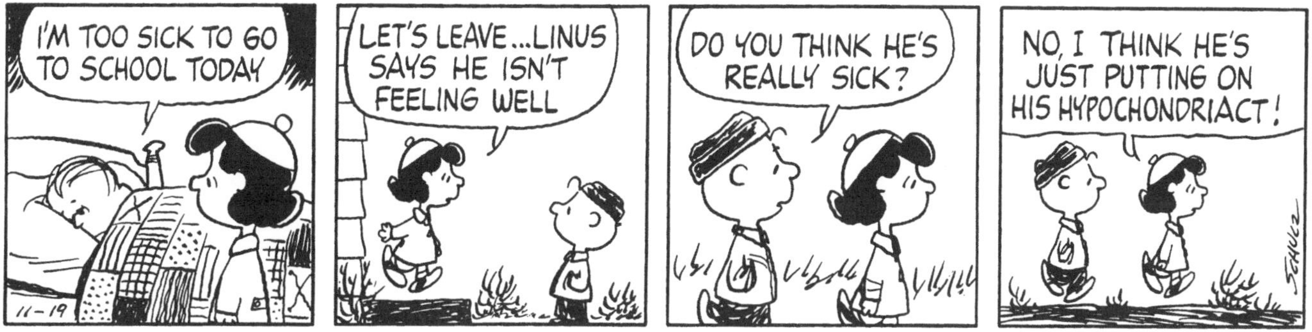
I'M TOO SICK TO GO TO SCHOOL TODAY
LET'S LEAVE...LINUS SAYS HE ISN'T FEELING WELL
DO YOU THINK HE'S REALLY SICK?
NO, I THINK HE'S JUST PUTTING ON HIS HYPOCHONDRIACT!
11-19
SCHULZ

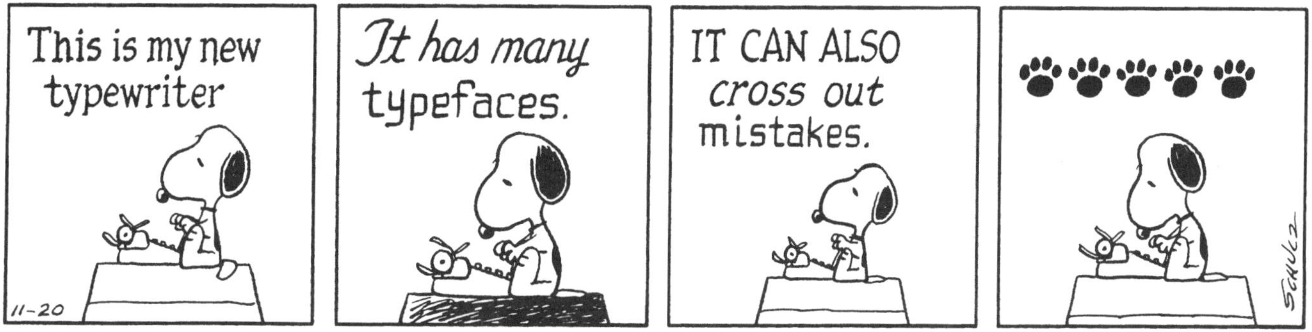
This is my new typewriter
It has many typefaces.
IT CAN ALSO cross out mistakes.
11-20
SCHULZ

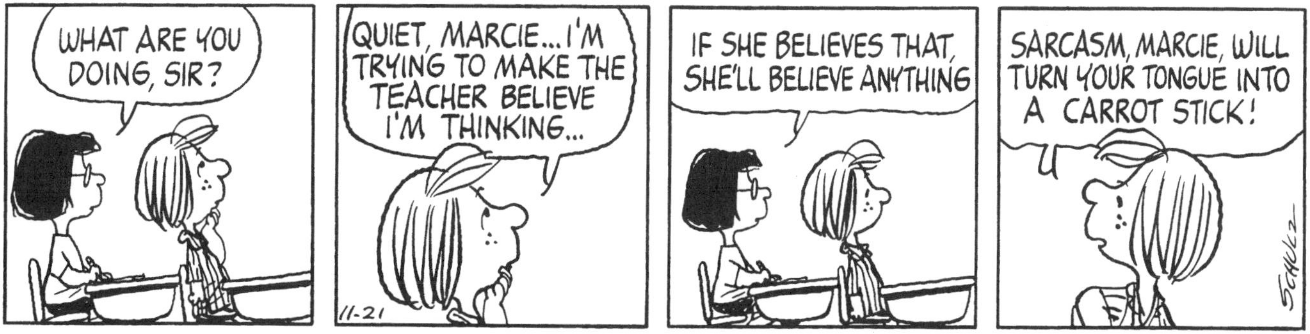
WHAT ARE YOU DOING, SIR?
QUIET, MARCIE...I'M TRYING TO MAKE THE TEACHER BELIEVE I'M THINKING...
IF SHE BELIEVES THAT, SHE'LL BELIEVE ANYTHING
SARCASM, MARCIE, WILL TURN YOUR TONGUE INTO A CARROT STICK!
11-21
SCHULZ

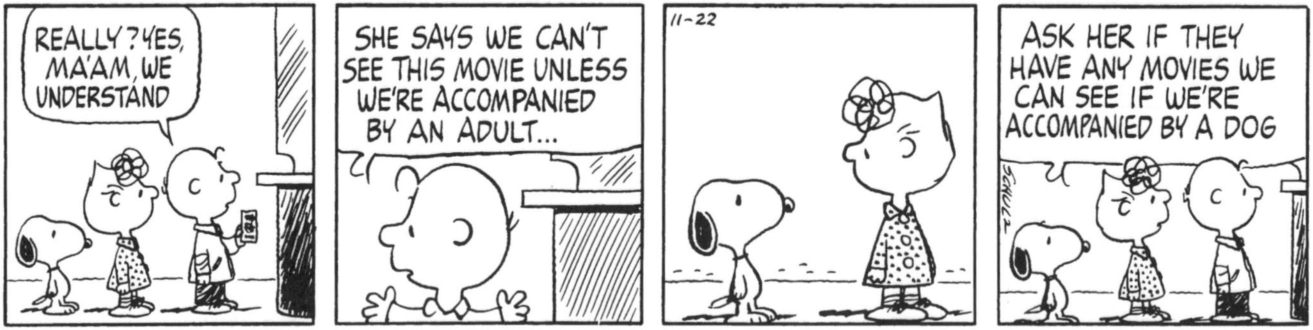
REALLY? YES, MA'AM, WE UNDERSTAND
SHE SAYS WE CAN'T SEE THIS MOVIE UNLESS WE'RE ACCOMPANIED BY AN ADULT...
11-22
ASK HER IF THEY HAVE ANY MOVIES WE CAN SEE IF WE'RE ACCOMPANIED BY A DOG
SCHULZ

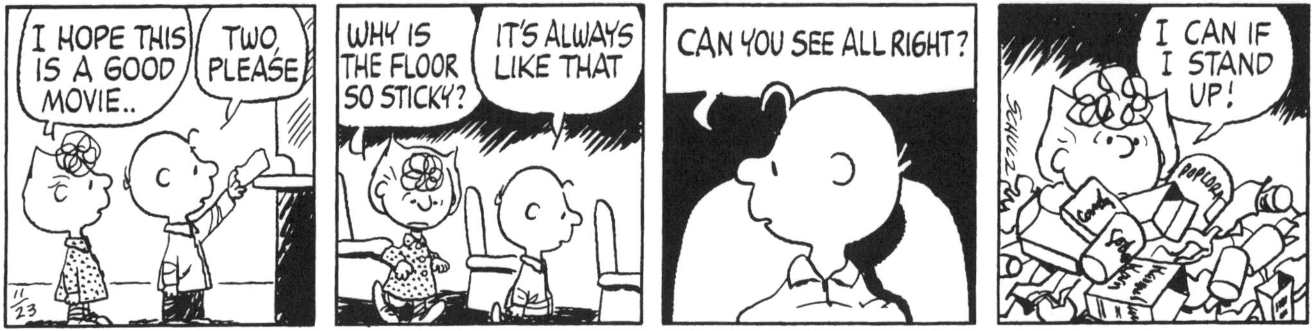
I HOPE THIS IS A GOOD MOVIE..
TWO, PLEASE
11/23
WHY IS THE FLOOR SO STICKY?
IT'S ALWAYS LIKE THAT
CAN YOU SEE ALL RIGHT?
SCHULZ
I CAN IF I STAND UP!

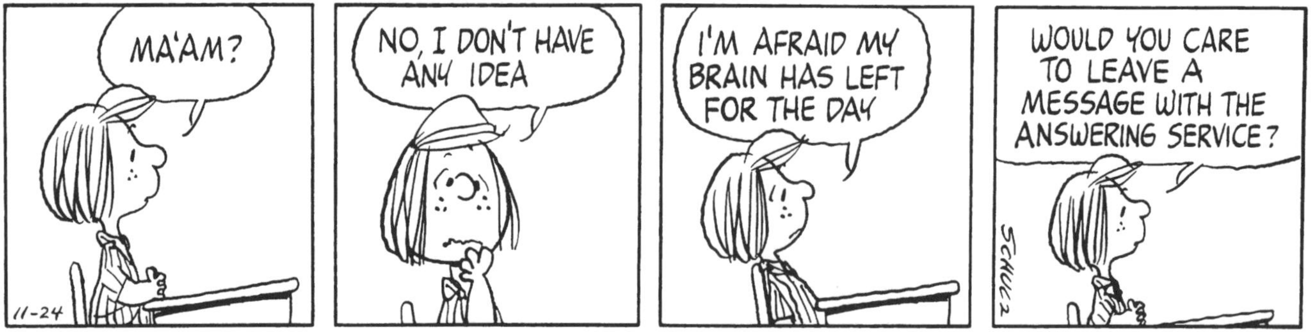
MA'AM?
11-24
NO, I DON'T HAVE ANY IDEA
I'M AFRAID MY BRAIN HAS LEFT FOR THE DAY
WOULD YOU CARE TO LEAVE A MESSAGE WITH THE ANSWERING SERVICE?
SCHULZ

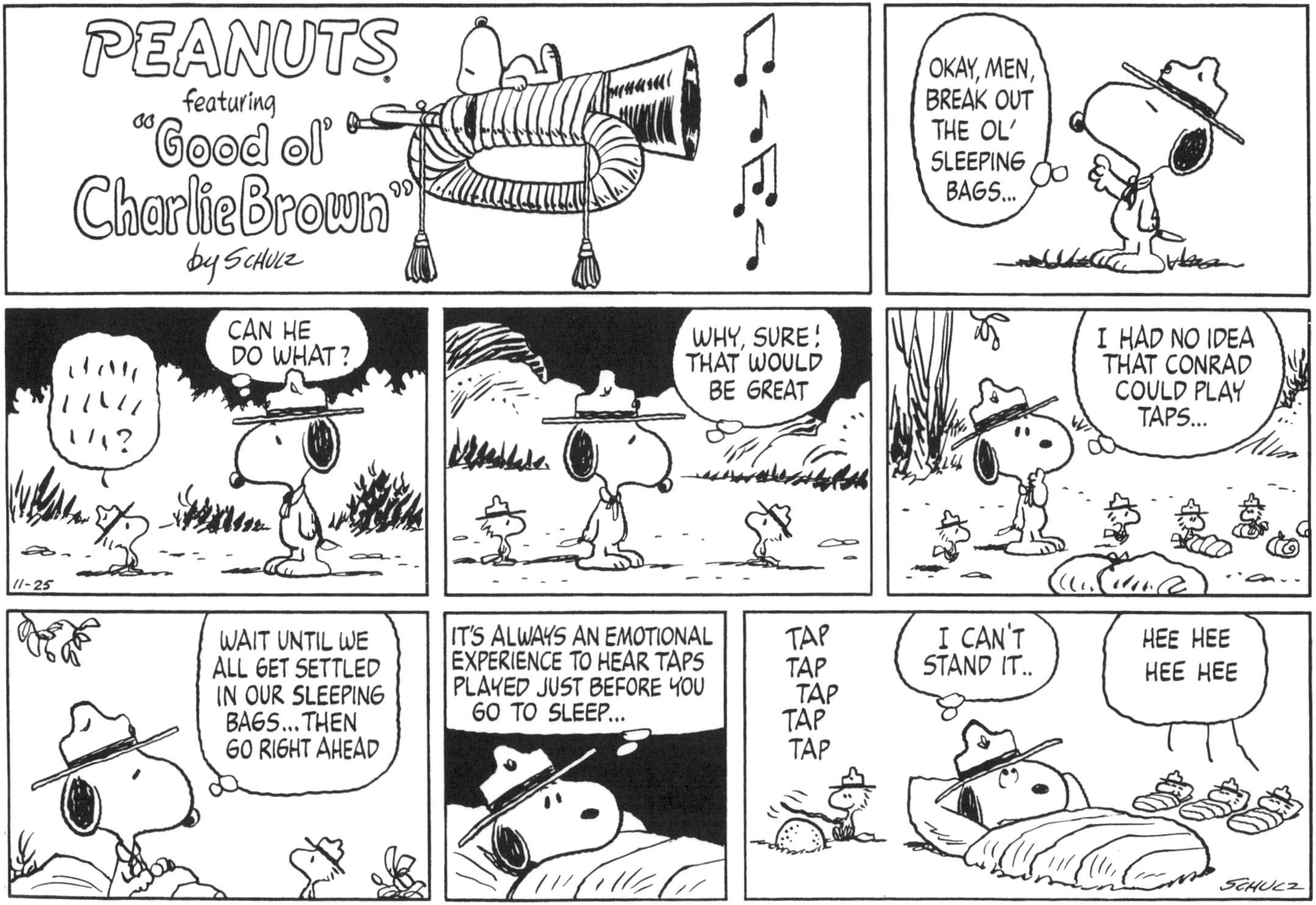
PEANUTS
featuring
"Good ol' Charlie Brown"
by SCHULZ
OKAY, MEN, BREAK OUT THE OL' SLEEPING BAGS...
11-25
CAN HE DO WHAT?
WHY, SURE! THAT WOULD BE GREAT
I HAD NO IDEA THAT CONRAD COULD PLAY TAPS...
WAIT UNTIL WE ALL GET SETTLED IN OUR SLEEPING BAGS...THEN GO RIGHT AHEAD
IT'S ALWAYS AN EMOTIONAL EXPERIENCE TO HEAR TAPS PLAYED JUST BEFORE YOU GO TO SLEEP...
TAP TAP TAP TAP TAP
I CAN'T STAND IT..
HEE HEE HEE HEE
SCHULZ

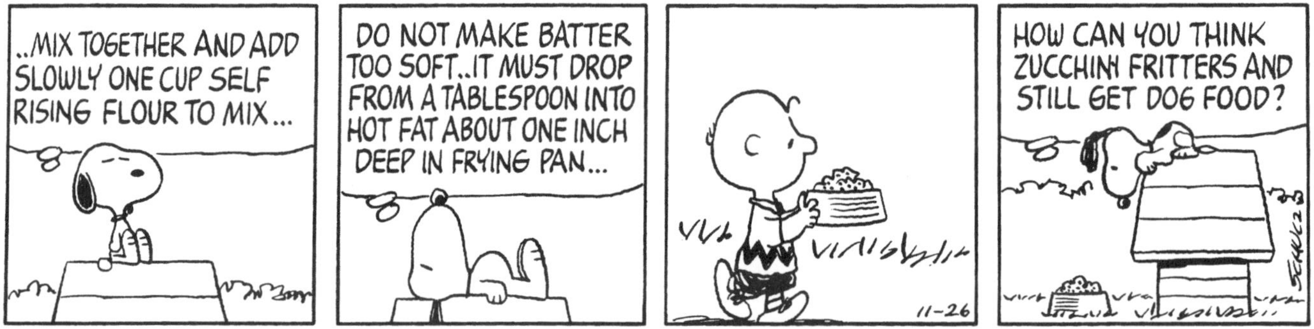
..MIX TOGETHER AND ADD SLOWLY ONE CUP SELF RISING FLOUR TO MIX...
DO NOT MAKE BATTER TOO SOFT..IT MUST DROP FROM A TABLESPOON INTO HOT FAT ABOUT ONE INCH DEEP IN FRYING PAN...
11-26
HOW CAN YOU THINK ZUCCHINI FRITTERS AND STILL GET DOG FOOD?
SCHULZ

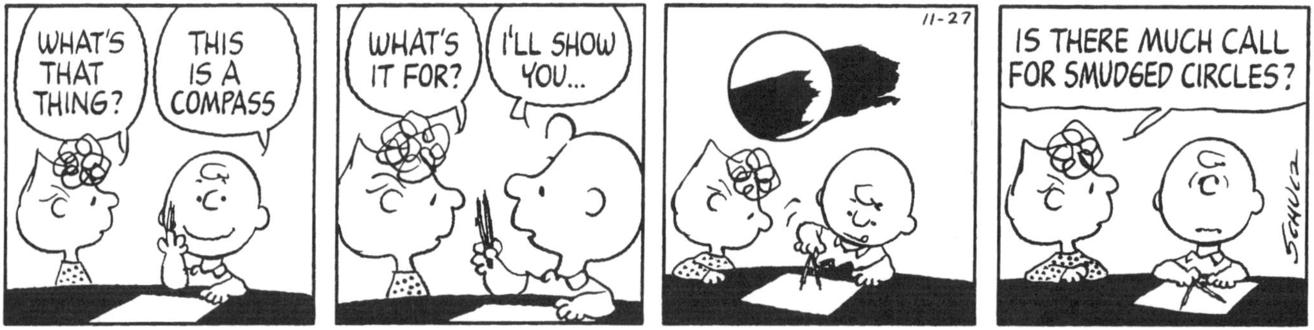
WHAT'S THAT THING?
THIS IS A COMPASS
WHAT'S IT FOR?
I'LL SHOW YOU...
11-27
IS THERE MUCH CALL FOR SMUDGED CIRCLES?
SCHULZ

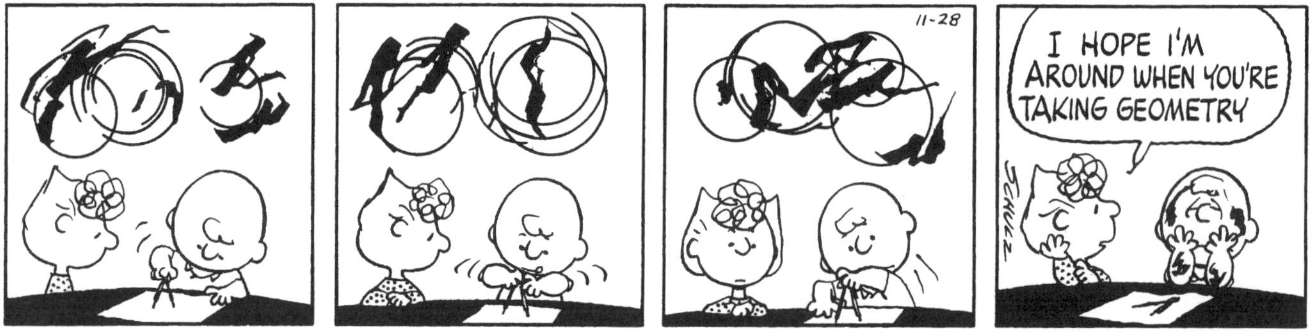
11-28
I HOPE I'M AROUND WHEN YOU'RE TAKING GEOMETRY
SCHULZ

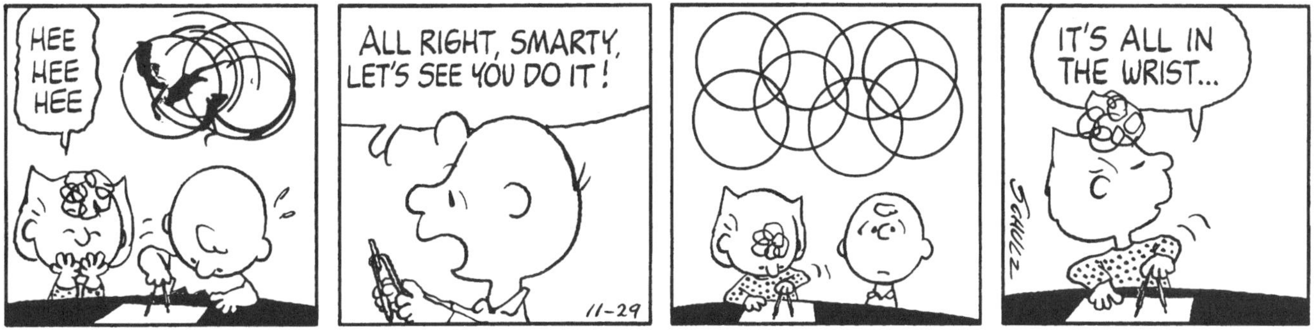
HEE HEE HEE
ALL RIGHT, SMARTY, LET'S SEE YOU DO IT!
11-29
IT'S ALL IN THE WRIST...
SCHULZ

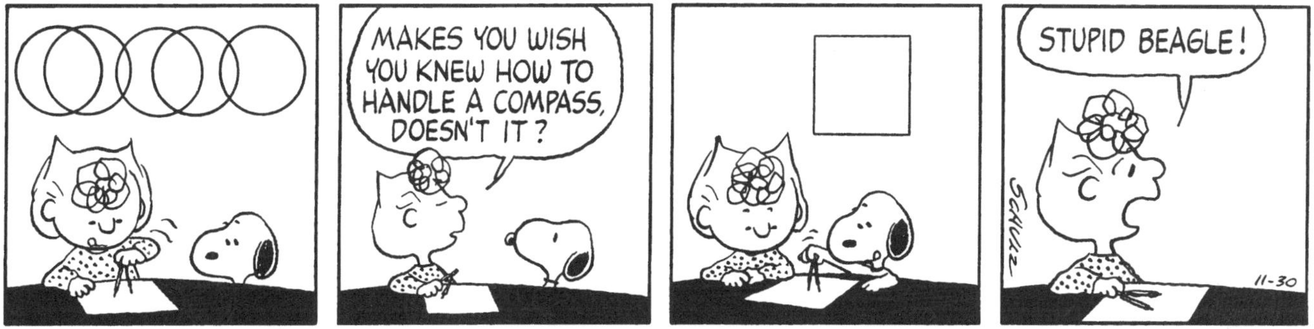
MAKES YOU WISH YOU KNEW HOW TO HANDLE A COMPASS, DOESN'T IT?
STUPID BEAGLE!
SCHULZ
11-30

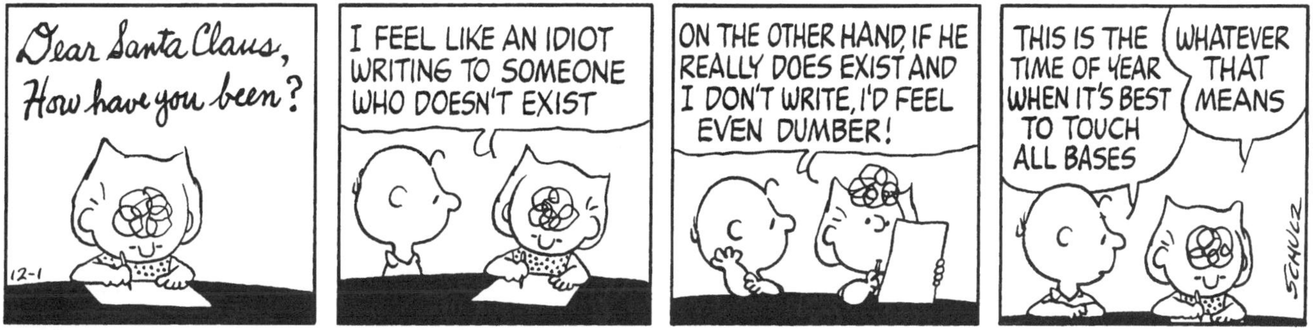
Dear Santa Claus, How have you been?
12-1
I FEEL LIKE AN IDIOT WRITING TO SOMEONE WHO DOESN'T EXIST
ON THE OTHER HAND, IF HE REALLY DOES EXIST AND I DON'T WRITE, I'D FEEL EVEN DUMBER!
THIS IS THE TIME OF YEAR WHEN IT'S BEST TO TOUCH ALL BASES
WHATEVER THAT MEANS
SCHULZ

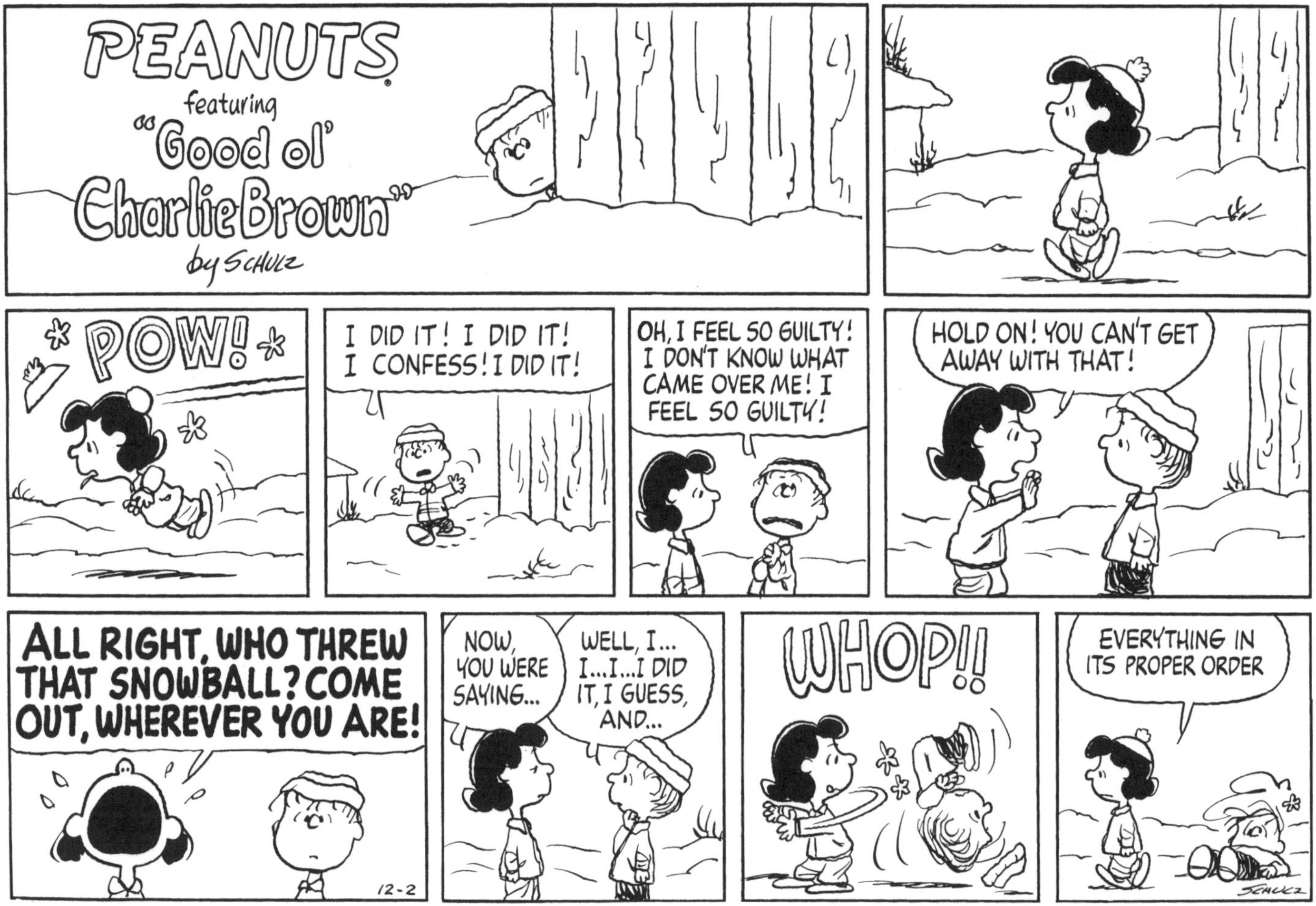
PEANUTS
featuring
"Good ol' Charlie Brown"
by SCHULZ
POW!
I DID IT! I DID IT! I CONFESS! I DID IT!
OH, I FEEL SO GUILTY! I DON'T KNOW WHAT CAME OVER ME! I FEEL SO GUILTY!
HOLD ON! YOU CAN'T GET AWAY WITH THAT!
ALL RIGHT, WHO THREW THAT SNOWBALL? COME OUT, WHEREVER YOU ARE!
12-2
NOW, YOU WERE SAYING...
WELL, I... I...I...I DID IT, I GUESS, AND...
WHOP!!
EVERYTHING IN ITS PROPER ORDER
SCHULZ

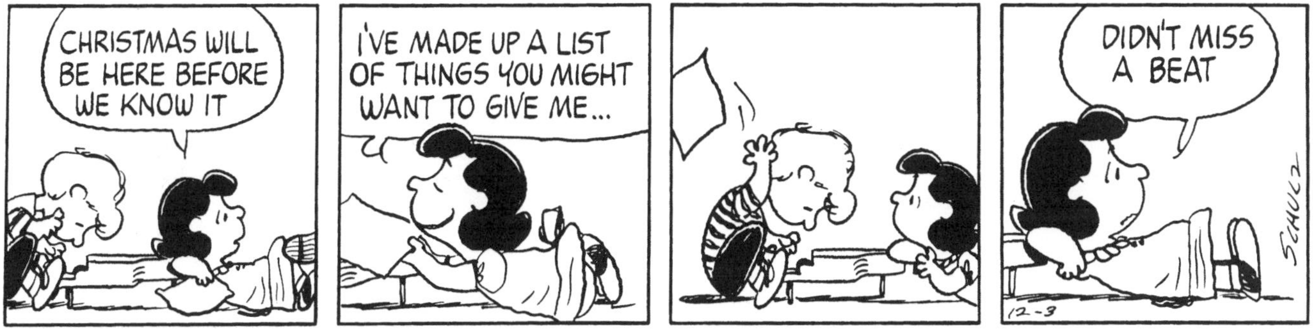
CHRISTMAS WILL BE HERE BEFORE WE KNOW IT
I'VE MADE UP A LIST OF THINGS YOU MIGHT WANT TO GIVE ME...
DIDN'T MISS A BEAT
SCHULZ
12-3

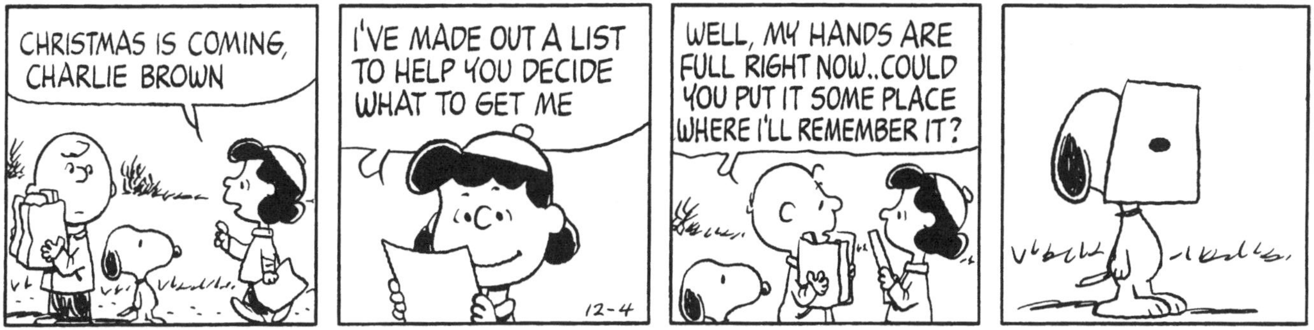
CHRISTMAS IS COMING, CHARLIE BROWN
I'VE MADE OUT A LIST TO HELP YOU DECIDE WHAT TO GET ME
12-4
WELL, MY HANDS ARE FULL RIGHT NOW..COULD YOU PUT IT SOME PLACE WHERE I'LL REMEMBER IT?

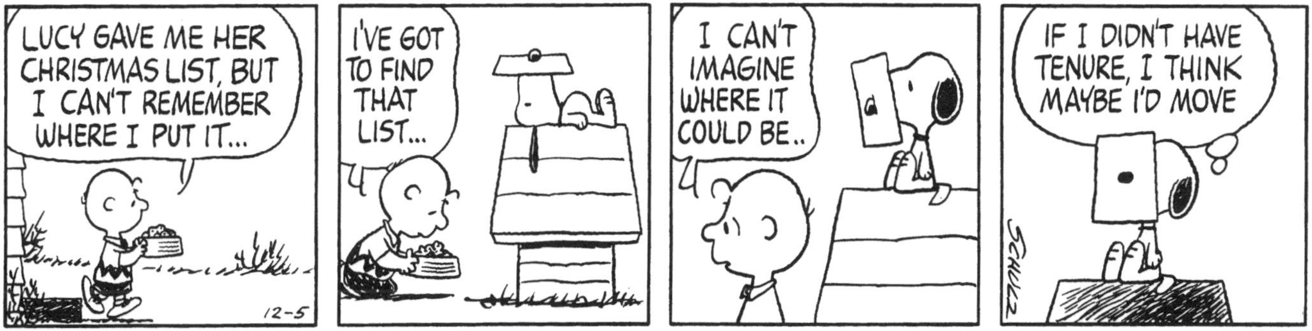
LUCY GAVE ME HER CHRISTMAS LIST, BUT I CAN'T REMEMBER WHERE I PUT IT...
12-5
I'VE GOT TO FIND THAT LIST...
I CAN'T IMAGINE WHERE IT COULD BE..
SCHULZ
IF I DIDN'T HAVE TENURE, I THINK MAYBE I'D MOVE

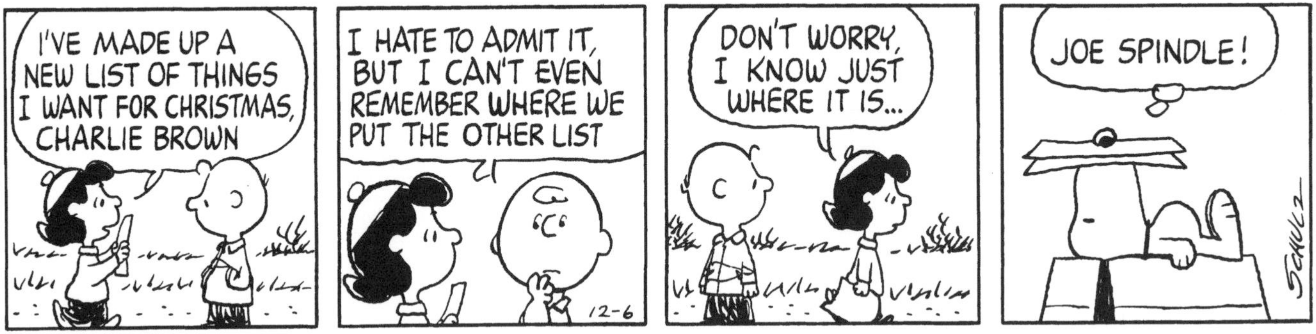
I'VE MADE UP A NEW LIST OF THINGS I WANT FOR CHRISTMAS, CHARLIE BROWN
I HATE TO ADMIT IT, BUT I CAN'T EVEN REMEMBER WHERE WE PUT THE OTHER LIST
DON'T WORRY, I KNOW JUST WHERE IT IS...
JOE SPINDLE!

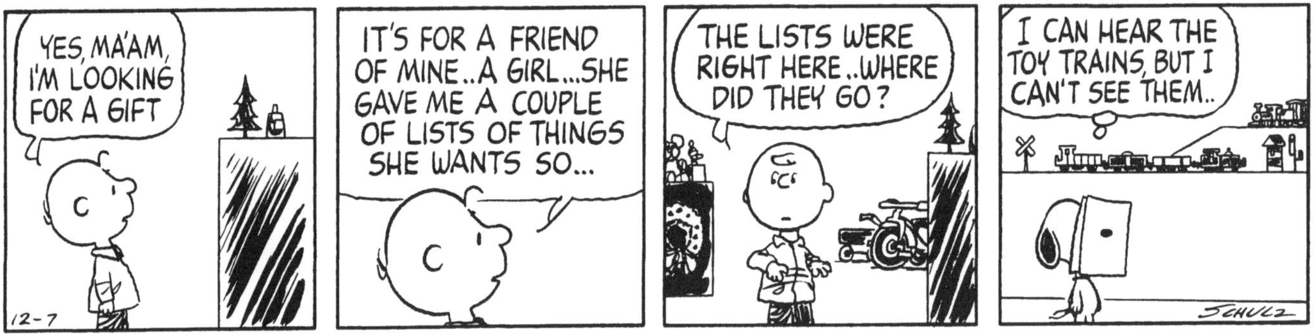
YES, MA'AM, I'M LOOKING FOR A GIFT
IT'S FOR A FRIEND OF MINE..A GIRL...SHE GAVE ME A COUPLE OF LISTS OF THINGS SHE WANTS SO...
THE LISTS WERE RIGHT HERE..WHERE DID THEY GO?
I CAN HEAR THE TOY TRAINS, BUT I CAN'T SEE THEM..

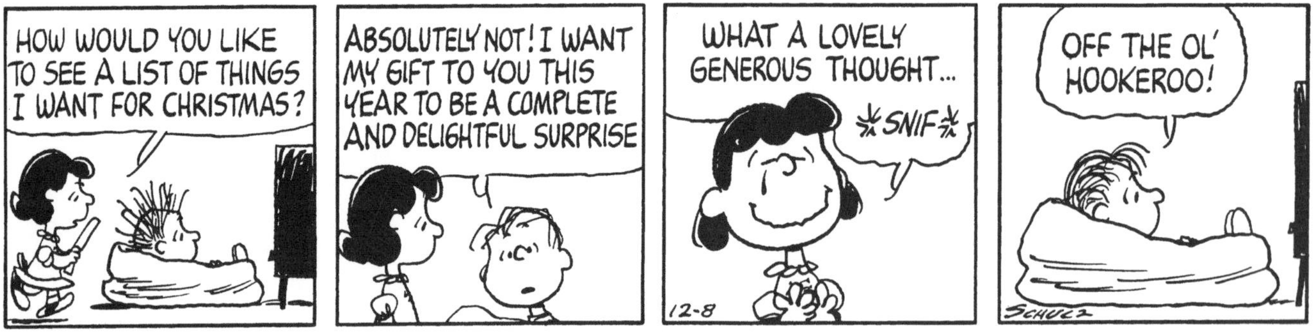
HOW WOULD YOU LIKE TO SEE A LIST OF THINGS I WANT FOR CHRISTMAS?
ABSOLUTELY NOT! I WANT MY GIFT TO YOU THIS YEAR TO BE A COMPLETE AND DELIGHTFUL SURPRISE
WHAT A LOVELY GENEROUS THOUGHT...
SNIF
OFF THE OL' HOOKEROO!

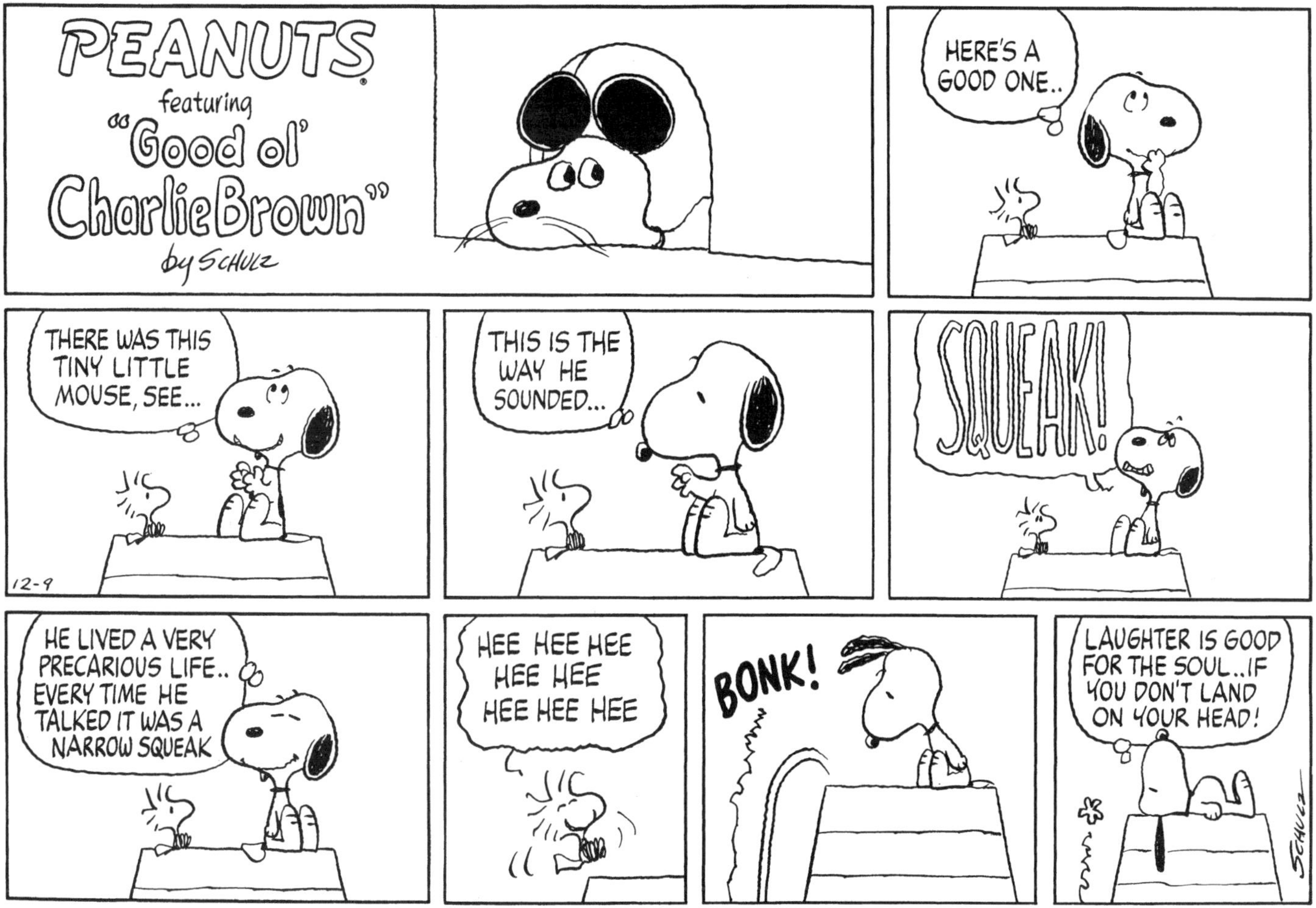
PEANUTS
featuring
"Good ol' CharlieBrown"
by SCHULZ
HERE'S A GOOD ONE..
THERE WAS THIS TINY LITTLE MOUSE, SEE...
12-9
THIS IS THE WAY HE SOUNDED...
SQUEAK!
HE LIVED A VERY PRECARIOUS LIFE.. EVERY TIME HE TALKED IT WAS A NARROW SQUEAK
HEE HEE HEE HEE HEE HEE HEE HEE
BONK!
LAUGHTER IS GOOD FOR THE SOUL...IF YOU DON'T LAND ON YOUR HEAD!
SCHULZ

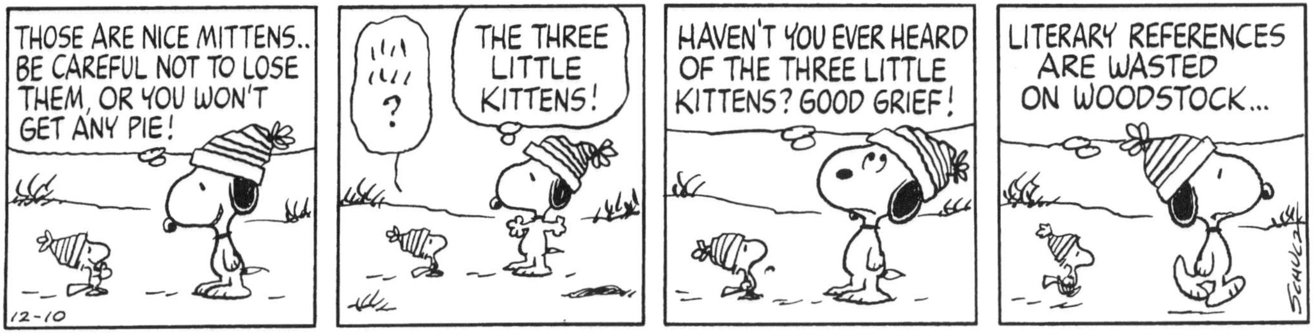
THOSE ARE NICE MITTENS.. BE CAREFUL NOT TO LOSE THEM, OR YOU WON'T GET ANY PIE!
12-10
?
THE THREE LITTLE KITTENS!
HAVEN'T YOU EVER HEARD OF THE THREE LITTLE KITTENS? GOOD GRIEF!
LITERARY REFERENCES ARE WASTED ON WOODSTOCK...
SCHULZ

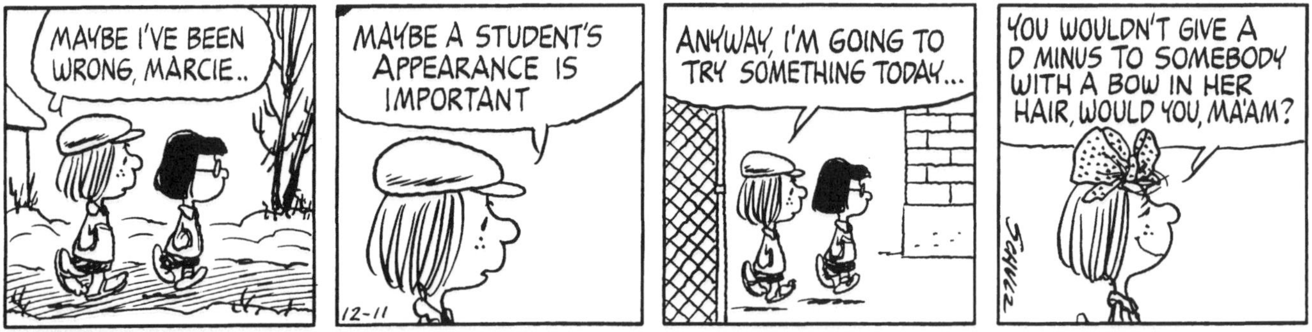
MAYBE I'VE BEEN WRONG, MARCIE..
MAYBE A STUDENT'S APPEARANCE IS IMPORTANT
12-11
ANYWAY, I'M GOING TO TRY SOMETHING TODAY...
YOU WOULDN'T GIVE A D MINUS TO SOMEBODY WITH A BOW IN HER HAIR, WOULD YOU, MA'AM?
SCHULZ

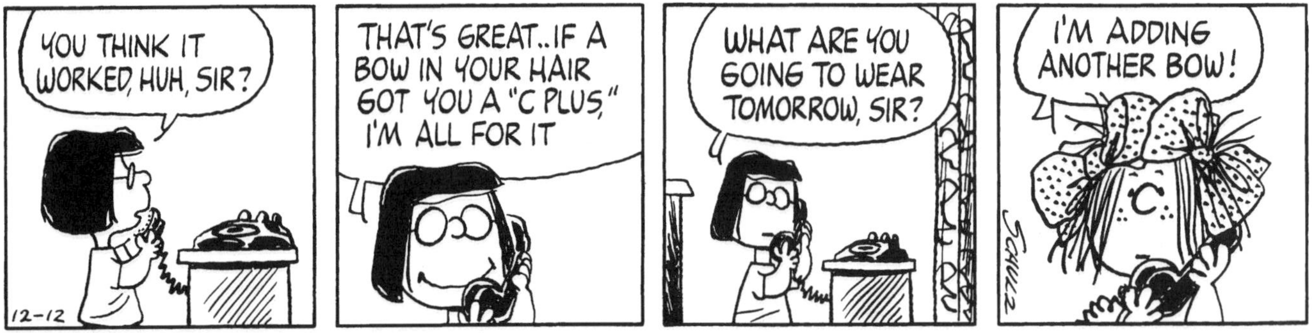
YOU THINK IT WORKED, HUH, SIR?
12-12
THAT'S GREAT..IF A BOW IN YOUR HAIR GOT YOU A "C PLUS," I'M ALL FOR IT
WHAT ARE YOU GOING TO WEAR TOMORROW, SIR?
I'M ADDING ANOTHER BOW!
SCHULZ

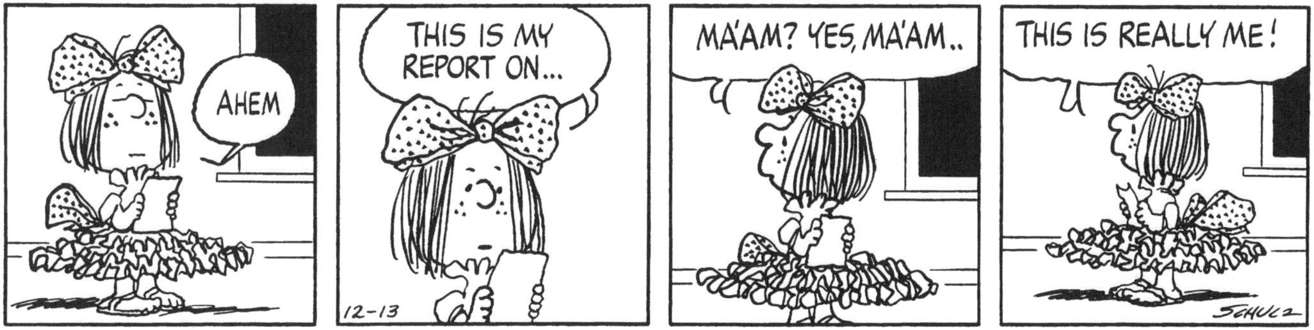
AHEM
THIS IS MY REPORT ON...
12-13
MA'AM? YES, MA'AM..
THIS IS REALLY ME!
SCHULZ

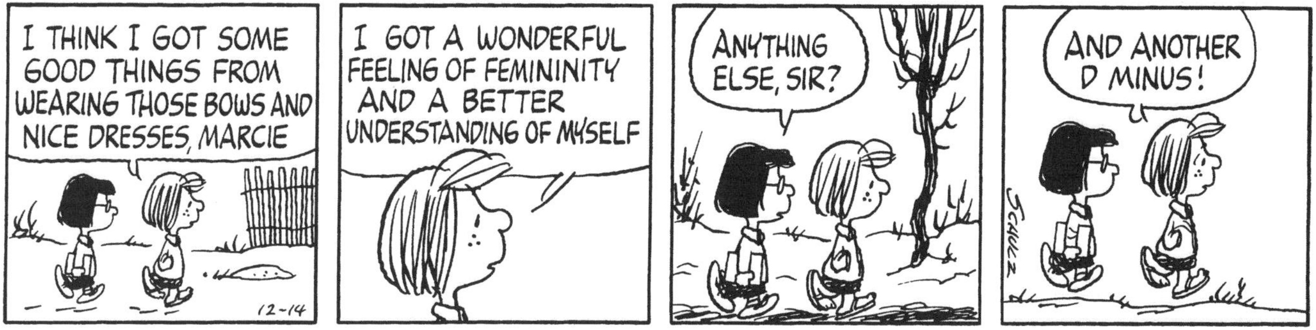
I THINK I GOT SOME GOOD THINGS FROM WEARING THOSE BOWS AND NICE DRESSES, MARCIE
12-14
I GOT A WONDERFUL FEELING OF FEMININITY AND A BETTER UNDERSTANDING OF MYSELF
ANYTHING ELSE, SIR?
AND ANOTHER D MINUS!
SCHULZ

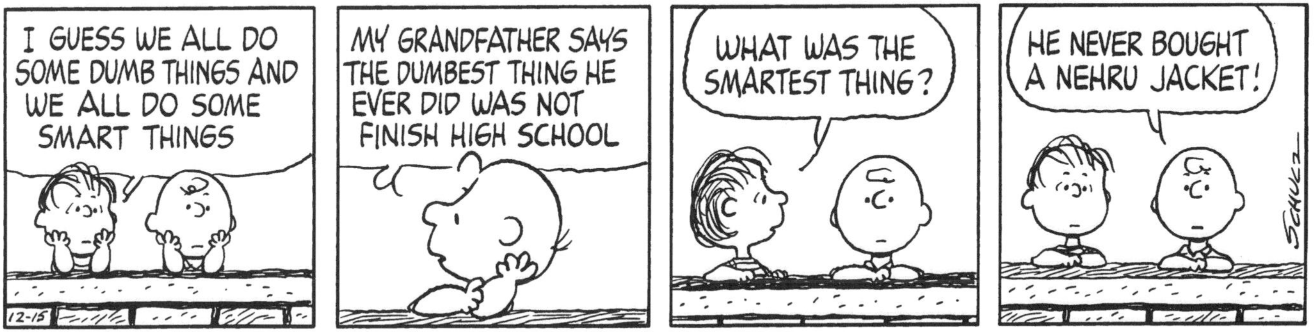
I GUESS WE ALL DO SOME DUMB THINGS AND WE ALL DO SOME SMART THINGS
12-15
MY GRANDFATHER SAYS THE DUMBEST THING HE EVER DID WAS NOT FINISH HIGH SCHOOL
WHAT WAS THE SMARTEST THING?
HE NEVER BOUGHT A NEHRU JACKET!
SCHULZ

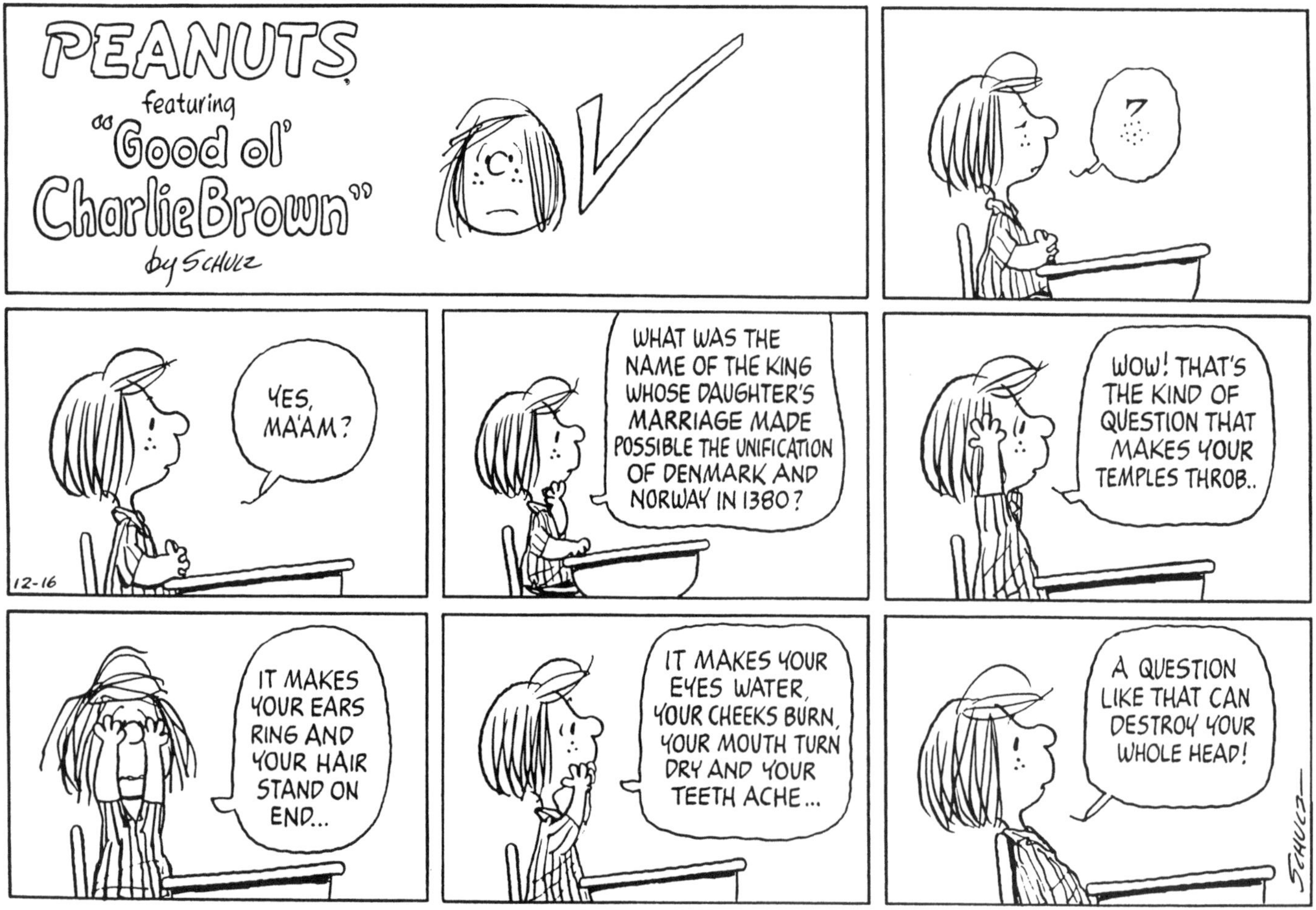
PEANUTS
featuring
"Good ol' CharlieBrown"
by SCHULZ
?
YES, MA'AM?
WHAT WAS THE NAME OF THE KING WHOSE DAUGHTER'S MARRIAGE MADE POSSIBLE THE UNIFICATION OF DENMARK AND NORWAY IN 1380?
WOW! THAT'S THE KIND OF QUESTION THAT MAKES YOUR TEMPLES THROB..
IT MAKES YOUR EARS RING AND YOUR HAIR STAND ON END...
IT MAKES YOUR EYES WATER, YOUR CHEEKS BURN, YOUR MOUTH TURN DRY AND YOUR TEETH ACHE...
A QUESTION LIKE THAT CAN DESTROY YOUR WHOLE HEAD!
12-16
SCHULZ

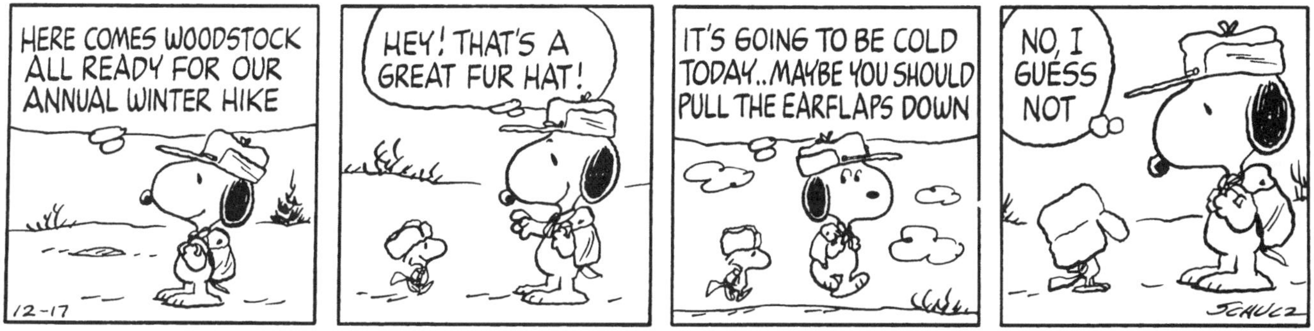
HERE COMES WOODSTOCK ALL READY FOR OUR ANNUAL WINTER HIKE
12-17
HEY! THAT'S A GREAT FUR HAT!
IT'S GOING TO BE COLD TODAY..MAYBE YOU SHOULD PULL THE EARFLAPS DOWN
NO, I GUESS NOT
SCHULZ

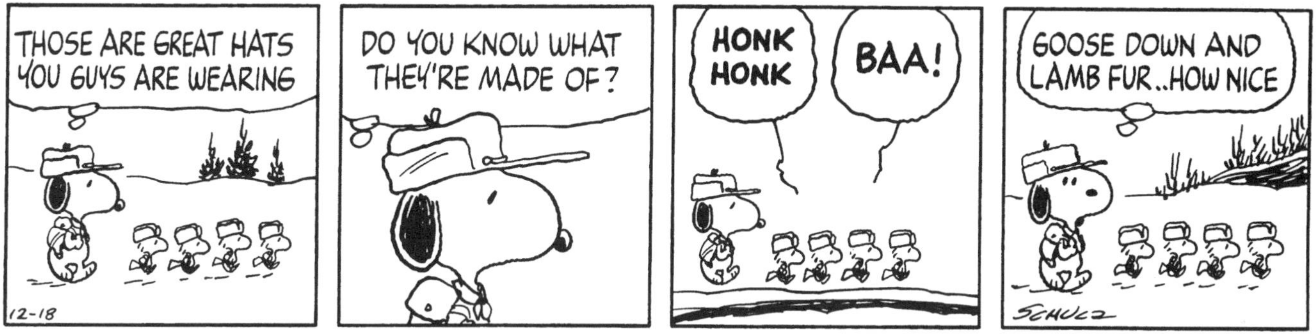
THOSE ARE GREAT HATS YOU GUYS ARE WEARING
12-18
DO YOU KNOW WHAT THEY'RE MADE OF?
HONK HONK
BAA!
GOOSE DOWN AND LAMB FUR..HOW NICE
SCHULZ

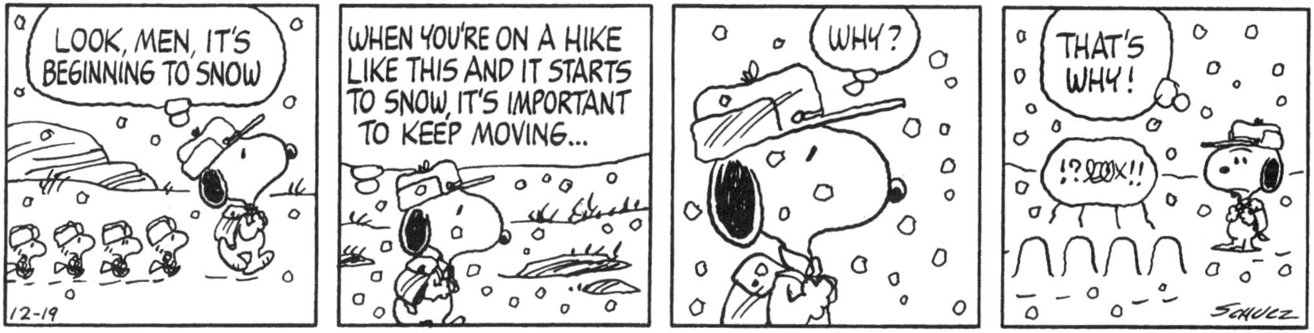
LOOK, MEN, IT'S BEGINNING TO SNOW
12-19
WHEN YOU'RE ON A HIKE LIKE THIS AND IT STARTS TO SNOW, IT'S IMPORTANT TO KEEP MOVING...
WHY?
THAT'S WHY!
SCHULZ

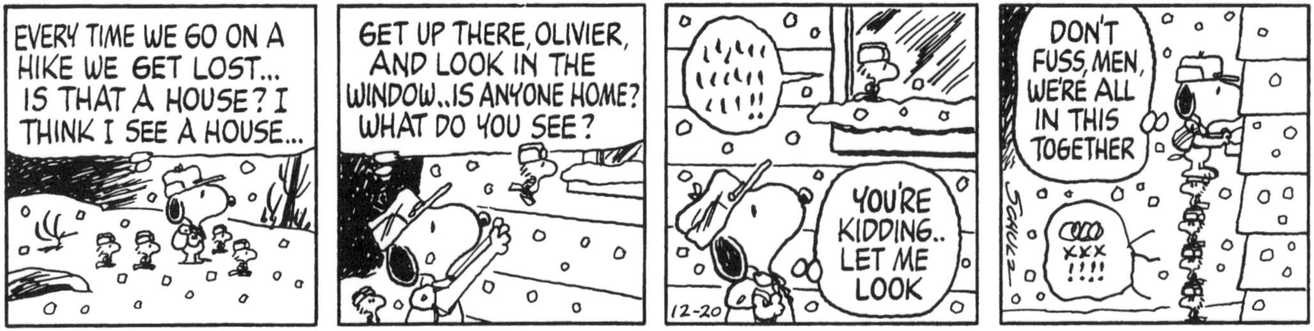
EVERY TIME WE GO ON A HIKE WE GET LOST... IS THAT A HOUSE? I THINK I SEE A HOUSE...
GET UP THERE, OLIVIER, AND LOOK IN THE WINDOW..IS ANYONE HOME? WHAT DO YOU SEE?
YOU'RE KIDDING.. LET ME LOOK
12-20
DON'T FUSS, MEN, WE'RE ALL IN THIS TOGETHER
SCHULZ

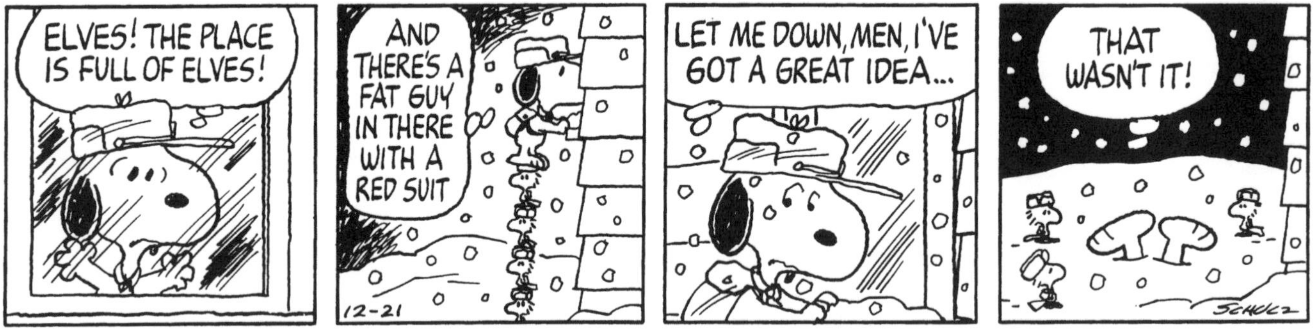
ELVES! THE PLACE IS FULL OF ELVES!
AND THERE'S A FAT GUY IN THERE WITH A RED SUIT
12-21
LET ME DOWN, MEN, I'VE GOT A GREAT IDEA...
THAT WASN'T IT!
SCHULZ

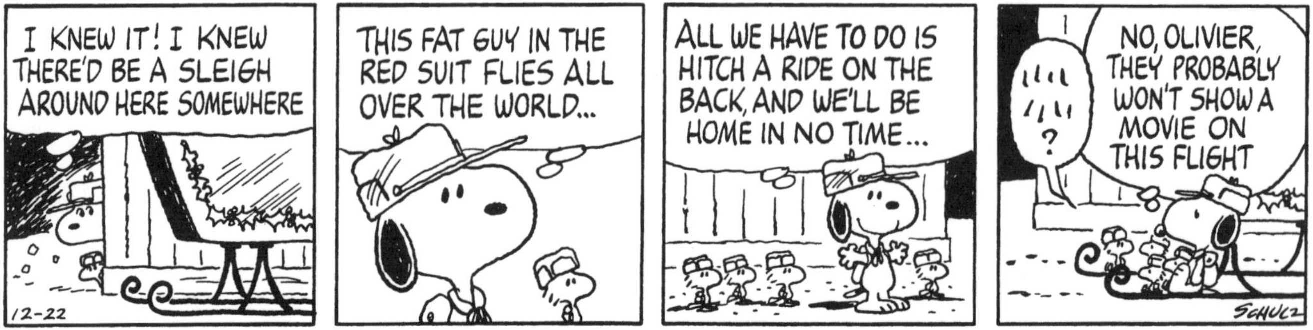
I KNEW IT! I KNEW THERE'D BE A SLEIGH AROUND HERE SOMEWHERE
12-22
THIS FAT GUY IN THE RED SUIT FLIES ALL OVER THE WORLD...
ALL WE HAVE TO DO IS HITCH A RIDE ON THE BACK, AND WE'LL BE HOME IN NO TIME...
NO, OLIVIER, THEY PROBABLY WON'T SHOW A MOVIE ON THIS FLIGHT
SCHULZ

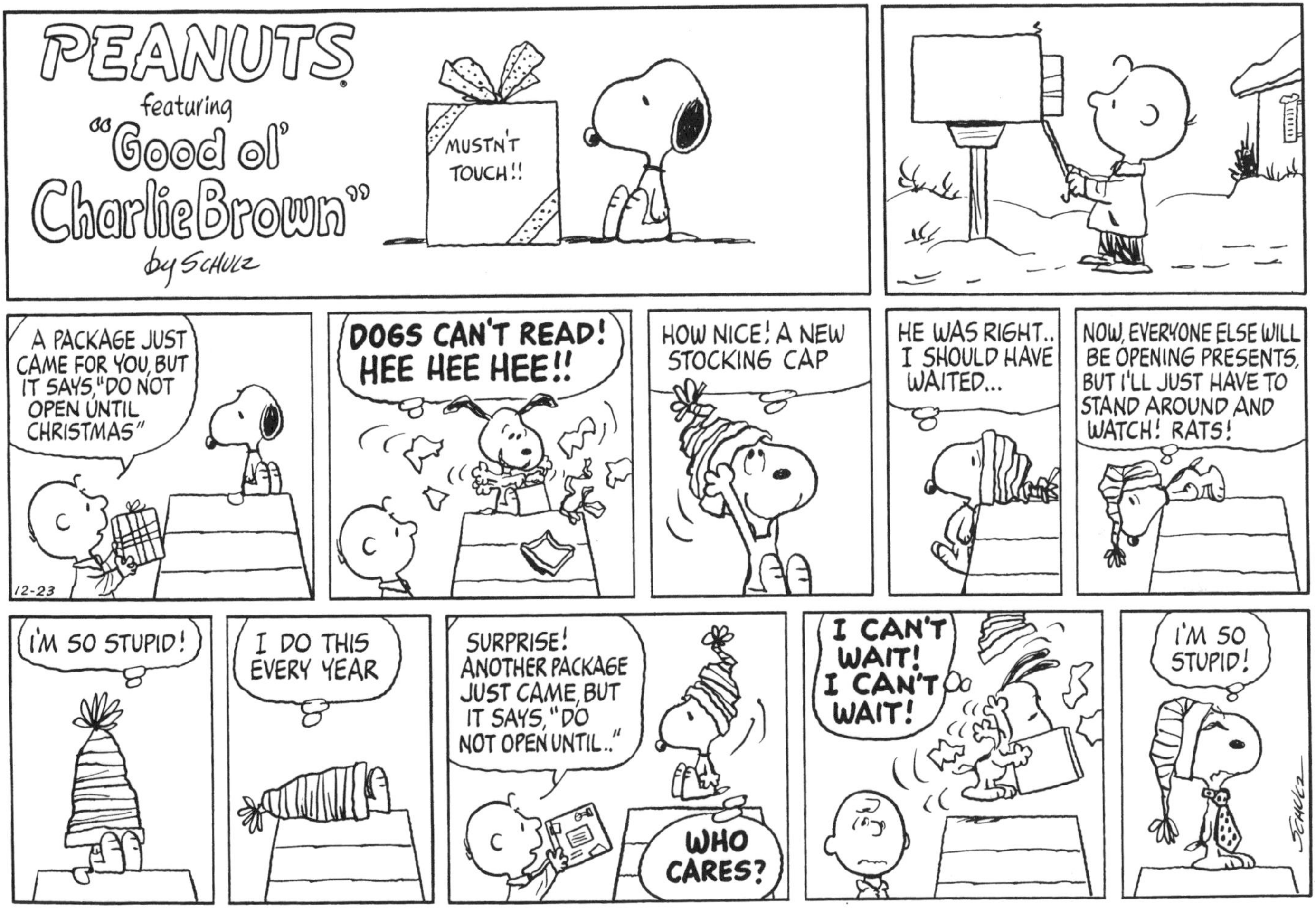
PEANUTS
featuring
"Good ol' Charlie Brown"
by SCHULZ
MUSTN'T TOUCH!!
A PACKAGE JUST CAME FOR YOU, BUT IT SAYS, "DO NOT OPEN UNTIL CHRISTMAS"
12-23
DOGS CAN'T READ! HEE HEE HEE!!
HOW NICE! A NEW STOCKING CAP
HE WAS RIGHT.. I SHOULD HAVE WAITED...
NOW, EVERYONE ELSE WILL BE OPENING PRESENTS, BUT I'LL JUST HAVE TO STAND AROUND AND WATCH! RATS!
I'M SO STUPID!
I DO THIS EVERY YEAR
SURPRISE! ANOTHER PACKAGE JUST CAME, BUT IT SAYS, "DO NOT OPEN UNTIL.."
WHO CARES?
I CAN'T WAIT! I CAN'T WAIT!
I'M SO STUPID!
SCHULZ

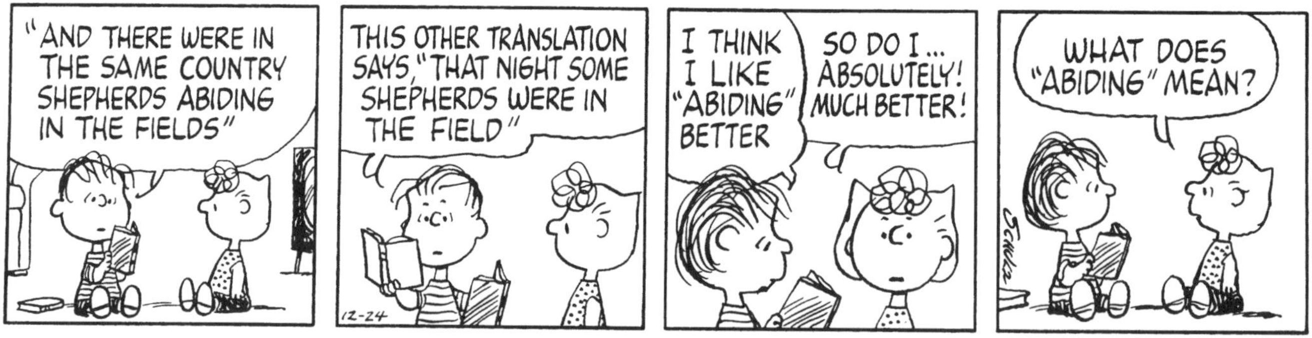
"AND THERE WERE IN THE SAME COUNTRY SHEPHERDS ABIDING IN THE FIELDS"
THIS OTHER TRANSLATION SAYS, "THAT NIGHT SOME SHEPHERDS WERE IN THE FIELD"
12-24
I THINK I LIKE "ABIDING" BETTER
SO DO I... ABSOLUTELY! MUCH BETTER!
WHAT DOES "ABIDING" MEAN?
SCHULZ

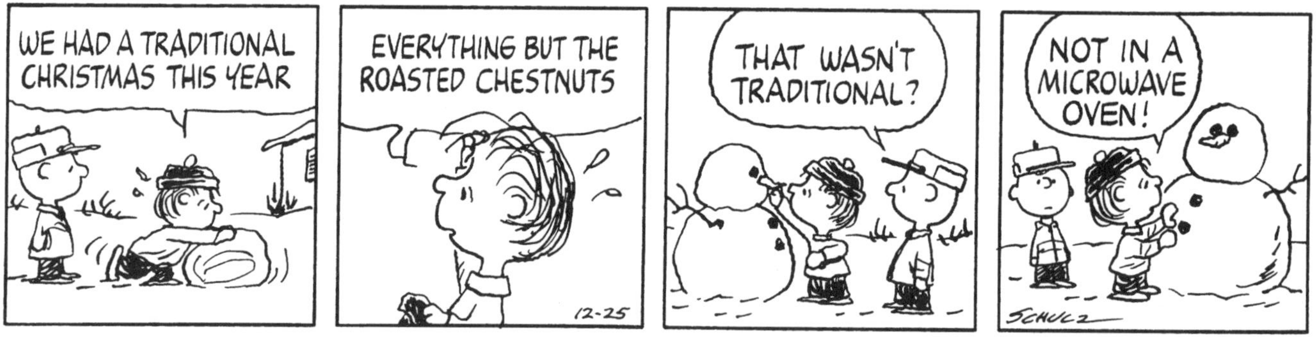
WE HAD A TRADITIONAL CHRISTMAS THIS YEAR
EVERYTHING BUT THE ROASTED CHESTNUTS
12-25
THAT WASN'T TRADITIONAL?
NOT IN A MICROWAVE OVEN!
SCHULZ

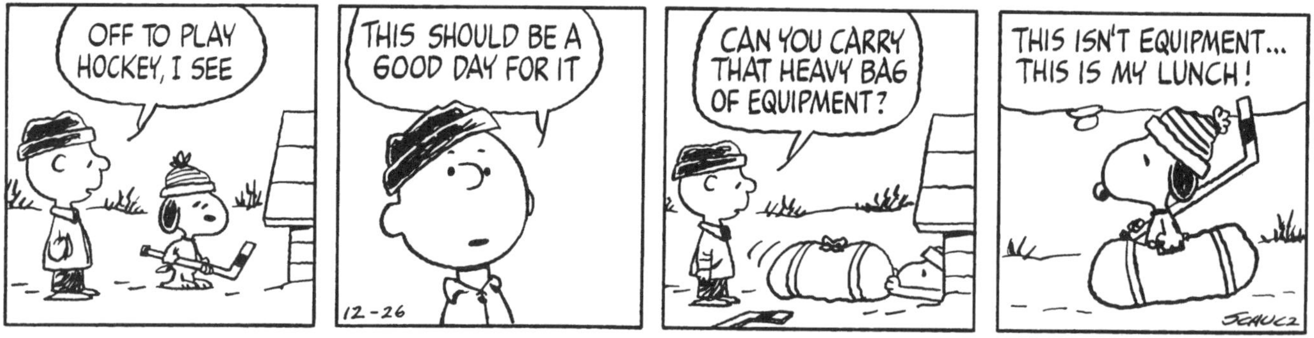
OFF TO PLAY HOCKEY, I SEE
THIS SHOULD BE A GOOD DAY FOR IT
12-26
CAN YOU CARRY THAT HEAVY BAG OF EQUIPMENT?
THIS ISN'T EQUIPMENT... THIS IS MY LUNCH!
SCHULZ

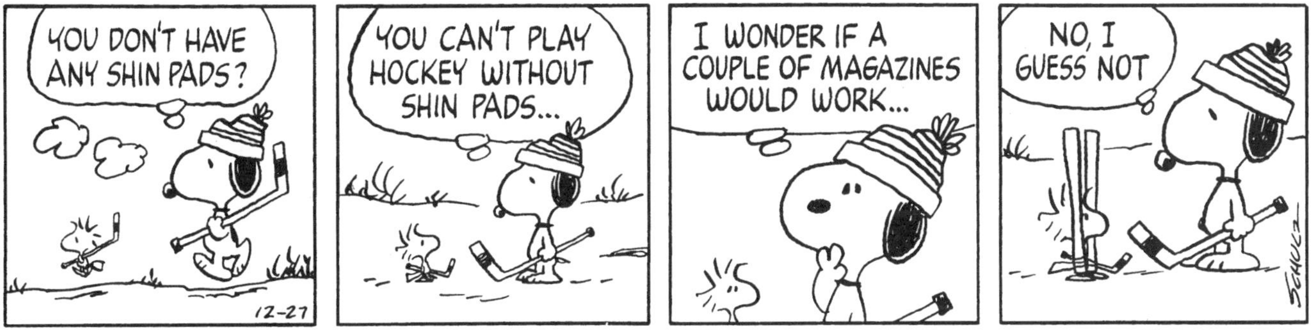
YOU DON'T HAVE ANY SHIN PADS?
12-27
YOU CAN'T PLAY HOCKEY WITHOUT SHIN PADS...
I WONDER IF A COUPLE OF MAGAZINES WOULD WORK...
NO, I GUESS NOT
SCHULZ

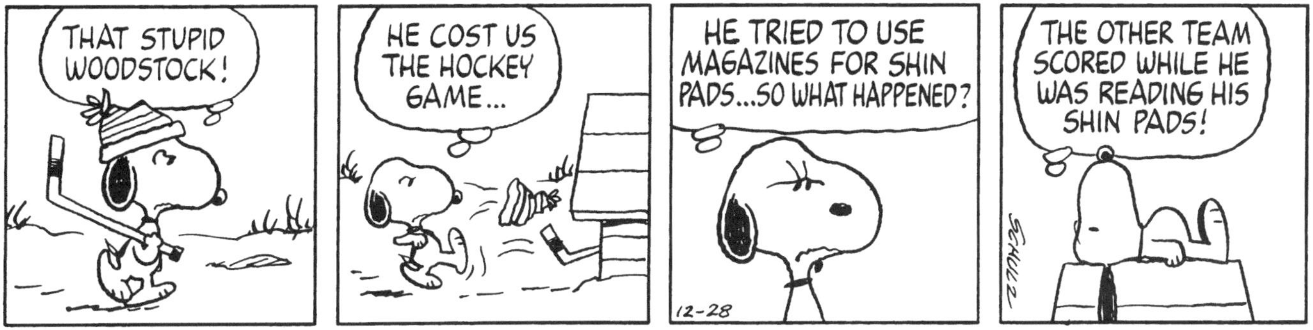
THAT STUPID WOODSTOCK!
HE COST US THE HOCKEY GAME...
HE TRIED TO USE MAGAZINES FOR SHIN PADS...SO WHAT HAPPENED?
12-28
THE OTHER TEAM SCORED WHILE HE WAS READING HIS SHIN PADS!
SCHULZ

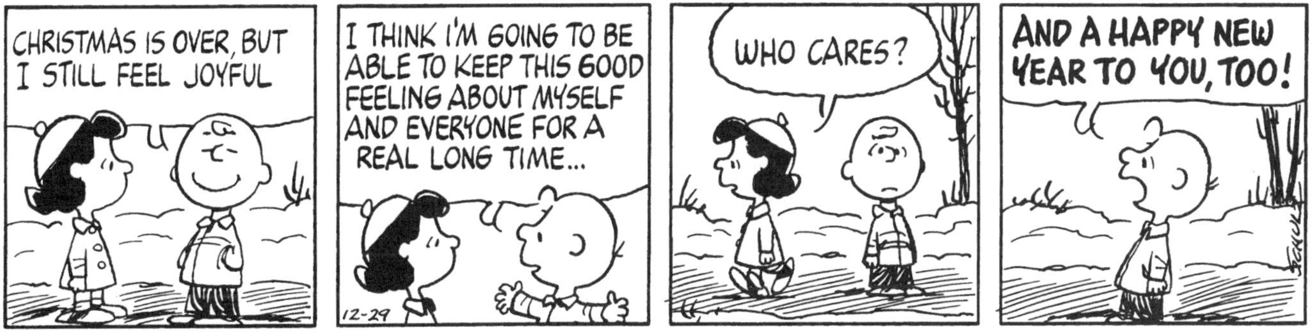
CHRISTMAS IS OVER, BUT I STILL FEEL JOYFUL
I THINK I'M GOING TO BE ABLE TO KEEP THIS GOOD FEELING ABOUT MYSELF AND EVERYONE FOR A REAL LONG TIME...
12-29
WHO CARES?
AND A HAPPY NEW YEAR TO YOU, TOO!
SCHULZ

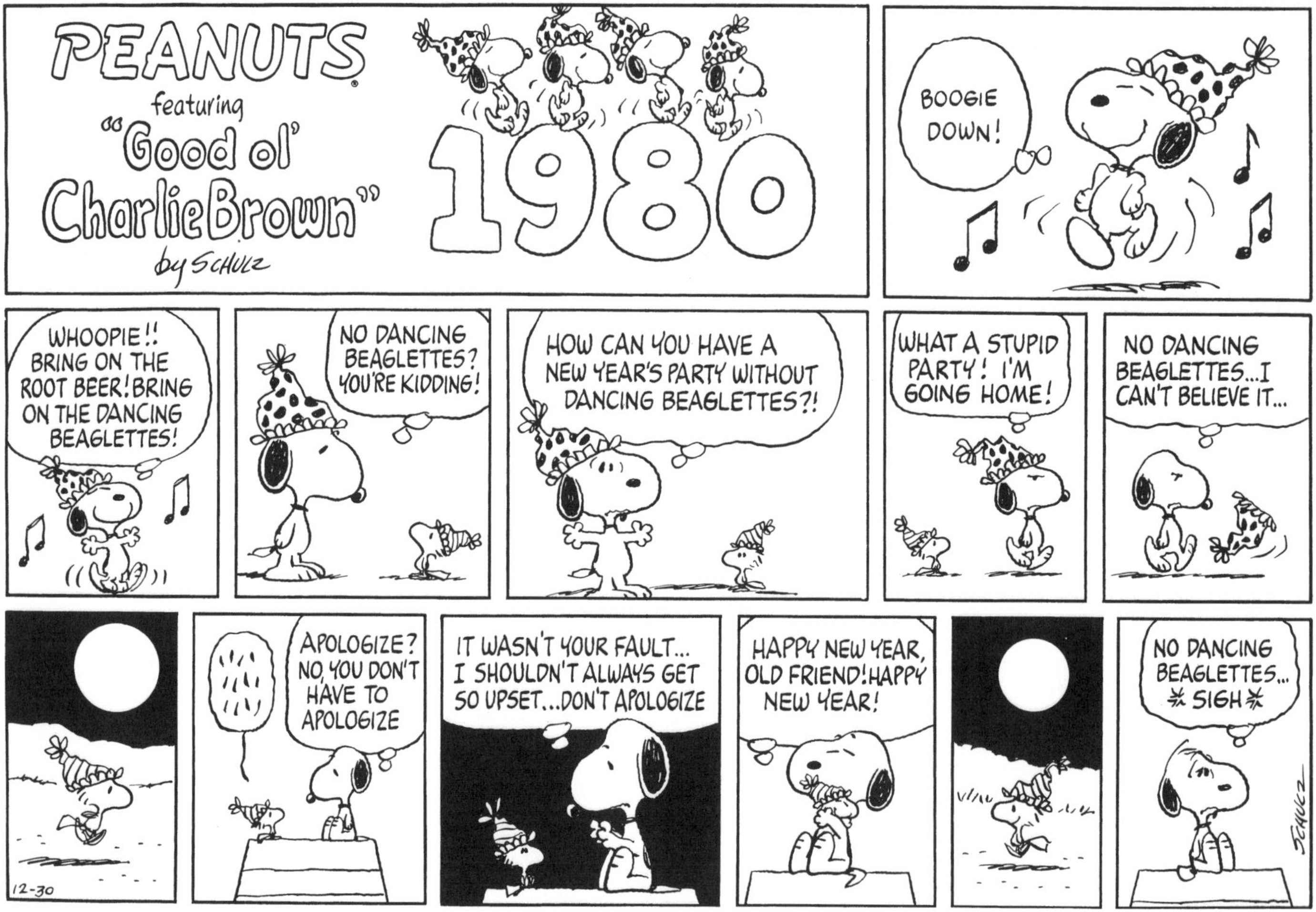
PEANUTS
featuring "Good ol' Charlie Brown"
by SCHULZ
1980
BOOGIE DOWN!
WHOOPIE!! BRING ON THE ROOT BEER! BRING ON THE DANCING BEAGLETTES!
NO DANCING BEAGLETTES? YOU'RE KIDDING!
HOW CAN YOU HAVE A NEW YEAR'S PARTY WITHOUT DANCING BEAGLETTES?!
WHAT A STUPID PARTY! I'M GOING HOME!
NO DANCING BEAGLETTES...I CAN'T BELIEVE IT...
12-30
APOLOGIZE? NO, YOU DON'T HAVE TO APOLOGIZE
IT WASN'T YOUR FAULT... I SHOULDN'T ALWAYS GET SO UPSET...DON'T APOLOGIZE
HAPPY NEW YEAR, OLD FRIEND! HAPPY NEW YEAR!
NO DANCING BEAGLETTES... *SIGH*
SCHULZ

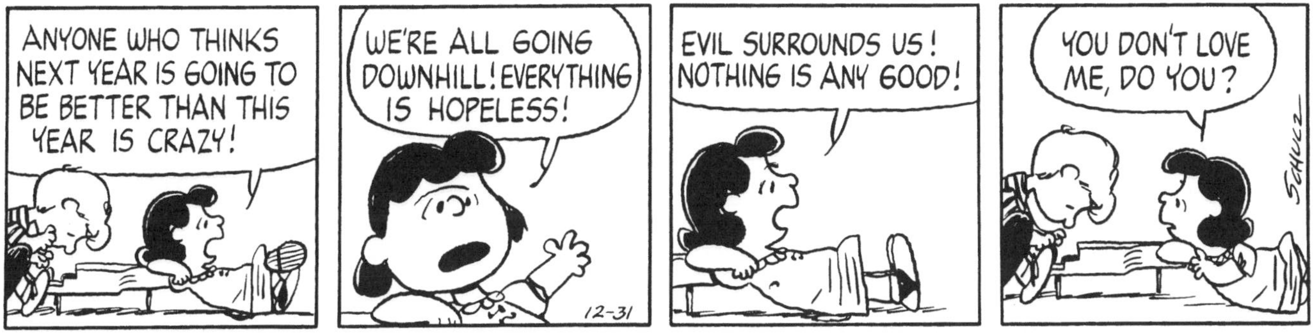
ANYONE WHO THINKS NEXT YEAR IS GOING TO BE BETTER THAN THIS YEAR IS CRAZY!
WE'RE ALL GOING DOWNHILL! EVERYTHING IS HOPELESS!
12-31
EVIL SURROUNDS US! NOTHING IS ANY GOOD!
YOU DON'T LOVE ME, DO YOU?

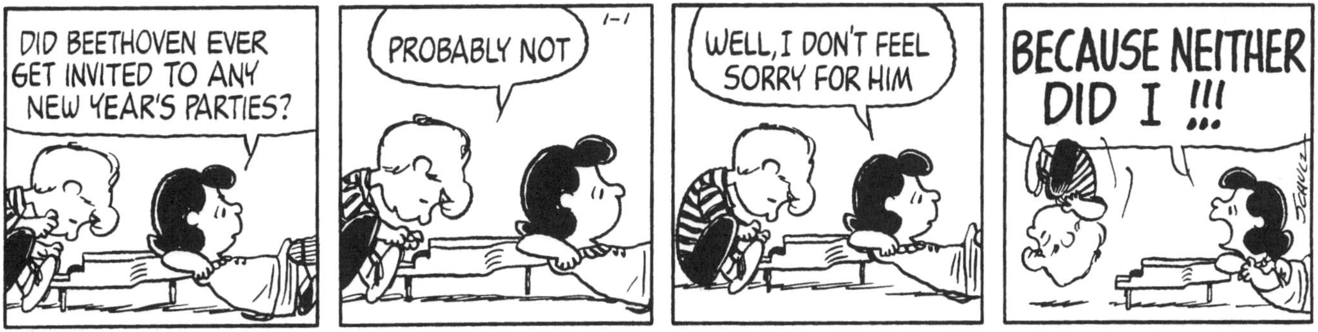
DID BEETHOVEN EVER GET INVITED TO ANY NEW YEAR'S PARTIES?
PROBABLY NOT
1-1
WELL, I DON'T FEEL SORRY FOR HIM
BECAUSE NEITHER DID I !!!

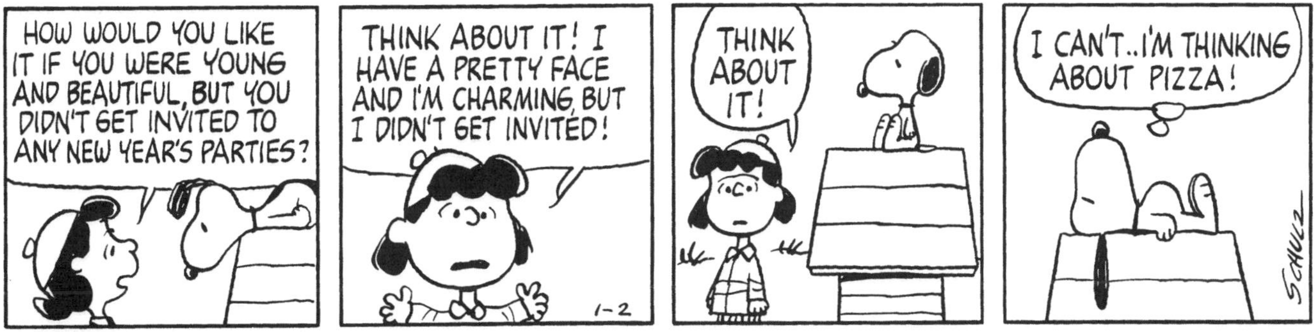
HOW WOULD YOU LIKE IT IF YOU WERE YOUNG AND BEAUTIFUL, BUT YOU DIDN'T GET INVITED TO ANY NEW YEAR'S PARTIES?
THINK ABOUT IT! I HAVE A PRETTY FACE AND I'M CHARMING, BUT I DIDN'T GET INVITED!
1-2
THINK ABOUT IT!
I CAN'T..I'M THINKING ABOUT PIZZA!

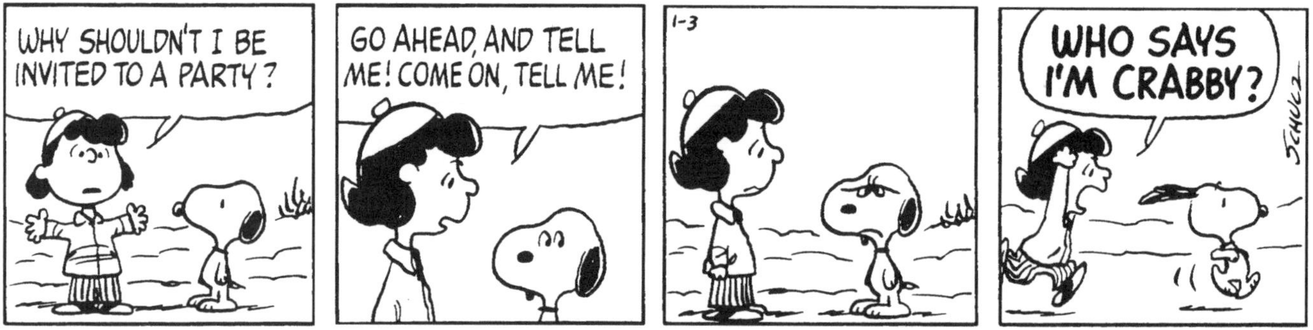
WHY SHOULDN'T I BE INVITED TO A PARTY?
GO AHEAD, AND TELL ME! COME ON, TELL ME!
1-3
WHO SAYS I'M CRABBY?
SCHULZ

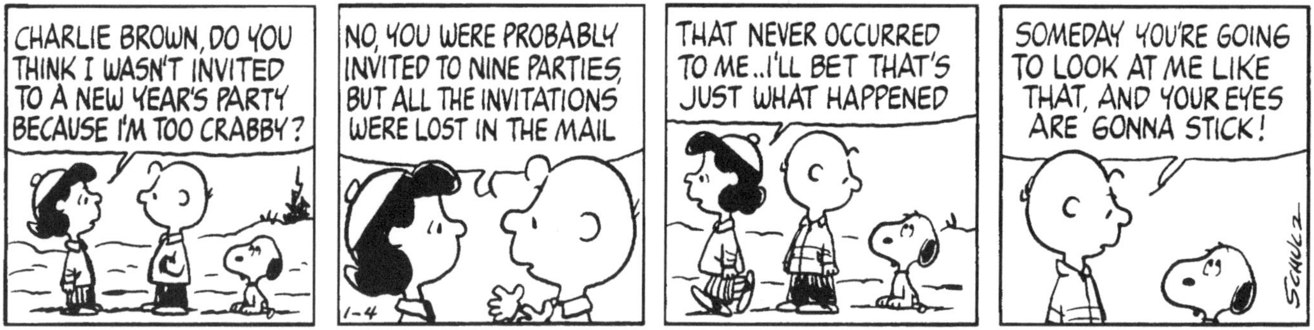
CHARLIE BROWN, DO YOU THINK I WASN'T INVITED TO A NEW YEAR'S PARTY BECAUSE I'M TOO CRABBY?
NO, YOU WERE PROBABLY INVITED TO NINE PARTIES, BUT ALL THE INVITATIONS WERE LOST IN THE MAIL
1-4
THAT NEVER OCCURRED TO ME..I'LL BET THAT'S JUST WHAT HAPPENED
SOMEDAY YOU'RE GOING TO LOOK AT ME LIKE THAT, AND YOUR EYES ARE GONNA STICK!
SCHULZ

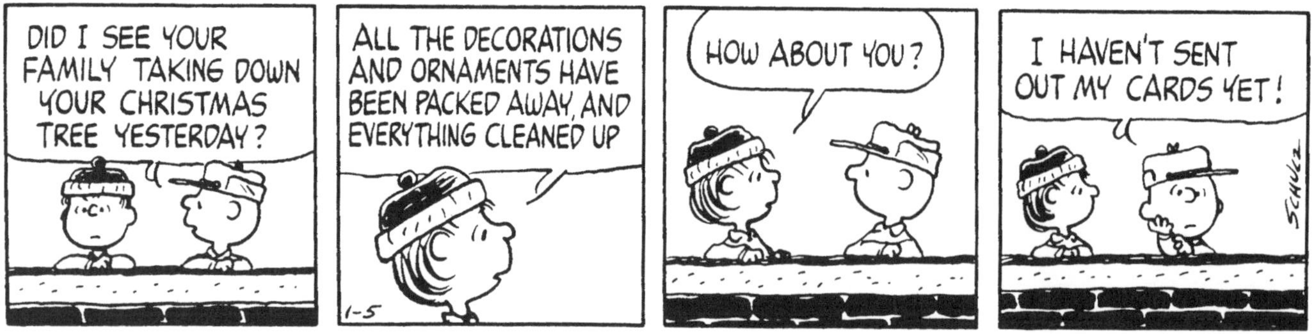
DID I SEE YOUR FAMILY TAKING DOWN YOUR CHRISTMAS TREE YESTERDAY?
ALL THE DECORATIONS AND ORNAMENTS HAVE BEEN PACKED AWAY, AND EVERYTHING CLEANED UP
1-5
HOW ABOUT YOU?
I HAVEN'T SENT OUT MY CARDS YET!
SCHULZ

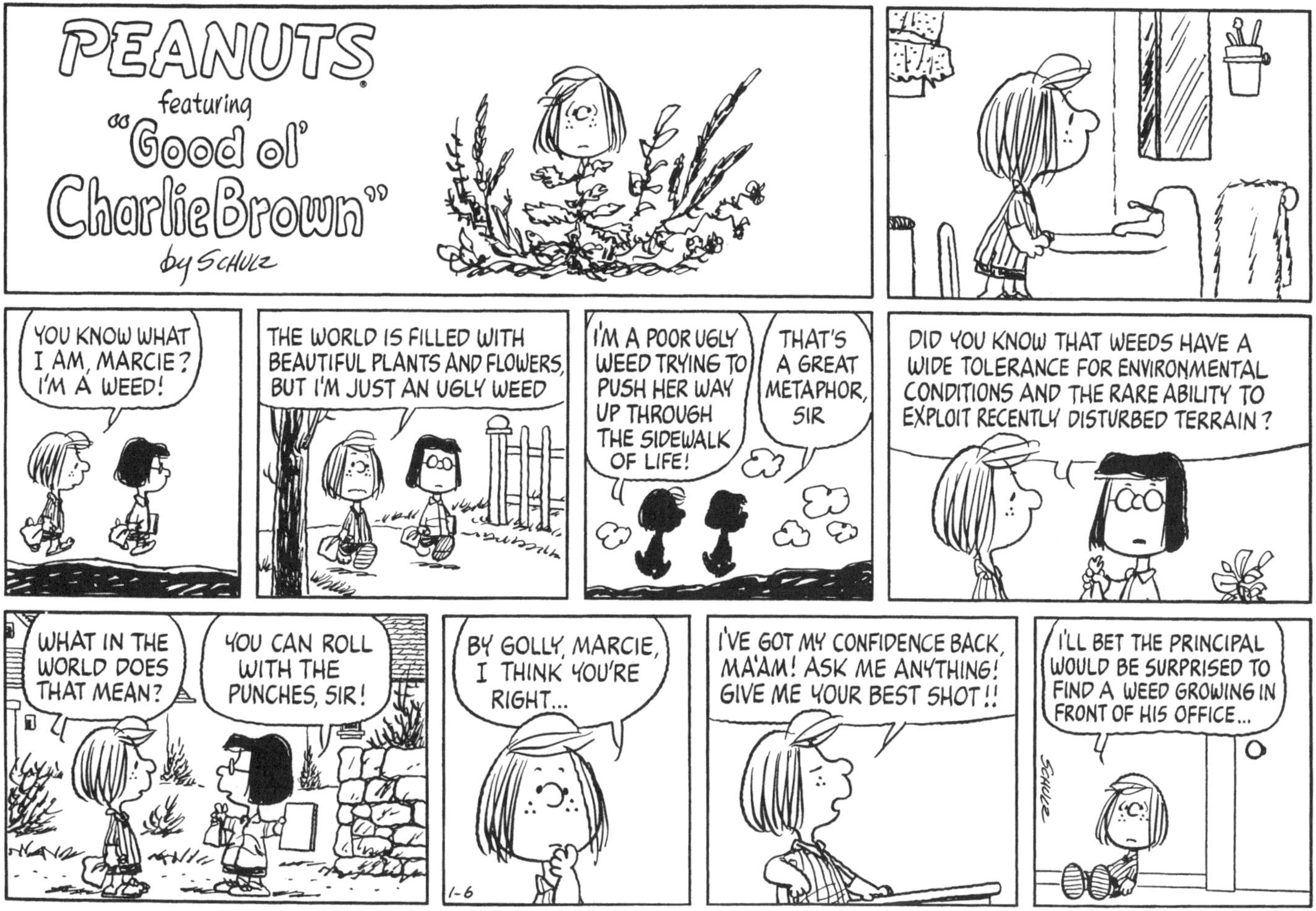
PEANUTS
featuring
"Good ol' CharlieBrown"
by SCHULZ
YOU KNOW WHAT I AM, MARCIE? I'M A WEED!
THE WORLD IS FILLED WITH BEAUTIFUL PLANTS AND FLOWERS, BUT I'M JUST AN UGLY WEED
I'M A POOR UGLY WEED TRYING TO PUSH HER WAY UP THROUGH THE SIDEWALK OF LIFE!
THAT'S A GREAT METAPHOR, SIR
DID YOU KNOW THAT WEEDS HAVE A WIDE TOLERANCE FOR ENVIRONMENTAL CONDITIONS AND THE RARE ABILITY TO EXPLOIT RECENTLY DISTURBED TERRAIN?
WHAT IN THE WORLD DOES THAT MEAN?
YOU CAN ROLL WITH THE PUNCHES, SIR!
BY GOLLY, MARCIE, I THINK YOU'RE RIGHT...
1-6
I'VE GOT MY CONFIDENCE BACK, MA'AM! ASK ME ANYTHING! GIVE ME YOUR BEST SHOT!!
I'LL BET THE PRINCIPAL WOULD BE SURPRISED TO FIND A WEED GROWING IN FRONT OF HIS OFFICE...
SCHULZ

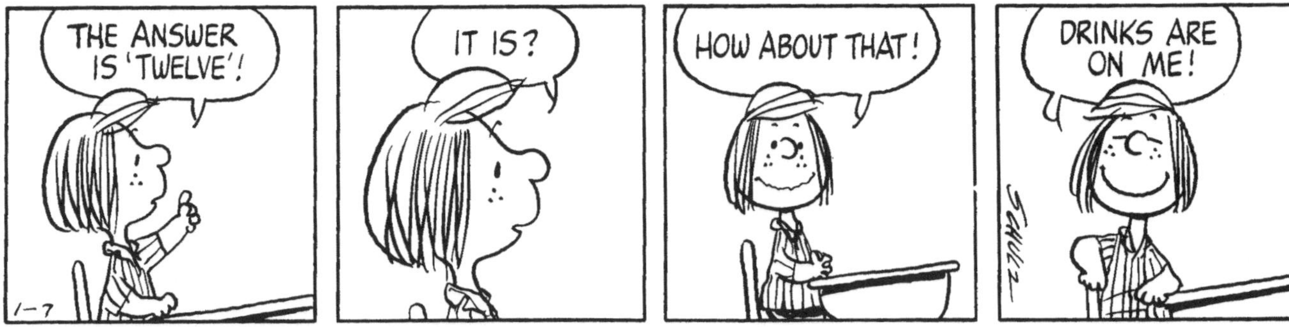
THE ANSWER IS 'TWELVE'!
IT IS?
HOW ABOUT THAT!
DRINKS ARE ON ME!

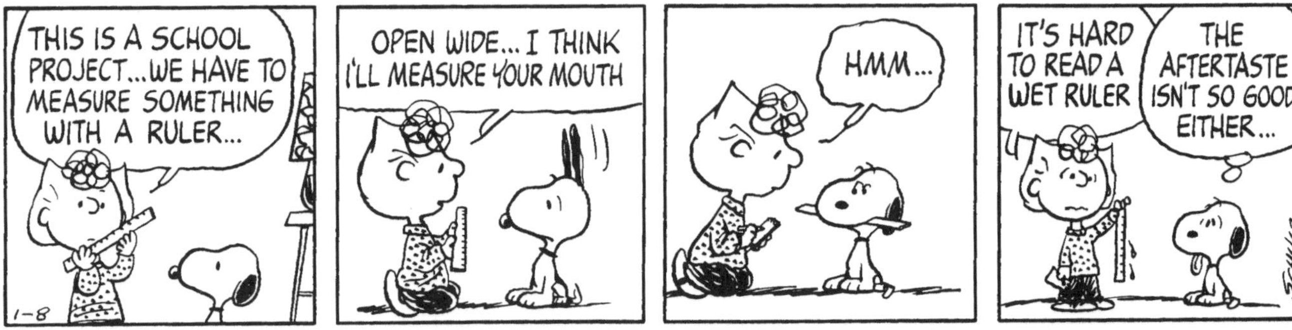
THIS IS A SCHOOL PROJECT...WE HAVE TO MEASURE SOMETHING WITH A RULER...
OPEN WIDE... I THINK I'LL MEASURE YOUR MOUTH
HMM...
IT'S HARD TO READ A WET RULER
THE AFTERTASTE ISN'T SO GOOD EITHER...

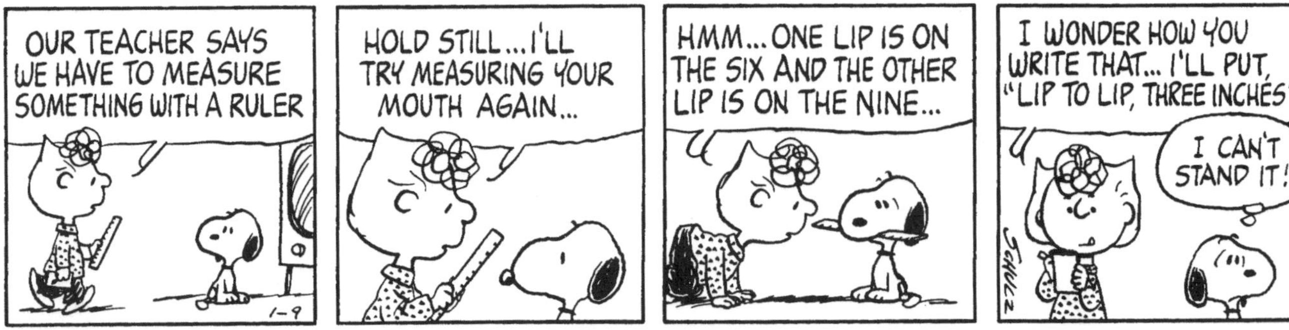
OUR TEACHER SAYS WE HAVE TO MEASURE SOMETHING WITH A RULER
HOLD STILL... I'LL TRY MEASURING YOUR MOUTH AGAIN...
HMM... ONE LIP IS ON THE SIX AND THE OTHER LIP IS ON THE NINE...
I WONDER HOW YOU WRITE THAT... I'LL PUT, "LIP TO LIP, THREE INCHES"
I CAN'T STAND IT!

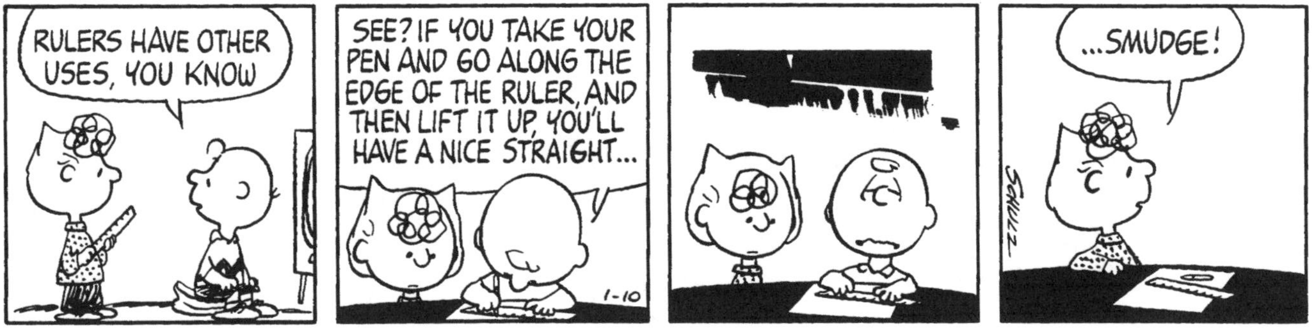
RULERS HAVE OTHER USES, YOU KNOW
SEE? IF YOU TAKE YOUR PEN AND GO ALONG THE EDGE OF THE RULER, AND THEN LIFT IT UP, YOU'LL HAVE A NICE STRAIGHT...
1-10
...SMUDGE!
SCHULZ

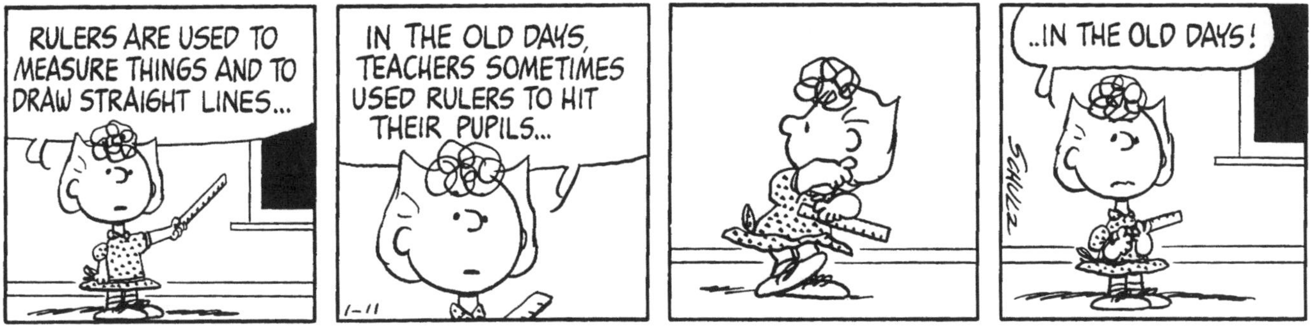
RULERS ARE USED TO MEASURE THINGS AND TO DRAW STRAIGHT LINES...
IN THE OLD DAYS, TEACHERS SOMETIMES USED RULERS TO HIT THEIR PUPILS...
1-11
..IN THE OLD DAYS!
SCHULZ

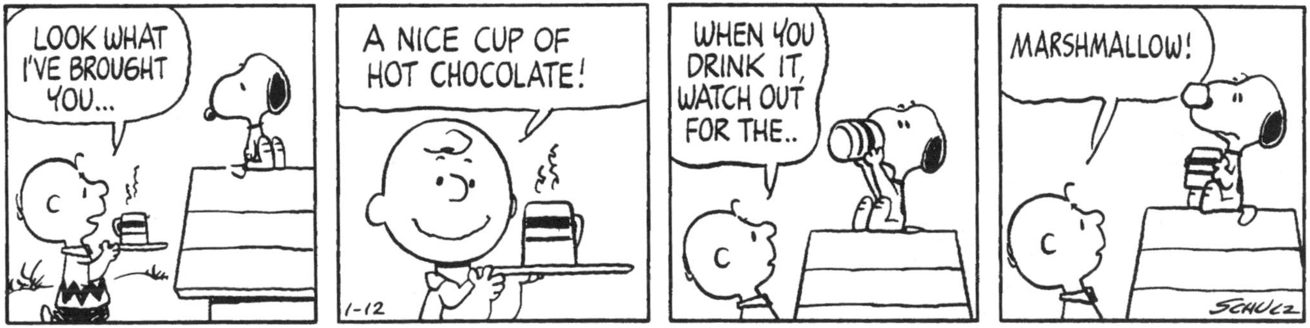
LOOK WHAT I'VE BROUGHT YOU...
A NICE CUP OF HOT CHOCOLATE!
1-12
WHEN YOU DRINK IT, WATCH OUT FOR THE..
MARSHMALLOW!
SCHULZ

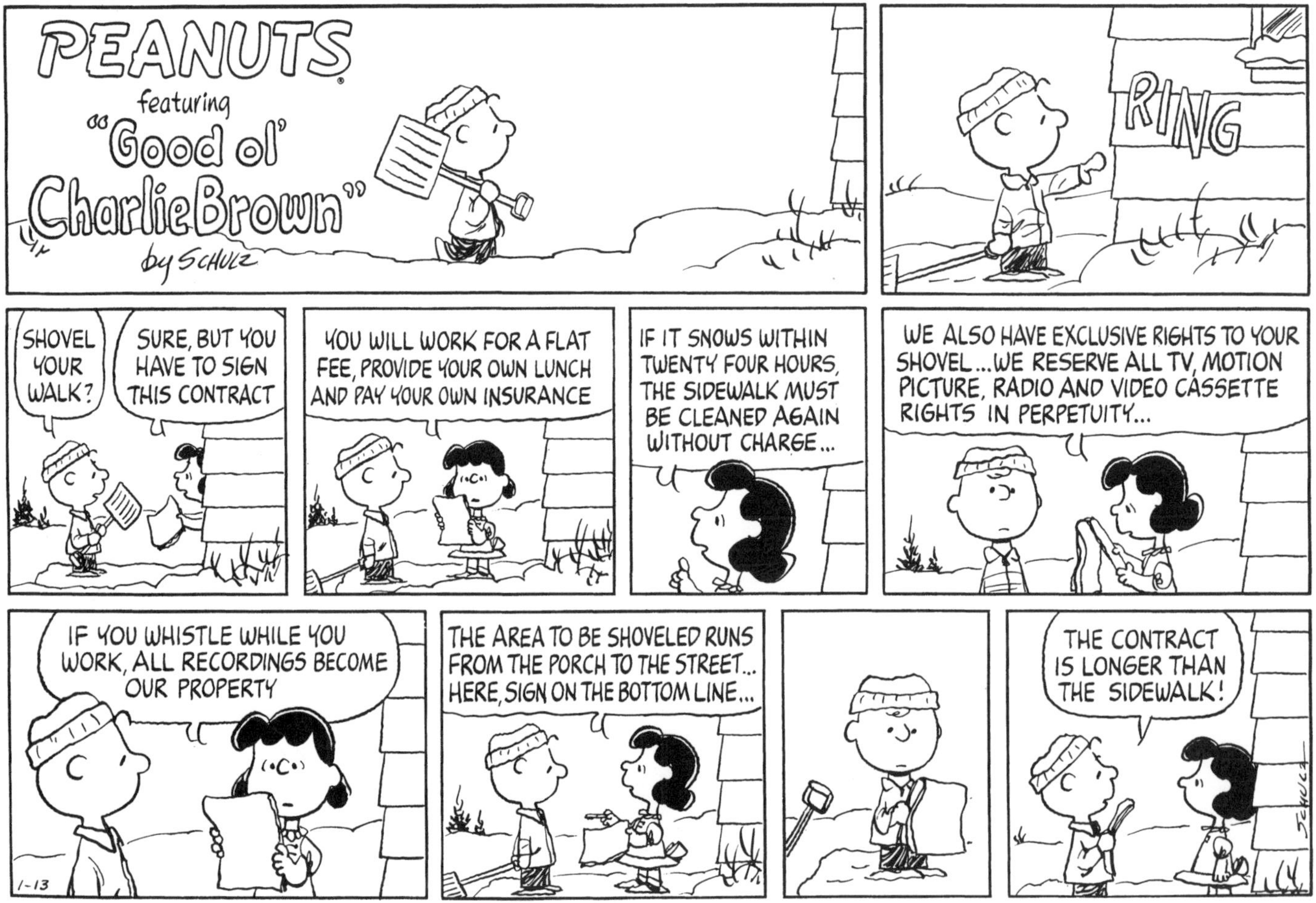
PEANUTS
featuring "Good ol' Charlie Brown"
by SCHULZ
RING
SHOVEL YOUR WALK?
SURE, BUT YOU HAVE TO SIGN THIS CONTRACT
YOU WILL WORK FOR A FLAT FEE, PROVIDE YOUR OWN LUNCH AND PAY YOUR OWN INSURANCE
IF IT SNOWS WITHIN TWENTY FOUR HOURS, THE SIDEWALK MUST BE CLEANED AGAIN WITHOUT CHARGE...
WE ALSO HAVE EXCLUSIVE RIGHTS TO YOUR SHOVEL...WE RESERVE ALL TV, MOTION PICTURE, RADIO AND VIDEO CASSETTE RIGHTS IN PERPETUITY...
IF YOU WHISTLE WHILE YOU WORK, ALL RECORDINGS BECOME OUR PROPERTY
1-13
THE AREA TO BE SHOVELED RUNS FROM THE PORCH TO THE STREET... HERE, SIGN ON THE BOTTOM LINE...
THE CONTRACT IS LONGER THAN THE SIDEWALK!
SCHULZ

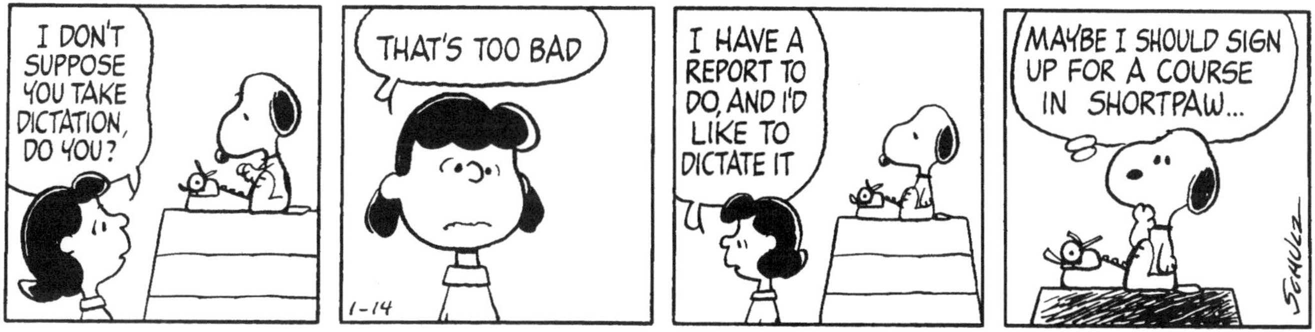
I DON'T SUPPOSE YOU TAKE DICTATION, DO YOU?
THAT'S TOO BAD
1-14
I HAVE A REPORT TO DO, AND I'D LIKE TO DICTATE IT
MAYBE I SHOULD SIGN UP FOR A COURSE IN SHORTPAW...
SCHULZ

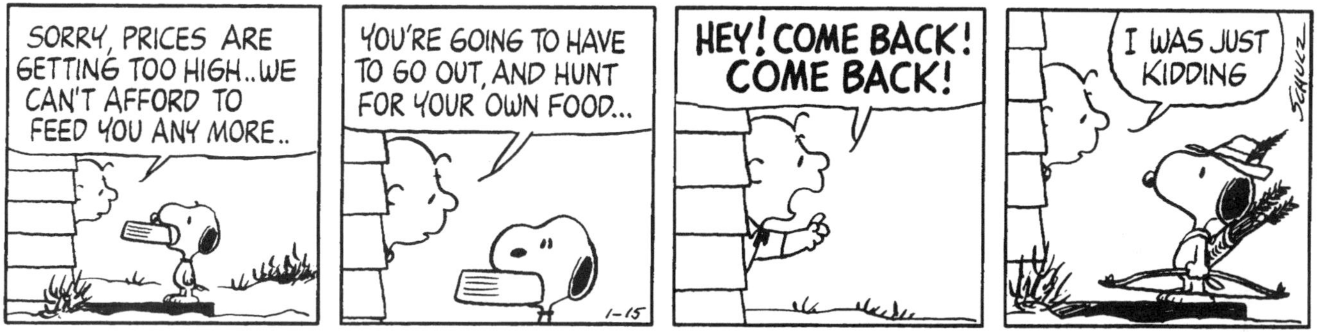
SORRY, PRICES ARE GETTING TOO HIGH..WE CAN'T AFFORD TO FEED YOU ANY MORE..
YOU'RE GOING TO HAVE TO GO OUT, AND HUNT FOR YOUR OWN FOOD...
1-15
HEY! COME BACK! COME BACK!
I WAS JUST KIDDING
SCHULZ

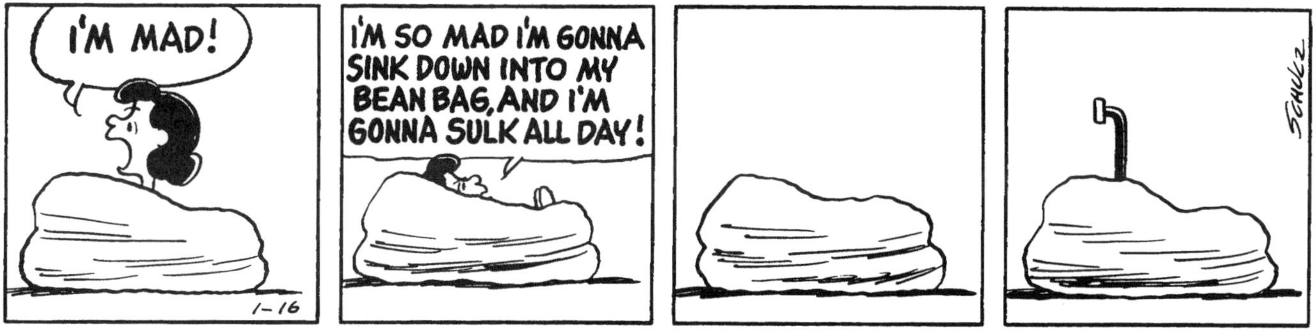
I'M MAD!
1-16
I'M SO MAD I'M GONNA SINK DOWN INTO MY BEAN BAG, AND I'M GONNA SULK ALL DAY!
SCHULZ

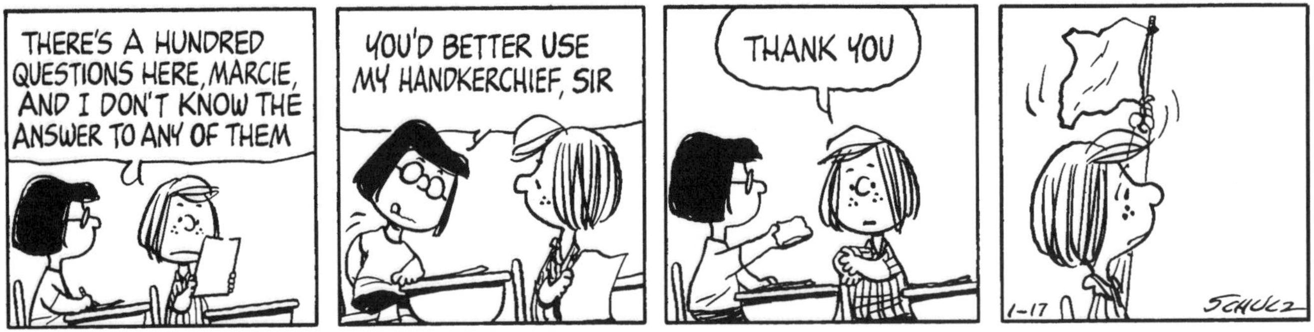
THERE'S A HUNDRED QUESTIONS HERE, MARCIE, AND I DON'T KNOW THE ANSWER TO ANY OF THEM
YOU'D BETTER USE MY HANDKERCHIEF, SIR
THANK YOU
1-17
SCHULZ

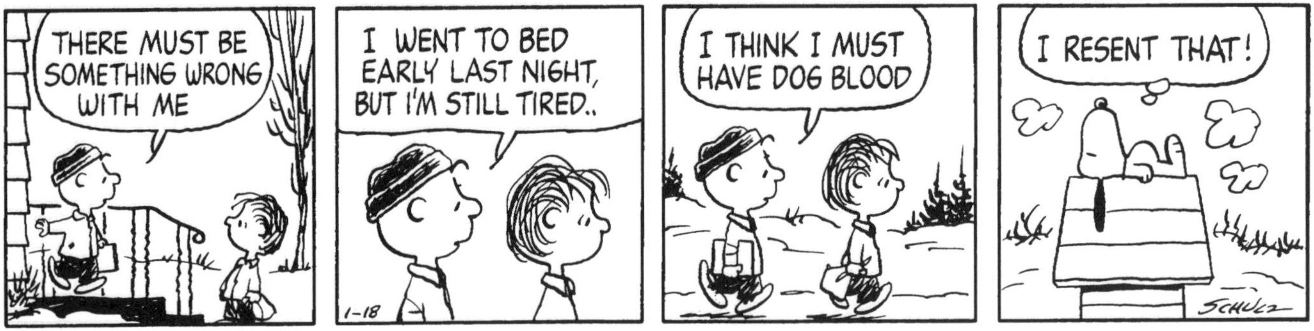
THERE MUST BE SOMETHING WRONG WITH ME
I WENT TO BED EARLY LAST NIGHT, BUT I'M STILL TIRED..
1-18
I THINK I MUST HAVE DOG BLOOD
I RESENT THAT!
SCHULZ

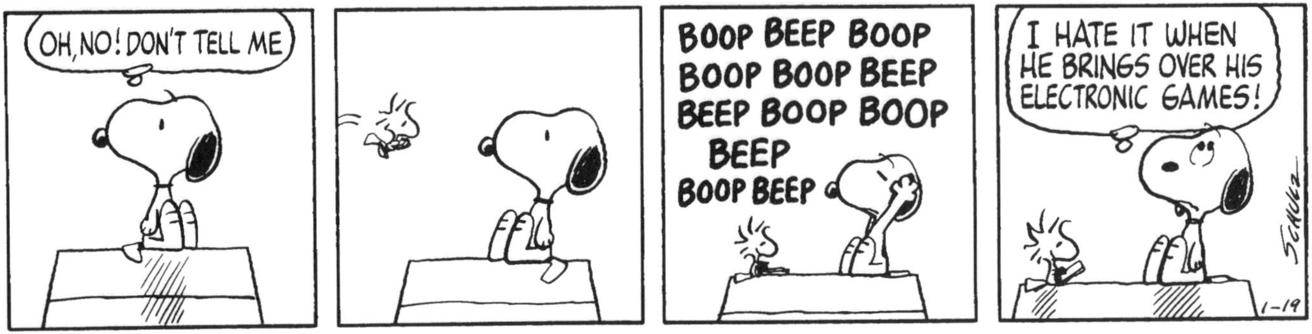
OH, NO! DON'T TELL ME
BOOP BEEP BOOP BOOP BOOP BEEP BEEP BOOP BOOP BEEP BOOP BEEP
I HATE IT WHEN HE BRINGS OVER HIS ELECTRONIC GAMES!
SCHULZ
1-19

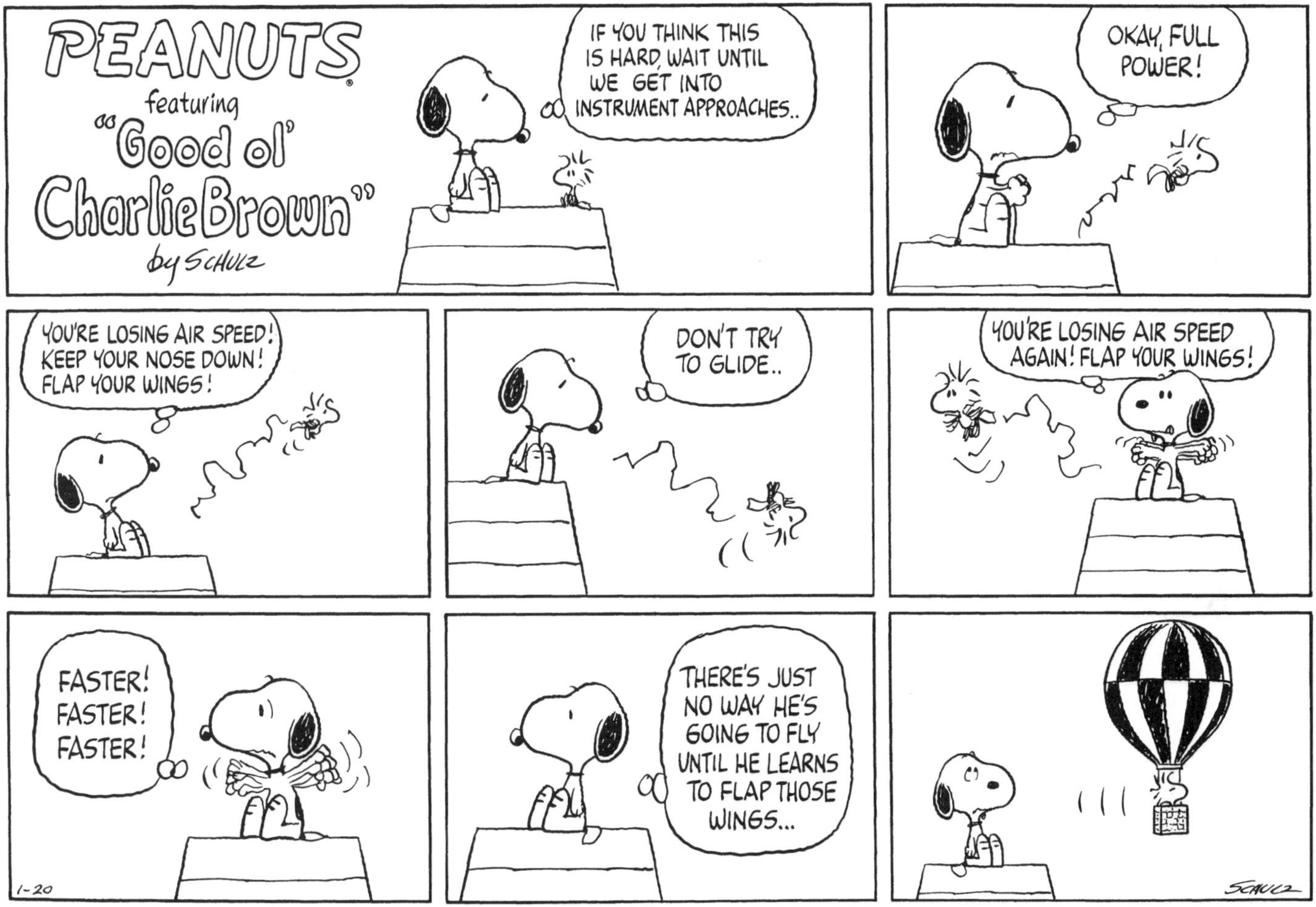
PEANUTS
featuring
"Good ol' Charlie Brown"
by SCHULZ
IF YOU THINK THIS IS HARD, WAIT UNTIL WE GET INTO INSTRUMENT APPROACHES..
OKAY, FULL POWER!
YOU'RE LOSING AIR SPEED! KEEP YOUR NOSE DOWN! FLAP YOUR WINGS!
DON'T TRY TO GLIDE..
YOU'RE LOSING AIR SPEED AGAIN! FLAP YOUR WINGS!
FASTER! FASTER! FASTER!
THERE'S JUST NO WAY HE'S GOING TO FLY UNTIL HE LEARNS TO FLAP THOSE WINGS...
1-20
SCHULZ

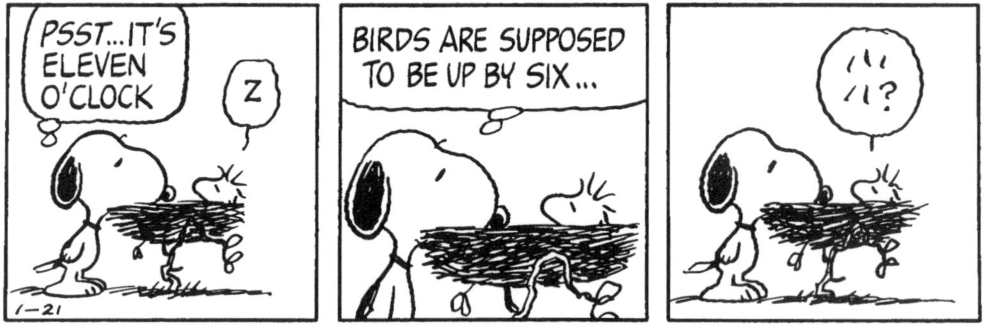
PSST...IT'S ELEVEN O'CLOCK
Z
1-21
BIRDS ARE SUPPOSED TO BE UP BY SIX...
?
HE HAS A POINT THERE...I DON'T KNOW WHO SAYS SO!
SCHULZ

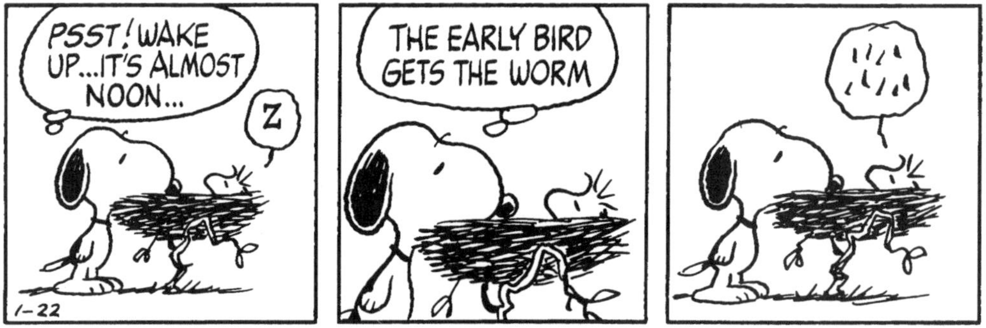
PSST! WAKE UP...IT'S ALMOST NOON...
Z
1-22
THE EARLY BIRD GETS THE WORM
THAT'S TRUE...YOU CAN GET PIZZA UNTIL MIDNIGHT!
SCHULZ

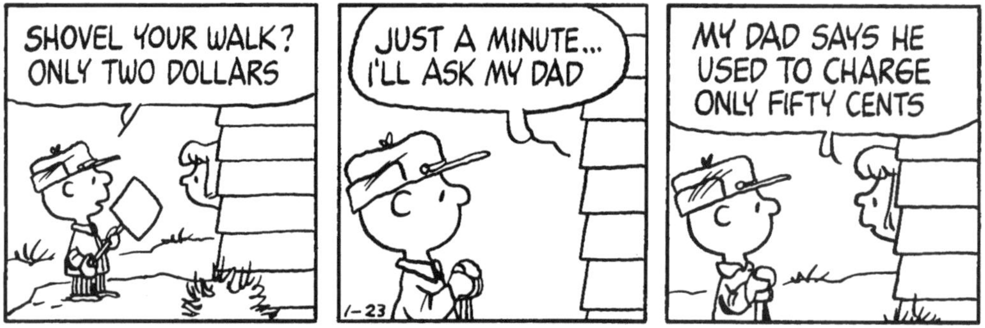
SHOVEL YOUR WALK? ONLY TWO DOLLARS
JUST A MINUTE... I'LL ASK MY DAD
1-23
MY DAD SAYS HE USED TO CHARGE ONLY FIFTY CENTS
DID THEY HAVE SIDEWALKS IN THOSE DAYS?
SCHULZ

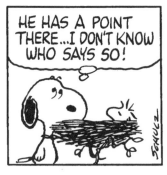

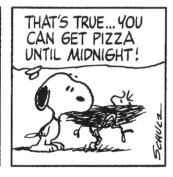

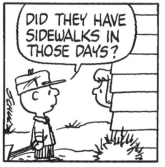

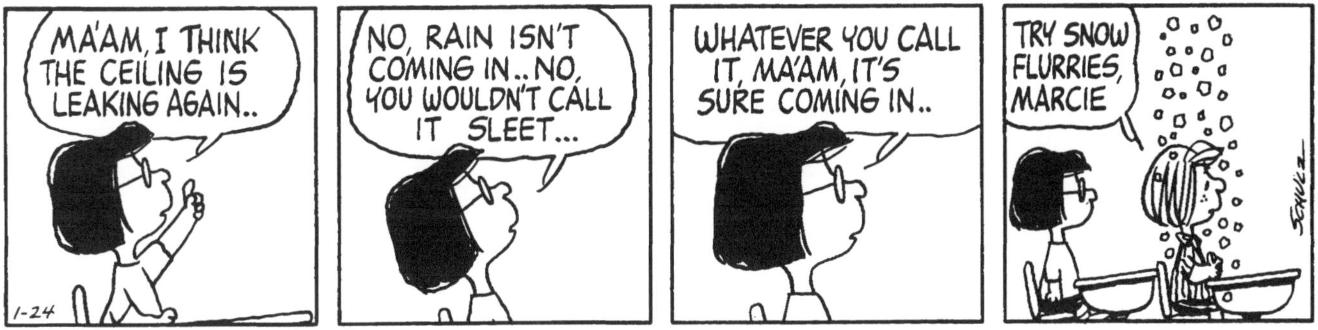
MA'AM, I THINK THE CEILING IS LEAKING AGAIN..
1-24
NO, RAIN ISN'T COMING IN..NO, YOU WOULDN'T CALL IT SLEET...
WHATEVER YOU CALL IT, MA'AM, IT'S SURE COMING IN..
TRY SNOW FLURRIES, MARCIE
SCHULZ

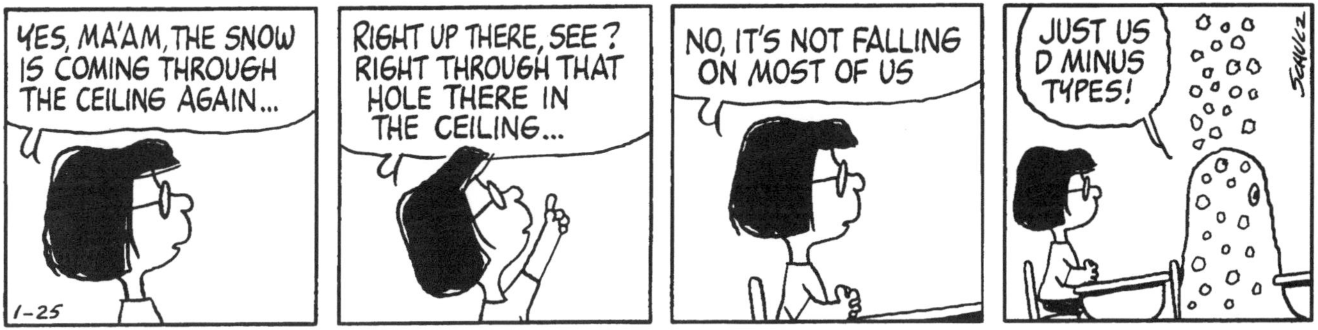
YES, MA'AM, THE SNOW IS COMING THROUGH THE CEILING AGAIN...
1-25
RIGHT UP THERE, SEE? RIGHT THROUGH THAT HOLE THERE IN THE CEILING...
NO, IT'S NOT FALLING ON MOST OF US
JUST US D MINUS TYPES!
SCHULZ

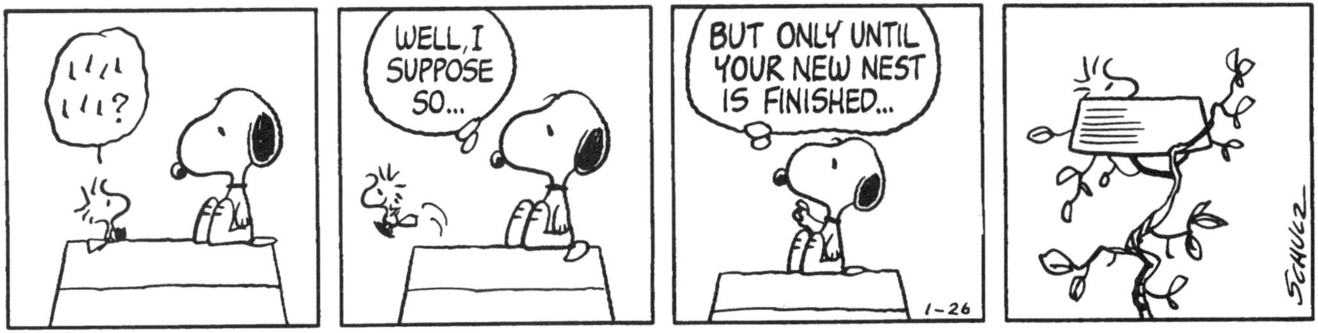
WELL, I SUPPOSE SO...
BUT ONLY UNTIL YOUR NEW NEST IS FINISHED...
1-26
SCHULZ

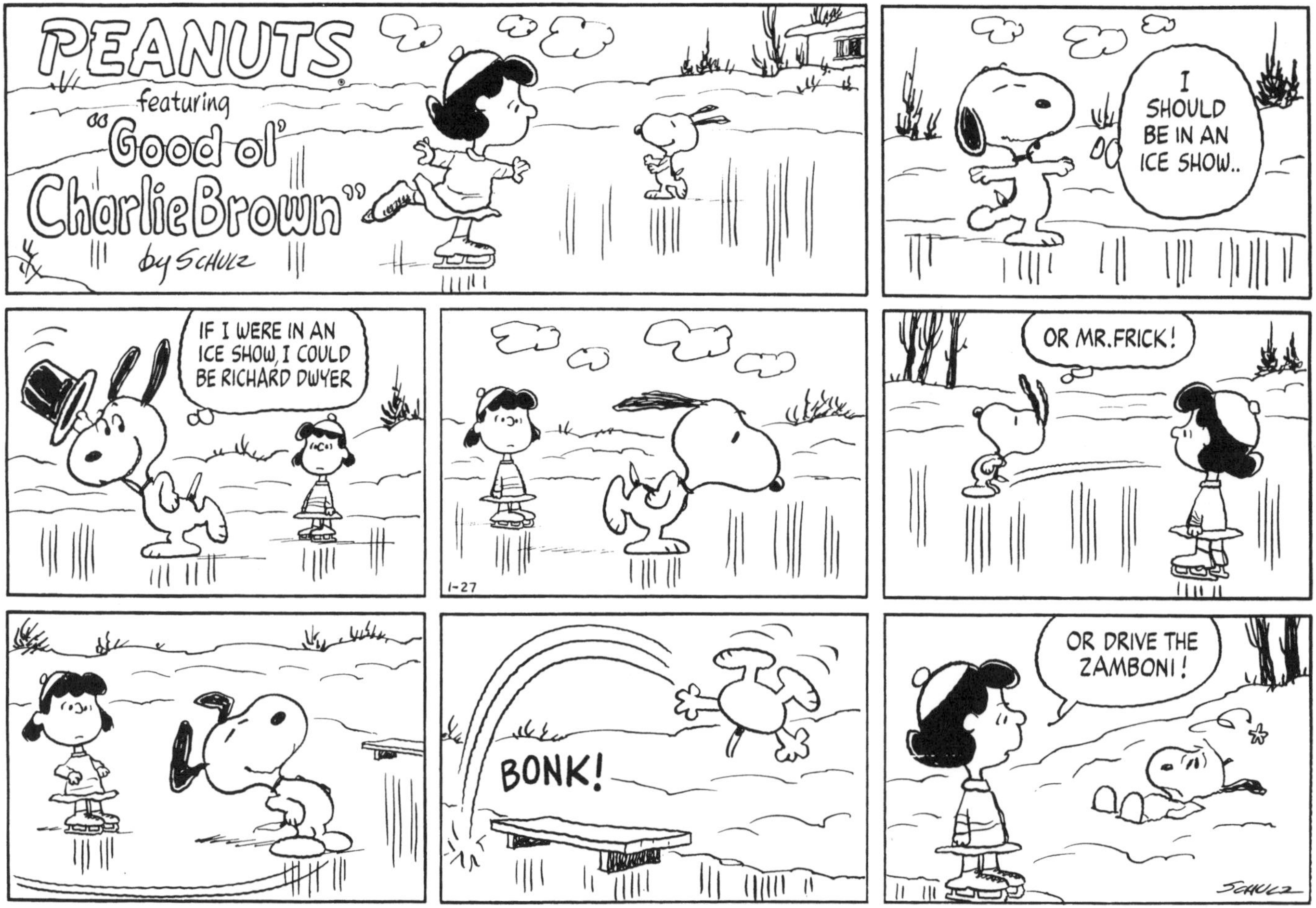
PEANUTS
featuring "Good ol' Charlie Brown"
by SCHULZ
I SHOULD BE IN AN ICE SHOW..
IF I WERE IN AN ICE SHOW, I COULD BE RICHARD DWYER
1-27
OR MR. FRICK!
BONK!
OR DRIVE THE ZAMBONI!
SCHULZ

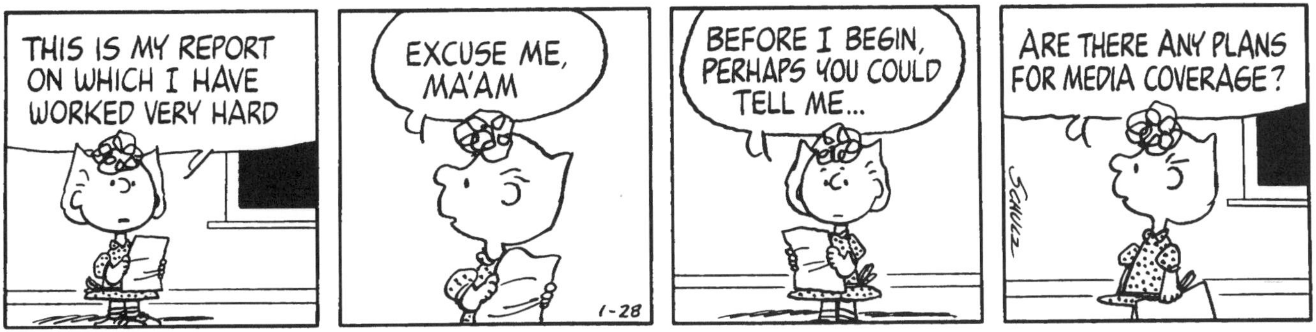
THIS IS MY REPORT ON WHICH I HAVE WORKED VERY HARD
EXCUSE ME, MA'AM
1-28
BEFORE I BEGIN, PERHAPS YOU COULD TELL ME...
ARE THERE ANY PLANS FOR MEDIA COVERAGE?
SCHULZ

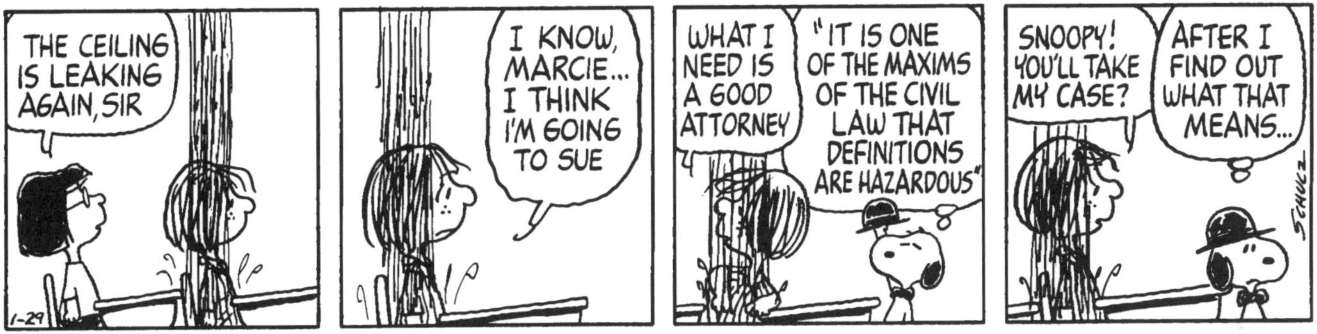
THE CEILING IS LEAKING AGAIN, SIR
1-29
I KNOW, MARCIE... I THINK I'M GOING TO SUE
WHAT I NEED IS A GOOD ATTORNEY
"IT IS ONE OF THE MAXIMS OF THE CIVIL LAW THAT DEFINITIONS ARE HAZARDOUS"
SNOOPY! YOU'LL TAKE MY CASE?
AFTER I FIND OUT WHAT THAT MEANS...
SCHULZ

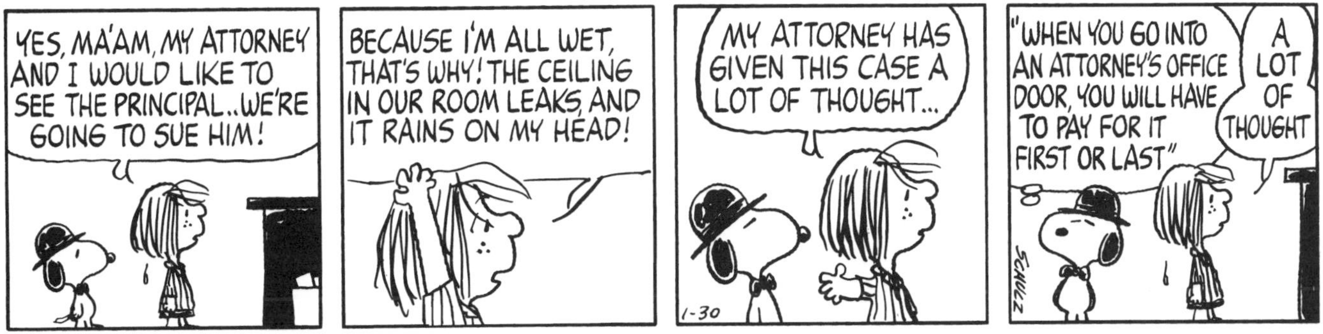
YES, MA'AM, MY ATTORNEY AND I WOULD LIKE TO SEE THE PRINCIPAL..WE'RE GOING TO SUE HIM!
BECAUSE I'M ALL WET, THAT'S WHY! THE CEILING IN OUR ROOM LEAKS, AND IT RAINS ON MY HEAD!
MY ATTORNEY HAS GIVEN THIS CASE A LOT OF THOUGHT...
1-30
"WHEN YOU GO INTO AN ATTORNEY'S OFFICE DOOR, YOU WILL HAVE TO PAY FOR IT FIRST OR LAST"
A LOT OF THOUGHT
SCHULZ

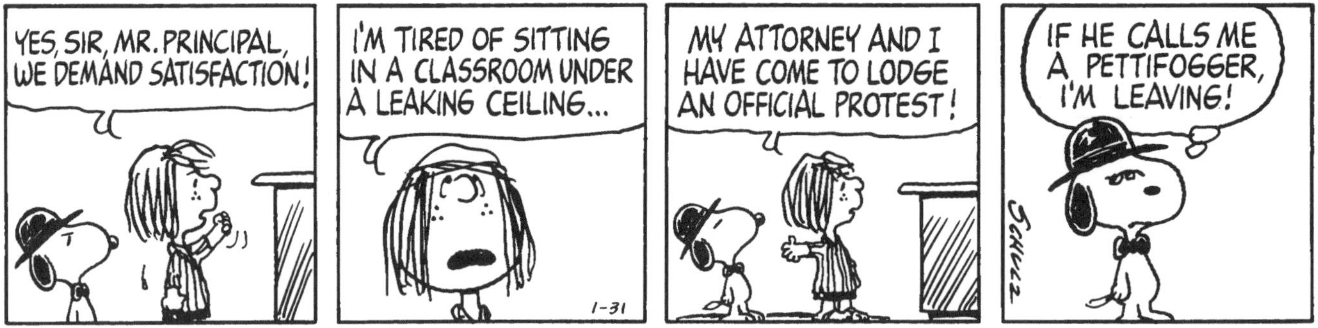
YES, SIR, MR. PRINCIPAL, WE DEMAND SATISFACTION!
I'M TIRED OF SITTING IN A CLASSROOM UNDER A LEAKING CEILING...
1-31
MY ATTORNEY AND I HAVE COME TO LODGE AN OFFICIAL PROTEST!
IF HE CALLS ME A PETTIFOGGER, I'M LEAVING!
SCHULZ

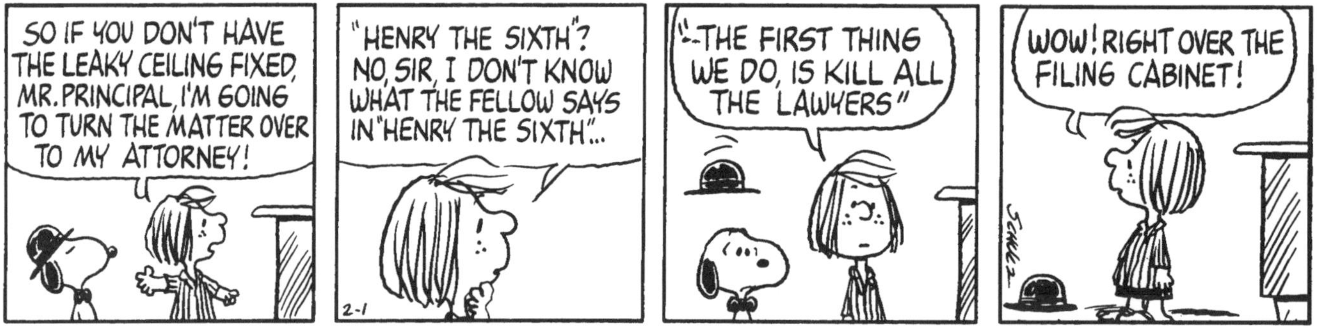
SO IF YOU DON'T HAVE THE LEAKY CEILING FIXED, MR. PRINCIPAL, I'M GOING TO TURN THE MATTER OVER TO MY ATTORNEY!
"HENRY THE SIXTH"? NO, SIR, I DON'T KNOW WHAT THE FELLOW SAYS IN "HENRY THE SIXTH"...
2-1
"...THE FIRST THING WE DO, IS KILL ALL THE LAWYERS"
WOW! RIGHT OVER THE FILING CABINET!
SCHULZ

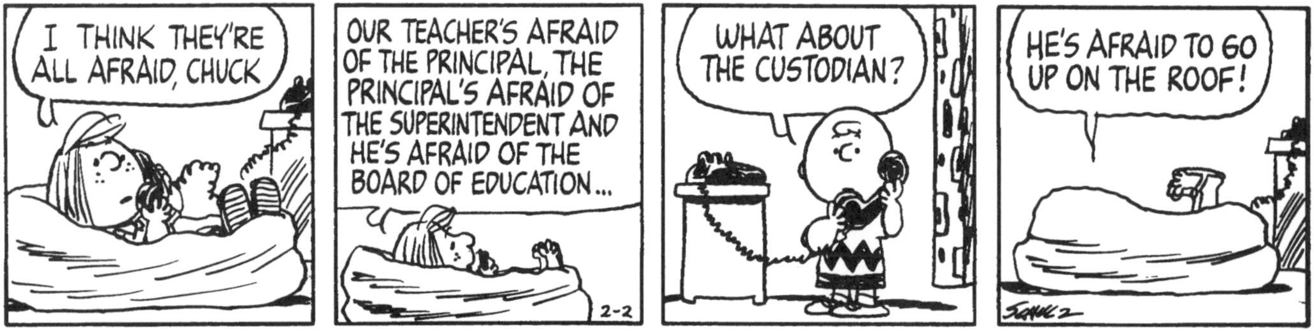
I THINK THEY'RE ALL AFRAID, CHUCK
OUR TEACHER'S AFRAID OF THE PRINCIPAL, THE PRINCIPAL'S AFRAID OF THE SUPERINTENDENT AND HE'S AFRAID OF THE BOARD OF EDUCATION...
2-2
WHAT ABOUT THE CUSTODIAN?
HE'S AFRAID TO GO UP ON THE ROOF!
SCHULZ

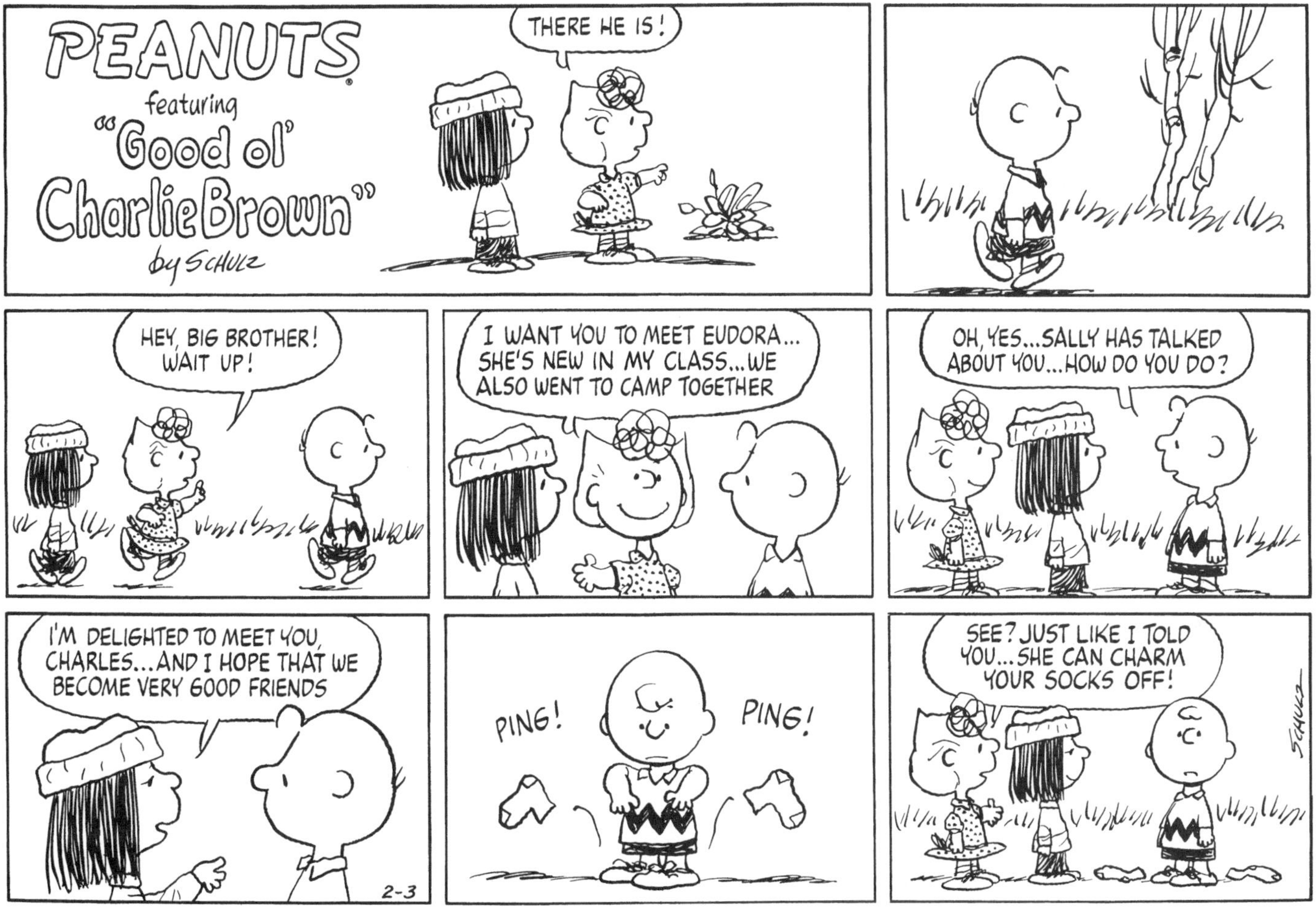
PEANUTS
featuring "Good ol' CharlieBrown"
by SCHULZ
THERE HE IS!
HEY, BIG BROTHER! WAIT UP!
I WANT YOU TO MEET EUDORA... SHE'S NEW IN MY CLASS...WE ALSO WENT TO CAMP TOGETHER
OH, YES...SALLY HAS TALKED ABOUT YOU...HOW DO YOU DO?
I'M DELIGHTED TO MEET YOU, CHARLES...AND I HOPE THAT WE BECOME VERY GOOD FRIENDS
2-3
PING!
PING!
SEE? JUST LIKE I TOLD YOU...SHE CAN CHARM YOUR SOCKS OFF!
SCHULZ

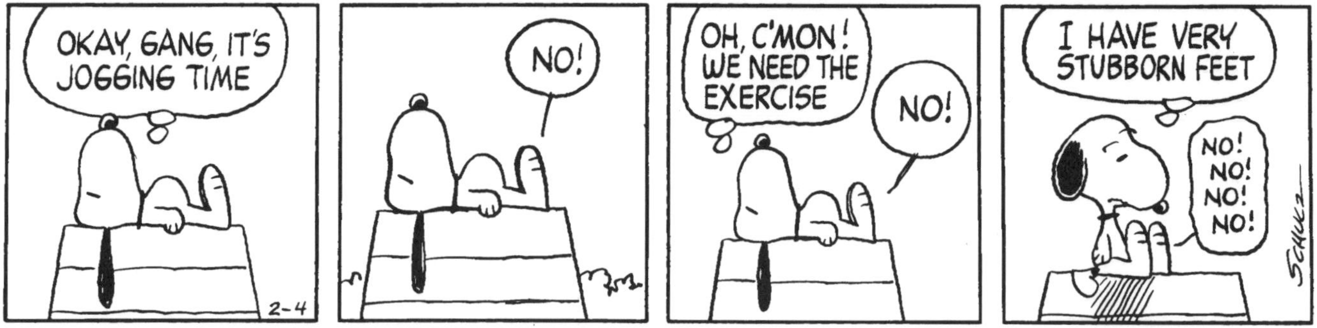
OKAY, GANG, IT'S JOGGING TIME
NO!
OH, C'MON! WE NEED THE EXERCISE
NO!
I HAVE VERY STUBBORN FEET
NO! NO! NO! NO!

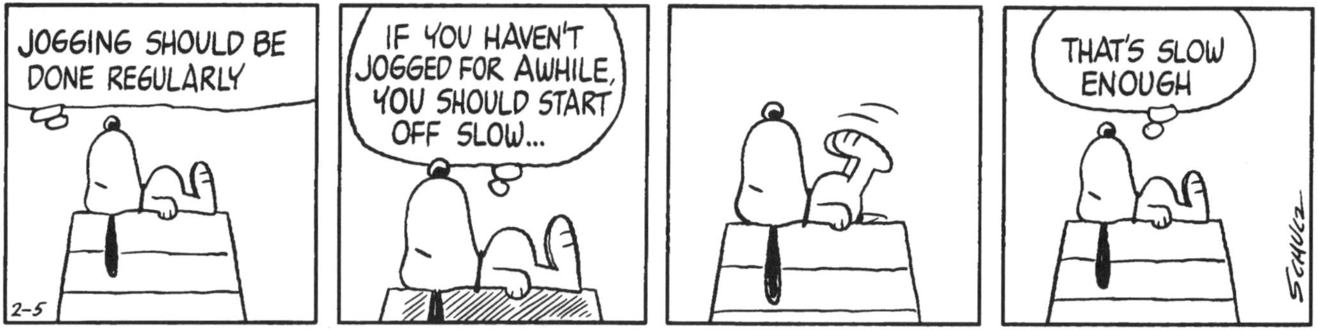
JOGGING SHOULD BE DONE REGULARLY
IF YOU HAVEN'T JOGGED FOR AWHILE, YOU SHOULD START OFF SLOW...
THAT'S SLOW ENOUGH

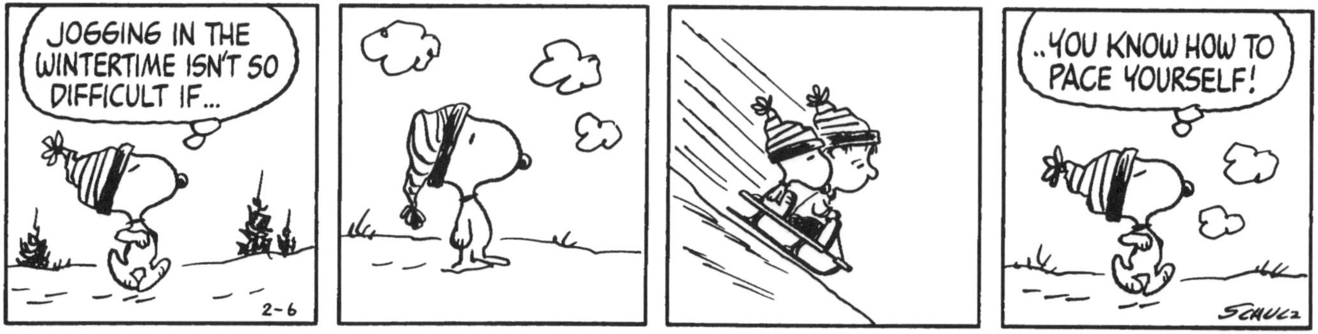
JOGGING IN THE WINTERTIME ISN'T SO DIFFICULT IF...
..YOU KNOW HOW TO PACE YOURSELF!

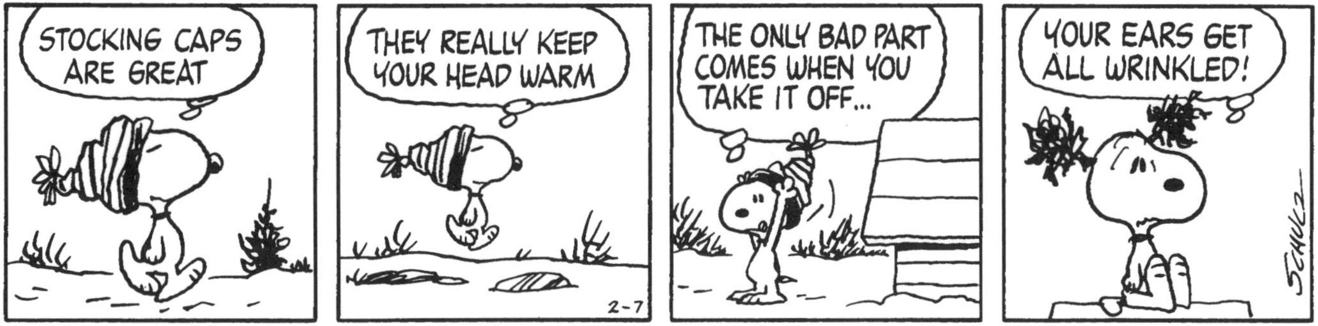
STOCKING CAPS ARE GREAT
THEY REALLY KEEP YOUR HEAD WARM
2-7
THE ONLY BAD PART COMES WHEN YOU TAKE IT OFF...
YOUR EARS GET ALL WRINKLED!
SCHULZ

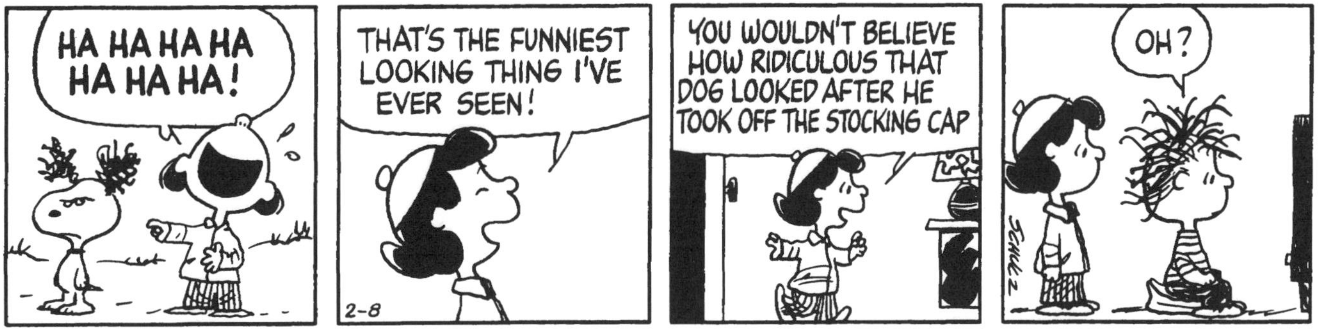
HA HA HA HA HA HA HA!
THAT'S THE FUNNIEST LOOKING THING I'VE EVER SEEN!
2-8
YOU WOULDN'T BELIEVE HOW RIDICULOUS THAT DOG LOOKED AFTER HE TOOK OFF THE STOCKING CAP
SCHULZ
OH?

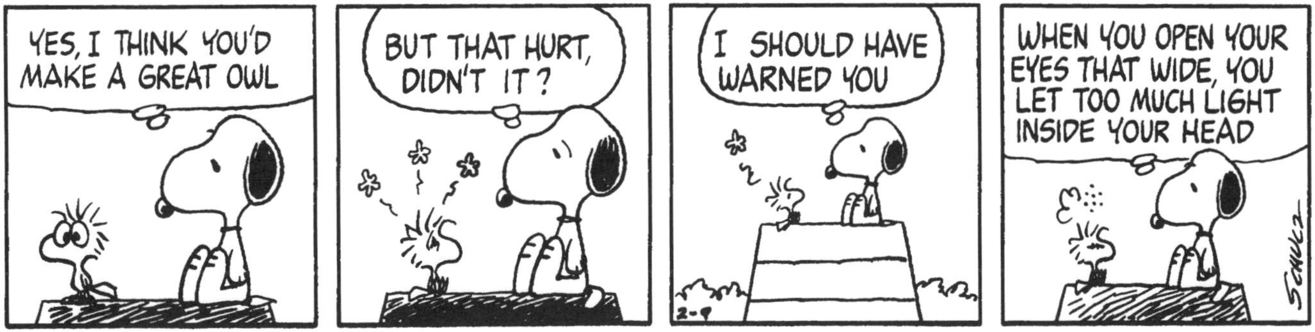
YES, I THINK YOU'D MAKE A GREAT OWL
BUT THAT HURT, DIDN'T IT?
I SHOULD HAVE WARNED YOU
2-9
WHEN YOU OPEN YOUR EYES THAT WIDE, YOU LET TOO MUCH LIGHT INSIDE YOUR HEAD
SCHULZ

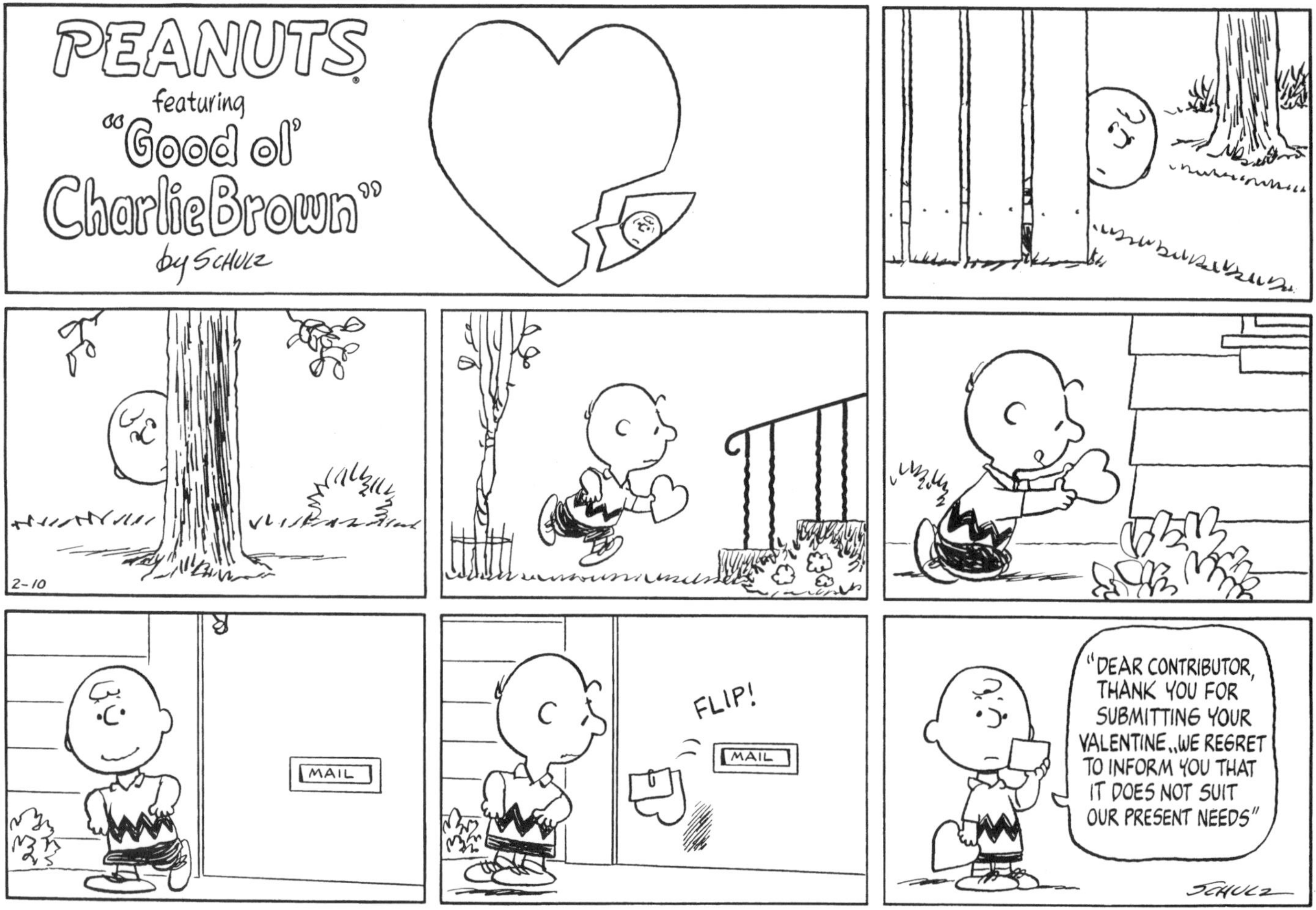
PEANUTS
featuring
"Good ol' CharlieBrown"
by SCHULZ
2-10
FLIP!
MAIL
MAIL
"DEAR CONTRIBUTOR, THANK YOU FOR SUBMITTING YOUR VALENTINE.. WE REGRET TO INFORM YOU THAT IT DOES NOT SUIT OUR PRESENT NEEDS"
SCHULZ

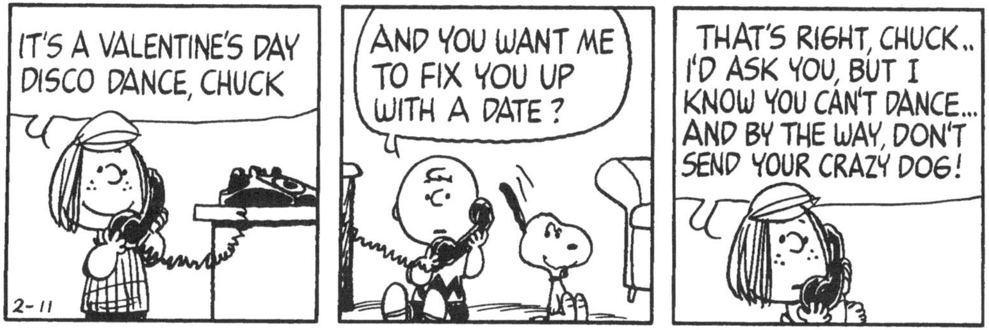
IT'S A VALENTINE'S DAY DISCO DANCE, CHUCK
2-11
AND YOU WANT ME TO FIX YOU UP WITH A DATE ?
THAT'S RIGHT, CHUCK.. I'D ASK YOU, BUT I KNOW YOU CAN'T DANCE... AND BY THE WAY, DON'T SEND YOUR CRAZY DOG!
RATS! I LOVE DISCO!

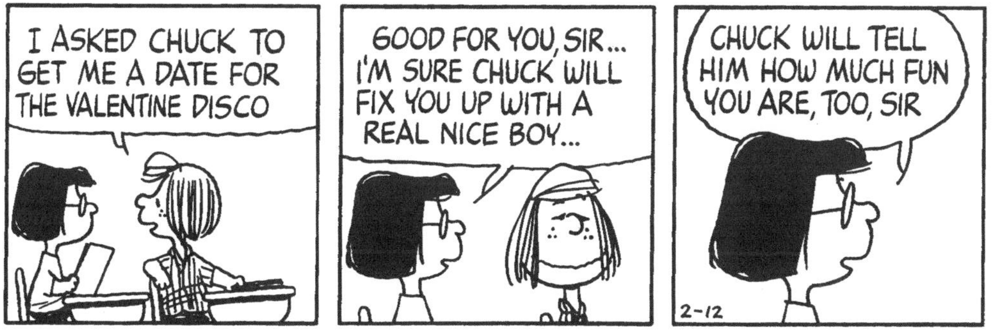
I ASKED CHUCK TO GET ME A DATE FOR THE VALENTINE DISCO
GOOD FOR YOU, SIR... I'M SURE CHUCK WILL FIX YOU UP WITH A REAL NICE BOY...
CHUCK WILL TELL HIM HOW MUCH FUN YOU ARE, TOO, SIR
2-12
YOU HAVE TO BE A LOT OF FUN, MARCIE, WHEN YOU HAVE A BIG NOSE!

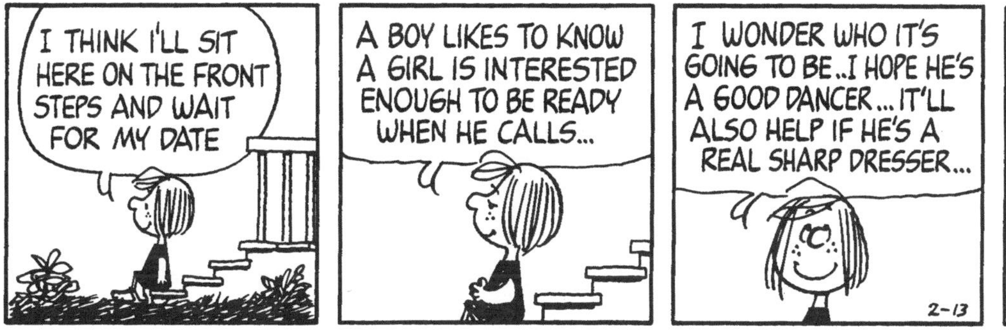
I THINK I'LL SIT HERE ON THE FRONT STEPS AND WAIT FOR MY DATE
A BOY LIKES TO KNOW A GIRL IS INTERESTED ENOUGH TO BE READY WHEN HE CALLS...
I WONDER WHO IT'S GOING TO BE..I HOPE HE'S A GOOD DANCER... IT'LL ALSO HELP IF HE'S A REAL SHARP DRESSER...
2-13
HI, MY NAME IS PIG-PEN
AAUGH!

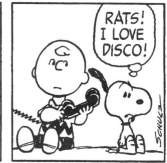

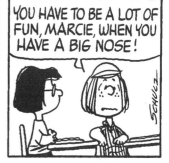

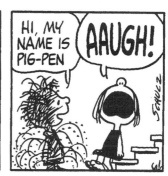

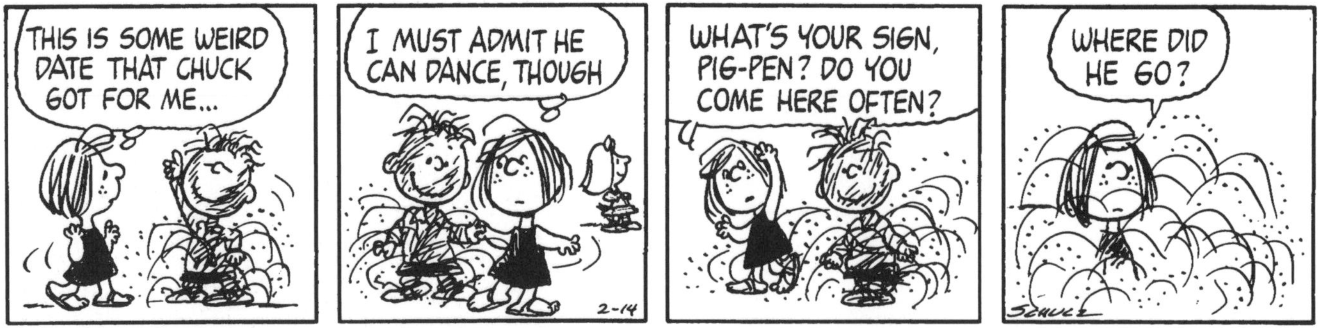
THIS IS SOME WEIRD DATE THAT CHUCK GOT FOR ME...
I MUST ADMIT HE CAN DANCE, THOUGH
2-14
WHAT'S YOUR SIGN, PIG-PEN? DO YOU COME HERE OFTEN?
WHERE DID HE GO?
SCHULZ

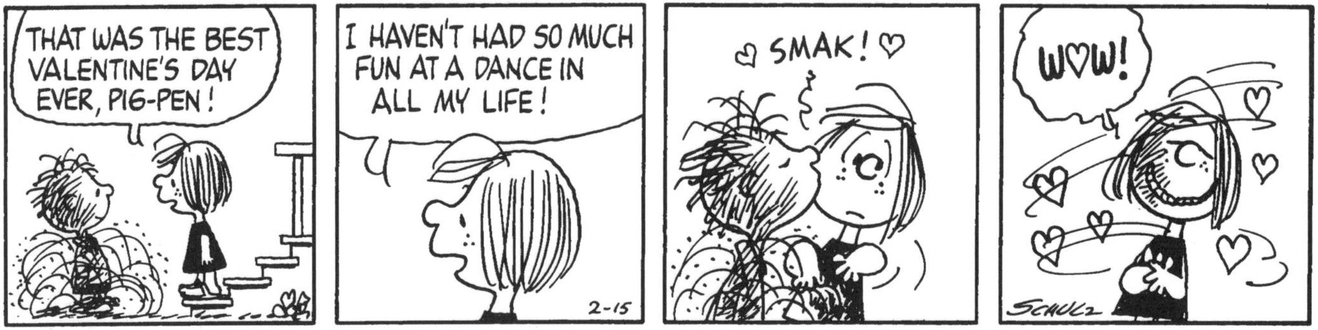
THAT WAS THE BEST VALENTINE'S DAY EVER, PIG-PEN!
I HAVEN'T HAD SO MUCH FUN AT A DANCE IN ALL MY LIFE!
2-15
SMAK!
WOW!
SCHULZ

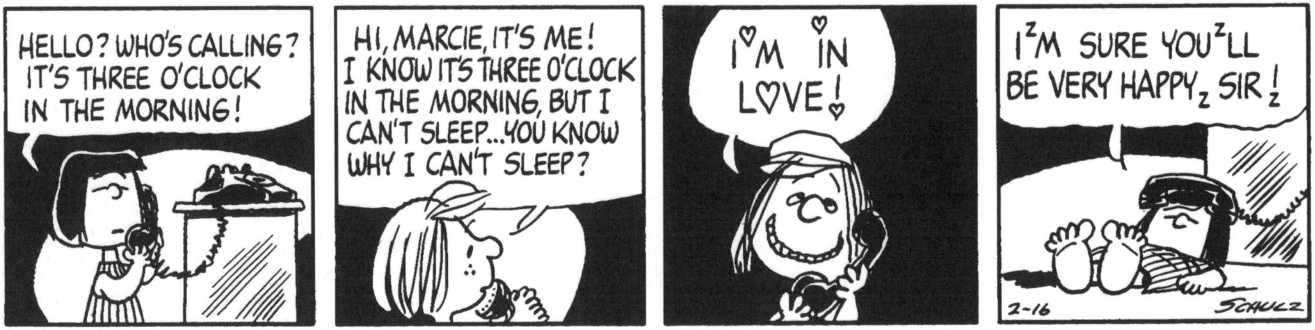
HELLO? WHO'S CALLING? IT'S THREE O'CLOCK IN THE MORNING!
HI, MARCIE, IT'S ME! I KNOW IT'S THREE O'CLOCK IN THE MORNING, BUT I CAN'T SLEEP...YOU KNOW WHY I CAN'T SLEEP?
I'M IN LOVE!
I'M SURE YOU'LL BE VERY HAPPY, SIR!
2-16
SCHULZ

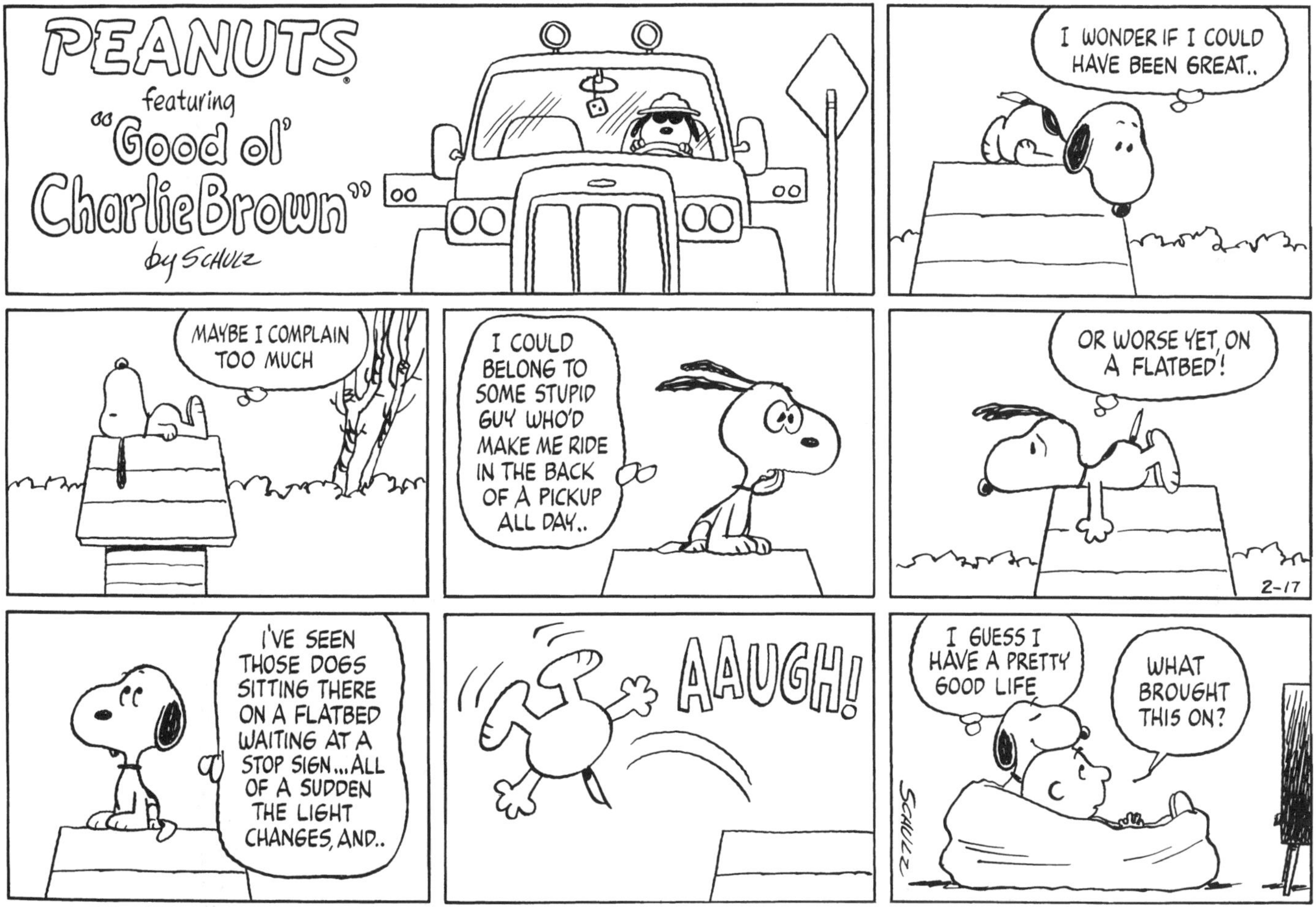
PEANUTS
featuring "Good ol' Charlie Brown"
by SCHULZ
I WONDER IF I COULD HAVE BEEN GREAT..
MAYBE I COMPLAIN TOO MUCH
I COULD BELONG TO SOME STUPID GUY WHO'D MAKE ME RIDE IN THE BACK OF A PICKUP ALL DAY..
OR WORSE YET, ON A FLATBED!
2-17
I'VE SEEN THOSE DOGS SITTING THERE ON A FLATBED WAITING AT A STOP SIGN...ALL OF A SUDDEN THE LIGHT CHANGES, AND..
AAUGH!
I GUESS I HAVE A PRETTY GOOD LIFE
WHAT BROUGHT THIS ON?
SCHULZ

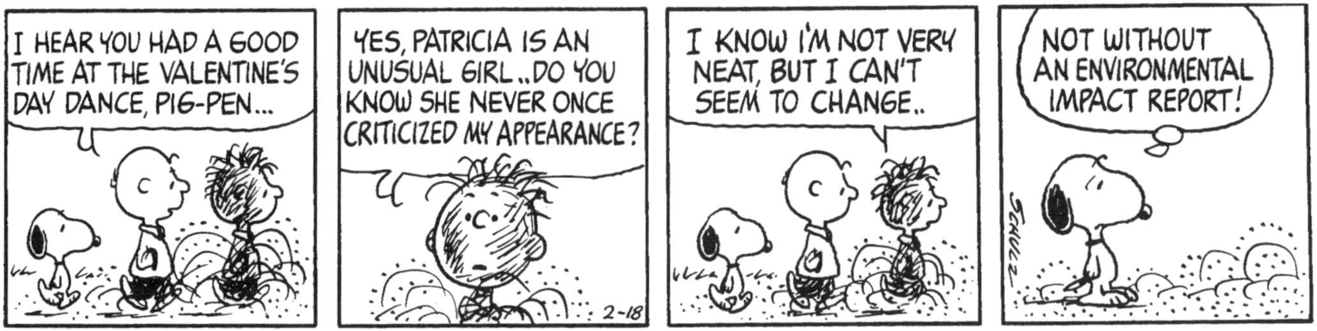
I HEAR YOU HAD A GOOD TIME AT THE VALENTINE'S DAY DANCE, PIG-PEN...
YES, PATRICIA IS AN UNUSUAL GIRL..DO YOU KNOW SHE NEVER ONCE CRITICIZED MY APPEARANCE?
2-18
I KNOW I'M NOT VERY NEAT, BUT I CAN'T SEEM TO CHANGE..
NOT WITHOUT AN ENVIRONMENTAL IMPACT REPORT!
SCHULZ

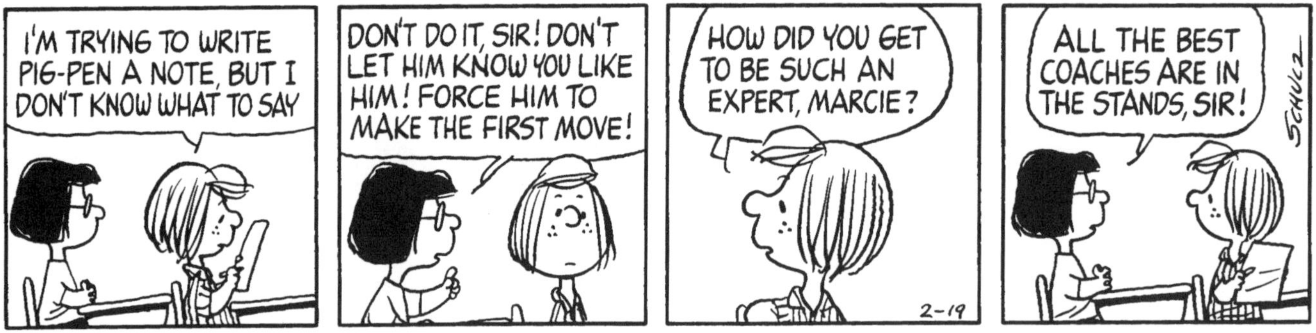
I'M TRYING TO WRITE PIG-PEN A NOTE, BUT I DON'T KNOW WHAT TO SAY
DON'T DO IT, SIR! DON'T LET HIM KNOW YOU LIKE HIM! FORCE HIM TO MAKE THE FIRST MOVE!
HOW DID YOU GET TO BE SUCH AN EXPERT, MARCIE?
2-19
ALL THE BEST COACHES ARE IN THE STANDS, SIR!
SCHULZ

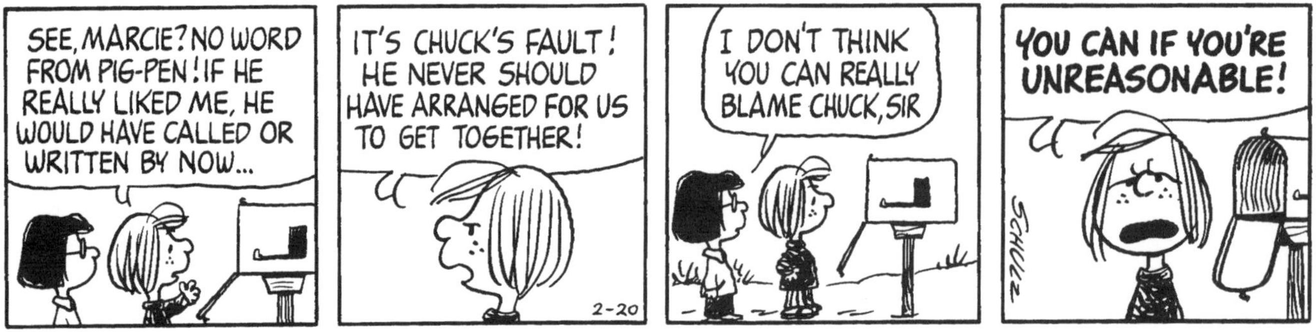
SEE, MARCIE? NO WORD FROM PIG-PEN! IF HE REALLY LIKED ME, HE WOULD HAVE CALLED OR WRITTEN BY NOW...
IT'S CHUCK'S FAULT! HE NEVER SHOULD HAVE ARRANGED FOR US TO GET TOGETHER!
2-20
I DON'T THINK YOU CAN REALLY BLAME CHUCK, SIR
SCHULZ
YOU CAN IF YOU'RE UNREASONABLE!

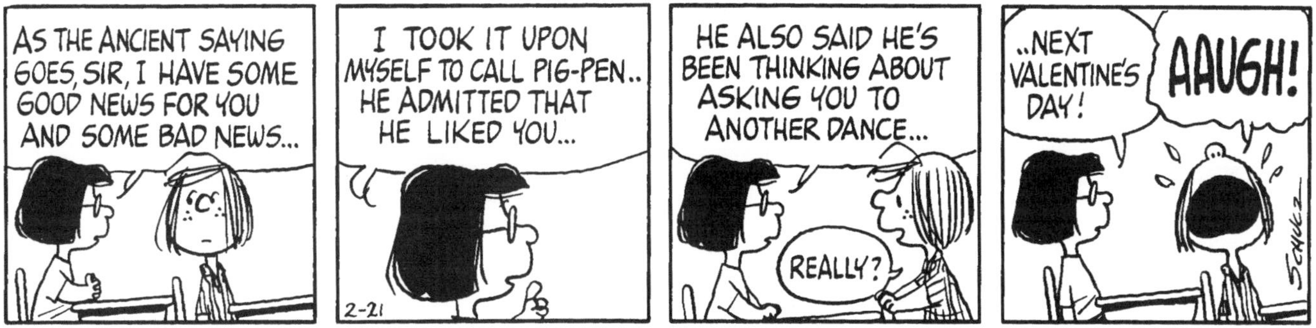
AS THE ANCIENT SAYING GOES, SIR, I HAVE SOME GOOD NEWS FOR YOU AND SOME BAD NEWS...
I TOOK IT UPON MYSELF TO CALL PIG-PEN.. HE ADMITTED THAT HE LIKED YOU...
2-21
HE ALSO SAID HE'S BEEN THINKING ABOUT ASKING YOU TO ANOTHER DANCE...
REALLY?
..NEXT VALENTINE'S DAY!
AAUGH!
SCHULZ

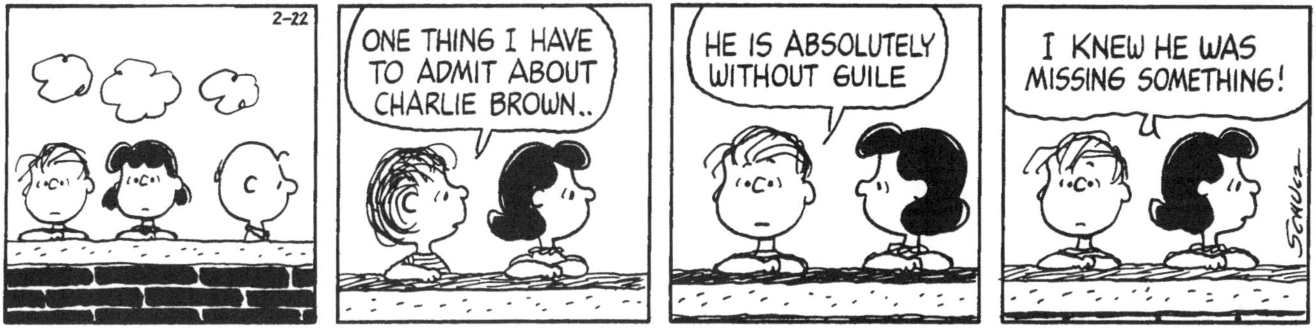
2-22
ONE THING I HAVE TO ADMIT ABOUT CHARLIE BROWN..
HE IS ABSOLUTELY WITHOUT GUILE
I KNEW HE WAS MISSING SOMETHING!
SCHULZ

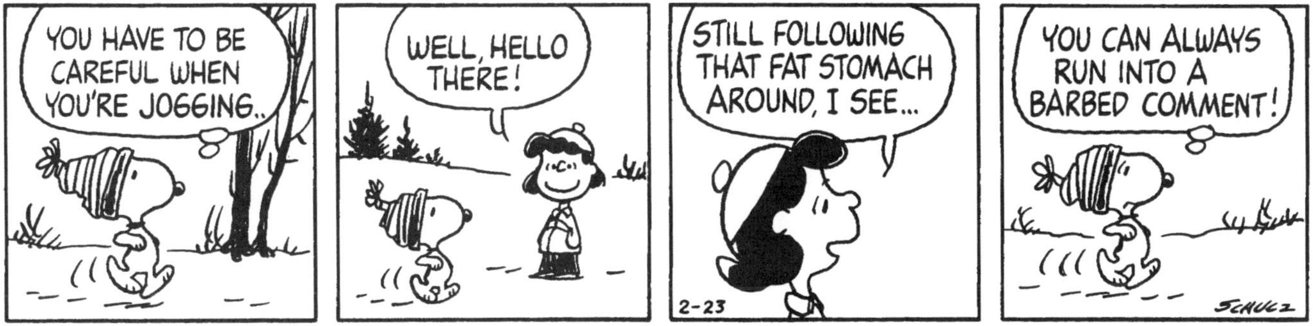
YOU HAVE TO BE CAREFUL WHEN YOU'RE JOGGING..
WELL, HELLO THERE!
STILL FOLLOWING THAT FAT STOMACH AROUND, I SEE...
2-23
YOU CAN ALWAYS RUN INTO A BARBED COMMENT!
SCHULZ

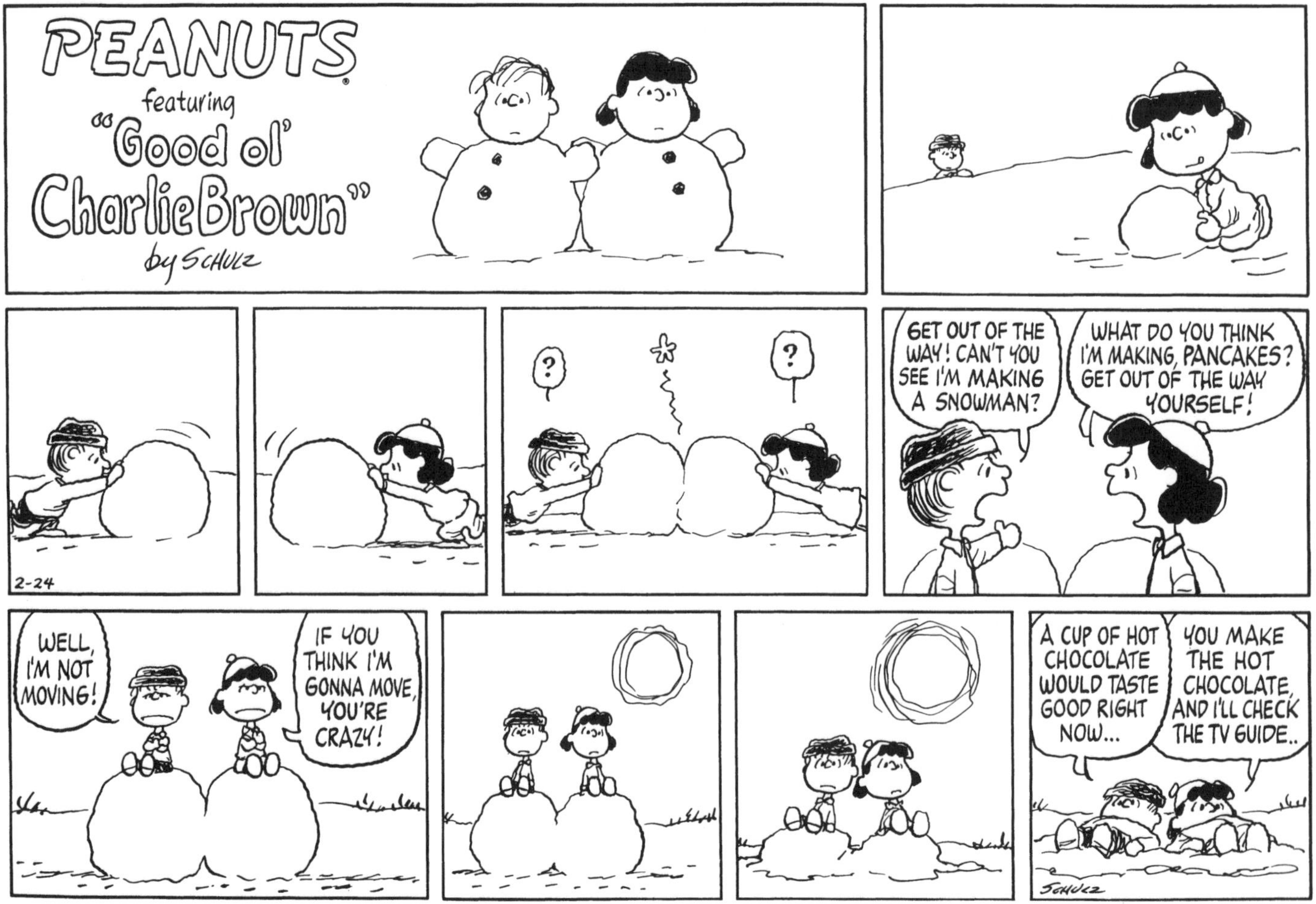
PEANUTS
featuring
"Good ol' Charlie Brown"
by SCHULZ
2-24
?
?
GET OUT OF THE WAY! CAN'T YOU SEE I'M MAKING A SNOWMAN?
WHAT DO YOU THINK I'M MAKING, PANCAKES? GET OUT OF THE WAY YOURSELF!
WELL, I'M NOT MOVING!
IF YOU THINK I'M GONNA MOVE, YOU'RE CRAZY!
A CUP OF HOT CHOCOLATE WOULD TASTE GOOD RIGHT NOW...
YOU MAKE THE HOT CHOCOLATE, AND I'LL CHECK THE TV GUIDE..
SCHULZ

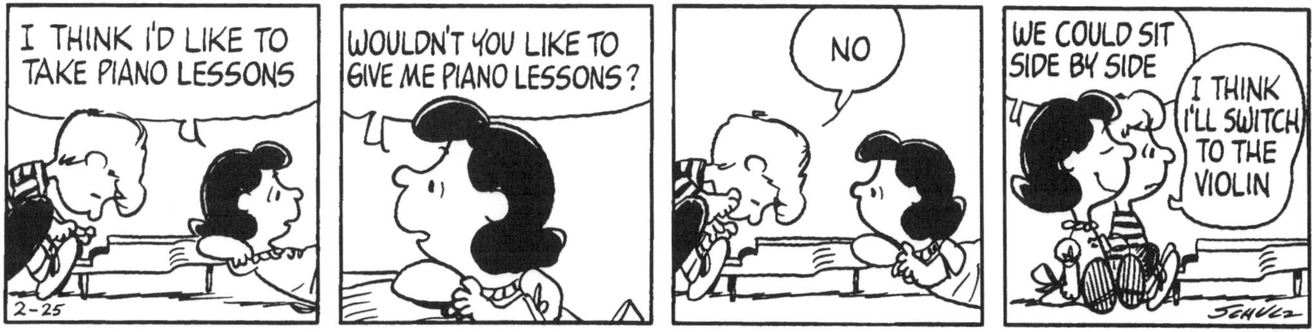
I THINK I'D LIKE TO TAKE PIANO LESSONS
WOULDN'T YOU LIKE TO GIVE ME PIANO LESSONS?
NO
WE COULD SIT SIDE BY SIDE
I THINK I'LL SWITCH TO THE VIOLIN
2-25
SCHULZ

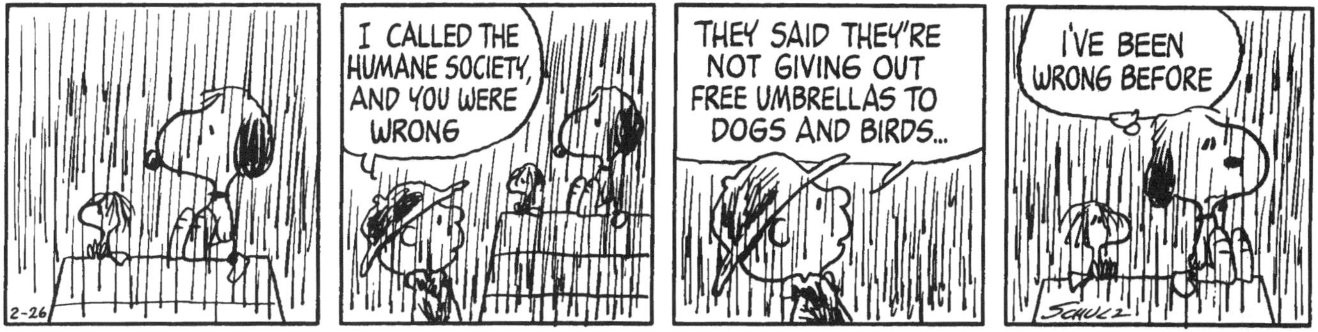
2-26
I CALLED THE HUMANE SOCIETY, AND YOU WERE WRONG
THEY SAID THEY'RE NOT GIVING OUT FREE UMBRELLAS TO DOGS AND BIRDS...
I'VE BEEN WRONG BEFORE
SCHULZ

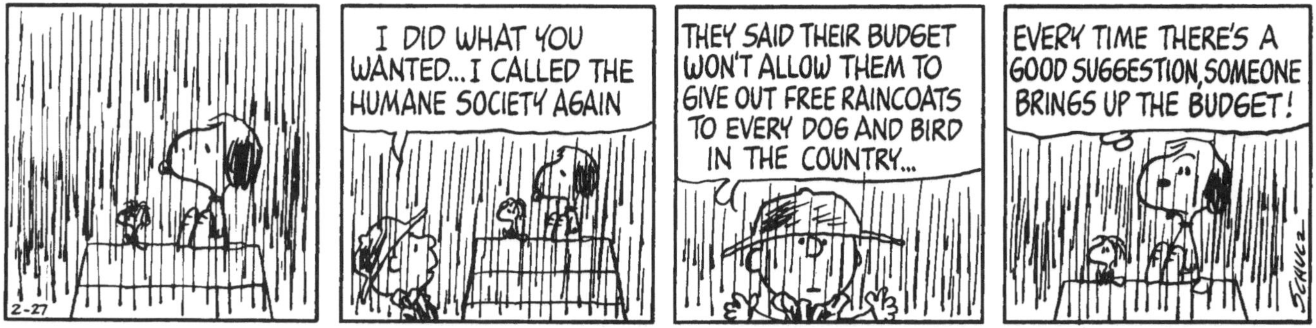
2-27
I DID WHAT YOU WANTED...I CALLED THE HUMANE SOCIETY AGAIN
THEY SAID THEIR BUDGET WON'T ALLOW THEM TO GIVE OUT FREE RAINCOATS TO EVERY DOG AND BIRD IN THE COUNTRY...
EVERY TIME THERE'S A GOOD SUGGESTION, SOMEONE BRINGS UP THE BUDGET!
SCHULZ

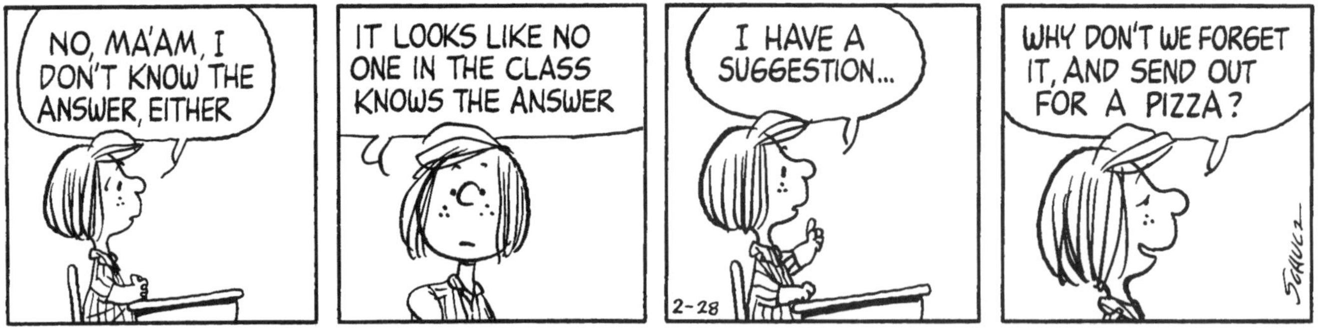
NO, MA'AM, I DON'T KNOW THE ANSWER, EITHER
IT LOOKS LIKE NO ONE IN THE CLASS KNOWS THE ANSWER
I HAVE A SUGGESTION...
WHY DON'T WE FORGET IT, AND SEND OUT FOR A PIZZA?

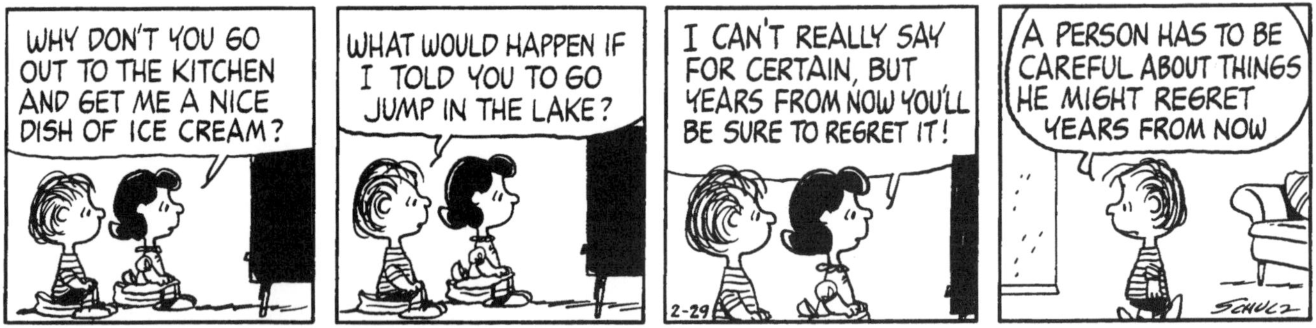
WHY DON'T YOU GO OUT TO THE KITCHEN AND GET ME A NICE DISH OF ICE CREAM?
WHAT WOULD HAPPEN IF I TOLD YOU TO GO JUMP IN THE LAKE?
I CAN'T REALLY SAY FOR CERTAIN, BUT YEARS FROM NOW YOU'LL BE SURE TO REGRET IT!
A PERSON HAS TO BE CAREFUL ABOUT THINGS HE MIGHT REGRET YEARS FROM NOW

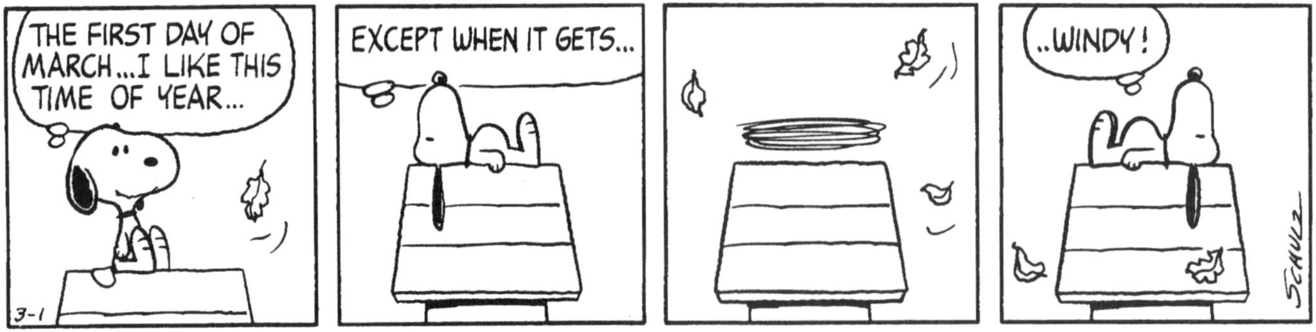
THE FIRST DAY OF MARCH...I LIKE THIS TIME OF YEAR...
EXCEPT WHEN IT GETS...
..WINDY!

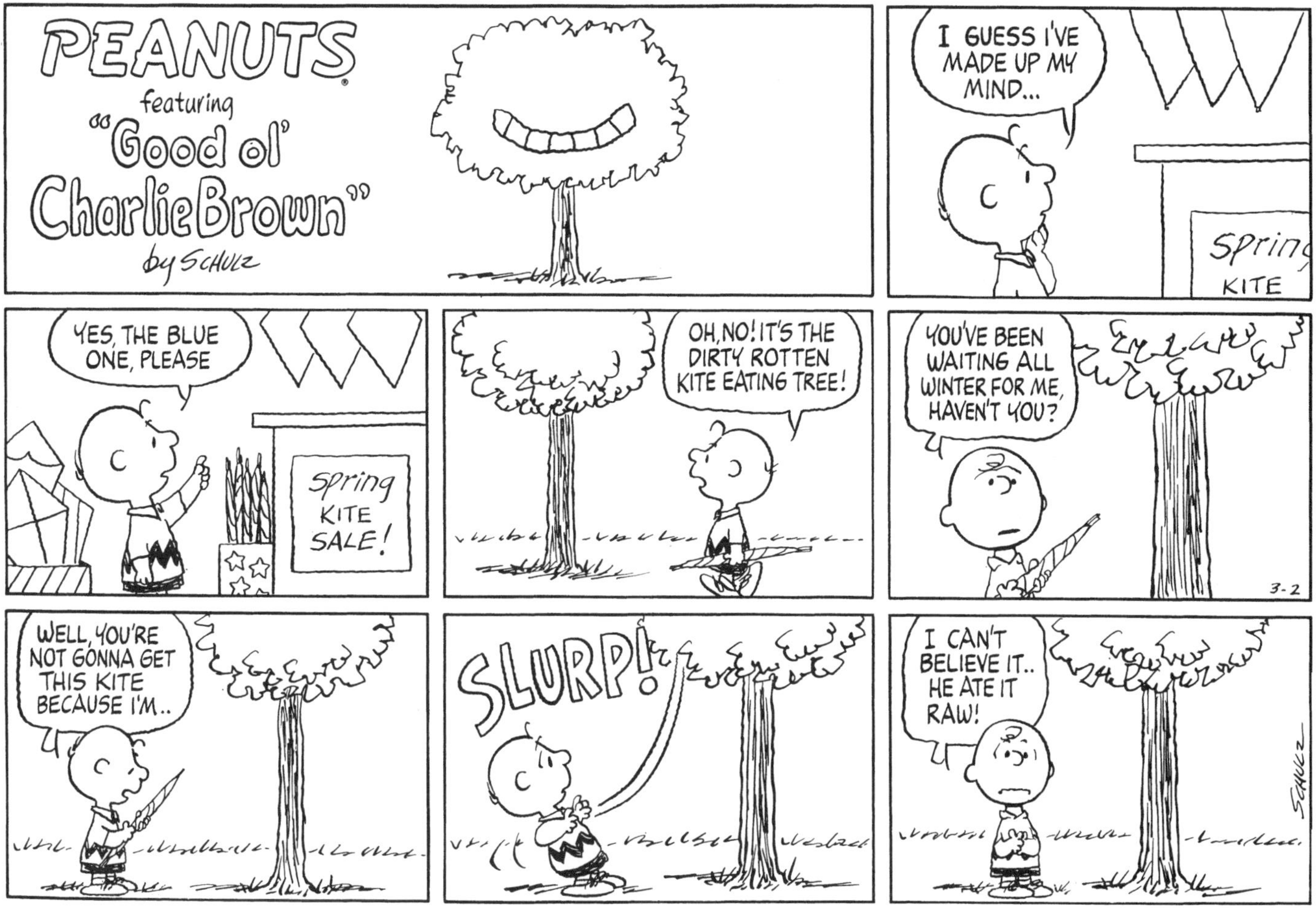
PEANUTS
featuring "Good ol' Charlie Brown"
by SCHULZ
I GUESS I'VE MADE UP MY MIND...
Spring KITE
YES, THE BLUE ONE, PLEASE
Spring KITE SALE!
OH, NO! IT'S THE DIRTY ROTTEN KITE EATING TREE!
YOU'VE BEEN WAITING ALL WINTER FOR ME, HAVEN'T YOU?
3-2
WELL, YOU'RE NOT GONNA GET THIS KITE BECAUSE I'M..
SLURP!
I CAN'T BELIEVE IT.. HE ATE IT RAW!
SCHULZ

Panel 1: YOU AND PEPPERMINT PATTY HAVE BEEN SEEING A LOT OF EACH OTHER, HAVEN'T YOU?

Panel 2: YES, I THINK WHAT I LIKE ABOUT HER IS THAT SHE HASN'T TRIED TO CHANGE ME

Panel 3 (3-3): (no dialogue)

Panel 4: I WONDER IF I COULD CHANGE HIM...

Panel 5: MARCIE, I CAME OVER BECAUSE I HAD TO TELL YOU THE CUTE THING PIG-PEN SAID TO ME

Panel 6 (3-4): I'M NOT INTERESTED IN YOUR ROMANCE, SIR, AND I'M VERY BUSY PRACTICING THE ORGAN

Panel 7: (no dialogue)

Panel 8: MAY ALL YOUR HEMIDEMISEMIQUAVERS BE FLAT!!!

Panel 9: HEY, LUCILLE, YOU WANNA HEAR THE CUTE THING THAT PIG-PEN SAID TO ME YESTERDAY?

Panel 10 (3-5): THIS WAS CUTE..THIS WAS REALLY CUTE...

Panel 11: HE......

Panel 12: RATS!

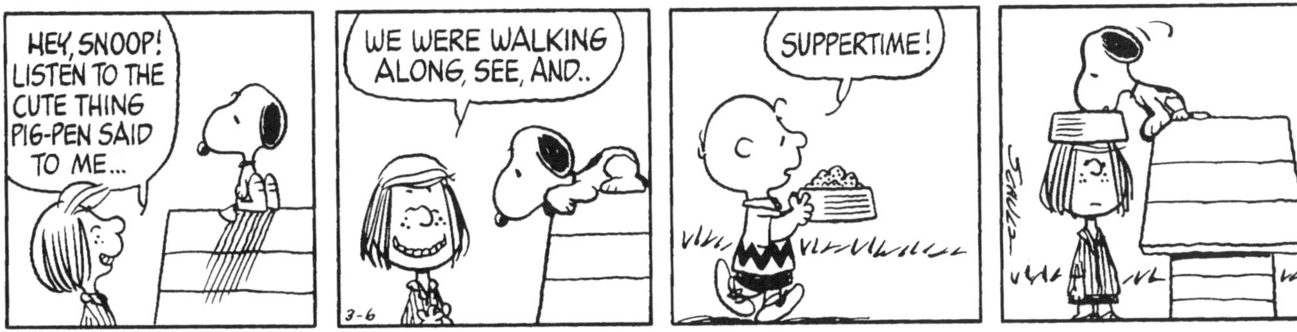
HEY, SNOOP! LISTEN TO THE CUTE THING PIG-PEN SAID TO ME...
WE WERE WALKING ALONG, SEE, AND..
3-6
SUPPERTIME!

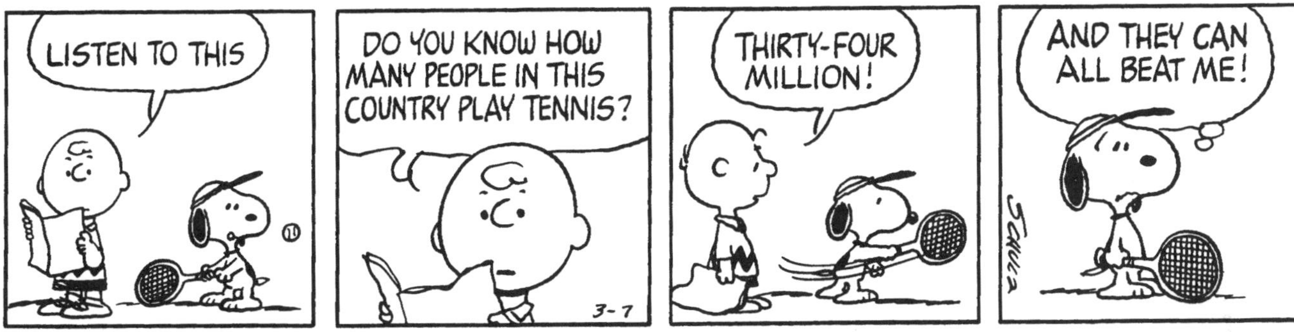
LISTEN TO THIS
DO YOU KNOW HOW MANY PEOPLE IN THIS COUNTRY PLAY TENNIS?
3-7
THIRTY-FOUR MILLION!
AND THEY CAN ALL BEAT ME!

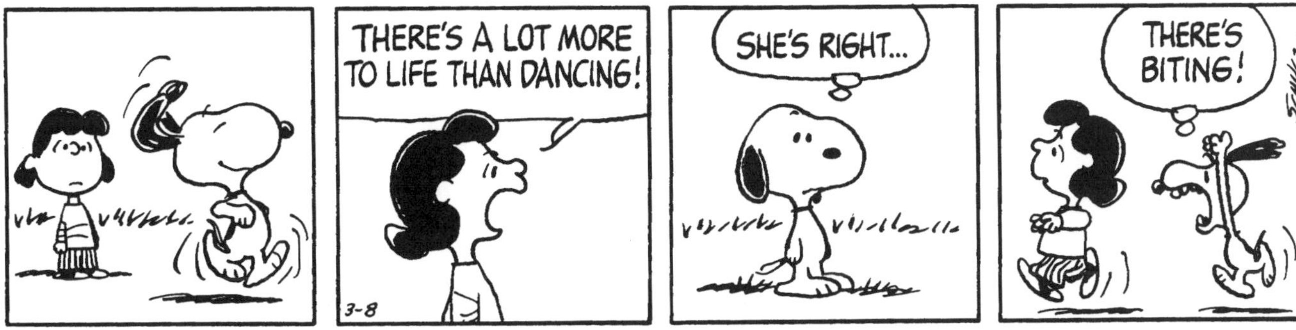
THERE'S A LOT MORE TO LIFE THAN DANCING!
3-8
SHE'S RIGHT...
THERE'S BITING!

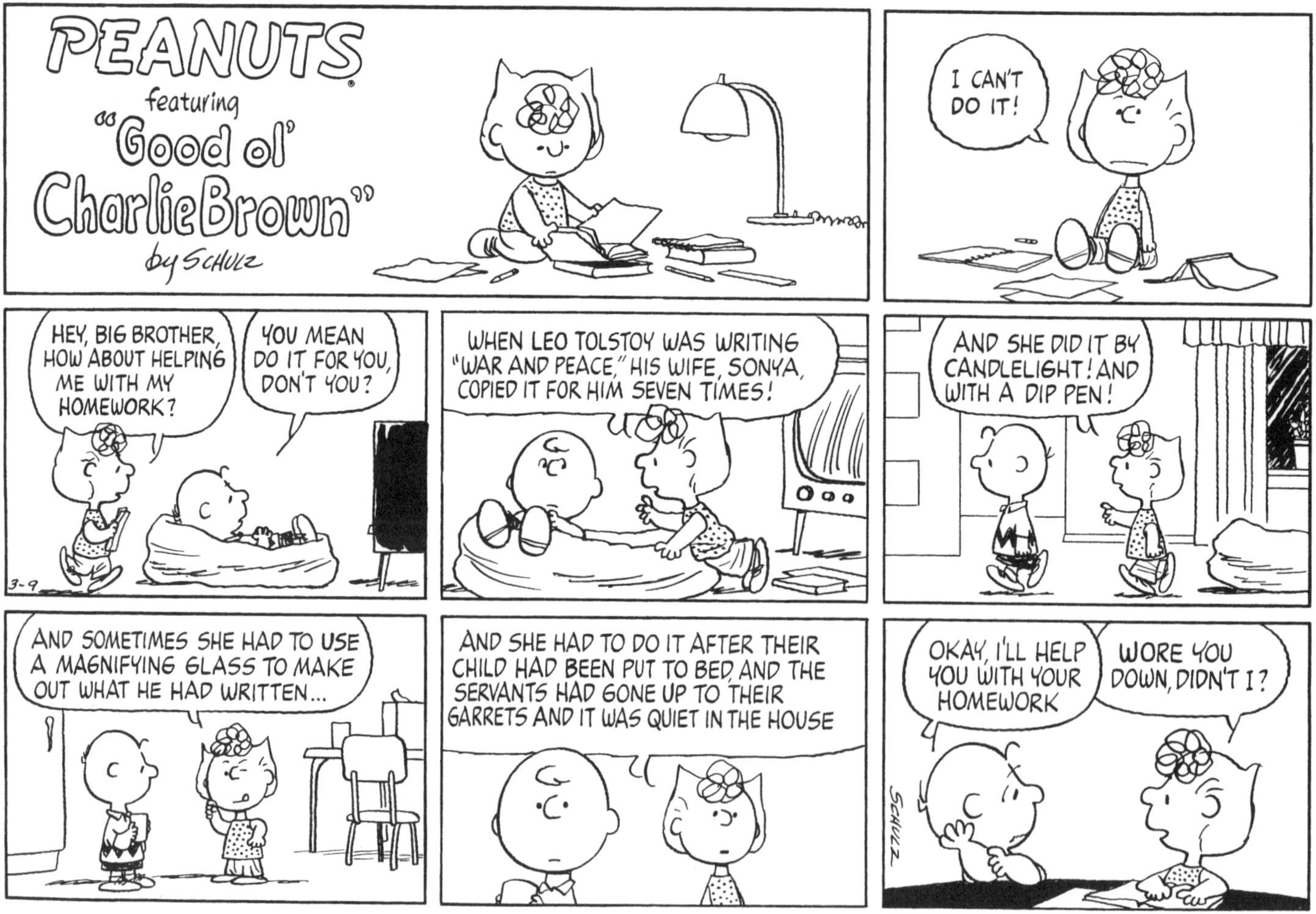
PEANUTS
featuring
"Good ol' Charlie Brown"
by SCHULZ
I CAN'T DO IT!
HEY, BIG BROTHER, HOW ABOUT HELPING ME WITH MY HOMEWORK?
YOU MEAN DO IT FOR YOU, DON'T YOU?
3-9
WHEN LEO TOLSTOY WAS WRITING "WAR AND PEACE," HIS WIFE, SONYA, COPIED IT FOR HIM SEVEN TIMES!
AND SHE DID IT BY CANDLELIGHT! AND WITH A DIP PEN!
AND SOMETIMES SHE HAD TO USE A MAGNIFYING GLASS TO MAKE OUT WHAT HE HAD WRITTEN...
AND SHE HAD TO DO IT AFTER THEIR CHILD HAD BEEN PUT TO BED, AND THE SERVANTS HAD GONE UP TO THEIR GARRETS AND IT WAS QUIET IN THE HOUSE
OKAY, I'LL HELP YOU WITH YOUR HOMEWORK
WORE YOU DOWN, DIDN'T I?
SCHULZ

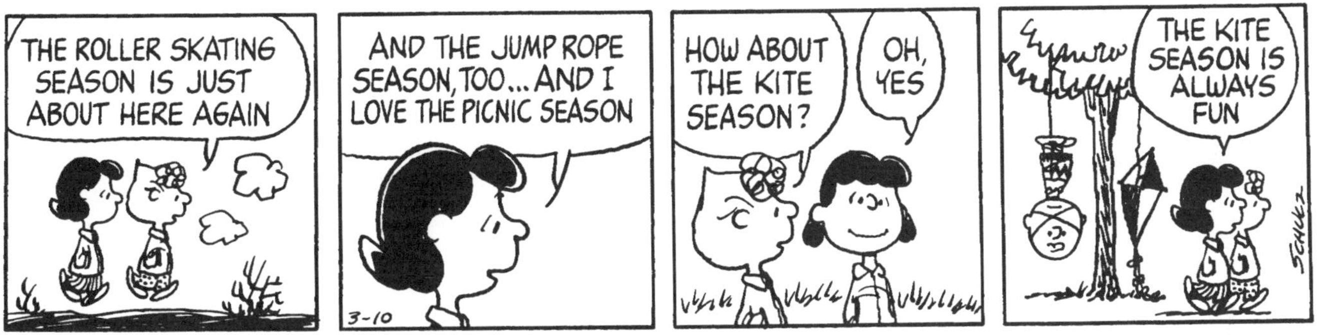
THE ROLLER SKATING SEASON IS JUST ABOUT HERE AGAIN
AND THE JUMP ROPE SEASON, TOO... AND I LOVE THE PICNIC SEASON
3-10
HOW ABOUT THE KITE SEASON?
OH, YES
THE KITE SEASON IS ALWAYS FUN
SCHULZ

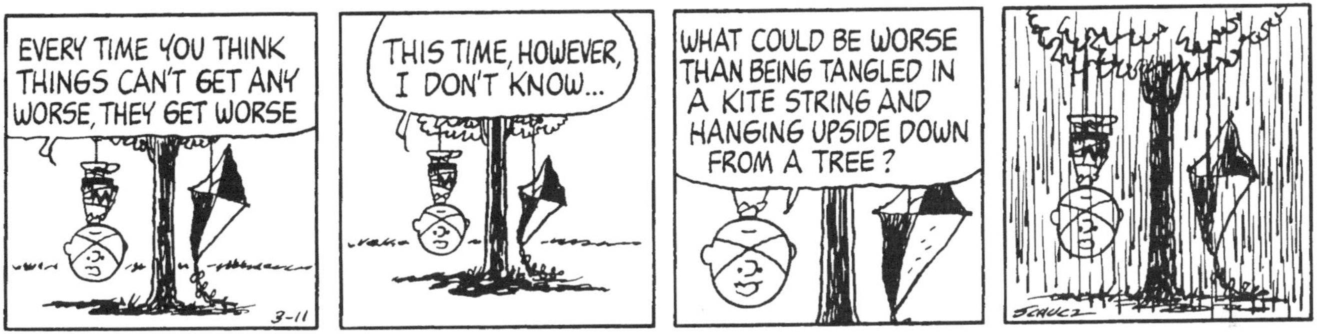
EVERY TIME YOU THINK THINGS CAN'T GET ANY WORSE, THEY GET WORSE
3-11
THIS TIME, HOWEVER, I DON'T KNOW...
WHAT COULD BE WORSE THAN BEING TANGLED IN A KITE STRING AND HANGING UPSIDE DOWN FROM A TREE?
SCHULZ

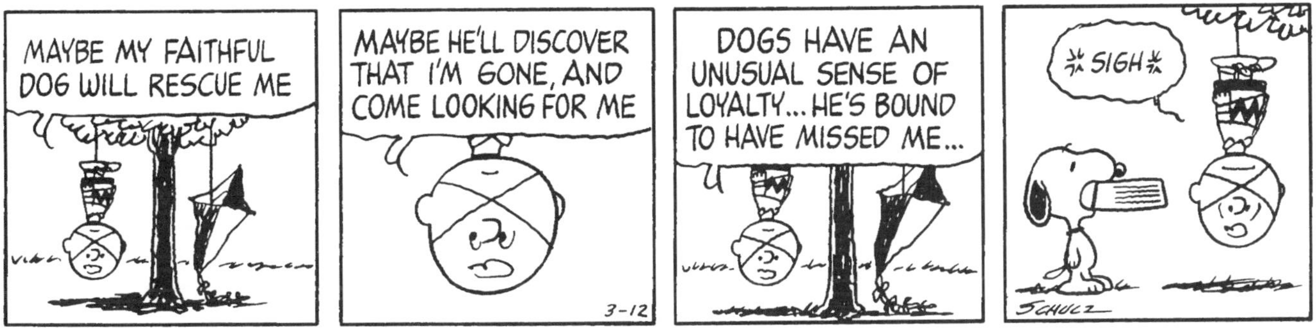
MAYBE MY FAITHFUL DOG WILL RESCUE ME
MAYBE HE'LL DISCOVER THAT I'M GONE, AND COME LOOKING FOR ME
3-12
DOGS HAVE AN UNUSUAL SENSE OF LOYALTY... HE'S BOUND TO HAVE MISSED ME...
SIGH
SCHULZ

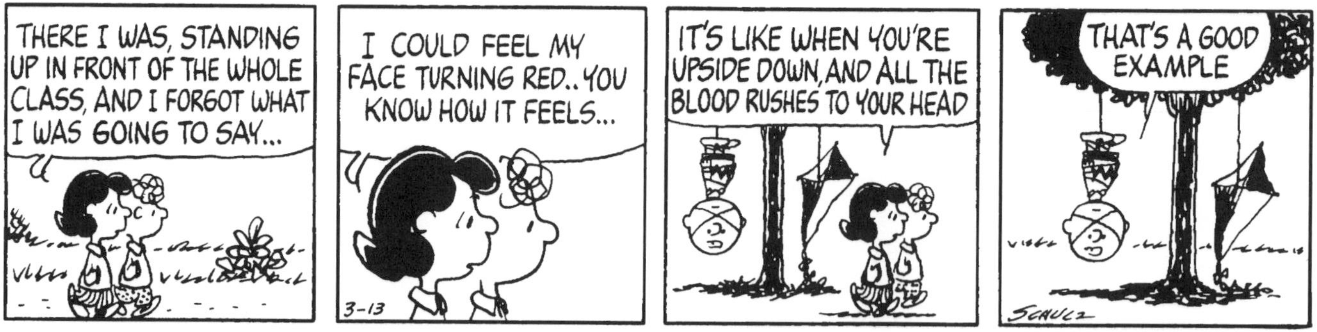
THERE I WAS, STANDING UP IN FRONT OF THE WHOLE CLASS, AND I FORGOT WHAT I WAS GOING TO SAY...
I COULD FEEL MY FACE TURNING RED.. YOU KNOW HOW IT FEELS...
IT'S LIKE WHEN YOU'RE UPSIDE DOWN, AND ALL THE BLOOD RUSHES TO YOUR HEAD
THAT'S A GOOD EXAMPLE

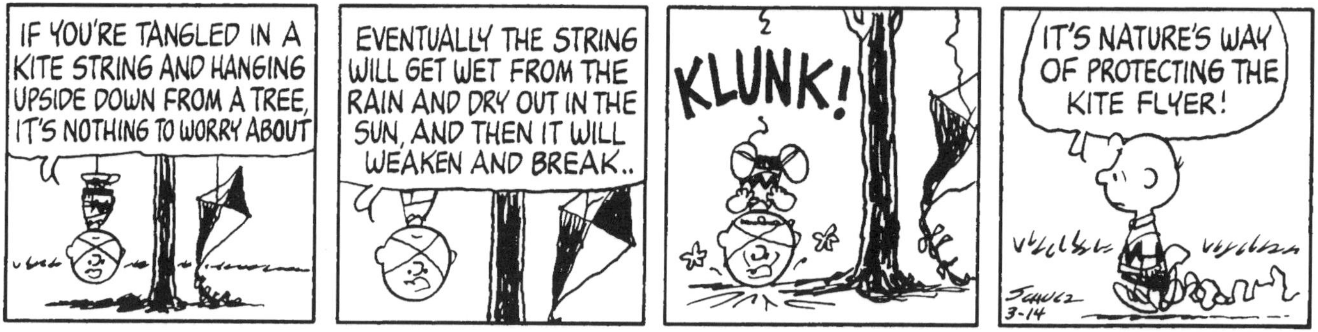
IF YOU'RE TANGLED IN A KITE STRING AND HANGING UPSIDE DOWN FROM A TREE, IT'S NOTHING TO WORRY ABOUT
EVENTUALLY THE STRING WILL GET WET FROM THE RAIN AND DRY OUT IN THE SUN, AND THEN IT WILL WEAKEN AND BREAK..
KLUNK!
IT'S NATURE'S WAY OF PROTECTING THE KITE FLYER!

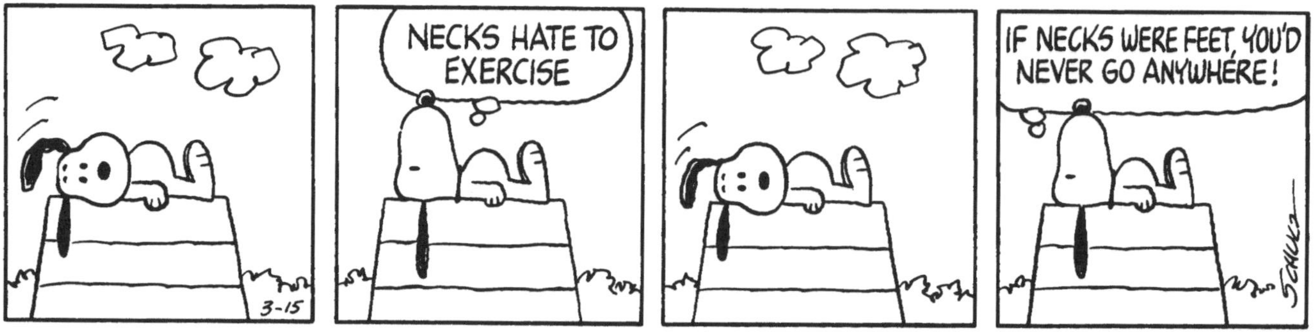
NECKS HATE TO EXERCISE
IF NECKS WERE FEET, YOU'D NEVER GO ANYWHERE!

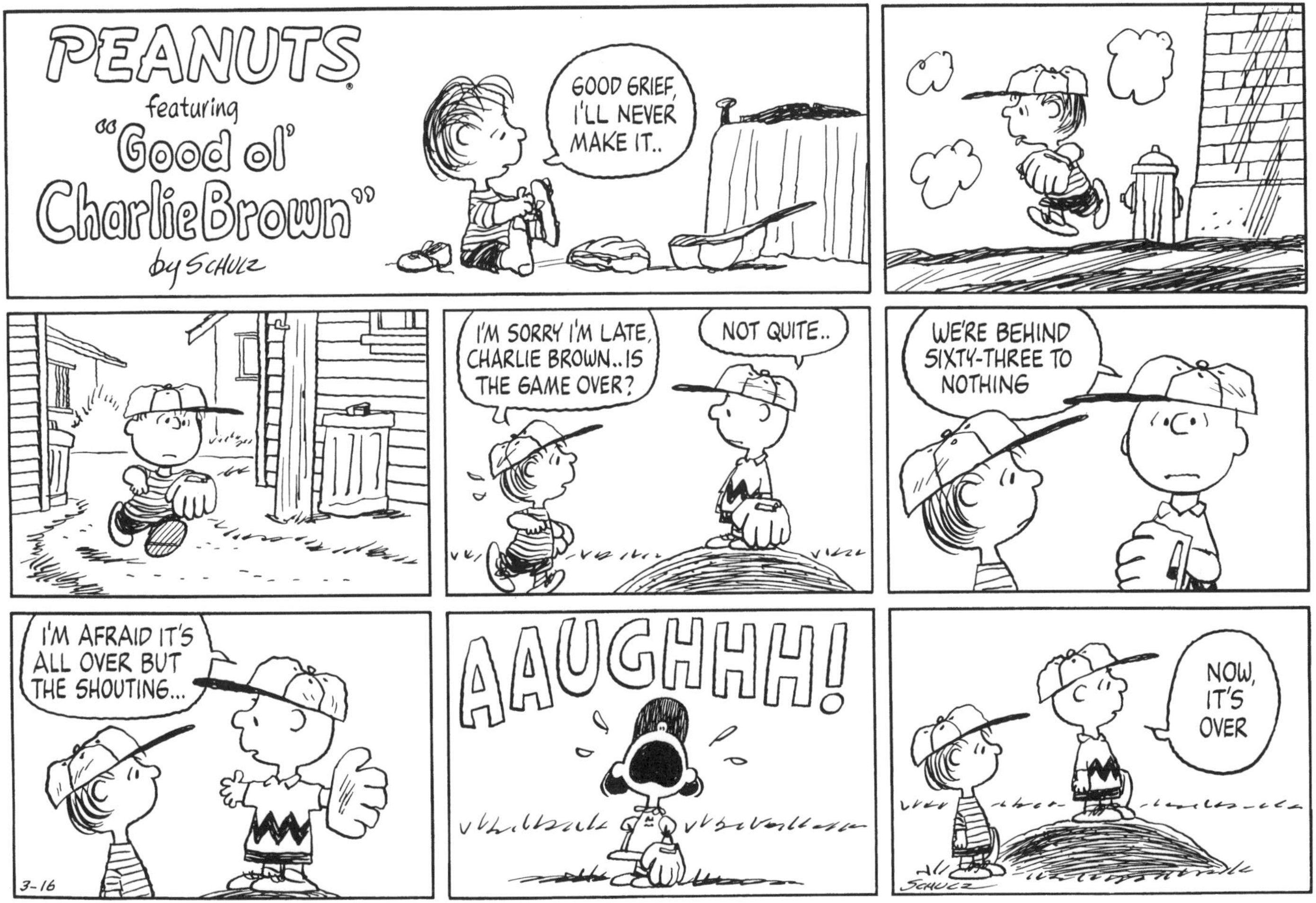
PEANUTS
featuring "Good ol' Charlie Brown"
by SCHULZ
GOOD GRIEF, I'LL NEVER MAKE IT..
I'M SORRY I'M LATE, CHARLIE BROWN..IS THE GAME OVER?
NOT QUITE..
WE'RE BEHIND SIXTY-THREE TO NOTHING
I'M AFRAID IT'S ALL OVER BUT THE SHOUTING...
3-16
AAUGHHH!
NOW, IT'S OVER
SCHULZ

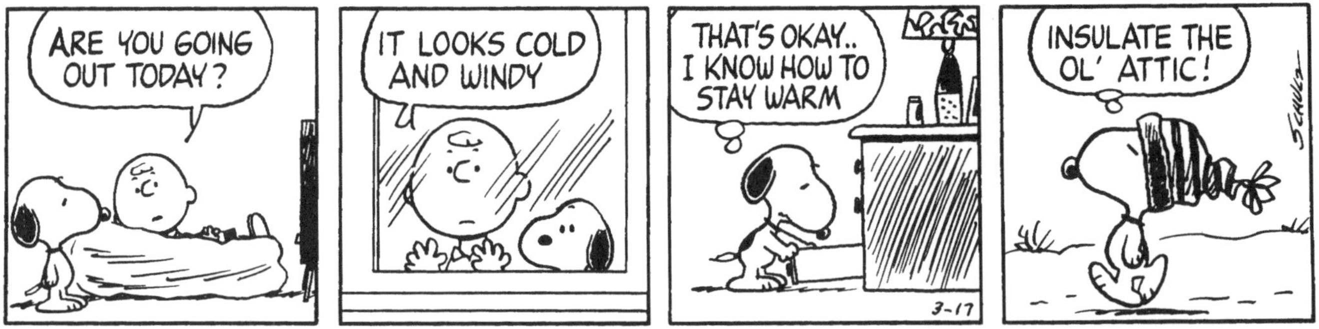
ARE YOU GOING OUT TODAY?
IT LOOKS COLD AND WINDY
THAT'S OKAY.. I KNOW HOW TO STAY WARM
3-17
INSULATE THE OL' ATTIC!
SCHULZ

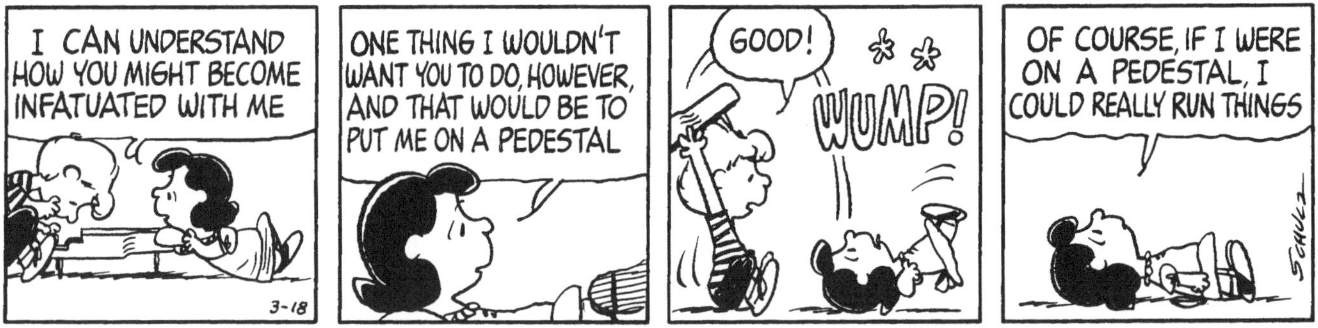
I CAN UNDERSTAND HOW YOU MIGHT BECOME INFATUATED WITH ME
3-18
ONE THING I WOULDN'T WANT YOU TO DO, HOWEVER, AND THAT WOULD BE TO PUT ME ON A PEDESTAL
GOOD!
WUMP!
OF COURSE, IF I WERE ON A PEDESTAL, I COULD REALLY RUN THINGS
SCHULZ

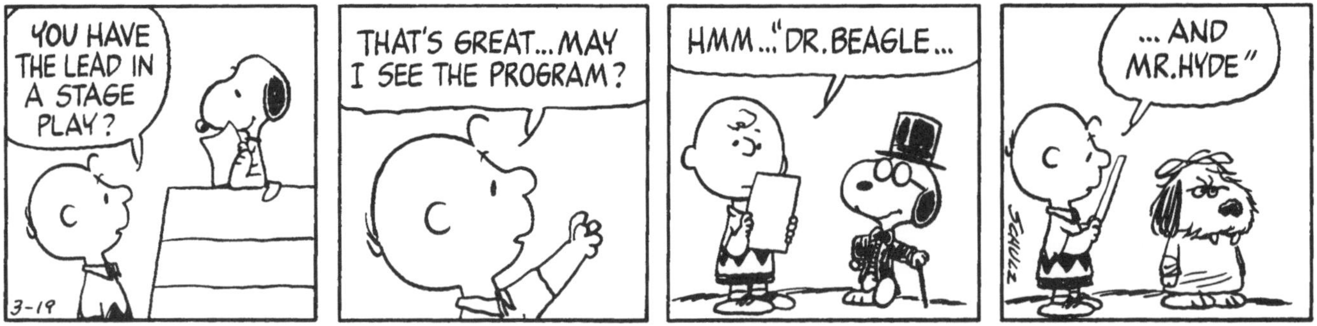
YOU HAVE THE LEAD IN A STAGE PLAY?
3-19
THAT'S GREAT... MAY I SEE THE PROGRAM?
HMM..."DR. BEAGLE...
... AND MR. HYDE"
SCHULZ

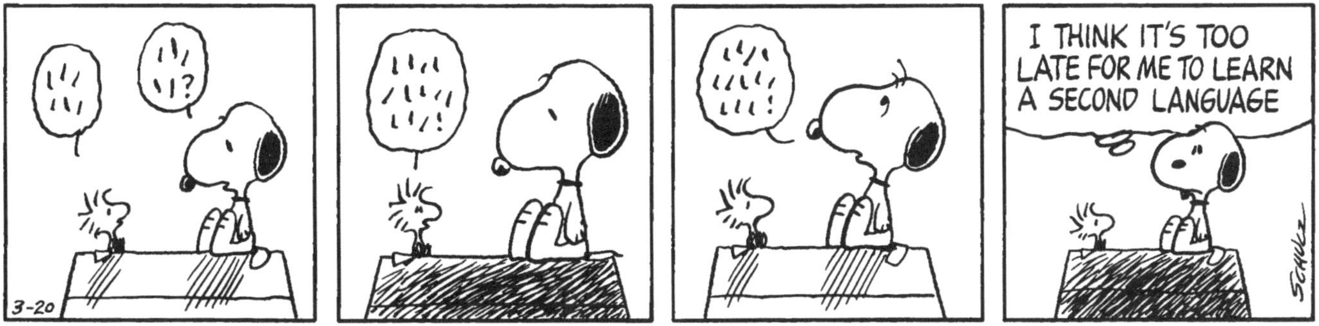
3-20
I THINK IT'S TOO LATE FOR ME TO LEARN A SECOND LANGUAGE
SCHULZ

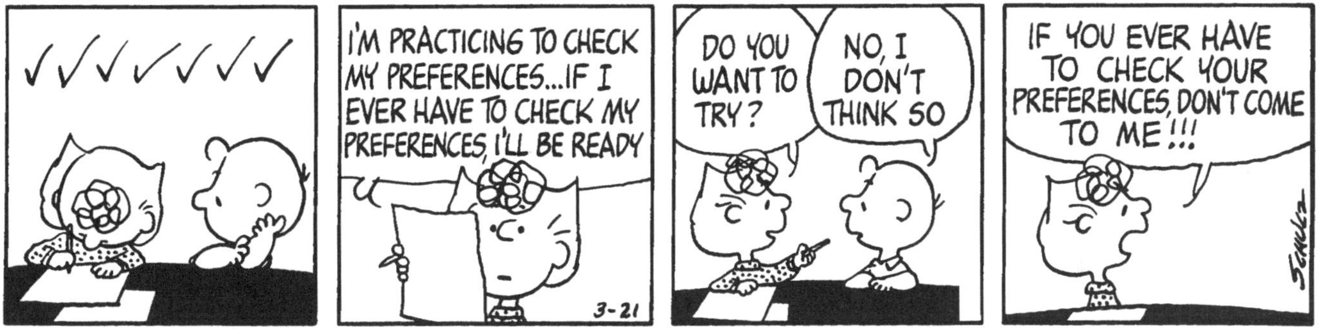
I'M PRACTICING TO CHECK MY PREFERENCES...IF I EVER HAVE TO CHECK MY PREFERENCES, I'LL BE READY
3-21
DO YOU WANT TO TRY?
NO, I DON'T THINK SO
IF YOU EVER HAVE TO CHECK YOUR PREFERENCES, DON'T COME TO ME!!!
SCHULZ

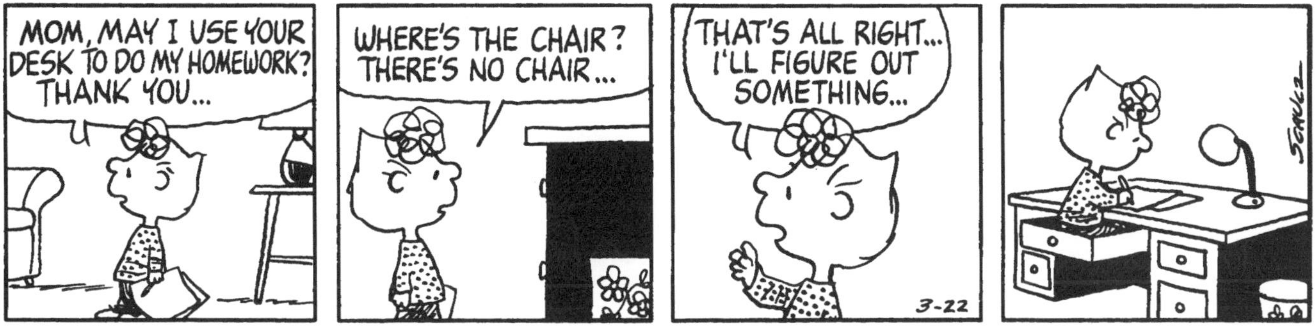
MOM, MAY I USE YOUR DESK TO DO MY HOMEWORK? THANK YOU...
WHERE'S THE CHAIR? THERE'S NO CHAIR...
THAT'S ALL RIGHT... I'LL FIGURE OUT SOMETHING...
3-22
SCHULZ

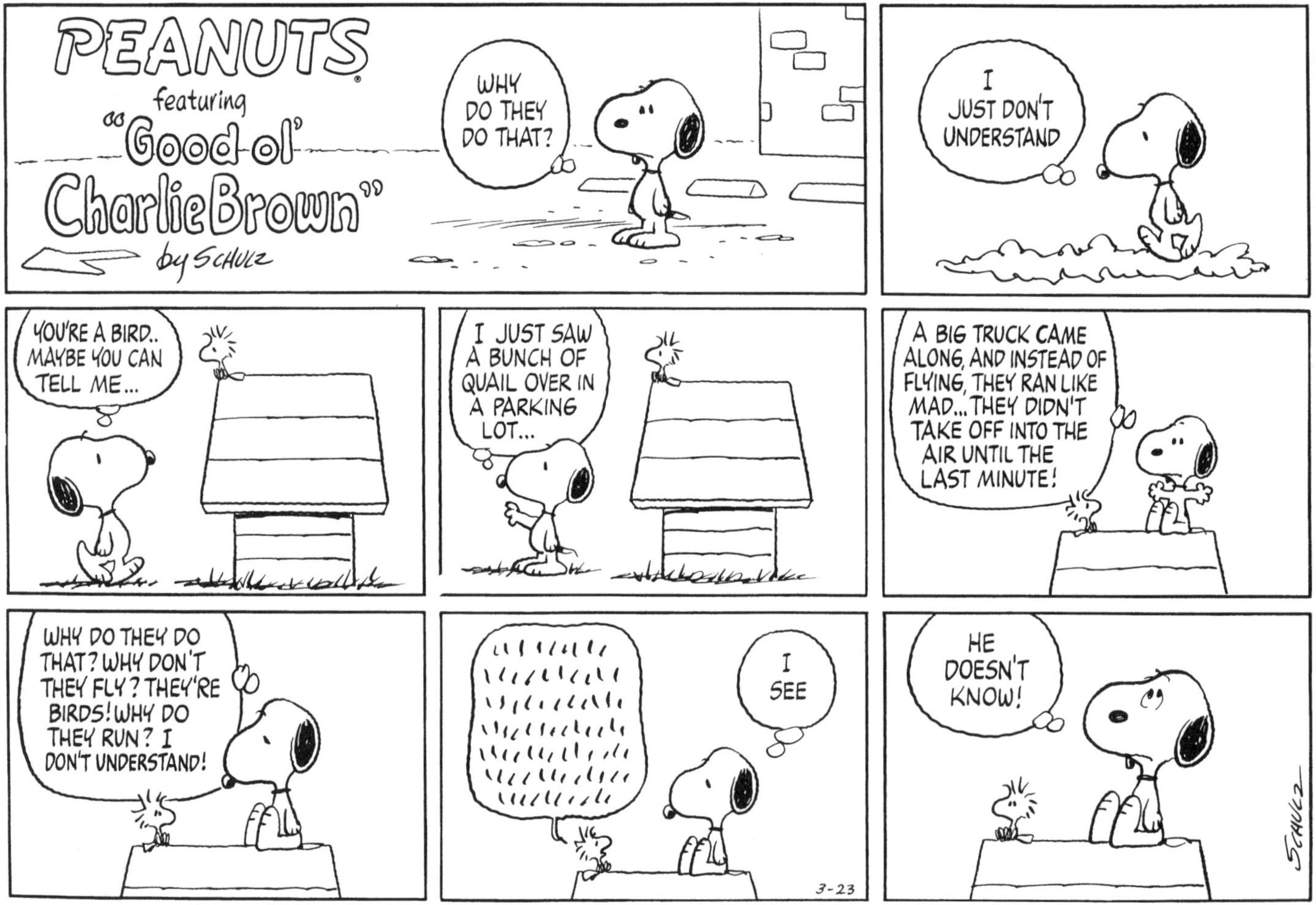
PEANUTS®
featuring
"Good ol' Charlie Brown"
by SCHULZ
WHY DO THEY DO THAT?
I JUST DON'T UNDERSTAND
YOU'RE A BIRD.. MAYBE YOU CAN TELL ME...
I JUST SAW A BUNCH OF QUAIL OVER IN A PARKING LOT...
A BIG TRUCK CAME ALONG, AND INSTEAD OF FLYING, THEY RAN LIKE MAD... THEY DIDN'T TAKE OFF INTO THE AIR UNTIL THE LAST MINUTE!
WHY DO THEY DO THAT? WHY DON'T THEY FLY? THEY'RE BIRDS! WHY DO THEY RUN? I DON'T UNDERSTAND!
I SEE
3-23
HE DOESN'T KNOW!
SCHULZ

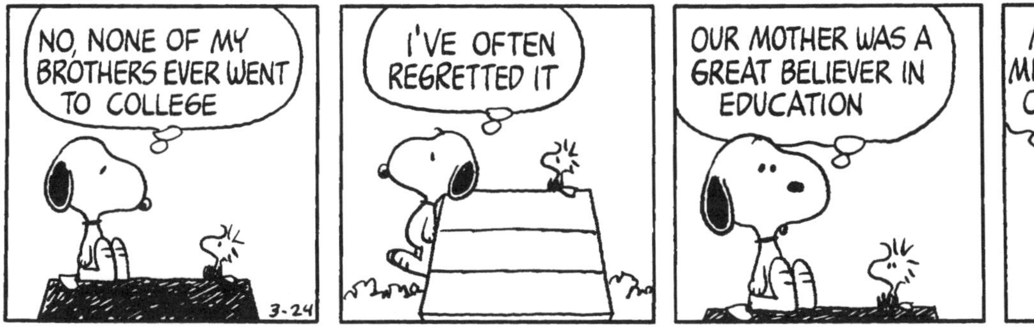
NO, NONE OF MY BROTHERS EVER WENT TO COLLEGE
3-24
I'VE OFTEN REGRETTED IT
OUR MOTHER WAS A GREAT BELIEVER IN EDUCATION
MOM ALWAYS WANTED ME TO GET A BEAGLE OF ARTS DEGREE

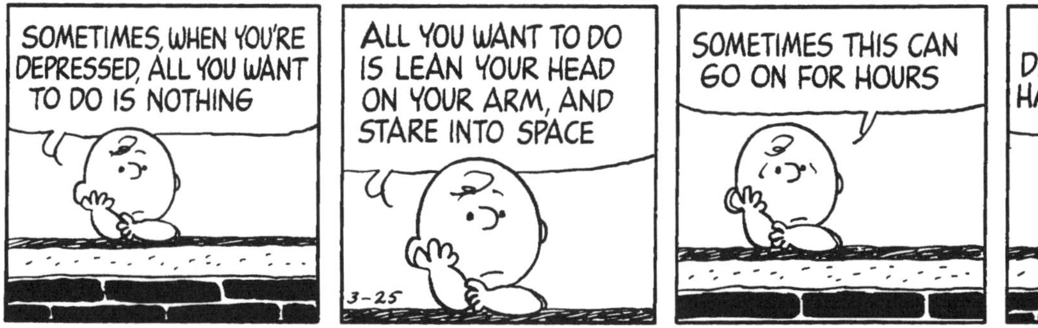
SOMETIMES, WHEN YOU'RE DEPRESSED, ALL YOU WANT TO DO IS NOTHING
ALL YOU WANT TO DO IS LEAN YOUR HEAD ON YOUR ARM, AND STARE INTO SPACE
3-25
SOMETIMES THIS CAN GO ON FOR HOURS
IF YOU'RE UNUSUALLY DEPRESSED, YOU MAY HAVE TO CHANGE ARMS

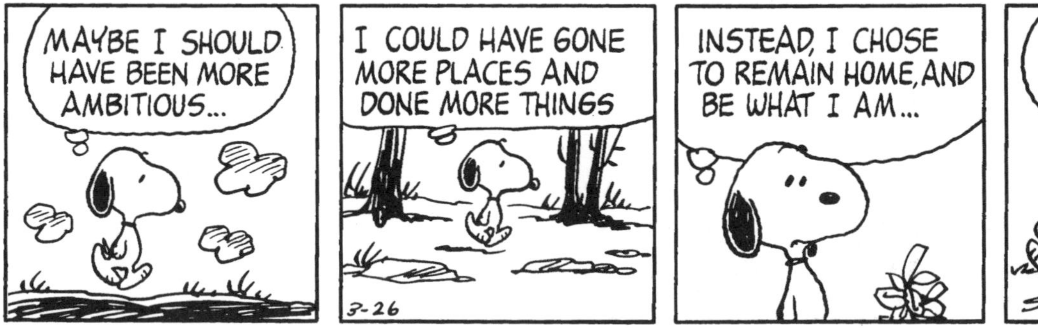
MAYBE I SHOULD HAVE BEEN MORE AMBITIOUS...
I COULD HAVE GONE MORE PLACES AND DONE MORE THINGS
3-26
INSTEAD, I CHOSE TO REMAIN HOME, AND BE WHAT I AM...
JUST YOUR BASIC BEAGLE!

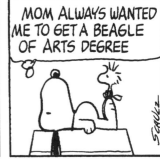

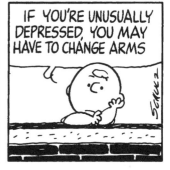

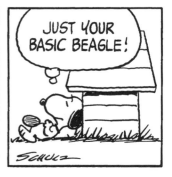

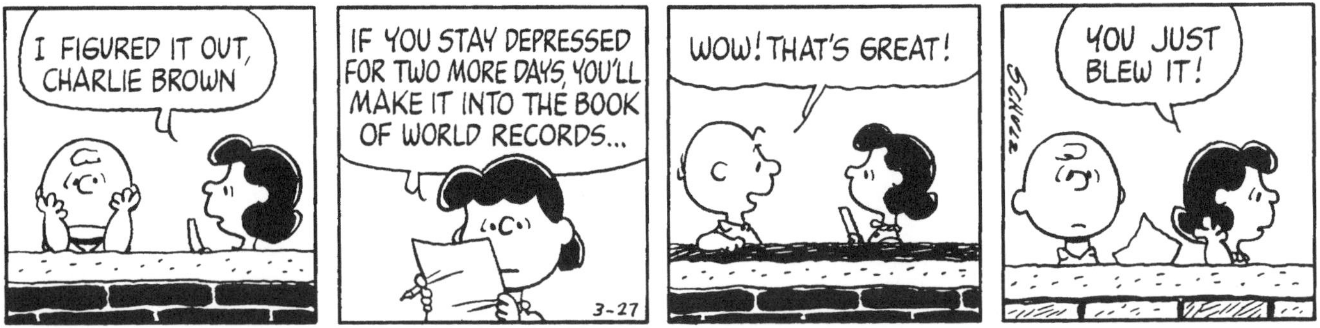
I FIGURED IT OUT, CHARLIE BROWN
IF YOU STAY DEPRESSED FOR TWO MORE DAYS, YOU'LL MAKE IT INTO THE BOOK OF WORLD RECORDS...
3-27
WOW! THAT'S GREAT!
YOU JUST BLEW IT!
SCHULZ

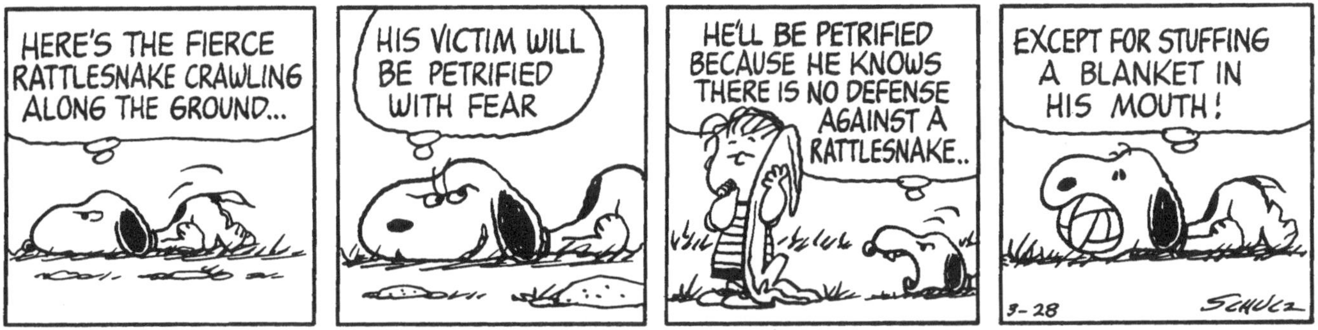
HERE'S THE FIERCE RATTLESNAKE CRAWLING ALONG THE GROUND...
HIS VICTIM WILL BE PETRIFIED WITH FEAR
HE'LL BE PETRIFIED BECAUSE HE KNOWS THERE IS NO DEFENSE AGAINST A RATTLESNAKE..
EXCEPT FOR STUFFING A BLANKET IN HIS MOUTH!
3-28
SCHULZ

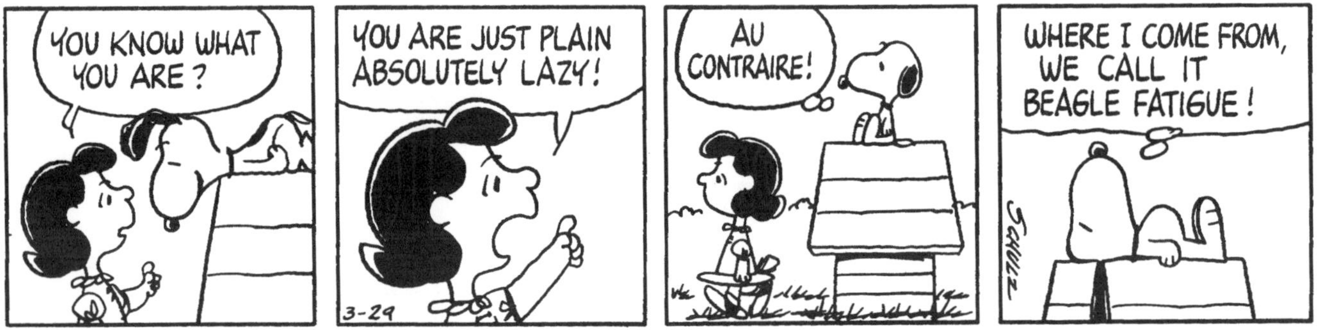
YOU KNOW WHAT YOU ARE?
YOU ARE JUST PLAIN ABSOLUTELY LAZY!
3-29
AU CONTRAIRE!
WHERE I COME FROM, WE CALL IT BEAGLE FATIGUE!
SCHULZ

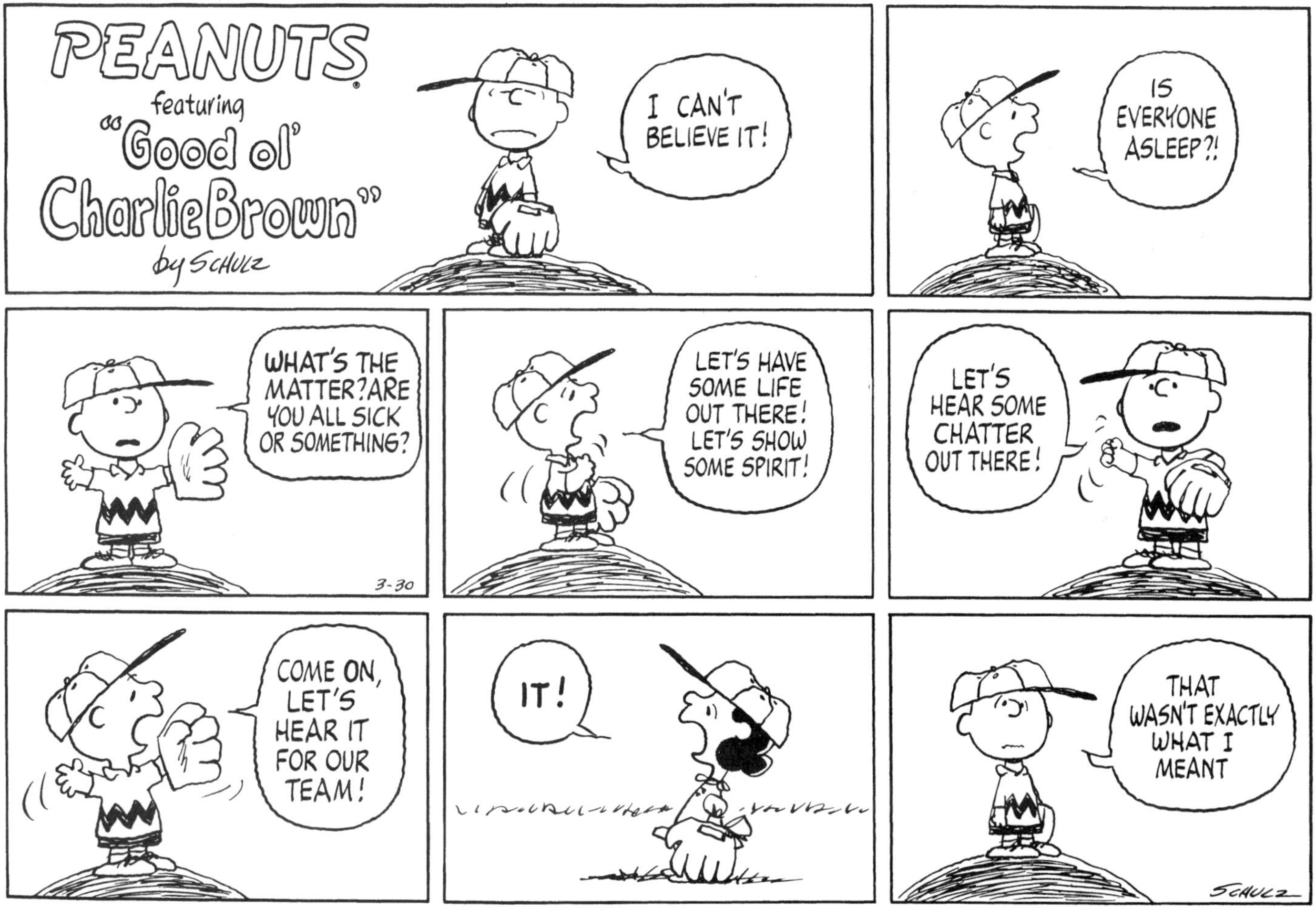
PEANUTS
featuring "Good ol' Charlie Brown"
by SCHULZ
I CAN'T BELIEVE IT!
IS EVERYONE ASLEEP?!
WHAT'S THE MATTER? ARE YOU ALL SICK OR SOMETHING?
3-30
LET'S HAVE SOME LIFE OUT THERE! LET'S SHOW SOME SPIRIT!
LET'S HEAR SOME CHATTER OUT THERE!
COME ON, LET'S HEAR IT FOR OUR TEAM!
IT!
THAT WASN'T EXACTLY WHAT I MEANT
SCHULZ

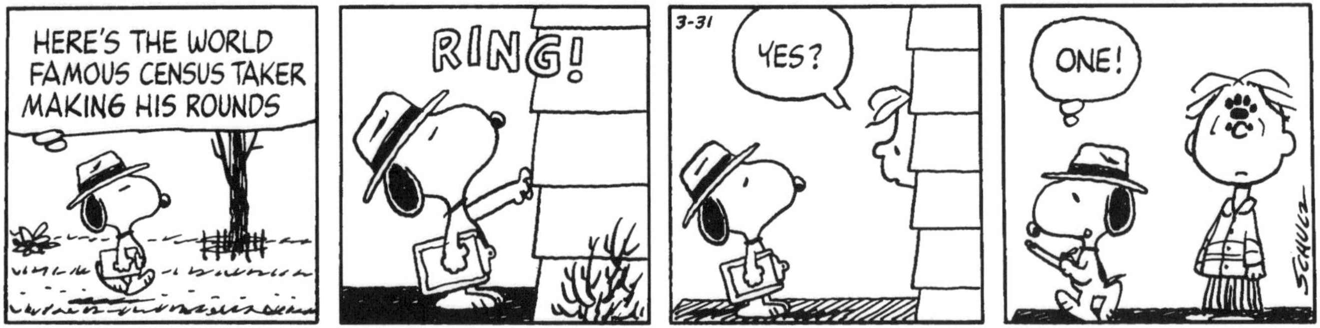
3-31
HERE'S THE WORLD FAMOUS CENSUS TAKER MAKING HIS ROUNDS
RING!
YES?
ONE!
SCHULZ

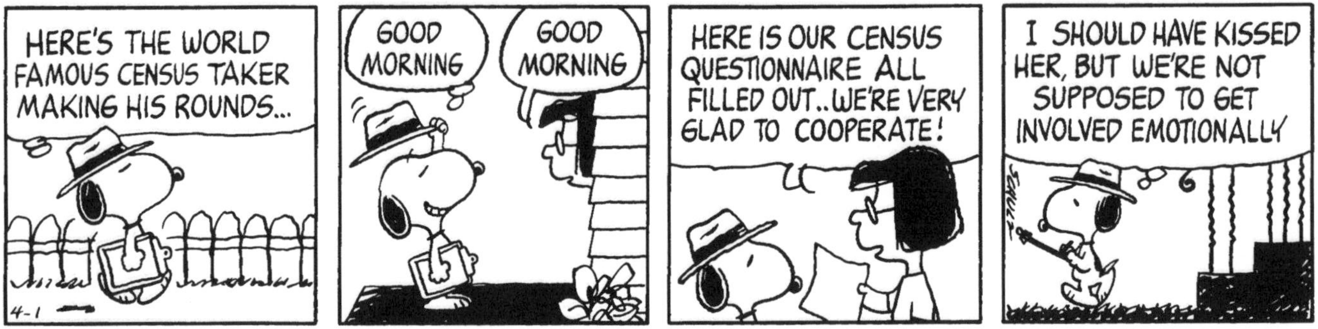
4-1
HERE'S THE WORLD FAMOUS CENSUS TAKER MAKING HIS ROUNDS...
GOOD MORNING
GOOD MORNING
HERE IS OUR CENSUS QUESTIONNAIRE ALL FILLED OUT..WE'RE VERY GLAD TO COOPERATE!
I SHOULD HAVE KISSED HER, BUT WE'RE NOT SUPPOSED TO GET INVOLVED EMOTIONALLY
SCHULZ

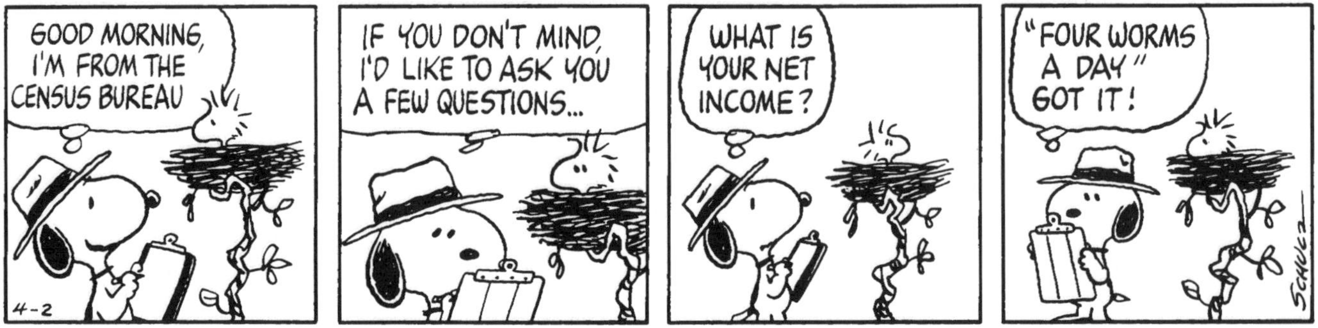
4-2
GOOD MORNING, I'M FROM THE CENSUS BUREAU
IF YOU DON'T MIND, I'D LIKE TO ASK YOU A FEW QUESTIONS...
WHAT IS YOUR NET INCOME?
"FOUR WORMS A DAY" GOT IT!
SCHULZ

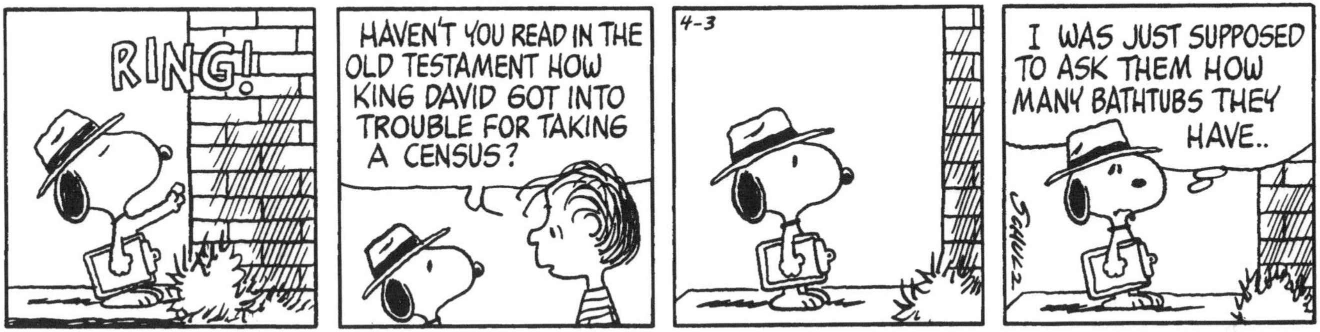
RING!
HAVEN'T YOU READ IN THE OLD TESTAMENT HOW KING DAVID GOT INTO TROUBLE FOR TAKING A CENSUS?
4-3
I WAS JUST SUPPOSED TO ASK THEM HOW MANY BATHTUBS THEY HAVE..

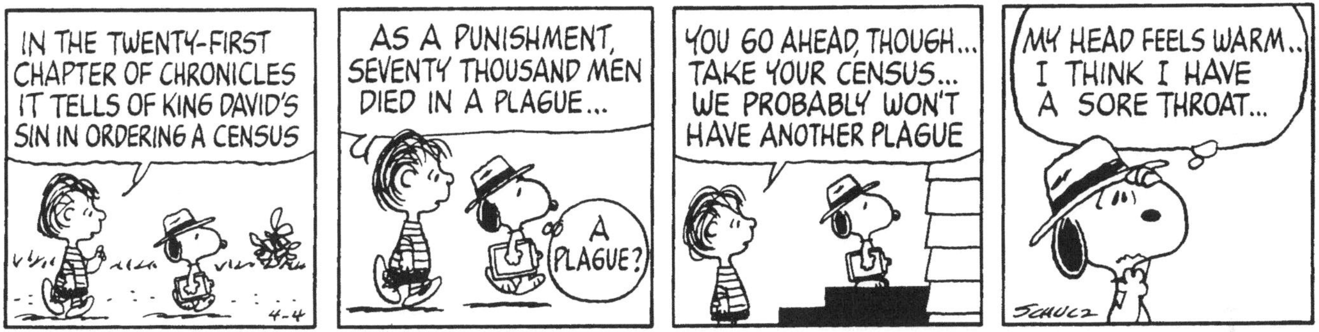
IN THE TWENTY-FIRST CHAPTER OF CHRONICLES IT TELLS OF KING DAVID'S SIN IN ORDERING A CENSUS
4-4
AS A PUNISHMENT, SEVENTY THOUSAND MEN DIED IN A PLAGUE...
A PLAGUE?
YOU GO AHEAD, THOUGH... TAKE YOUR CENSUS... WE PROBABLY WON'T HAVE ANOTHER PLAGUE
MY HEAD FEELS WARM.. I THINK I HAVE A SORE THROAT...

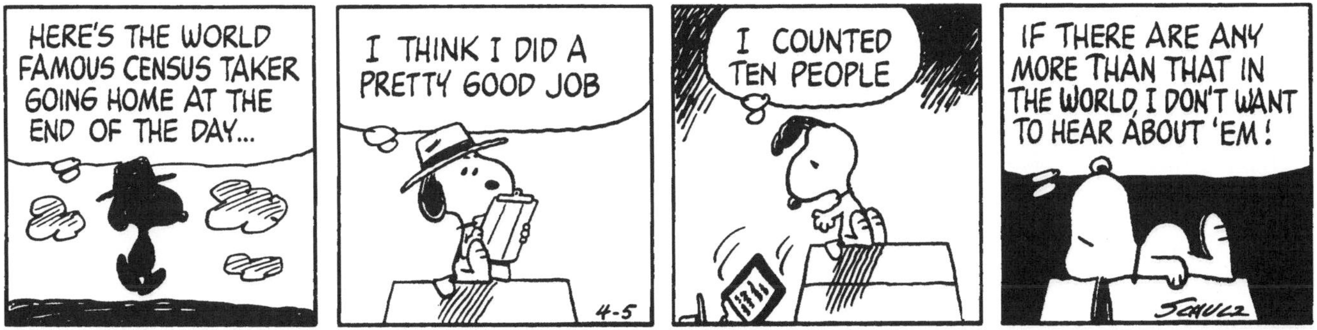
HERE'S THE WORLD FAMOUS CENSUS TAKER GOING HOME AT THE END OF THE DAY...
I THINK I DID A PRETTY GOOD JOB
4-5
I COUNTED TEN PEOPLE
IF THERE ARE ANY MORE THAN THAT IN THE WORLD, I DON'T WANT TO HEAR ABOUT 'EM!

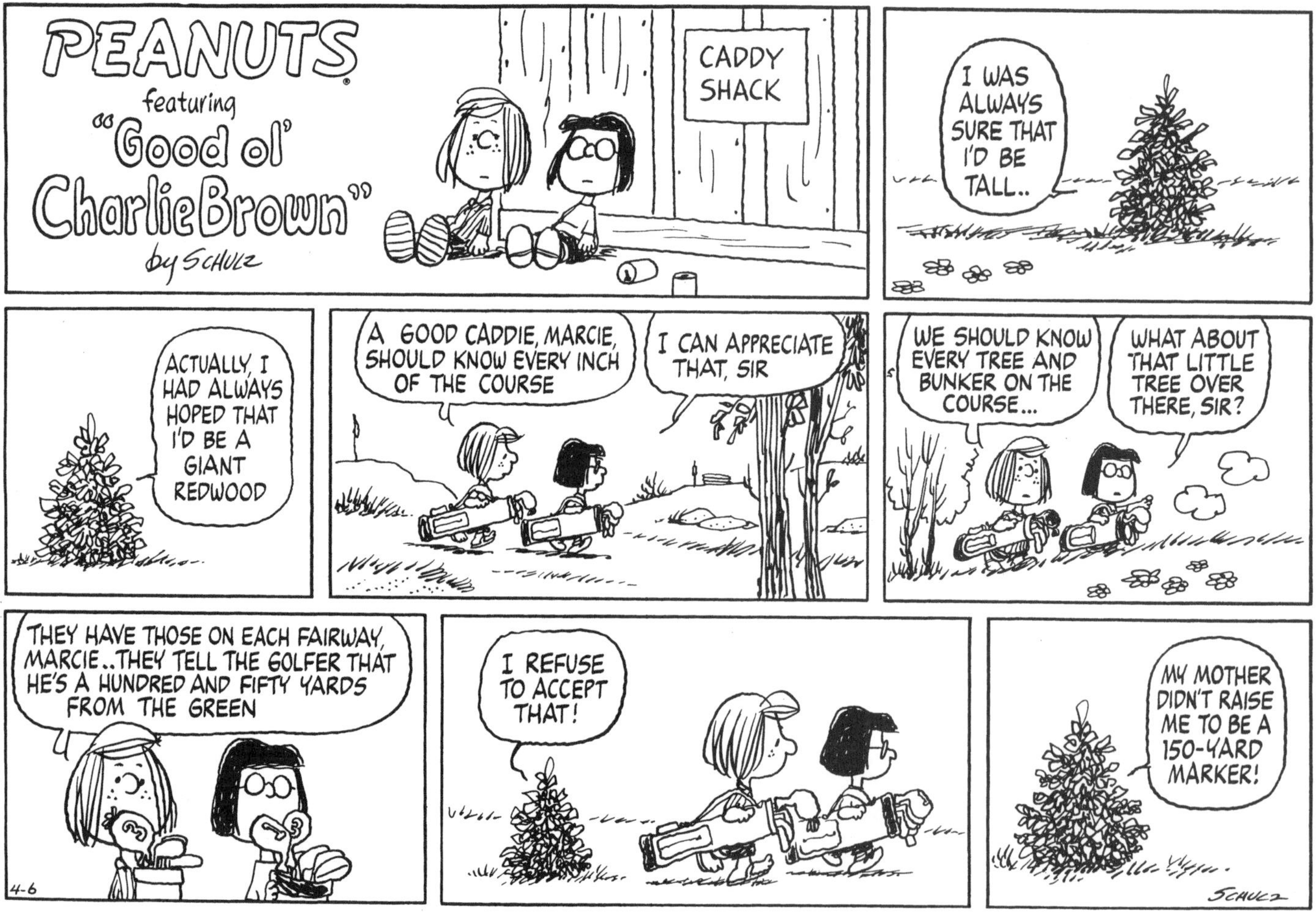
PEANUTS
featuring "Good ol' CharlieBrown"
by SCHULZ
CADDY SHACK
I WAS ALWAYS SURE THAT I'D BE TALL..
ACTUALLY, I HAD ALWAYS HOPED THAT I'D BE A GIANT REDWOOD
A GOOD CADDIE, MARCIE, SHOULD KNOW EVERY INCH OF THE COURSE
I CAN APPRECIATE THAT, SIR
WE SHOULD KNOW EVERY TREE AND BUNKER ON THE COURSE...
WHAT ABOUT THAT LITTLE TREE OVER THERE, SIR?
THEY HAVE THOSE ON EACH FAIRWAY, MARCIE..THEY TELL THE GOLFER THAT HE'S A HUNDRED AND FIFTY YARDS FROM THE GREEN
4-6
I REFUSE TO ACCEPT THAT!
MY MOTHER DIDN'T RAISE ME TO BE A 150-YARD MARKER!
SCHULZ

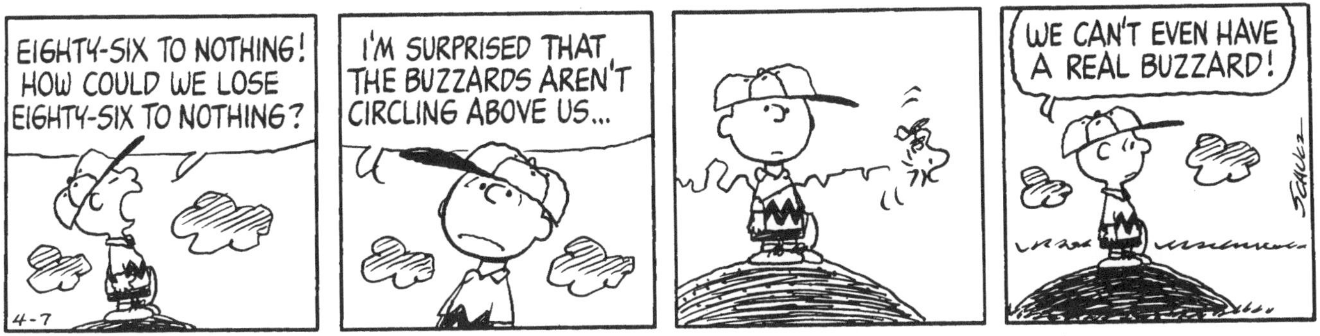
EIGHTY-SIX TO NOTHING! HOW COULD WE LOSE EIGHTY-SIX TO NOTHING?
4-7
I'M SURPRISED THAT THE BUZZARDS AREN'T CIRCLING ABOVE US...
WE CAN'T EVEN HAVE A REAL BUZZARD!
SCHULZ

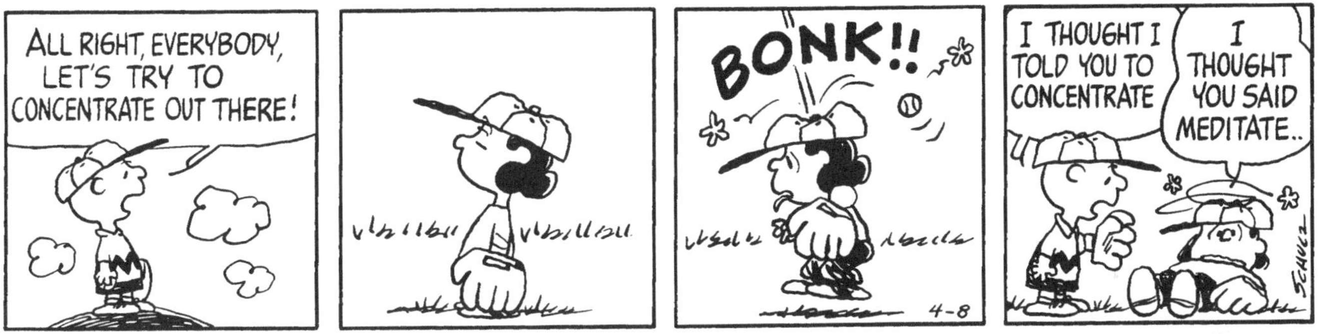
ALL RIGHT, EVERYBODY, LET'S TRY TO CONCENTRATE OUT THERE!
BONK!!
4-8
I THOUGHT I TOLD YOU TO CONCENTRATE
I THOUGHT YOU SAID MEDITATE..
SCHULZ

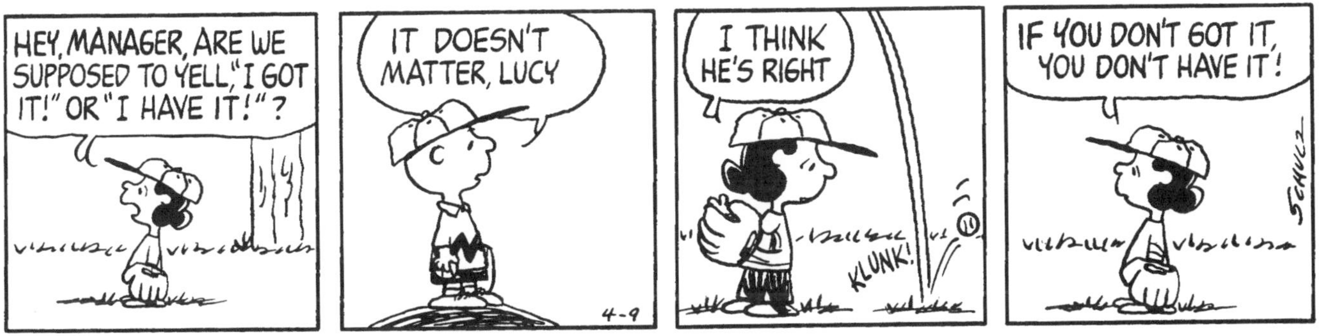
HEY, MANAGER, ARE WE SUPPOSED TO YELL, "I GOT IT!" OR "I HAVE IT!"?
IT DOESN'T MATTER, LUCY
4-9
I THINK HE'S RIGHT
KLUNK!
IF YOU DON'T GOT IT, YOU DON'T HAVE IT!
SCHULZ

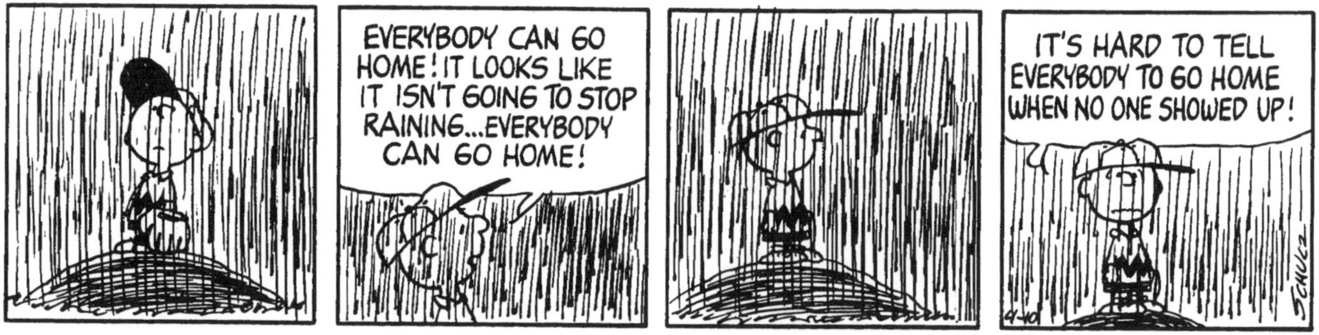
EVERYBODY CAN GO HOME! IT LOOKS LIKE IT ISN'T GOING TO STOP RAINING...EVERYBODY CAN GO HOME!
IT'S HARD TO TELL EVERYBODY TO GO HOME WHEN NO ONE SHOWED UP!
4-10
SCHULZ

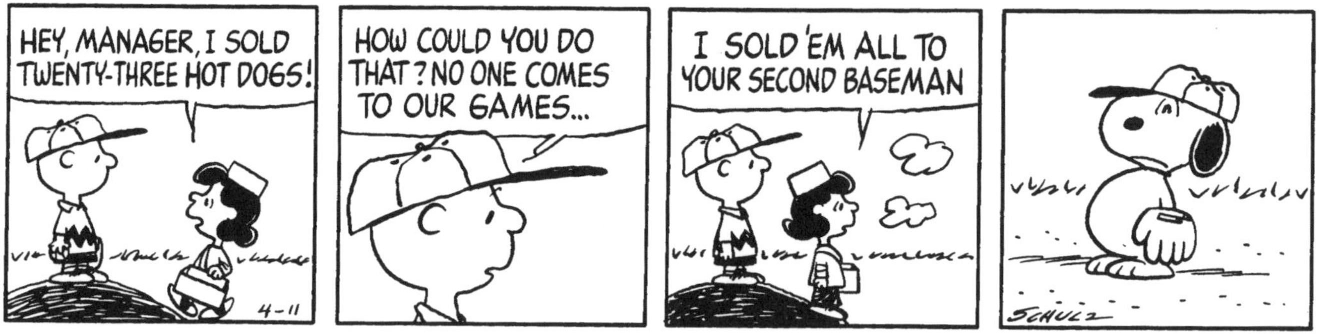
HEY, MANAGER, I SOLD TWENTY-THREE HOT DOGS!
4-11
HOW COULD YOU DO THAT? NO ONE COMES TO OUR GAMES...
I SOLD 'EM ALL TO YOUR SECOND BASEMAN
SCHULZ

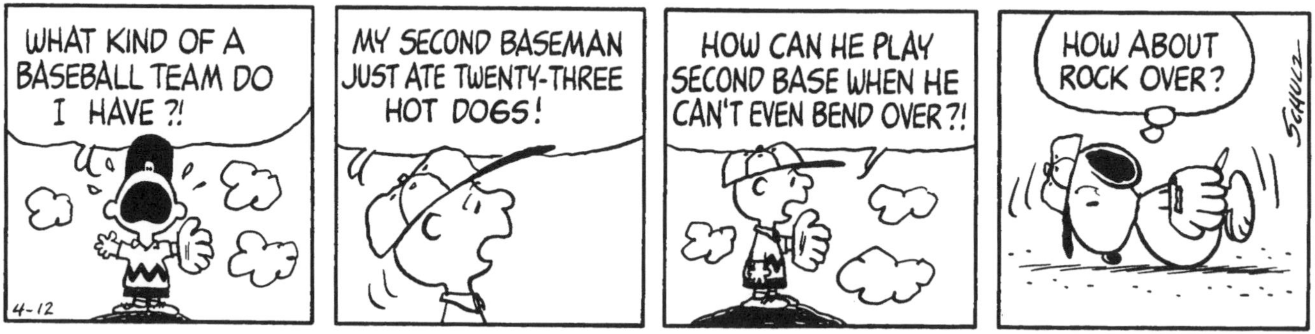
WHAT KIND OF A BASEBALL TEAM DO I HAVE ?!
4-12
MY SECOND BASEMAN JUST ATE TWENTY-THREE HOT DOGS!
HOW CAN HE PLAY SECOND BASE WHEN HE CAN'T EVEN BEND OVER?!
HOW ABOUT ROCK OVER?
SCHULZ

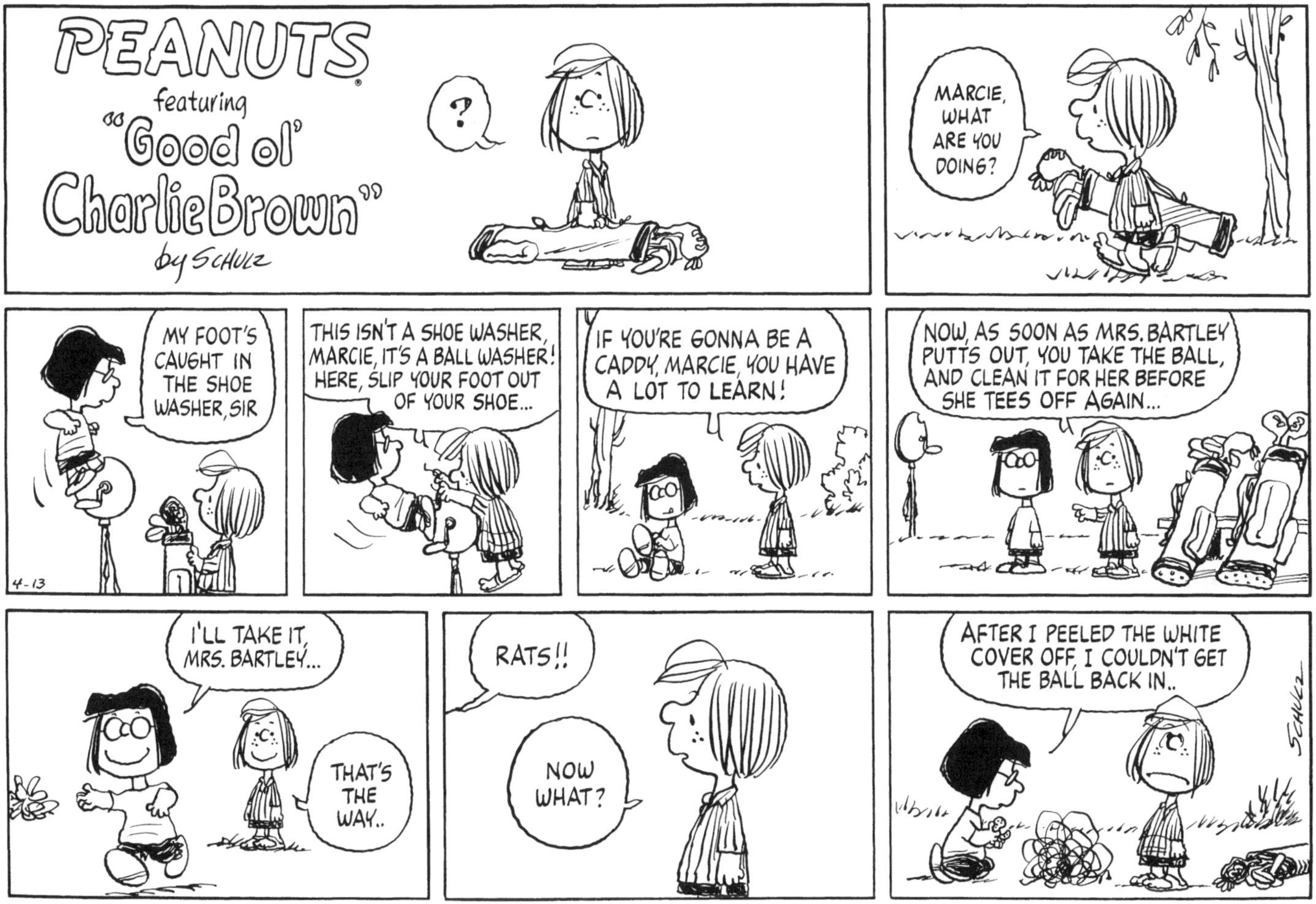
PEANUTS
featuring "Good ol' CharlieBrown"
by SCHULZ
?
MARCIE, WHAT ARE YOU DOING?
MY FOOT'S CAUGHT IN THE SHOE WASHER, SIR
4-13
THIS ISN'T A SHOE WASHER, MARCIE, IT'S A BALL WASHER! HERE, SLIP YOUR FOOT OUT OF YOUR SHOE...
IF YOU'RE GONNA BE A CADDY, MARCIE, YOU HAVE A LOT TO LEARN!
NOW, AS SOON AS MRS. BARTLEY PUTTS OUT, YOU TAKE THE BALL, AND CLEAN IT FOR HER BEFORE SHE TEES OFF AGAIN...
I'LL TAKE IT, MRS. BARTLEY...
THAT'S THE WAY..
RATS!!
NOW WHAT?
AFTER I PEELED THE WHITE COVER OFF, I COULDN'T GET THE BALL BACK IN..
SCHULZ

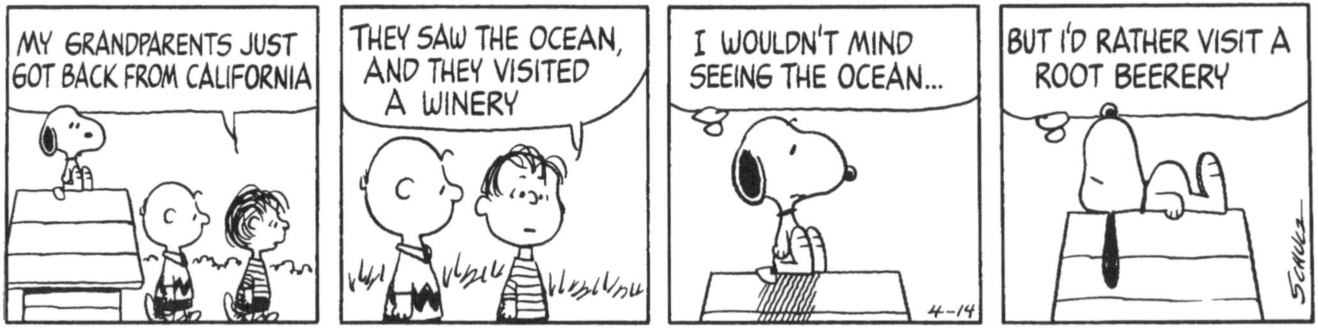
MY GRANDPARENTS JUST GOT BACK FROM CALIFORNIA
THEY SAW THE OCEAN, AND THEY VISITED A WINERY
I WOULDN'T MIND SEEING THE OCEAN...
4-14
BUT I'D RATHER VISIT A ROOT BEERERY
SCHULZ

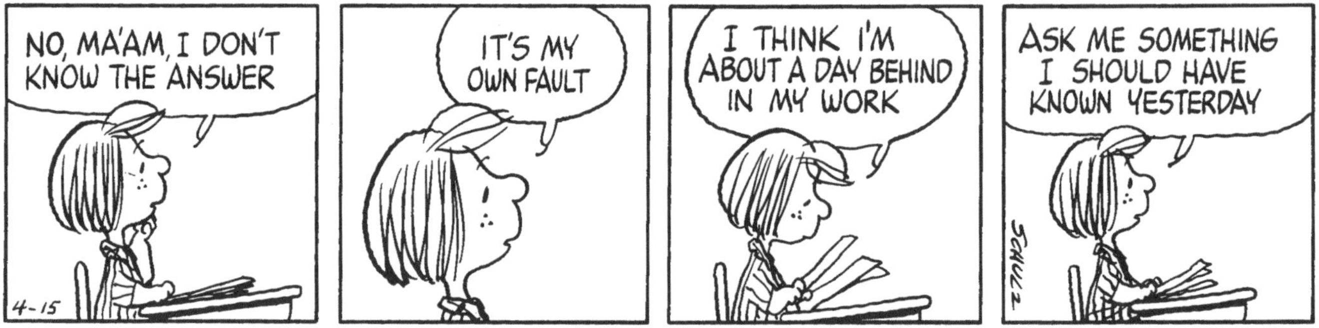
NO, MA'AM, I DON'T KNOW THE ANSWER
4-15
IT'S MY OWN FAULT
I THINK I'M ABOUT A DAY BEHIND IN MY WORK
ASK ME SOMETHING I SHOULD HAVE KNOWN YESTERDAY
SCHULZ

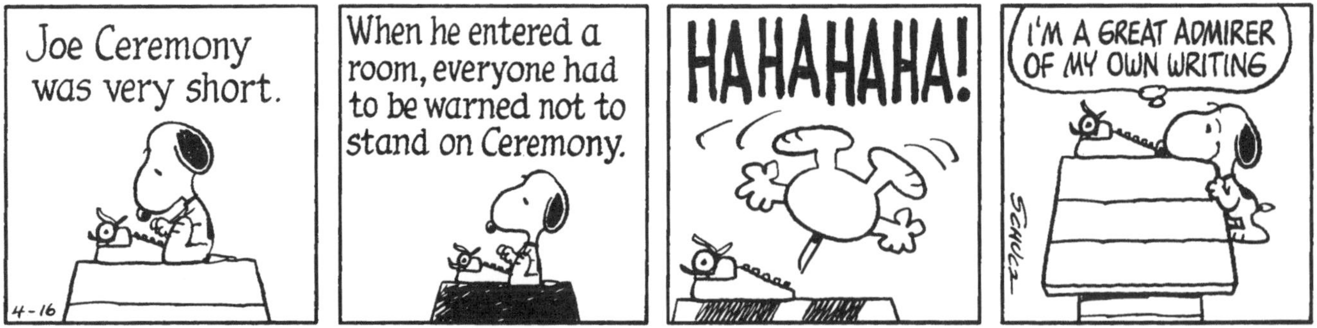
Joe Ceremony was very short.
4-16
When he entered a room, everyone had to be warned not to stand on Ceremony.
HAHAHAHA!
I'M A GREAT ADMIRER OF MY OWN WRITING
SCHULZ

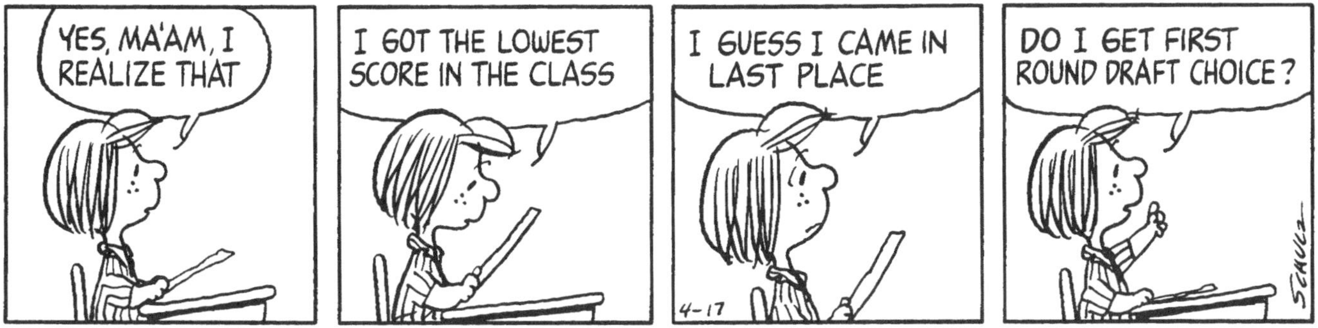
YES, MA'AM, I REALIZE THAT
I GOT THE LOWEST SCORE IN THE CLASS
I GUESS I CAME IN LAST PLACE
4-17
DO I GET FIRST ROUND DRAFT CHOICE?
SCHULZ

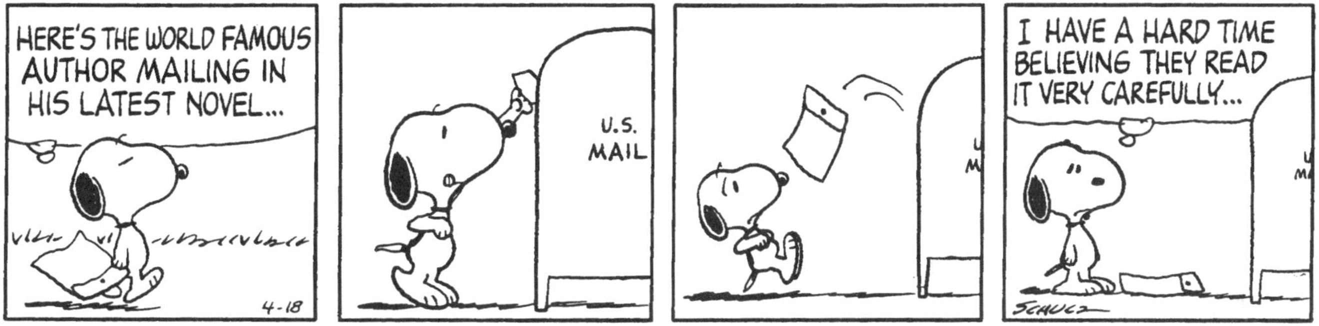
HERE'S THE WORLD FAMOUS AUTHOR MAILING IN HIS LATEST NOVEL...
4-18
U.S. MAIL
I HAVE A HARD TIME BELIEVING THEY READ IT VERY CAREFULLY...
SCHULZ

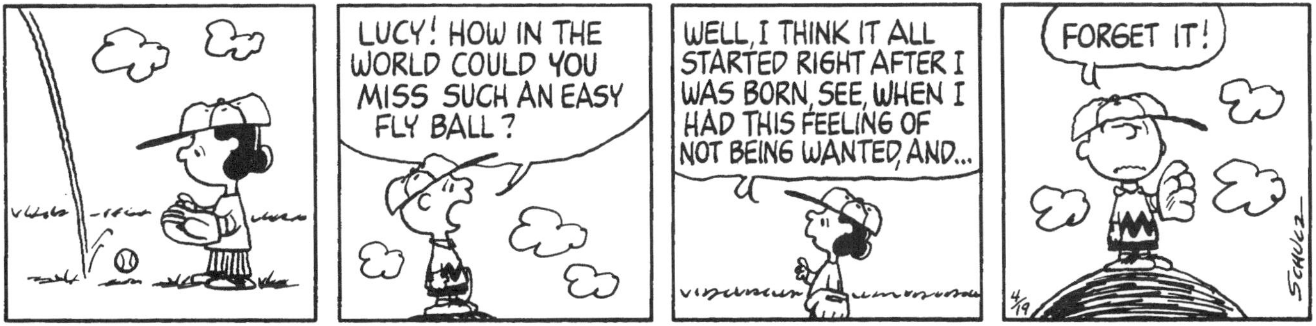
LUCY! HOW IN THE WORLD COULD YOU MISS SUCH AN EASY FLY BALL?
WELL, I THINK IT ALL STARTED RIGHT AFTER I WAS BORN, SEE, WHEN I HAD THIS FEELING OF NOT BEING WANTED, AND...
FORGET IT!
4/19
SCHULZ

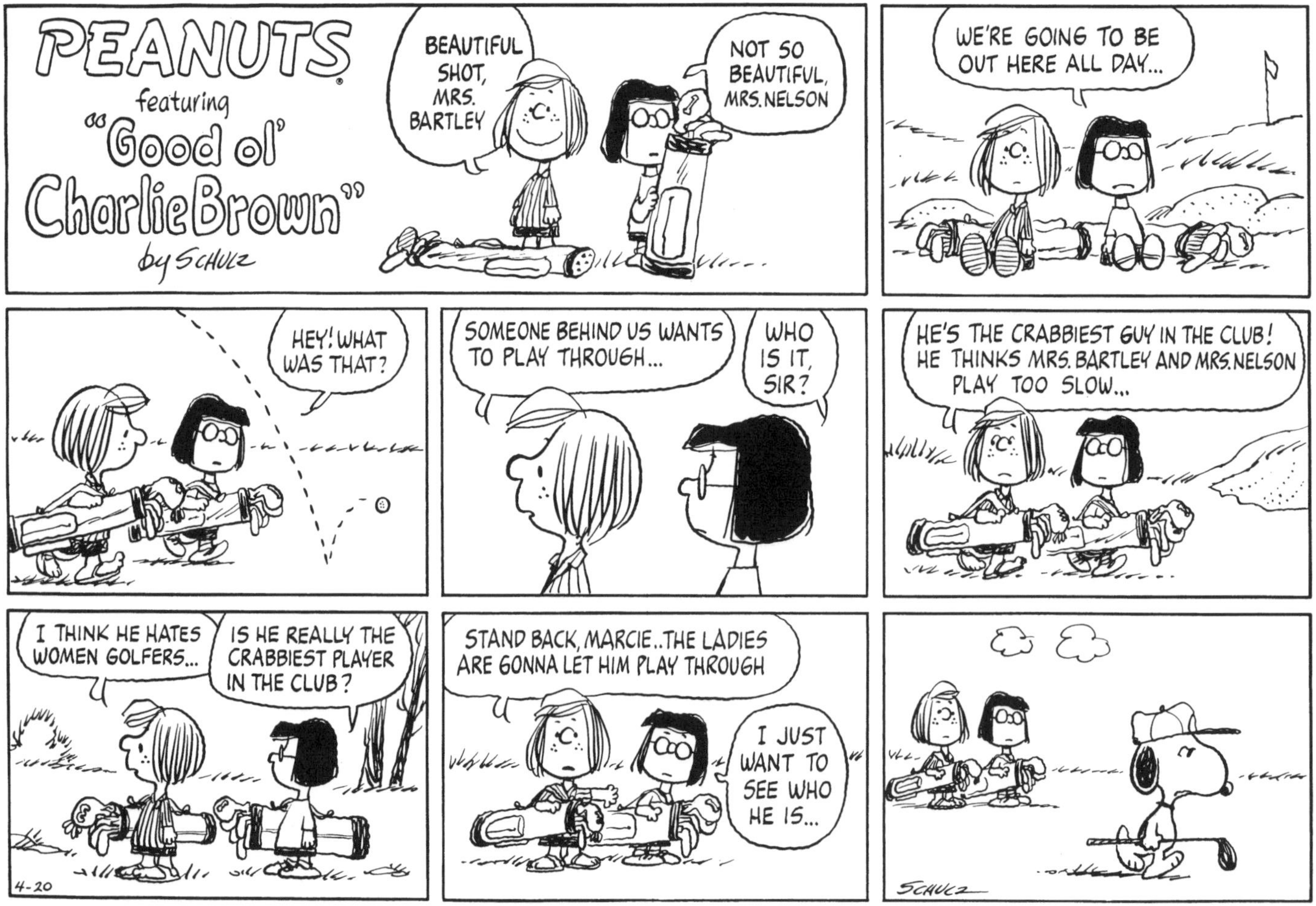
PEANUTS
featuring "Good ol' Charlie Brown"
by SCHULZ
BEAUTIFUL SHOT, MRS. BARTLEY
NOT SO BEAUTIFUL, MRS. NELSON
WE'RE GOING TO BE OUT HERE ALL DAY...
HEY! WHAT WAS THAT?
SOMEONE BEHIND US WANTS TO PLAY THROUGH...
WHO IS IT, SIR?
HE'S THE CRABBIEST GUY IN THE CLUB! HE THINKS MRS. BARTLEY AND MRS. NELSON PLAY TOO SLOW...
I THINK HE HATES WOMEN GOLFERS...
IS HE REALLY THE CRABBIEST PLAYER IN THE CLUB?
4-20
STAND BACK, MARCIE..THE LADIES ARE GONNA LET HIM PLAY THROUGH
I JUST WANT TO SEE WHO HE IS...
SCHULZ

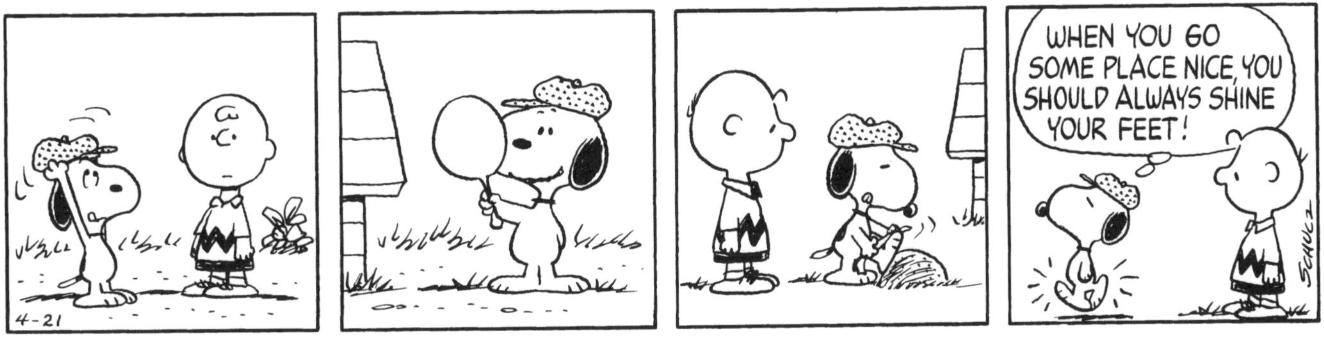
4-21
WHEN YOU GO SOME PLACE NICE, YOU SHOULD ALWAYS SHINE YOUR FEET!
SCHULZ

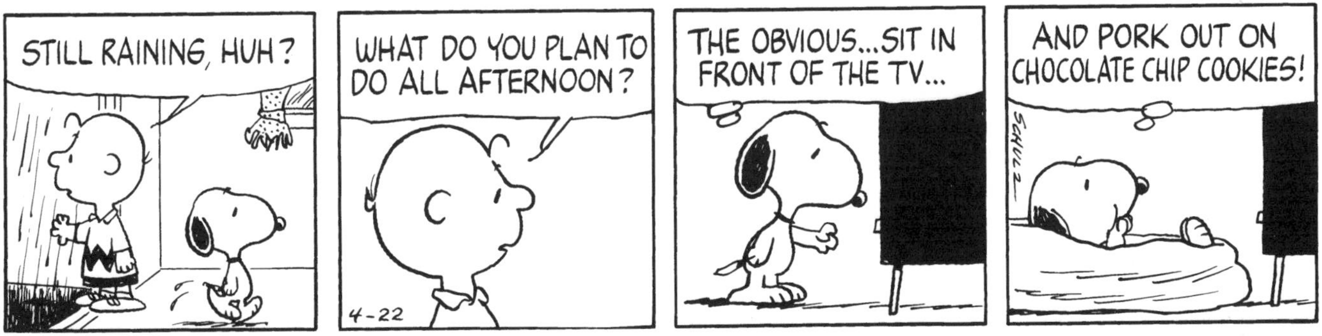
STILL RAINING, HUH?
WHAT DO YOU PLAN TO DO ALL AFTERNOON?
4-22
THE OBVIOUS...SIT IN FRONT OF THE TV...
AND PORK OUT ON CHOCOLATE CHIP COOKIES!
SCHULZ

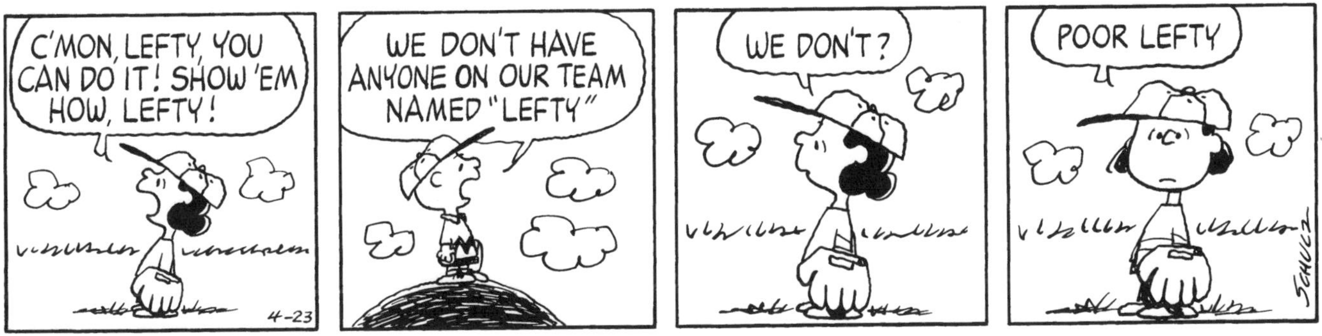
C'MON, LEFTY, YOU CAN DO IT! SHOW 'EM HOW, LEFTY!
4-23
WE DON'T HAVE ANYONE ON OUR TEAM NAMED "LEFTY"
WE DON'T?
POOR LEFTY
SCHULZ

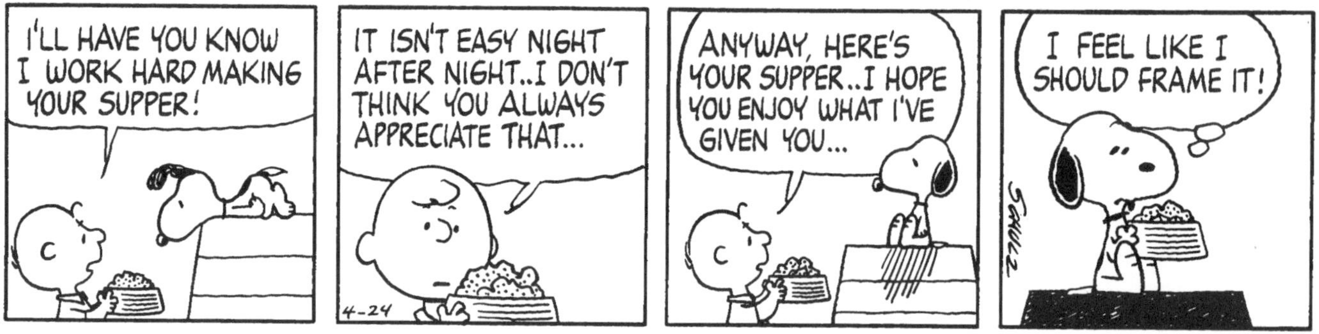
I'LL HAVE YOU KNOW I WORK HARD MAKING YOUR SUPPER!
IT ISN'T EASY NIGHT AFTER NIGHT..I DON'T THINK YOU ALWAYS APPRECIATE THAT...
4-24
ANYWAY, HERE'S YOUR SUPPER..I HOPE YOU ENJOY WHAT I'VE GIVEN YOU...
I FEEL LIKE I SHOULD FRAME IT!
SCHULZ

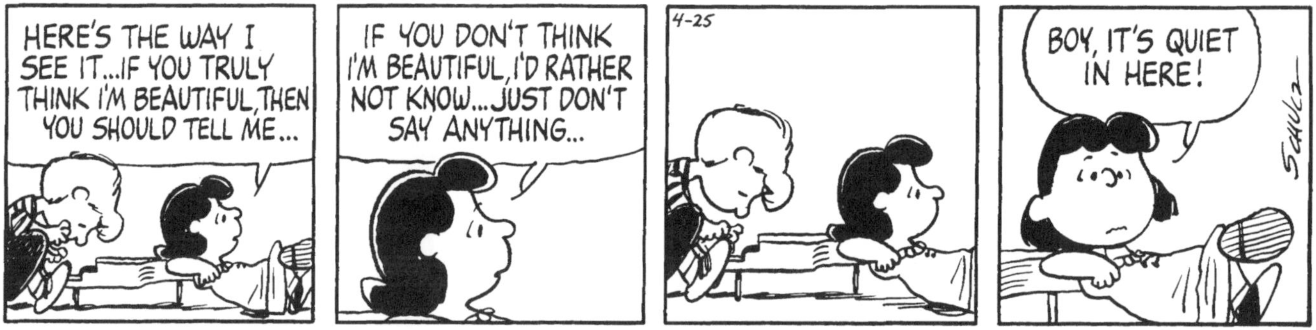
HERE'S THE WAY I SEE IT...IF YOU TRULY THINK I'M BEAUTIFUL, THEN YOU SHOULD TELL ME...
IF YOU DON'T THINK I'M BEAUTIFUL, I'D RATHER NOT KNOW...JUST DON'T SAY ANYTHING...
4-25
BOY, IT'S QUIET IN HERE!
SCHULZ

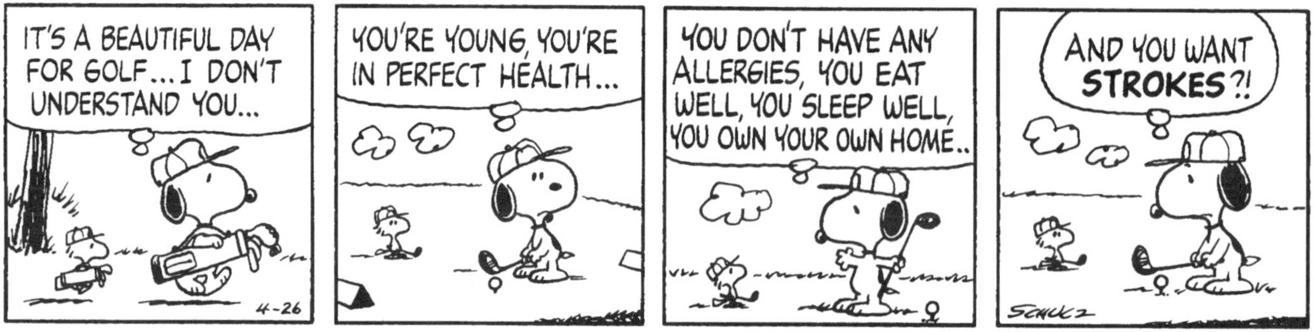
IT'S A BEAUTIFUL DAY FOR GOLF...I DON'T UNDERSTAND YOU...
4-26
YOU'RE YOUNG, YOU'RE IN PERFECT HEALTH...
YOU DON'T HAVE ANY ALLERGIES, YOU EAT WELL, YOU SLEEP WELL, YOU OWN YOUR OWN HOME..
AND YOU WANT **STROKES**?!
SCHULZ

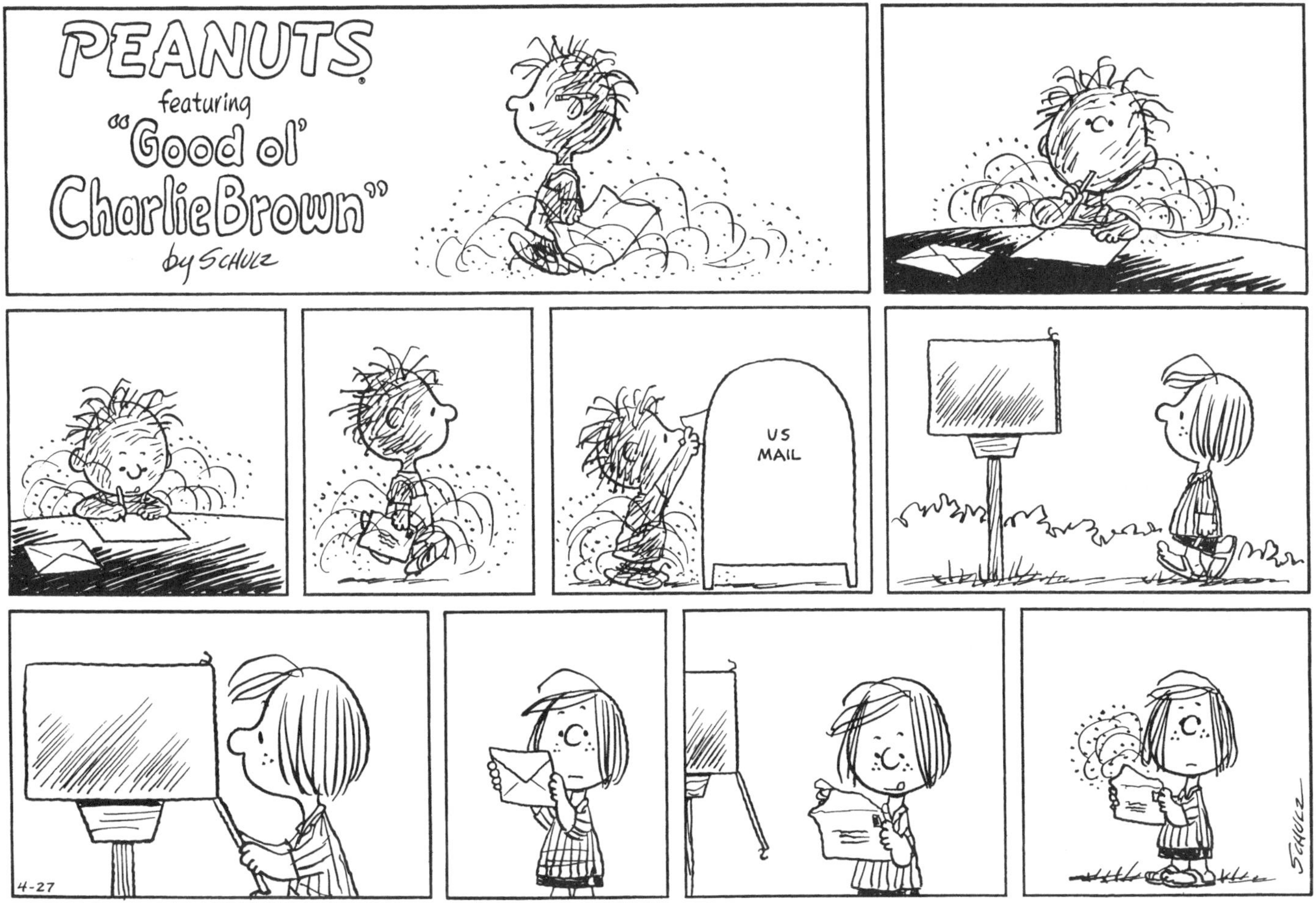
PEANUTS
featuring
"Good ol' Charlie Brown"
by SCHULZ
US MAIL
4-27
SCHULZ

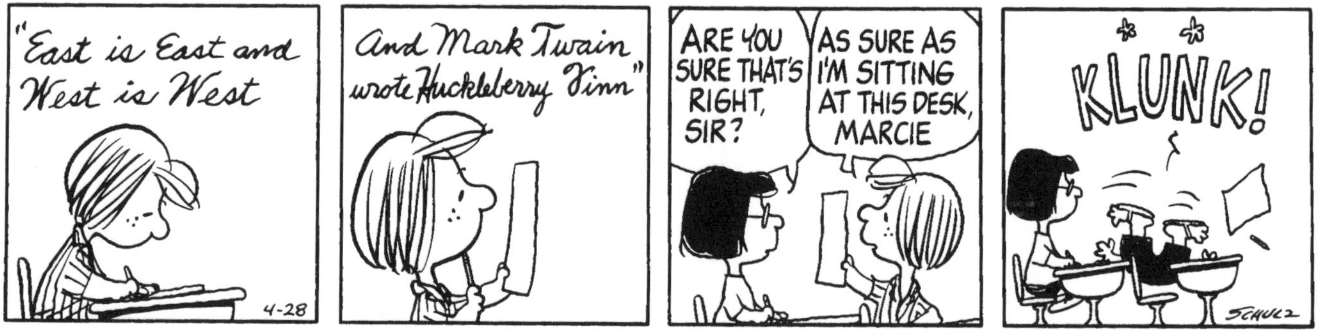
"East is East and West is West
4-28
And Mark Twain wrote Huckleberry Finn"
ARE YOU SURE THAT'S RIGHT, SIR?
AS SURE AS I'M SITTING AT THIS DESK, MARCIE
KLUNK!
SCHULZ

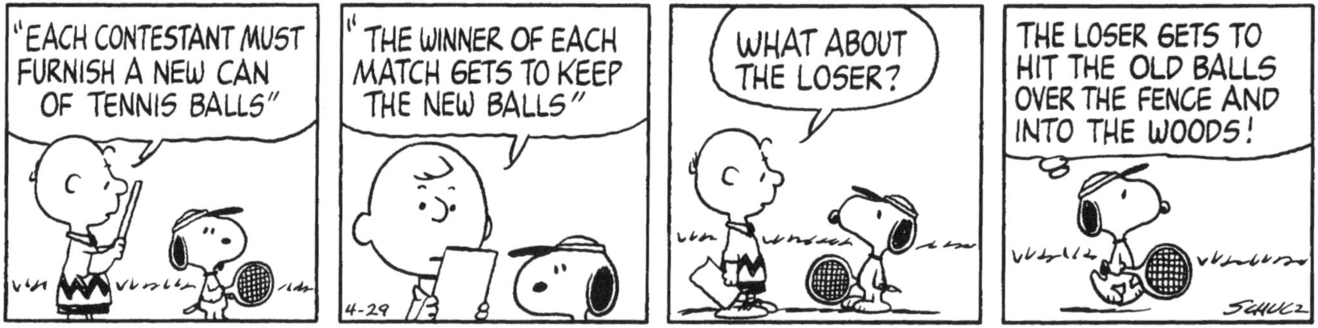
"EACH CONTESTANT MUST FURNISH A NEW CAN OF TENNIS BALLS"
"THE WINNER OF EACH MATCH GETS TO KEEP THE NEW BALLS"
4-29
WHAT ABOUT THE LOSER?
THE LOSER GETS TO HIT THE OLD BALLS OVER THE FENCE AND INTO THE WOODS!
SCHULZ

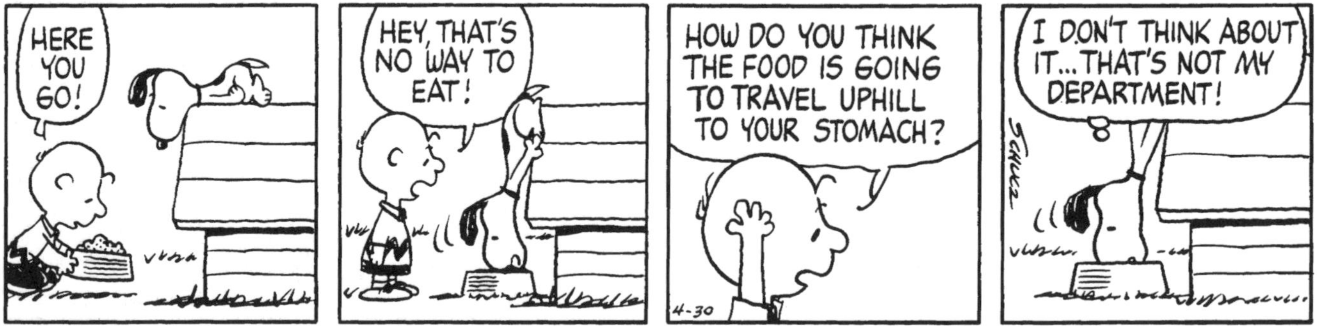
HERE YOU GO!
HEY, THAT'S NO WAY TO EAT!
HOW DO YOU THINK THE FOOD IS GOING TO TRAVEL UPHILL TO YOUR STOMACH?
4-30
SCHULZ
I DON'T THINK ABOUT IT... THAT'S NOT MY DEPARTMENT!

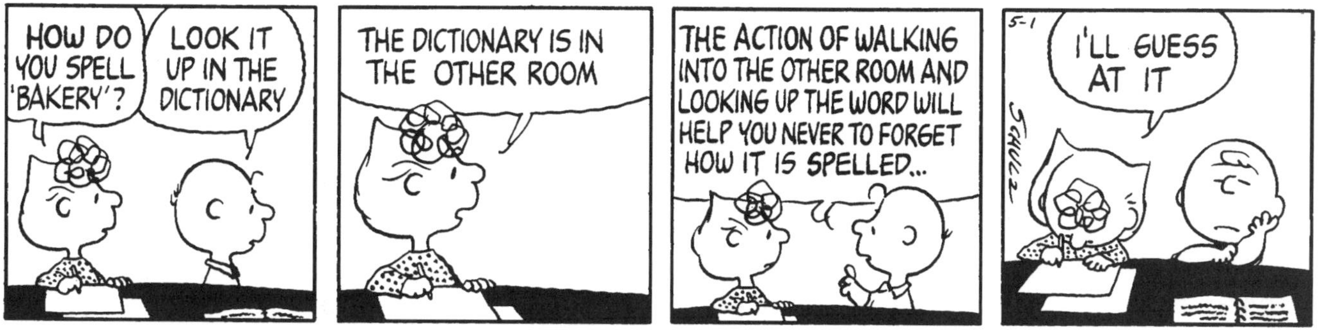
HOW DO YOU SPELL 'BAKERY'?
LOOK IT UP IN THE DICTIONARY
THE DICTIONARY IS IN THE OTHER ROOM
THE ACTION OF WALKING INTO THE OTHER ROOM AND LOOKING UP THE WORD WILL HELP YOU NEVER TO FORGET HOW IT IS SPELLED...
5-1
I'LL GUESS AT IT
SCHULZ

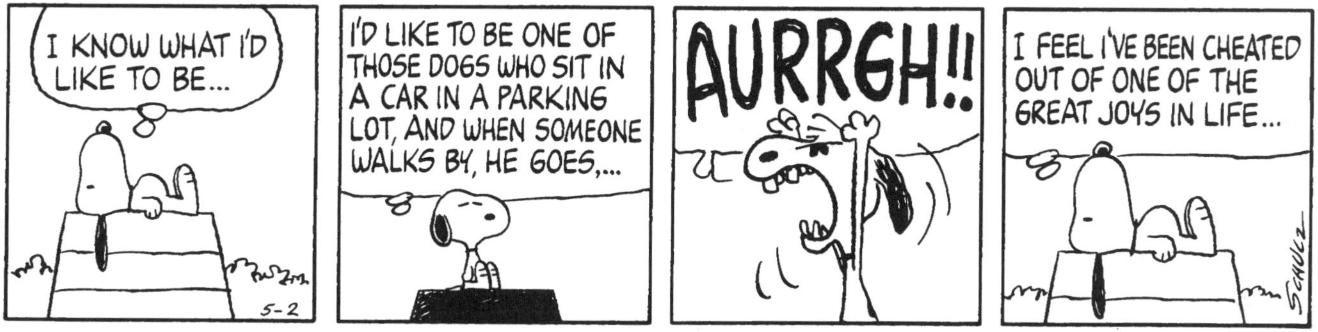
I KNOW WHAT I'D LIKE TO BE...
5-2
I'D LIKE TO BE ONE OF THOSE DOGS WHO SIT IN A CAR IN A PARKING LOT, AND WHEN SOMEONE WALKS BY, HE GOES,...
AURRGH!!
I FEEL I'VE BEEN CHEATED OUT OF ONE OF THE GREAT JOYS IN LIFE...
SCHULZ

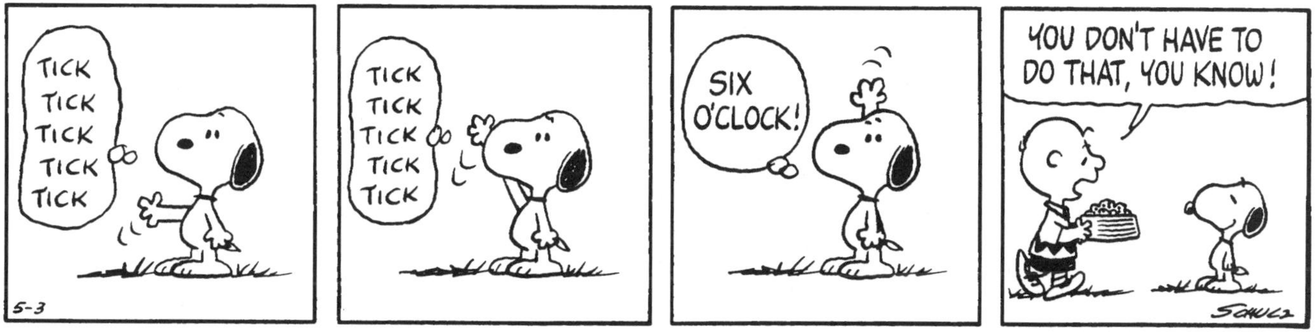
TICK TICK TICK TICK TICK
5-3
TICK TICK TICK TICK TICK
SIX O'CLOCK!
YOU DON'T HAVE TO DO THAT, YOU KNOW!
SCHULZ

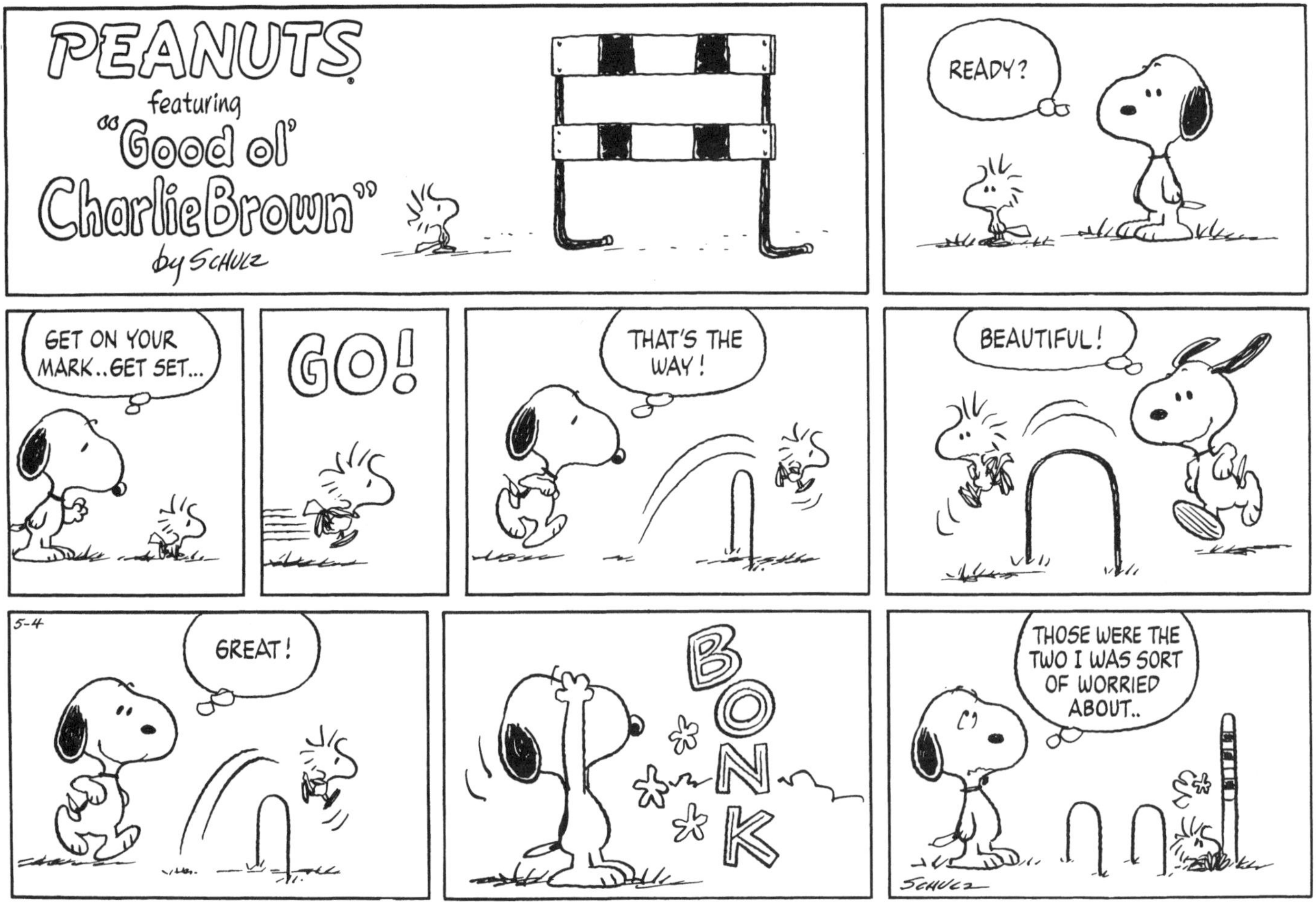
PEANUTS
featuring
"Good ol' Charlie Brown"
by SCHULZ
READY?
GET ON YOUR MARK..GET SET...
GO!
THAT'S THE WAY!
BEAUTIFUL!
5-4
GREAT!
BONK
THOSE WERE THE TWO I WAS SORT OF WORRIED ABOUT..
SCHULZ

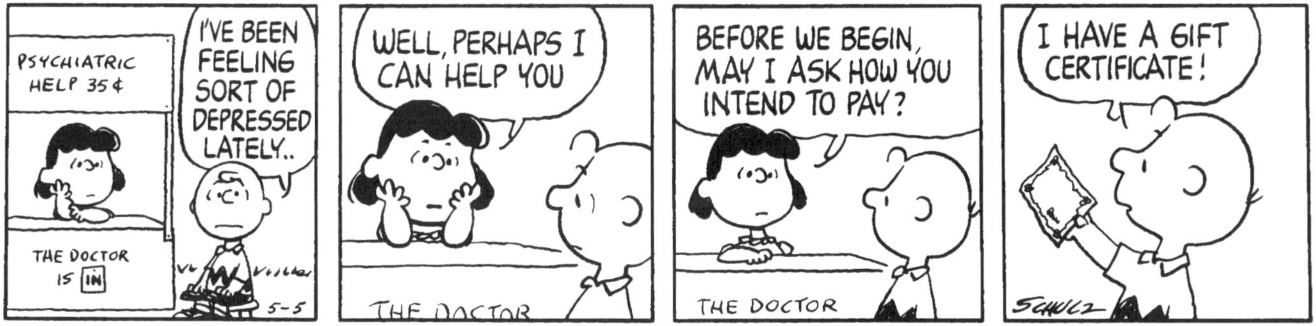
PSYCHIATRIC HELP 35¢
THE DOCTOR IS IN
I'VE BEEN FEELING SORT OF DEPRESSED LATELY..
WELL, PERHAPS I CAN HELP YOU
BEFORE WE BEGIN, MAY I ASK HOW YOU INTEND TO PAY?
THE DOCTOR
I HAVE A GIFT CERTIFICATE!

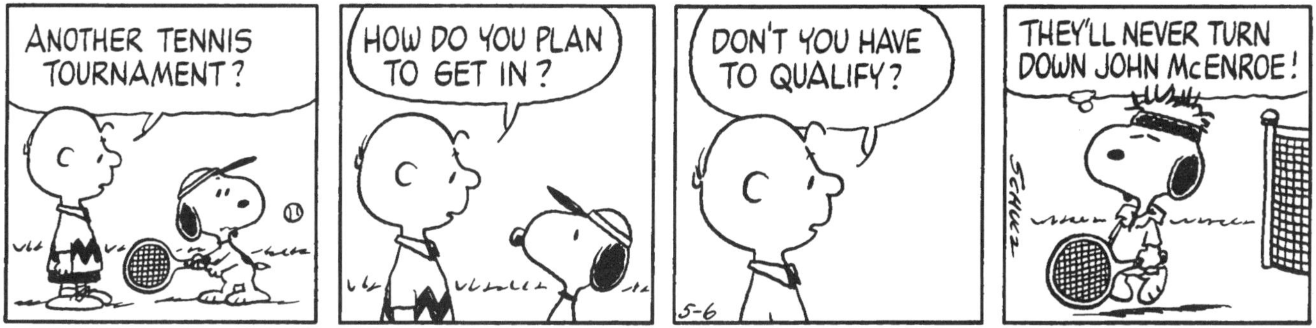
ANOTHER TENNIS TOURNAMENT?
HOW DO YOU PLAN TO GET IN?
DON'T YOU HAVE TO QUALIFY?
THEY'LL NEVER TURN DOWN JOHN McENROE!

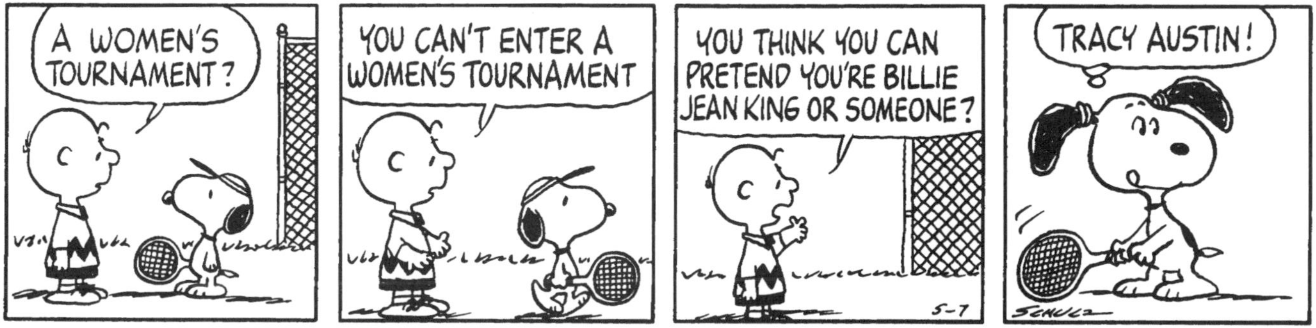
A WOMEN'S TOURNAMENT?
YOU CAN'T ENTER A WOMEN'S TOURNAMENT
YOU THINK YOU CAN PRETEND YOU'RE BILLIE JEAN KING OR SOMEONE?
TRACY AUSTIN!

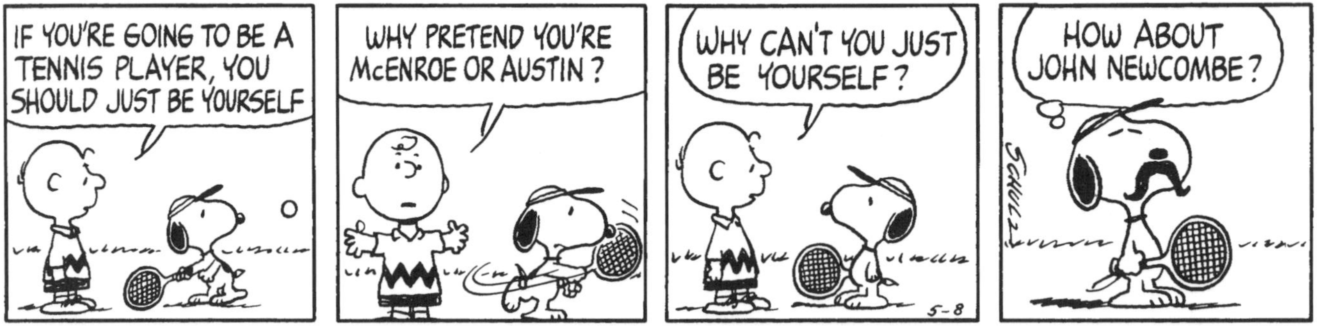
IF YOU'RE GOING TO BE A TENNIS PLAYER, YOU SHOULD JUST BE YOURSELF
WHY PRETEND YOU'RE McENROE OR AUSTIN ?
WHY CAN'T YOU JUST BE YOURSELF ?
5-8
HOW ABOUT JOHN NEWCOMBE ?
SCHULZ

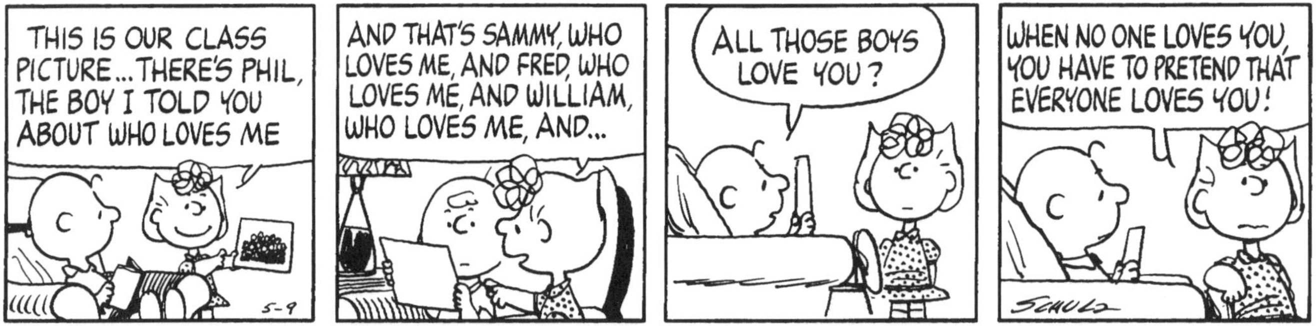
THIS IS OUR CLASS PICTURE...THERE'S PHIL, THE BOY I TOLD YOU ABOUT WHO LOVES ME
5-9
AND THAT'S SAMMY, WHO LOVES ME, AND FRED, WHO LOVES ME, AND WILLIAM, WHO LOVES ME, AND...
ALL THOSE BOYS LOVE YOU ?
WHEN NO ONE LOVES YOU, YOU HAVE TO PRETEND THAT EVERYONE LOVES YOU !
SCHULZ

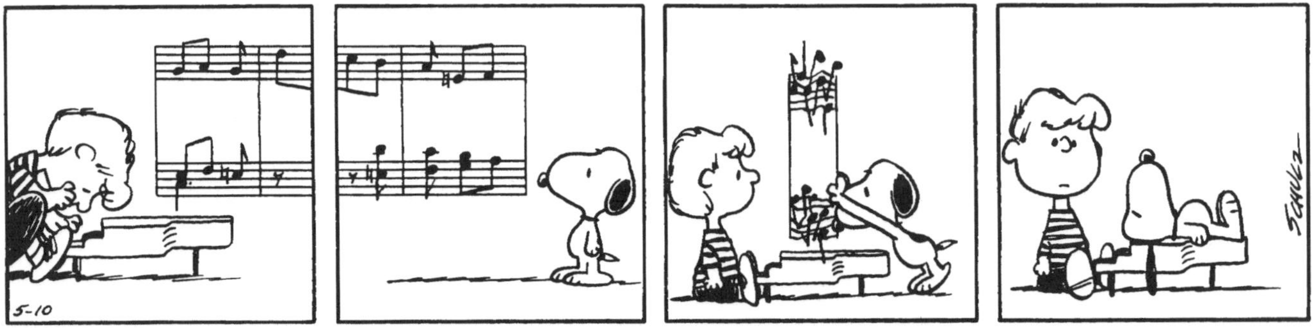
5-10
SCHULZ

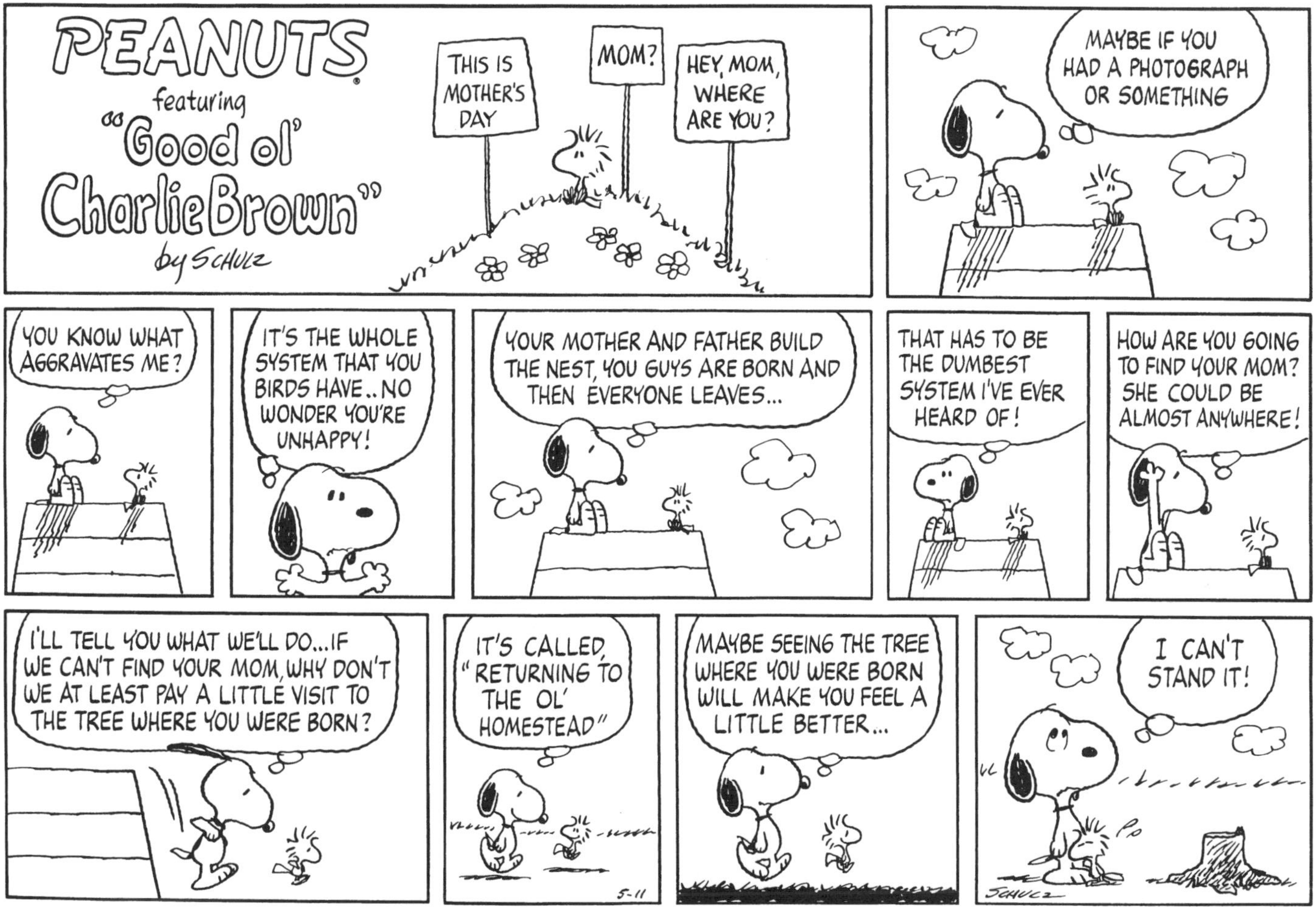
PEANUTS
featuring "Good ol' Charlie Brown"
by SCHULZ
THIS IS MOTHER'S DAY
MOM?
HEY, MOM, WHERE ARE YOU?
MAYBE IF YOU HAD A PHOTOGRAPH OR SOMETHING
YOU KNOW WHAT AGGRAVATES ME?
IT'S THE WHOLE SYSTEM THAT YOU BIRDS HAVE..NO WONDER YOU'RE UNHAPPY!
YOUR MOTHER AND FATHER BUILD THE NEST, YOU GUYS ARE BORN AND THEN EVERYONE LEAVES...
THAT HAS TO BE THE DUMBEST SYSTEM I'VE EVER HEARD OF!
HOW ARE YOU GOING TO FIND YOUR MOM? SHE COULD BE ALMOST ANYWHERE!
I'LL TELL YOU WHAT WE'LL DO...IF WE CAN'T FIND YOUR MOM, WHY DON'T WE AT LEAST PAY A LITTLE VISIT TO THE TREE WHERE YOU WERE BORN?
IT'S CALLED, "RETURNING TO THE OL' HOMESTEAD"
5-11
MAYBE SEEING THE TREE WHERE YOU WERE BORN WILL MAKE YOU FEEL A LITTLE BETTER...
I CAN'T STAND IT!
SCHULZ

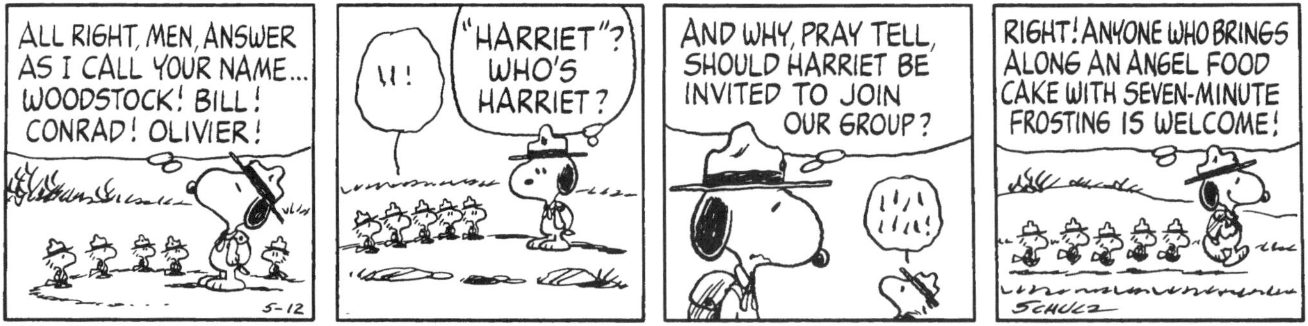
ALL RIGHT, MEN, ANSWER AS I CALL YOUR NAME... WOODSTOCK! BILL! CONRAD! OLIVIER!
5-12
"HARRIET"? WHO'S HARRIET?
AND WHY, PRAY TELL, SHOULD HARRIET BE INVITED TO JOIN OUR GROUP?
RIGHT! ANYONE WHO BRINGS ALONG AN ANGEL FOOD CAKE WITH SEVEN-MINUTE FROSTING IS WELCOME!
SCHULZ

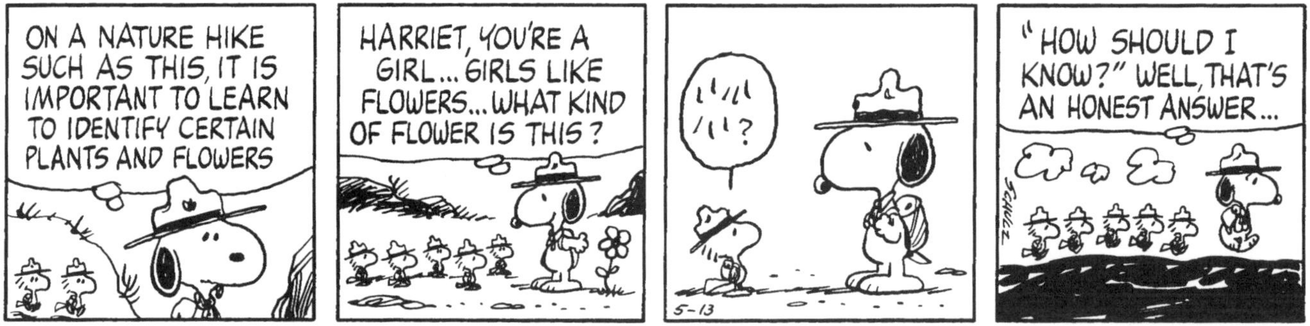
ON A NATURE HIKE SUCH AS THIS, IT IS IMPORTANT TO LEARN TO IDENTIFY CERTAIN PLANTS AND FLOWERS
HARRIET, YOU'RE A GIRL... GIRLS LIKE FLOWERS... WHAT KIND OF FLOWER IS THIS?
5-13
"HOW SHOULD I KNOW?" WELL, THAT'S AN HONEST ANSWER...
SCHULZ

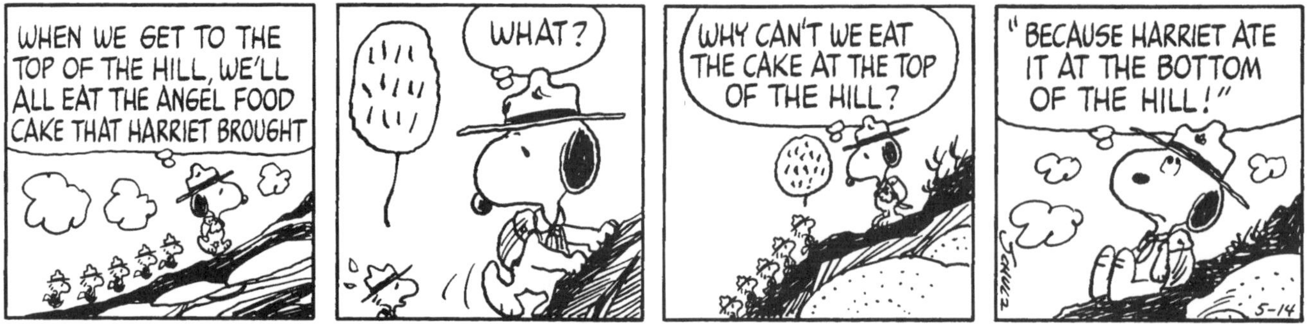
WHEN WE GET TO THE TOP OF THE HILL, WE'LL ALL EAT THE ANGEL FOOD CAKE THAT HARRIET BROUGHT
WHAT?
WHY CAN'T WE EAT THE CAKE AT THE TOP OF THE HILL?
"BECAUSE HARRIET ATE IT AT THE BOTTOM OF THE HILL!"
SCHULZ
5-14

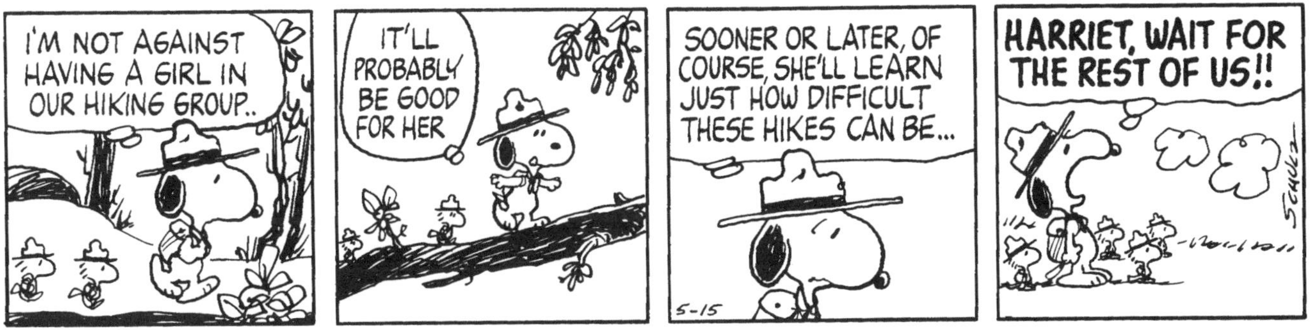
I'M NOT AGAINST HAVING A GIRL IN OUR HIKING GROUP..
IT'LL PROBABLY BE GOOD FOR HER
SOONER OR LATER, OF COURSE, SHE'LL LEARN JUST HOW DIFFICULT THESE HIKES CAN BE...
5-15
HARRIET, WAIT FOR THE REST OF US!!
SCHULZ

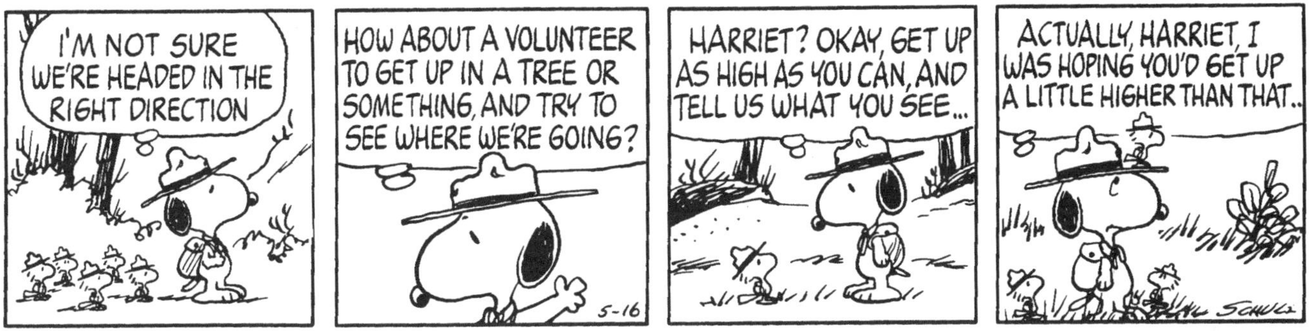
I'M NOT SURE WE'RE HEADED IN THE RIGHT DIRECTION
HOW ABOUT A VOLUNTEER TO GET UP IN A TREE OR SOMETHING, AND TRY TO SEE WHERE WE'RE GOING?
5-16
HARRIET? OKAY, GET UP AS HIGH AS YOU CAN, AND TELL US WHAT YOU SEE...
ACTUALLY, HARRIET, I WAS HOPING YOU'D GET UP A LITTLE HIGHER THAN THAT..
SCHULZ

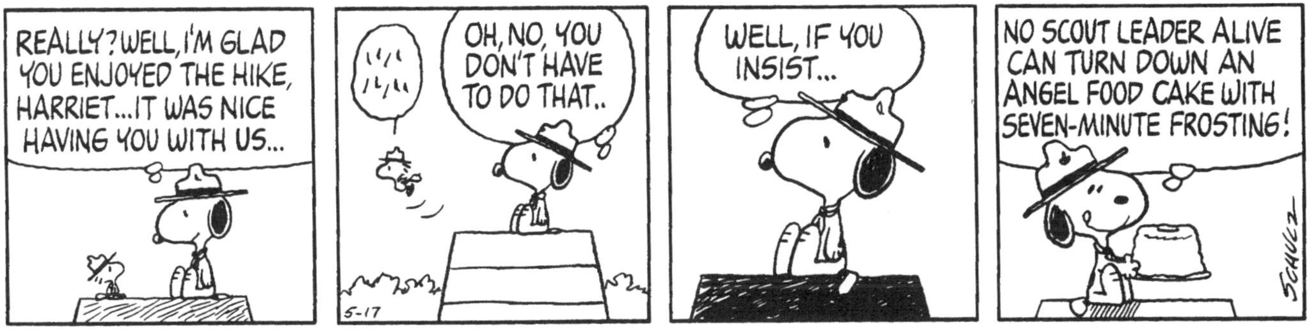
REALLY? WELL, I'M GLAD YOU ENJOYED THE HIKE, HARRIET...IT WAS NICE HAVING YOU WITH US...
OH, NO, YOU DON'T HAVE TO DO THAT..
5-17
WELL, IF YOU INSIST...
NO SCOUT LEADER ALIVE CAN TURN DOWN AN ANGEL FOOD CAKE WITH SEVEN-MINUTE FROSTING!
SCHULZ

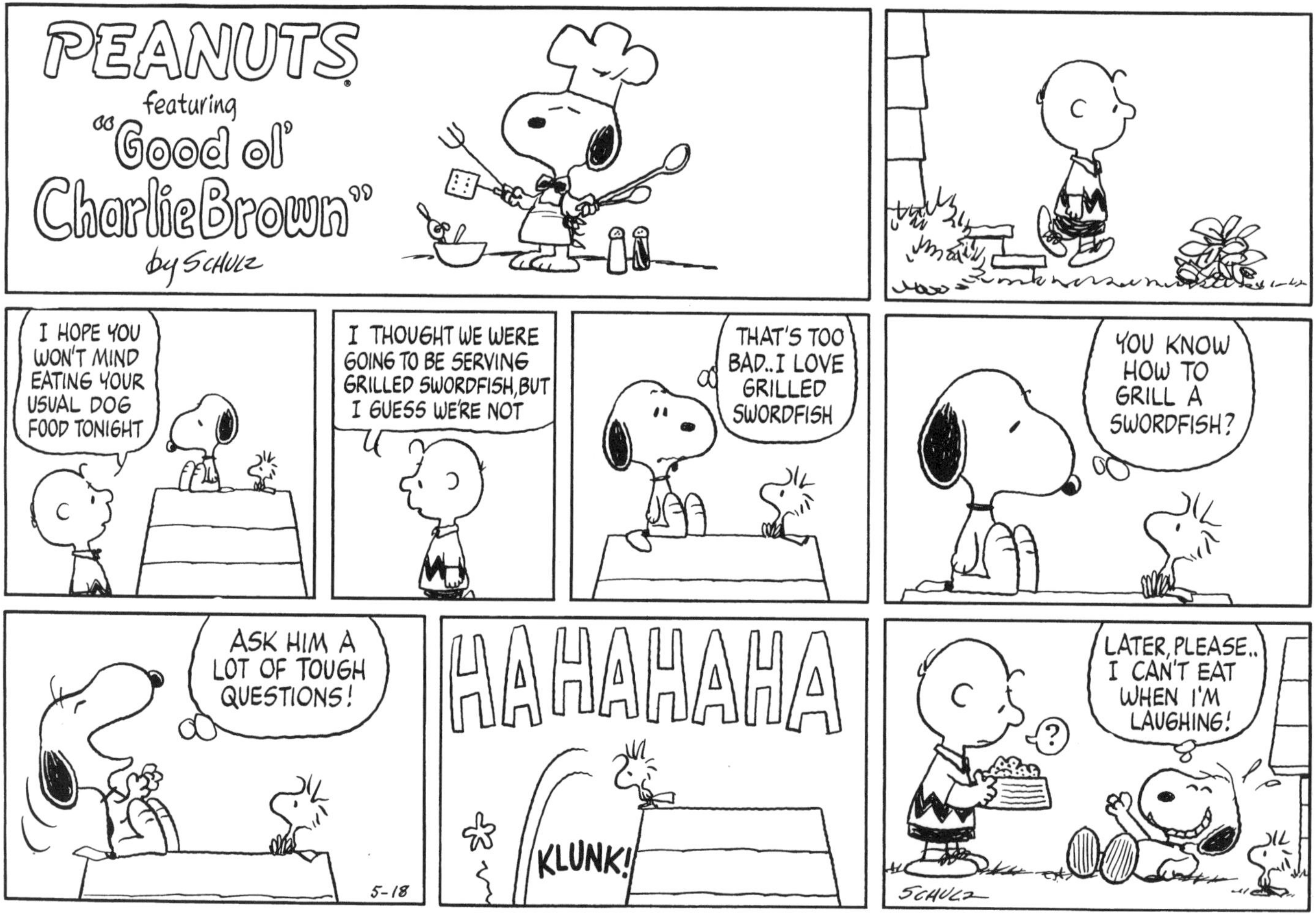
PEANUTS
featuring
"Good ol' Charlie Brown"
by SCHULZ
I HOPE YOU WON'T MIND EATING YOUR USUAL DOG FOOD TONIGHT
I THOUGHT WE WERE GOING TO BE SERVING GRILLED SWORDFISH, BUT I GUESS WE'RE NOT
THAT'S TOO BAD..I LOVE GRILLED SWORDFISH
YOU KNOW HOW TO GRILL A SWORDFISH?
ASK HIM A LOT OF TOUGH QUESTIONS!
5-18
HAHAHAHA
KLUNK!
?
LATER, PLEASE.. I CAN'T EAT WHEN I'M LAUGHING!
SCHULZ

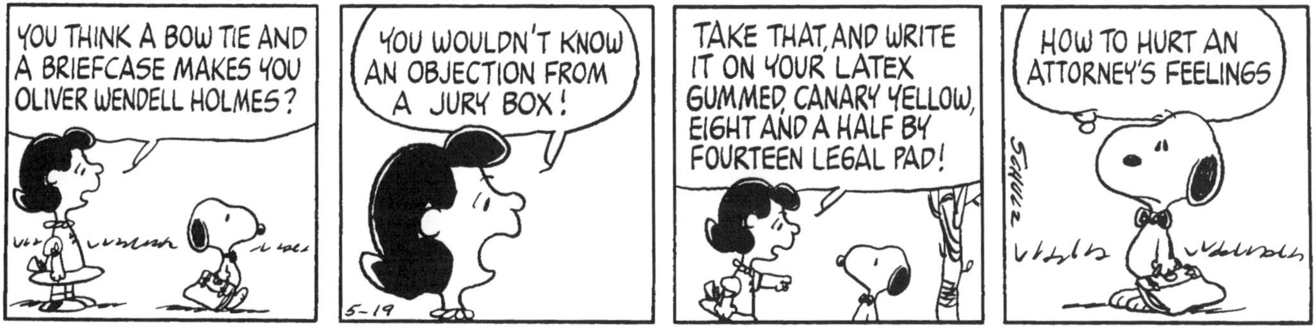
YOU THINK A BOW TIE AND A BRIEFCASE MAKES YOU OLIVER WENDELL HOLMES?
YOU WOULDN'T KNOW AN OBJECTION FROM A JURY BOX!
5-19
TAKE THAT, AND WRITE IT ON YOUR LATEX GUMMED, CANARY YELLOW, EIGHT AND A HALF BY FOURTEEN LEGAL PAD!
HOW TO HURT AN ATTORNEY'S FEELINGS
SCHULZ

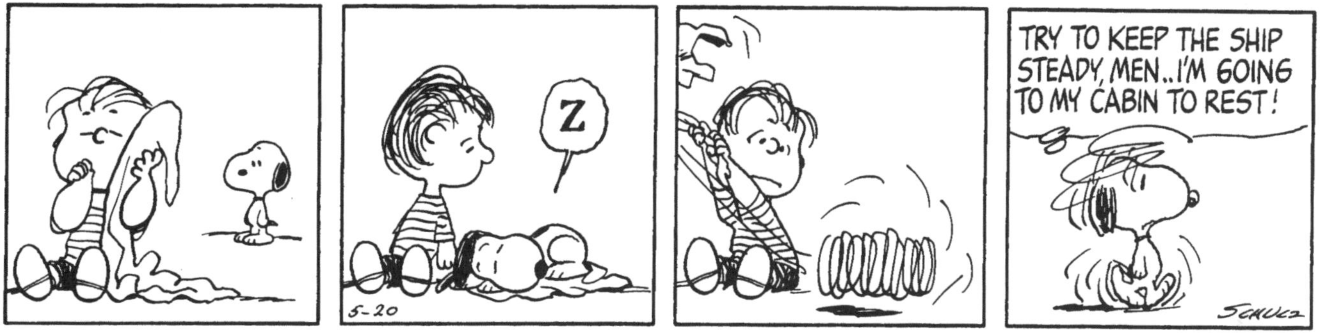
Z
5-20
TRY TO KEEP THE SHIP STEADY, MEN..I'M GOING TO MY CABIN TO REST!
SCHULZ

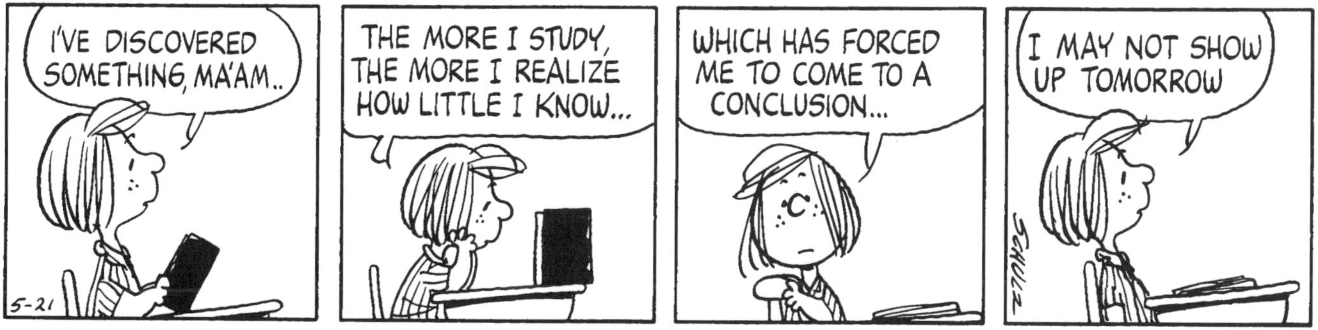
I'VE DISCOVERED SOMETHING, MA'AM..
5-21
THE MORE I STUDY, THE MORE I REALIZE HOW LITTLE I KNOW...
WHICH HAS FORCED ME TO COME TO A CONCLUSION...
I MAY NOT SHOW UP TOMORROW
SCHULZ

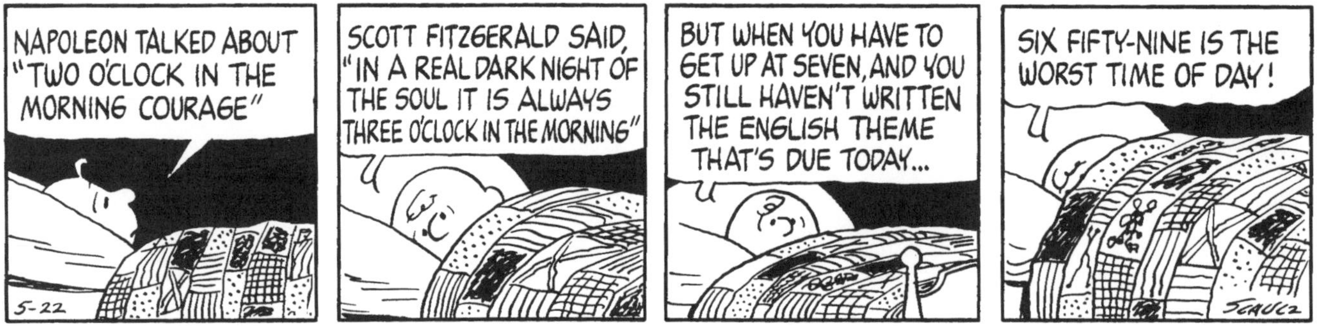
NAPOLEON TALKED ABOUT "TWO O'CLOCK IN THE MORNING COURAGE"
SCOTT FITZGERALD SAID, "IN A REAL DARK NIGHT OF THE SOUL IT IS ALWAYS THREE O'CLOCK IN THE MORNING"
BUT WHEN YOU HAVE TO GET UP AT SEVEN, AND YOU STILL HAVEN'T WRITTEN THE ENGLISH THEME THAT'S DUE TODAY...
SIX FIFTY-NINE IS THE WORST TIME OF DAY!
5-22

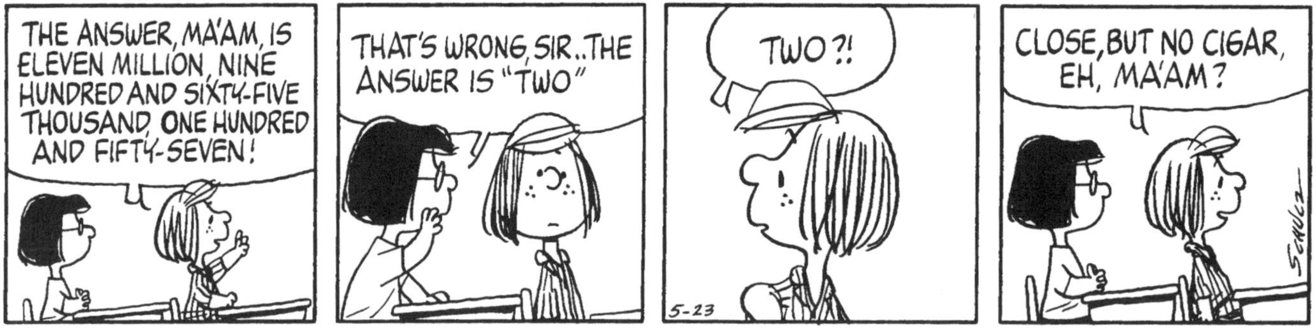
THE ANSWER, MA'AM, IS ELEVEN MILLION, NINE HUNDRED AND SIXTY-FIVE THOUSAND, ONE HUNDRED AND FIFTY-SEVEN!
THAT'S WRONG, SIR..THE ANSWER IS "TWO"
TWO?!
CLOSE, BUT NO CIGAR, EH, MA'AM?
5-23

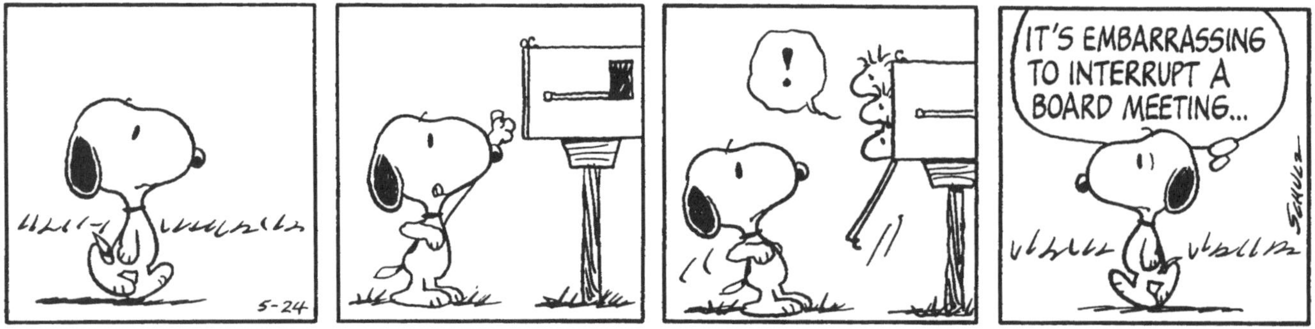
!
IT'S EMBARRASSING TO INTERRUPT A BOARD MEETING...
5-24

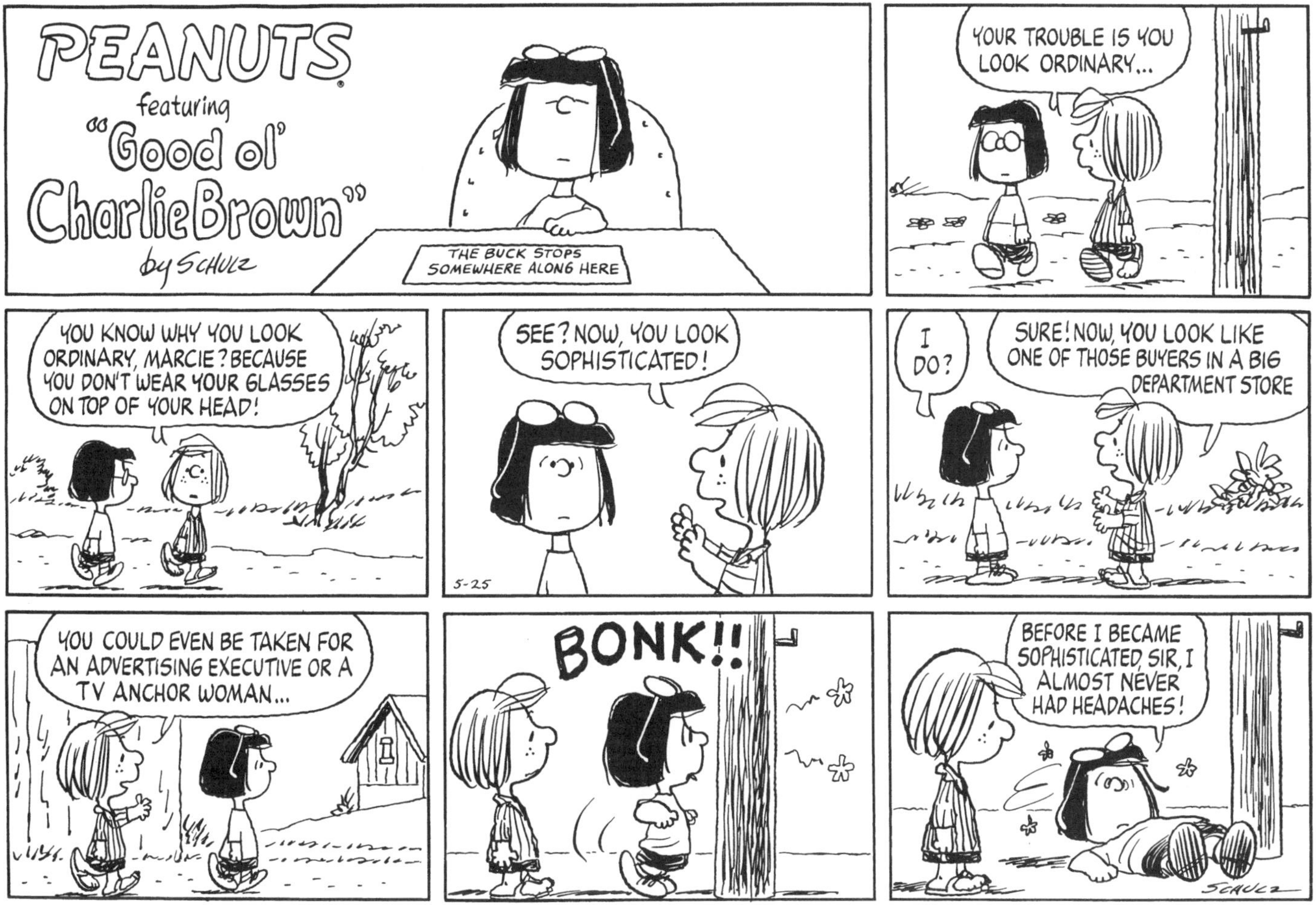
PEANUTS
featuring
"Good ol' CharlieBrown"
by SCHULZ
THE BUCK STOPS SOMEWHERE ALONG HERE
YOUR TROUBLE IS YOU LOOK ORDINARY...
YOU KNOW WHY YOU LOOK ORDINARY, MARCIE? BECAUSE YOU DON'T WEAR YOUR GLASSES ON TOP OF YOUR HEAD!
SEE? NOW, YOU LOOK SOPHISTICATED!
5-25
I DO?
SURE! NOW, YOU LOOK LIKE ONE OF THOSE BUYERS IN A BIG DEPARTMENT STORE
YOU COULD EVEN BE TAKEN FOR AN ADVERTISING EXECUTIVE OR A TV ANCHOR WOMAN...
BONK!!
BEFORE I BECAME SOPHISTICATED, SIR, I ALMOST NEVER HAD HEADACHES!
SCHULZ

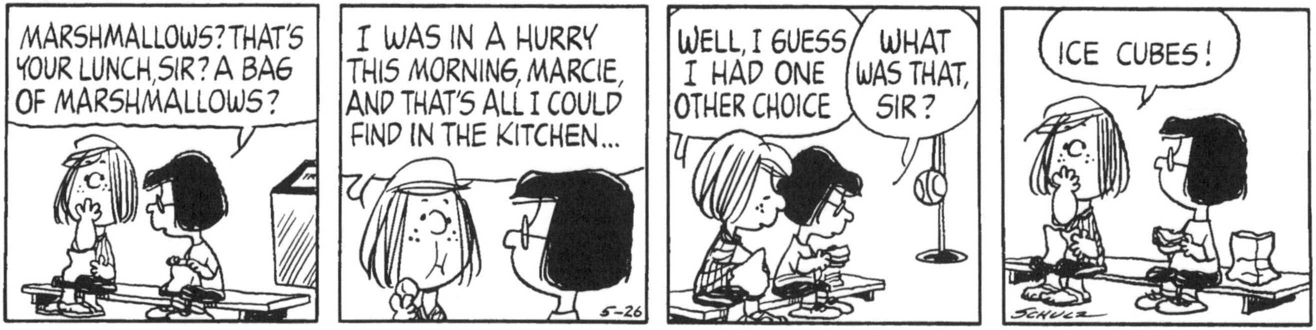
MARSHMALLOWS? THAT'S YOUR LUNCH, SIR? A BAG OF MARSHMALLOWS?
I WAS IN A HURRY THIS MORNING, MARCIE, AND THAT'S ALL I COULD FIND IN THE KITCHEN...
5-26
WELL, I GUESS I HAD ONE OTHER CHOICE
WHAT WAS THAT, SIR?
ICE CUBES!
SCHULZ

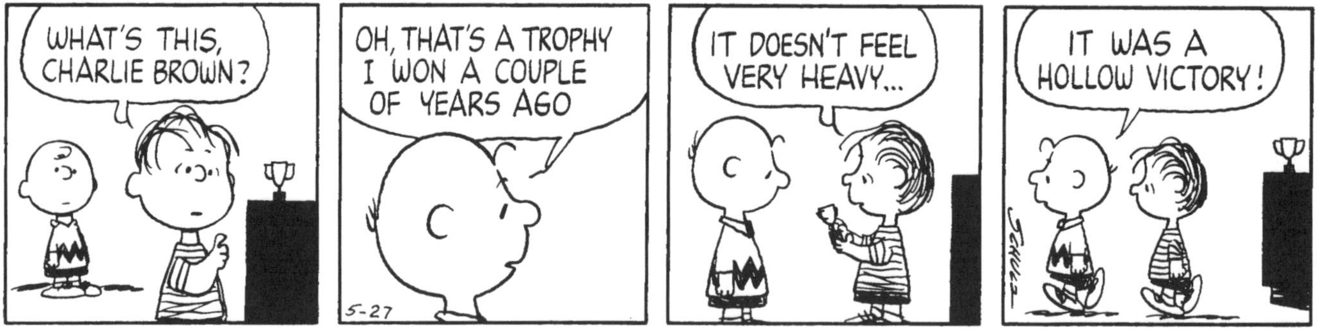
WHAT'S THIS, CHARLIE BROWN?
OH, THAT'S A TROPHY I WON A COUPLE OF YEARS AGO
5-27
IT DOESN'T FEEL VERY HEAVY...
IT WAS A HOLLOW VICTORY!
SCHULZ

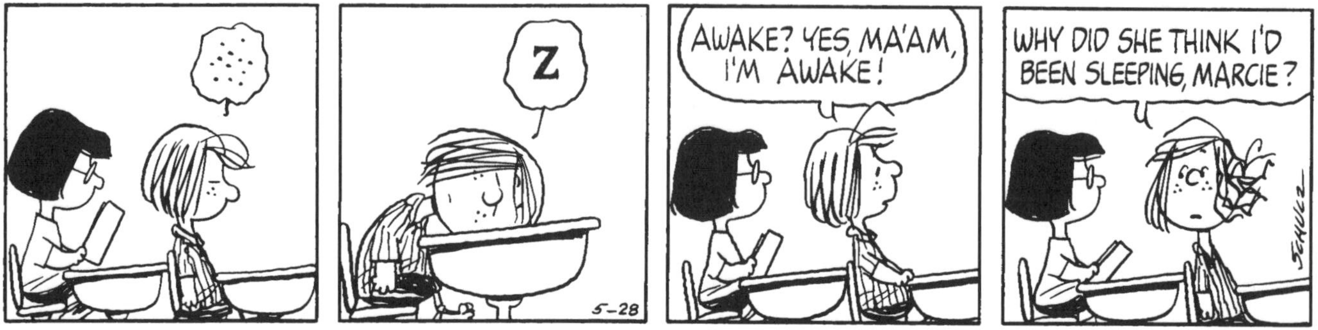
Z
5-28
AWAKE? YES, MA'AM, I'M AWAKE!
WHY DID SHE THINK I'D BEEN SLEEPING, MARCIE?
SCHULZ

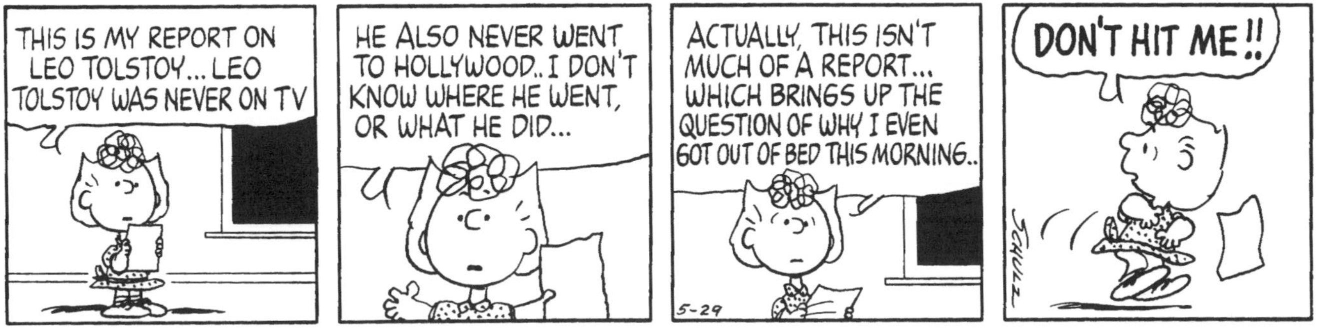
THIS IS MY REPORT ON LEO TOLSTOY... LEO TOLSTOY WAS NEVER ON TV
HE ALSO NEVER WENT TO HOLLYWOOD.. I DON'T KNOW WHERE HE WENT, OR WHAT HE DID...
ACTUALLY, THIS ISN'T MUCH OF A REPORT... WHICH BRINGS UP THE QUESTION OF WHY I EVEN GOT OUT OF BED THIS MORNING..
5-29
DON'T HIT ME!!
SCHULZ

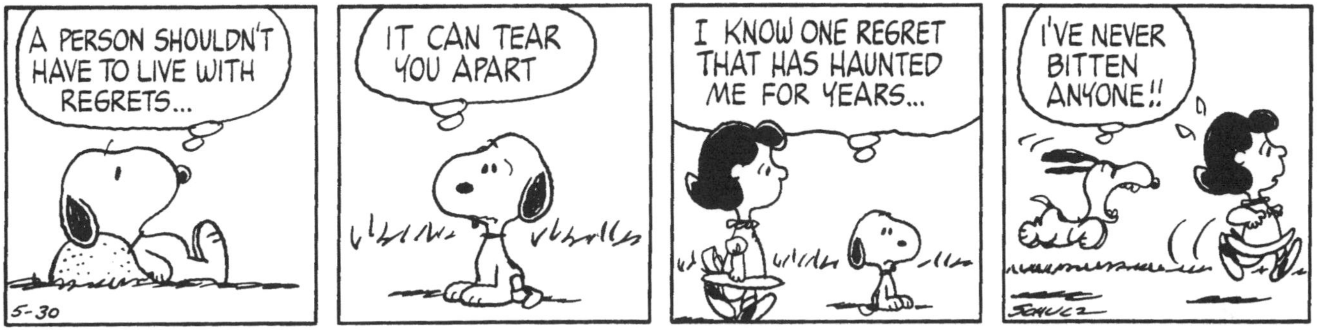
A PERSON SHOULDN'T HAVE TO LIVE WITH REGRETS...
5-30
IT CAN TEAR YOU APART
I KNOW ONE REGRET THAT HAS HAUNTED ME FOR YEARS...
I'VE NEVER BITTEN ANYONE!!
SCHULZ

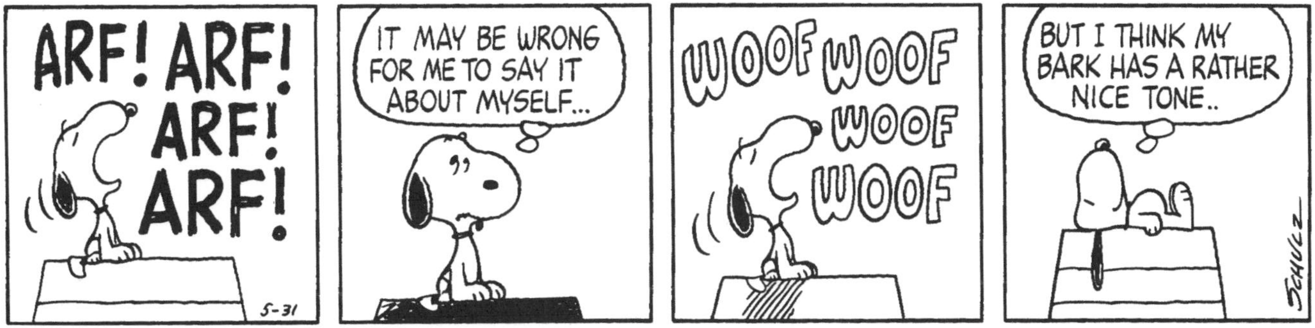
ARF! ARF! ARF! ARF!
5-31
IT MAY BE WRONG FOR ME TO SAY IT ABOUT MYSELF...
WOOF WOOF WOOF WOOF
BUT I THINK MY BARK HAS A RATHER NICE TONE..
SCHULZ

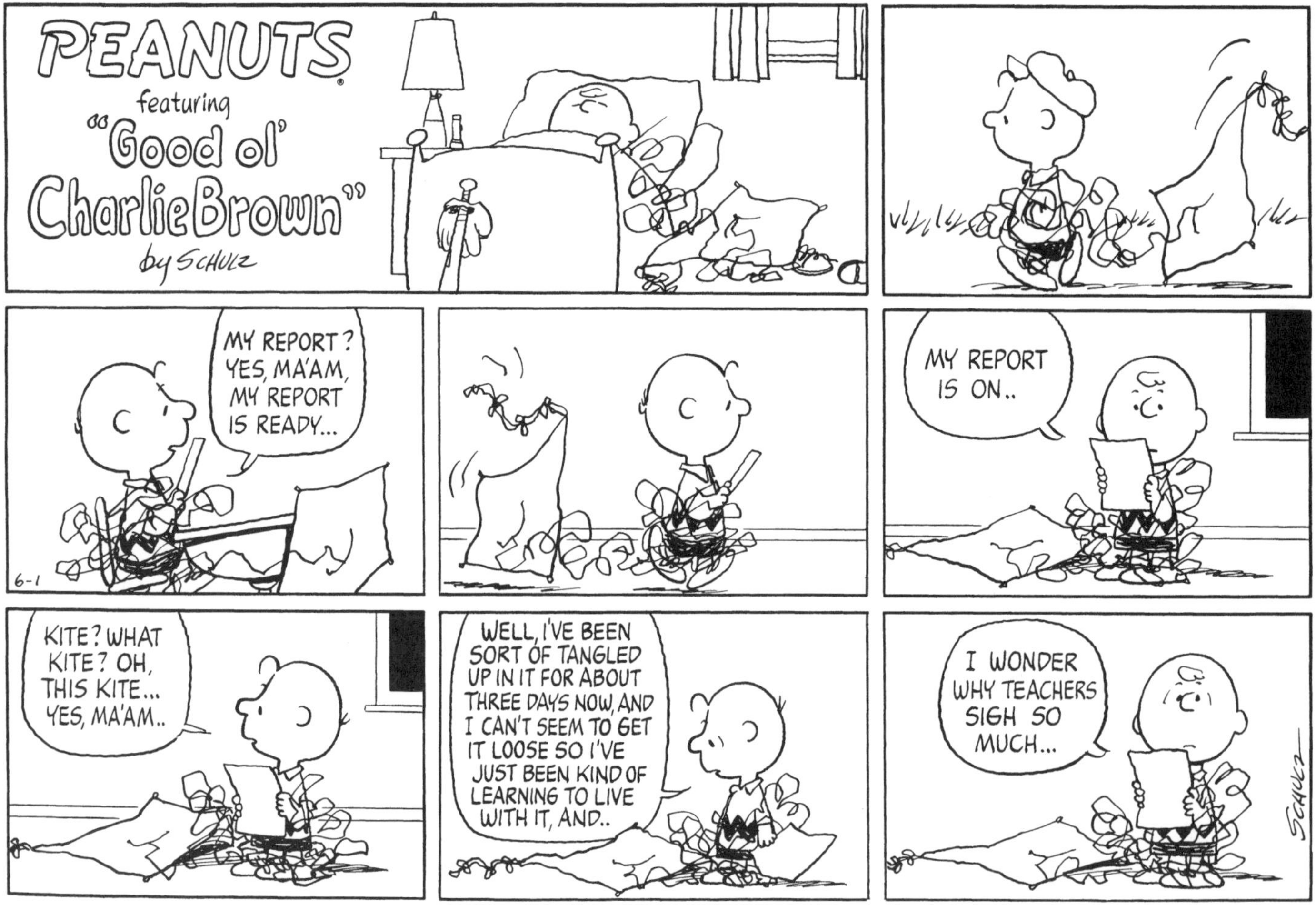
PEANUTS
featuring "Good ol' Charlie Brown" by SCHULZ
6-1
MY REPORT? YES, MA'AM, MY REPORT IS READY...
MY REPORT IS ON..
KITE? WHAT KITE? OH, THIS KITE... YES, MA'AM..
WELL, I'VE BEEN SORT OF TANGLED UP IN IT FOR ABOUT THREE DAYS NOW, AND I CAN'T SEEM TO GET IT LOOSE SO I'VE JUST BEEN KIND OF LEARNING TO LIVE WITH IT, AND..
I WONDER WHY TEACHERS SIGH SO MUCH...
SCHULZ

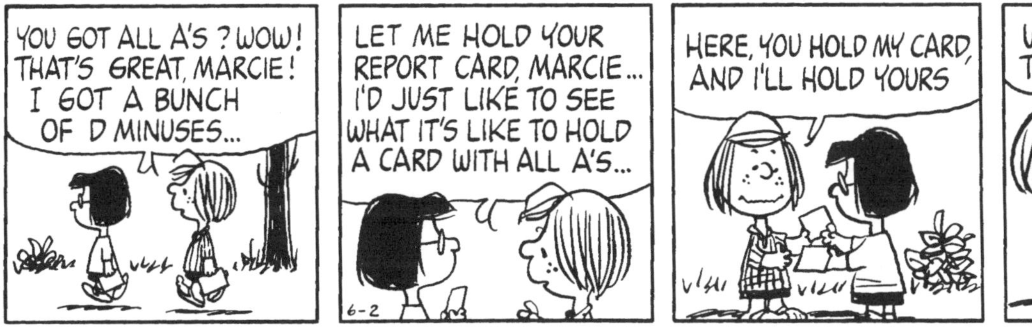
YOU GOT ALL A'S ? WOW! THAT'S GREAT, MARCIE! I GOT A BUNCH OF D MINUSES...
LET ME HOLD YOUR REPORT CARD, MARCIE... I'D JUST LIKE TO SEE WHAT IT'S LIKE TO HOLD A CARD WITH ALL A'S...
HERE, YOU HOLD MY CARD, AND I'LL HOLD YOURS
WELL, YOU DON'T HAVE TO HOLD IT LIKE **THAT**!

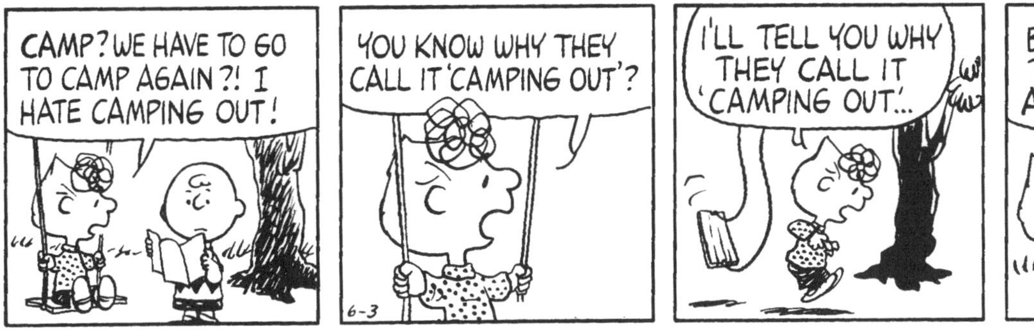
CAMP? WE HAVE TO GO TO CAMP AGAIN ?! I HATE CAMPING OUT!
YOU KNOW WHY THEY CALL IT 'CAMPING OUT'?
I'LL TELL YOU WHY THEY CALL IT 'CAMPING OUT'...
BY THE TIME YOU GET TO MY AGE YOU'RE ALL CAMPED OUT!!

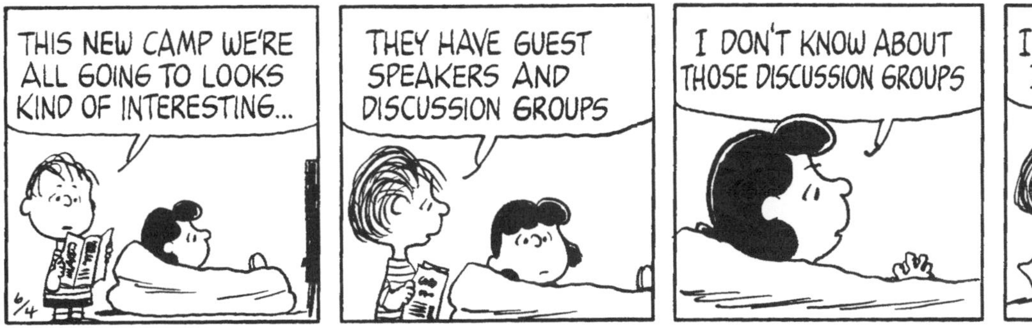
THIS NEW CAMP WE'RE ALL GOING TO LOOKS KIND OF INTERESTING...
THEY HAVE GUEST SPEAKERS AND DISCUSSION GROUPS
I DON'T KNOW ABOUT THOSE DISCUSSION GROUPS
I LIKE TALKING, BUT I HATE LISTENING!

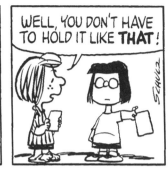

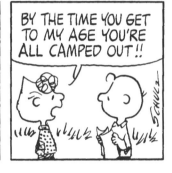

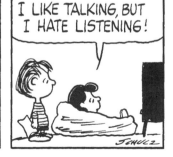

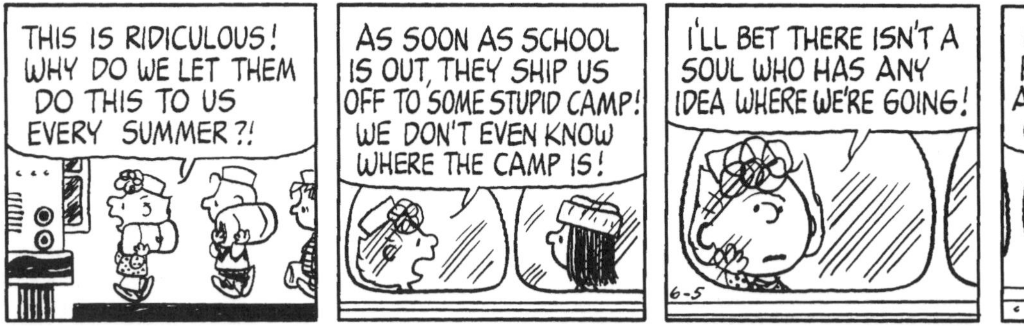
THIS IS RIDICULOUS! WHY DO WE LET THEM DO THIS TO US EVERY SUMMER?!
AS SOON AS SCHOOL IS OUT, THEY SHIP US OFF TO SOME STUPID CAMP! WE DON'T EVEN KNOW WHERE THE CAMP IS!
I'LL BET THERE ISN'T A SOUL WHO HAS ANY IDEA WHERE WE'RE GOING!
6-5
HERE'S THE WORLD WAR I FLYING ACE RIDING ACROSS NORTHERN FRANCE ON A TROOP TRAIN...
SCHULZ

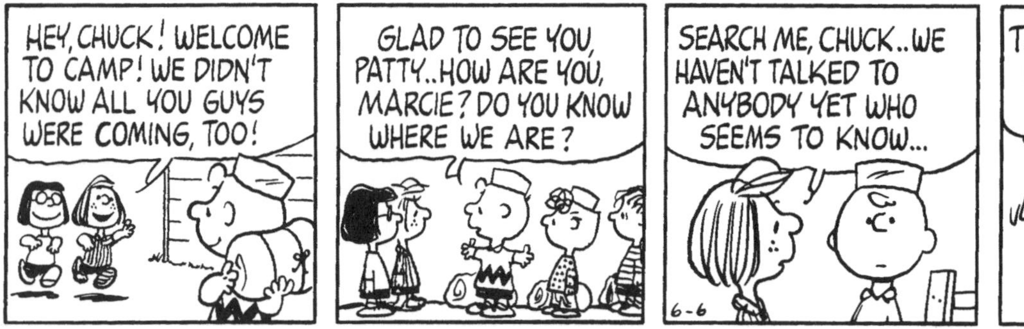
HEY, CHUCK! WELCOME TO CAMP! WE DIDN'T KNOW ALL YOU GUYS WERE COMING, TOO!
GLAD TO SEE YOU, PATTY..HOW ARE YOU, MARCIE? DO YOU KNOW WHERE WE ARE?
SEARCH ME, CHUCK..WE HAVEN'T TALKED TO ANYBODY YET WHO SEEMS TO KNOW...
6-6
THE SKY ABOVE NORMANDY IS VERY BLUE THIS TIME OF YEAR...
SCHULZ

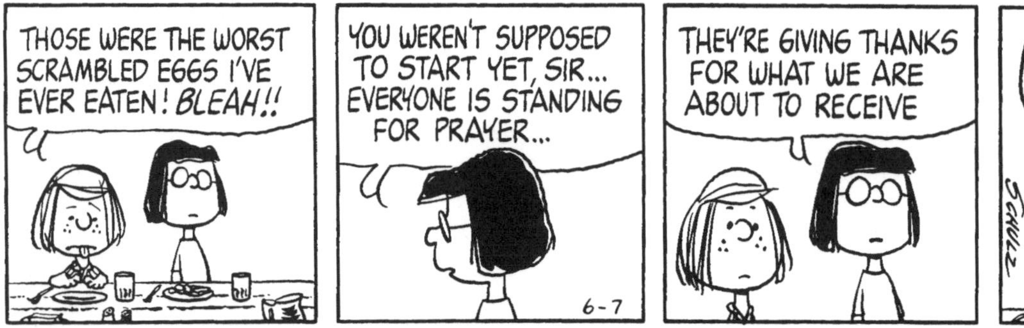
THOSE WERE THE WORST SCRAMBLED EGGS I'VE EVER EATEN! BLEAH!!
YOU WEREN'T SUPPOSED TO START YET, SIR... EVERYONE IS STANDING FOR PRAYER...
6-7
THEY'RE GIVING THANKS FOR WHAT WE ARE ABOUT TO RECEIVE
SCHULZ
I'VE ALREADY RECEIVED IT, AND IT WAS TERRIBLE!

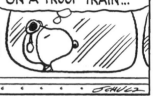

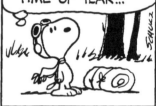

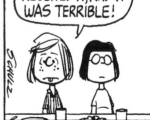

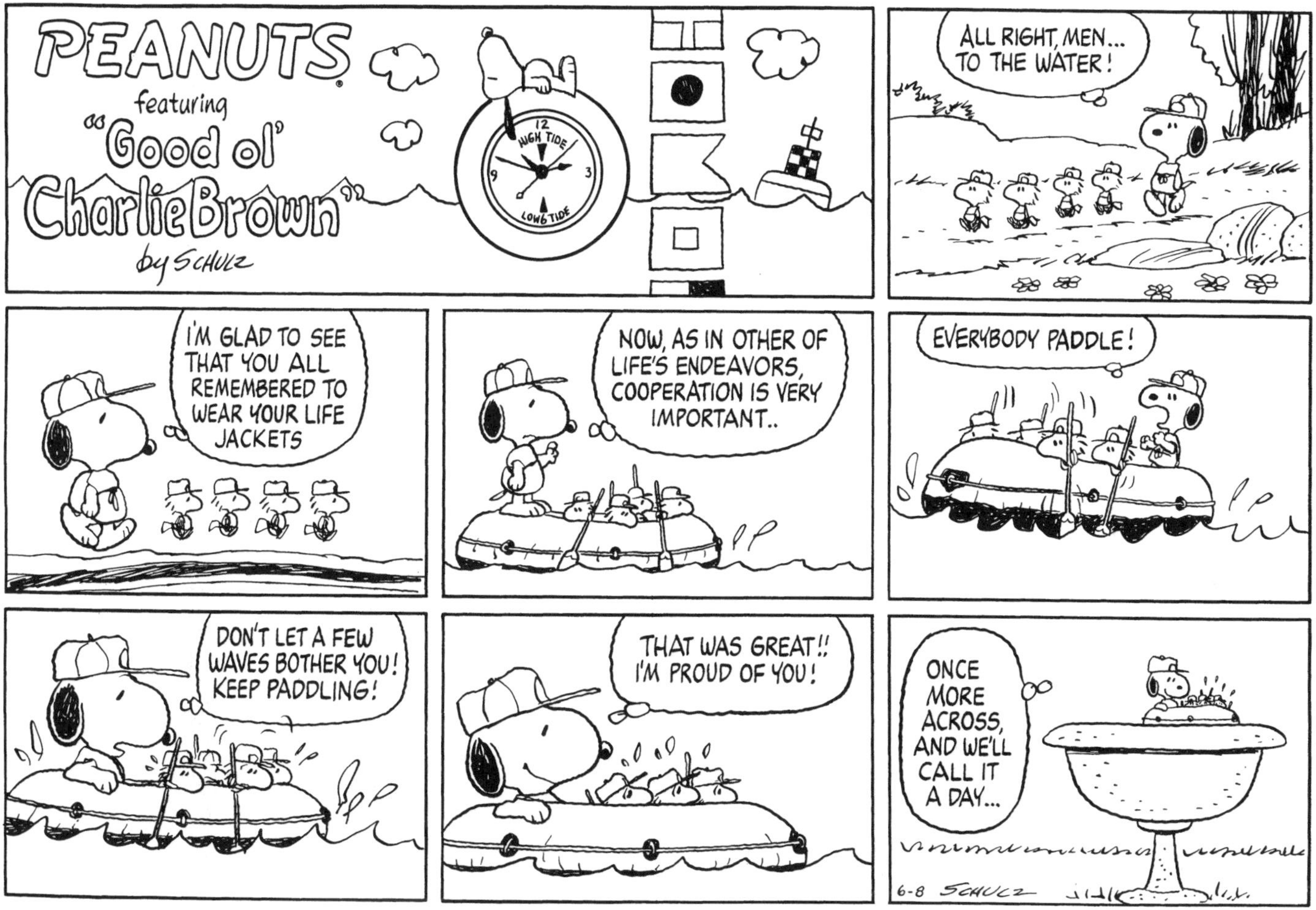
PEANUTS
featuring "Good ol' Charlie Brown"
by SCHULZ
12
HIGH TIDE
9
3
LOW TIDE
ALL RIGHT, MEN... TO THE WATER!
I'M GLAD TO SEE THAT YOU ALL REMEMBERED TO WEAR YOUR LIFE JACKETS
NOW, AS IN OTHER OF LIFE'S ENDEAVORS, COOPERATION IS VERY IMPORTANT..
EVERYBODY PADDLE!
DON'T LET A FEW WAVES BOTHER YOU! KEEP PADDLING!
THAT WAS GREAT!! I'M PROUD OF YOU!
ONCE MORE ACROSS, AND WE'LL CALL IT A DAY...
6-8 SCHULZ

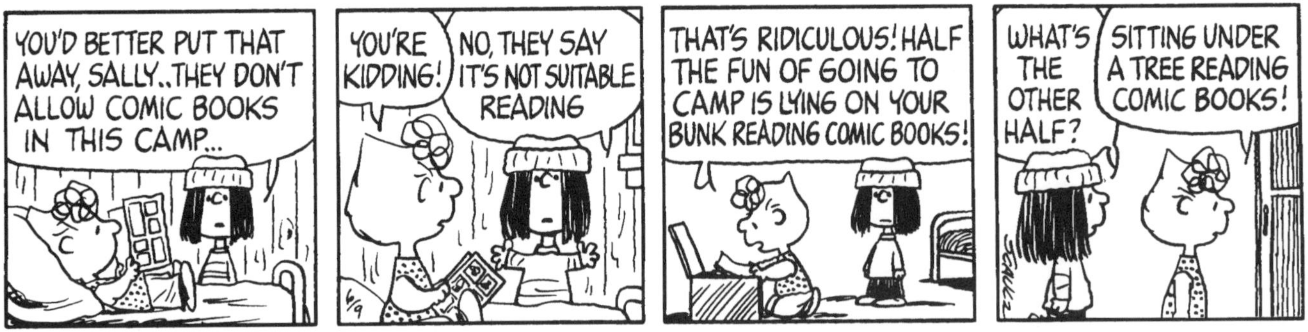
YOU'D BETTER PUT THAT AWAY, SALLY..THEY DON'T ALLOW COMIC BOOKS IN THIS CAMP...
YOU'RE KIDDING!
NO, THEY SAY IT'S NOT SUITABLE READING
6/9
THAT'S RIDICULOUS! HALF THE FUN OF GOING TO CAMP IS LYING ON YOUR BUNK READING COMIC BOOKS!
WHAT'S THE OTHER HALF?
SITTING UNDER A TREE READING COMIC BOOKS!
SCHULZ

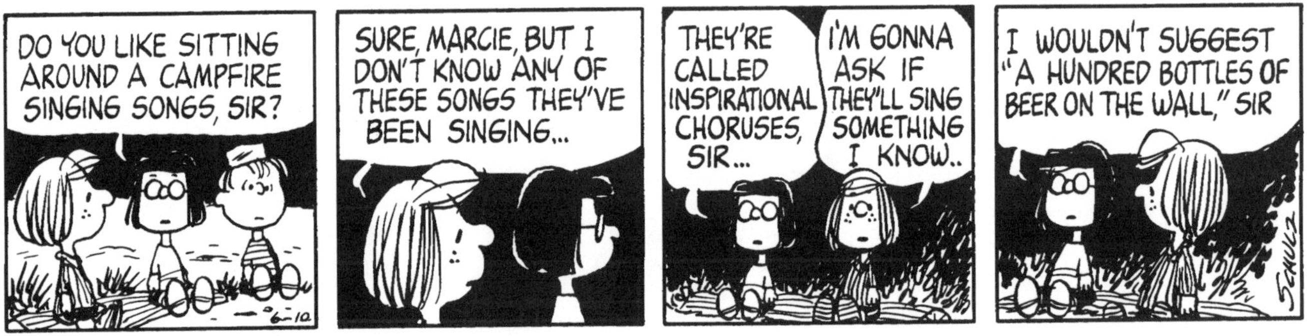
DO YOU LIKE SITTING AROUND A CAMPFIRE SINGING SONGS, SIR?
6-10
SURE, MARCIE, BUT I DON'T KNOW ANY OF THESE SONGS THEY'VE BEEN SINGING...
THEY'RE CALLED INSPIRATIONAL CHORUSES, SIR...
I'M GONNA ASK IF THEY'LL SING SOMETHING I KNOW..
I WOULDN'T SUGGEST "A HUNDRED BOTTLES OF BEER ON THE WALL," SIR
SCHULZ

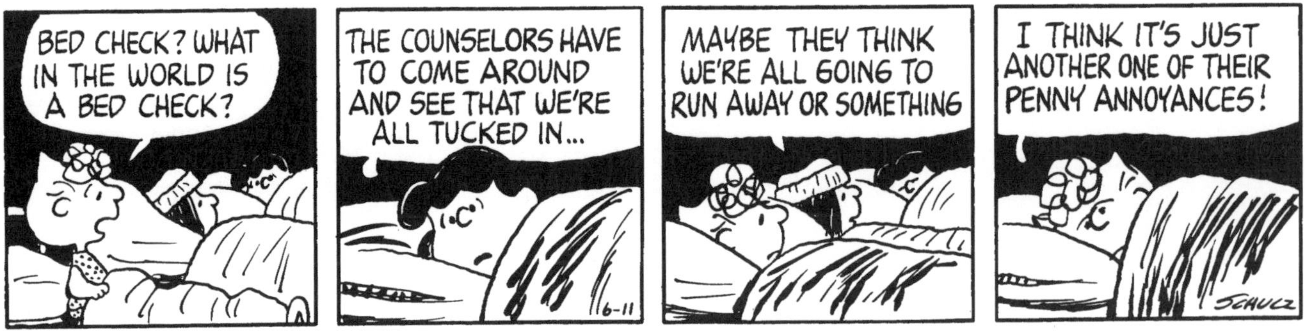
BED CHECK? WHAT IN THE WORLD IS A BED CHECK?
THE COUNSELORS HAVE TO COME AROUND AND SEE THAT WE'RE ALL TUCKED IN...
6-11
MAYBE THEY THINK WE'RE ALL GOING TO RUN AWAY OR SOMETHING
I THINK IT'S JUST ANOTHER ONE OF THEIR PENNY ANNOYANCES!
SCHULZ

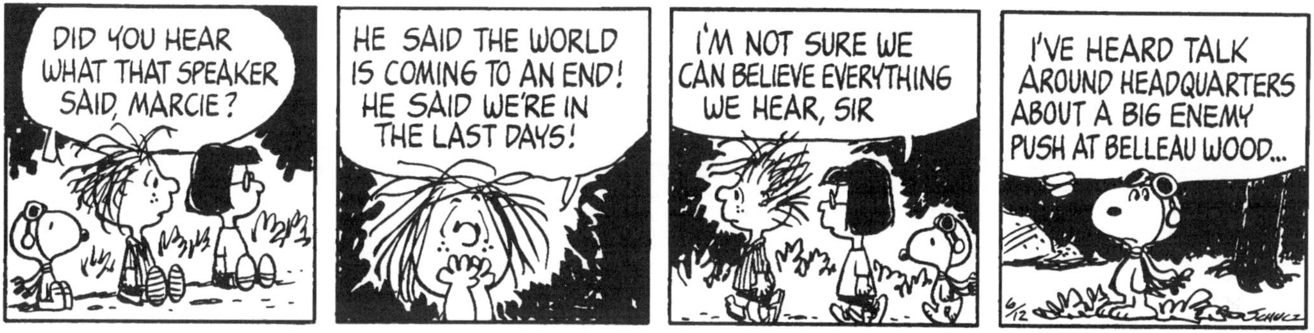
DID YOU HEAR WHAT THAT SPEAKER SAID, MARCIE?
HE SAID THE WORLD IS COMING TO AN END! HE SAID WE'RE IN THE LAST DAYS!
I'M NOT SURE WE CAN BELIEVE EVERYTHING WE HEAR, SIR
I'VE HEARD TALK AROUND HEADQUARTERS ABOUT A BIG ENEMY PUSH AT BELLEAU WOOD...
6/12
SCHULZ

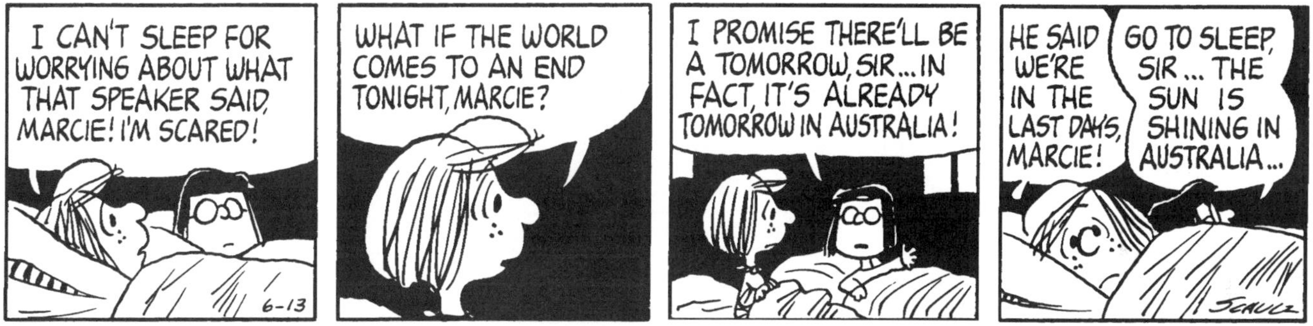
I CAN'T SLEEP FOR WORRYING ABOUT WHAT THAT SPEAKER SAID, MARCIE! I'M SCARED!
6-13
WHAT IF THE WORLD COMES TO AN END TONIGHT, MARCIE?
I PROMISE THERE'LL BE A TOMORROW, SIR... IN FACT, IT'S ALREADY TOMORROW IN AUSTRALIA!
HE SAID WE'RE IN THE LAST DAYS, MARCIE!
GO TO SLEEP, SIR... THE SUN IS SHINING IN AUSTRALIA...
SCHULZ

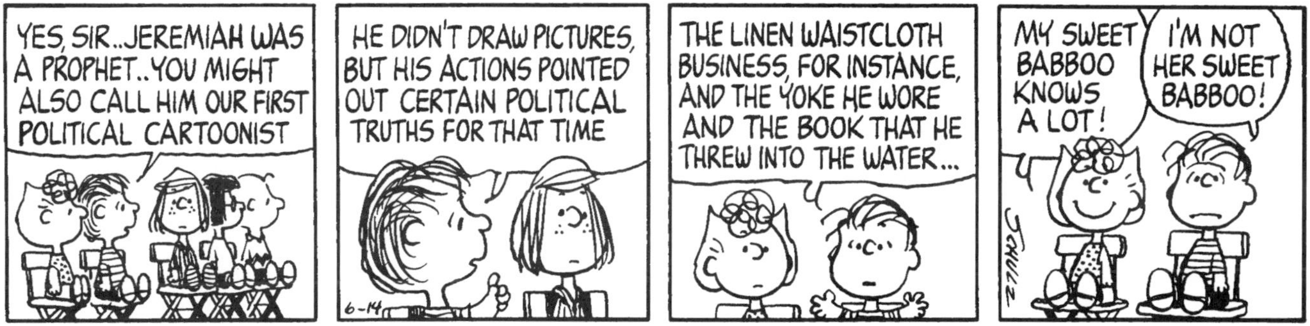
YES, SIR..JEREMIAH WAS A PROPHET..YOU MIGHT ALSO CALL HIM OUR FIRST POLITICAL CARTOONIST
HE DIDN'T DRAW PICTURES, BUT HIS ACTIONS POINTED OUT CERTAIN POLITICAL TRUTHS FOR THAT TIME
6-14
THE LINEN WAISTCLOTH BUSINESS, FOR INSTANCE, AND THE YOKE HE WORE AND THE BOOK THAT HE THREW INTO THE WATER...
MY SWEET BABBOO KNOWS A LOT!
I'M NOT HER SWEET BABBOO!
SCHULZ

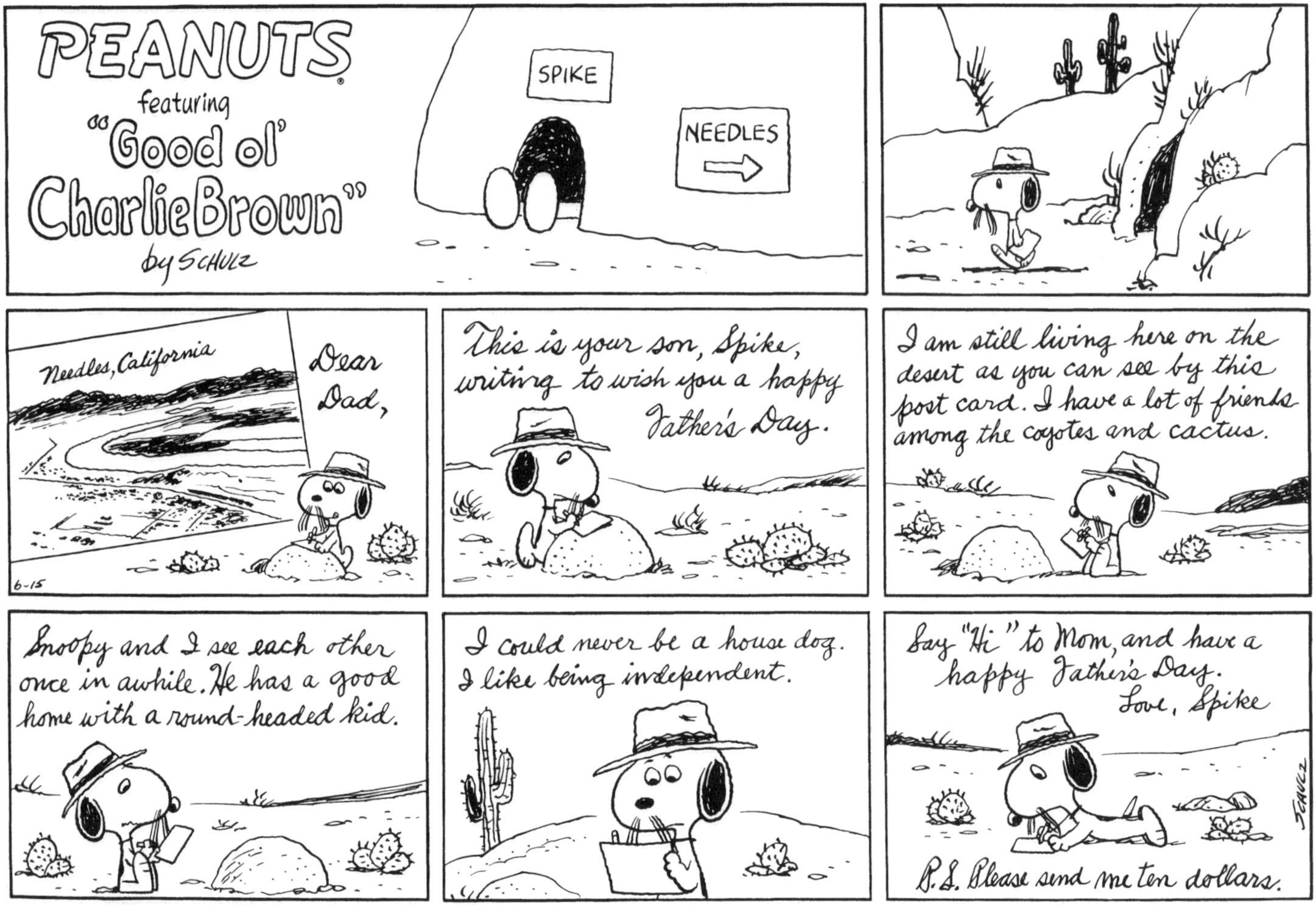
PEANUTS
featuring
"Good ol' CharlieBrown"
by SCHULZ
SPIKE
NEEDLES
Needles, California
Dear Dad,
This is your son, Spike, writing to wish you a happy Father's Day.
I am still living here on the desert as you can see by this post card. I have a lot of friends among the coyotes and cactus.
Snoopy and I see each other once in awhile. He has a good home with a round-headed kid.
I could never be a house dog. I like being independent.
Say "Hi" to Mom, and have a happy Father's Day.
Love, Spike
P.S. Please send me ten dollars.
6-15
SCHULZ

YOU HEARD WHAT THAT SPEAKER SAID, CHUCK.. HE SAID WE'RE IN THE LAST DAYS!

I KNOW..I HEARD HIM SAY THE WORLD IS COMING TO AN END...

6-16

MARCIE SAID THE WORLD CAN'T END TODAY BECAUSE IT'S ALREADY TOMORROW IN AUSTRALIA...

MAYBE WE SHOULD GO TO AUSTRALIA

DON'T MAKE JOKES, CHUCK!

HE SAID IT AGAIN, MARCIE! YOU HEARD HIM! HE SAID WE'RE IN THE LAST DAYS!

6-17

HE STOOD THERE RIGHT IN FRONT OF ALL OF US TONIGHT, AND SAID THE WORLD IS COMING TO AN END!

AREN'T YOU SCARED, MARCIE? DOESN'T THAT BOTHER YOU? AREN'T YOU TERRIFIED?!

SHE'S NOT TERRIFIED..

Z

I HATE THESE DISCUSSION GROUPS! I NEVER KNOW WHAT THEY'RE TALKING ABOUT! I SHOULD BE HOME WATCHING TV!

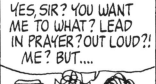

YES, SIR? YOU WANT ME TO WHAT? LEAD IN PRAYER? OUT LOUD?! ME? BUT....

GO AHEAD, SALLY... YOU CAN DO IT..

6/18

"NOW I LAY US DOWN TO SLEEP..."

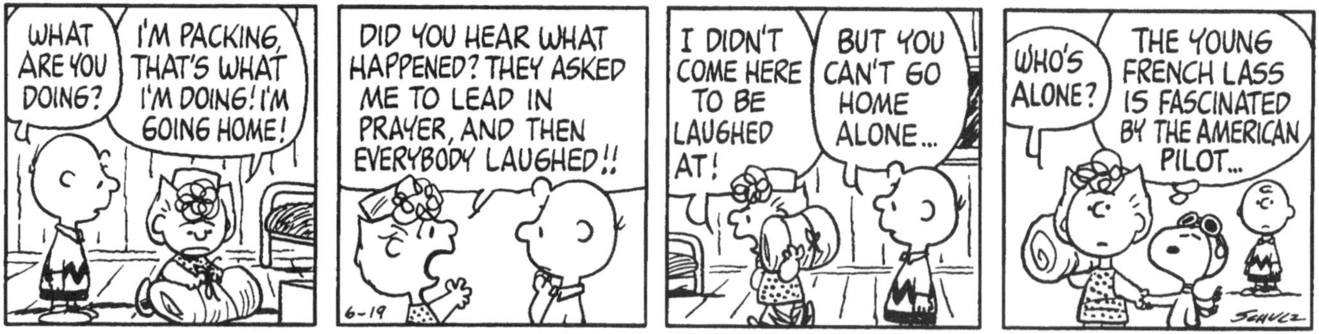
WHAT ARE YOU DOING?
I'M PACKING, THAT'S WHAT I'M DOING! I'M GOING HOME!
DID YOU HEAR WHAT HAPPENED? THEY ASKED ME TO LEAD IN PRAYER, AND THEN EVERYBODY LAUGHED!!
6-19
I DIDN'T COME HERE TO BE LAUGHED AT!
BUT YOU CAN'T GO HOME ALONE...
WHO'S ALONE?
THE YOUNG FRENCH LASS IS FASCINATED BY THE AMERICAN PILOT...
SCHULZ

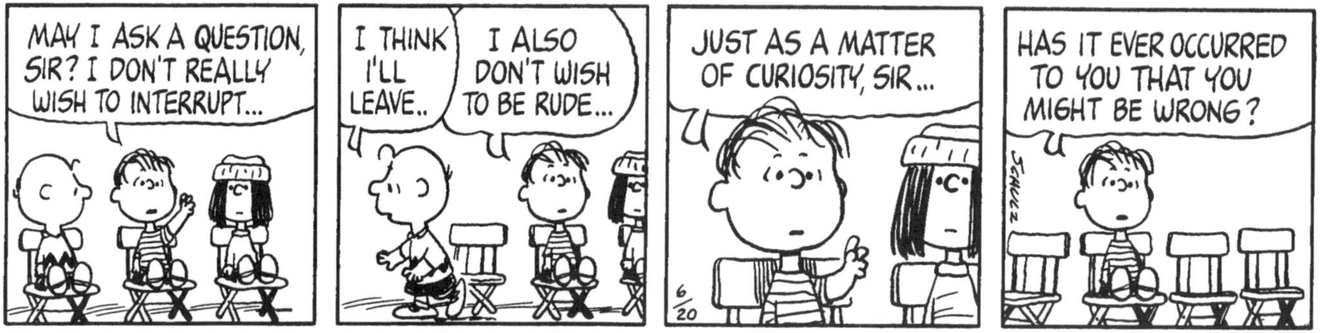
MAY I ASK A QUESTION, SIR? I DON'T REALLY WISH TO INTERRUPT...
I THINK I'LL LEAVE..
I ALSO DON'T WISH TO BE RUDE...
JUST AS A MATTER OF CURIOSITY, SIR...
6/20
HAS IT EVER OCCURRED TO YOU THAT YOU MIGHT BE WRONG?
SCHULZ

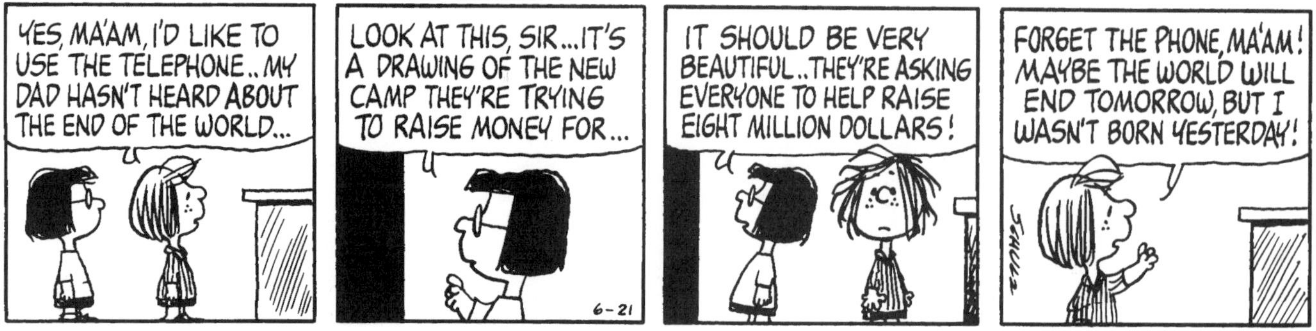
YES, MA'AM, I'D LIKE TO USE THE TELEPHONE.. MY DAD HASN'T HEARD ABOUT THE END OF THE WORLD...
LOOK AT THIS, SIR...IT'S A DRAWING OF THE NEW CAMP THEY'RE TRYING TO RAISE MONEY FOR...
6-21
IT SHOULD BE VERY BEAUTIFUL..THEY'RE ASKING EVERYONE TO HELP RAISE EIGHT MILLION DOLLARS!
FORGET THE PHONE, MA'AM! MAYBE THE WORLD WILL END TOMORROW, BUT I WASN'T BORN YESTERDAY!
SCHULZ

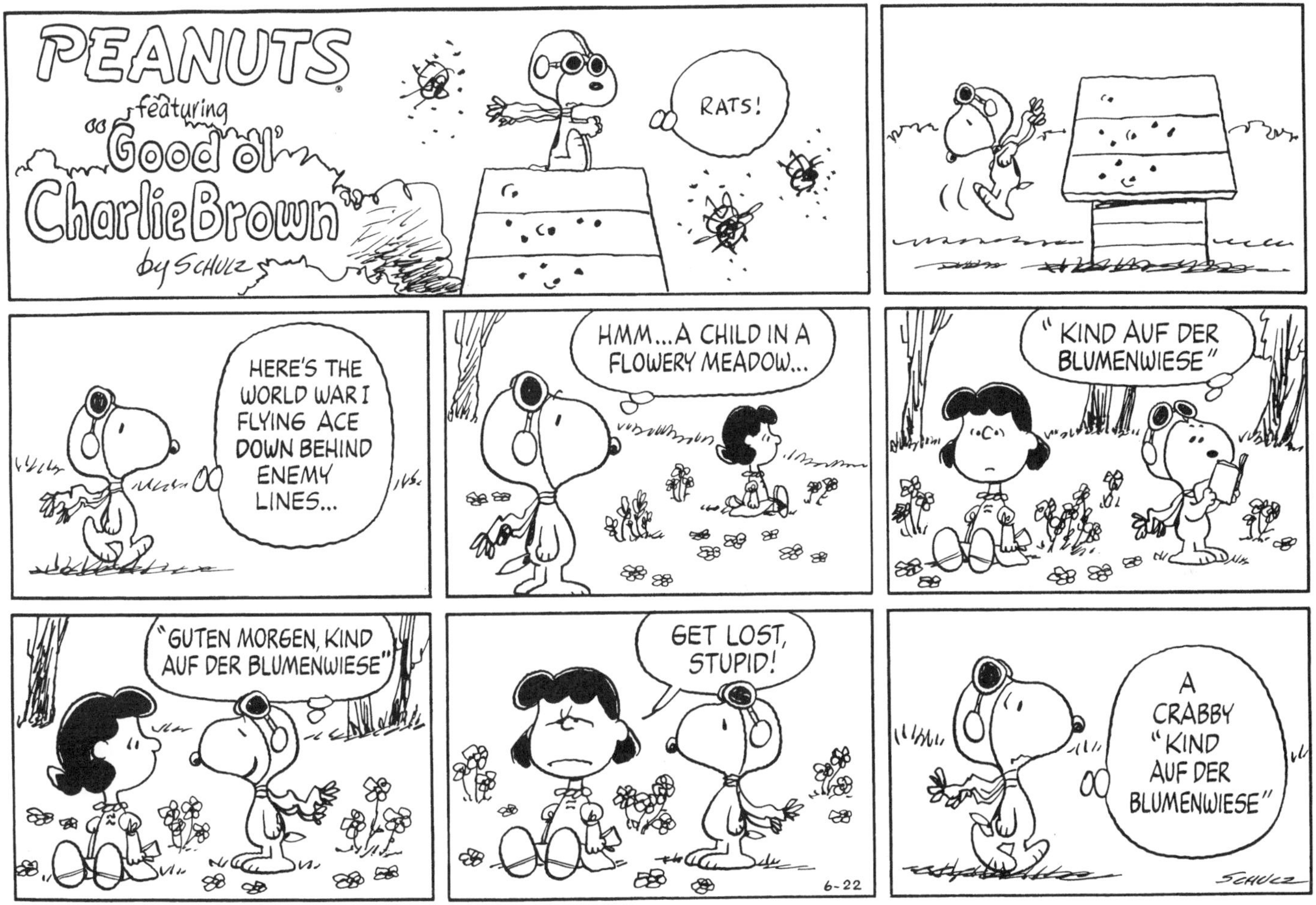
PEANUTS
featuring
"Good ol' Charlie Brown"
by SCHULZ
RATS!
HERE'S THE WORLD WAR I FLYING ACE DOWN BEHIND ENEMY LINES...
HMM...A CHILD IN A FLOWERY MEADOW...
"KIND AUF DER BLUMENWIESE"
"GUTEN MORGEN, KIND AUF DER BLUMENWIESE"
GET LOST, STUPID!
6-22
A CRABBY "KIND AUF DER BLUMENWIESE"
SCHULZ

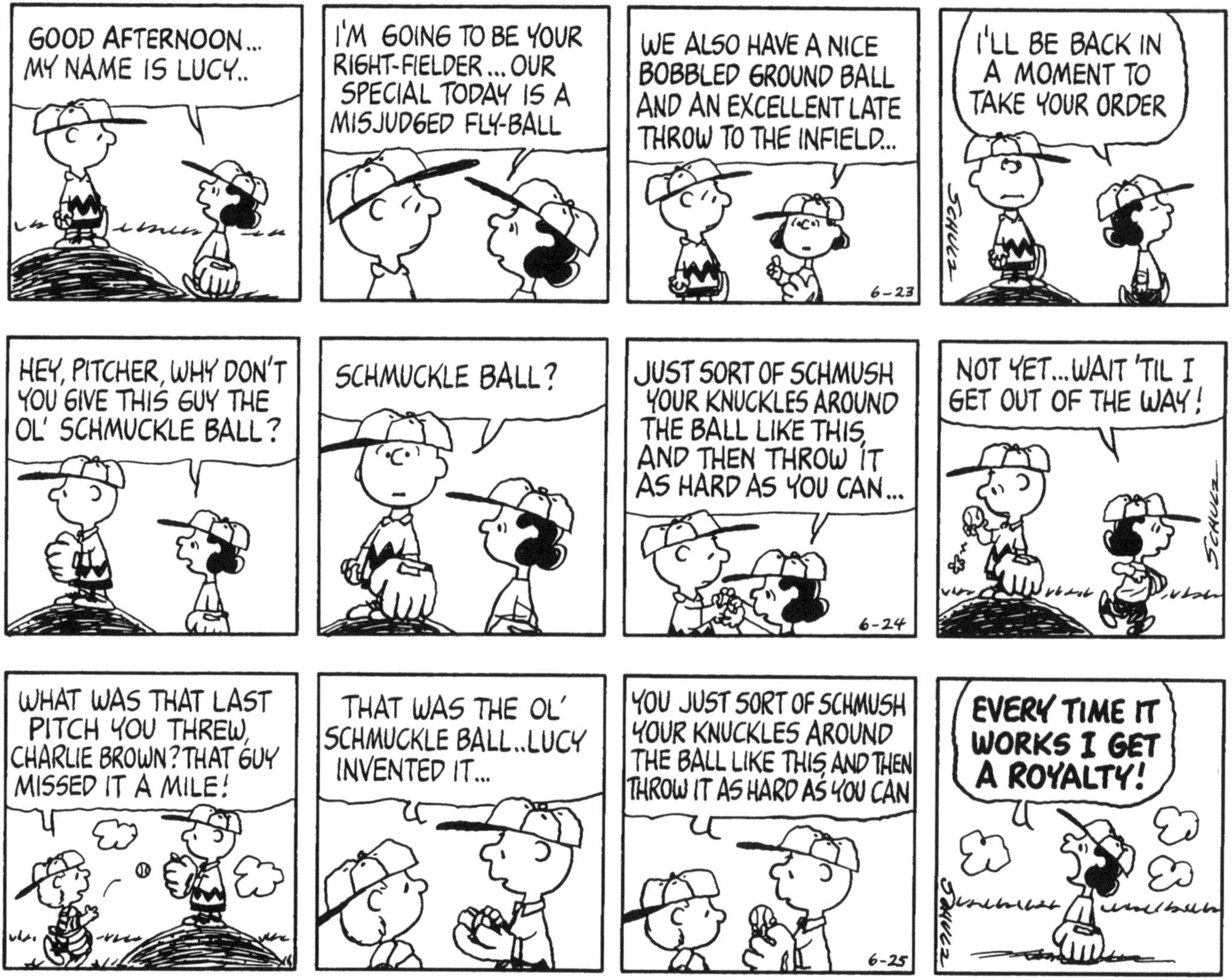

GOOD AFTERNOON... MY NAME IS LUCY..
I'M GOING TO BE YOUR RIGHT-FIELDER... OUR SPECIAL TODAY IS A MISJUDGED FLY-BALL
WE ALSO HAVE A NICE BOBBLED GROUND BALL AND AN EXCELLENT LATE THROW TO THE INFIELD...
6-23
I'LL BE BACK IN A MOMENT TO TAKE YOUR ORDER
SCHULZ
HEY, PITCHER, WHY DON'T YOU GIVE THIS GUY THE OL' SCHMUCKLE BALL?
SCHMUCKLE BALL?
JUST SORT OF SCHMUSH YOUR KNUCKLES AROUND THE BALL LIKE THIS, AND THEN THROW IT AS HARD AS YOU CAN...
6-24
NOT YET...WAIT 'TIL I GET OUT OF THE WAY!
SCHULZ
WHAT WAS THAT LAST PITCH YOU THREW, CHARLIE BROWN? THAT GUY MISSED IT A MILE!
THAT WAS THE OL' SCHMUCKLE BALL..LUCY INVENTED IT...
YOU JUST SORT OF SCHMUSH YOUR KNUCKLES AROUND THE BALL LIKE THIS, AND THEN THROW IT AS HARD AS YOU CAN
6-25
EVERY TIME IT WORKS I GET A ROYALTY!
SCHULZ

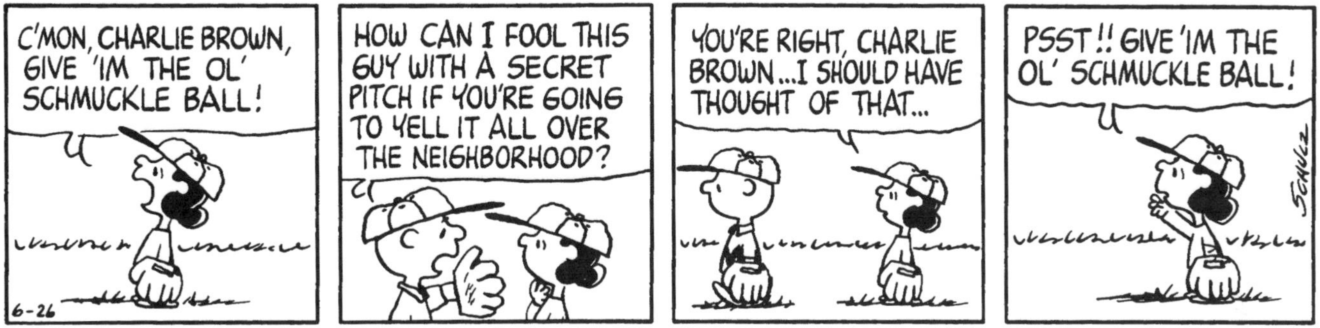
C'MON, CHARLIE BROWN, GIVE 'IM THE OL' SCHMUCKLE BALL!
6-26
HOW CAN I FOOL THIS GUY WITH A SECRET PITCH IF YOU'RE GOING TO YELL IT ALL OVER THE NEIGHBORHOOD?
YOU'RE RIGHT, CHARLIE BROWN...I SHOULD HAVE THOUGHT OF THAT...
PSST!! GIVE 'IM THE OL' SCHMUCKLE BALL!
SCHULZ

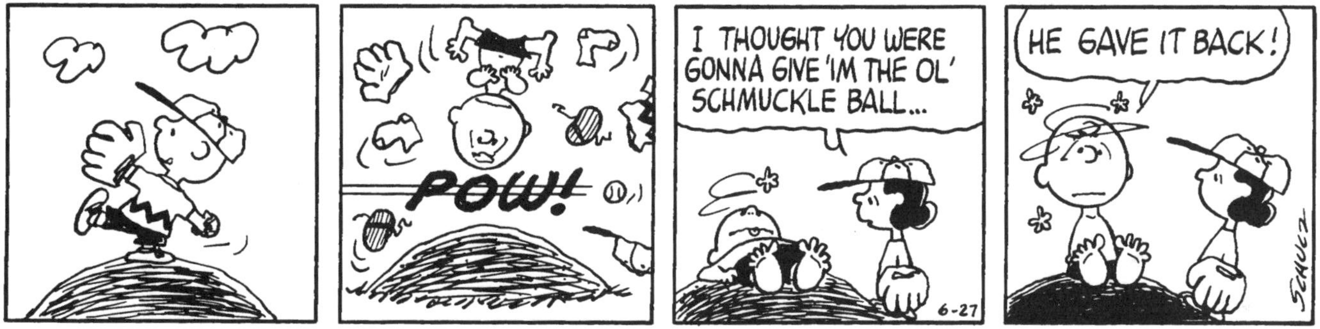
POW!
I THOUGHT YOU WERE GONNA GIVE 'IM THE OL' SCHMUCKLE BALL...
6-27
HE GAVE IT BACK!
SCHULZ

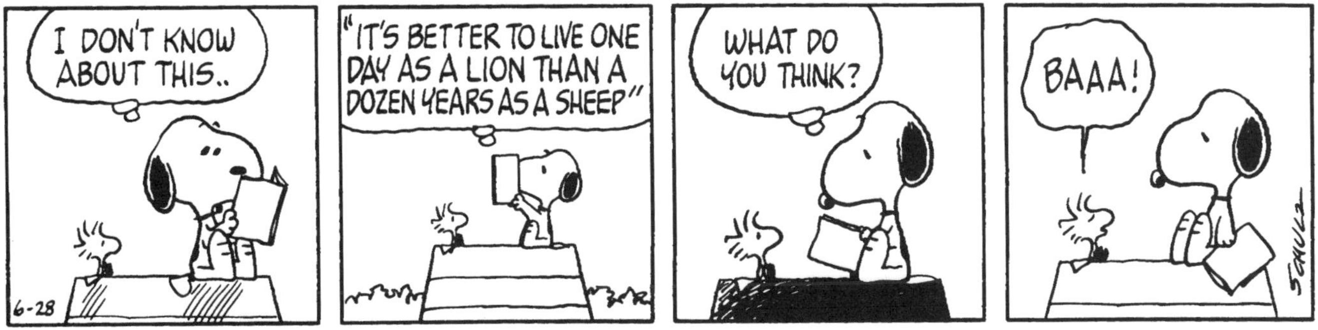
I DON'T KNOW ABOUT THIS..
6-28
"IT'S BETTER TO LIVE ONE DAY AS A LION THAN A DOZEN YEARS AS A SHEEP"
WHAT DO YOU THINK?
BAAA!
SCHULZ

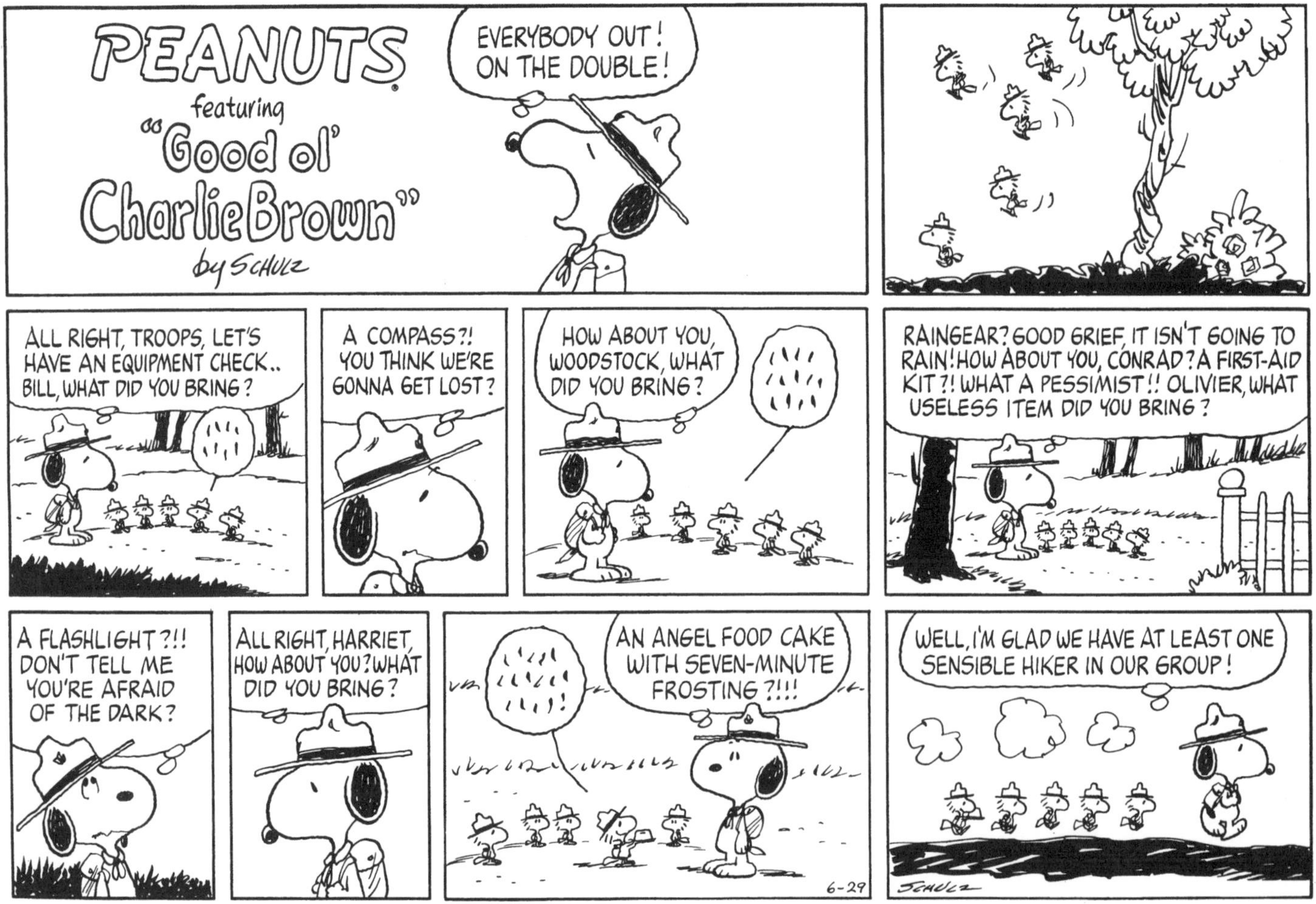
PEANUTS
featuring
"Good ol' Charlie Brown"
by SCHULZ
EVERYBODY OUT! ON THE DOUBLE!
ALL RIGHT, TROOPS, LET'S HAVE AN EQUIPMENT CHECK.. BILL, WHAT DID YOU BRING?
A COMPASS?! YOU THINK WE'RE GONNA GET LOST?
HOW ABOUT YOU, WOODSTOCK, WHAT DID YOU BRING?
RAINGEAR? GOOD GRIEF, IT ISN'T GOING TO RAIN! HOW ABOUT YOU, CONRAD? A FIRST-AID KIT?! WHAT A PESSIMIST!! OLIVIER, WHAT USELESS ITEM DID YOU BRING?
A FLASHLIGHT?!! DON'T TELL ME YOU'RE AFRAID OF THE DARK?
ALL RIGHT, HARRIET, HOW ABOUT YOU? WHAT DID YOU BRING?
AN ANGEL FOOD CAKE WITH SEVEN-MINUTE FROSTING?!!!
6-29
WELL, I'M GLAD WE HAVE AT LEAST ONE SENSIBLE HIKER IN OUR GROUP!
SCHULZ

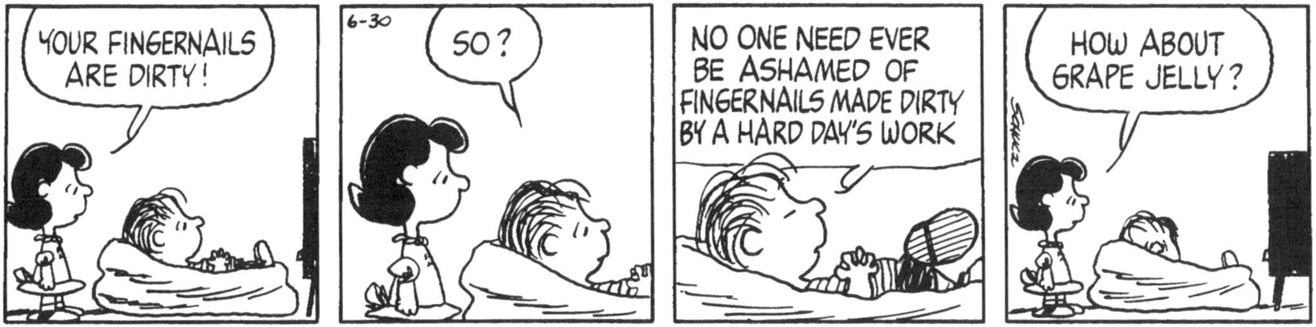
YOUR FINGERNAILS ARE DIRTY!
6-30
SO?
NO ONE NEED EVER BE ASHAMED OF FINGERNAILS MADE DIRTY BY A HARD DAY'S WORK
HOW ABOUT GRAPE JELLY?

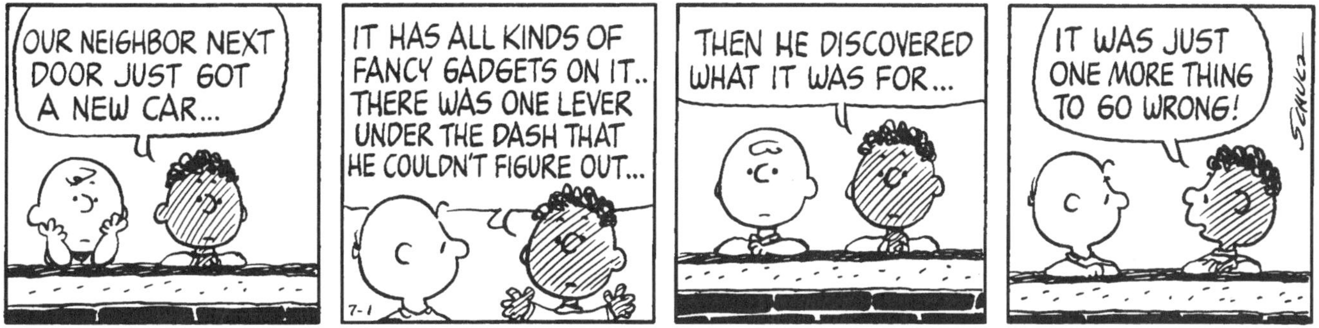
OUR NEIGHBOR NEXT DOOR JUST GOT A NEW CAR...
IT HAS ALL KINDS OF FANCY GADGETS ON IT.. THERE WAS ONE LEVER UNDER THE DASH THAT HE COULDN'T FIGURE OUT...
7-1
THEN HE DISCOVERED WHAT IT WAS FOR...
IT WAS JUST ONE MORE THING TO GO WRONG!

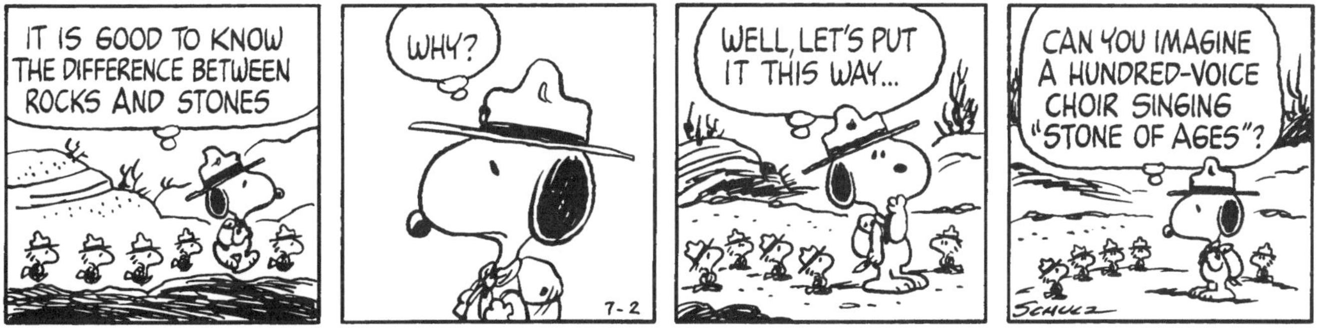
IT IS GOOD TO KNOW THE DIFFERENCE BETWEEN ROCKS AND STONES
WHY?
7-2
WELL, LET'S PUT IT THIS WAY...
CAN YOU IMAGINE A HUNDRED-VOICE CHOIR SINGING "STONE OF AGES"?

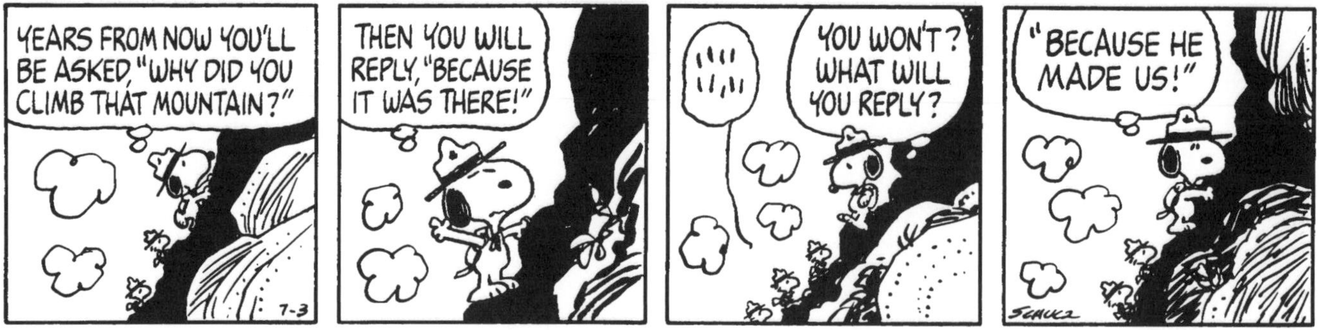
YEARS FROM NOW YOU'LL BE ASKED, "WHY DID YOU CLIMB THAT MOUNTAIN?"
THEN YOU WILL REPLY, "BECAUSE IT WAS THERE!"
YOU WON'T? WHAT WILL YOU REPLY?
"BECAUSE HE MADE US!"

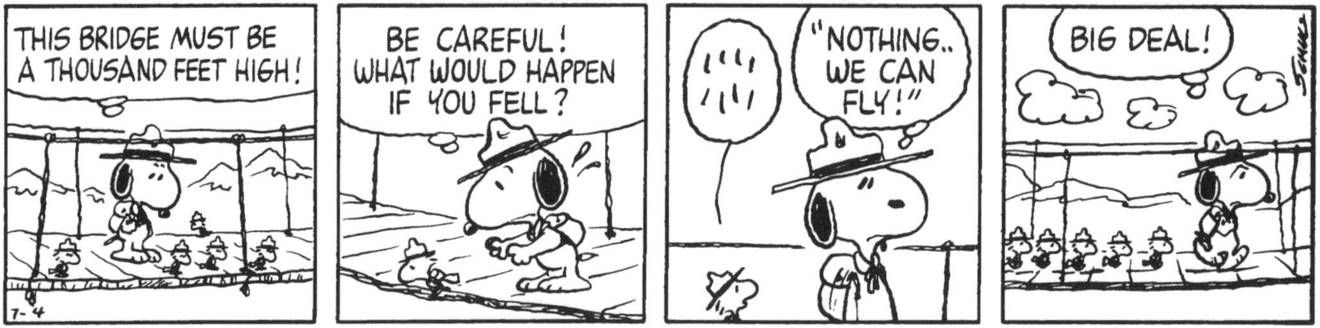
THIS BRIDGE MUST BE A THOUSAND FEET HIGH!
BE CAREFUL! WHAT WOULD HAPPEN IF YOU FELL?
"NOTHING.. WE CAN FLY!"
BIG DEAL!

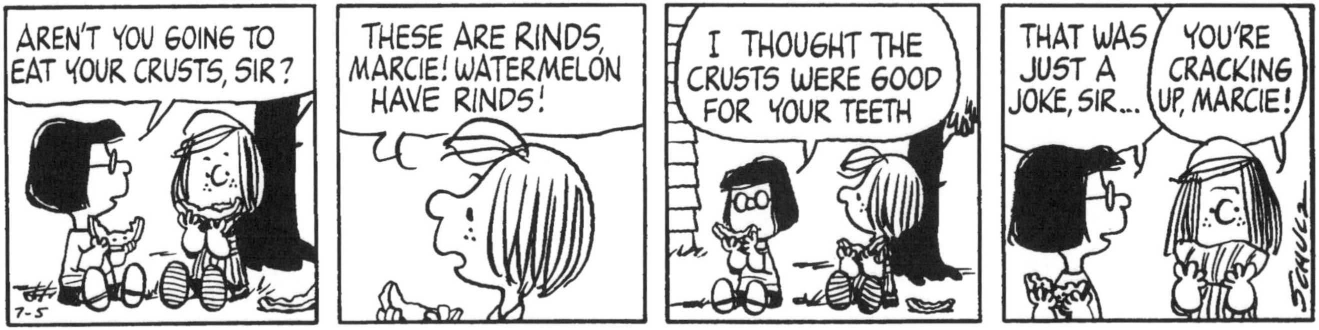
AREN'T YOU GOING TO EAT YOUR CRUSTS, SIR?
THESE ARE RINDS, MARCIE! WATERMELON HAVE RINDS!
I THOUGHT THE CRUSTS WERE GOOD FOR YOUR TEETH
THAT WAS JUST A JOKE, SIR...
YOU'RE CRACKING UP, MARCIE!

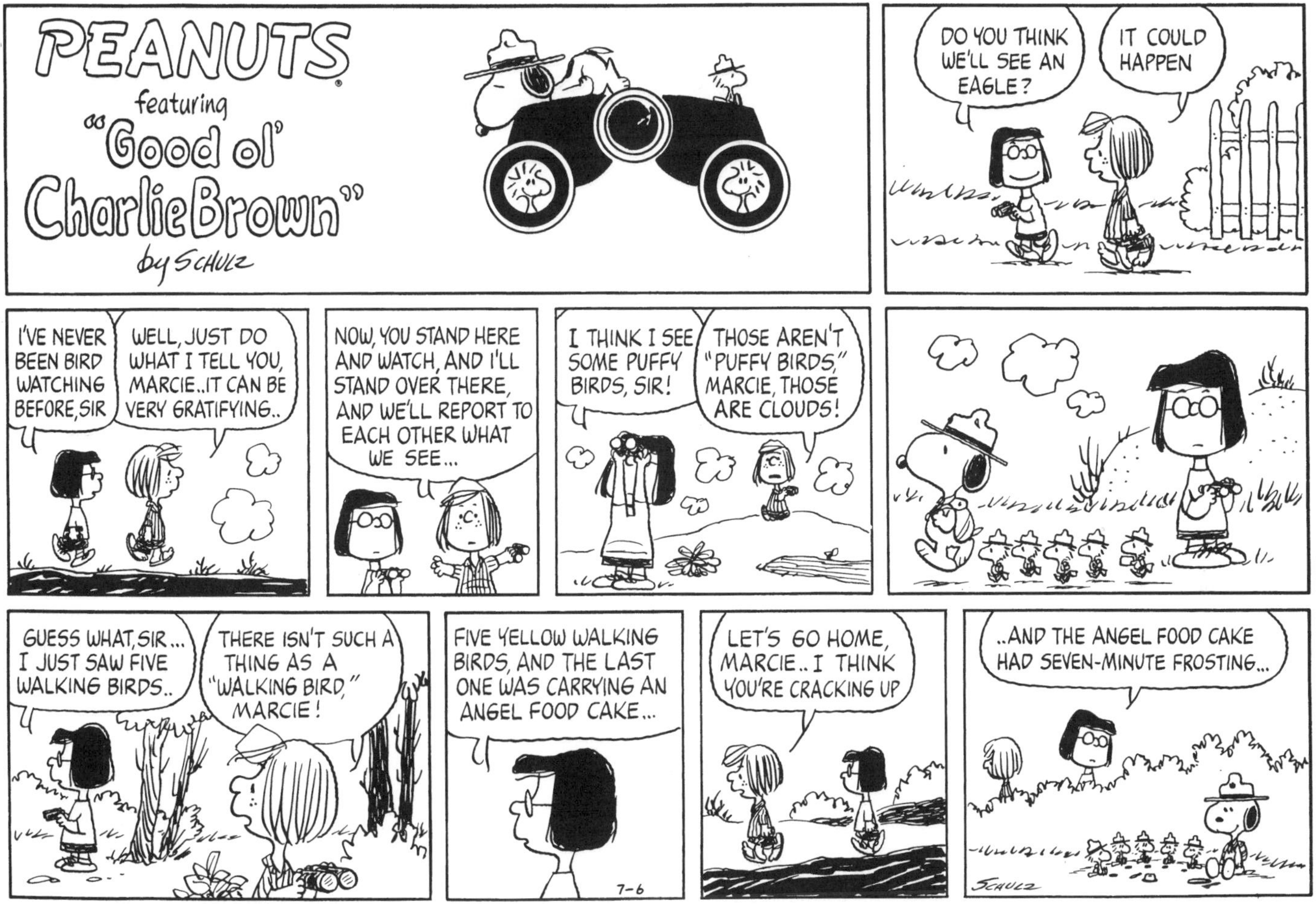
PEANUTS®
featuring
"Good ol' Charlie Brown"
by SCHULZ
DO YOU THINK WE'LL SEE AN EAGLE?
IT COULD HAPPEN
I'VE NEVER BEEN BIRD WATCHING BEFORE, SIR
WELL, JUST DO WHAT I TELL YOU, MARCIE.. IT CAN BE VERY GRATIFYING..
NOW, YOU STAND HERE AND WATCH, AND I'LL STAND OVER THERE, AND WE'LL REPORT TO EACH OTHER WHAT WE SEE...
I THINK I SEE SOME PUFFY BIRDS, SIR!
THOSE AREN'T "PUFFY BIRDS," MARCIE, THOSE ARE CLOUDS!
GUESS WHAT, SIR... I JUST SAW FIVE WALKING BIRDS..
THERE ISN'T SUCH A THING AS A "WALKING BIRD," MARCIE!
FIVE YELLOW WALKING BIRDS, AND THE LAST ONE WAS CARRYING AN ANGEL FOOD CAKE...
7-6
LET'S GO HOME, MARCIE.. I THINK YOU'RE CRACKING UP
..AND THE ANGEL FOOD CAKE HAD SEVEN-MINUTE FROSTING...
SCHULZ

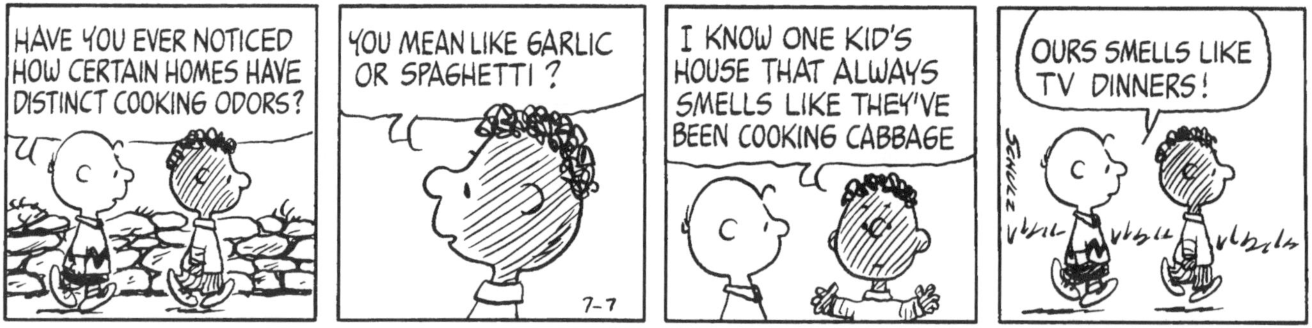
HAVE YOU EVER NOTICED HOW CERTAIN HOMES HAVE DISTINCT COOKING ODORS?
YOU MEAN LIKE GARLIC OR SPAGHETTI ?
7-7
I KNOW ONE KID'S HOUSE THAT ALWAYS SMELLS LIKE THEY'VE BEEN COOKING CABBAGE
OURS SMELLS LIKE TV DINNERS!
SCHULZ

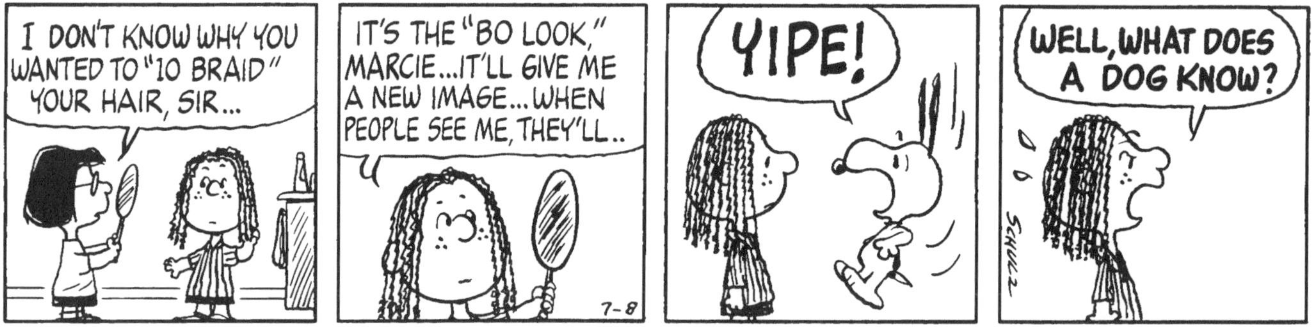
I DON'T KNOW WHY YOU WANTED TO "10 BRAID" YOUR HAIR, SIR...
IT'S THE "BO LOOK," MARCIE...IT'LL GIVE ME A NEW IMAGE...WHEN PEOPLE SEE ME, THEY'LL..
7-8
YIPE!
WELL, WHAT DOES A DOG KNOW?
SCHULZ

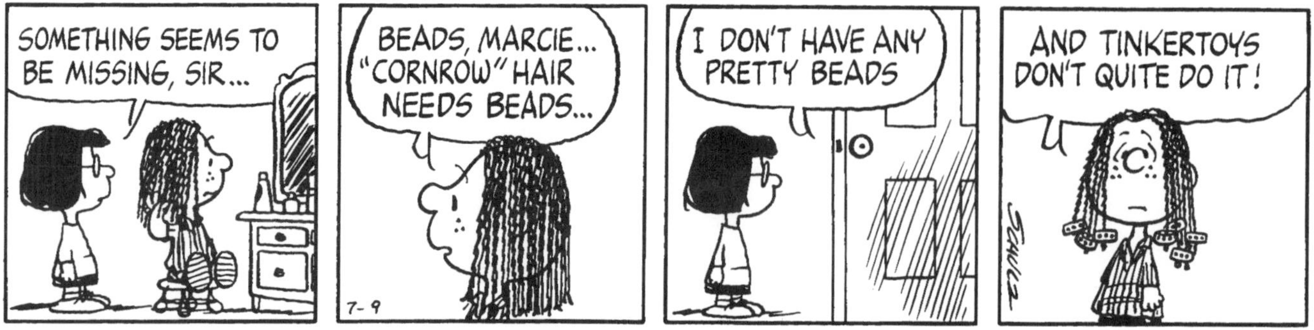
SOMETHING SEEMS TO BE MISSING, SIR...
BEADS, MARCIE... "CORNROW" HAIR NEEDS BEADS...
7-9
I DON'T HAVE ANY PRETTY BEADS
AND TINKERTOYS DON'T QUITE DO IT!
SCHULZ

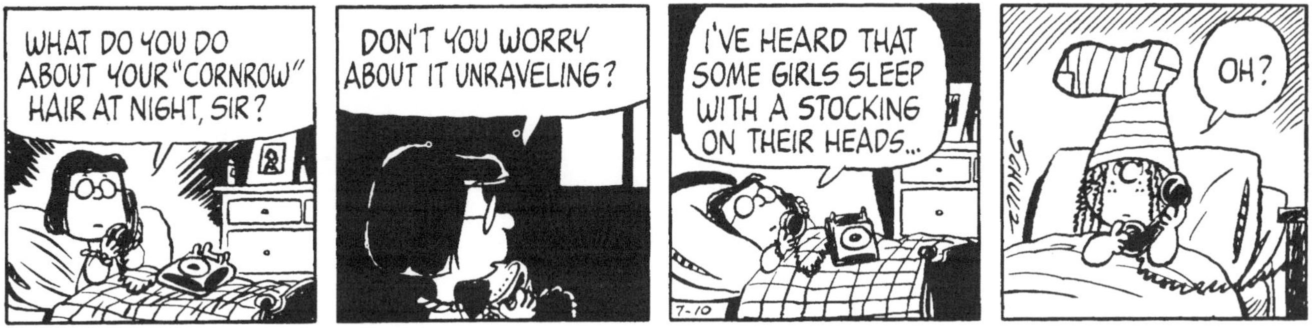
WHAT DO YOU DO ABOUT YOUR "CORNROW" HAIR AT NIGHT, SIR?
DON'T YOU WORRY ABOUT IT UNRAVELING?
I'VE HEARD THAT SOME GIRLS SLEEP WITH A STOCKING ON THEIR HEADS...
OH?
7-10
SCHULZ

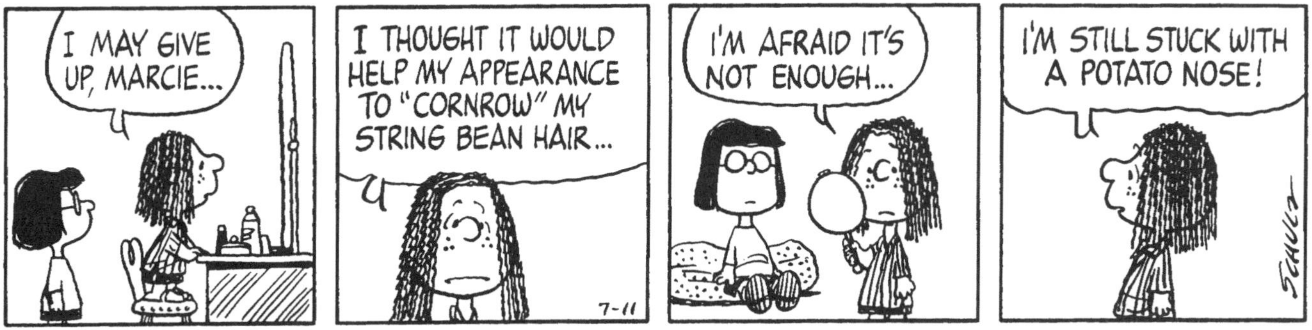
I MAY GIVE UP, MARCIE...
I THOUGHT IT WOULD HELP MY APPEARANCE TO "CORNROW" MY STRING BEAN HAIR...
7-11
I'M AFRAID IT'S NOT ENOUGH...
I'M STILL STUCK WITH A POTATO NOSE!
SCHULZ

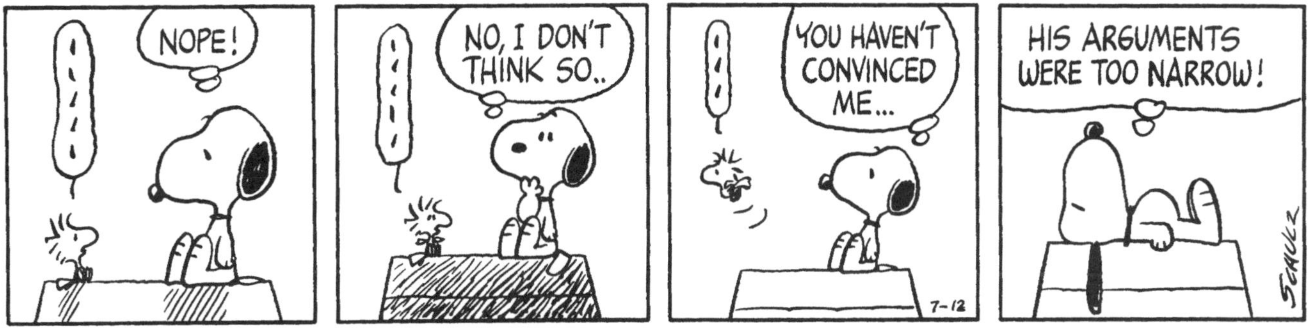
NOPE!
NO, I DON'T THINK SO..
YOU HAVEN'T CONVINCED ME...
7-12
HIS ARGUMENTS WERE TOO NARROW!
SCHULZ

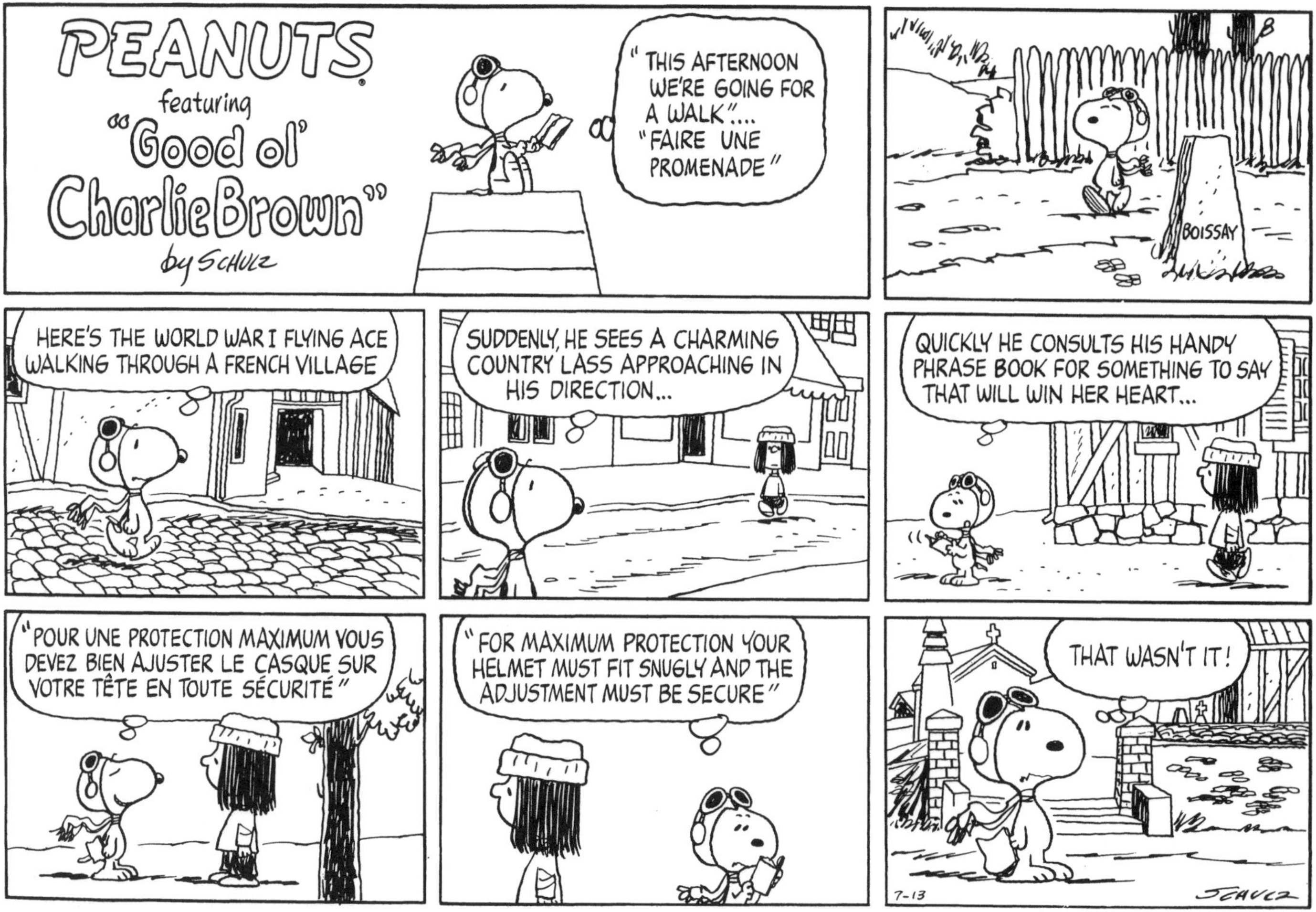
PEANUTS
featuring "Good ol' Charlie Brown"
by SCHULZ
"THIS AFTERNOON WE'RE GOING FOR A WALK"....
"FAIRE UNE PROMENADE"
BOISSAY
HERE'S THE WORLD WAR I FLYING ACE WALKING THROUGH A FRENCH VILLAGE
SUDDENLY, HE SEES A CHARMING COUNTRY LASS APPROACHING IN HIS DIRECTION...
QUICKLY HE CONSULTS HIS HANDY PHRASE BOOK FOR SOMETHING TO SAY THAT WILL WIN HER HEART...
"POUR UNE PROTECTION MAXIMUM VOUS DEVEZ BIEN AJUSTER LE CASQUE SUR VOTRE TÊTE EN TOUTE SÉCURITÉ"
"FOR MAXIMUM PROTECTION YOUR HELMET MUST FIT SNUGLY AND THE ADJUSTMENT MUST BE SECURE"
THAT WASN'T IT!
7-13
SCHULZ

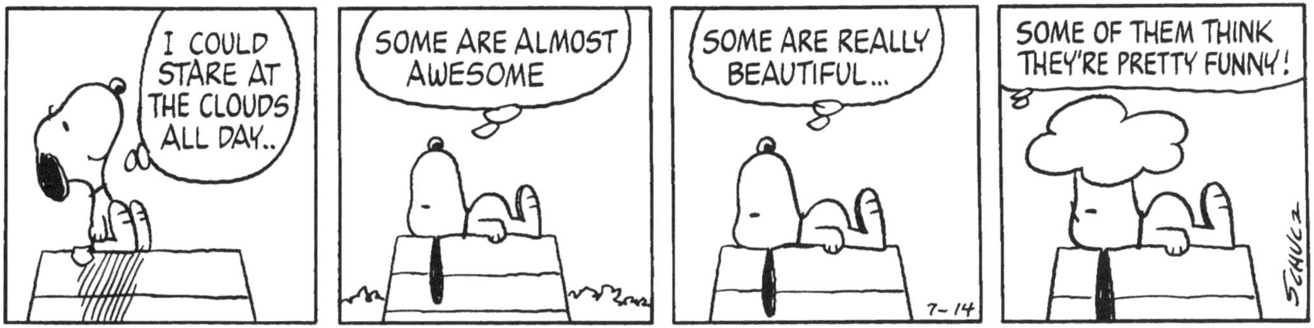
I COULD STARE AT THE CLOUDS ALL DAY..
SOME ARE ALMOST AWESOME
SOME ARE REALLY BEAUTIFUL...
SOME OF THEM THINK THEY'RE PRETTY FUNNY!
7-14
SCHULZ

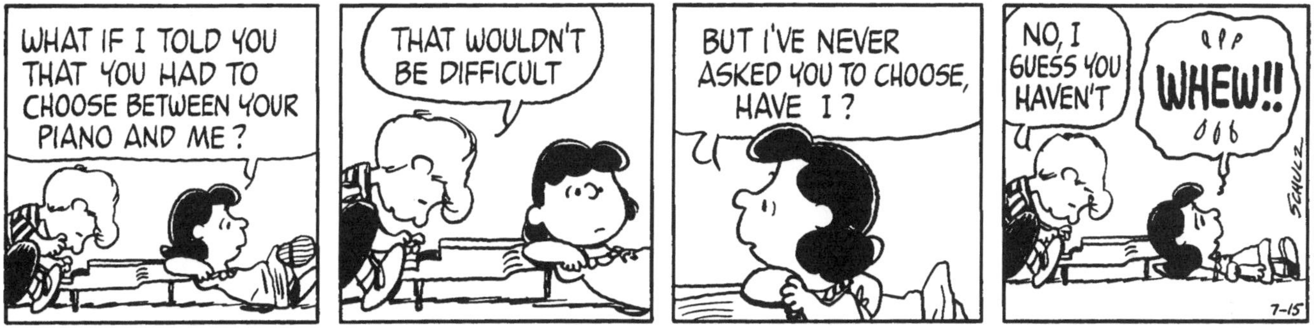
WHAT IF I TOLD YOU THAT YOU HAD TO CHOOSE BETWEEN YOUR PIANO AND ME?
THAT WOULDN'T BE DIFFICULT
BUT I'VE NEVER ASKED YOU TO CHOOSE, HAVE I?
NO, I GUESS YOU HAVEN'T
WHEW!!
SCHULZ
7-15

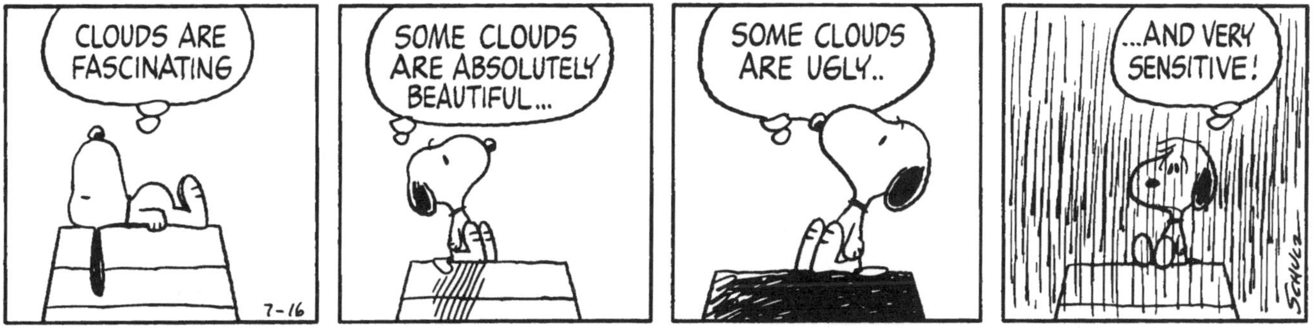
CLOUDS ARE FASCINATING
7-16
SOME CLOUDS ARE ABSOLUTELY BEAUTIFUL...
SOME CLOUDS ARE UGLY..
...AND VERY SENSITIVE!
SCHULZ

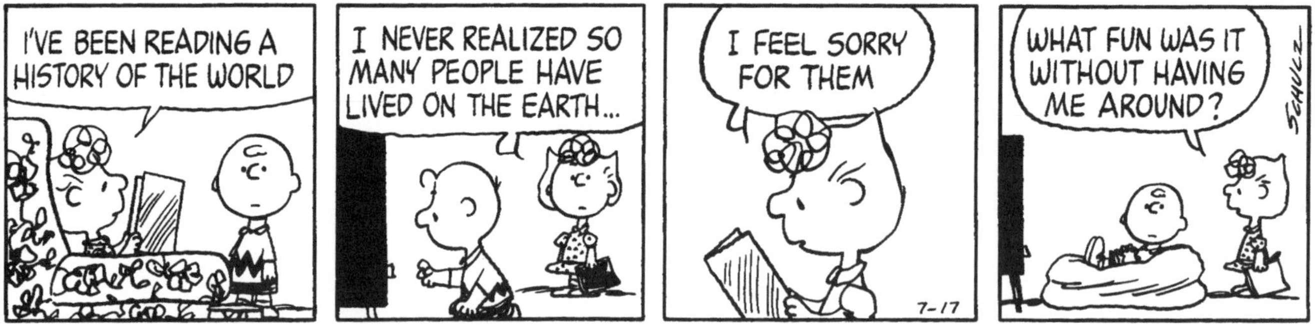
I'VE BEEN READING A HISTORY OF THE WORLD
I NEVER REALIZED SO MANY PEOPLE HAVE LIVED ON THE EARTH...
I FEEL SORRY FOR THEM
7-17
WHAT FUN WAS IT WITHOUT HAVING ME AROUND?
SCHULZ

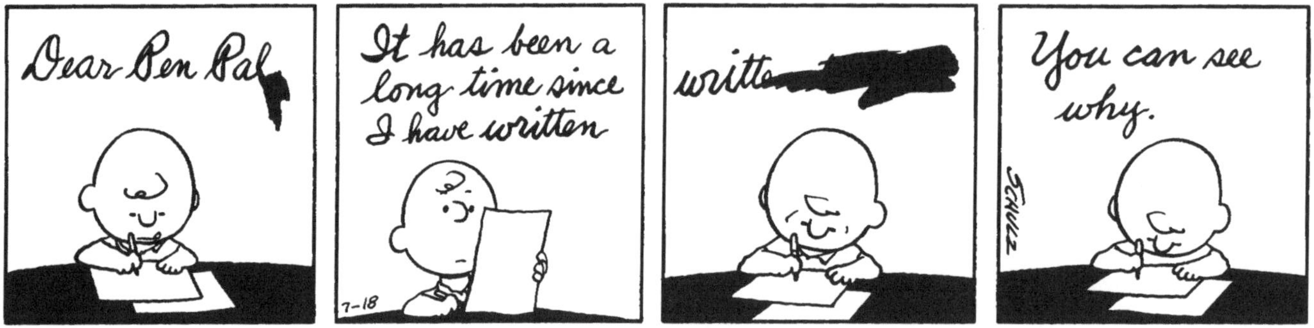
Dear Pen Pal
It has been a long time since I have written
7-18
writte
SCHULZ
You can see why.

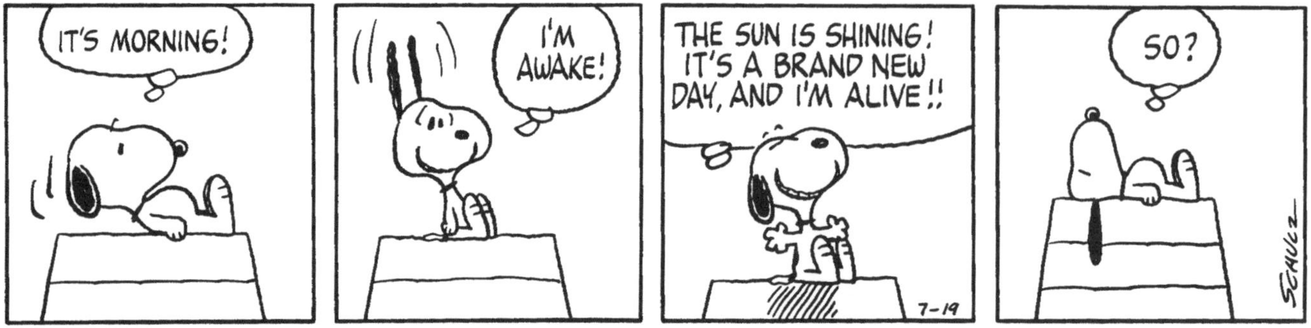
IT'S MORNING!
I'M AWAKE!
THE SUN IS SHINING! IT'S A BRAND NEW DAY, AND I'M ALIVE!!
7-19
SO?
SCHULZ

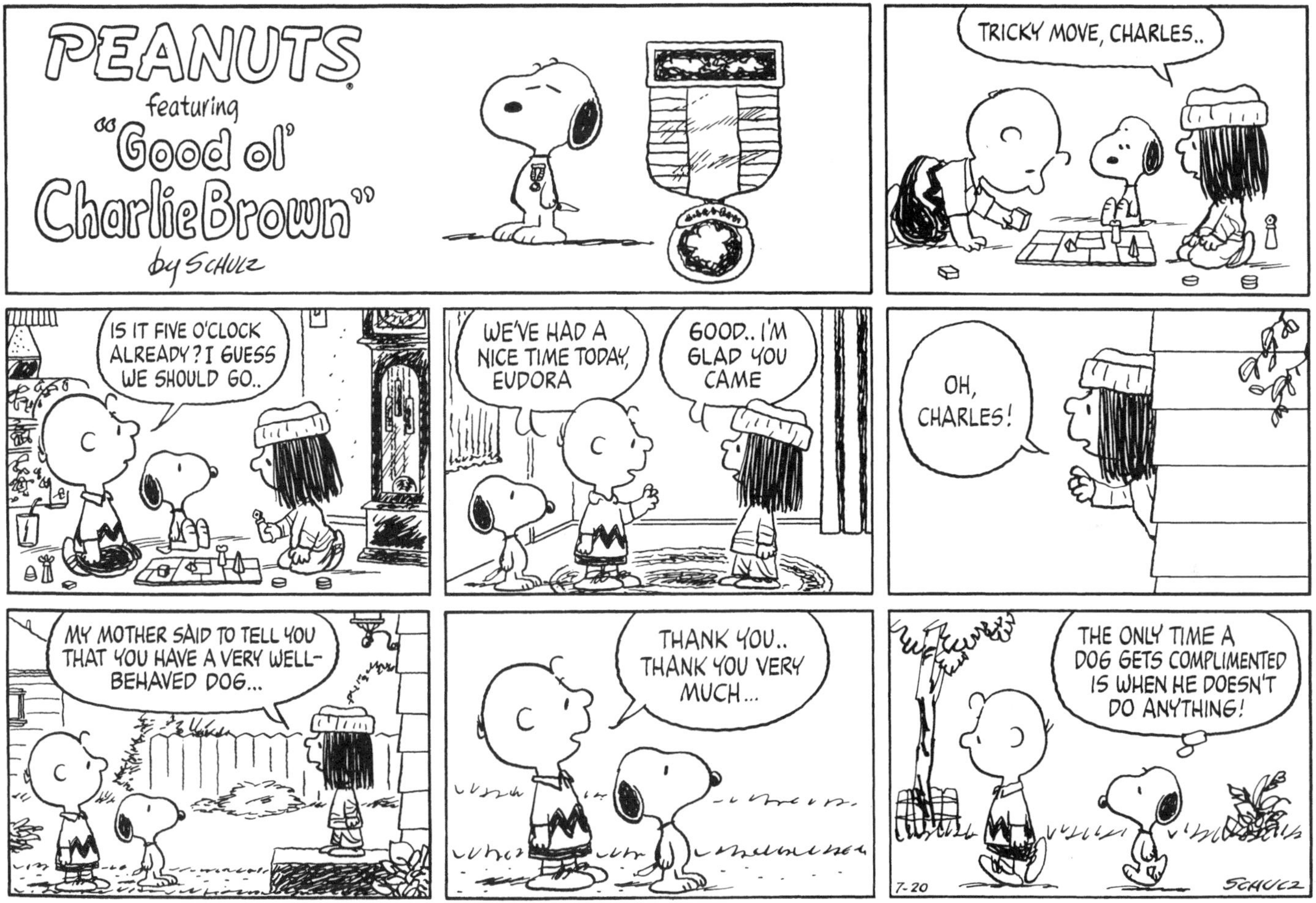
PEANUTS
featuring
"Good ol' CharlieBrown"
by SCHULZ
TRICKY MOVE, CHARLES..
IS IT FIVE O'CLOCK ALREADY? I GUESS WE SHOULD GO..
WE'VE HAD A NICE TIME TODAY, EUDORA
GOOD.. I'M GLAD YOU CAME
OH, CHARLES!
MY MOTHER SAID TO TELL YOU THAT YOU HAVE A VERY WELL-BEHAVED DOG...
THANK YOU.. THANK YOU VERY MUCH...
THE ONLY TIME A DOG GETS COMPLIMENTED IS WHEN HE DOESN'T DO ANYTHING!
7-20
SCHULZ

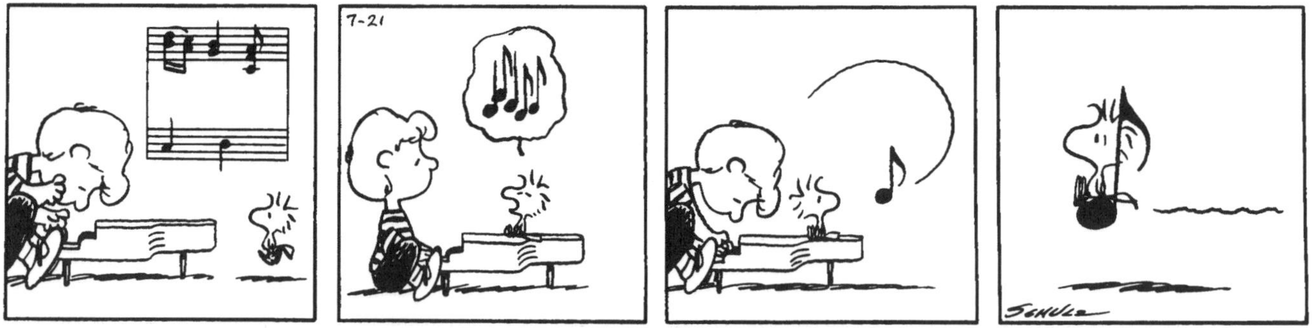
7-21

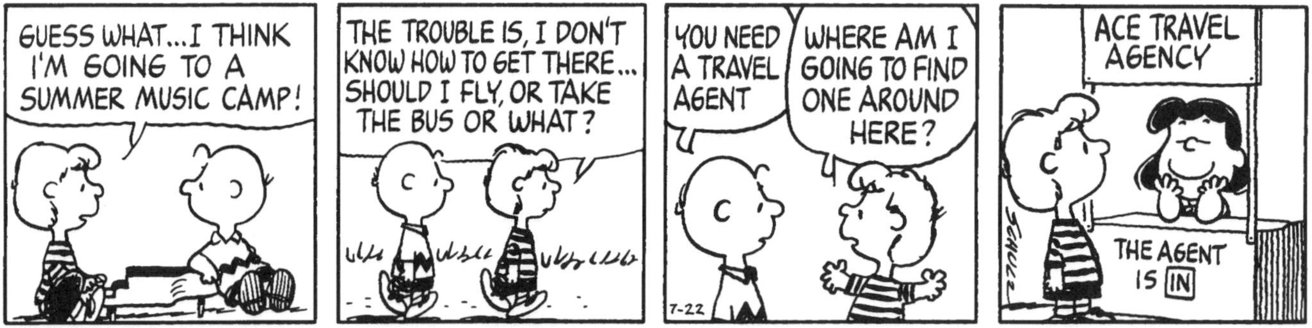
GUESS WHAT...I THINK I'M GOING TO A SUMMER MUSIC CAMP!
THE TROUBLE IS, I DON'T KNOW HOW TO GET THERE... SHOULD I FLY, OR TAKE THE BUS OR WHAT?
YOU NEED A TRAVEL AGENT
WHERE AM I GOING TO FIND ONE AROUND HERE?
7-22
ACE TRAVEL AGENCY
THE AGENT IS IN

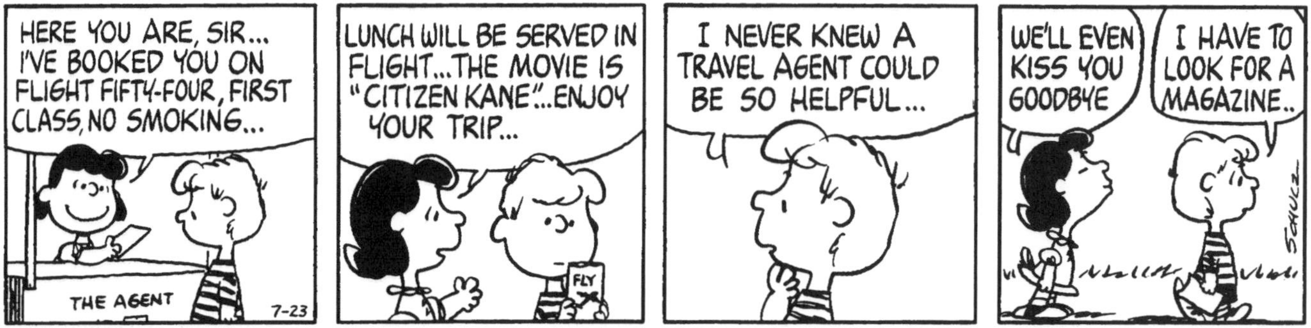
HERE YOU ARE, SIR... I'VE BOOKED YOU ON FLIGHT FIFTY-FOUR, FIRST CLASS, NO SMOKING...
THE AGENT
7-23
LUNCH WILL BE SERVED IN FLIGHT...THE MOVIE IS "CITIZEN KANE"...ENJOY YOUR TRIP...
FLY
I NEVER KNEW A TRAVEL AGENT COULD BE SO HELPFUL...
WE'LL EVEN KISS YOU GOODBYE
I HAVE TO LOOK FOR A MAGAZINE..

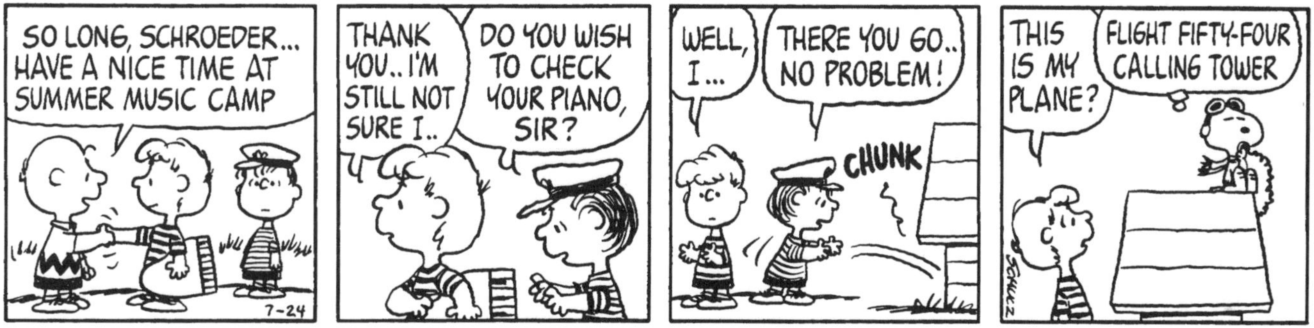
SO LONG, SCHROEDER... HAVE A NICE TIME AT SUMMER MUSIC CAMP
7-24
THANK YOU.. I'M STILL NOT SURE I..
DO YOU WISH TO CHECK YOUR PIANO, SIR?
WELL, I...
THERE YOU GO.. NO PROBLEM!
CHUNK
THIS IS MY PLANE?
FLIGHT FIFTY-FOUR CALLING TOWER

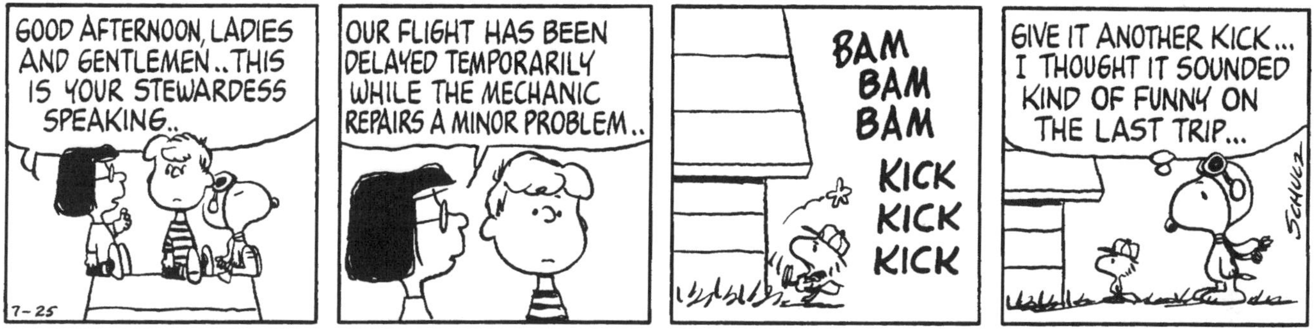
GOOD AFTERNOON, LADIES AND GENTLEMEN.. THIS IS YOUR STEWARDESS SPEAKING..
7-25
OUR FLIGHT HAS BEEN DELAYED TEMPORARILY WHILE THE MECHANIC REPAIRS A MINOR PROBLEM..
BAM
BAM
BAM
KICK
KICK
KICK
GIVE IT ANOTHER KICK... I THOUGHT IT SOUNDED KIND OF FUNNY ON THE LAST TRIP...
SCHULZ

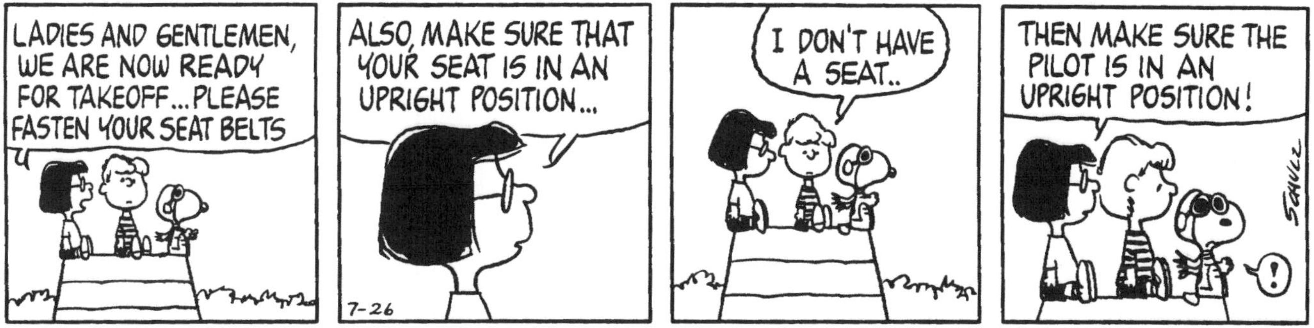
LADIES AND GENTLEMEN, WE ARE NOW READY FOR TAKEOFF... PLEASE FASTEN YOUR SEAT BELTS
ALSO, MAKE SURE THAT YOUR SEAT IS IN AN UPRIGHT POSITION...
7-26
I DON'T HAVE A SEAT..
THEN MAKE SURE THE PILOT IS IN AN UPRIGHT POSITION!
!
SCHULZ

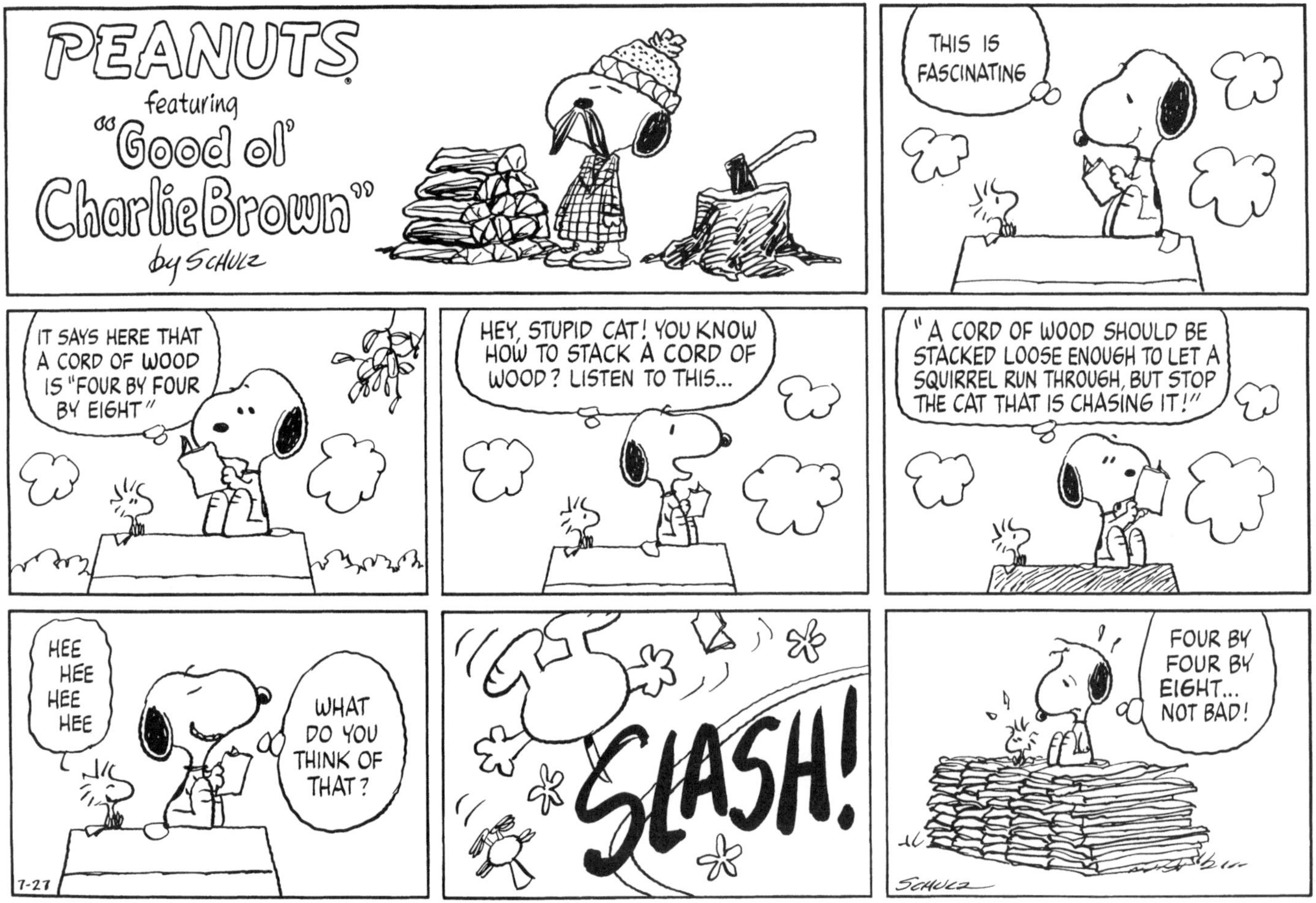
PEANUTS
featuring
"Good ol' Charlie Brown"
by SCHULZ
THIS IS FASCINATING
IT SAYS HERE THAT A CORD OF WOOD IS "FOUR BY FOUR BY EIGHT"
HEY, STUPID CAT! YOU KNOW HOW TO STACK A CORD OF WOOD? LISTEN TO THIS...
"A CORD OF WOOD SHOULD BE STACKED LOOSE ENOUGH TO LET A SQUIRREL RUN THROUGH, BUT STOP THE CAT THAT IS CHASING IT!"
HEE HEE HEE HEE
WHAT DO YOU THINK OF THAT?
7-27
SLASH!
FOUR BY FOUR BY EIGHT... NOT BAD!
SCHULZ

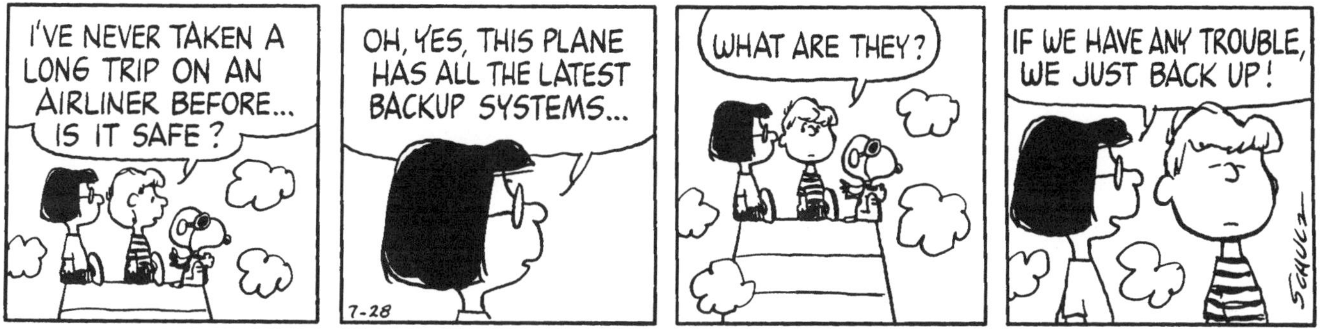
I'VE NEVER TAKEN A LONG TRIP ON AN AIRLINER BEFORE... IS IT SAFE?
OH, YES, THIS PLANE HAS ALL THE LATEST BACKUP SYSTEMS...
7-28
WHAT ARE THEY?
IF WE HAVE ANY TROUBLE, WE JUST BACK UP!
SCHULZ

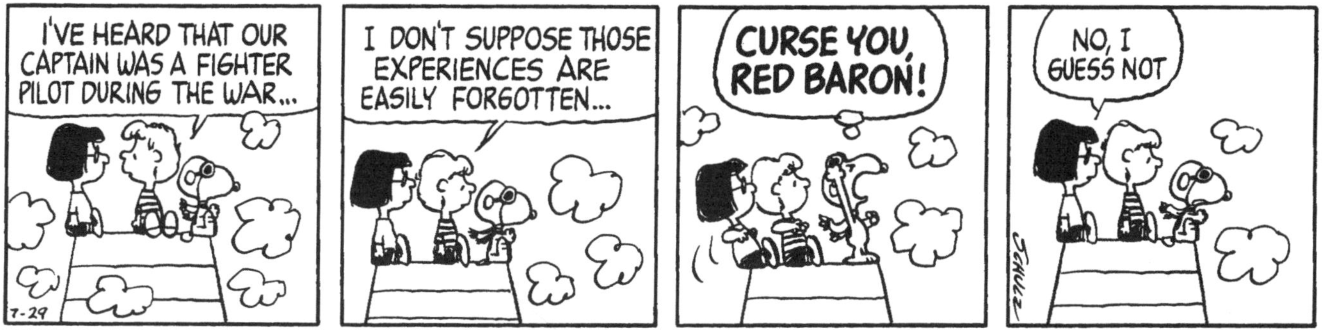
I'VE HEARD THAT OUR CAPTAIN WAS A FIGHTER PILOT DURING THE WAR...
7-29
I DON'T SUPPOSE THOSE EXPERIENCES ARE EASILY FORGOTTEN...
CURSE YOU, RED BARON!
SCHULZ
NO, I GUESS NOT

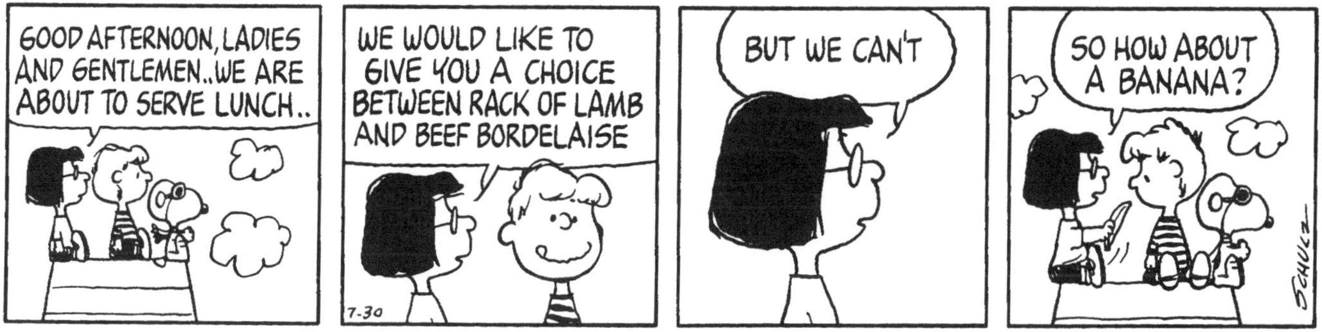
GOOD AFTERNOON, LADIES AND GENTLEMEN..WE ARE ABOUT TO SERVE LUNCH..
WE WOULD LIKE TO GIVE YOU A CHOICE BETWEEN RACK OF LAMB AND BEEF BORDELAISE
7-30
BUT WE CAN'T
SO HOW ABOUT A BANANA?
SCHULZ

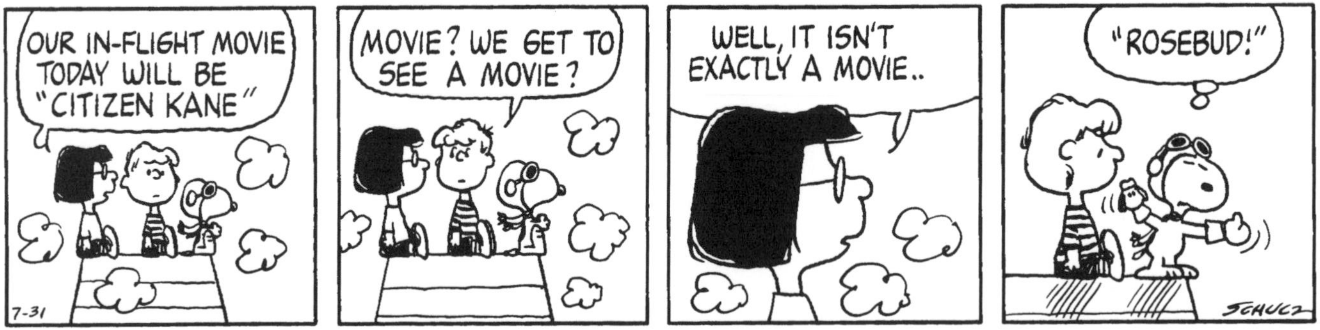
OUR IN-FLIGHT MOVIE TODAY WILL BE "CITIZEN KANE"
MOVIE? WE GET TO SEE A MOVIE?
WELL, IT ISN'T EXACTLY A MOVIE..
"ROSEBUD!"

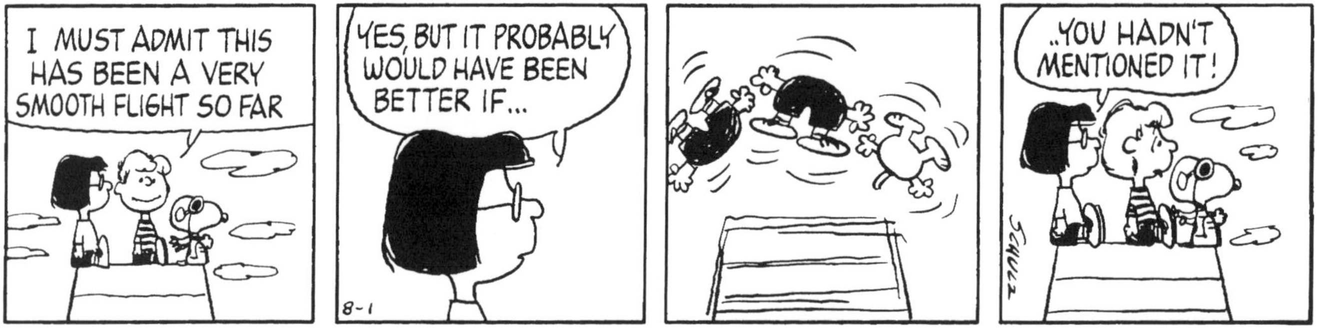
I MUST ADMIT THIS HAS BEEN A VERY SMOOTH FLIGHT SO FAR
YES, BUT IT PROBABLY WOULD HAVE BEEN BETTER IF...
..YOU HADN'T MENTIONED IT!

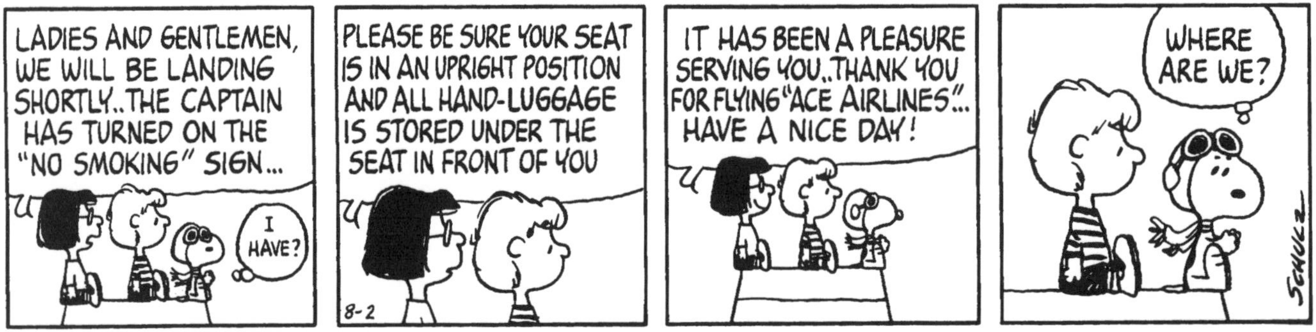
LADIES AND GENTLEMEN, WE WILL BE LANDING SHORTLY..THE CAPTAIN HAS TURNED ON THE "NO SMOKING" SIGN...
I HAVE?
PLEASE BE SURE YOUR SEAT IS IN AN UPRIGHT POSITION AND ALL HAND-LUGGAGE IS STORED UNDER THE SEAT IN FRONT OF YOU
IT HAS BEEN A PLEASURE SERVING YOU..THANK YOU FOR FLYING "ACE AIRLINES"... HAVE A NICE DAY!
WHERE ARE WE?

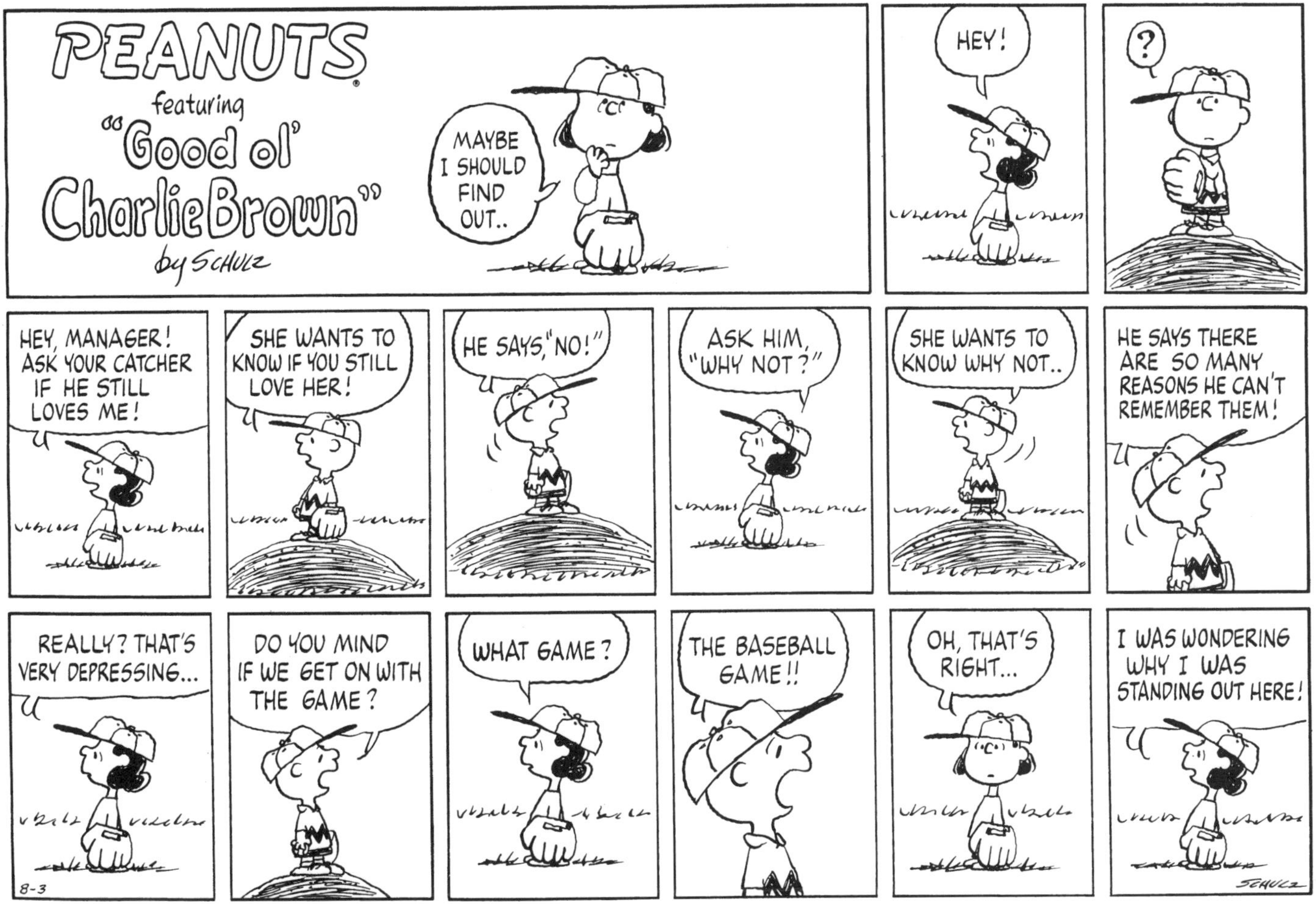
PEANUTS
featuring
"Good ol' Charlie Brown"
by SCHULZ
MAYBE I SHOULD FIND OUT..
HEY!
?
HEY, MANAGER! ASK YOUR CATCHER IF HE STILL LOVES ME!
SHE WANTS TO KNOW IF YOU STILL LOVE HER!
HE SAYS, "NO!"
ASK HIM, "WHY NOT?"
SHE WANTS TO KNOW WHY NOT..
HE SAYS THERE ARE SO MANY REASONS HE CAN'T REMEMBER THEM!
REALLY? THAT'S VERY DEPRESSING...
DO YOU MIND IF WE GET ON WITH THE GAME?
WHAT GAME?
THE BASEBALL GAME!!
OH, THAT'S RIGHT...
I WAS WONDERING WHY I WAS STANDING OUT HERE!
8-3
SCHULZ

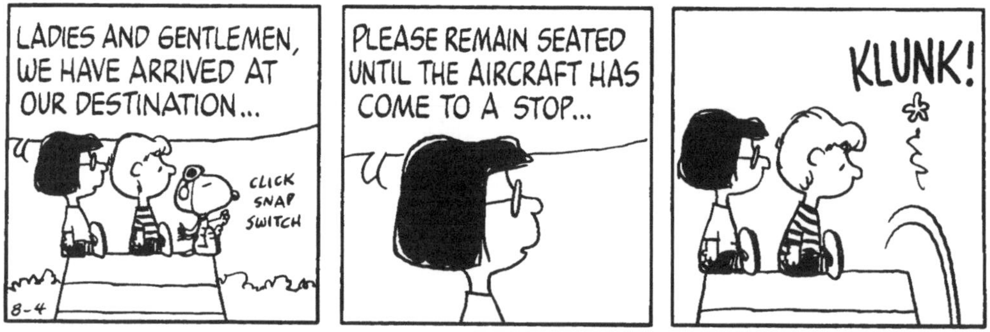
LADIES AND GENTLEMEN, WE HAVE ARRIVED AT OUR DESTINATION...
CLICK SNAP SWITCH
8-4
PLEASE REMAIN SEATED UNTIL THE AIRCRAFT HAS COME TO A STOP...
KLUNK!
DON'T MIND HIM, SIR.. HE FAINTS AFTER EVERY LANDING!
SCHULZ

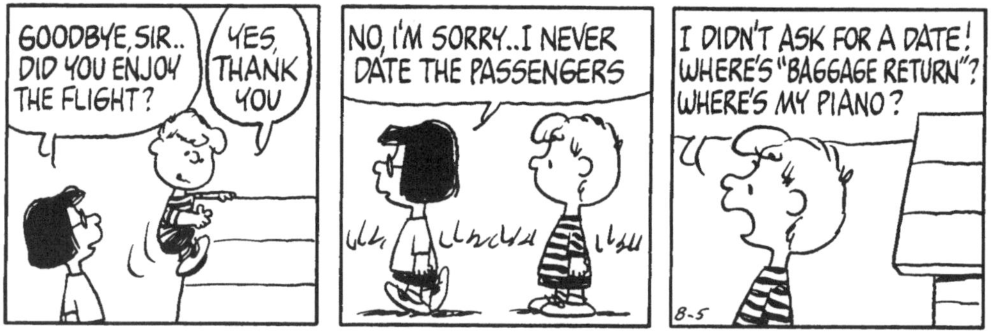
GOODBYE, SIR.. DID YOU ENJOY THE FLIGHT?
YES, THANK YOU
NO, I'M SORRY..I NEVER DATE THE PASSENGERS
I DIDN'T ASK FOR A DATE! WHERE'S "BAGGAGE RETURN"? WHERE'S MY PIANO?
8-5
SCHULZ
BONK!!

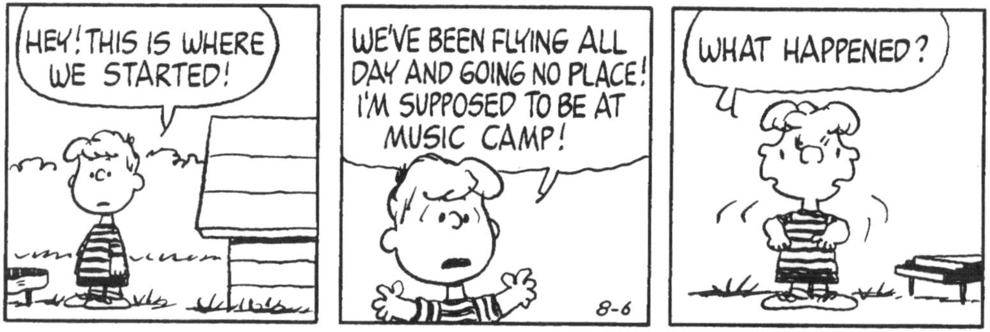
HEY! THIS IS WHERE WE STARTED!
WE'VE BEEN FLYING ALL DAY AND GOING NO PLACE! I'M SUPPOSED TO BE AT MUSIC CAMP!
8-6
WHAT HAPPENED?
SORRY, SIR..THIS SECTION OF THE AIRPORT TERMINAL IS CLOSED FOR REPAIRS!
SCHULZ

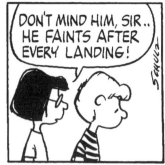

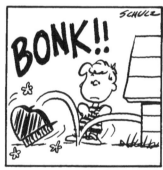

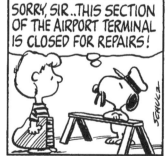

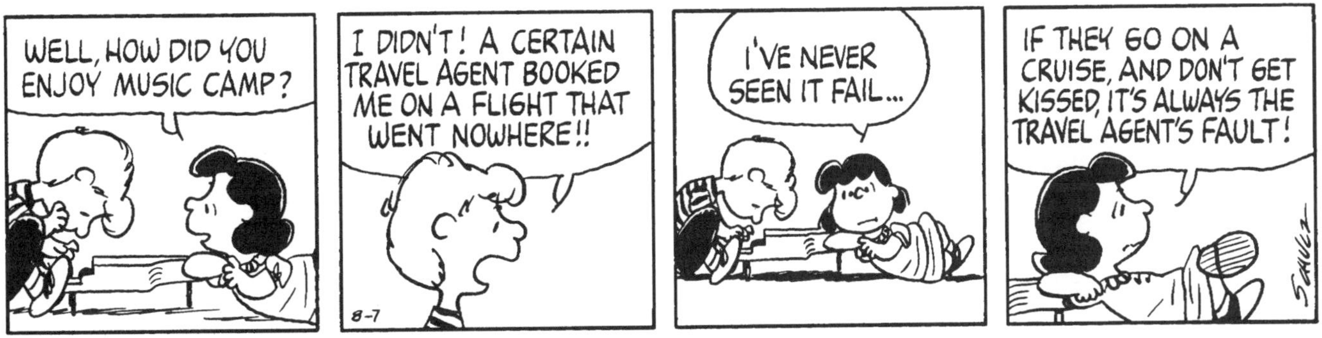
WELL, HOW DID YOU ENJOY MUSIC CAMP?
I DIDN'T! A CERTAIN TRAVEL AGENT BOOKED ME ON A FLIGHT THAT WENT NOWHERE!!
8-7
I'VE NEVER SEEN IT FAIL...
IF THEY GO ON A CRUISE, AND DON'T GET KISSED, IT'S ALWAYS THE TRAVEL AGENT'S FAULT!
SCHULZ

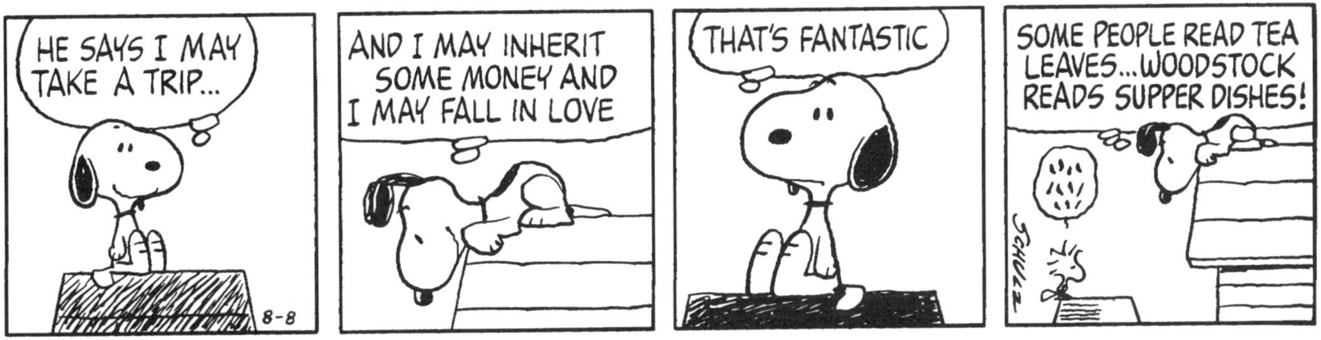
HE SAYS I MAY TAKE A TRIP...
8-8
AND I MAY INHERIT SOME MONEY AND I MAY FALL IN LOVE
THAT'S FANTASTIC
SOME PEOPLE READ TEA LEAVES...WOODSTOCK READS SUPPER DISHES!
SCHULZ

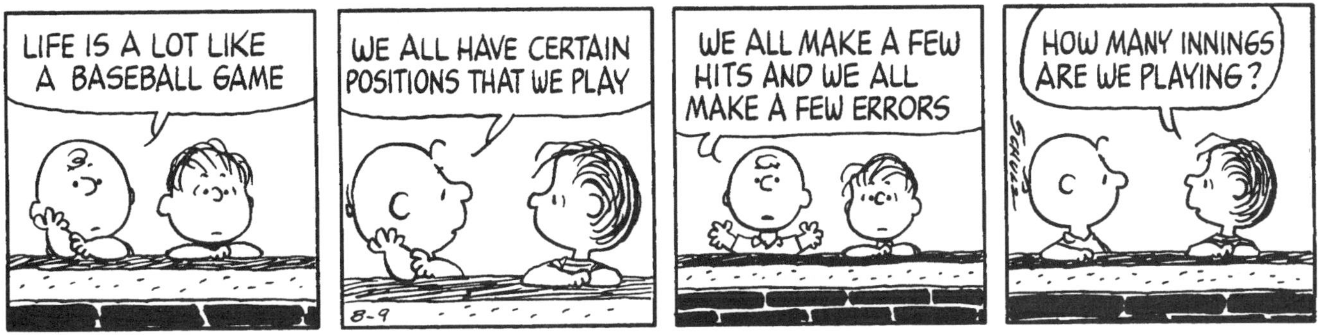
LIFE IS A LOT LIKE A BASEBALL GAME
WE ALL HAVE CERTAIN POSITIONS THAT WE PLAY
8-9
WE ALL MAKE A FEW HITS AND WE ALL MAKE A FEW ERRORS
HOW MANY INNINGS ARE WE PLAYING?
SCHULZ

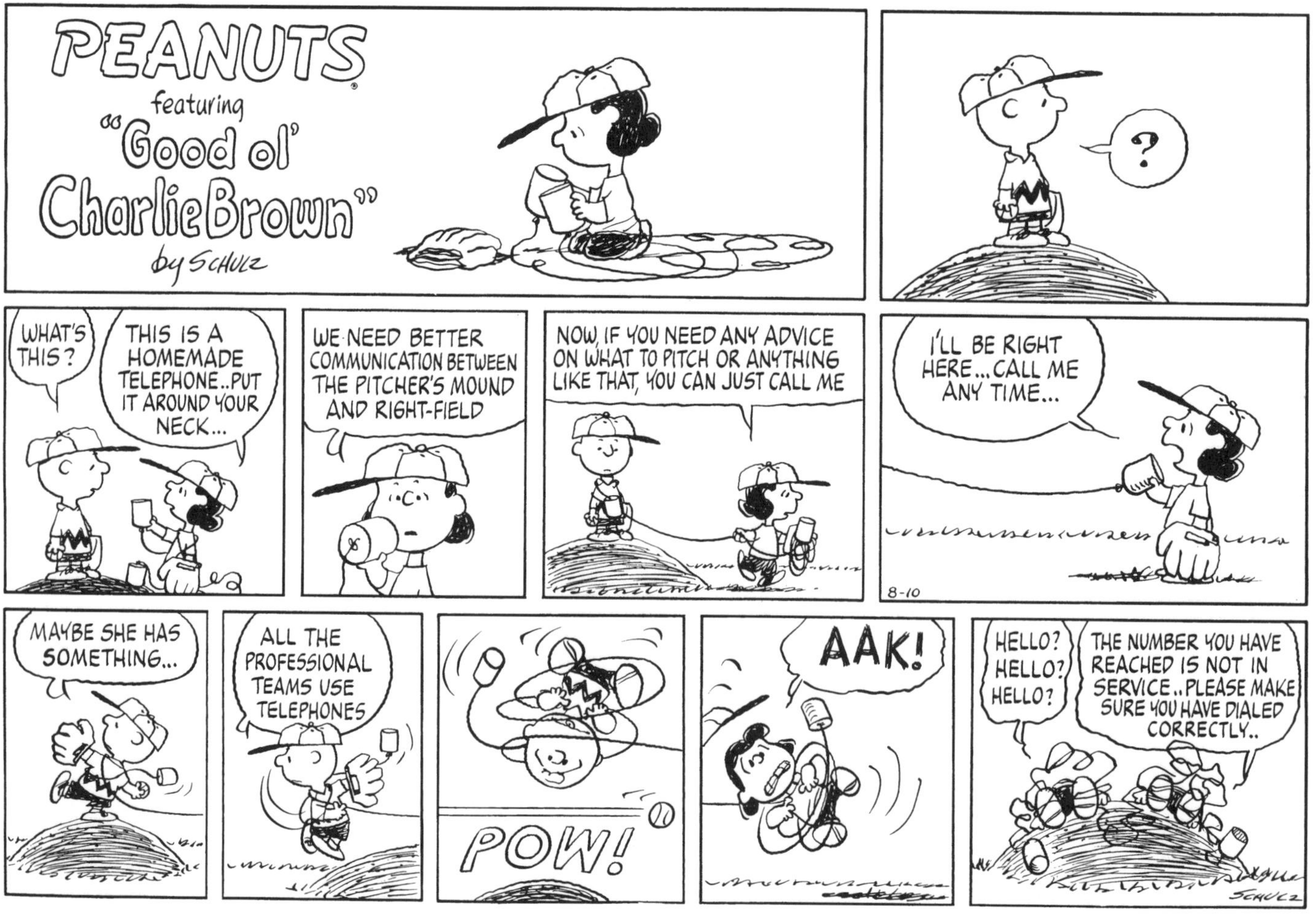

PEANUTS
featuring
"Good ol' Charlie Brown"
by SCHULZ
?
WHAT'S THIS?
THIS IS A HOMEMADE TELEPHONE..PUT IT AROUND YOUR NECK...
WE NEED BETTER COMMUNICATION BETWEEN THE PITCHER'S MOUND AND RIGHT-FIELD
NOW, IF YOU NEED ANY ADVICE ON WHAT TO PITCH OR ANYTHING LIKE THAT, YOU CAN JUST CALL ME
I'LL BE RIGHT HERE...CALL ME ANY TIME...
8-10
MAYBE SHE HAS SOMETHING...
ALL THE PROFESSIONAL TEAMS USE TELEPHONES
POW!
AAK!
HELLO? HELLO? HELLO?
THE NUMBER YOU HAVE REACHED IS NOT IN SERVICE..PLEASE MAKE SURE YOU HAVE DIALED CORRECTLY..
SCHULZ

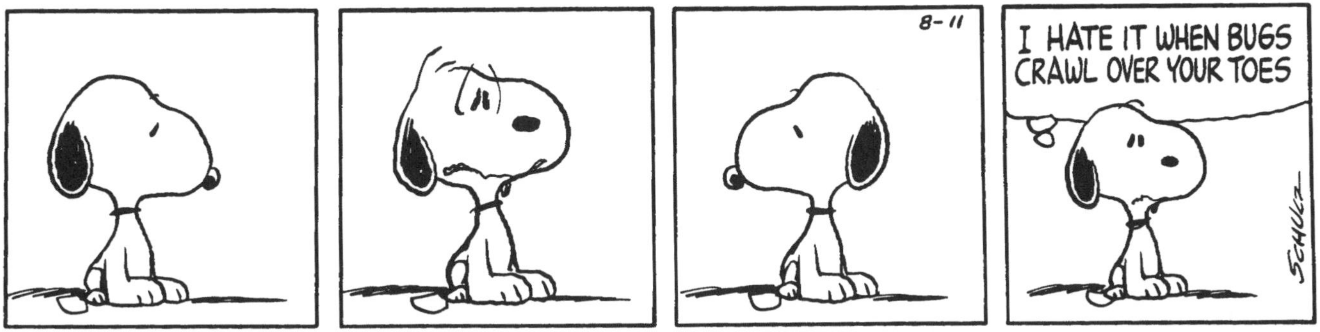
8-11
I HATE IT WHEN BUGS CRAWL OVER YOUR TOES
SCHULZ

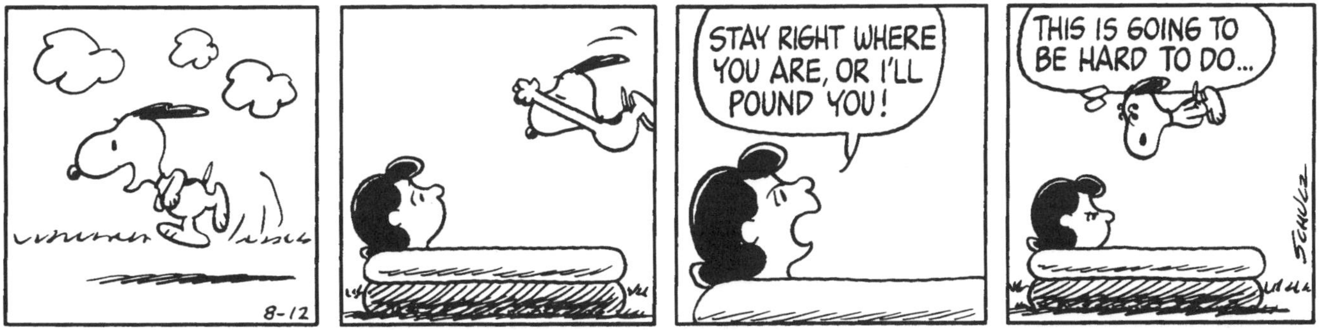
8-12
STAY RIGHT WHERE YOU ARE, OR I'LL POUND YOU!
THIS IS GOING TO BE HARD TO DO...
SCHULZ

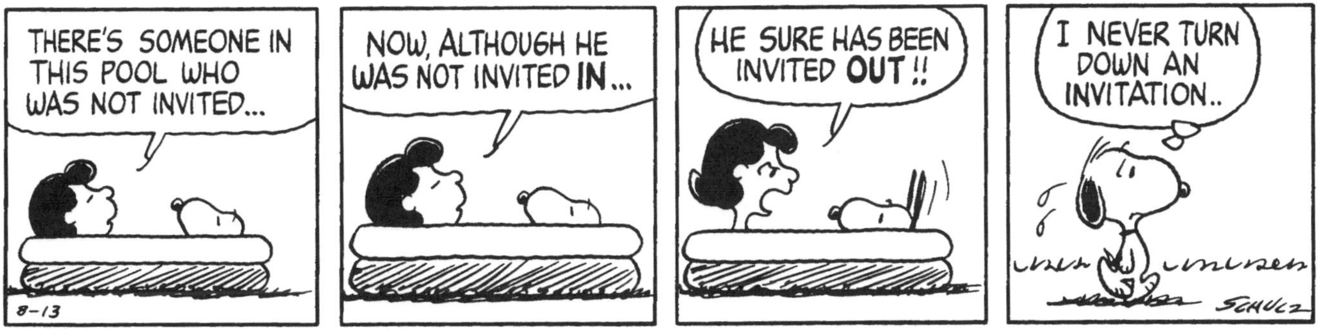
THERE'S SOMEONE IN THIS POOL WHO WAS NOT INVITED...
8-13
NOW, ALTHOUGH HE WAS NOT INVITED IN...
HE SURE HAS BEEN INVITED OUT!!
I NEVER TURN DOWN AN INVITATION..
SCHULZ

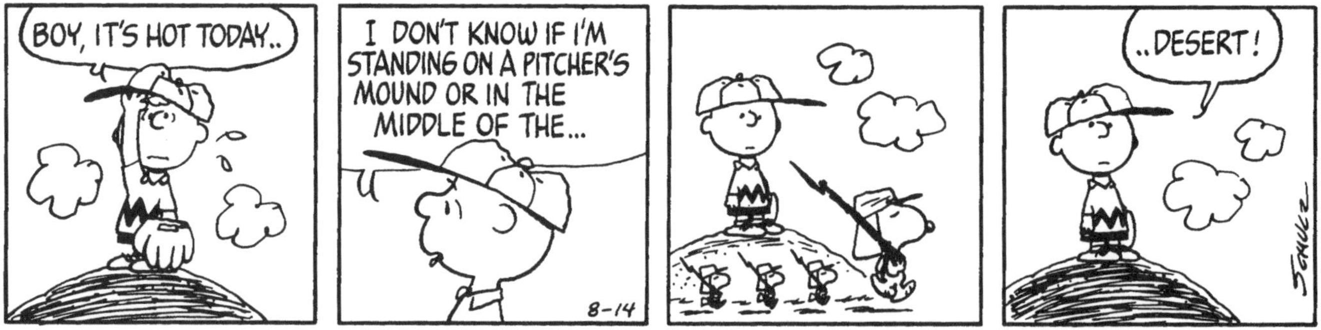
BOY, IT'S HOT TODAY..
I DON'T KNOW IF I'M STANDING ON A PITCHER'S MOUND OR IN THE MIDDLE OF THE...
8-14
..DESERT!
SCHULZ

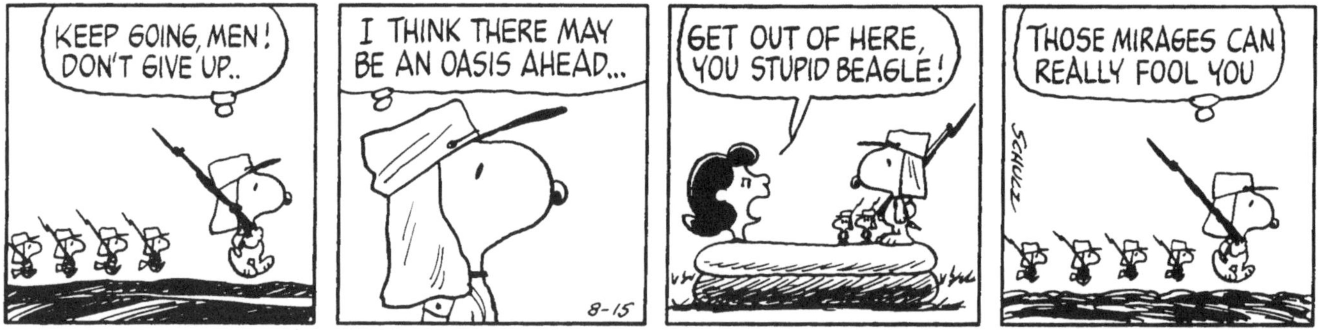
KEEP GOING, MEN! DON'T GIVE UP..
I THINK THERE MAY BE AN OASIS AHEAD...
8-15
GET OUT OF HERE, YOU STUPID BEAGLE!
SCHULZ
THOSE MIRAGES CAN REALLY FOOL YOU

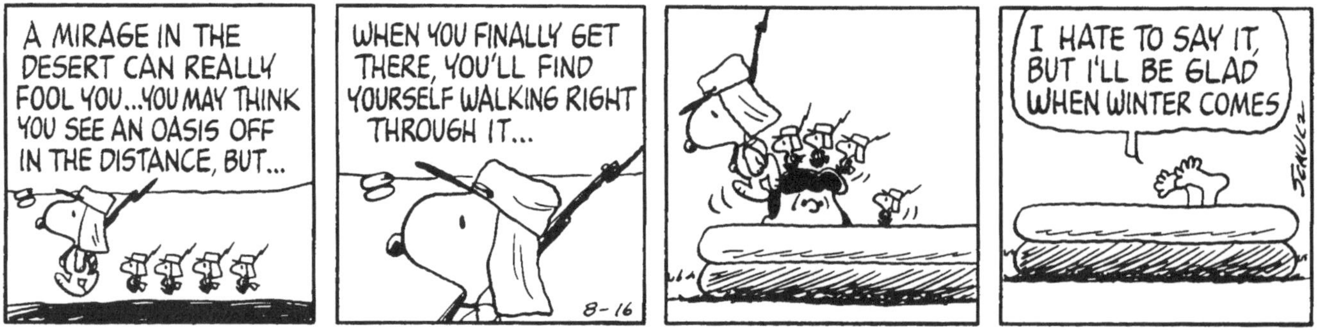
A MIRAGE IN THE DESERT CAN REALLY FOOL YOU...YOU MAY THINK YOU SEE AN OASIS OFF IN THE DISTANCE, BUT...
WHEN YOU FINALLY GET THERE, YOU'LL FIND YOURSELF WALKING RIGHT THROUGH IT...
8-16
I HATE TO SAY IT, BUT I'LL BE GLAD WHEN WINTER COMES
SCHULZ

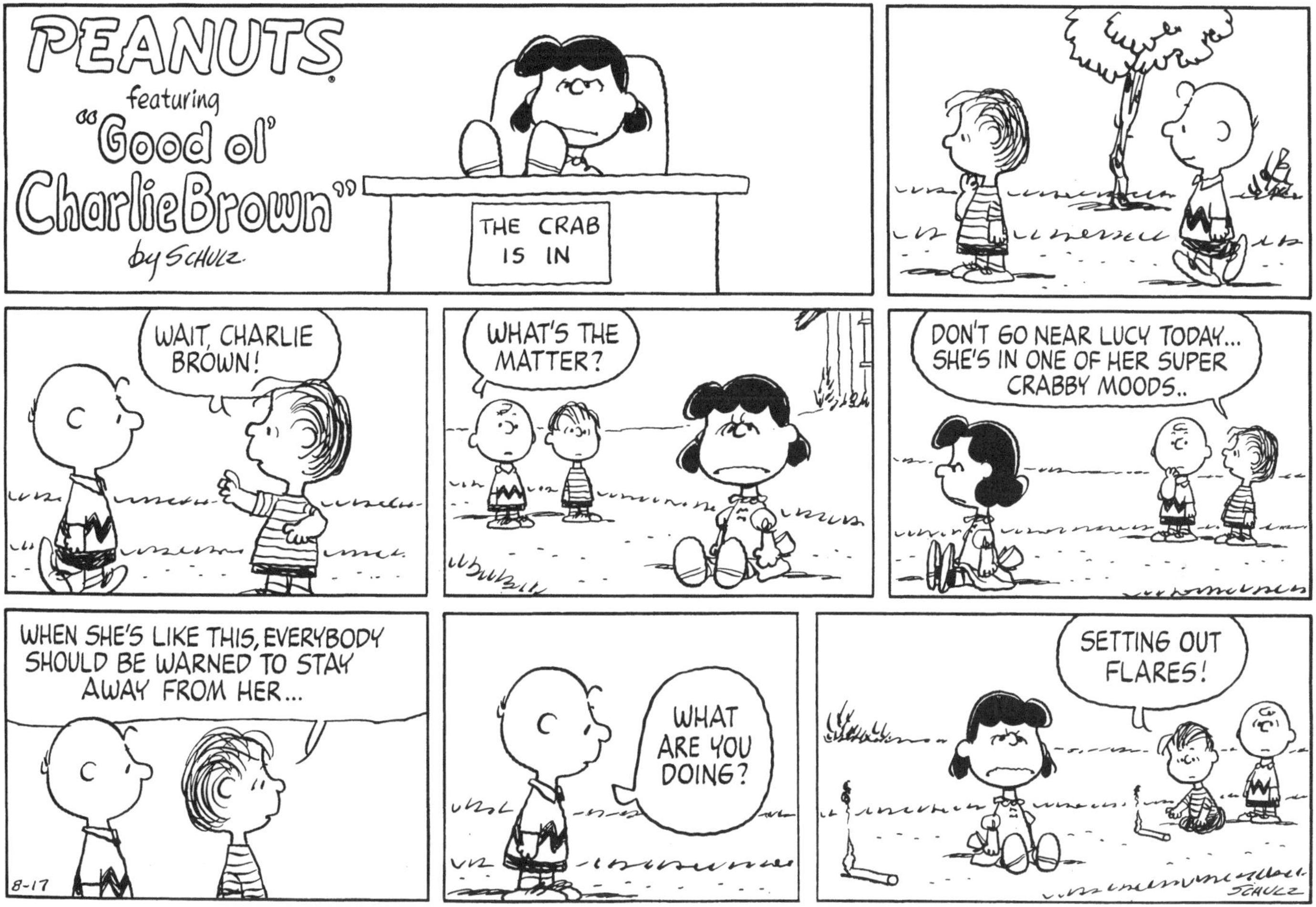
PEANUTS
featuring
"Good ol' Charlie Brown"
by SCHULZ
THE CRAB IS IN
WAIT, CHARLIE BROWN!
WHAT'S THE MATTER?
DON'T GO NEAR LUCY TODAY... SHE'S IN ONE OF HER SUPER CRABBY MOODS..
WHEN SHE'S LIKE THIS, EVERYBODY SHOULD BE WARNED TO STAY AWAY FROM HER...
8-17
WHAT ARE YOU DOING?
SETTING OUT FLARES!
SCHULZ

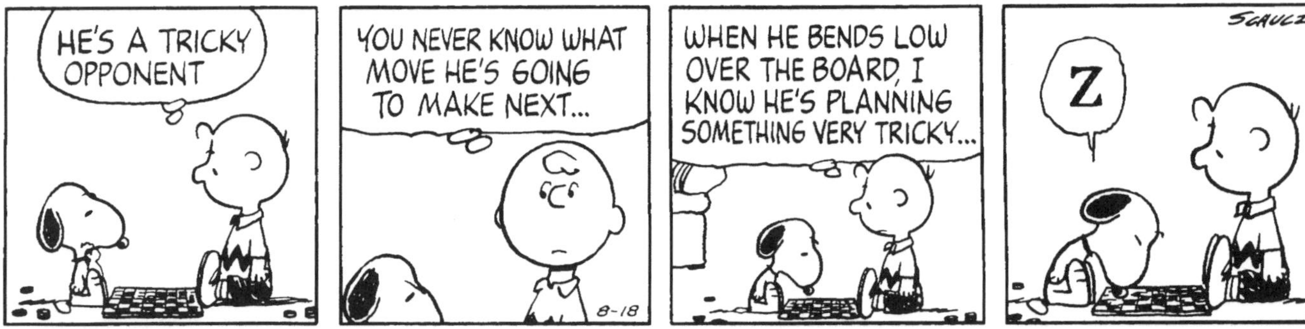
HE'S A TRICKY OPPONENT
YOU NEVER KNOW WHAT MOVE HE'S GOING TO MAKE NEXT...
8-18
WHEN HE BENDS LOW OVER THE BOARD, I KNOW HE'S PLANNING SOMETHING VERY TRICKY...
SCHULZ
Z

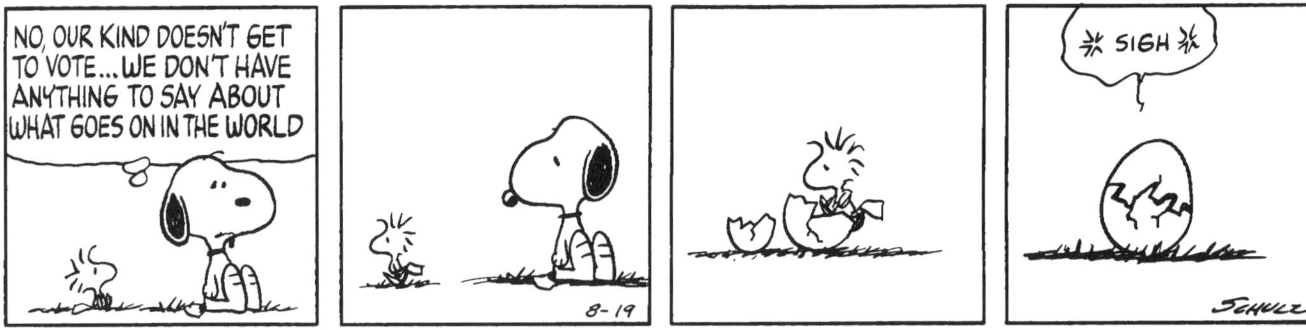
NO, OUR KIND DOESN'T GET TO VOTE... WE DON'T HAVE ANYTHING TO SAY ABOUT WHAT GOES ON IN THE WORLD
8-19
SIGH
SCHULZ

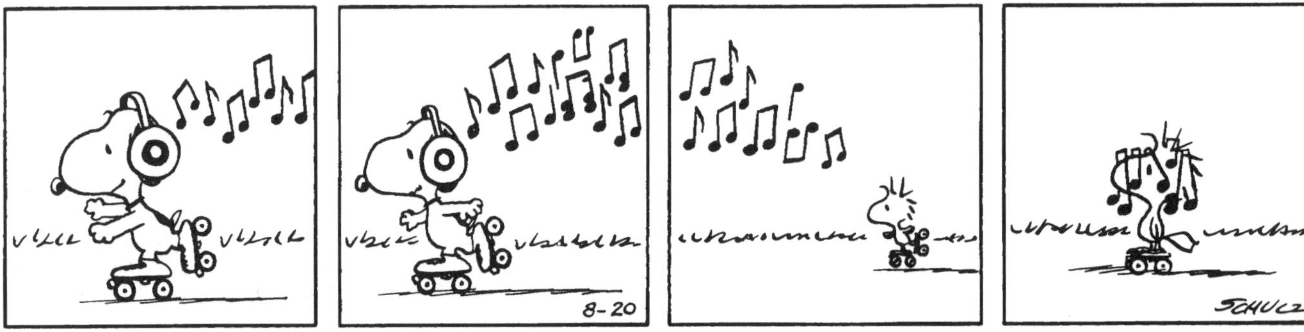
8-20
SCHULZ

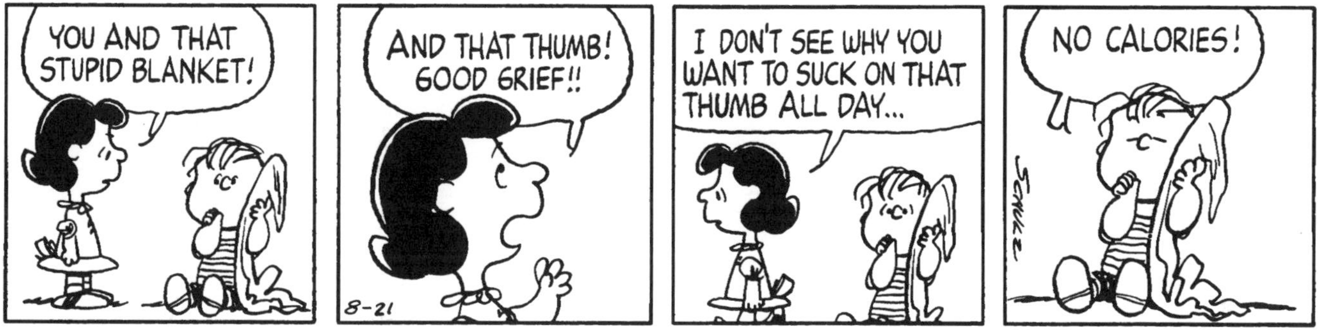
YOU AND THAT STUPID BLANKET!
AND THAT THUMB! GOOD GRIEF!!
8-21
I DON'T SEE WHY YOU WANT TO SUCK ON THAT THUMB ALL DAY...
NO CALORIES!

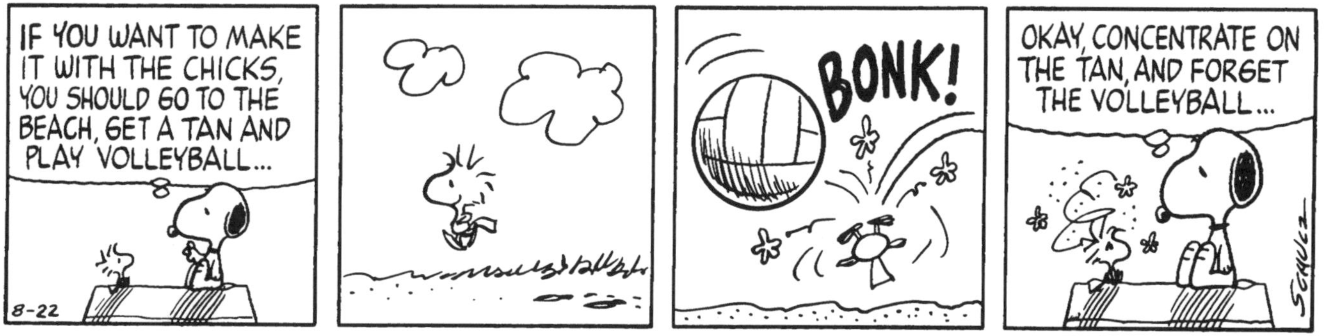
IF YOU WANT TO MAKE IT WITH THE CHICKS, YOU SHOULD GO TO THE BEACH, GET A TAN AND PLAY VOLLEYBALL...
8-22
BONK!
OKAY, CONCENTRATE ON THE TAN, AND FORGET THE VOLLEYBALL...

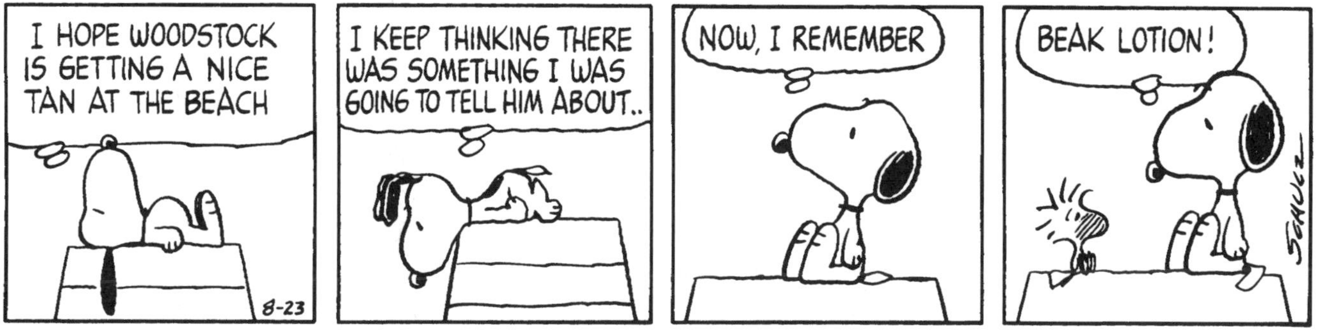
I HOPE WOODSTOCK IS GETTING A NICE TAN AT THE BEACH
8-23
I KEEP THINKING THERE WAS SOMETHING I WAS GOING TO TELL HIM ABOUT..
NOW, I REMEMBER
BEAK LOTION!

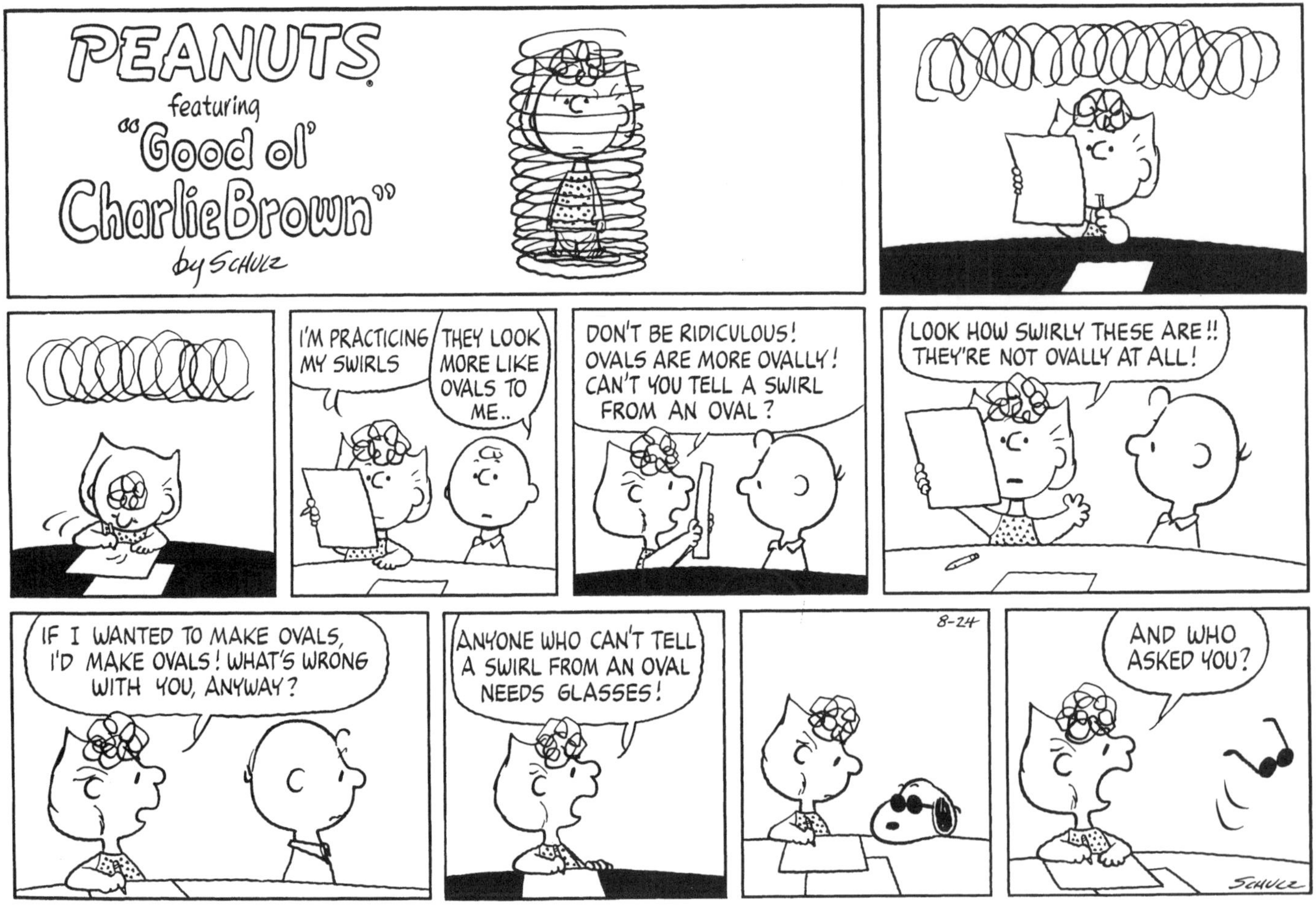
PEANUTS
featuring
"Good ol' CharlieBrown"
by SCHULZ
I'M PRACTICING MY SWIRLS
THEY LOOK MORE LIKE OVALS TO ME..
DON'T BE RIDICULOUS! OVALS ARE MORE OVALLY! CAN'T YOU TELL A SWIRL FROM AN OVAL?
LOOK HOW SWIRLY THESE ARE!! THEY'RE NOT OVALLY AT ALL!
IF I WANTED TO MAKE OVALS, I'D MAKE OVALS! WHAT'S WRONG WITH YOU, ANYWAY?
ANYONE WHO CAN'T TELL A SWIRL FROM AN OVAL NEEDS GLASSES!
8-24
AND WHO ASKED YOU?
SCHULZ

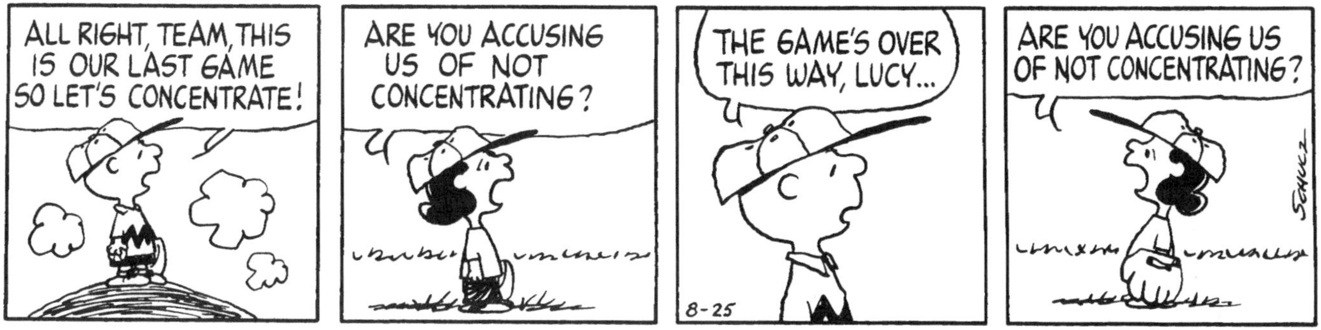
ALL RIGHT, TEAM, THIS IS OUR LAST GAME SO LET'S CONCENTRATE!
ARE YOU ACCUSING US OF NOT CONCENTRATING?
THE GAME'S OVER THIS WAY, LUCY...
ARE YOU ACCUSING US OF NOT CONCENTRATING?
SCHULZ
8-25

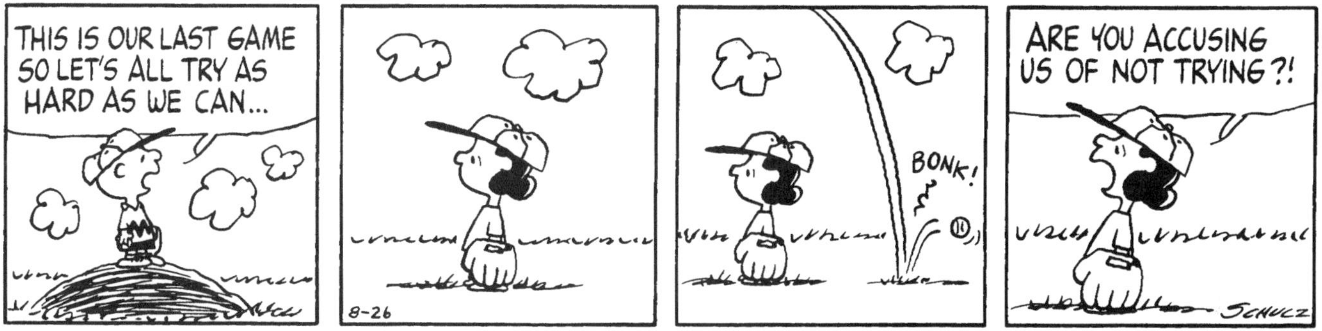
THIS IS OUR LAST GAME SO LET'S ALL TRY AS HARD AS WE CAN...
BONK!
ARE YOU ACCUSING US OF NOT TRYING?!
SCHULZ
8-26

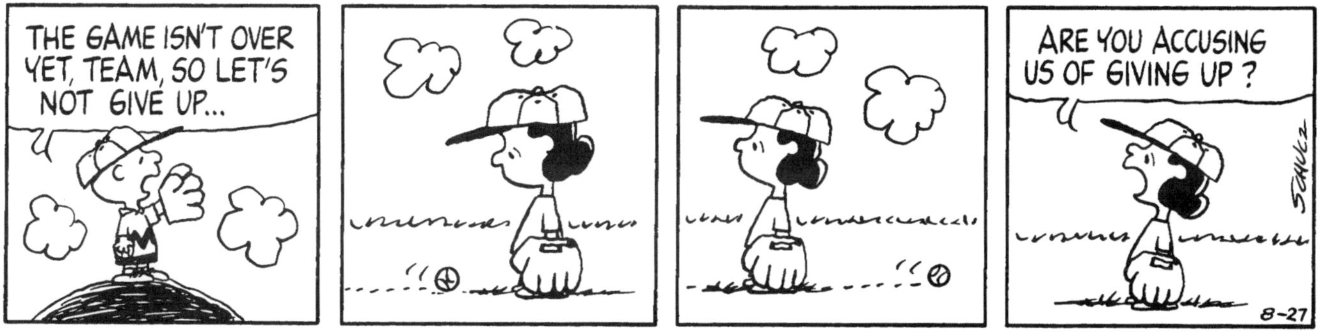
THE GAME ISN'T OVER YET, TEAM, SO LET'S NOT GIVE UP...
ARE YOU ACCUSING US OF GIVING UP?
SCHULZ
8-27

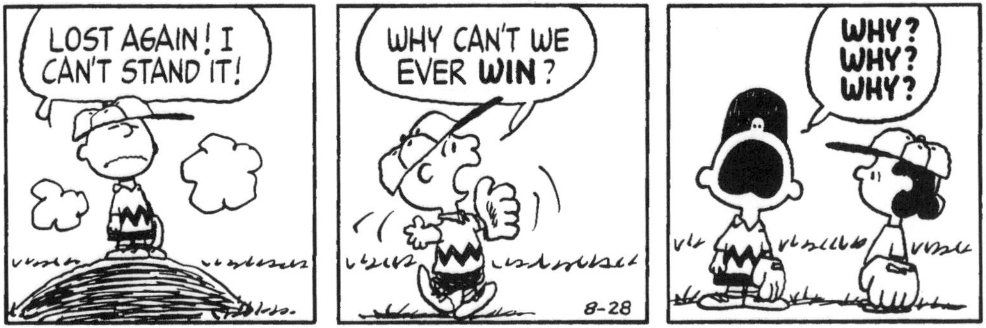
LOST AGAIN! I CAN'T STAND IT!
WHY CAN'T WE EVER **WIN**?
8-28
WHY? WHY? WHY?
BECAUSE WE'RE NO GOOD... BECAUSE WE'RE NO GOOD... BECAUSE WE'RE NO GOOD!
SCHULZ

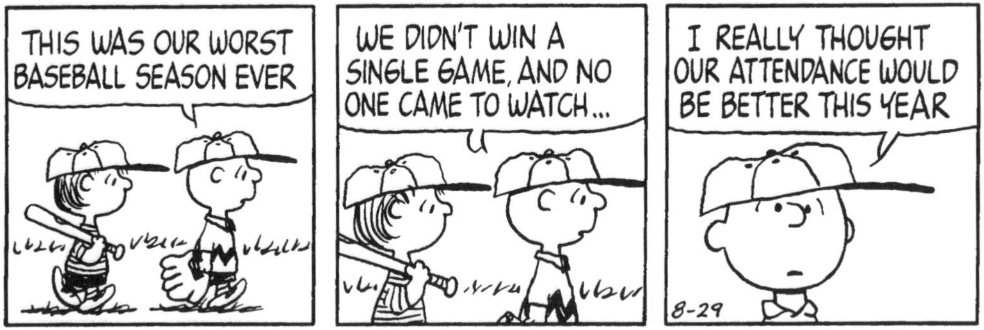
THIS WAS OUR WORST BASEBALL SEASON EVER
WE DIDN'T WIN A SINGLE GAME, AND NO ONE CAME TO WATCH...
I REALLY THOUGHT OUR ATTENDANCE WOULD BE BETTER THIS YEAR
8-29
WHAT SHOULD I DO WITH THE TICKET WE HAD PRINTED?
SCHULZ

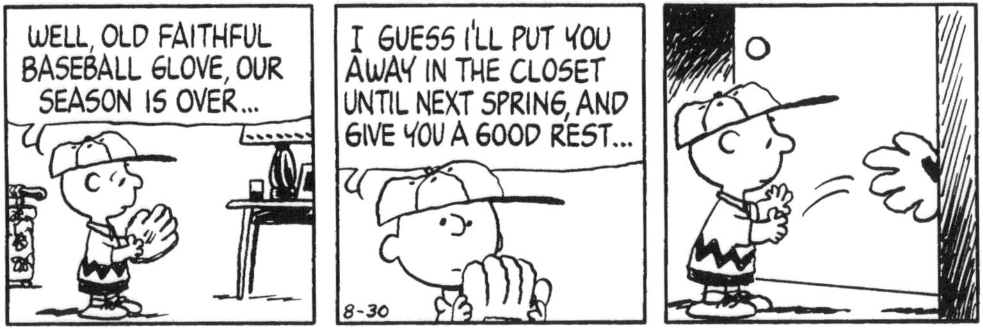
WELL, OLD FAITHFUL BASEBALL GLOVE, OUR SEASON IS OVER...
I GUESS I'LL PUT YOU AWAY IN THE CLOSET UNTIL NEXT SPRING, AND GIVE YOU A GOOD REST...
8-30
I KNOW WHAT'LL HAPPEN.. I'LL WAKE UP IN DECEMBER, AND WON'T BE ABLE TO GO BACK TO SLEEP!
SCHULZ

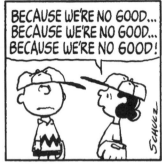

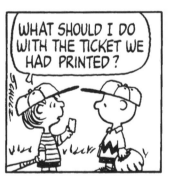

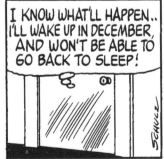

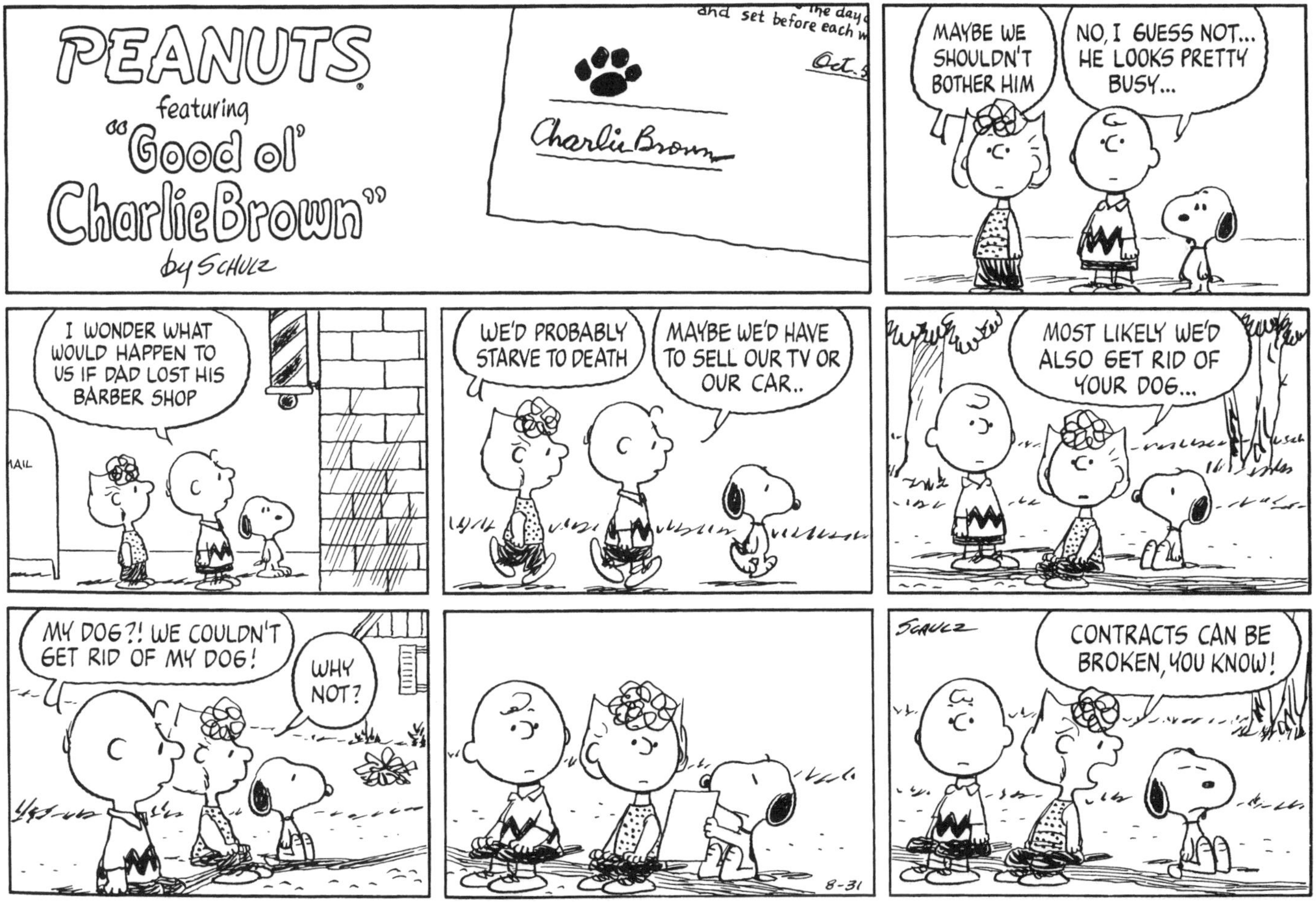
PEANUTS
featuring
"Good ol' CharlieBrown"
by SCHULZ
and set before each
Oct. 5
Charlie Brown
MAYBE WE SHOULDN'T BOTHER HIM
NO, I GUESS NOT... HE LOOKS PRETTY BUSY...
I WONDER WHAT WOULD HAPPEN TO US IF DAD LOST HIS BARBER SHOP
WE'D PROBABLY STARVE TO DEATH
MAYBE WE'D HAVE TO SELL OUR TV OR OUR CAR..
MOST LIKELY WE'D ALSO GET RID OF YOUR DOG...
MY DOG?! WE COULDN'T GET RID OF MY DOG!
WHY NOT?
8-31
SCHULZ
CONTRACTS CAN BE BROKEN, YOU KNOW!

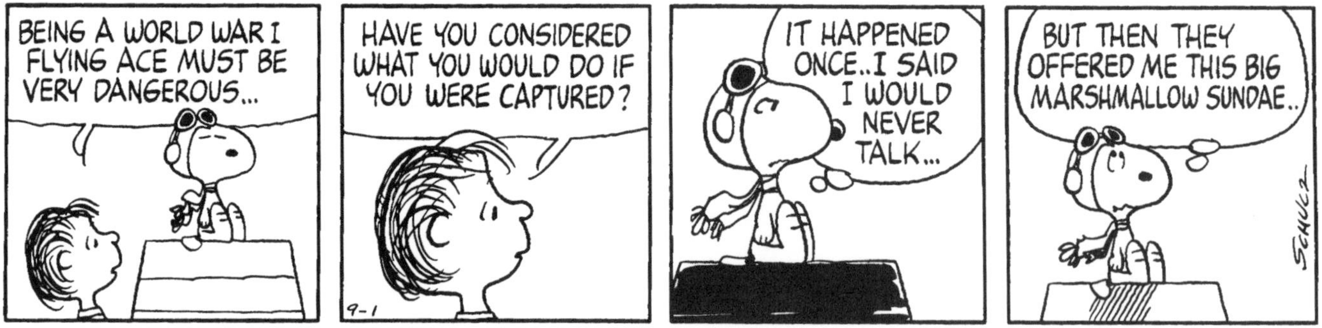
BEING A WORLD WAR I FLYING ACE MUST BE VERY DANGEROUS...
HAVE YOU CONSIDERED WHAT YOU WOULD DO IF YOU WERE CAPTURED?
IT HAPPENED ONCE..I SAID I WOULD NEVER TALK...
BUT THEN THEY OFFERED ME THIS BIG MARSHMALLOW SUNDAE..
9-1
SCHULZ

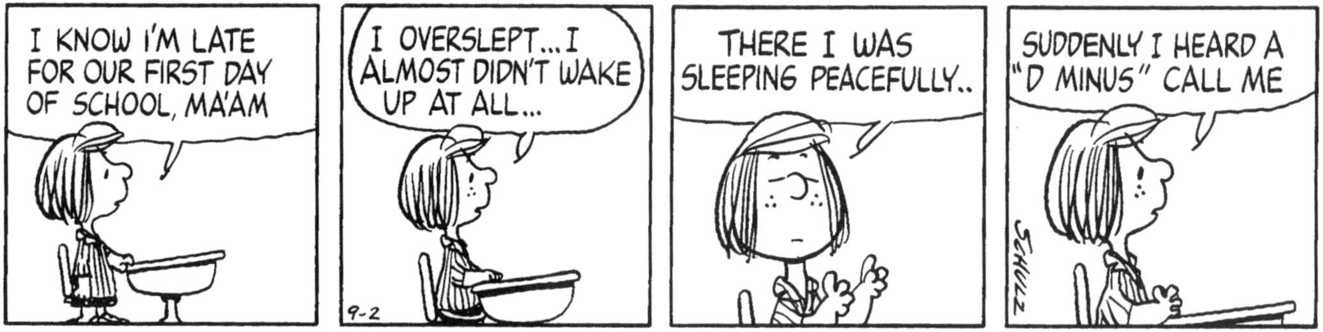
I KNOW I'M LATE FOR OUR FIRST DAY OF SCHOOL, MA'AM
I OVERSLEPT...I ALMOST DIDN'T WAKE UP AT ALL...
THERE I WAS SLEEPING PEACEFULLY..
SUDDENLY I HEARD A "D MINUS" CALL ME
9-2
SCHULZ

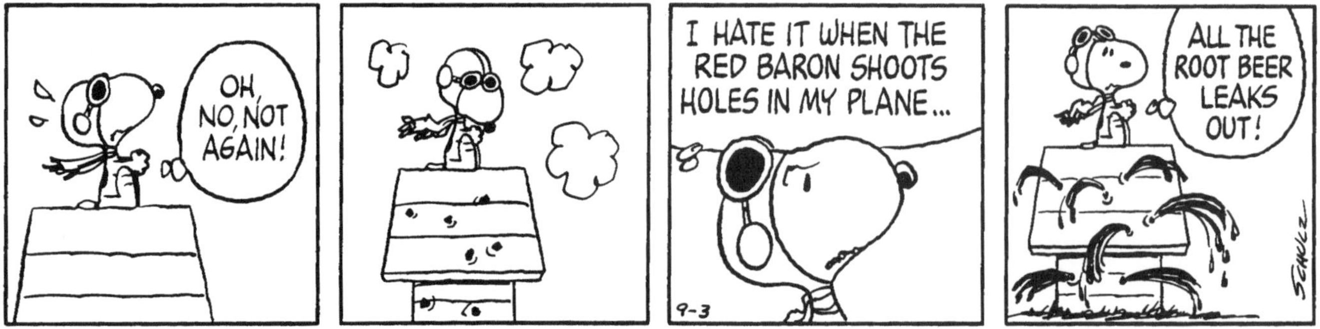
OH, NO, NOT AGAIN!
I HATE IT WHEN THE RED BARON SHOOTS HOLES IN MY PLANE...
ALL THE ROOT BEER LEAKS OUT!
9-3
SCHULZ

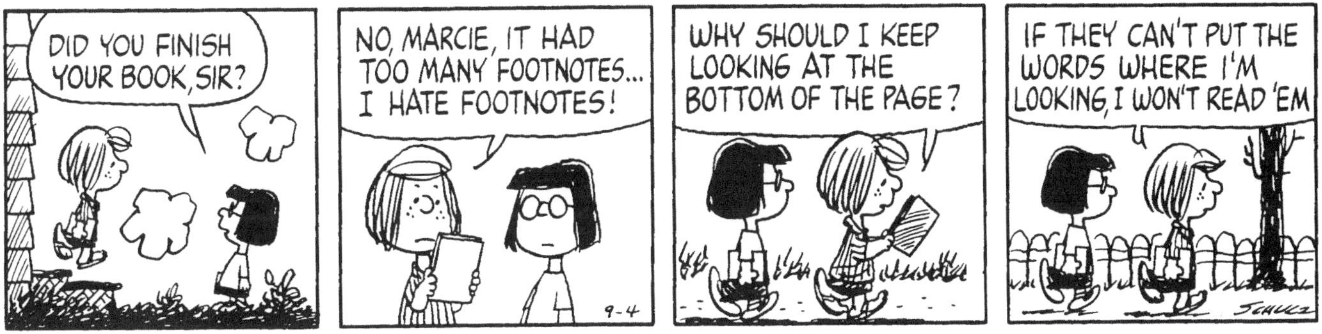

DID YOU FINISH YOUR BOOK, SIR?
NO, MARCIE, IT HAD TOO MANY FOOTNOTES... I HATE FOOTNOTES!
9-4
WHY SHOULD I KEEP LOOKING AT THE BOTTOM OF THE PAGE?
IF THEY CAN'T PUT THE WORDS WHERE I'M LOOKING, I WON'T READ 'EM
SCHULZ

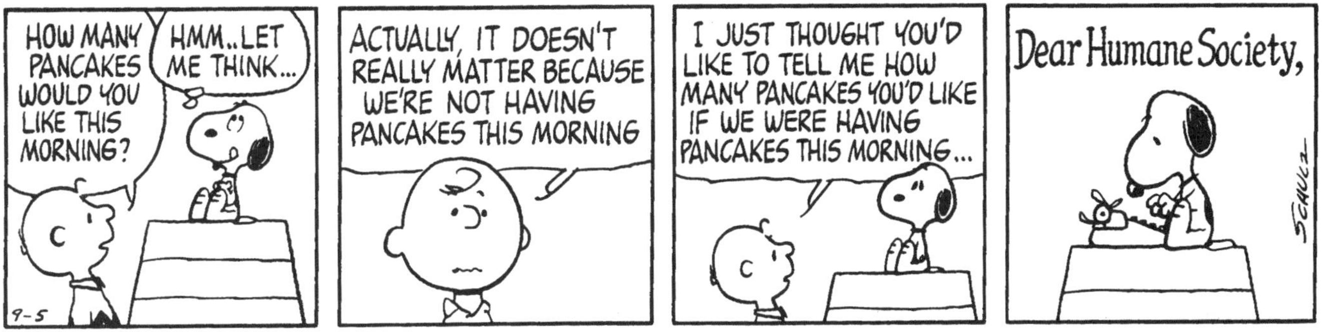

HOW MANY PANCAKES WOULD YOU LIKE THIS MORNING?
HMM..LET ME THINK...
9-5
ACTUALLY, IT DOESN'T REALLY MATTER BECAUSE WE'RE NOT HAVING PANCAKES THIS MORNING
I JUST THOUGHT YOU'D LIKE TO TELL ME HOW MANY PANCAKES YOU'D LIKE IF WE WERE HAVING PANCAKES THIS MORNING...
Dear Humane Society,
SCHULZ

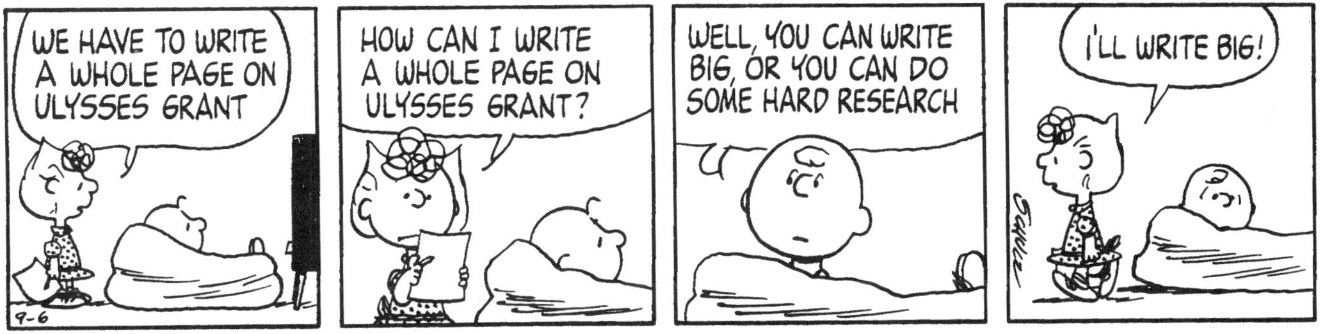

WE HAVE TO WRITE A WHOLE PAGE ON ULYSSES GRANT
9-6
HOW CAN I WRITE A WHOLE PAGE ON ULYSSES GRANT?
WELL, YOU CAN WRITE BIG, OR YOU CAN DO SOME HARD RESEARCH
I'LL WRITE BIG!
SCHULZ

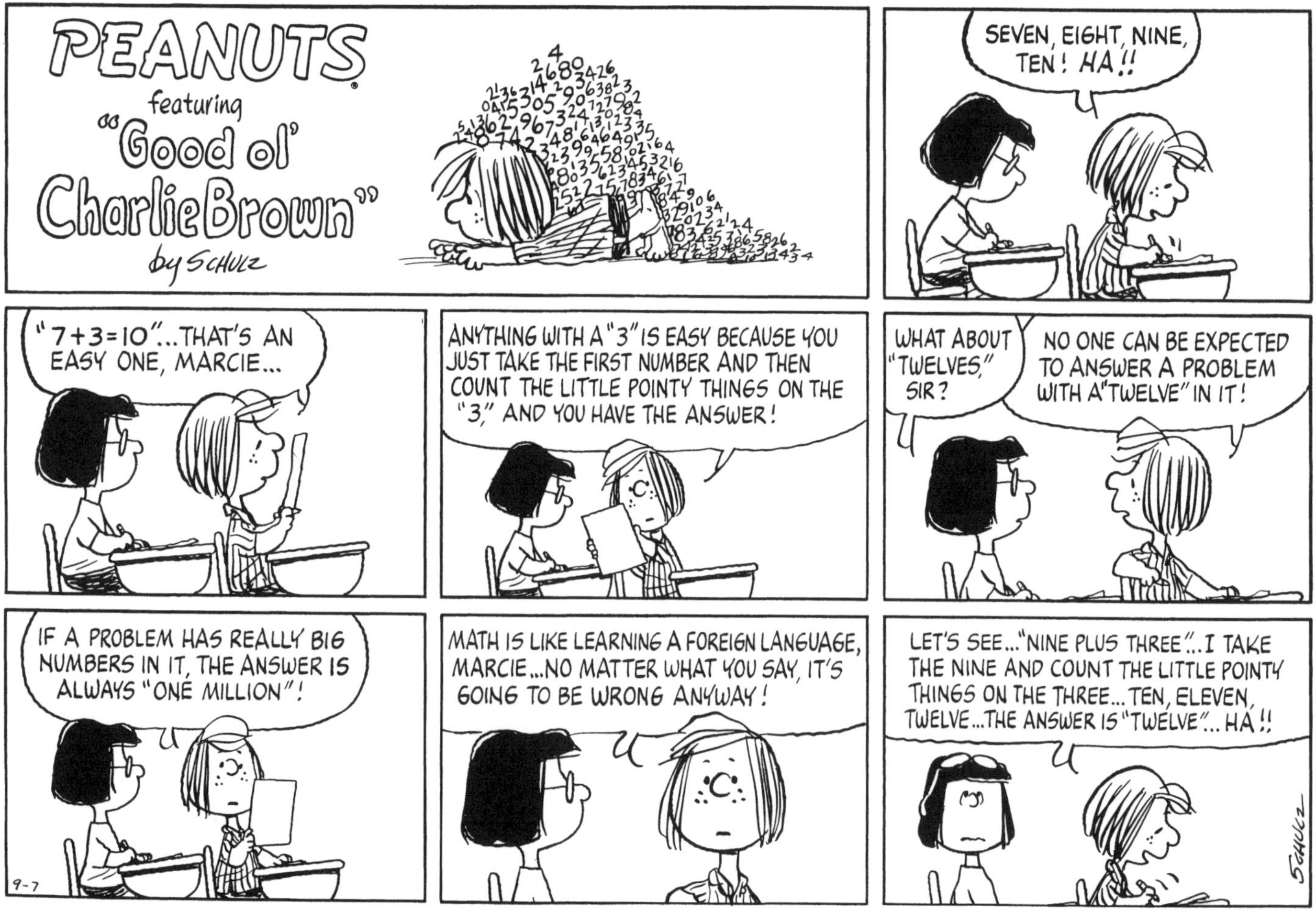
PEANUTS featuring "Good ol' Charlie Brown" by SCHULZ
SEVEN, EIGHT, NINE, TEN! HA!!
"7+3=10"...THAT'S AN EASY ONE, MARCIE...
ANYTHING WITH A "3" IS EASY BECAUSE YOU JUST TAKE THE FIRST NUMBER AND THEN COUNT THE LITTLE POINTY THINGS ON THE "3," AND YOU HAVE THE ANSWER!
WHAT ABOUT "TWELVES," SIR?
NO ONE CAN BE EXPECTED TO ANSWER A PROBLEM WITH A "TWELVE" IN IT!
IF A PROBLEM HAS REALLY BIG NUMBERS IN IT, THE ANSWER IS ALWAYS "ONE MILLION"!
9-7
MATH IS LIKE LEARNING A FOREIGN LANGUAGE, MARCIE...NO MATTER WHAT YOU SAY, IT'S GOING TO BE WRONG ANYWAY!
LET'S SEE..."NINE PLUS THREE"...I TAKE THE NINE AND COUNT THE LITTLE POINTY THINGS ON THE THREE...TEN, ELEVEN, TWELVE...THE ANSWER IS "TWELVE"... HA!!
SCHULZ

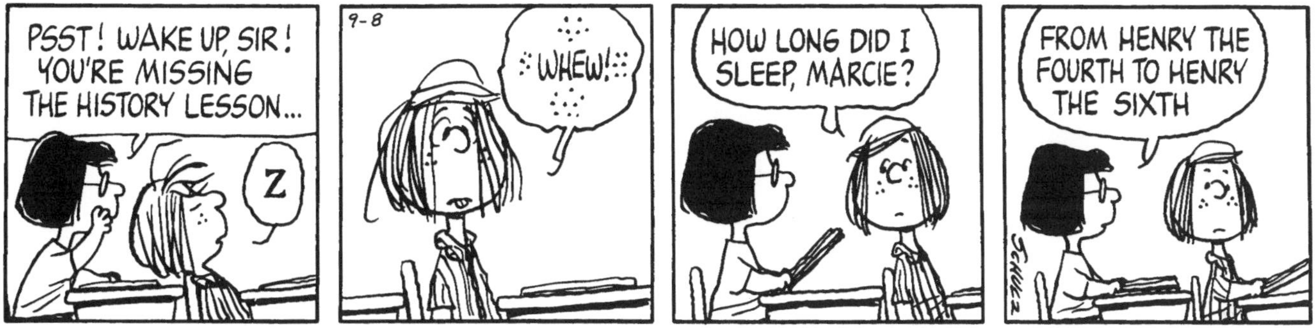
PSST! WAKE UP, SIR! YOU'RE MISSING THE HISTORY LESSON...
Z
9-8
WHEW!
HOW LONG DID I SLEEP, MARCIE?
FROM HENRY THE FOURTH TO HENRY THE SIXTH

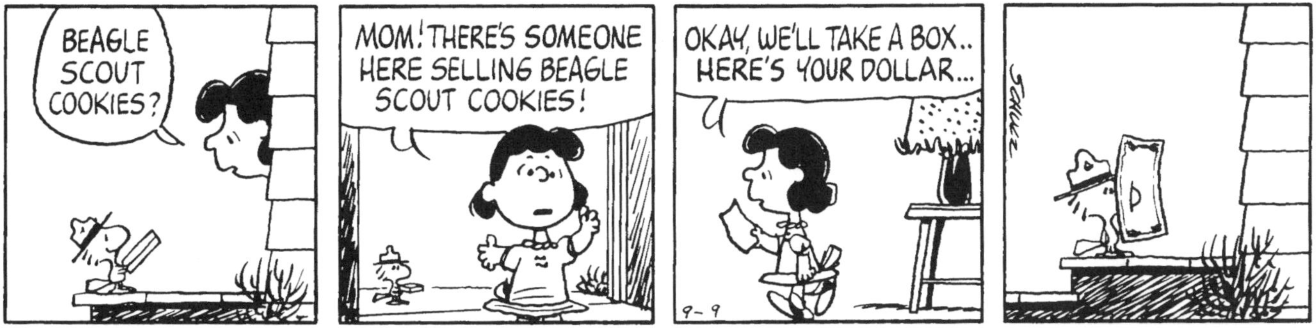
BEAGLE SCOUT COOKIES?
MOM! THERE'S SOMEONE HERE SELLING BEAGLE SCOUT COOKIES!
OKAY, WE'LL TAKE A BOX.. HERE'S YOUR DOLLAR...
9-9

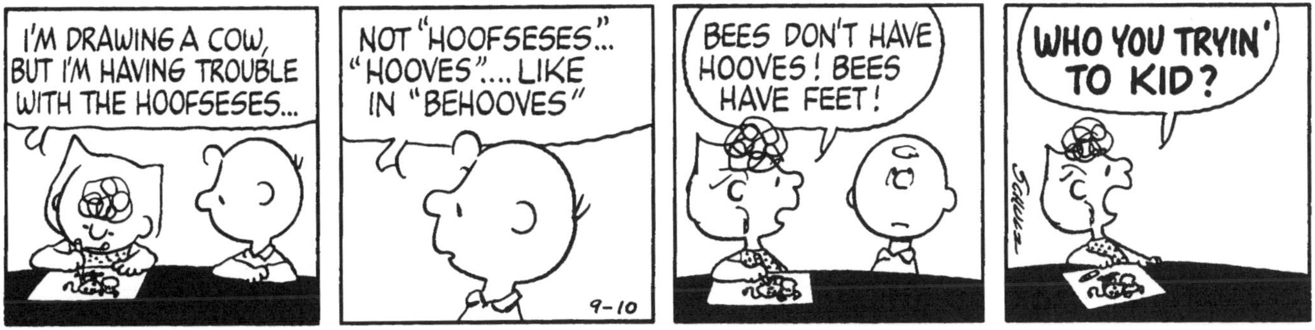
I'M DRAWING A COW, BUT I'M HAVING TROUBLE WITH THE HOOFSESES...
NOT "HOOFSESES"... "HOOVES"... LIKE IN "BEHOOVES"
9-10
BEES DON'T HAVE HOOVES! BEES HAVE FEET!
WHO YOU TRYIN' TO KID?

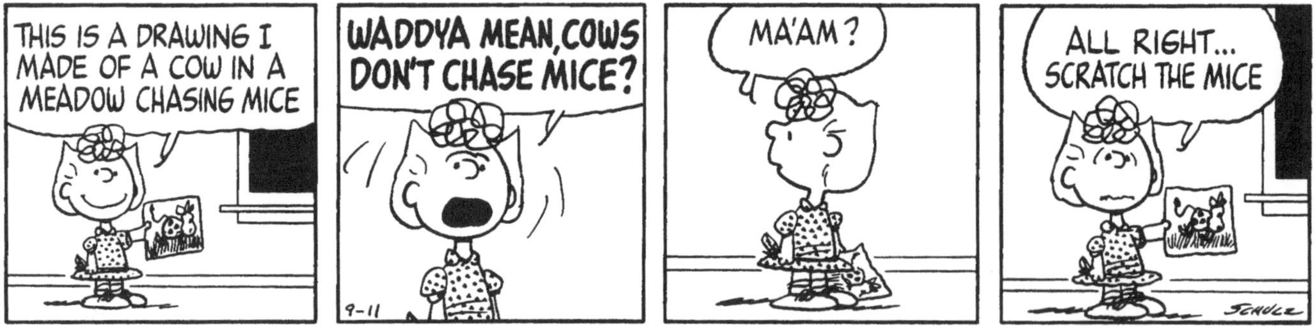
THIS IS A DRAWING I MADE OF A COW IN A MEADOW CHASING MICE
WADDYA MEAN, COWS DON'T CHASE MICE?
9-11
MA'AM?
ALL RIGHT... SCRATCH THE MICE
SCHULZ

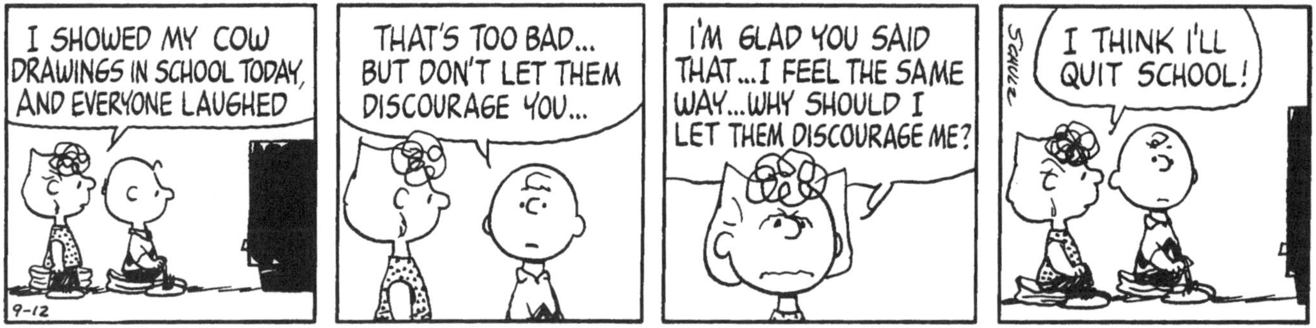
I SHOWED MY COW DRAWINGS IN SCHOOL TODAY, AND EVERYONE LAUGHED
9-12
THAT'S TOO BAD... BUT DON'T LET THEM DISCOURAGE YOU...
I'M GLAD YOU SAID THAT...I FEEL THE SAME WAY...WHY SHOULD I LET THEM DISCOURAGE ME?
SCHULZ
I THINK I'LL QUIT SCHOOL!

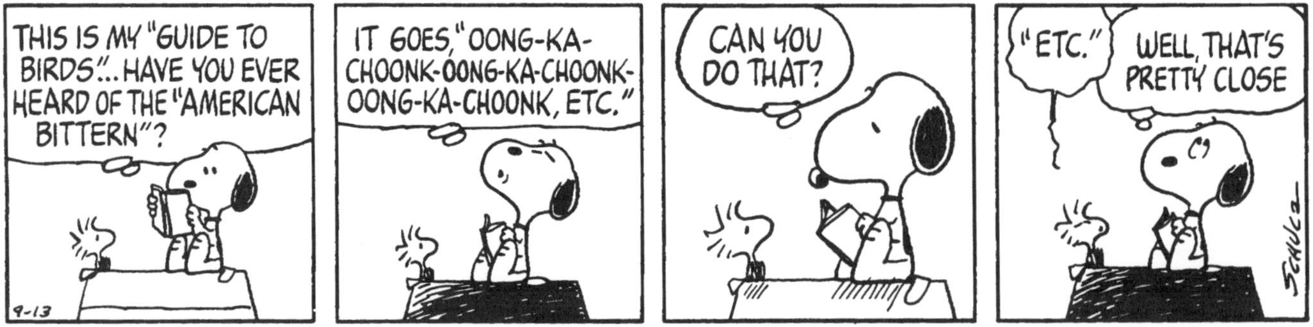
THIS IS MY "GUIDE TO BIRDS"...HAVE YOU EVER HEARD OF THE "AMERICAN BITTERN"?
9-13
IT GOES, "OONG-KA-CHOONK-OONG-KA-CHOONK-OONG-KA-CHOONK, ETC."
CAN YOU DO THAT?
"ETC."
WELL, THAT'S PRETTY CLOSE
SCHULZ

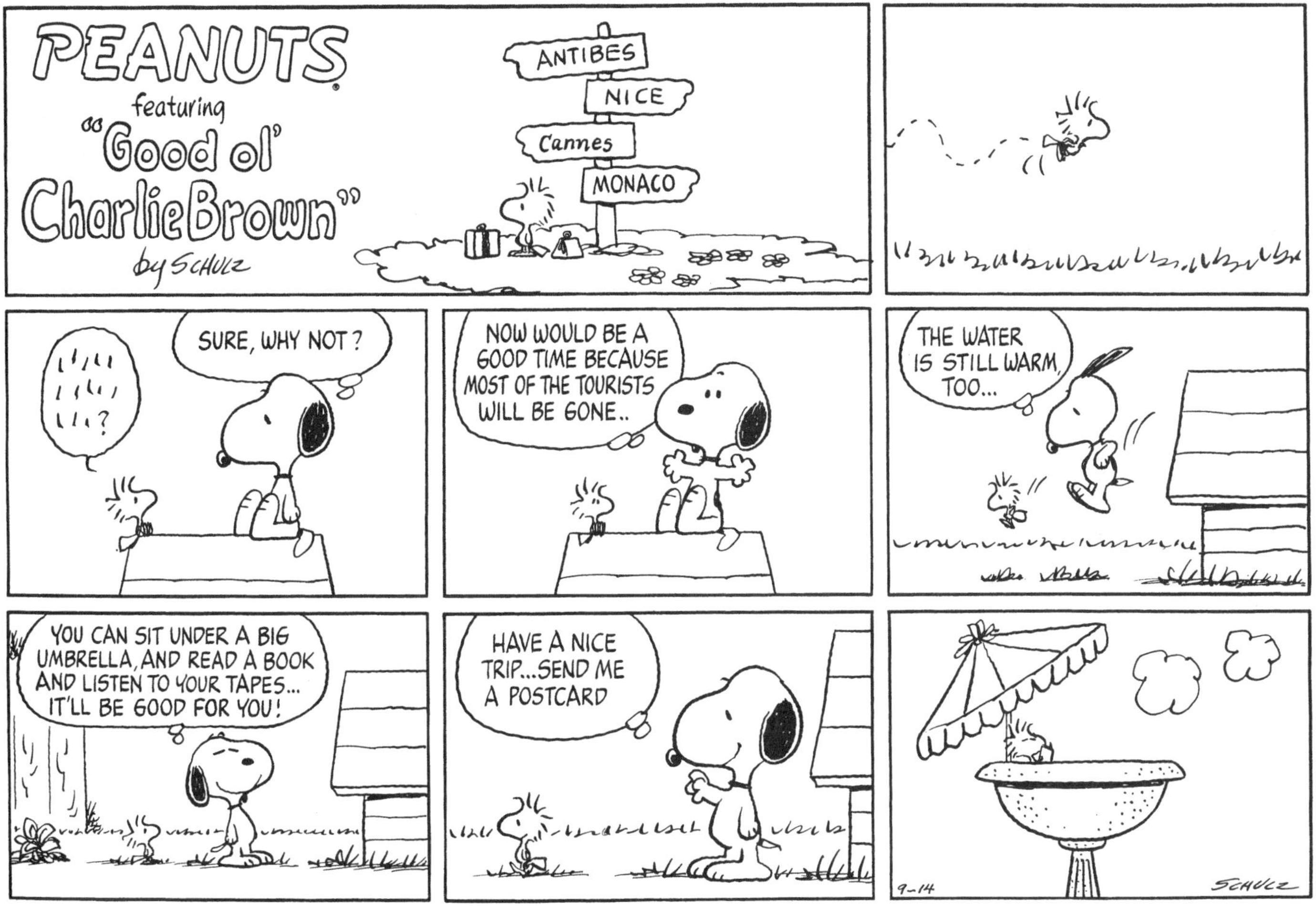
PEANUTS
featuring
"Good ol' Charlie Brown"
by SCHULZ
ANTIBES
NICE
Cannes
MONACO
SURE, WHY NOT?
NOW WOULD BE A GOOD TIME BECAUSE MOST OF THE TOURISTS WILL BE GONE..
THE WATER IS STILL WARM, TOO...
YOU CAN SIT UNDER A BIG UMBRELLA, AND READ A BOOK AND LISTEN TO YOUR TAPES... IT'LL BE GOOD FOR YOU!
HAVE A NICE TRIP...SEND ME A POSTCARD
9-14
SCHULZ

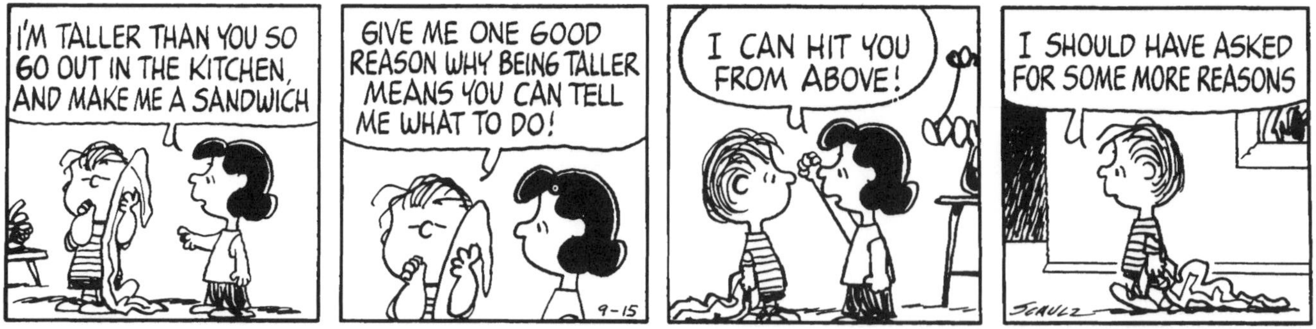
I'M TALLER THAN YOU SO GO OUT IN THE KITCHEN, AND MAKE ME A SANDWICH
GIVE ME ONE GOOD REASON WHY BEING TALLER MEANS YOU CAN TELL ME WHAT TO DO!
9-15
I CAN HIT YOU FROM ABOVE!
I SHOULD HAVE ASKED FOR SOME MORE REASONS
SCHULZ

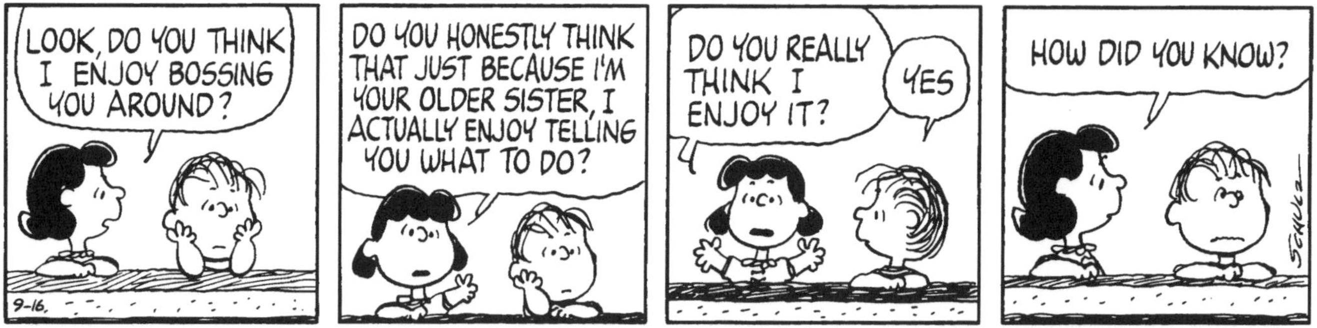
LOOK, DO YOU THINK I ENJOY BOSSING YOU AROUND?
9-16
DO YOU HONESTLY THINK THAT JUST BECAUSE I'M YOUR OLDER SISTER, I ACTUALLY ENJOY TELLING YOU WHAT TO DO?
DO YOU REALLY THINK I ENJOY IT?
YES
HOW DID YOU KNOW?
SCHULZ

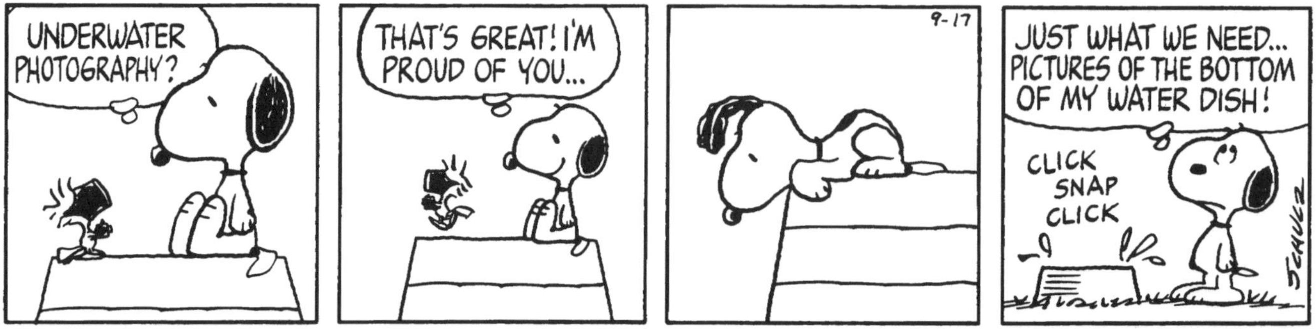
UNDERWATER PHOTOGRAPHY?
THAT'S GREAT! I'M PROUD OF YOU...
9-17
JUST WHAT WE NEED... PICTURES OF THE BOTTOM OF MY WATER DISH!
CLICK
SNAP
CLICK
SCHULZ

Panel 1: DO YOU KNOW THAT GIRL'S NAME, CHARLIE BROWN?

Panel 2: NO, BUT I REMEMBER HER

9-18

Panel 3: ONE DAY LAST MONTH I OFFERED HER HALF OF MY CANDY BAR, AND SHE JUST WALKED AWAY...

Panel 4: I CAN'T REMEMBER NAMES, BUT I NEVER FORGET A SLIGHT!

Panel 5: YOU KNOW WHAT YOU NEED TO DO? YOU NEED TO LEARN TO OBEY COMMANDS

Panel 6: SIT!

9-19

Panel 8: (Snoopy in chair)

Panel 9: MY DOG NEVER OBEYS COMMANDS.. OTHER DOGS WILL "SIT" OR "HEEL"

9-20

Panel 10: MY DOG HAS ONLY OBEYED ONE COMMAND IN HIS LIFE...

Panel 11: I ONCE TOLD HIM TO "STAY," AND HE NEVER WENT HOME!

?

Panel 12: HOW EMBARRASSING! I'VE ALWAYS THOUGHT IT WAS AN INVITATION...

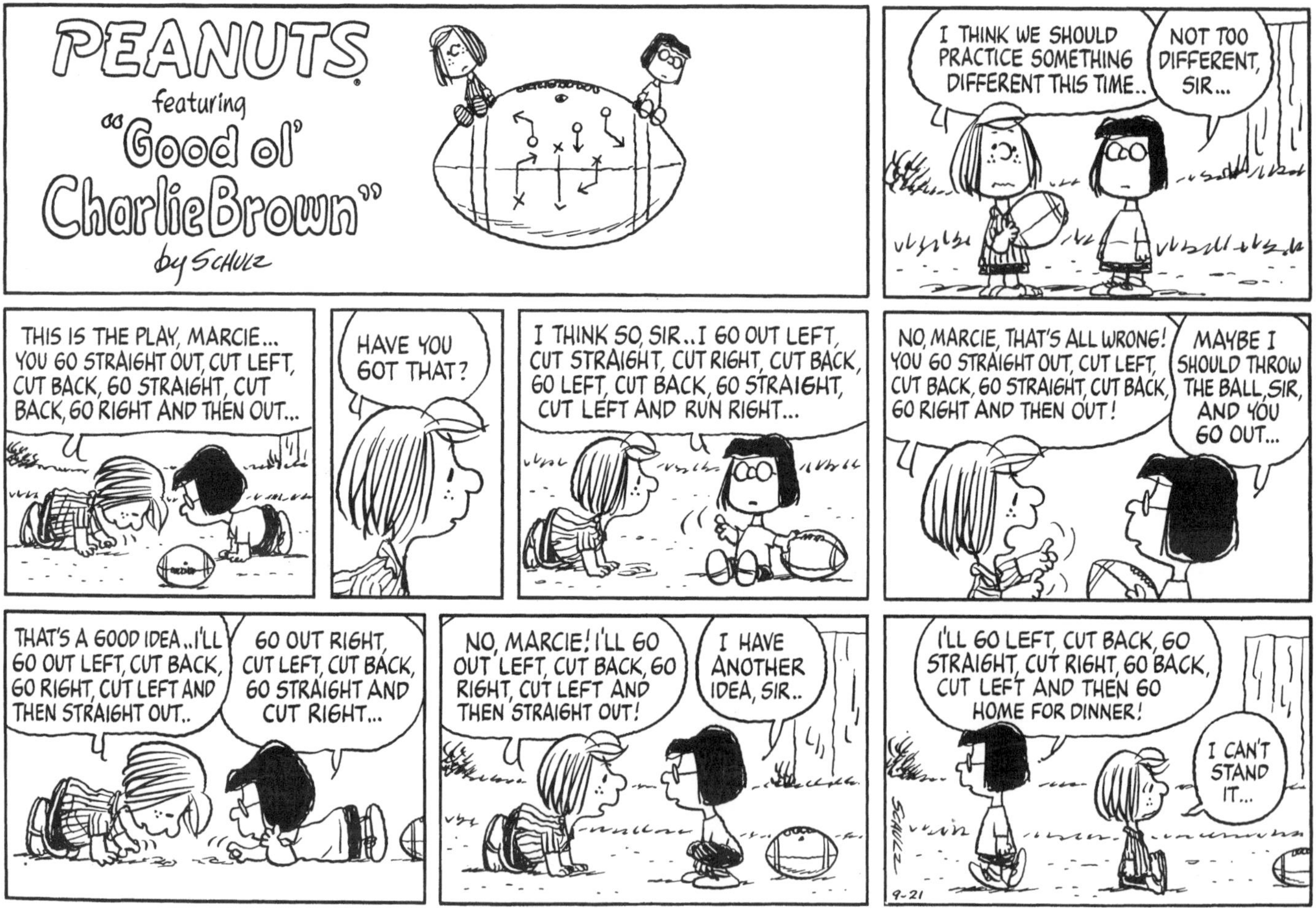
PEANUTS
featuring "Good ol' CharlieBrown"
by SCHULZ
I THINK WE SHOULD PRACTICE SOMETHING DIFFERENT THIS TIME..
NOT TOO DIFFERENT, SIR...
THIS IS THE PLAY, MARCIE... YOU GO STRAIGHT OUT, CUT LEFT, CUT BACK, GO STRAIGHT, CUT BACK, GO RIGHT AND THEN OUT...
HAVE YOU GOT THAT?
I THINK SO, SIR..I GO OUT LEFT, CUT STRAIGHT, CUT RIGHT, CUT BACK, GO LEFT, CUT BACK, GO STRAIGHT, CUT LEFT AND RUN RIGHT...
NO, MARCIE, THAT'S ALL WRONG! YOU GO STRAIGHT OUT, CUT LEFT, CUT BACK, GO STRAIGHT, CUT BACK, GO RIGHT AND THEN OUT!
MAYBE I SHOULD THROW THE BALL, SIR, AND YOU GO OUT...
THAT'S A GOOD IDEA..I'LL GO OUT LEFT, CUT BACK, GO RIGHT, CUT LEFT AND THEN STRAIGHT OUT..
GO OUT RIGHT, CUT LEFT, CUT BACK, GO STRAIGHT AND CUT RIGHT...
NO, MARCIE! I'LL GO OUT LEFT, CUT BACK, GO RIGHT, CUT LEFT AND THEN STRAIGHT OUT!
I HAVE ANOTHER IDEA, SIR..
I'LL GO LEFT, CUT BACK, GO STRAIGHT, CUT RIGHT, GO BACK, CUT LEFT AND THEN GO HOME FOR DINNER!
I CAN'T STAND IT...
SCHULZ
9-21

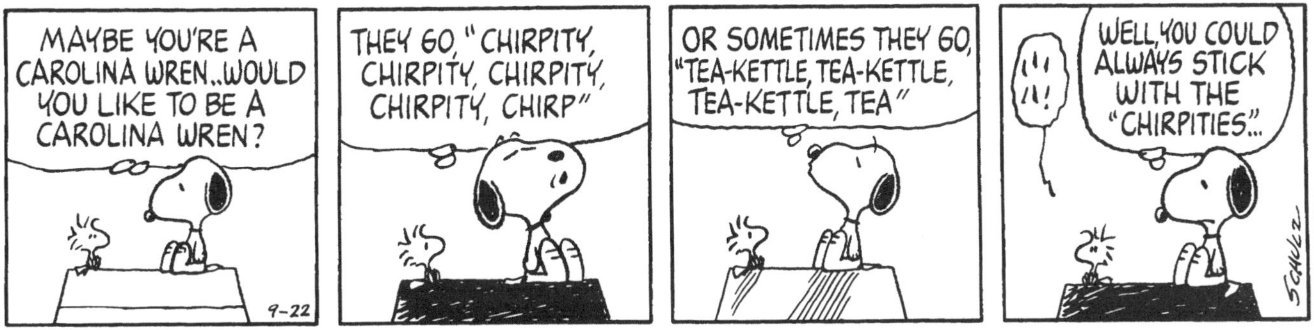
MAYBE YOU'RE A CAROLINA WREN..WOULD YOU LIKE TO BE A CAROLINA WREN?
9-22
THEY GO, "CHIRPITY, CHIRPITY, CHIRPITY, CHIRPITY, CHIRP"
OR SOMETIMES THEY GO, "TEA-KETTLE, TEA-KETTLE, TEA-KETTLE, TEA"
WELL, YOU COULD ALWAYS STICK WITH THE "CHIRPITIES"...
SCHULZ

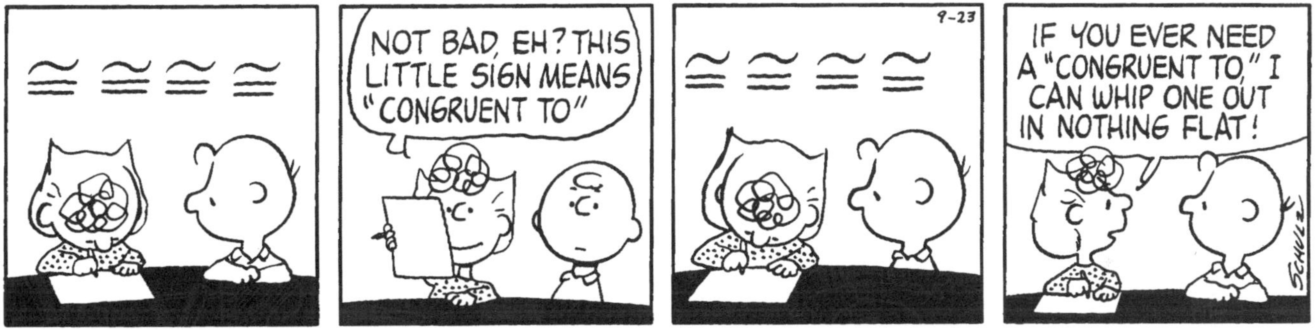
≅ ≅ ≅ ≅
NOT BAD, EH? THIS LITTLE SIGN MEANS "CONGRUENT TO"
9-23
≅ ≅ ≅ ≅
IF YOU EVER NEED A "CONGRUENT TO," I CAN WHIP ONE OUT IN NOTHING FLAT!
SCHULZ

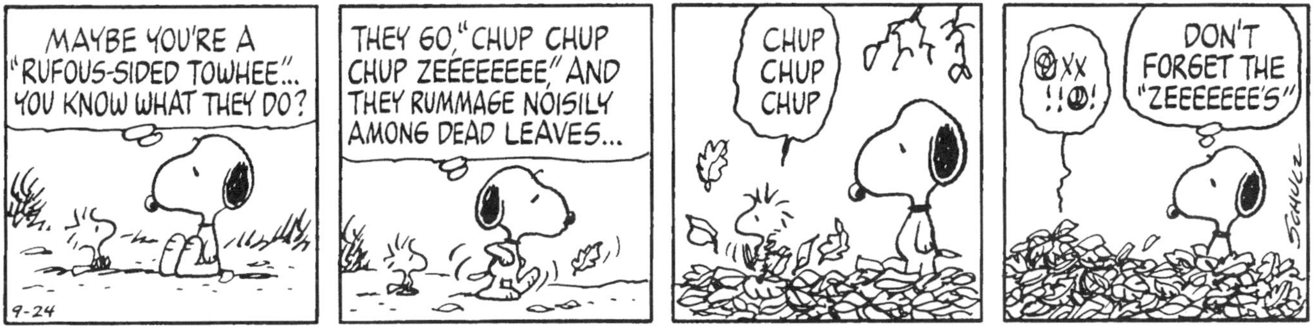
MAYBE YOU'RE A "RUFOUS-SIDED TOWHEE"... YOU KNOW WHAT THEY DO?
9-24
THEY GO, "CHUP CHUP CHUP ZEEEEEEEE," AND THEY RUMMAGE NOISILY AMONG DEAD LEAVES...
CHUP CHUP CHUP
DON'T FORGET THE "ZEEEEEEE'S"
SCHULZ

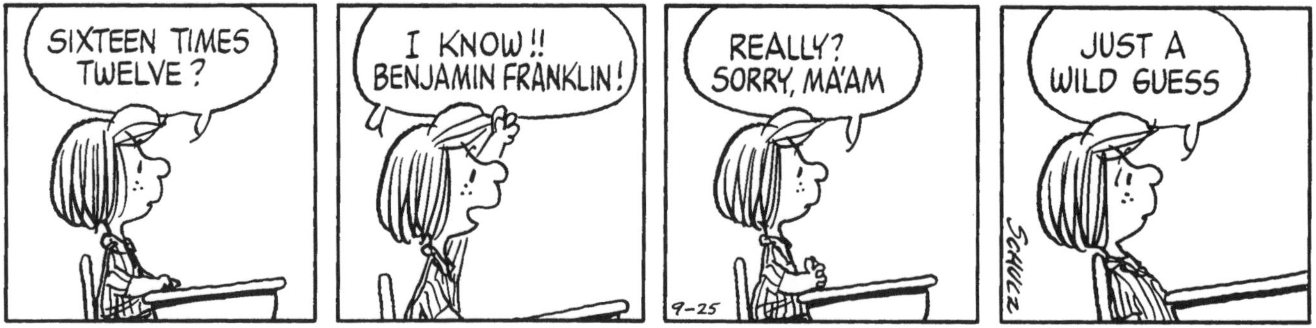
SIXTEEN TIMES TWELVE?
I KNOW!! BENJAMIN FRANKLIN!
REALLY? SORRY, MA'AM
JUST A WILD GUESS
9-25
SCHULZ

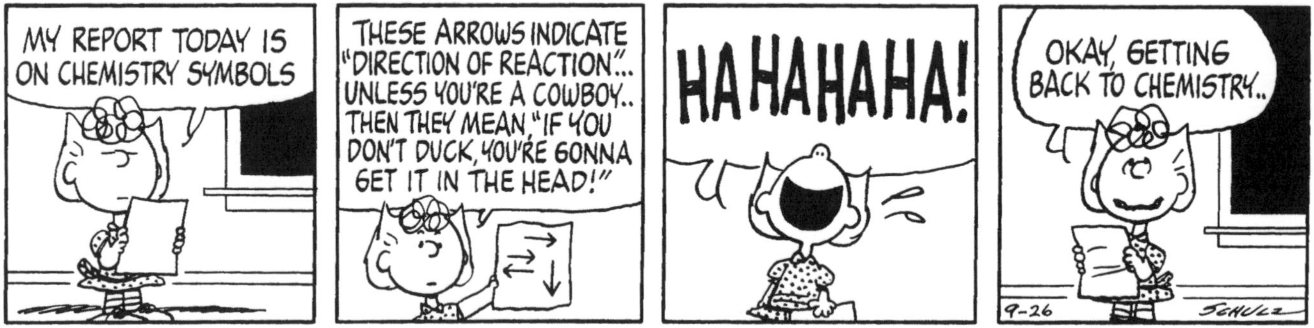
MY REPORT TODAY IS ON CHEMISTRY SYMBOLS
THESE ARROWS INDICATE "DIRECTION OF REACTION"... UNLESS YOU'RE A COWBOY.. THEN THEY MEAN, "IF YOU DON'T DUCK, YOU'RE GONNA GET IT IN THE HEAD!"
HAHAHAHA!
OKAY, GETTING BACK TO CHEMISTRY..
9-26
SCHULZ

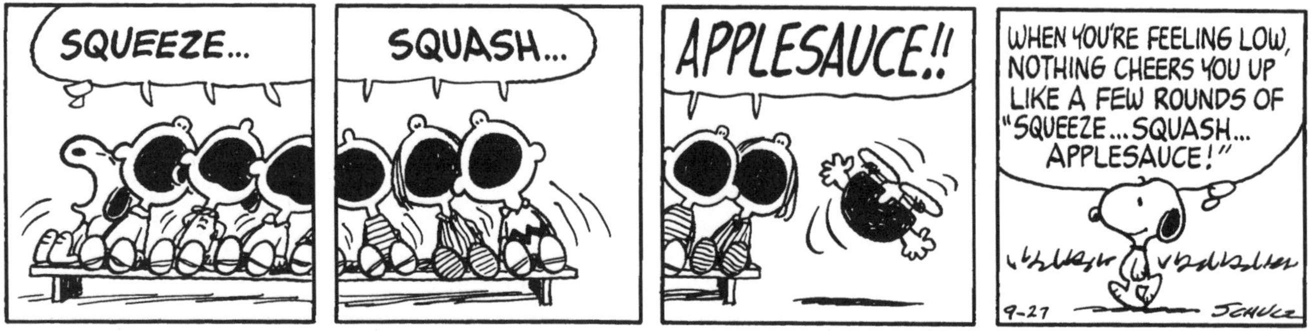
SQUEEZE...
SQUASH...
APPLESAUCE!!
WHEN YOU'RE FEELING LOW, NOTHING CHEERS YOU UP LIKE A FEW ROUNDS OF "SQUEEZE...SQUASH... APPLESAUCE!"
9-27
SCHULZ

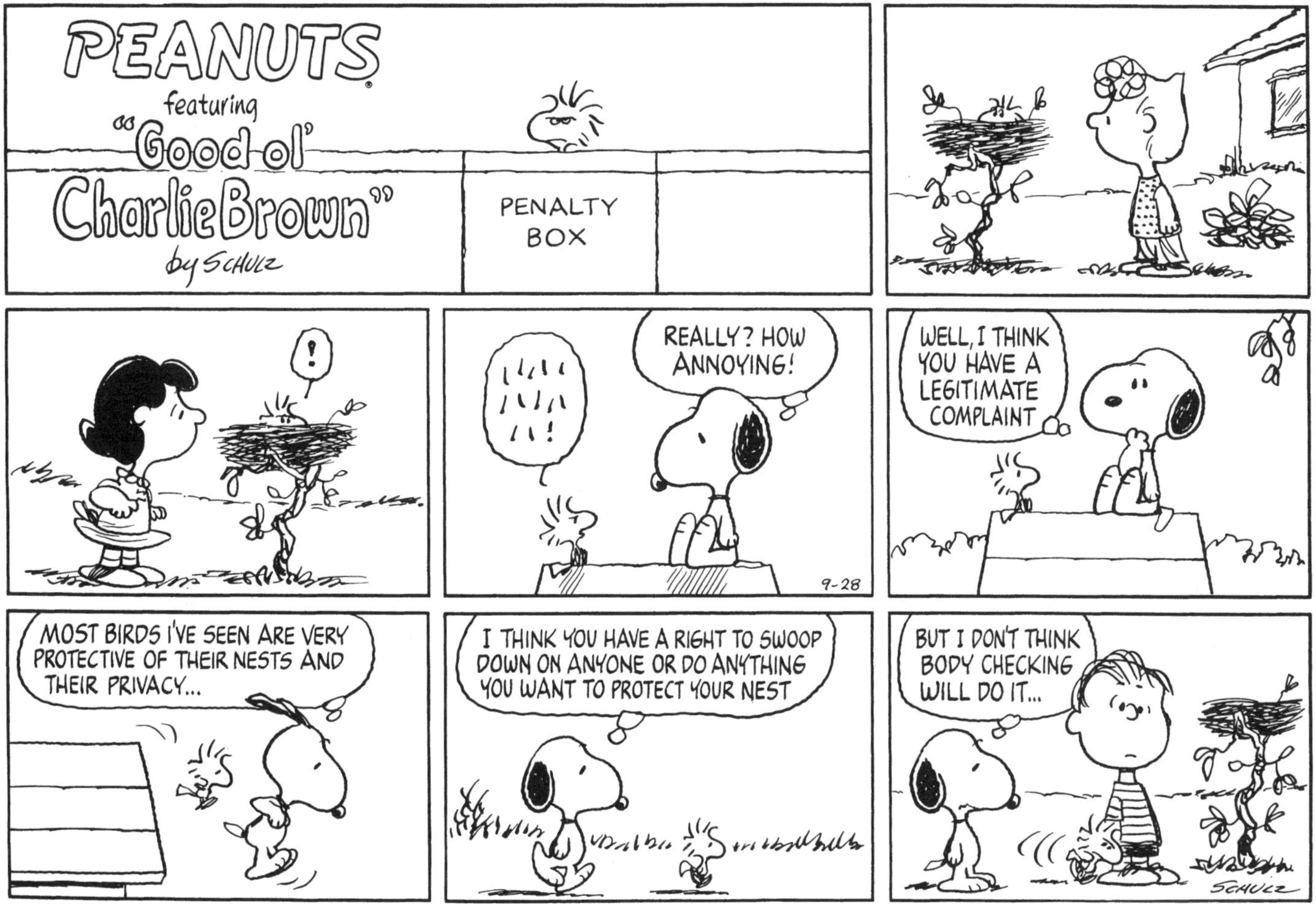
PEANUTS
featuring
"Good ol' CharlieBrown"
by SCHULZ
PENALTY BOX
!
REALLY? HOW ANNOYING!
9-28
WELL, I THINK YOU HAVE A LEGITIMATE COMPLAINT
MOST BIRDS I'VE SEEN ARE VERY PROTECTIVE OF THEIR NESTS AND THEIR PRIVACY...
I THINK YOU HAVE A RIGHT TO SWOOP DOWN ON ANYONE OR DO ANYTHING YOU WANT TO PROTECT YOUR NEST
BUT I DON'T THINK BODY CHECKING WILL DO IT...
SCHULZ

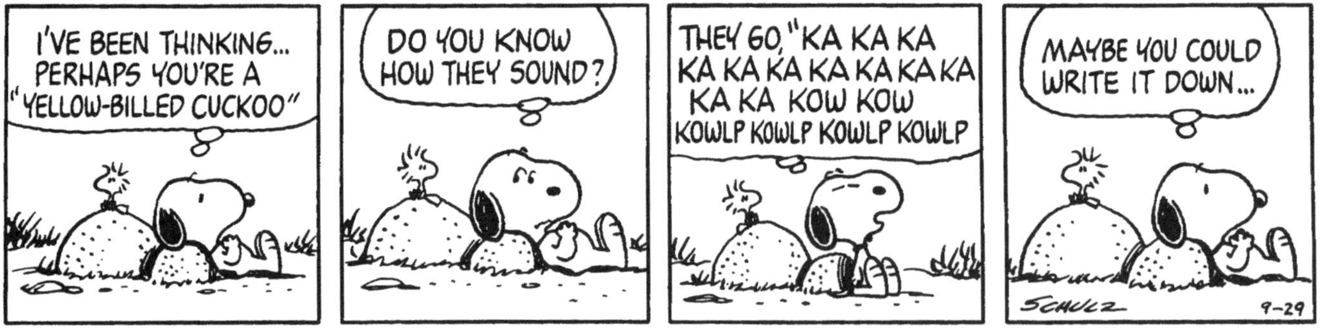
I'VE BEEN THINKING... PERHAPS YOU'RE A "YELLOW-BILLED CUCKOO"
DO YOU KNOW HOW THEY SOUND?
THEY GO, "KA KA KA KA KA KA KA KA KA KA KA KA KOW KOW KOWLP KOWLP KOWLP KOWLP
MAYBE YOU COULD WRITE IT DOWN...
SCHULZ
9-29

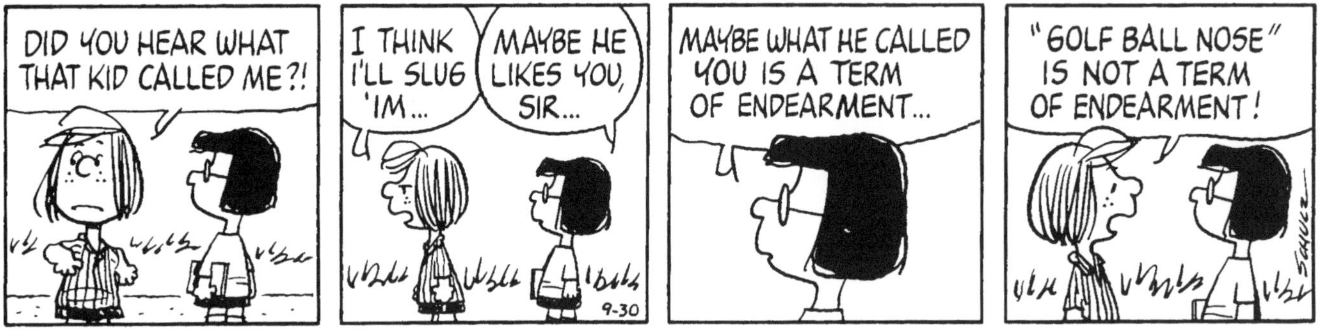
DID YOU HEAR WHAT THAT KID CALLED ME?!
I THINK I'LL SLUG 'IM...
MAYBE HE LIKES YOU, SIR...
9-30
MAYBE WHAT HE CALLED YOU IS A TERM OF ENDEARMENT...
"GOLF BALL NOSE" IS NOT A TERM OF ENDEARMENT!
SCHULZ

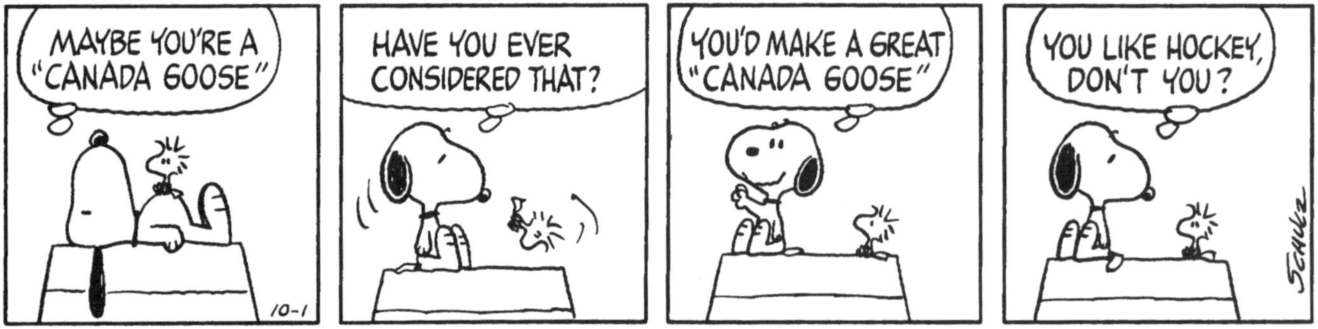
MAYBE YOU'RE A "CANADA GOOSE"
10-1
HAVE YOU EVER CONSIDERED THAT?
YOU'D MAKE A GREAT "CANADA GOOSE"
YOU LIKE HOCKEY, DON'T YOU?
SCHULZ

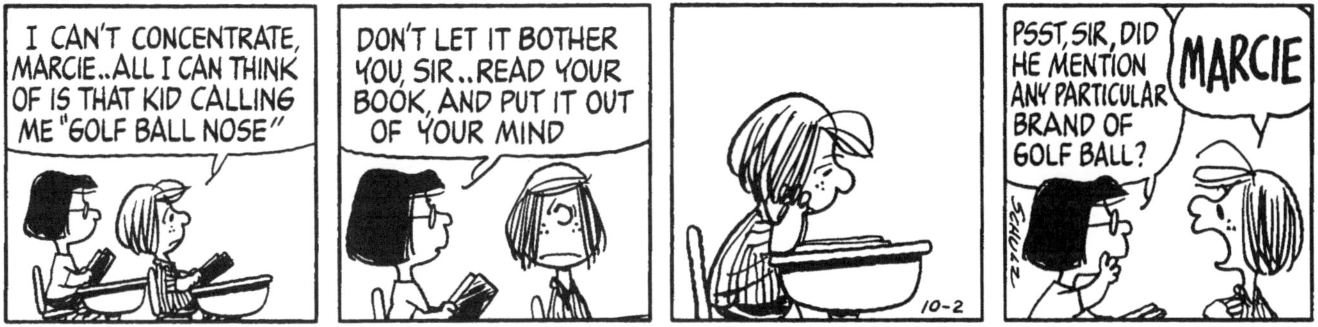
I CAN'T CONCENTRATE, MARCIE..ALL I CAN THINK OF IS THAT KID CALLING ME "GOLF BALL NOSE"
DON'T LET IT BOTHER YOU, SIR..READ YOUR BOOK, AND PUT IT OUT OF YOUR MIND
PSST, SIR, DID HE MENTION ANY PARTICULAR BRAND OF GOLF BALL?
MARCIE
SCHULZ
10-2

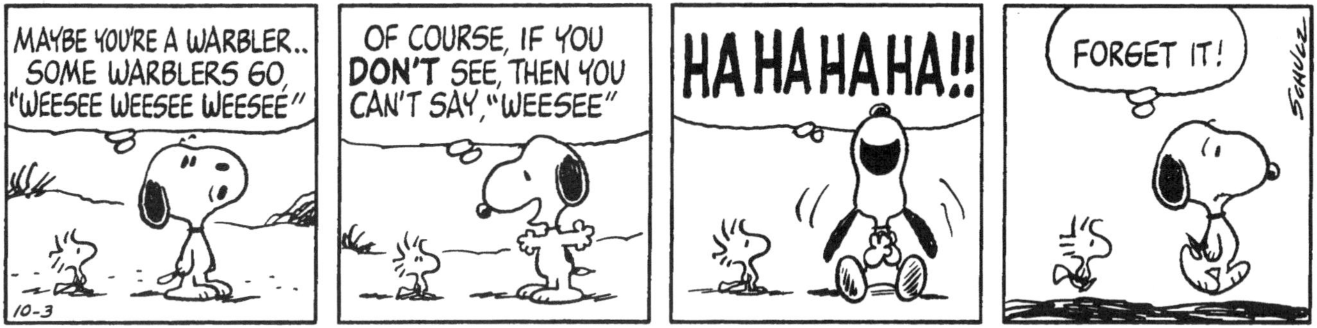
MAYBE YOU'RE A WARBLER.. SOME WARBLERS GO, "WEESEE WEESEE WEESEE"
10-3
OF COURSE, IF YOU **DON'T** SEE, THEN YOU CAN'T SAY, "WEESEE"
HA HA HA HA!!
FORGET IT!
SCHULZ

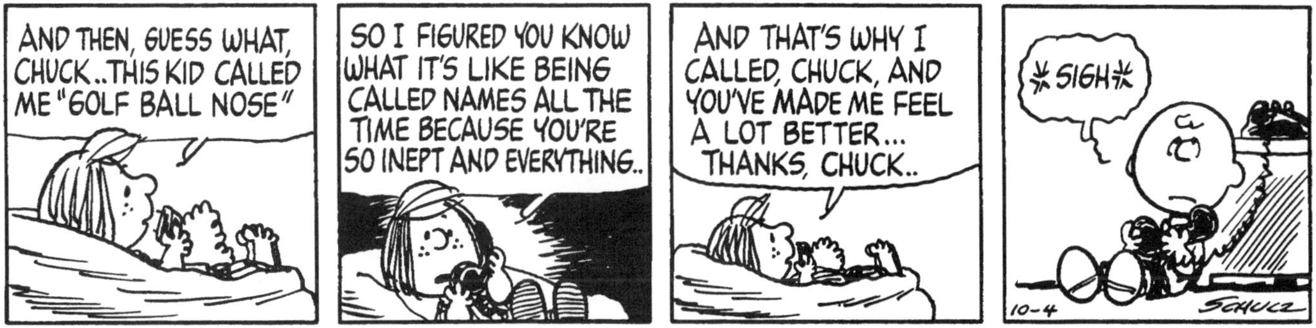
AND THEN, GUESS WHAT, CHUCK..THIS KID CALLED ME "GOLF BALL NOSE"
SO I FIGURED YOU KNOW WHAT IT'S LIKE BEING CALLED NAMES ALL THE TIME BECAUSE YOU'RE SO INEPT AND EVERYTHING..
AND THAT'S WHY I CALLED, CHUCK, AND YOU'VE MADE ME FEEL A LOT BETTER... THANKS, CHUCK..
SIGH
10-4
SCHULZ

PEANUTS featuring "Good ol' Charlie Brown" by Schulz

"HO HUM YAWN"

I WONDER...

I THINK MAYBE I'M A BORING PERSON

I WONDER IF THERE'S ANY SURE WAY OF FINDING OUT IF YOU'RE A BORING PERSON...

FOR INSTANCE, IF IT'S OBVIOUS THAT SOMEONE ISN'T LISTENING TO WHAT YOU'RE SAYING, YOU MIGHT SUSPECT THAT YOU'RE BORING...

OR IF SOMEONE FALLS ASLEEP WHILE YOU'RE TALKING TO HIM, YOU MIGHT ALSO SUSPECT THAT YOU'RE BORING

OR IF SOMEONE ACTUALLY WALKS AWAY WHILE YOU'RE TALKING TO HIM, YOU MIGHT SUSPECT THAT YOU'RE BORING...

10-5

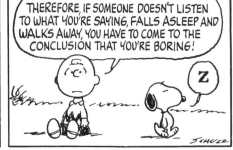

THEREFORE, IF SOMEONE DOESN'T LISTEN TO WHAT YOU'RE SAYING, FALLS ASLEEP AND WALKS AWAY, YOU HAVE TO COME TO THE CONCLUSION THAT YOU'RE BORING!

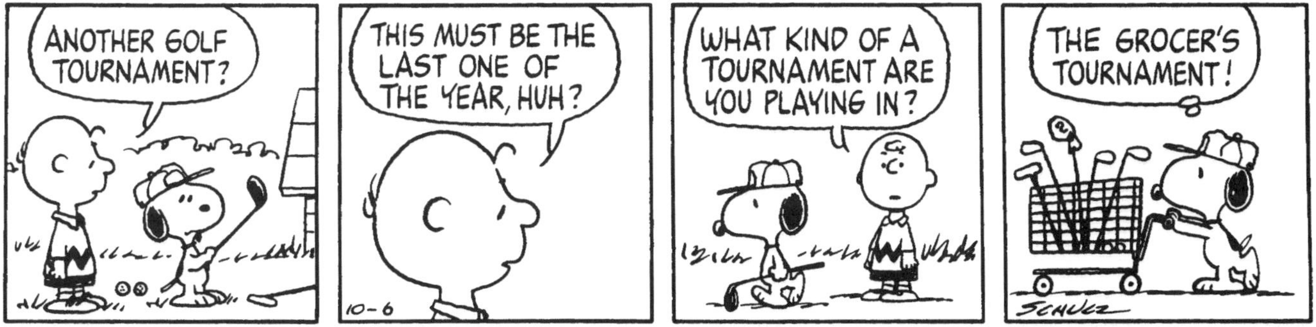
ANOTHER GOLF TOURNAMENT?
THIS MUST BE THE LAST ONE OF THE YEAR, HUH?
WHAT KIND OF A TOURNAMENT ARE YOU PLAYING IN?
THE GROCER'S TOURNAMENT!

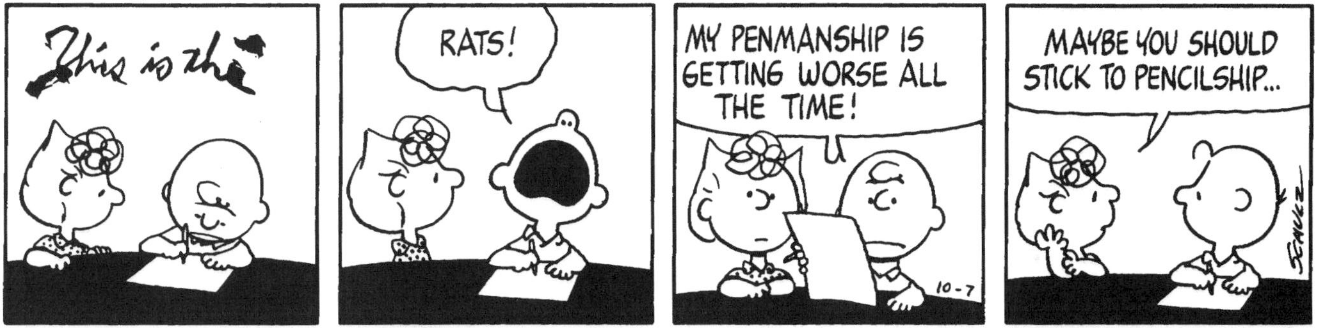
This is the
RATS!
MY PENMANSHIP IS GETTING WORSE ALL THE TIME!
MAYBE YOU SHOULD STICK TO PENCILSHIP...

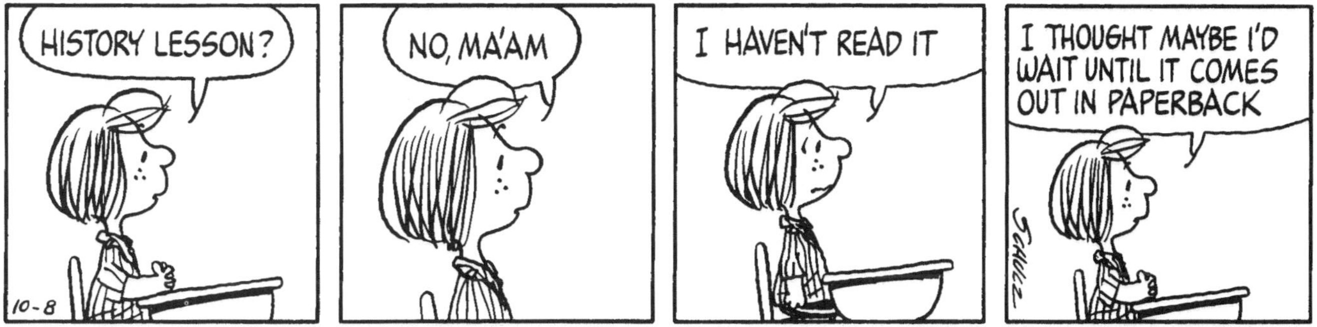
HISTORY LESSON?
NO, MA'AM
I HAVEN'T READ IT
I THOUGHT MAYBE I'D WAIT UNTIL IT COMES OUT IN PAPERBACK

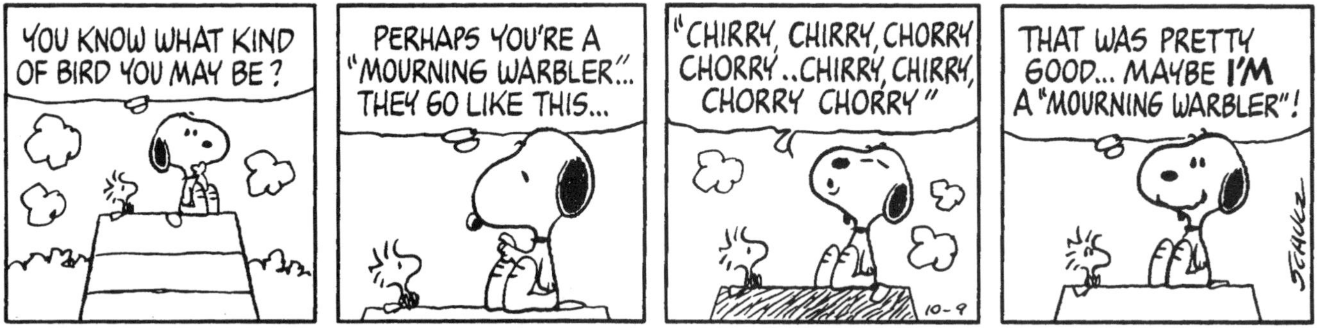
YOU KNOW WHAT KIND OF BIRD YOU MAY BE?
PERHAPS YOU'RE A "MOURNING WARBLER"... THEY GO LIKE THIS...
"CHIRRY, CHIRRY, CHORRY CHORRY..CHIRRY, CHIRRY, CHORRY CHORRY"
10-9
THAT WAS PRETTY GOOD... MAYBE **I'M** A "MOURNING WARBLER"!
SCHULZ

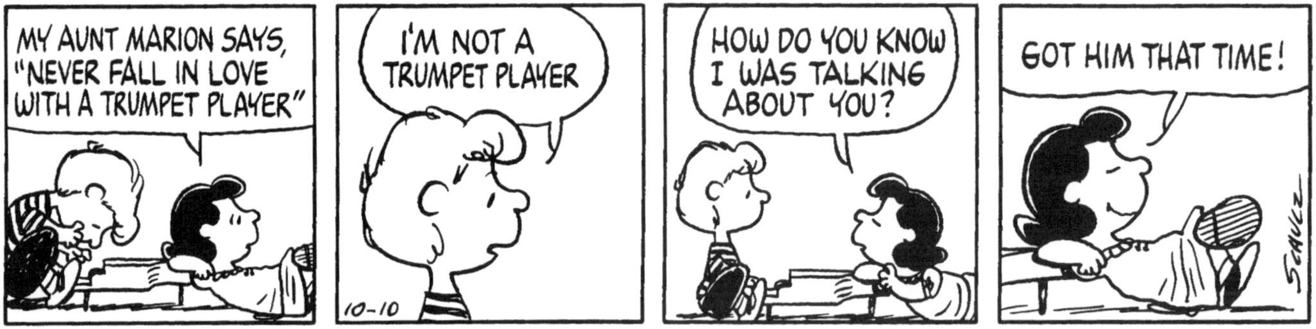
MY AUNT MARION SAYS, "NEVER FALL IN LOVE WITH A TRUMPET PLAYER"
I'M NOT A TRUMPET PLAYER
10-10
HOW DO YOU KNOW I WAS TALKING ABOUT YOU?
GOT HIM THAT TIME!
SCHULZ

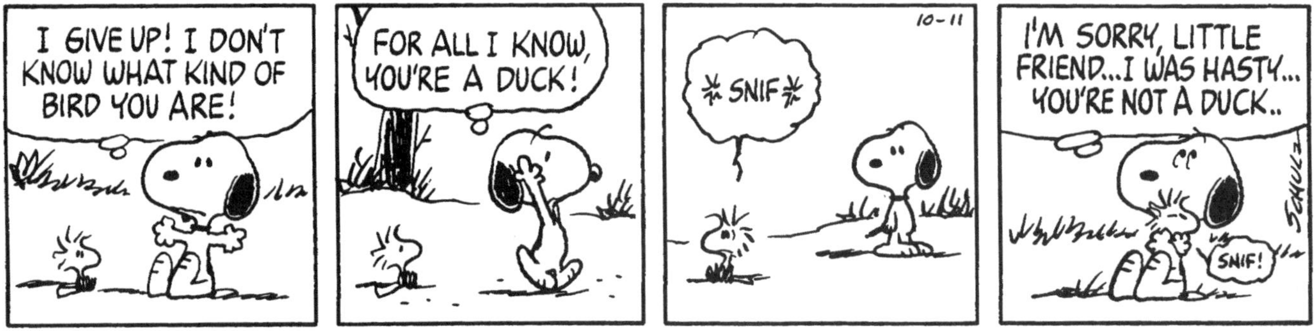
I GIVE UP! I DON'T KNOW WHAT KIND OF BIRD YOU ARE!
FOR ALL I KNOW, YOU'RE A DUCK!
10-11
* SNIF *
I'M SORRY, LITTLE FRIEND...I WAS HASTY... YOU'RE NOT A DUCK..
SNIF!
SCHULZ

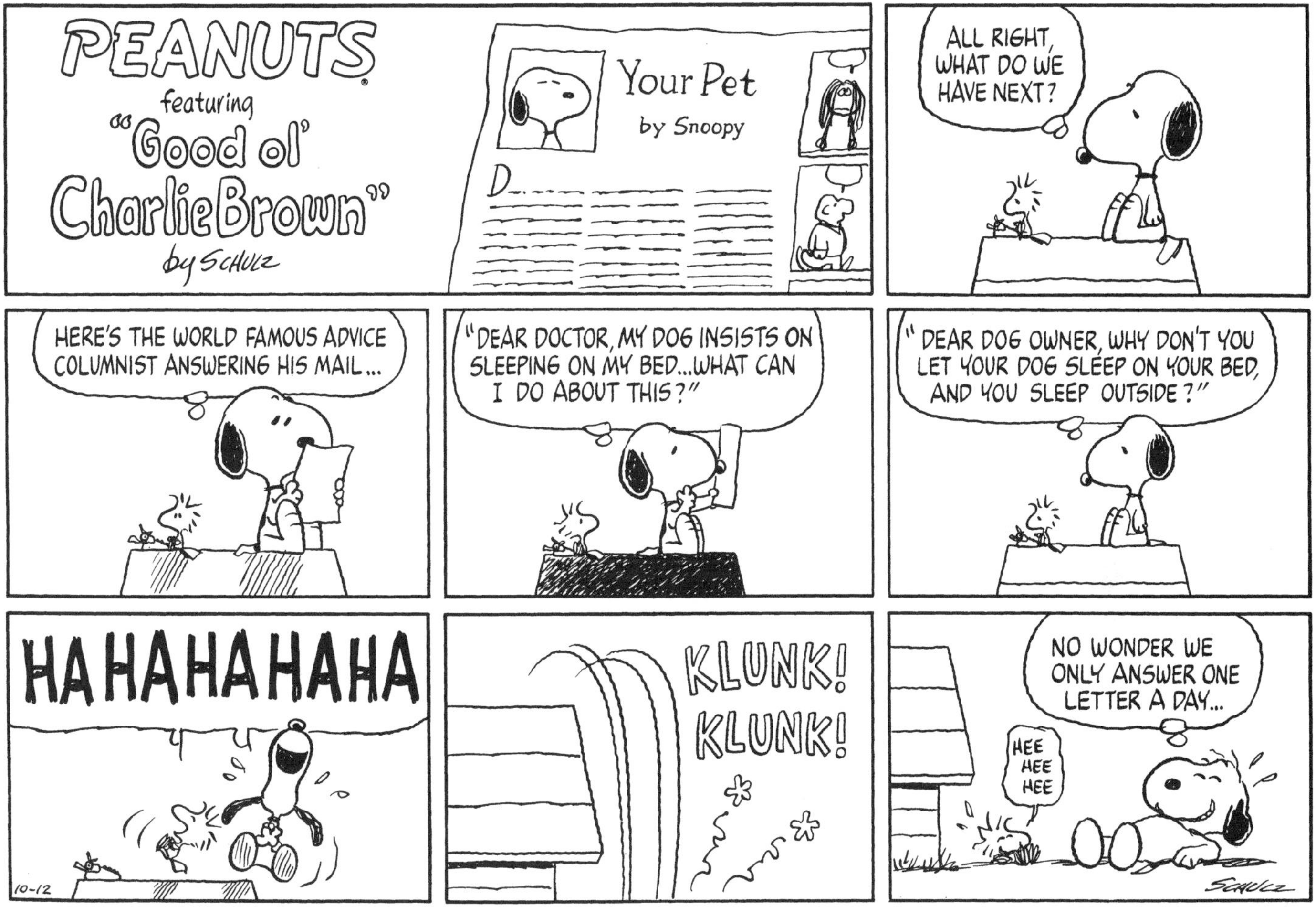
PEANUTS
featuring
"Good ol' CharlieBrown"
by SCHULZ
Your Pet
by Snoopy
ALL RIGHT, WHAT DO WE HAVE NEXT?
HERE'S THE WORLD FAMOUS ADVICE COLUMNIST ANSWERING HIS MAIL...
"DEAR DOCTOR, MY DOG INSISTS ON SLEEPING ON MY BED...WHAT CAN I DO ABOUT THIS?"
"DEAR DOG OWNER, WHY DON'T YOU LET YOUR DOG SLEEP ON YOUR BED, AND YOU SLEEP OUTSIDE?"
HAHAHAHAHAHA
10-12
KLUNK! KLUNK!
NO WONDER WE ONLY ANSWER ONE LETTER A DAY...
HEE HEE HEE
SCHULZ

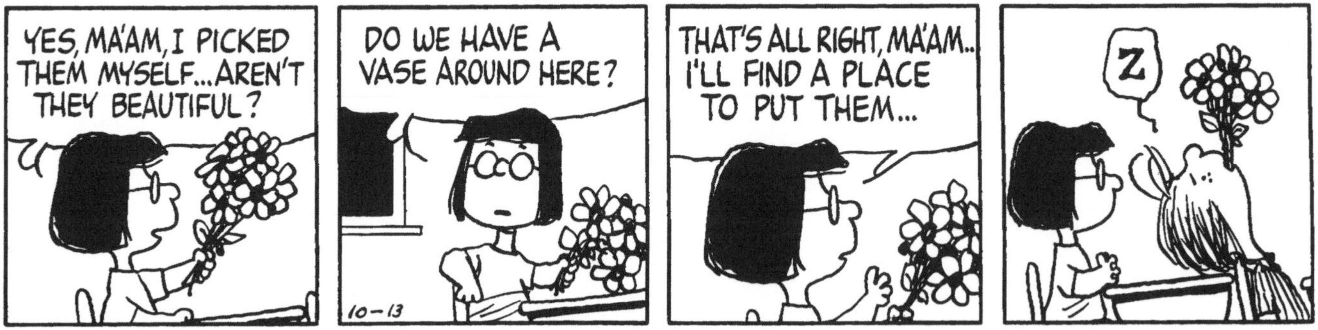
YES, MA'AM, I PICKED THEM MYSELF...AREN'T THEY BEAUTIFUL?
DO WE HAVE A VASE AROUND HERE?
10-13
THAT'S ALL RIGHT, MA'AM.. I'LL FIND A PLACE TO PUT THEM...
Z

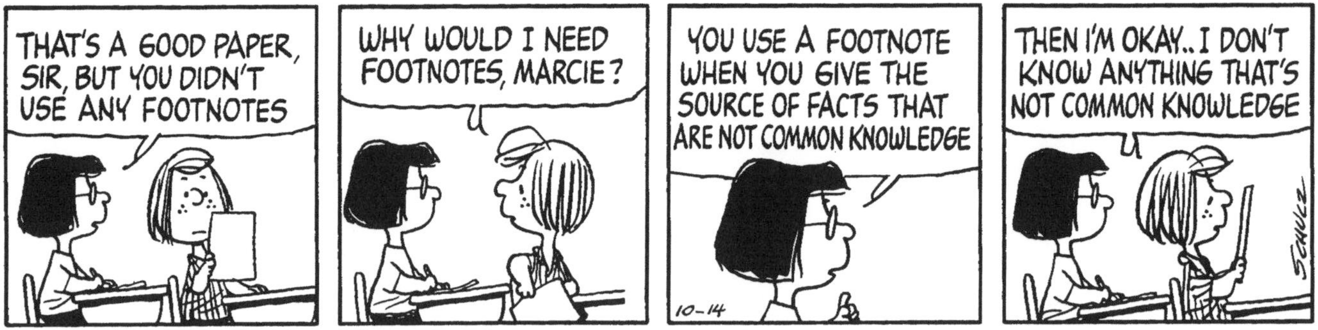
THAT'S A GOOD PAPER, SIR, BUT YOU DIDN'T USE ANY FOOTNOTES
WHY WOULD I NEED FOOTNOTES, MARCIE?
YOU USE A FOOTNOTE WHEN YOU GIVE THE SOURCE OF FACTS THAT ARE NOT COMMON KNOWLEDGE
10-14
THEN I'M OKAY.. I DON'T KNOW ANYTHING THAT'S NOT COMMON KNOWLEDGE
SCHULZ

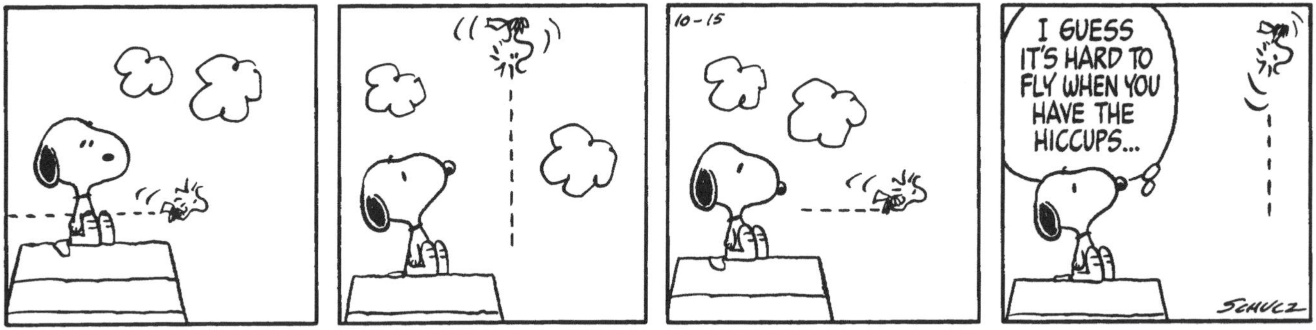
10-15
I GUESS IT'S HARD TO FLY WHEN YOU HAVE THE HICCUPS...
SCHULZ

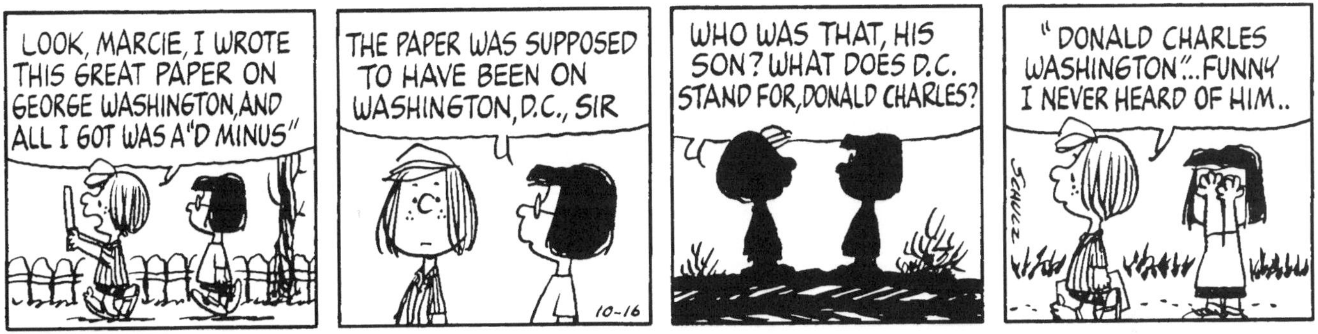
LOOK, MARCIE, I WROTE THIS GREAT PAPER ON GEORGE WASHINGTON, AND ALL I GOT WAS A "D MINUS"
THE PAPER WAS SUPPOSED TO HAVE BEEN ON WASHINGTON, D.C., SIR
10-16
WHO WAS THAT, HIS SON? WHAT DOES D.C. STAND FOR, DONALD CHARLES?
"DONALD CHARLES WASHINGTON"... FUNNY I NEVER HEARD OF HIM..
SCHULZ

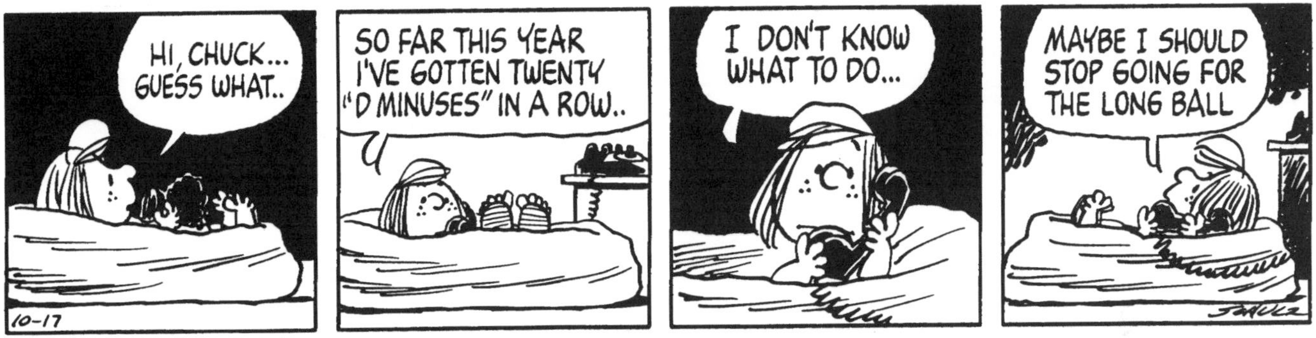
HI, CHUCK... GUESS WHAT..
10-17
SO FAR THIS YEAR I'VE GOTTEN TWENTY "D MINUSES" IN A ROW..
I DON'T KNOW WHAT TO DO...
MAYBE I SHOULD STOP GOING FOR THE LONG BALL
SCHULZ

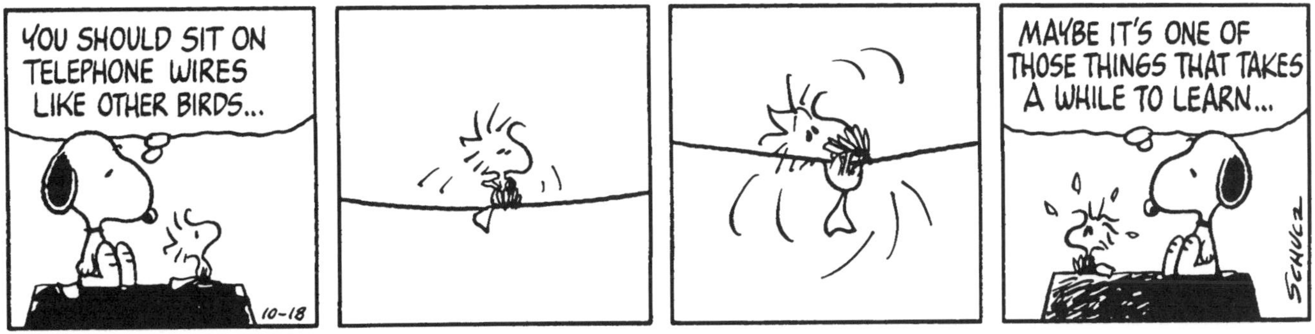
YOU SHOULD SIT ON TELEPHONE WIRES LIKE OTHER BIRDS...
10-18
MAYBE IT'S ONE OF THOSE THINGS THAT TAKES A WHILE TO LEARN...
SCHULZ

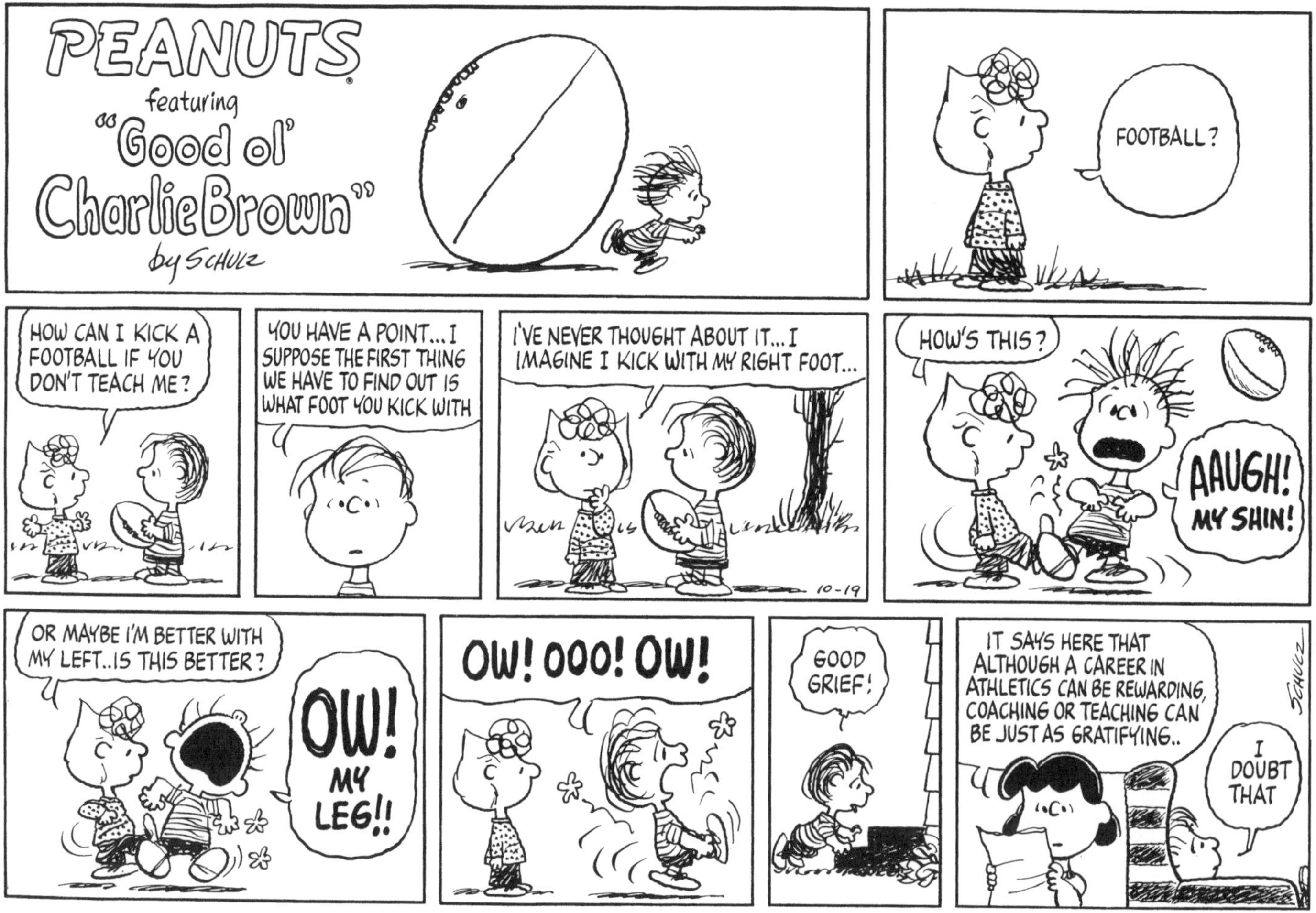
PEANUTS
featuring
"Good ol' Charlie Brown"
by SCHULZ
FOOTBALL?
HOW CAN I KICK A FOOTBALL IF YOU DON'T TEACH ME?
YOU HAVE A POINT... I SUPPOSE THE FIRST THING WE HAVE TO FIND OUT IS WHAT FOOT YOU KICK WITH
I'VE NEVER THOUGHT ABOUT IT... I IMAGINE I KICK WITH MY RIGHT FOOT...
10-19
HOW'S THIS?
AAUGH! MY SHIN!
OR MAYBE I'M BETTER WITH MY LEFT..IS THIS BETTER?
OW! MY LEG!!
OW! OOO! OW!
GOOD GRIEF!
IT SAYS HERE THAT ALTHOUGH A CAREER IN ATHLETICS CAN BE REWARDING, COACHING OR TEACHING CAN BE JUST AS GRATIFYING..
I DOUBT THAT
SCHULZ

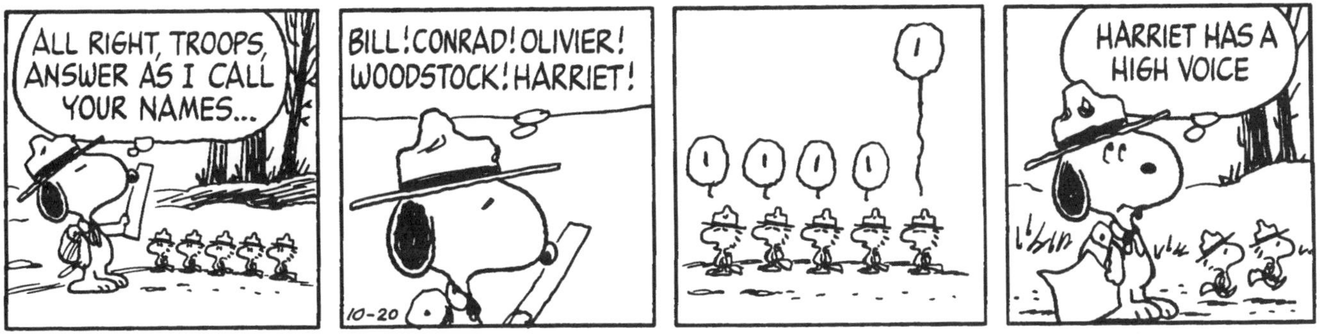
ALL RIGHT, TROOPS, ANSWER AS I CALL YOUR NAMES...
BILL! CONRAD! OLIVIER! WOODSTOCK! HARRIET!
10-20
HARRIET HAS A HIGH VOICE

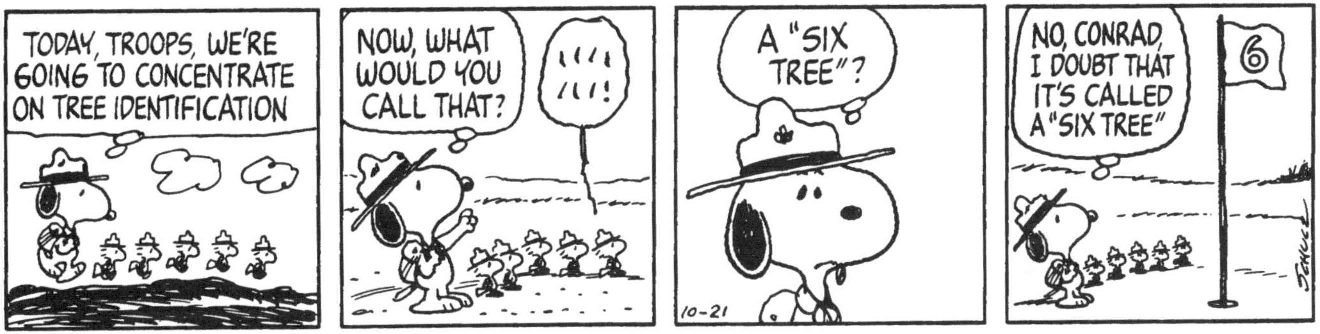
TODAY, TROOPS, WE'RE GOING TO CONCENTRATE ON TREE IDENTIFICATION
NOW, WHAT WOULD YOU CALL THAT?
A "SIX TREE"?
10-21
NO, CONRAD, I DOUBT THAT IT'S CALLED A "SIX TREE"
6
SCHULZ

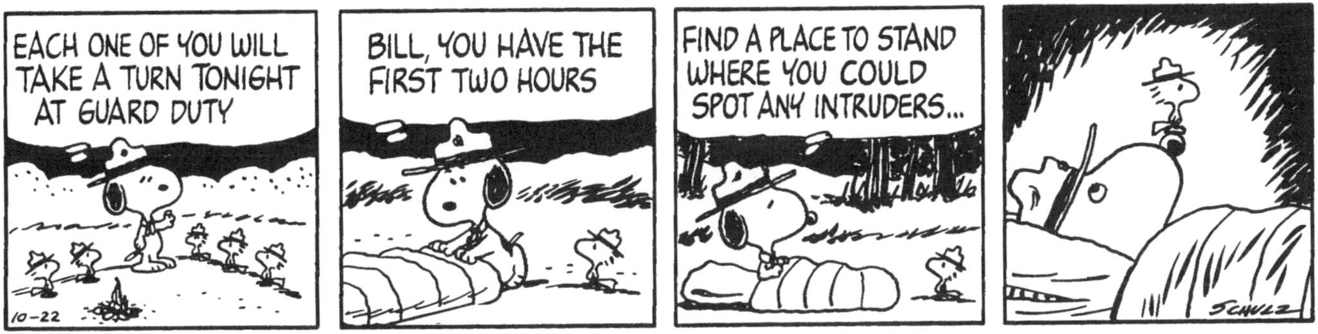
EACH ONE OF YOU WILL TAKE A TURN TONIGHT AT GUARD DUTY
10-22
BILL, YOU HAVE THE FIRST TWO HOURS
FIND A PLACE TO STAND WHERE YOU COULD SPOT ANY INTRUDERS...
SCHULZ

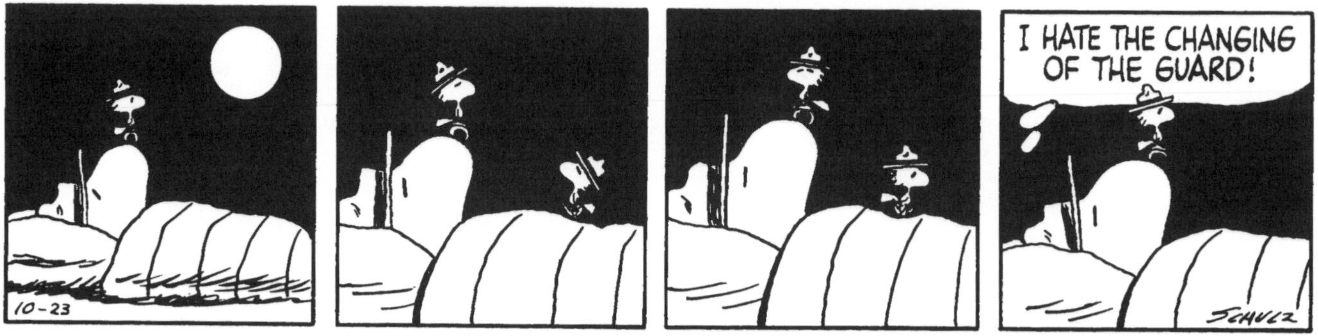
10-23
I HATE THE CHANGING OF THE GUARD!
SCHULZ

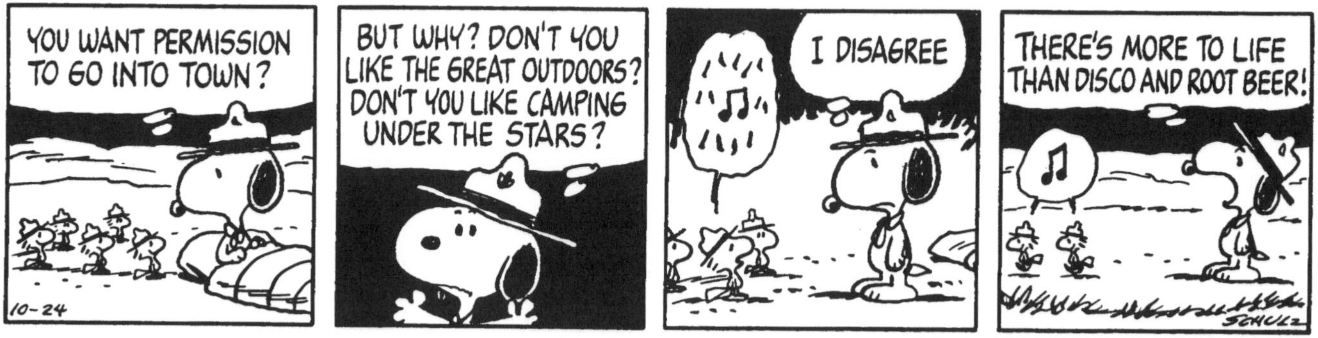
YOU WANT PERMISSION TO GO INTO TOWN?
10-24
BUT WHY? DON'T YOU LIKE THE GREAT OUTDOORS? DON'T YOU LIKE CAMPING UNDER THE STARS?
I DISAGREE
THERE'S MORE TO LIFE THAN DISCO AND ROOT BEER!
SCHULZ

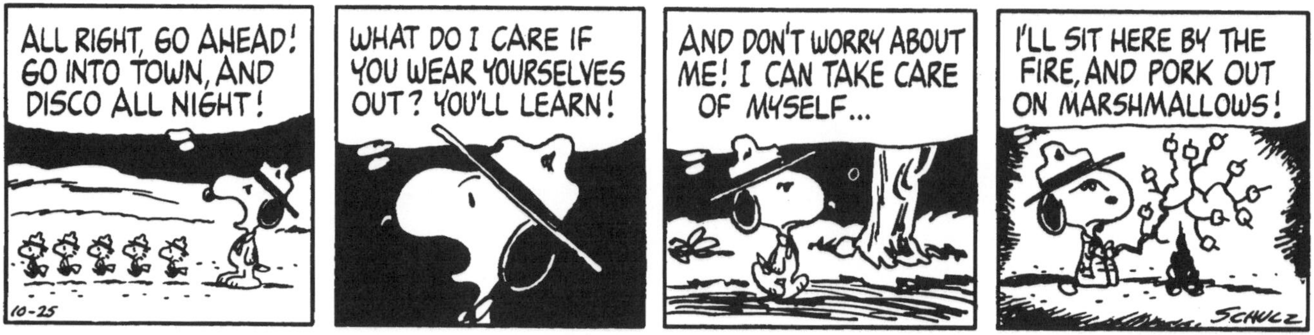
ALL RIGHT, GO AHEAD! GO INTO TOWN, AND DISCO ALL NIGHT!
10-25
WHAT DO I CARE IF YOU WEAR YOURSELVES OUT? YOU'LL LEARN!
AND DON'T WORRY ABOUT ME! I CAN TAKE CARE OF MYSELF...
I'LL SIT HERE BY THE FIRE, AND PORK OUT ON MARSHMALLOWS!
SCHULZ

PEANUTS
featuring
"Good ol' Charlie Brown"
by Schulz

12	13	14	15	16	17	18
19	20	21	22	23	24	25
	27	28	29	30		

LINUS, YOU REMEMBER EUDORA, DON'T YOU?

SURE... HOW ARE YOU?

HALLOWEEN IS COMING!

ON HALLOWEEN NIGHT THE GREAT PUMPKIN RISES OUT OF THE PUMPKIN PATCH AND BRINGS TOYS TO ALL THE CHILDREN IN THE WORLD

BUT FIRST HE LOOKS OVER ALL THE PUMPKIN PATCHES TO SEE WHICH ONE IS THE MOST SINCERE... IF HE CHOOSES THIS PUMPKIN PATCH, I'LL GET TO MEET HIM!

THIS YEAR I JUST KNOW HE'S GOING TO CHOOSE THIS PUMPKIN PATCH!! I JUST KNOW IT!

OH, WHAT A GLORIOUS MOMENT THAT WILL BE!!!

SEE?

10-26

HOW SHARPER THAN A SERPENT'S TOOTH IS A SISTER'S "SEE?"

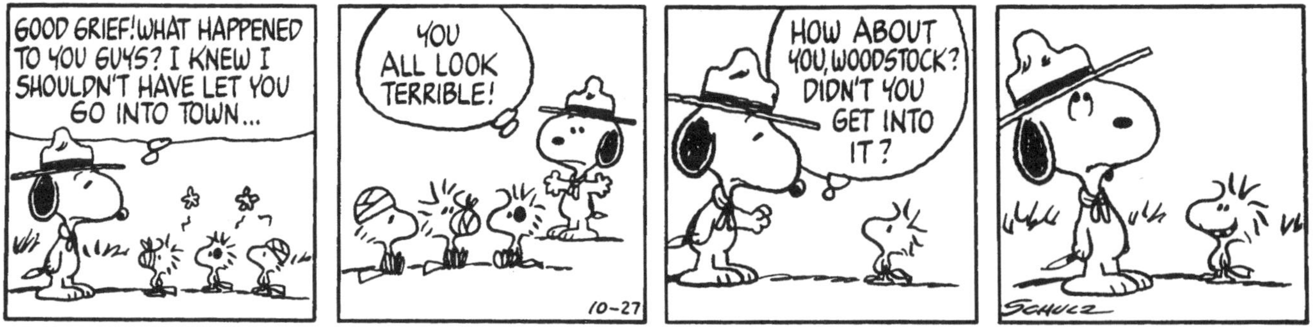
GOOD GRIEF! WHAT HAPPENED TO YOU GUYS? I KNEW I SHOULDN'T HAVE LET YOU GO INTO TOWN...
YOU ALL LOOK TERRIBLE!
10-27
HOW ABOUT YOU, WOODSTOCK? DIDN'T YOU GET INTO IT?
SCHULZ

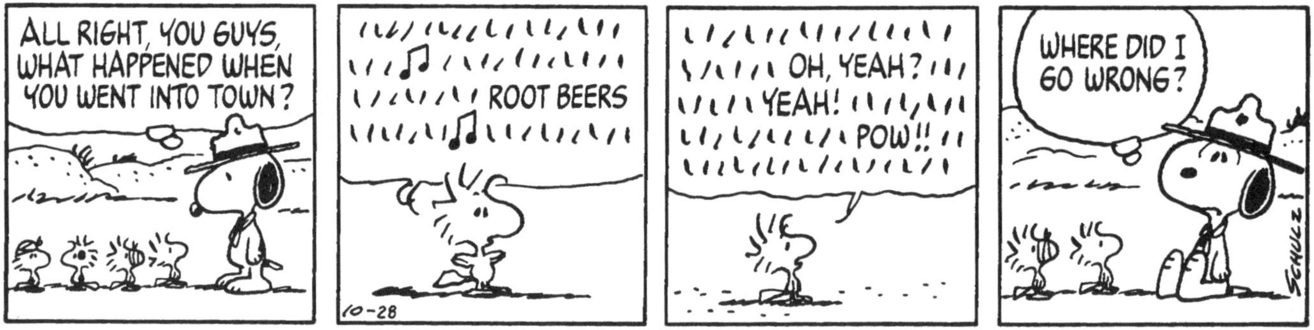
ALL RIGHT, YOU GUYS, WHAT HAPPENED WHEN YOU WENT INTO TOWN?
ROOT BEERS
10-28
OH, YEAH?
YEAH!
POW!!
WHERE DID I GO WRONG?
SCHULZ

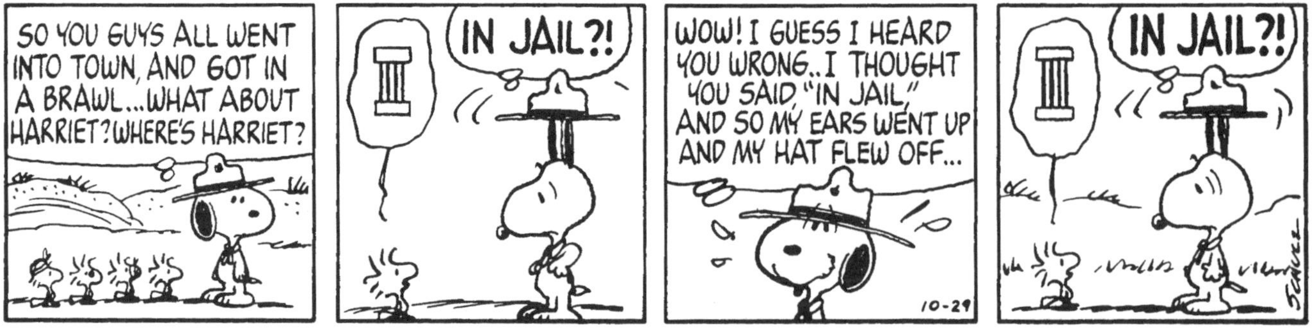
SO YOU GUYS ALL WENT INTO TOWN, AND GOT IN A BRAWL...WHAT ABOUT HARRIET? WHERE'S HARRIET?
IN JAIL?!
WOW! I GUESS I HEARD YOU WRONG..I THOUGHT YOU SAID, "IN JAIL," AND SO MY EARS WENT UP AND MY HAT FLEW OFF...
10-29
IN JAIL?!
SCHULZ

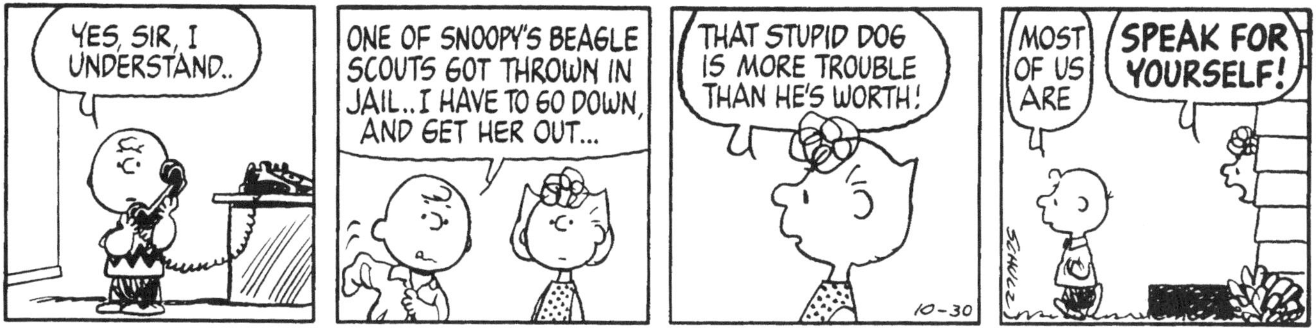
YES, SIR, I UNDERSTAND..
ONE OF SNOOPY'S BEAGLE SCOUTS GOT THROWN IN JAIL..I HAVE TO GO DOWN, AND GET HER OUT...
THAT STUPID DOG IS MORE TROUBLE THAN HE'S WORTH!
10-30
MOST OF US ARE
SPEAK FOR YOURSELF!
SCHULZ

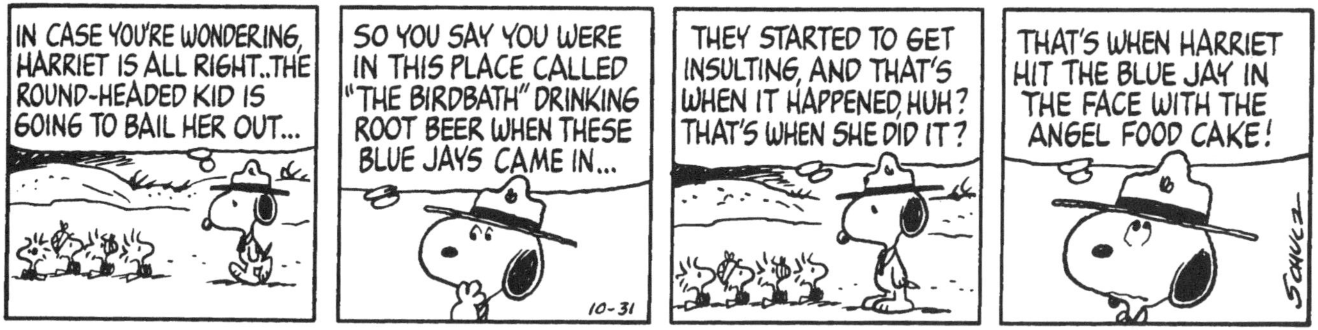
IN CASE YOU'RE WONDERING, HARRIET IS ALL RIGHT..THE ROUND-HEADED KID IS GOING TO BAIL HER OUT...
SO YOU SAY YOU WERE IN THIS PLACE CALLED "THE BIRDBATH" DRINKING ROOT BEER WHEN THESE BLUE JAYS CAME IN...
10-31
THEY STARTED TO GET INSULTING, AND THAT'S WHEN IT HAPPENED, HUH? THAT'S WHEN SHE DID IT?
THAT'S WHEN HARRIET HIT THE BLUE JAY IN THE FACE WITH THE ANGEL FOOD CAKE!
SCHULZ

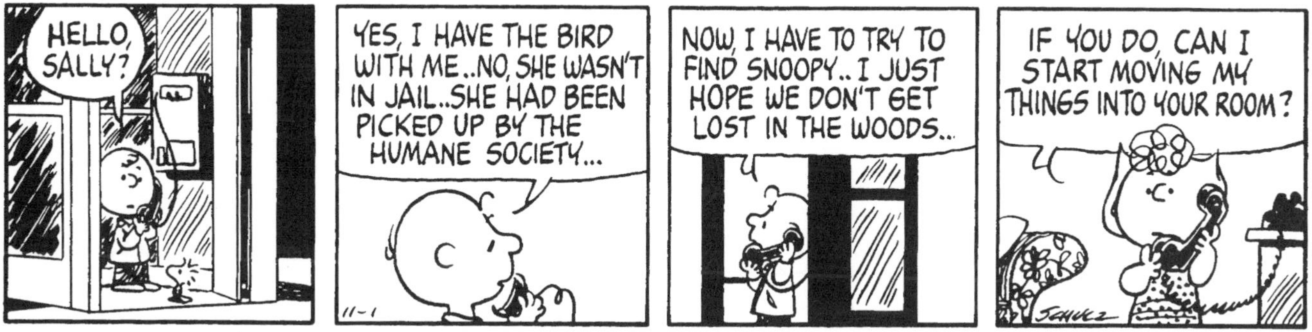
HELLO, SALLY?
YES, I HAVE THE BIRD WITH ME..NO, SHE WASN'T IN JAIL..SHE HAD BEEN PICKED UP BY THE HUMANE SOCIETY...
11-1
NOW, I HAVE TO TRY TO FIND SNOOPY.. I JUST HOPE WE DON'T GET LOST IN THE WOODS..
IF YOU DO, CAN I START MOVING MY THINGS INTO YOUR ROOM?
SCHULZ

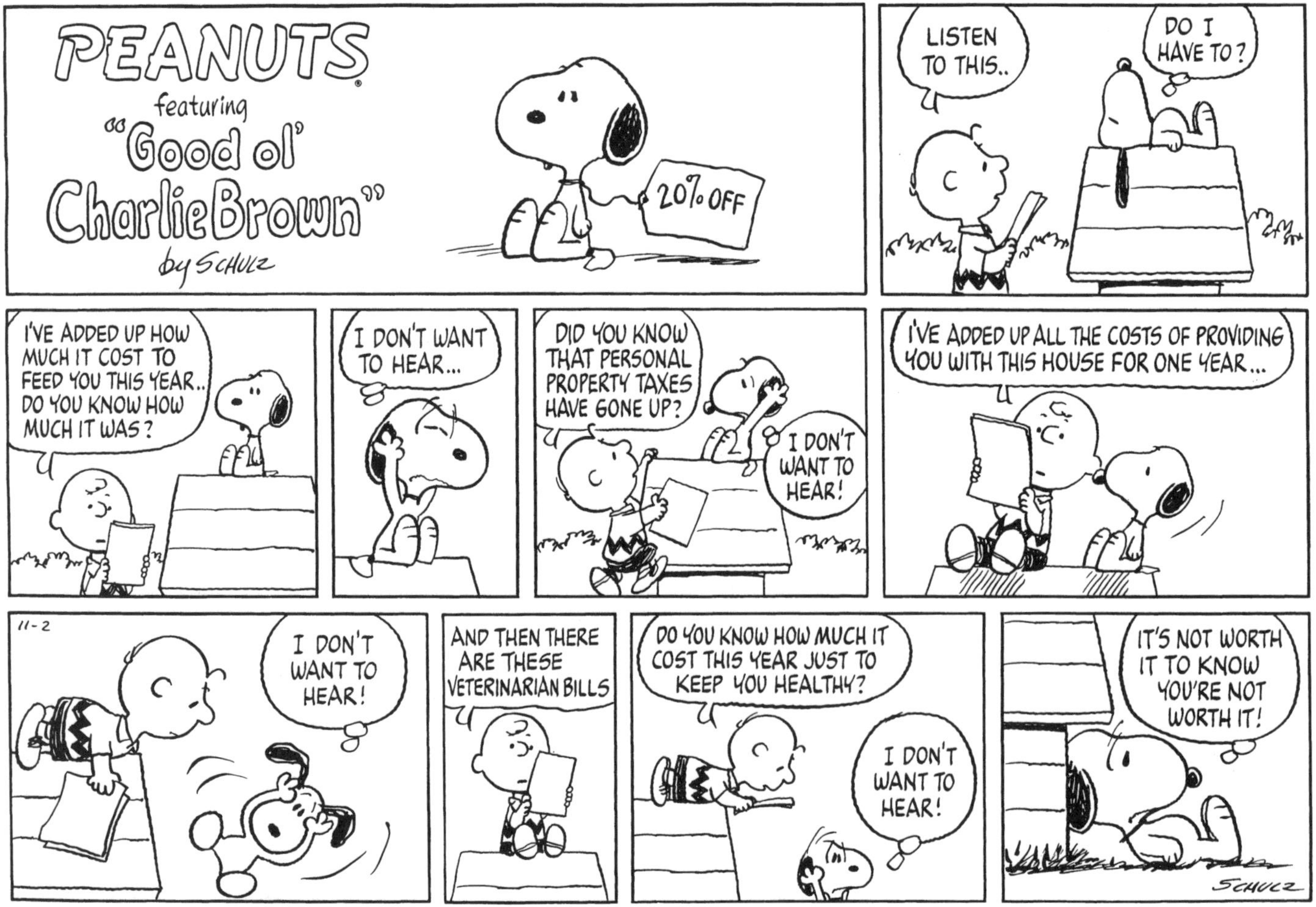
PEANUTS
featuring
"Good ol' Charlie Brown"
by SCHULZ
20% OFF
LISTEN TO THIS..
DO I HAVE TO?
I'VE ADDED UP HOW MUCH IT COST TO FEED YOU THIS YEAR.. DO YOU KNOW HOW MUCH IT WAS?
I DON'T WANT TO HEAR...
DID YOU KNOW THAT PERSONAL PROPERTY TAXES HAVE GONE UP?
I DON'T WANT TO HEAR!
I'VE ADDED UP ALL THE COSTS OF PROVIDING YOU WITH THIS HOUSE FOR ONE YEAR...
11-2
I DON'T WANT TO HEAR!
AND THEN THERE ARE THESE VETERINARIAN BILLS
DO YOU KNOW HOW MUCH IT COST THIS YEAR JUST TO KEEP YOU HEALTHY?
I DON'T WANT TO HEAR!
IT'S NOT WORTH IT TO KNOW YOU'RE NOT WORTH IT!
SCHULZ

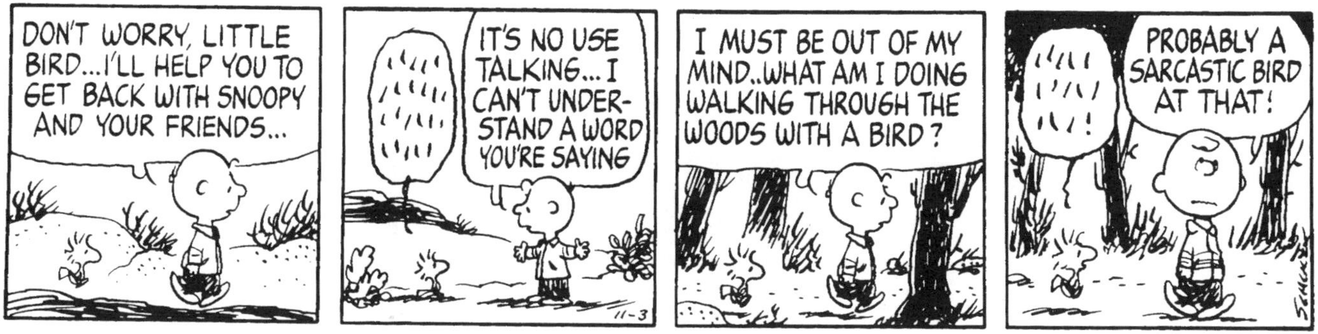
DON'T WORRY, LITTLE BIRD...I'LL HELP YOU TO GET BACK WITH SNOOPY AND YOUR FRIENDS...
IT'S NO USE TALKING... I CAN'T UNDER-STAND A WORD YOU'RE SAYING
11-3
I MUST BE OUT OF MY MIND..WHAT AM I DOING WALKING THROUGH THE WOODS WITH A BIRD ?
PROBABLY A SARCASTIC BIRD AT THAT!

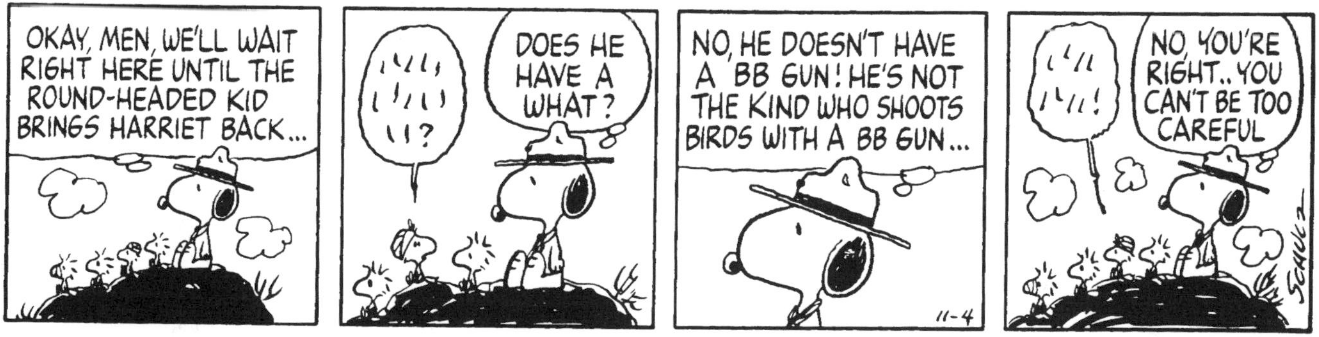
OKAY, MEN, WE'LL WAIT RIGHT HERE UNTIL THE ROUND-HEADED KID BRINGS HARRIET BACK...
DOES HE HAVE A WHAT?
NO, HE DOESN'T HAVE A BB GUN! HE'S NOT THE KIND WHO SHOOTS BIRDS WITH A BB GUN...
11-4
NO, YOU'RE RIGHT.. YOU CAN'T BE TOO CAREFUL

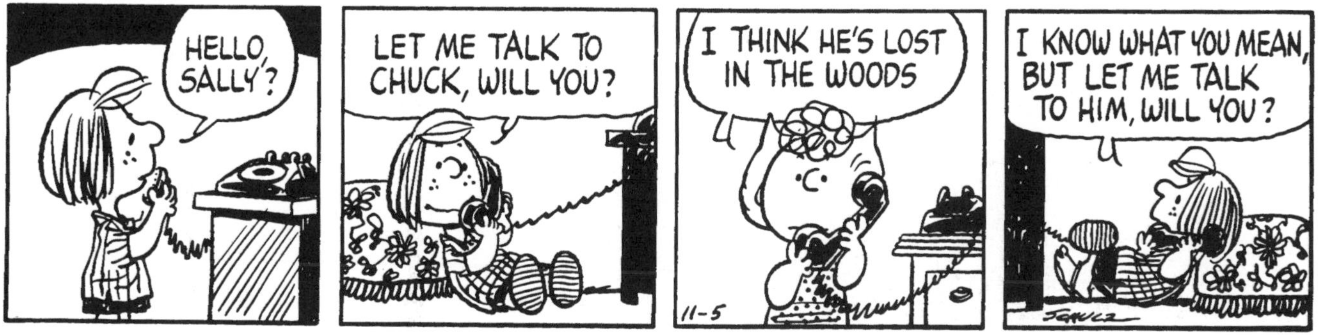
HELLO, SALLY?
LET ME TALK TO CHUCK, WILL YOU?
I THINK HE'S LOST IN THE WOODS
11-5
I KNOW WHAT YOU MEAN, BUT LET ME TALK TO HIM, WILL YOU?

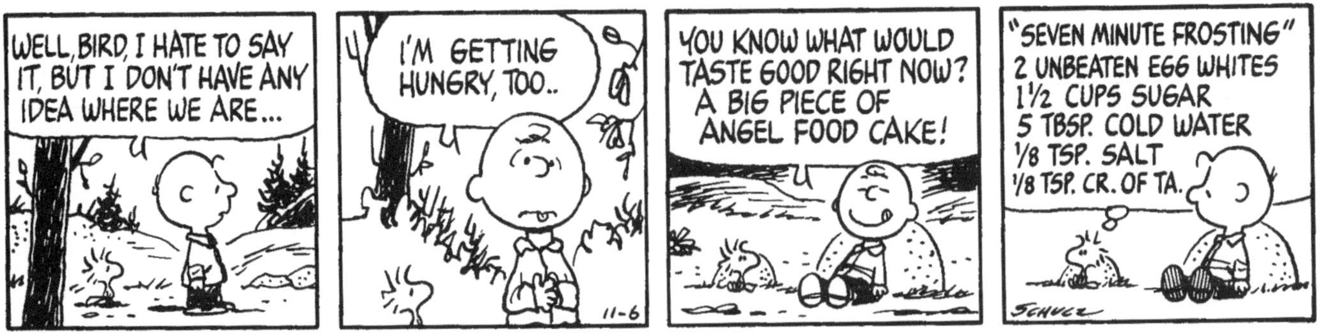
WELL, BIRD, I HATE TO SAY IT, BUT I DON'T HAVE ANY IDEA WHERE WE ARE...
I'M GETTING HUNGRY, TOO..
YOU KNOW WHAT WOULD TASTE GOOD RIGHT NOW? A BIG PIECE OF ANGEL FOOD CAKE!
"SEVEN MINUTE FROSTING"
2 UNBEATEN EGG WHITES
1½ CUPS SUGAR
5 TBSP. COLD WATER
1/8 TSP. SALT
1/8 TSP. CR. OF TA.
SCHULZ
11-6

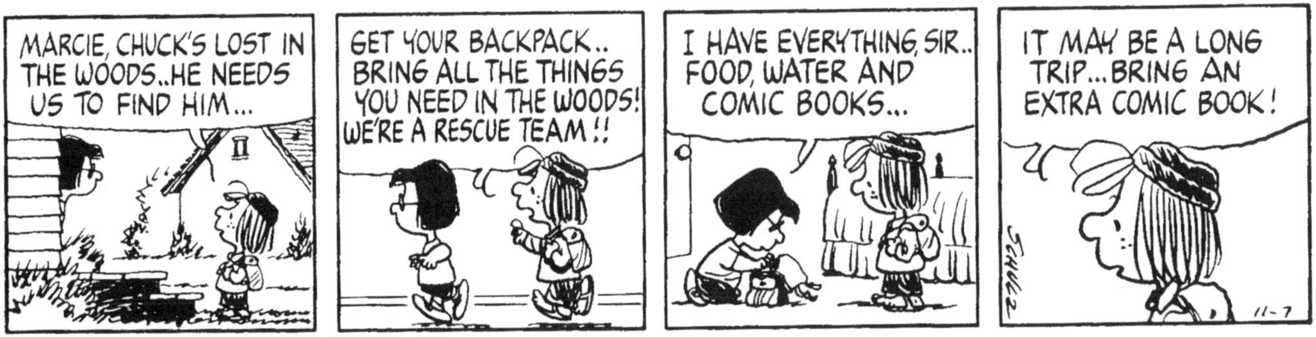
MARCIE, CHUCK'S LOST IN THE WOODS..HE NEEDS US TO FIND HIM...
GET YOUR BACKPACK.. BRING ALL THE THINGS YOU NEED IN THE WOODS! WE'RE A RESCUE TEAM!!
I HAVE EVERYTHING, SIR.. FOOD, WATER AND COMIC BOOKS...
IT MAY BE A LONG TRIP...BRING AN EXTRA COMIC BOOK!
SCHULZ
11-7

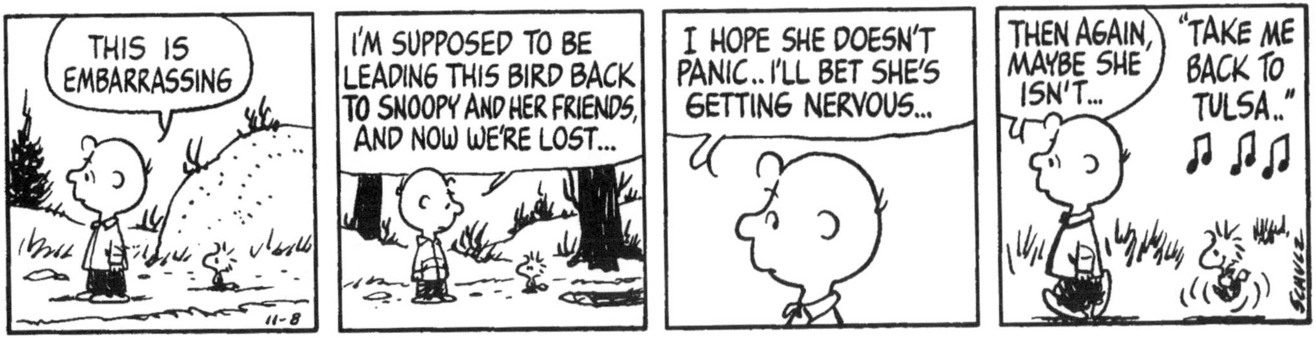
THIS IS EMBARRASSING
11-8
I'M SUPPOSED TO BE LEADING THIS BIRD BACK TO SNOOPY AND HER FRIENDS, AND NOW WE'RE LOST...
I HOPE SHE DOESN'T PANIC.. I'LL BET SHE'S GETTING NERVOUS...
THEN AGAIN, MAYBE SHE ISN'T...
"TAKE ME BACK TO TULSA.."
SCHULZ

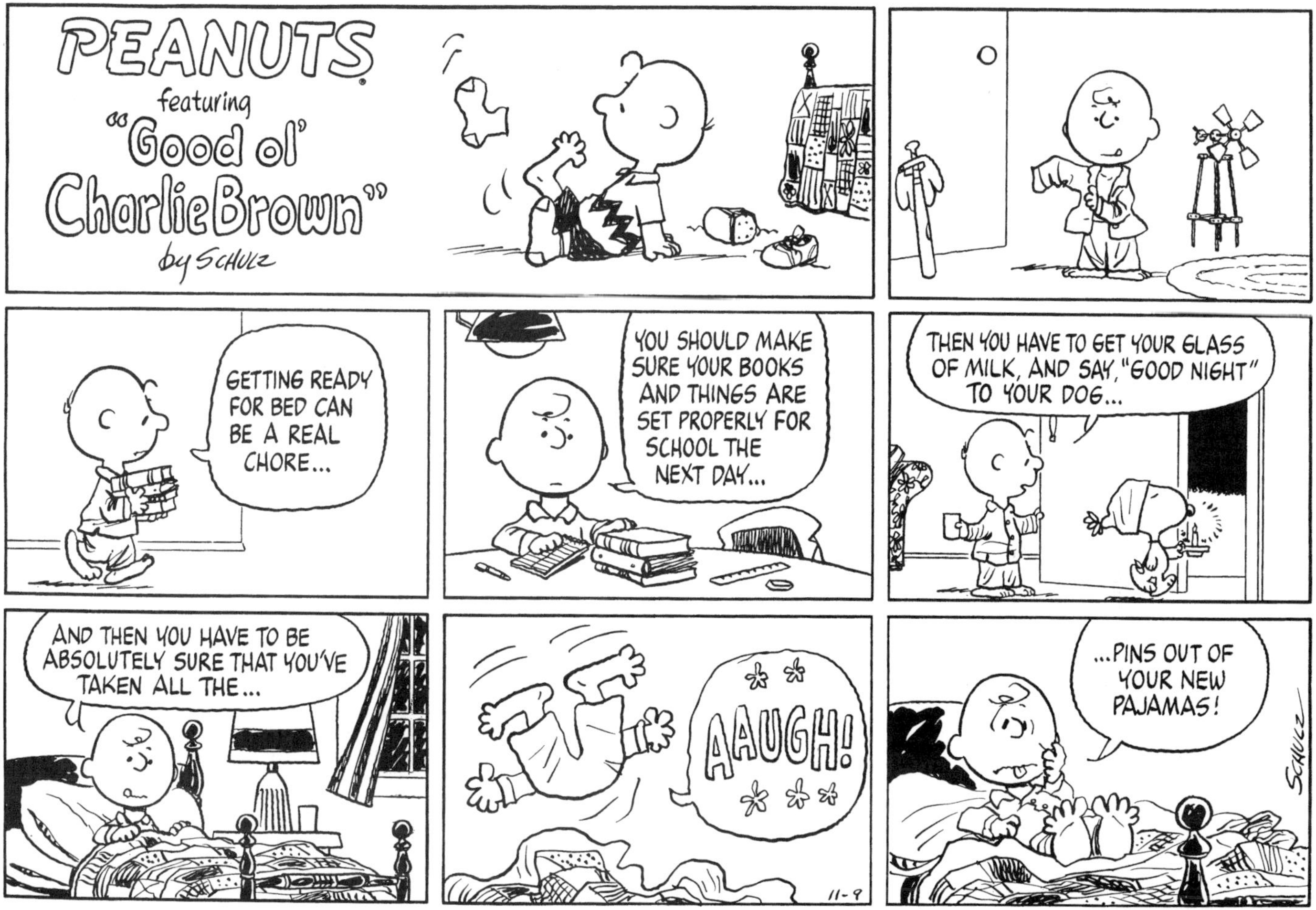
PEANUTS®
featuring
"Good ol' CharlieBrown"
by SCHULZ
GETTING READY FOR BED CAN BE A REAL CHORE...
YOU SHOULD MAKE SURE YOUR BOOKS AND THINGS ARE SET PROPERLY FOR SCHOOL THE NEXT DAY...
THEN YOU HAVE TO GET YOUR GLASS OF MILK, AND SAY, "GOOD NIGHT" TO YOUR DOG...
AND THEN YOU HAVE TO BE ABSOLUTELY SURE THAT YOU'VE TAKEN ALL THE...
AAUGH!
11-9
...PINS OUT OF YOUR NEW PAJAMAS!
SCHULZ

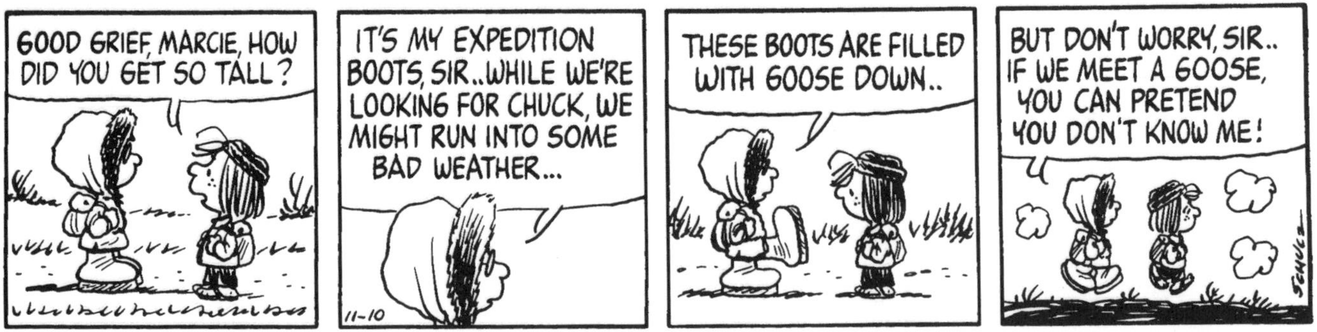
GOOD GRIEF, MARCIE, HOW DID YOU GET SO TALL?
IT'S MY EXPEDITION BOOTS, SIR..WHILE WE'RE LOOKING FOR CHUCK, WE MIGHT RUN INTO SOME BAD WEATHER...
11-10
THESE BOOTS ARE FILLED WITH GOOSE DOWN..
BUT DON'T WORRY, SIR.. IF WE MEET A GOOSE, YOU CAN PRETEND YOU DON'T KNOW ME!
SCHULZ

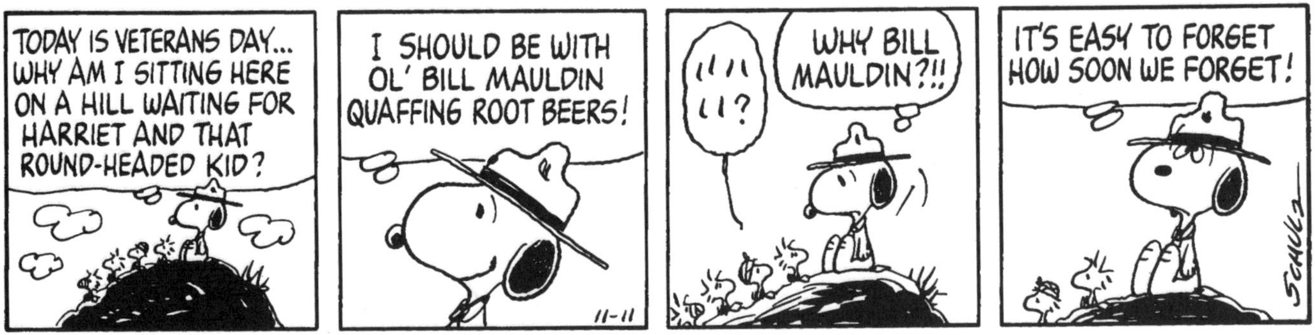
TODAY IS VETERANS DAY... WHY AM I SITTING HERE ON A HILL WAITING FOR HARRIET AND THAT ROUND-HEADED KID?
I SHOULD BE WITH OL' BILL MAULDIN QUAFFING ROOT BEERS!
11-11
WHY BILL MAULDIN?!!
IT'S EASY TO FORGET HOW SOON WE FORGET!
SCHULZ

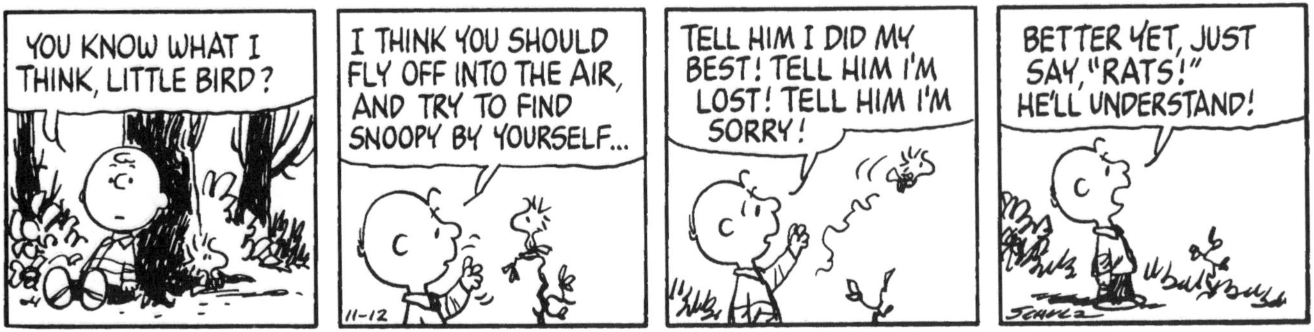
YOU KNOW WHAT I THINK, LITTLE BIRD?
I THINK YOU SHOULD FLY OFF INTO THE AIR, AND TRY TO FIND SNOOPY BY YOURSELF...
11-12
TELL HIM I DID MY BEST! TELL HIM I'M LOST! TELL HIM I'M SORRY!
BETTER YET, JUST SAY, "RATS!" HE'LL UNDERSTAND!
SCHULZ

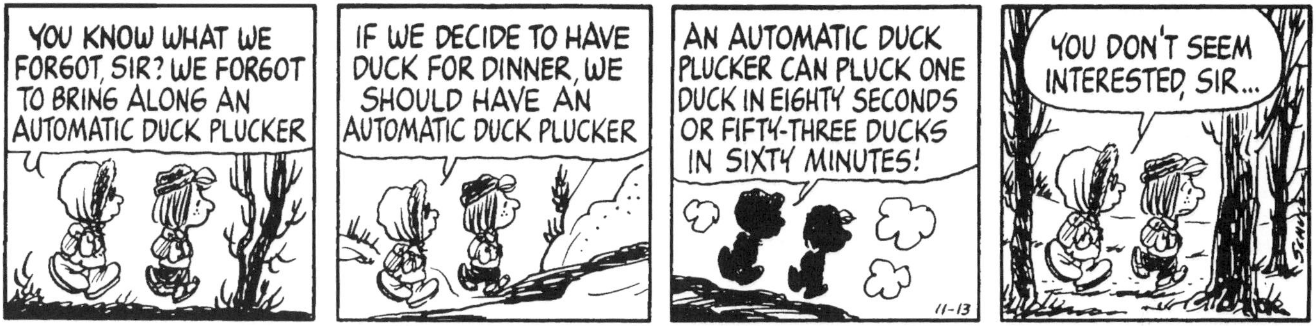
YOU KNOW WHAT WE FORGOT, SIR? WE FORGOT TO BRING ALONG AN AUTOMATIC DUCK PLUCKER
IF WE DECIDE TO HAVE DUCK FOR DINNER, WE SHOULD HAVE AN AUTOMATIC DUCK PLUCKER
AN AUTOMATIC DUCK PLUCKER CAN PLUCK ONE DUCK IN EIGHTY SECONDS OR FIFTY-THREE DUCKS IN SIXTY MINUTES!
11-13
YOU DON'T SEEM INTERESTED, SIR...
SCHULZ

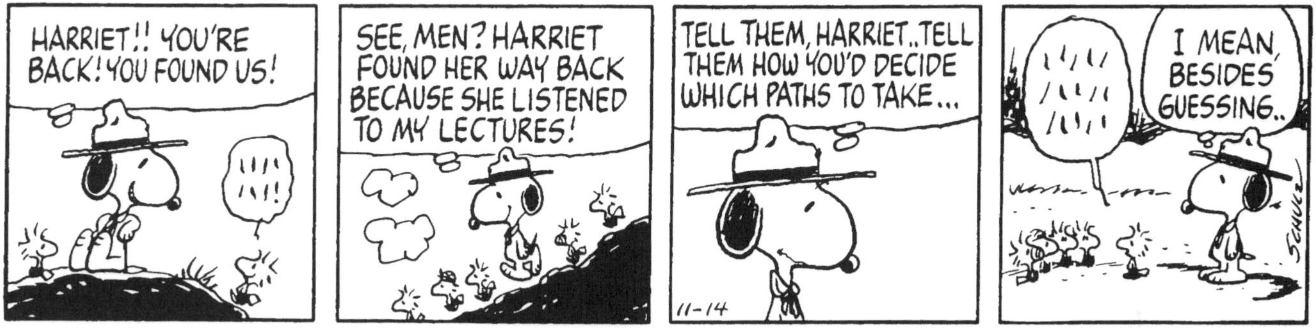
HARRIET!! YOU'RE BACK! YOU FOUND US!
SEE, MEN? HARRIET FOUND HER WAY BACK BECAUSE SHE LISTENED TO MY LECTURES!
TELL THEM, HARRIET..TELL THEM HOW YOU'D DECIDE WHICH PATHS TO TAKE...
11-14
I MEAN, BESIDES GUESSING..
SCHULZ

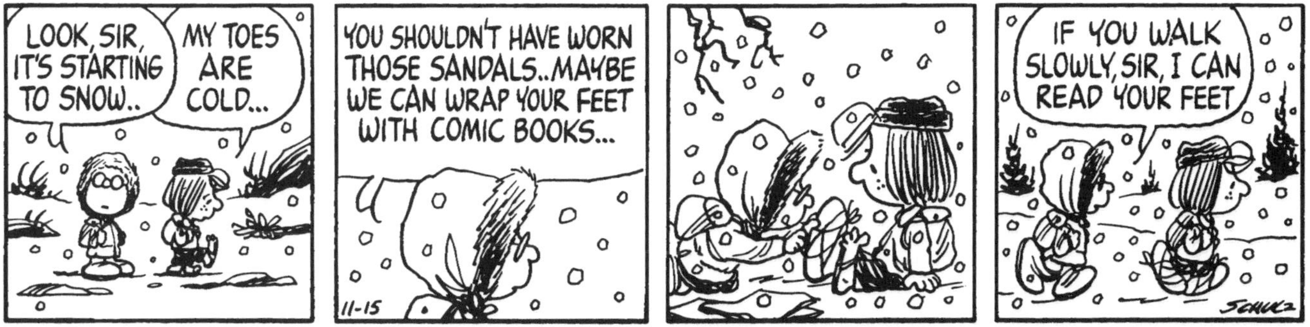
LOOK, SIR, IT'S STARTING TO SNOW..
MY TOES ARE COLD...
YOU SHOULDN'T HAVE WORN THOSE SANDALS..MAYBE WE CAN WRAP YOUR FEET WITH COMIC BOOKS...
11-15
IF YOU WALK SLOWLY, SIR, I CAN READ YOUR FEET
SCHULZ

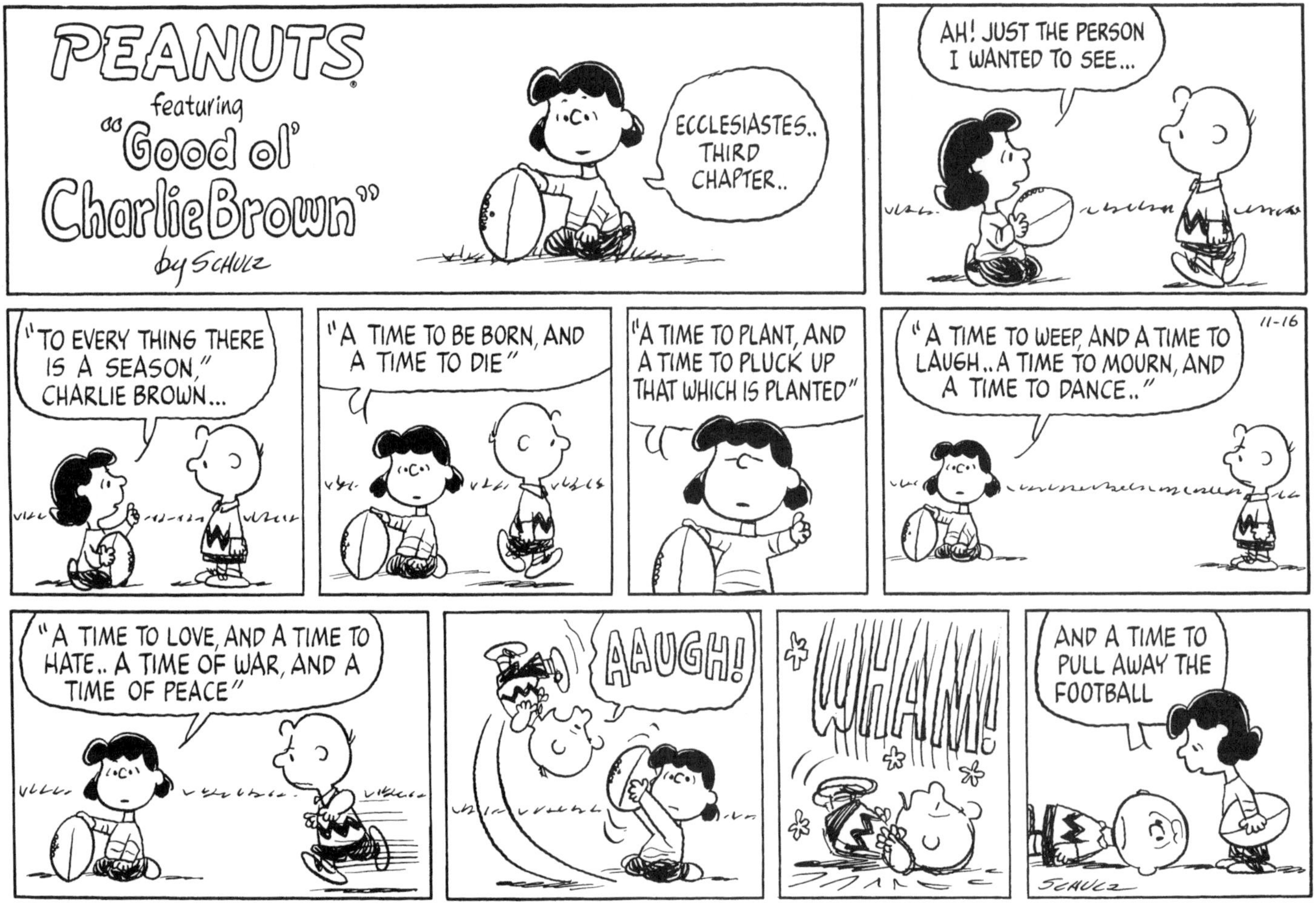
PEANUTS
featuring "Good ol' Charlie Brown"
by SCHULZ
ECCLESIASTES.. THIRD CHAPTER..
AH! JUST THE PERSON I WANTED TO SEE...
"TO EVERY THING THERE IS A SEASON," CHARLIE BROWN...
"A TIME TO BE BORN, AND A TIME TO DIE"
"A TIME TO PLANT, AND A TIME TO PLUCK UP THAT WHICH IS PLANTED"
11-16
"A TIME TO WEEP, AND A TIME TO LAUGH..A TIME TO MOURN, AND A TIME TO DANCE.."
"A TIME TO LOVE, AND A TIME TO HATE.. A TIME OF WAR, AND A TIME OF PEACE"
AAUGH!
WHAM!
AND A TIME TO PULL AWAY THE FOOTBALL
SCHULZ

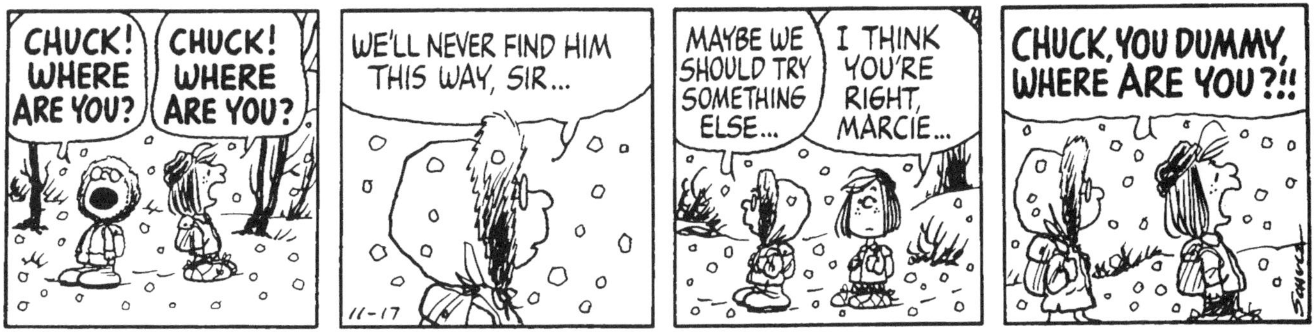
CHUCK! WHERE ARE YOU?
CHUCK! WHERE ARE YOU?
WE'LL NEVER FIND HIM THIS WAY, SIR...
11-17
MAYBE WE SHOULD TRY SOMETHING ELSE...
I THINK YOU'RE RIGHT, MARCIE...
CHUCK, YOU DUMMY, WHERE ARE YOU?!!
SCHULZ

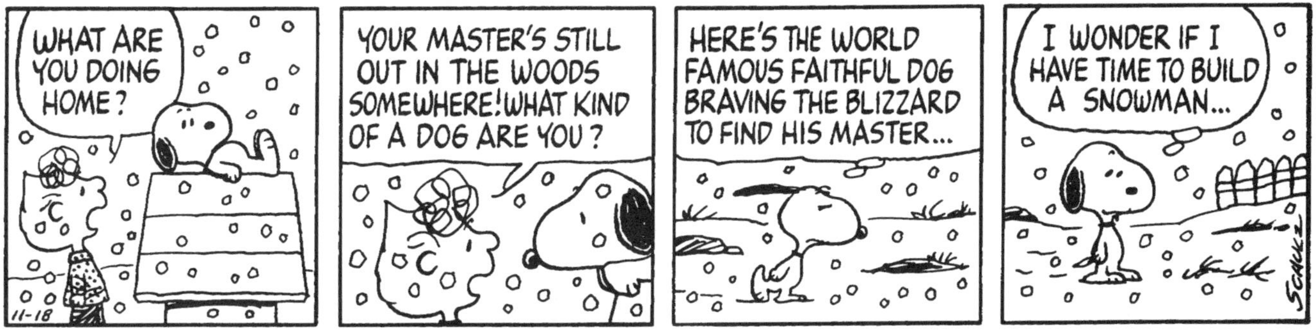
WHAT ARE YOU DOING HOME?
11-18
YOUR MASTER'S STILL OUT IN THE WOODS SOMEWHERE! WHAT KIND OF A DOG ARE YOU?
HERE'S THE WORLD FAMOUS FAITHFUL DOG BRAVING THE BLIZZARD TO FIND HIS MASTER...
I WONDER IF I HAVE TIME TO BUILD A SNOWMAN...
SCHULZ

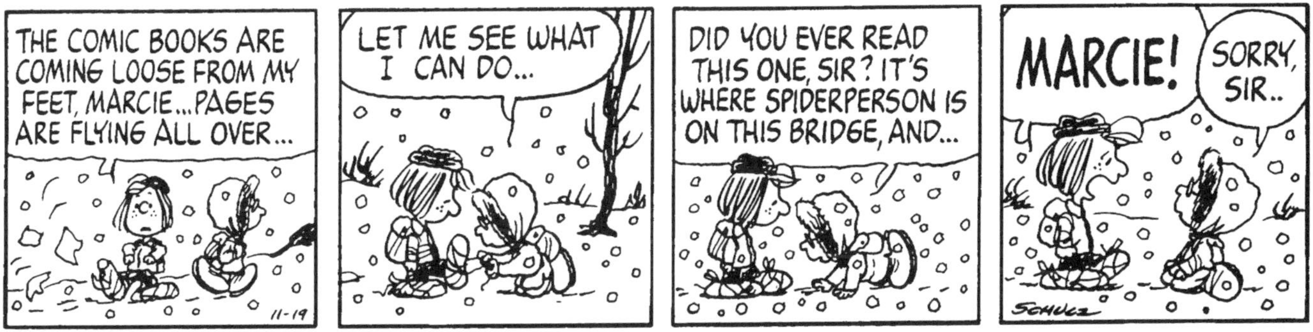
THE COMIC BOOKS ARE COMING LOOSE FROM MY FEET, MARCIE... PAGES ARE FLYING ALL OVER...
11-19
LET ME SEE WHAT I CAN DO...
DID YOU EVER READ THIS ONE, SIR? IT'S WHERE SPIDERPERSON IS ON THIS BRIDGE, AND...
SCHULZ
MARCIE!
SORRY, SIR..

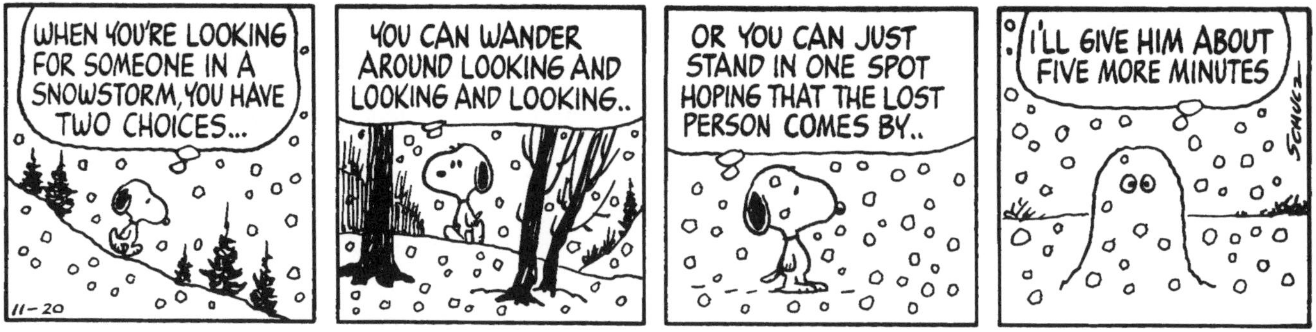
WHEN YOU'RE LOOKING FOR SOMEONE IN A SNOWSTORM, YOU HAVE TWO CHOICES...
11-20
YOU CAN WANDER AROUND LOOKING AND LOOKING AND LOOKING..
OR YOU CAN JUST STAND IN ONE SPOT HOPING THAT THE LOST PERSON COMES BY..
I'LL GIVE HIM ABOUT FIVE MORE MINUTES

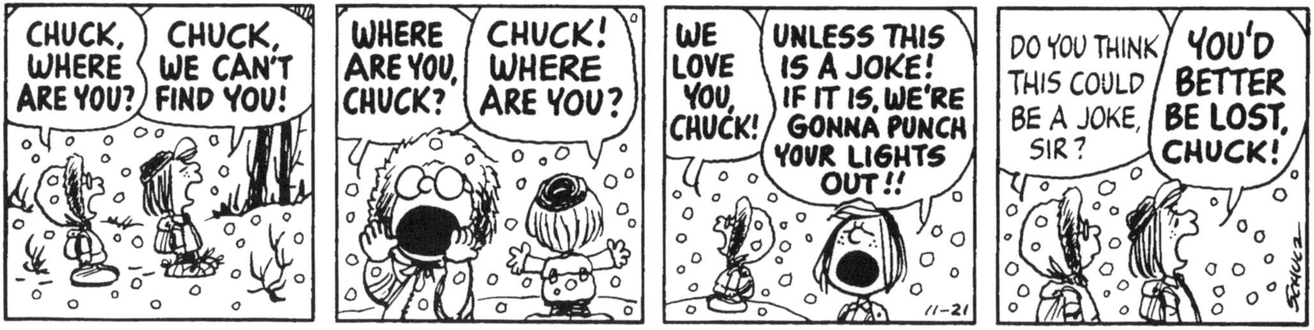
CHUCK, WHERE ARE YOU?
CHUCK, WE CAN'T FIND YOU!
WHERE ARE YOU, CHUCK?
CHUCK! WHERE ARE YOU?
WE LOVE YOU, CHUCK!
UNLESS THIS IS A JOKE! IF IT IS, WE'RE GONNA PUNCH YOUR LIGHTS OUT!!
11-21
DO YOU THINK THIS COULD BE A JOKE, SIR?
YOU'D BETTER BE LOST, CHUCK!

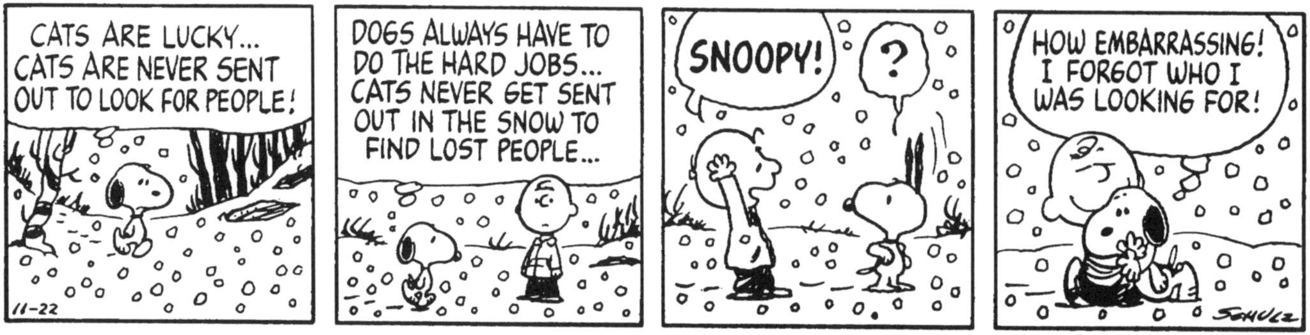
CATS ARE LUCKY... CATS ARE NEVER SENT OUT TO LOOK FOR PEOPLE!
11-22
DOGS ALWAYS HAVE TO DO THE HARD JOBS... CATS NEVER GET SENT OUT IN THE SNOW TO FIND LOST PEOPLE...
SNOOPY!
?
HOW EMBARRASSING! I FORGOT WHO I WAS LOOKING FOR!

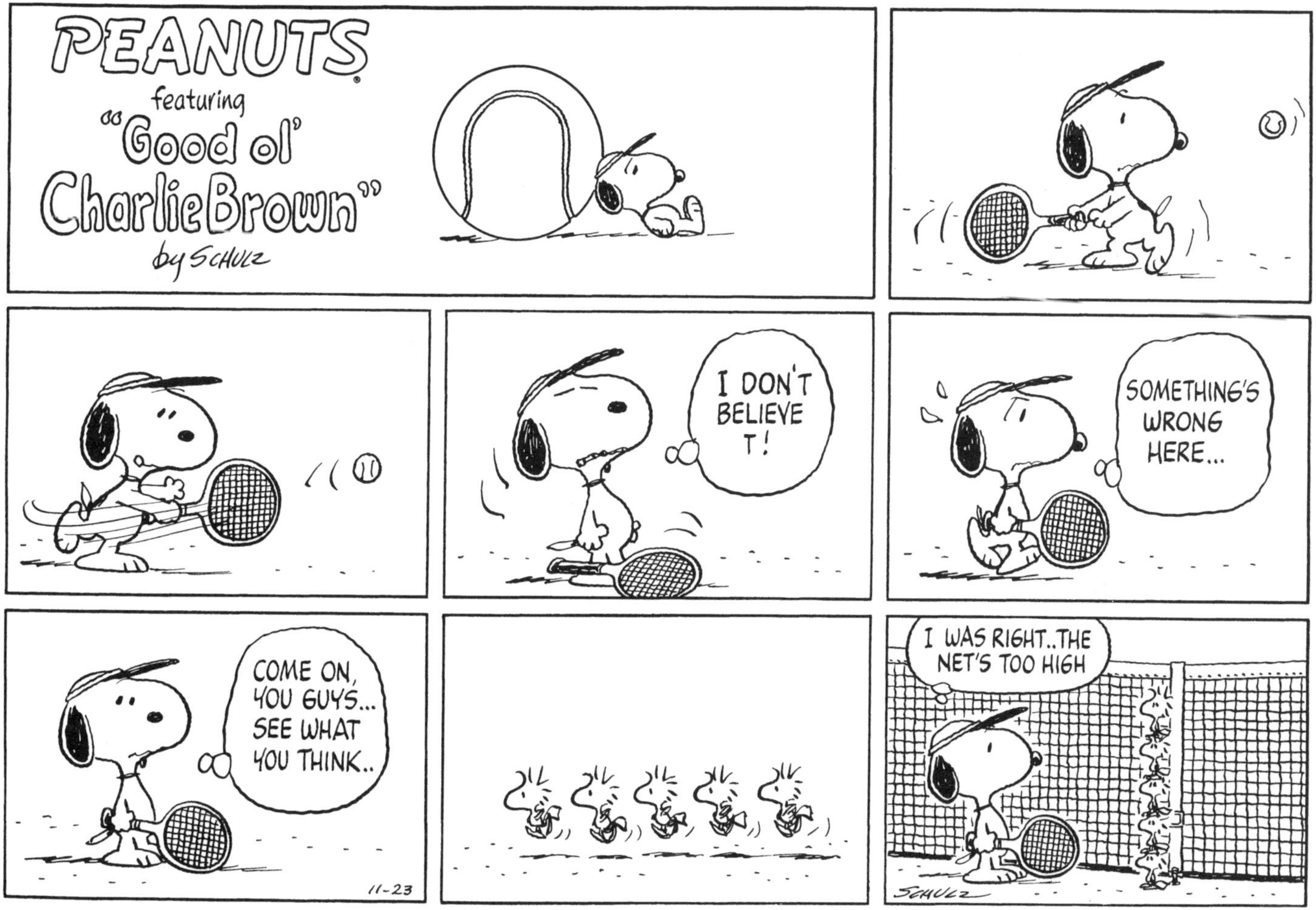
PEANUTS
featuring "Good ol' CharlieBrown"
by SCHULZ
I DON'T BELIEVE IT!
SOMETHING'S WRONG HERE...
COME ON, YOU GUYS... SEE WHAT YOU THINK..
11-23
I WAS RIGHT..THE NET'S TOO HIGH
SCHULZ

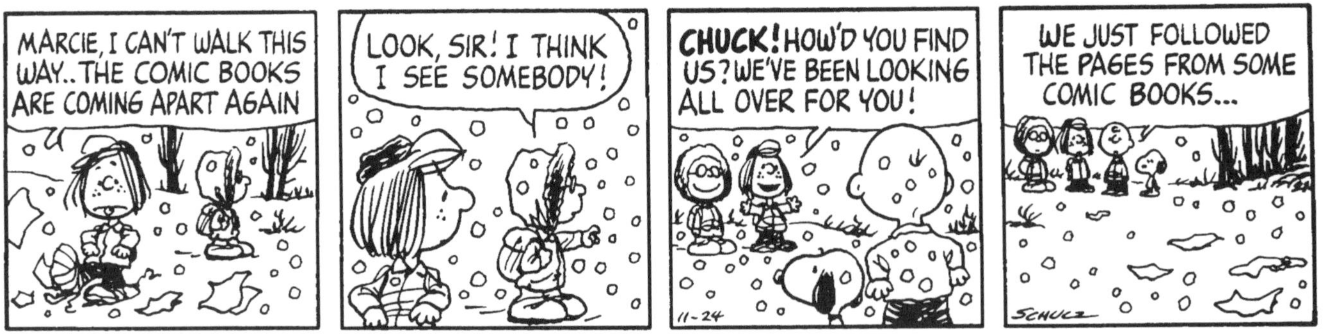
MARCIE, I CAN'T WALK THIS WAY.. THE COMIC BOOKS ARE COMING APART AGAIN
LOOK, SIR! I THINK I SEE SOMEBODY!
CHUCK! HOW'D YOU FIND US? WE'VE BEEN LOOKING ALL OVER FOR YOU!
11-24
WE JUST FOLLOWED THE PAGES FROM SOME COMIC BOOKS...
SCHULZ

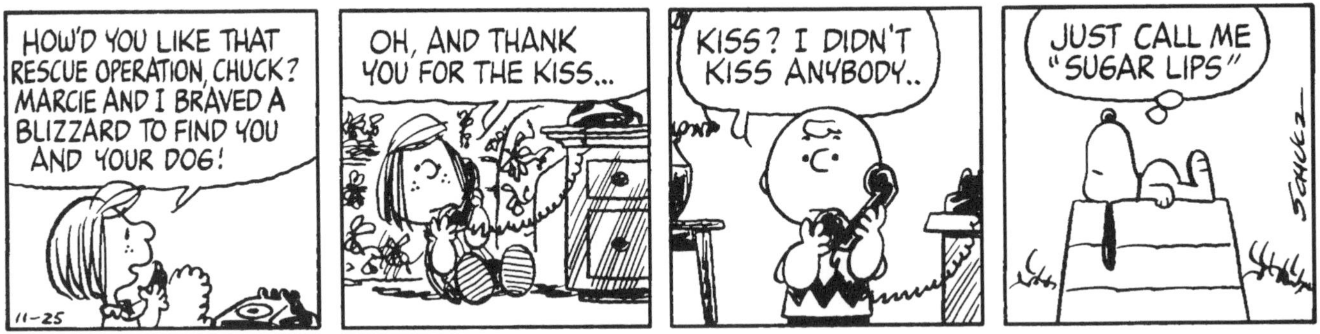
HOW'D YOU LIKE THAT RESCUE OPERATION, CHUCK? MARCIE AND I BRAVED A BLIZZARD TO FIND YOU AND YOUR DOG!
11-25
OH, AND THANK YOU FOR THE KISS...
KISS? I DIDN'T KISS ANYBODY..
JUST CALL ME "SUGAR LIPS"
SCHULZ

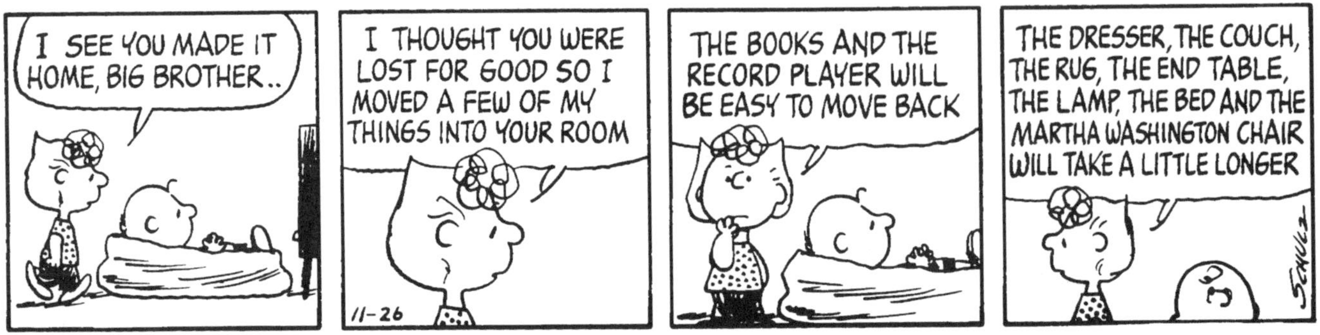
I SEE YOU MADE IT HOME, BIG BROTHER..
I THOUGHT YOU WERE LOST FOR GOOD SO I MOVED A FEW OF MY THINGS INTO YOUR ROOM
11-26
THE BOOKS AND THE RECORD PLAYER WILL BE EASY TO MOVE BACK
THE DRESSER, THE COUCH, THE RUG, THE END TABLE, THE LAMP, THE BED AND THE MARTHA WASHINGTON CHAIR WILL TAKE A LITTLE LONGER
SCHULZ

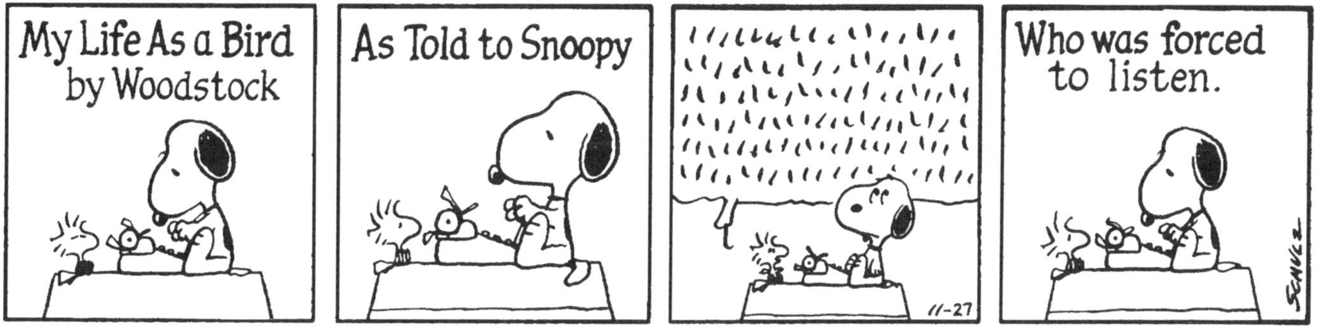
My Life As a Bird
by Woodstock
As Told to Snoopy
11-27
Who was forced
to listen.
SCHULZ

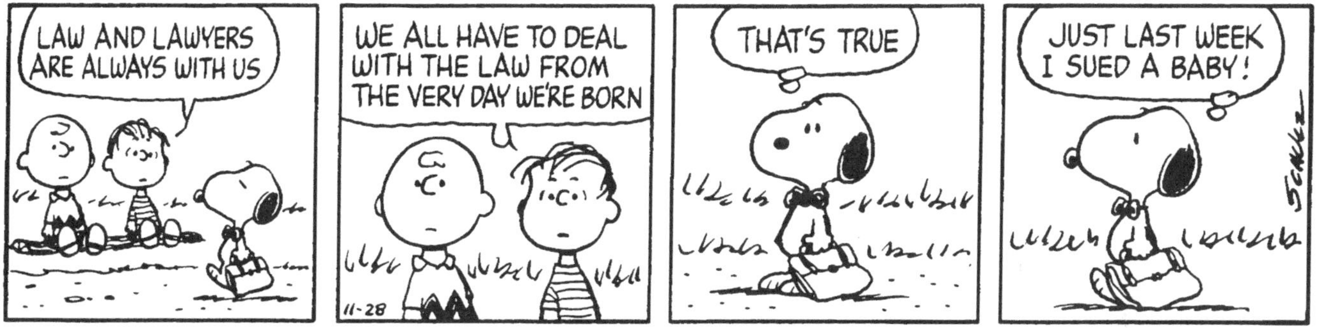
LAW AND LAWYERS
ARE ALWAYS WITH US
WE ALL HAVE TO DEAL
WITH THE LAW FROM
THE VERY DAY WE'RE BORN
11-28
THAT'S TRUE
JUST LAST WEEK
I SUED A BABY!
SCHULZ

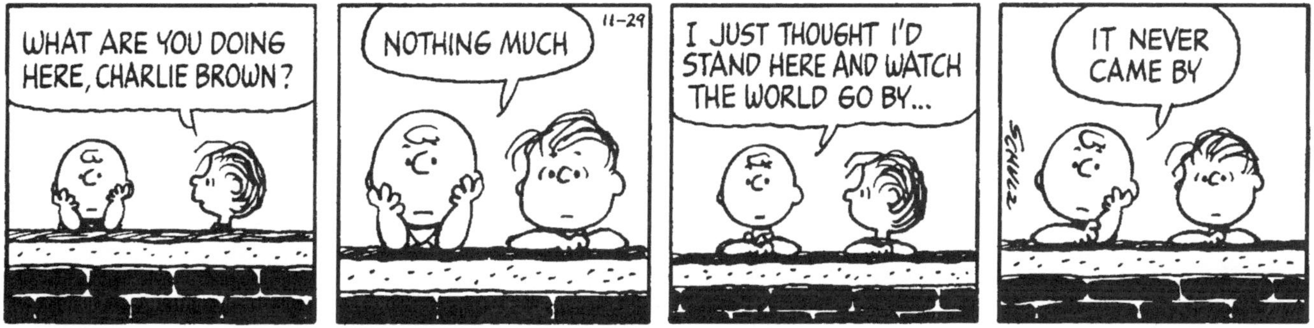
WHAT ARE YOU DOING
HERE, CHARLIE BROWN?
NOTHING MUCH
11-29
I JUST THOUGHT I'D
STAND HERE AND WATCH
THE WORLD GO BY...
SCHULZ
IT NEVER
CAME BY

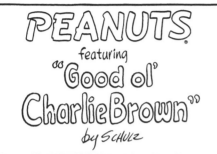

PEANUTS
featuring
"Good ol'
Charlie Brown"
by Schulz

FAIR

I HEAR FOOTSTEPS.. IS THERE NO PEACE?

YOU DOGS THINK YOU'RE SMART, DON'T YOU?

SPARE ME

WELL, YOU KNOW WHO'S REALLY SMART? A PIG!

A WHO?

PEOPLE ARE ALWAYS TALKING ABOUT HOW SMART THEIR DOGS ARE...

11-30

WELL, JUST REMEMBER, WHEN YOU'RE TALKING ABOUT SMART ANIMALS, PIGS ARE REALLY SMART!

IF THEY'RE SO SMART, WHY ARE THEY PIGS?

SCHULZ

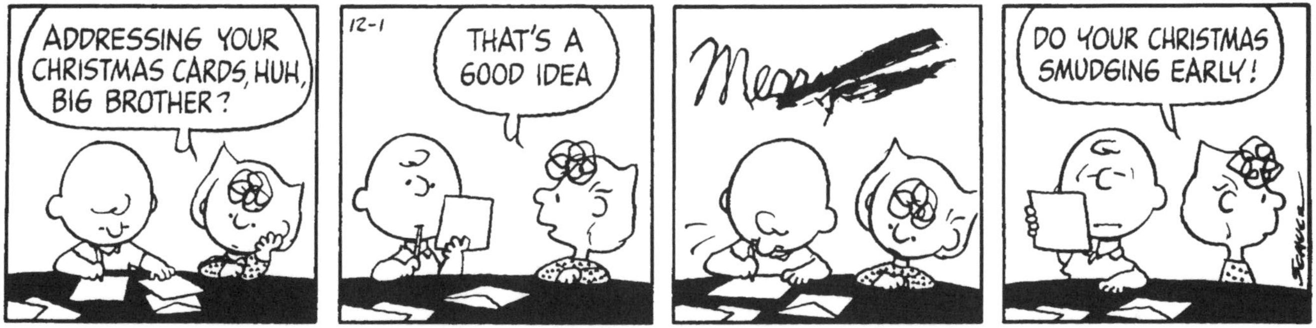
ADDRESSING YOUR CHRISTMAS CARDS, HUH, BIG BROTHER?
12-1
THAT'S A GOOD IDEA
DO YOUR CHRISTMAS SMUDGING EARLY!

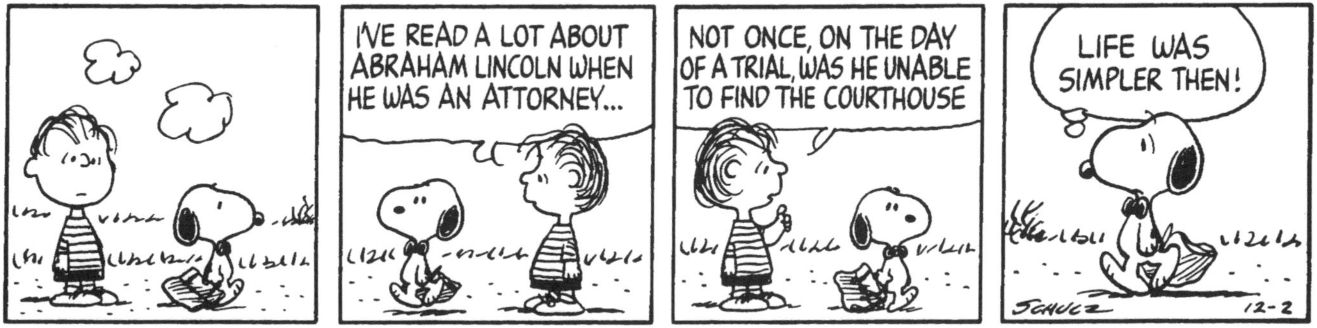
I'VE READ A LOT ABOUT ABRAHAM LINCOLN WHEN HE WAS AN ATTORNEY...
NOT ONCE, ON THE DAY OF A TRIAL, WAS HE UNABLE TO FIND THE COURTHOUSE
LIFE WAS SIMPLER THEN!
12-2

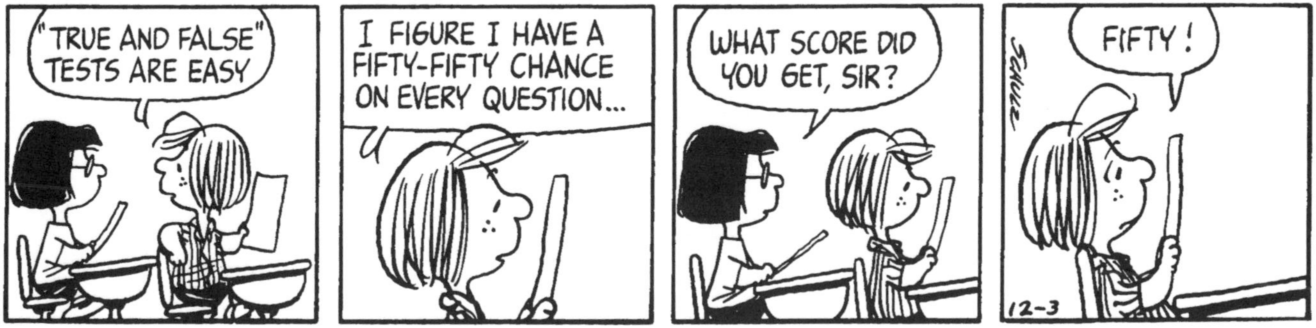
"TRUE AND FALSE" TESTS ARE EASY
I FIGURE I HAVE A FIFTY-FIFTY CHANCE ON EVERY QUESTION...
WHAT SCORE DID YOU GET, SIR?
FIFTY!
12-3

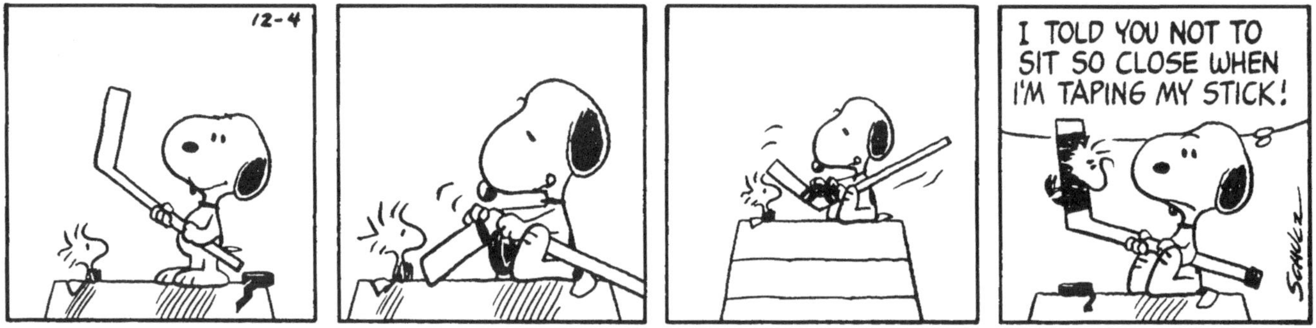
12-4
I TOLD YOU NOT TO SIT SO CLOSE WHEN I'M TAPING MY STICK!

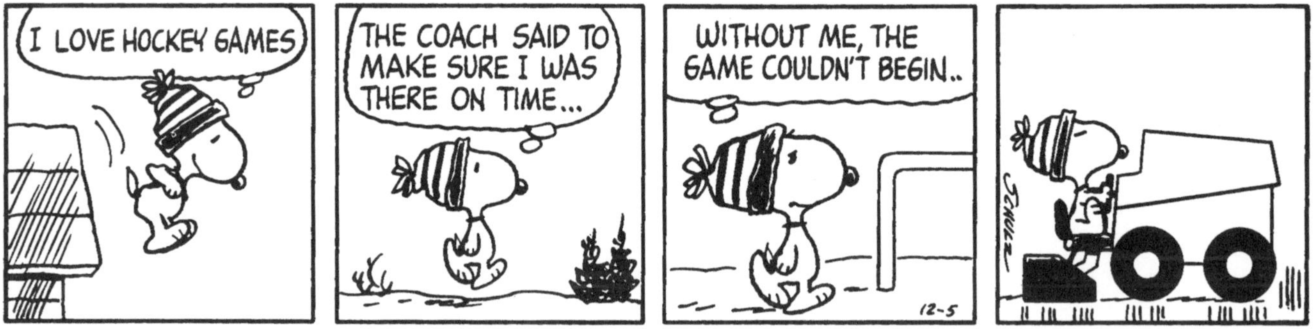
I LOVE HOCKEY GAMES
THE COACH SAID TO MAKE SURE I WAS THERE ON TIME...
WITHOUT ME, THE GAME COULDN'T BEGIN..
12-5

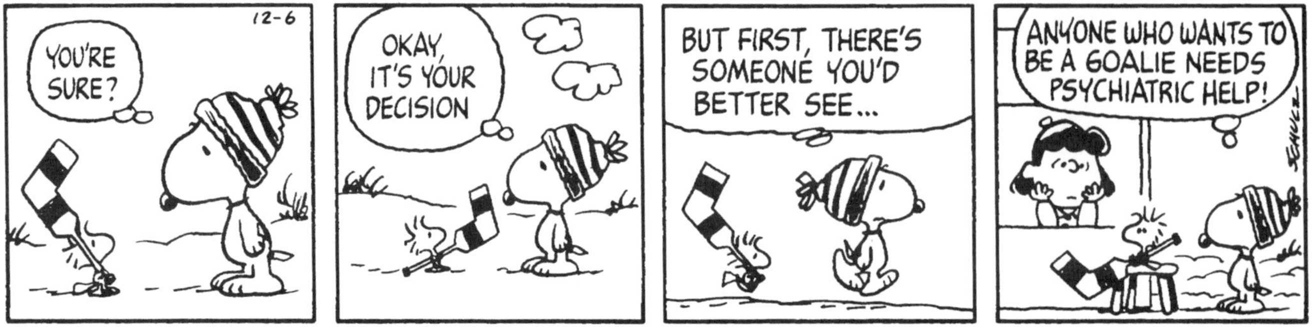
12-6
YOU'RE SURE?
OKAY, IT'S YOUR DECISION
BUT FIRST, THERE'S SOMEONE YOU'D BETTER SEE...
ANYONE WHO WANTS TO BE A GOALIE NEEDS PSYCHIATRIC HELP!

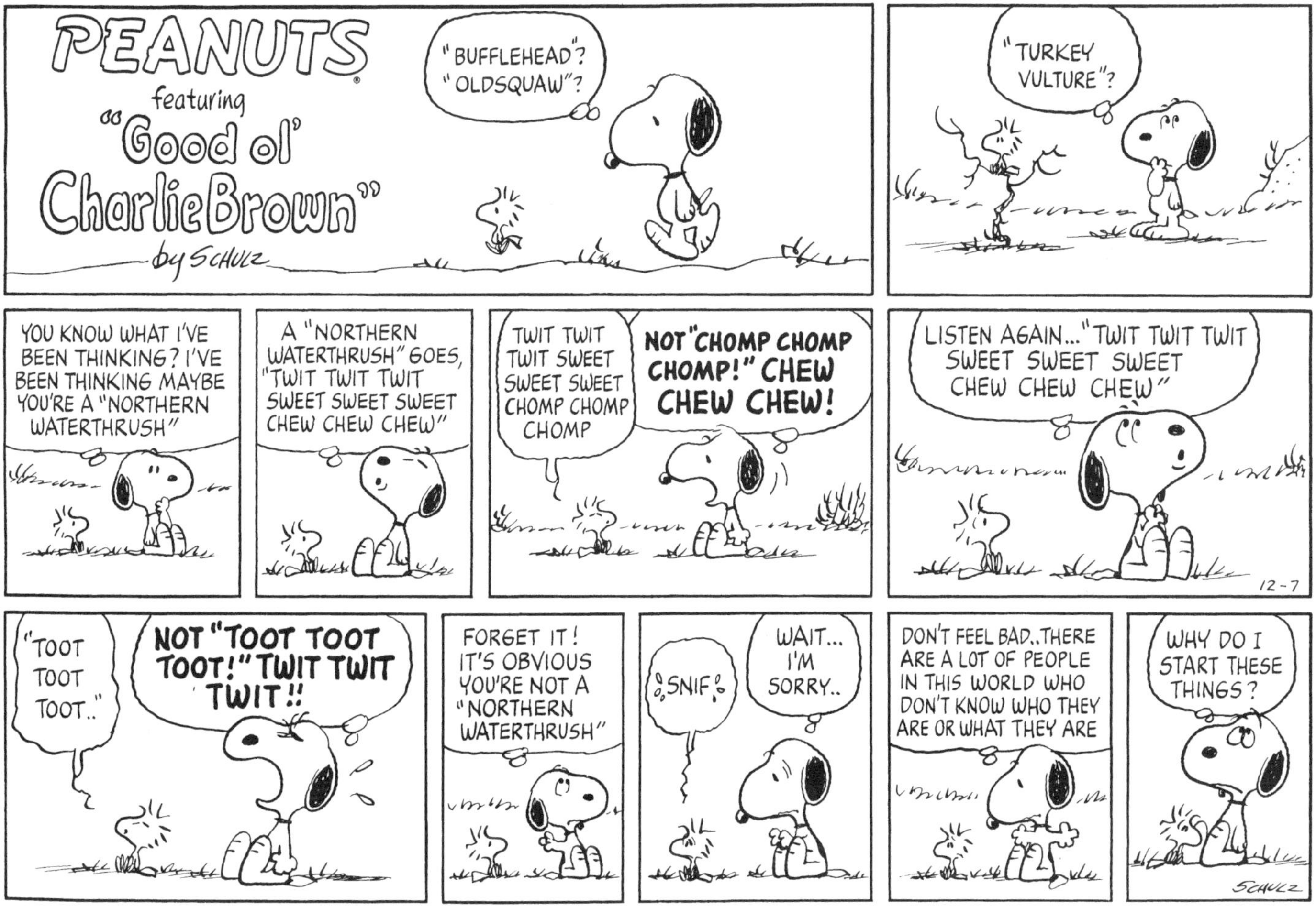
PEANUTS
featuring "Good ol' Charlie Brown"
by SCHULZ
"BUFFLEHEAD"? "OLDSQUAW"?
"TURKEY VULTURE"?
YOU KNOW WHAT I'VE BEEN THINKING? I'VE BEEN THINKING MAYBE YOU'RE A "NORTHERN WATERTHRUSH"
A "NORTHERN WATERTHRUSH" GOES, "TWIT TWIT TWIT SWEET SWEET SWEET CHEW CHEW CHEW"
TWIT TWIT TWIT SWEET SWEET SWEET CHOMP CHOMP CHOMP
NOT "CHOMP CHOMP CHOMP!" CHEW CHEW CHEW!
LISTEN AGAIN..."TWIT TWIT TWIT SWEET SWEET SWEET CHEW CHEW CHEW"
12-7
"TOOT TOOT TOOT.."
NOT "TOOT TOOT TOOT!" TWIT TWIT TWIT!!
FORGET IT! IT'S OBVIOUS YOU'RE NOT A "NORTHERN WATERTHRUSH"
SNIF
WAIT... I'M SORRY..
DON'T FEEL BAD..THERE ARE A LOT OF PEOPLE IN THIS WORLD WHO DON'T KNOW WHO THEY ARE OR WHAT THEY ARE
WHY DO I START THESE THINGS?
SCHULZ

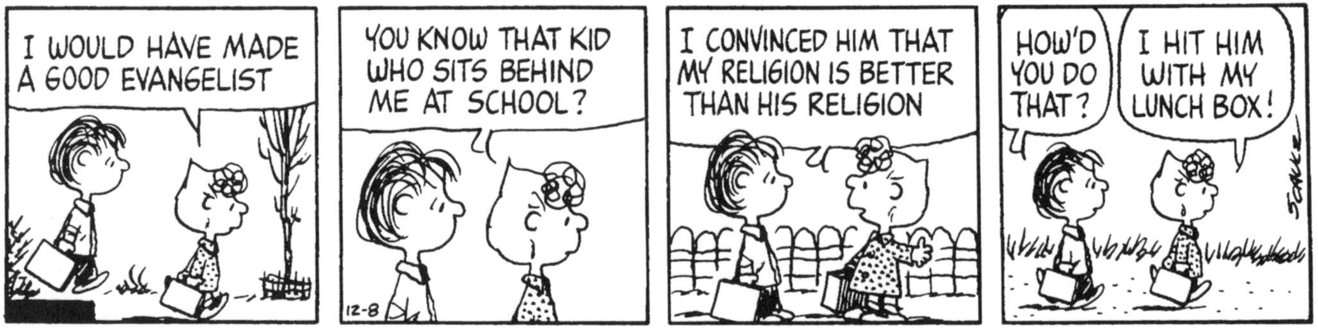
I WOULD HAVE MADE A GOOD EVANGELIST
YOU KNOW THAT KID WHO SITS BEHIND ME AT SCHOOL?
12-8
I CONVINCED HIM THAT MY RELIGION IS BETTER THAN HIS RELIGION
HOW'D YOU DO THAT?
I HIT HIM WITH MY LUNCH BOX!
SCHULZ

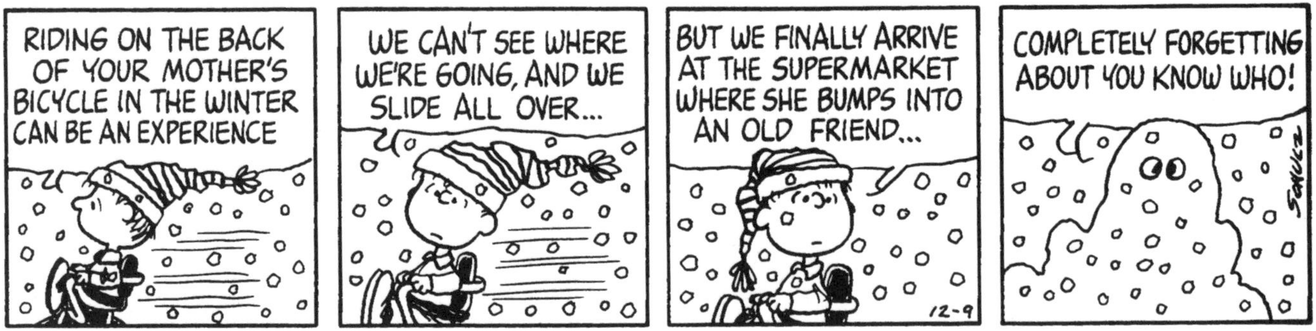
RIDING ON THE BACK OF YOUR MOTHER'S BICYCLE IN THE WINTER CAN BE AN EXPERIENCE
WE CAN'T SEE WHERE WE'RE GOING, AND WE SLIDE ALL OVER...
BUT WE FINALLY ARRIVE AT THE SUPERMARKET WHERE SHE BUMPS INTO AN OLD FRIEND...
12-9
COMPLETELY FORGETTING ABOUT YOU KNOW WHO!
SCHULZ

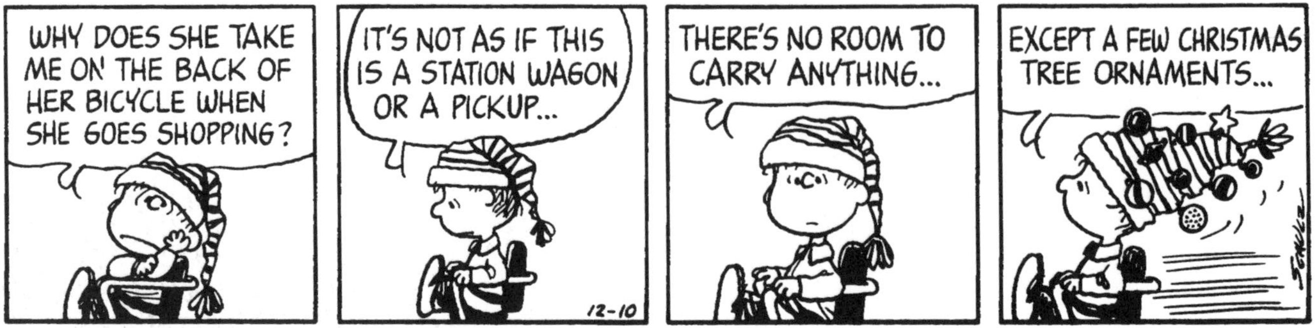
WHY DOES SHE TAKE ME ON THE BACK OF HER BICYCLE WHEN SHE GOES SHOPPING?
IT'S NOT AS IF THIS IS A STATION WAGON OR A PICKUP...
12-10
THERE'S NO ROOM TO CARRY ANYTHING...
EXCEPT A FEW CHRISTMAS TREE ORNAMENTS...
SCHULZ

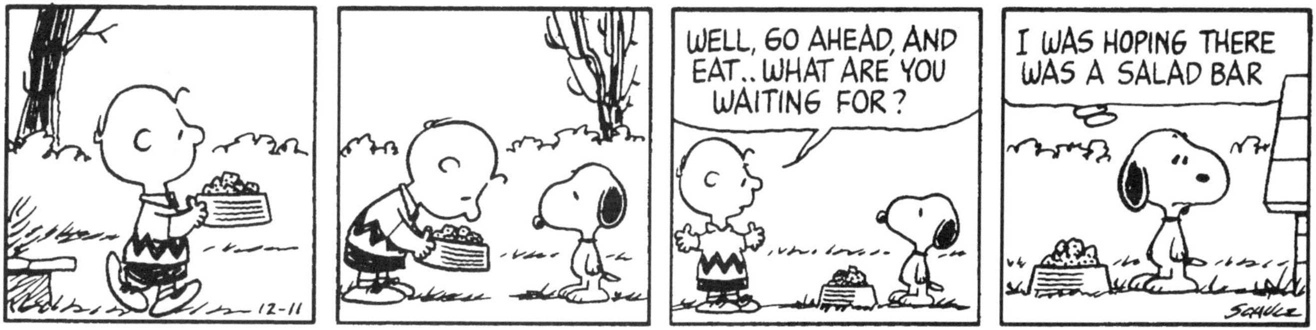
WELL, GO AHEAD, AND EAT.. WHAT ARE YOU WAITING FOR?
I WAS HOPING THERE WAS A SALAD BAR

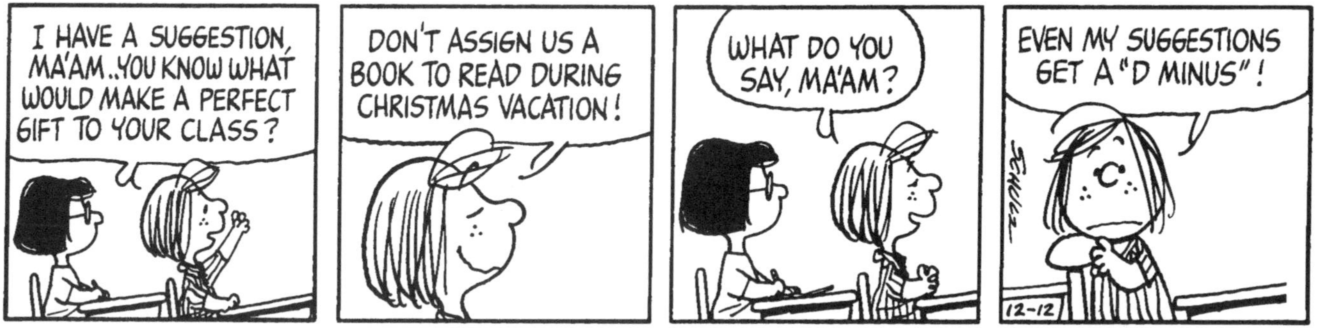
I HAVE A SUGGESTION, MA'AM..YOU KNOW WHAT WOULD MAKE A PERFECT GIFT TO YOUR CLASS?
DON'T ASSIGN US A BOOK TO READ DURING CHRISTMAS VACATION!
WHAT DO YOU SAY, MA'AM?
EVEN MY SUGGESTIONS GET A "D MINUS"!

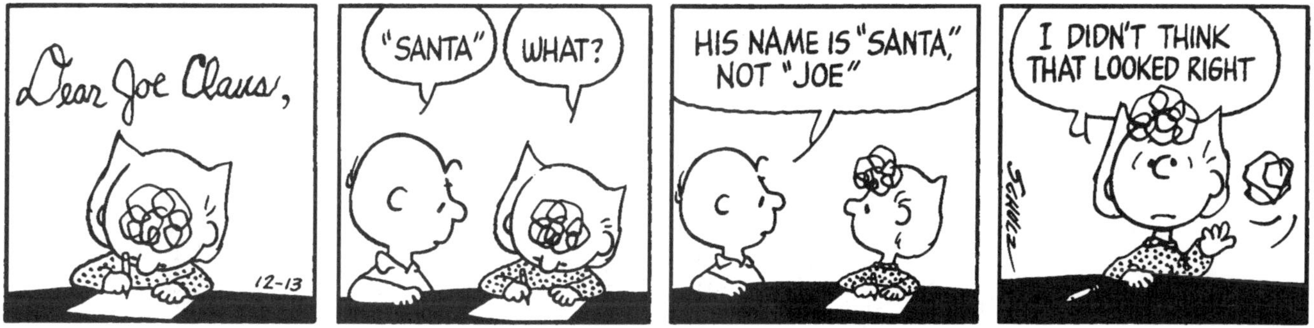
Dear Joe Claus,
"SANTA"
WHAT?
HIS NAME IS "SANTA," NOT "JOE"
I DIDN'T THINK THAT LOOKED RIGHT

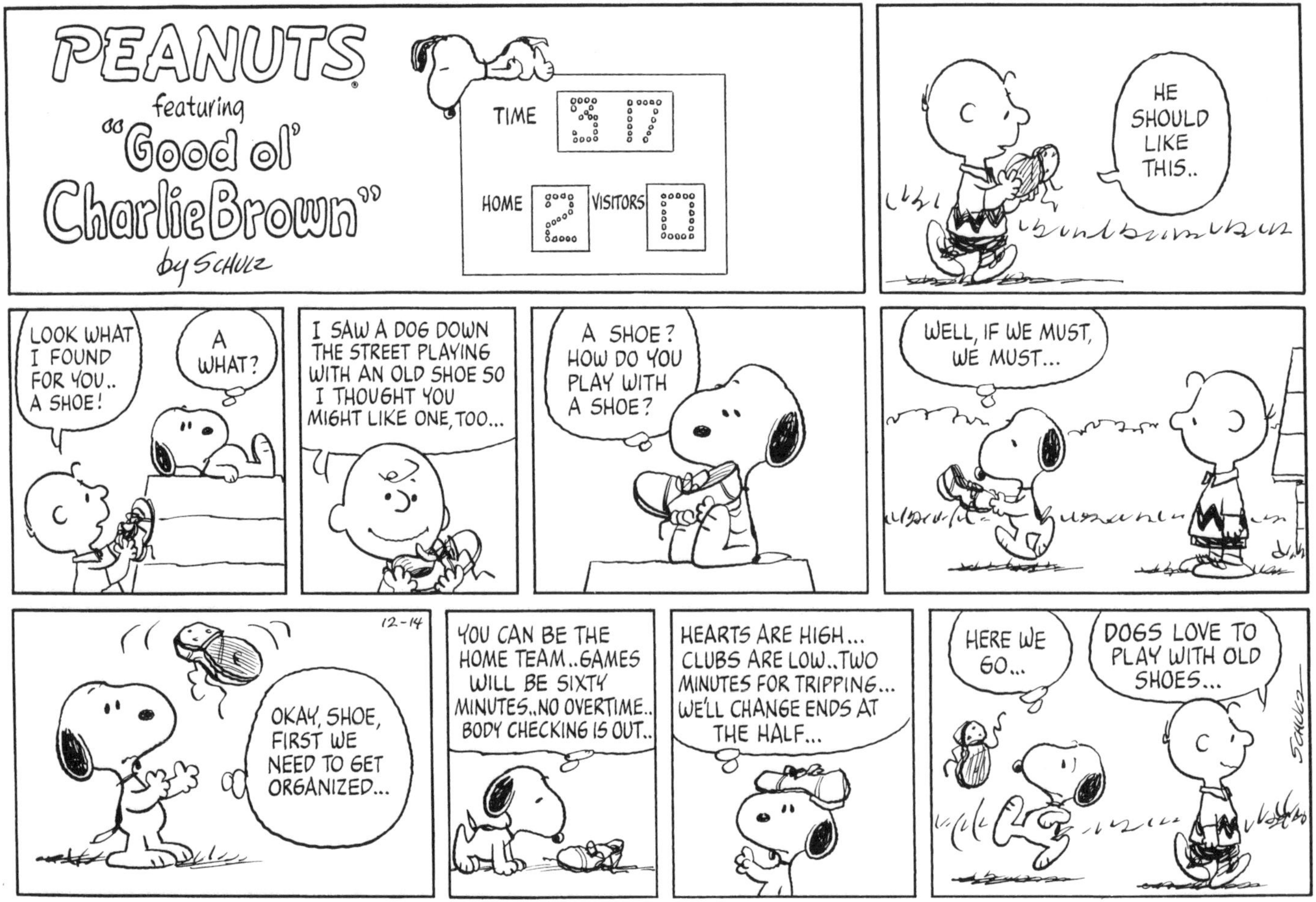
PEANUTS
featuring
"Good ol' CharlieBrown"
by SCHULZ
TIME 37
HOME 2 VISITORS 0
HE SHOULD LIKE THIS..
LOOK WHAT I FOUND FOR YOU.. A SHOE!
A WHAT?
I SAW A DOG DOWN THE STREET PLAYING WITH AN OLD SHOE SO I THOUGHT YOU MIGHT LIKE ONE, TOO...
A SHOE? HOW DO YOU PLAY WITH A SHOE?
WELL, IF WE MUST, WE MUST...
12-14
OKAY, SHOE, FIRST WE NEED TO GET ORGANIZED...
YOU CAN BE THE HOME TEAM..GAMES WILL BE SIXTY MINUTES..NO OVERTIME.. BODY CHECKING IS OUT..
HEARTS ARE HIGH... CLUBS ARE LOW..TWO MINUTES FOR TRIPPING... WE'LL CHANGE ENDS AT THE HALF...
HERE WE GO...
DOGS LOVE TO PLAY WITH OLD SHOES...
SCHULZ

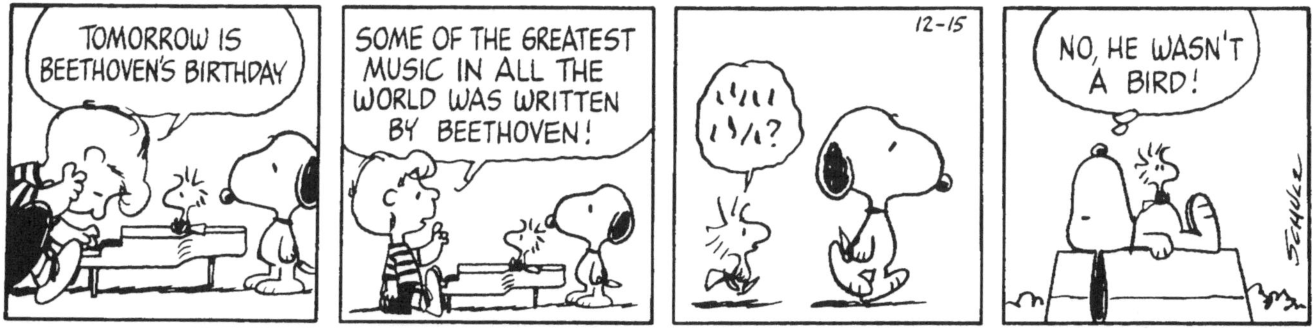
TOMORROW IS BEETHOVEN'S BIRTHDAY
SOME OF THE GREATEST MUSIC IN ALL THE WORLD WAS WRITTEN BY BEETHOVEN!
12-15
NO, HE WASN'T A BIRD!

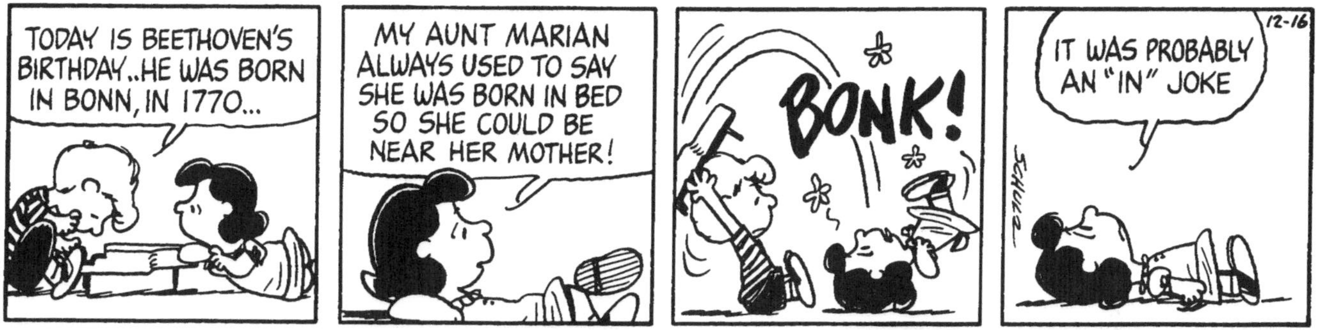
TODAY IS BEETHOVEN'S BIRTHDAY..HE WAS BORN IN BONN, IN 1770...
MY AUNT MARIAN ALWAYS USED TO SAY SHE WAS BORN IN BED SO SHE COULD BE NEAR HER MOTHER!
BONK!
12-16
IT WAS PROBABLY AN "IN" JOKE

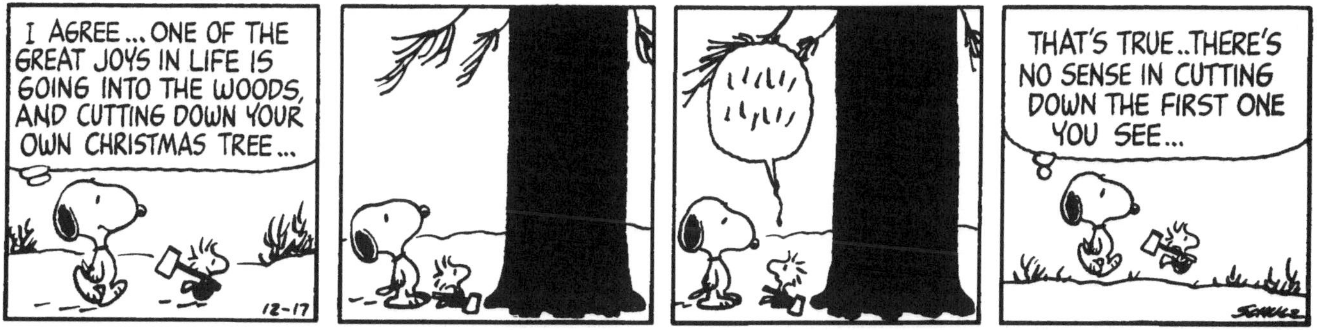
I AGREE... ONE OF THE GREAT JOYS IN LIFE IS GOING INTO THE WOODS, AND CUTTING DOWN YOUR OWN CHRISTMAS TREE...
12-17
THAT'S TRUE..THERE'S NO SENSE IN CUTTING DOWN THE FIRST ONE YOU SEE...

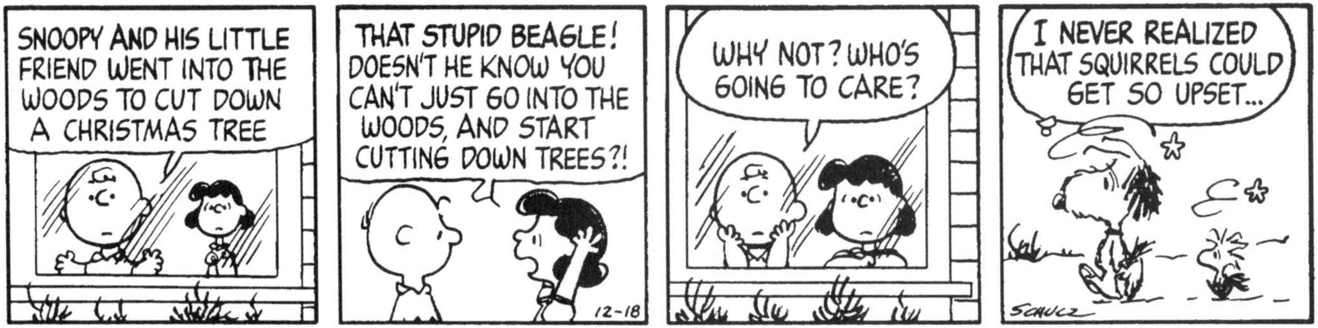
SNOOPY AND HIS LITTLE FRIEND WENT INTO THE WOODS TO CUT DOWN A CHRISTMAS TREE
THAT STUPID BEAGLE! DOESN'T HE KNOW YOU CAN'T JUST GO INTO THE WOODS, AND START CUTTING DOWN TREES?!
12-18
WHY NOT? WHO'S GOING TO CARE?
I NEVER REALIZED THAT SQUIRRELS COULD GET SO UPSET...
SCHULZ

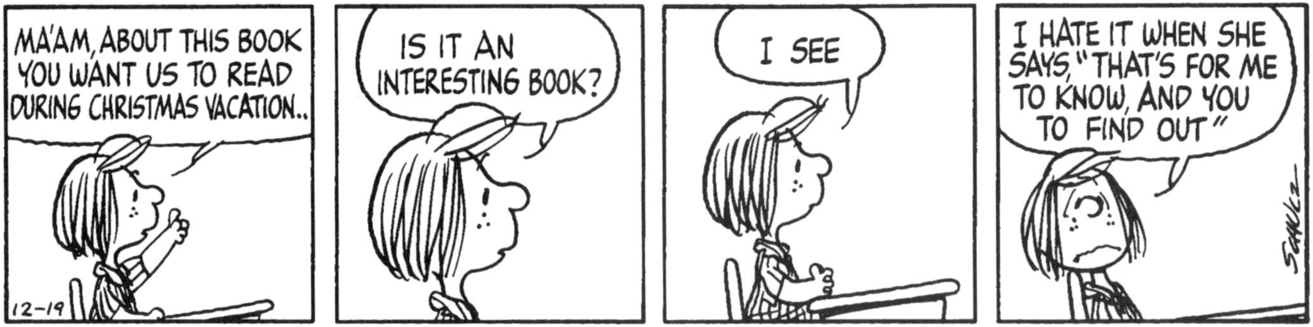
MA'AM, ABOUT THIS BOOK YOU WANT US TO READ DURING CHRISTMAS VACATION..
12-19
IS IT AN INTERESTING BOOK?
I SEE
I HATE IT WHEN SHE SAYS, "THAT'S FOR ME TO KNOW, AND YOU TO FIND OUT"
SCHULZ

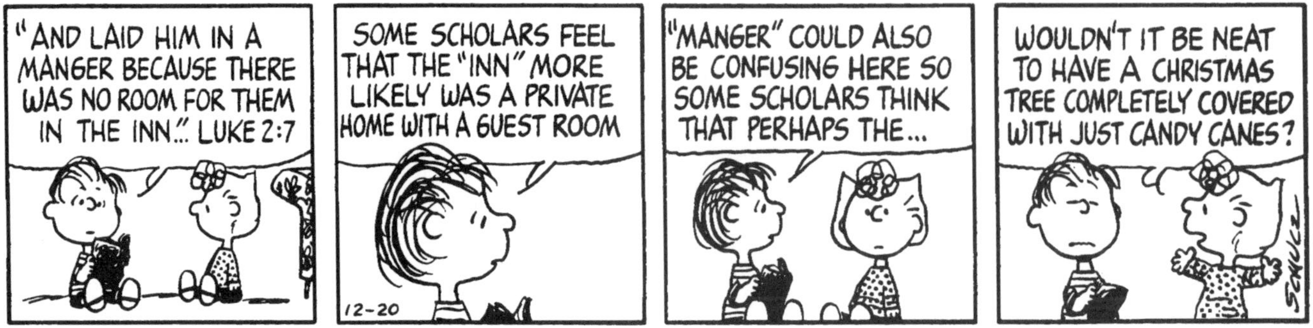
"AND LAID HIM IN A MANGER BECAUSE THERE WAS NO ROOM FOR THEM IN THE INN." LUKE 2:7
SOME SCHOLARS FEEL THAT THE "INN" MORE LIKELY WAS A PRIVATE HOME WITH A GUEST ROOM
12-20
"MANGER" COULD ALSO BE CONFUSING HERE SO SOME SCHOLARS THINK THAT PERHAPS THE...
WOULDN'T IT BE NEAT TO HAVE A CHRISTMAS TREE COMPLETELY COVERED WITH JUST CANDY CANES?
SCHULZ

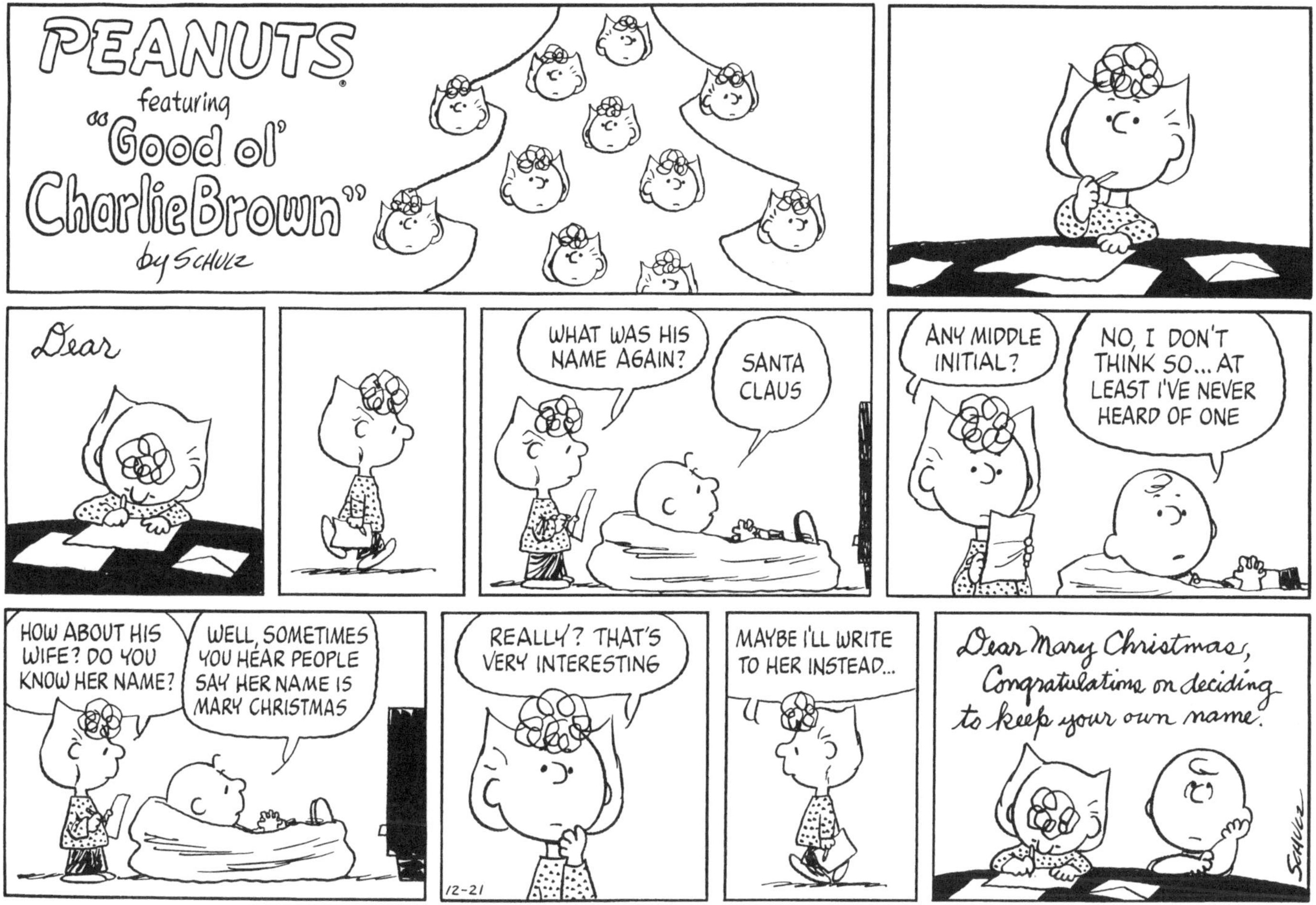
PEANUTS®
featuring "Good ol' Charlie Brown"
by SCHULZ
Dear
WHAT WAS HIS NAME AGAIN?
SANTA CLAUS
ANY MIDDLE INITIAL?
NO, I DON'T THINK SO... AT LEAST I'VE NEVER HEARD OF ONE
HOW ABOUT HIS WIFE? DO YOU KNOW HER NAME?
WELL, SOMETIMES YOU HEAR PEOPLE SAY HER NAME IS MARY CHRISTMAS
12-21
REALLY? THAT'S VERY INTERESTING
MAYBE I'LL WRITE TO HER INSTEAD...
Dear Mary Christmas,
Congratulations on deciding to keep your own name.
SCHULZ

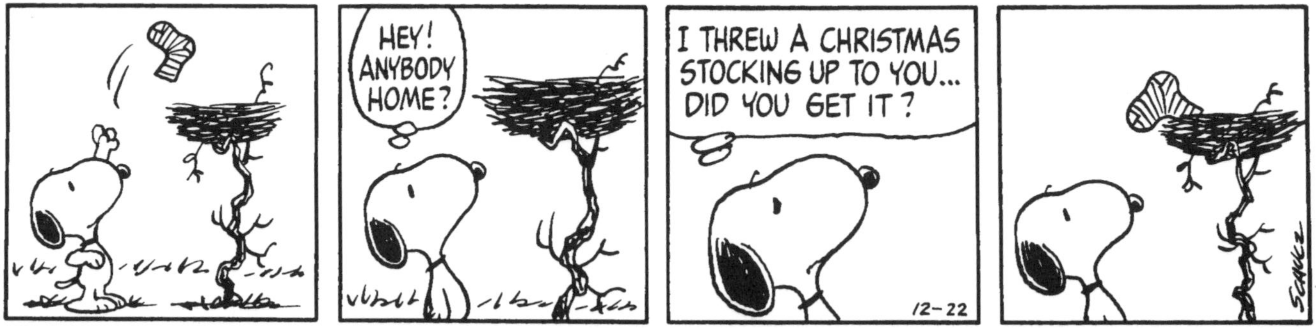
HEY! ANYBODY HOME?
I THREW A CHRISTMAS STOCKING UP TO YOU... DID YOU GET IT?
12-22
SCHULZ

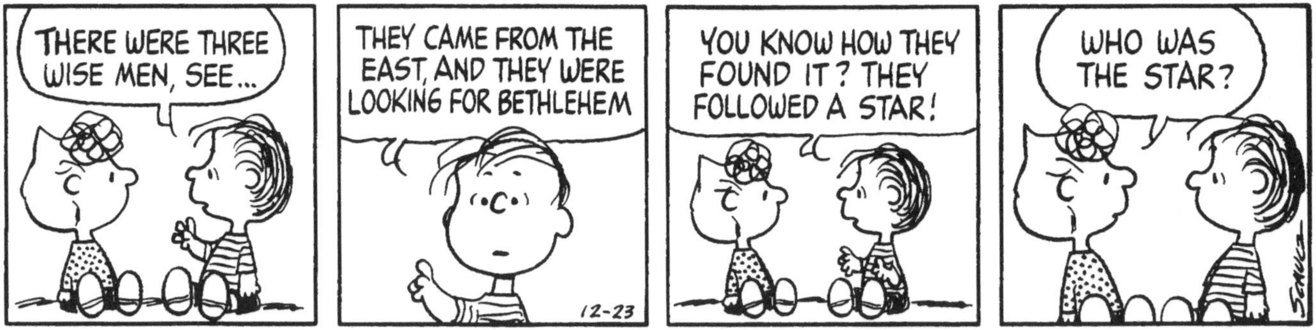
THERE WERE THREE WISE MEN, SEE...
THEY CAME FROM THE EAST, AND THEY WERE LOOKING FOR BETHLEHEM
12-23
YOU KNOW HOW THEY FOUND IT? THEY FOLLOWED A STAR!
WHO WAS THE STAR?
SCHULZ

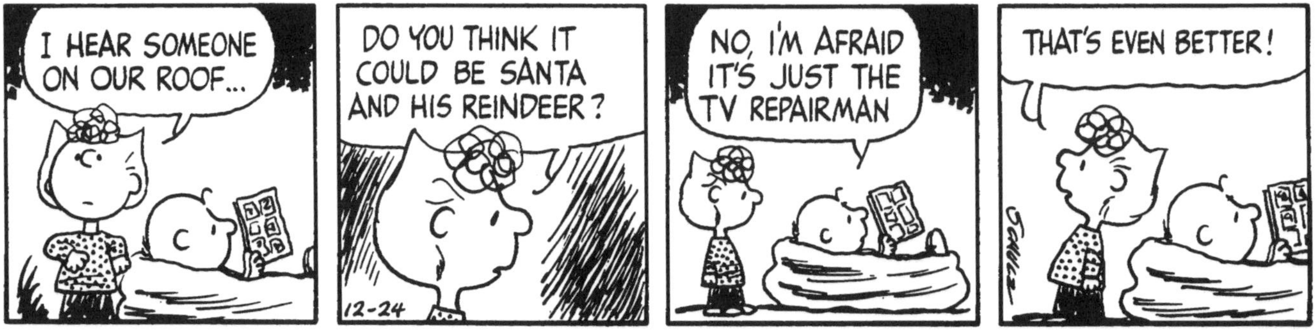
I HEAR SOMEONE ON OUR ROOF...
DO YOU THINK IT COULD BE SANTA AND HIS REINDEER?
12-24
NO, I'M AFRAID IT'S JUST THE TV REPAIRMAN
SCHULZ
THAT'S EVEN BETTER!

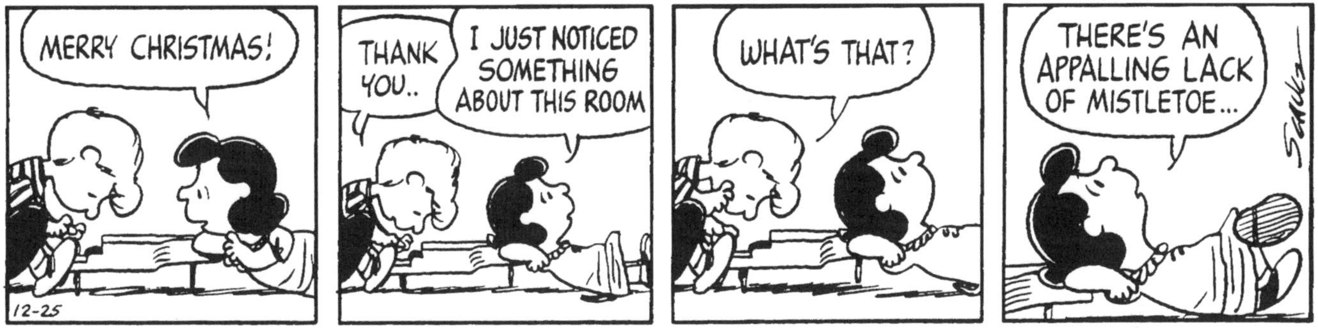
MERRY CHRISTMAS!
THANK YOU..
I JUST NOTICED SOMETHING ABOUT THIS ROOM
WHAT'S THAT?
THERE'S AN APPALLING LACK OF MISTLETOE...
SCHULZ
12-25

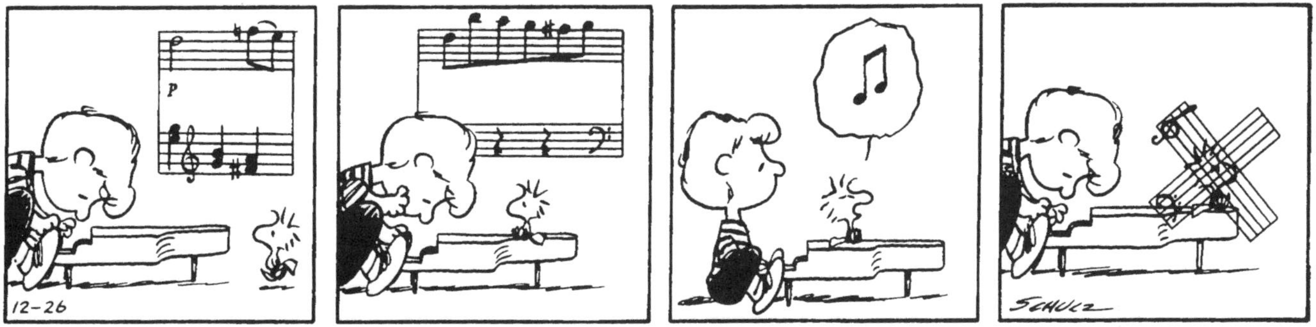
12-26
SCHULZ

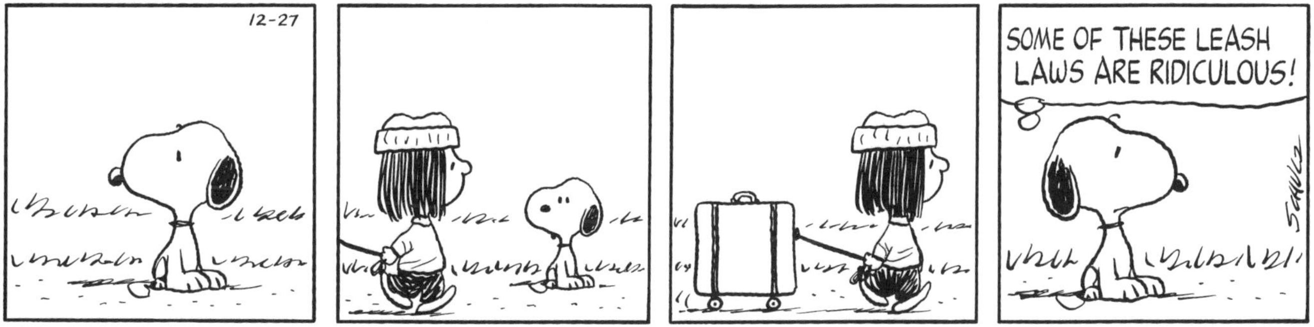
12-27
SOME OF THESE LEASH LAWS ARE RIDICULOUS!
SCHULZ

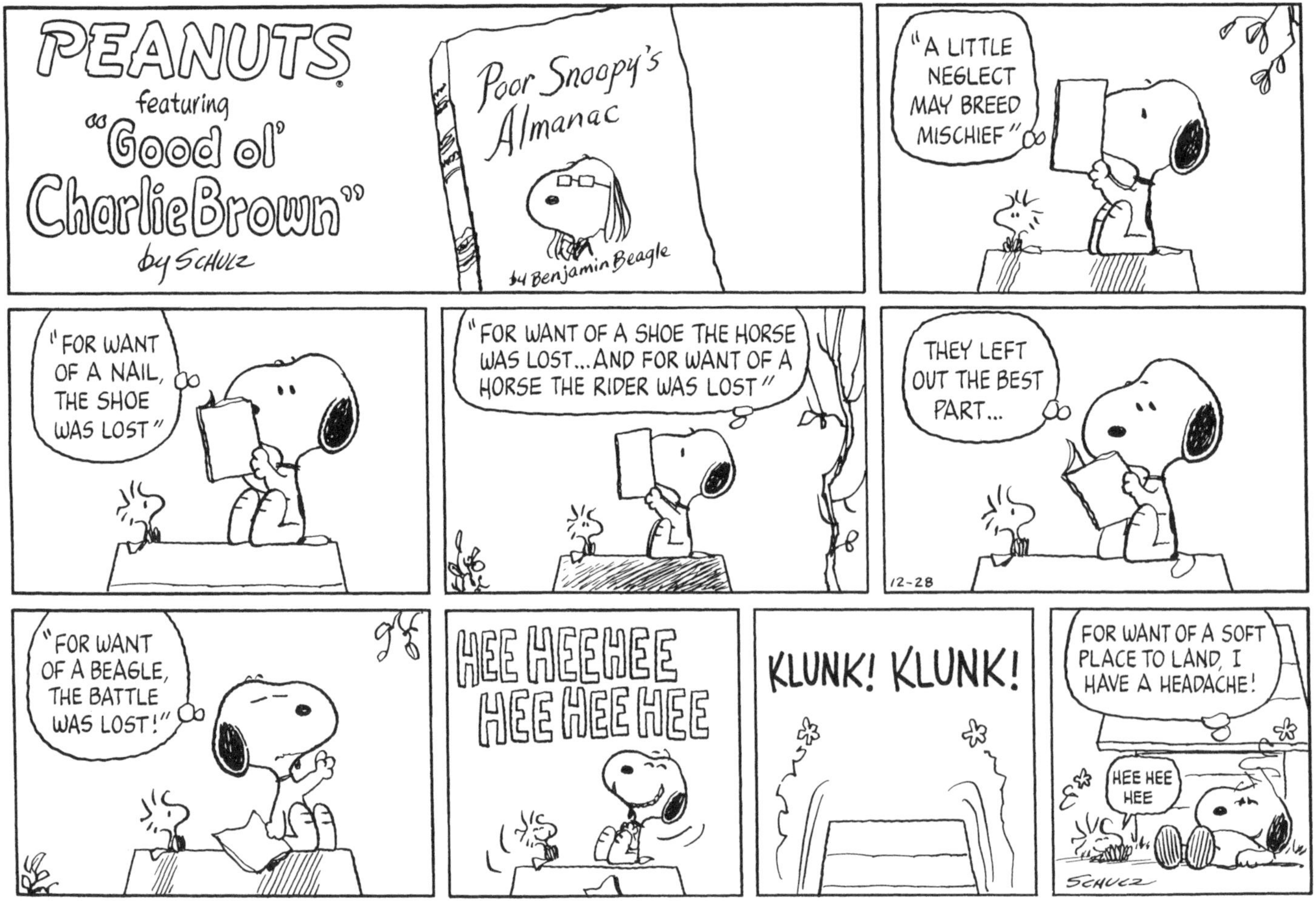

PEANUTS
featuring "Good ol' Charlie Brown"
by SCHULZ
Poor Snoopy's Almanac
by Benjamin Beagle
"A LITTLE NEGLECT MAY BREED MISCHIEF"
"FOR WANT OF A NAIL, THE SHOE WAS LOST"
"FOR WANT OF A SHOE THE HORSE WAS LOST...AND FOR WANT OF A HORSE THE RIDER WAS LOST"
THEY LEFT OUT THE BEST PART...
12-28
"FOR WANT OF A BEAGLE, THE BATTLE WAS LOST!"
HEE HEEHEE HEE HEE HEE
KLUNK! KLUNK!
FOR WANT OF A SOFT PLACE TO LAND, I HAVE A HEADACHE!
HEE HEE HEE
SCHULZ

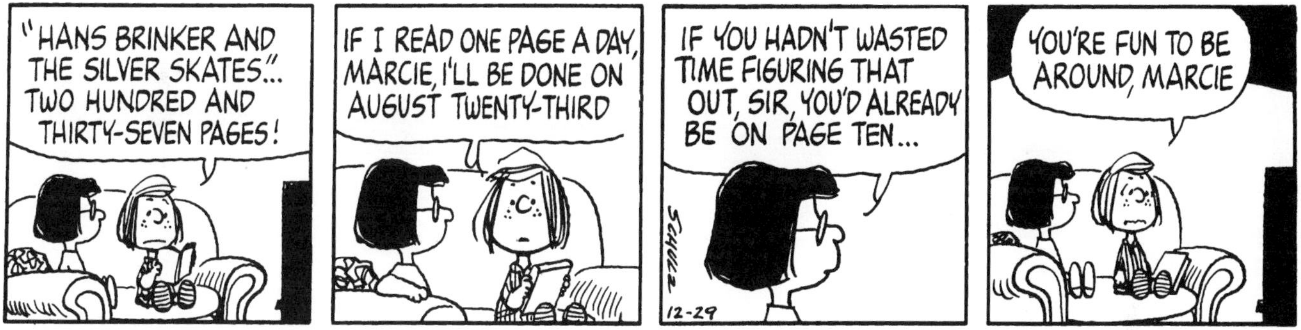
"HANS BRINKER AND THE SILVER SKATES"... TWO HUNDRED AND THIRTY-SEVEN PAGES!
IF I READ ONE PAGE A DAY, MARCIE, I'LL BE DONE ON AUGUST TWENTY-THIRD
IF YOU HADN'T WASTED TIME FIGURING THAT OUT, SIR, YOU'D ALREADY BE ON PAGE TEN...
SCHULZ
12-29
YOU'RE FUN TO BE AROUND, MARCIE

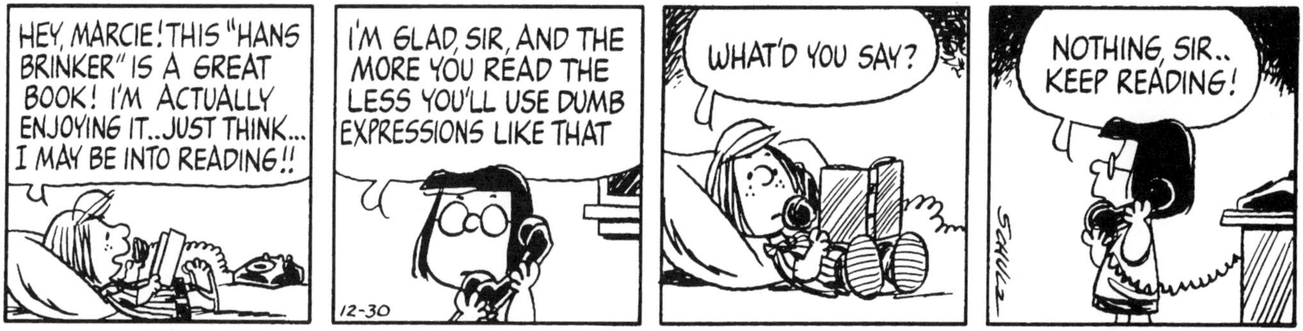
HEY, MARCIE! THIS "HANS BRINKER" IS A GREAT BOOK! I'M ACTUALLY ENJOYING IT...JUST THINK... I MAY BE INTO READING!!
I'M GLAD, SIR, AND THE MORE YOU READ THE LESS YOU'LL USE DUMB EXPRESSIONS LIKE THAT
12-30
WHAT'D YOU SAY?
NOTHING, SIR.. KEEP READING!
SCHULZ

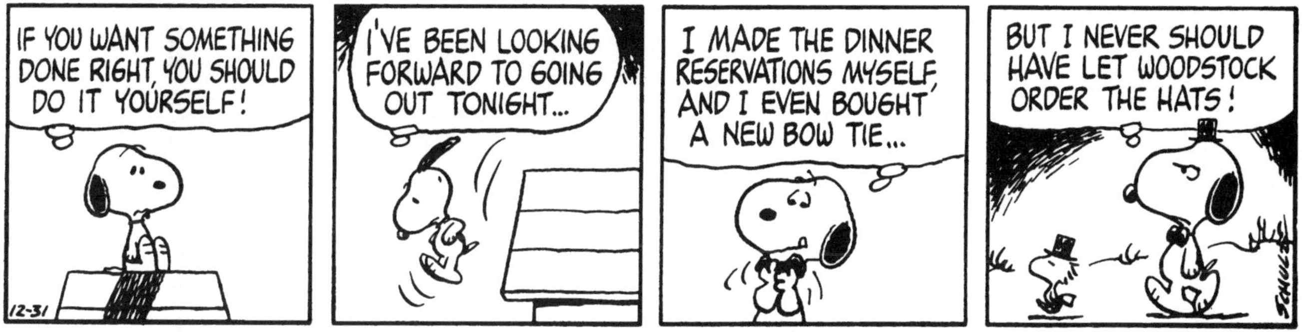
IF YOU WANT SOMETHING DONE RIGHT, YOU SHOULD DO IT YOURSELF!
12-31
I'VE BEEN LOOKING FORWARD TO GOING OUT TONIGHT...
I MADE THE DINNER RESERVATIONS MYSELF, AND I EVEN BOUGHT A NEW BOW TIE...
BUT I NEVER SHOULD HAVE LET WOODSTOCK ORDER THE HATS!
SCHULZ

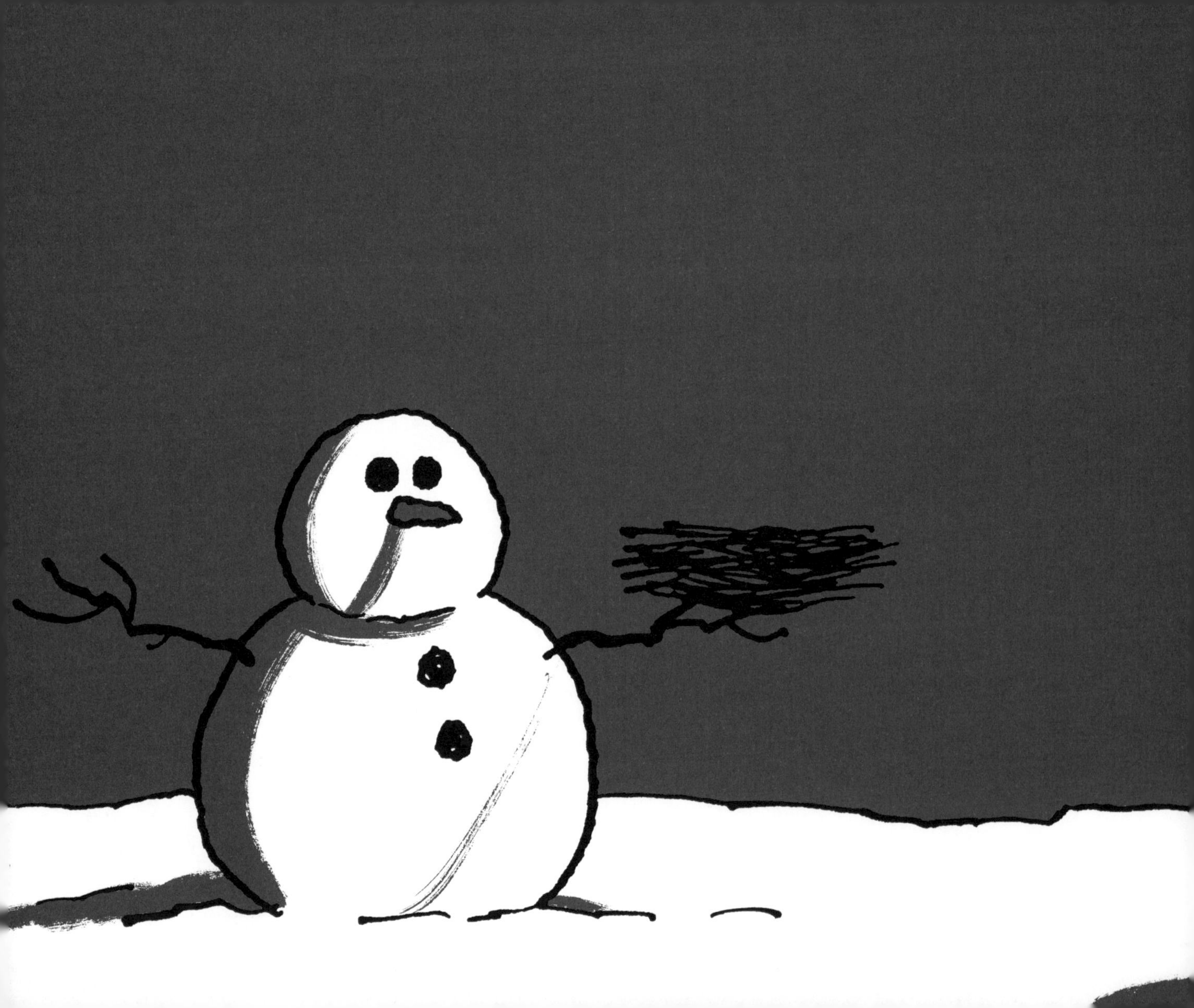

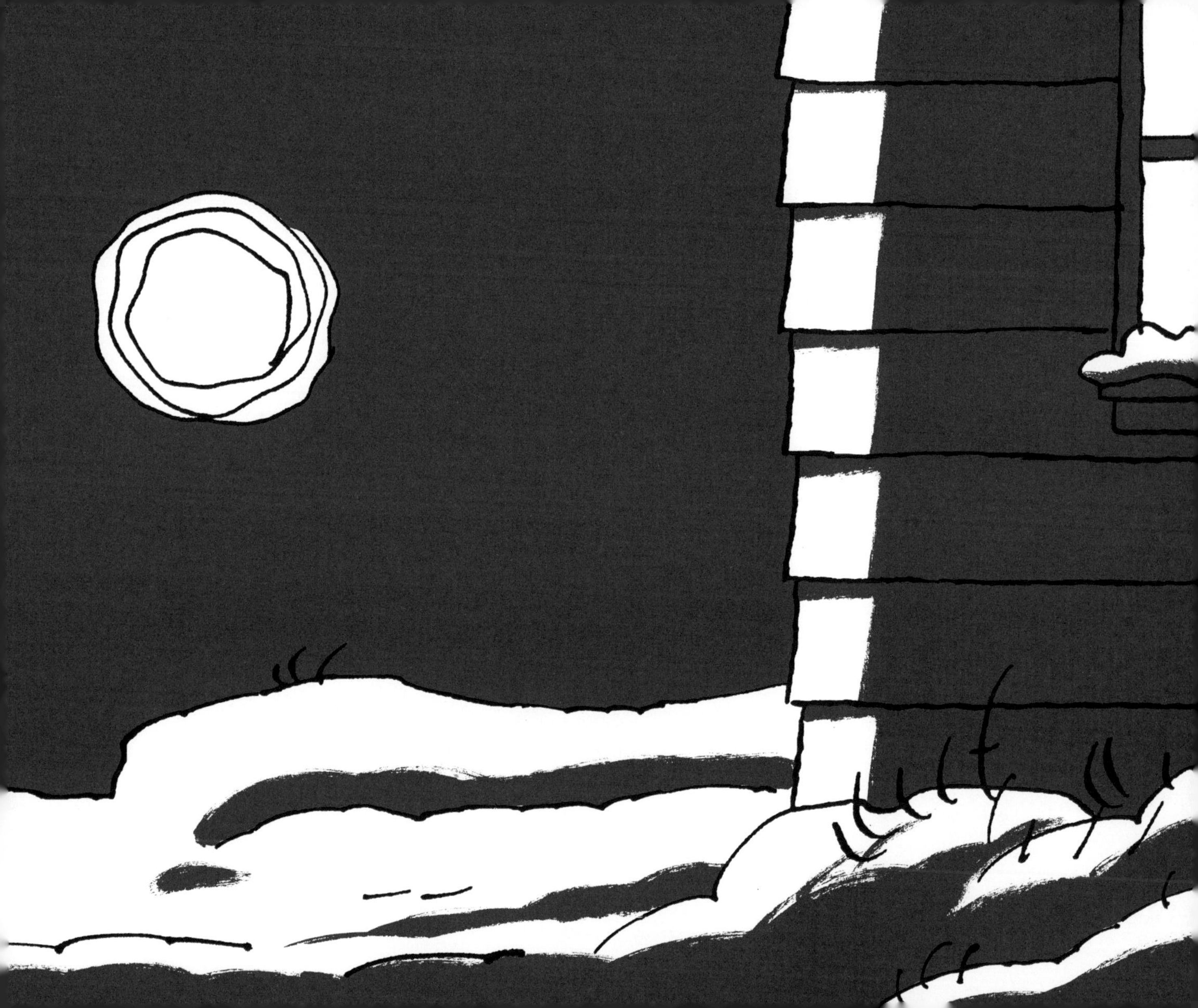

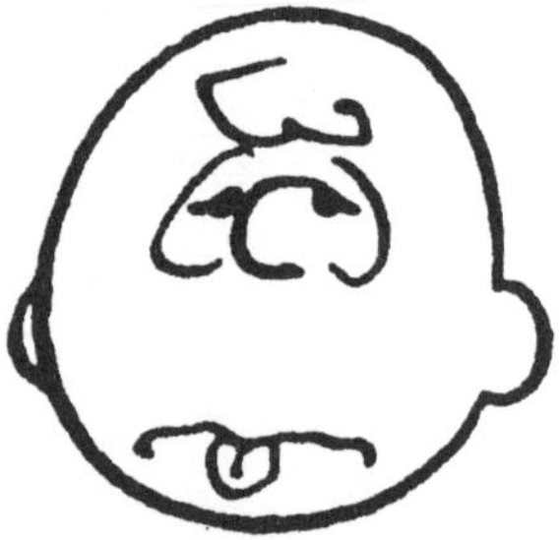

INDEX

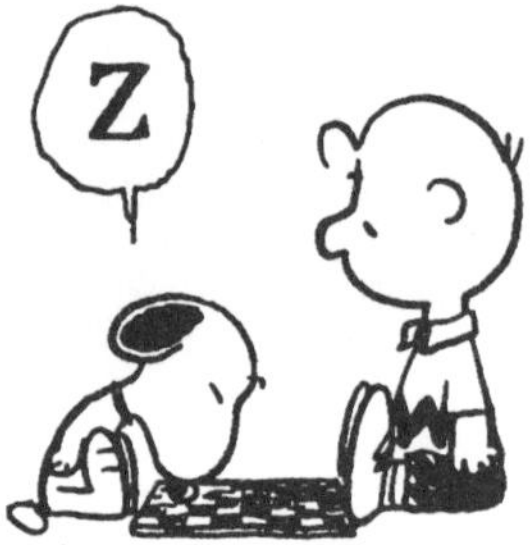

Z

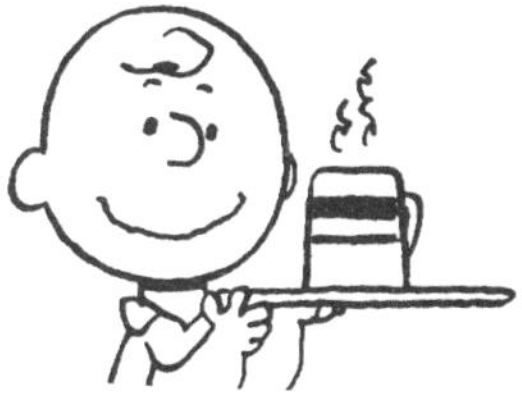

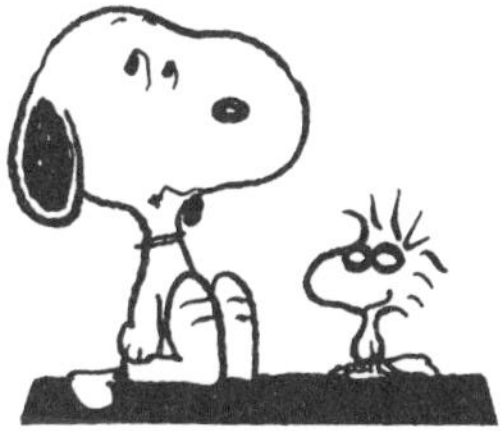

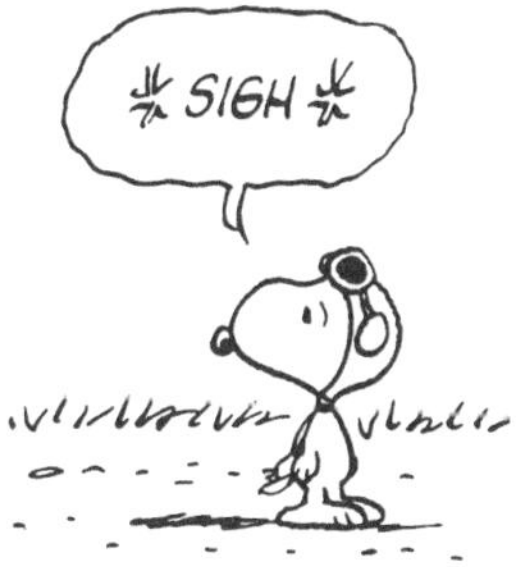
SIGH

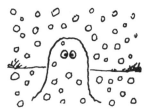

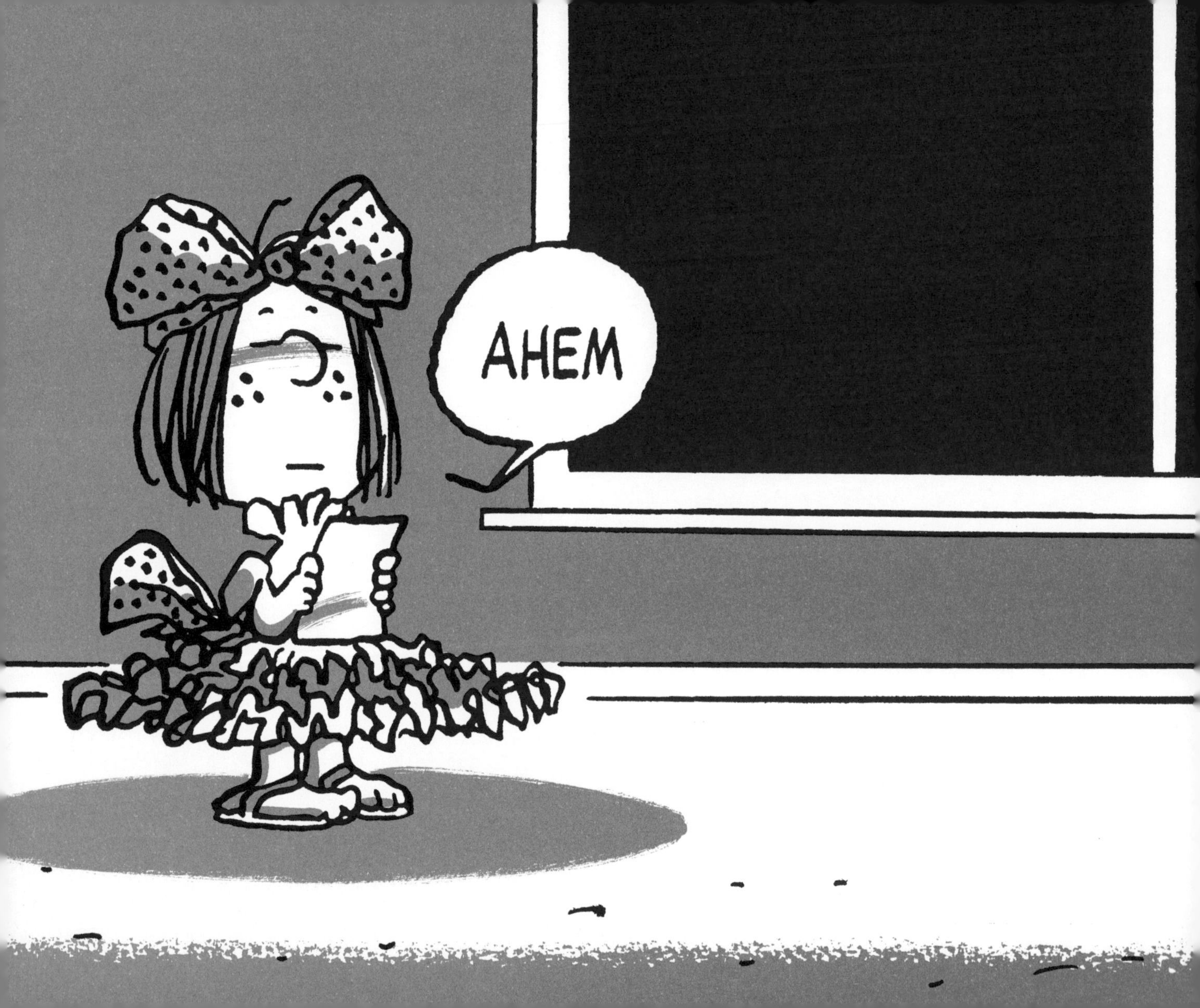
AHEM

CHARLES M. SCHULZ · 1922 To 2000

Charles M. Schulz was born November 25, 1922 in Minneapolis. His destiny was foreshadowed when an uncle gave him, at the age of two days, the nickname Sparky (after the racehorse Spark Plug in the newspaper strip *Barney Google*).

Schulz grew up in St. Paul. By all accounts, he led an unremarkable, albeit sheltered, childhood. He was an only child, close to both parents, his eventual career path nurtured by his father, who bought four Sunday papers every week — just for the comics.

An outstanding student, he skipped two grades early on, but began to flounder in high school — perhaps not so coincidentally at the same time kids are going through their cruelest, most status-conscious period of socialization. The pain, bitterness, insecurity, and failures chronicled in *Peanuts* appear to have originated from this period of Schulz's life.

Although Schulz enjoyed sports, he also found refuge in solitary activities: reading, drawing, and watching movies. He bought comic books and Big Little Books, pored over the newspaper strips, and copied his favorites — *Buck Rogers*, the Walt Disney characters, *Popeye, Tim Tyler's Luck*. He quickly became a connoisseur; his heroes were Milton Caniff, Roy Crane, Hal Foster, and Alex Raymond.

In his senior year in high school, his mother noticed an ad in a local newspaper for a correspondence school, Federal Schools (later called Art

Instruction Schools). Schulz passed the talent test, completed the course and began trying, unsuccessfully, to sell gag cartoons to magazines. (His first published drawing was of his dog, Spike, and appeared in a 1937 *Ripley's Believe It Or Not!* installment.)

After World War II had ended and Schulz was discharged from the army, he started submitting gag cartoons to the various magazines of the time; his first breakthrough, however, came when an editor at *Timeless Topix* hired him to letter adventure comics. Soon after that, he was hired by his alma mater, Art Instruction, to correct student lessons returned by mail.

Between 1948 and 1950, he succeeded in selling 17 cartoons to the *Saturday Evening Post* — as well as, to the local *St. Paul Pioneer Press*, a weekly comic feature called *Li'l Folks*. It was run in the women's section and paid $10 a week. After writing and drawing the feature for two years, Schulz asked for a better location in the paper or for daily exposure, as well as a raise. When he was turned down on all three counts, he quit.

He started submitting strips to the newspaper syndicates. In the Spring of 1950, he received a letter from the United Feature Syndicate, announcing their interest in his submission, *Li'l Folks*. Schulz boarded a train in June for New York City; more interested in doing a strip than a panel, he also brought along the first installments of what would become *Peanuts* — and that was what sold. (The title, which Schulz loathed to his dying day, was imposed by the syndicate). The first *Peanuts* daily appeared October 2, 1950; the first Sunday, January 6, 1952.

Prior to *Peanuts*, the province of the comics page had been that of gags, social and political observation, domestic comedy, soap opera, and various adventure genres. Although *Peanuts* changed, or evolved, during the 50 years Schulz wrote and drew it, it remained, as it began, an anomaly on the comics page — a comic strip about the interior crises of the cartoonist himself. After a painful divorce in 1973 from which he had not yet recovered, Schulz told a reporter, "Strangely, I've drawn better cartoons in the last six months — or as good as I've ever drawn. I don't know how the human mind works." Surely, it was this kind of humility in the face of profoundly irreducible human question that makes *Peanuts* as universally moving as it is.

Diagnosed with cancer, Schulz retired from *Peanuts* at the end of 1999. He died on February 12th 2000, the day before his last strip was published (and two days before Valentine's Day) — having completed 17,897 daily and Sunday strips, each and every one fully written, drawn, and lettered entirely by his own hand — an unmatched achievement in comics.

—*Gary Groth*

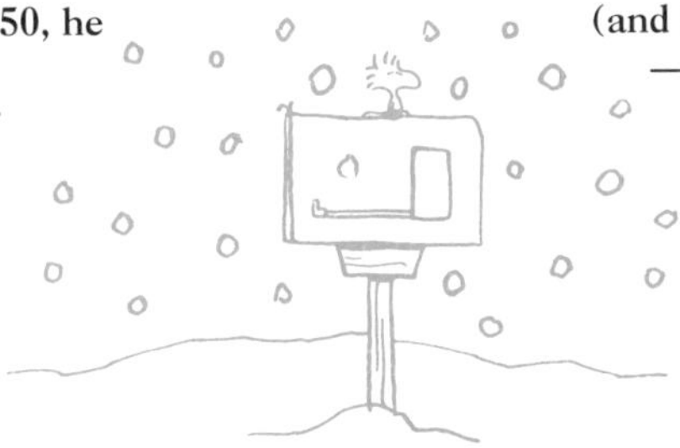

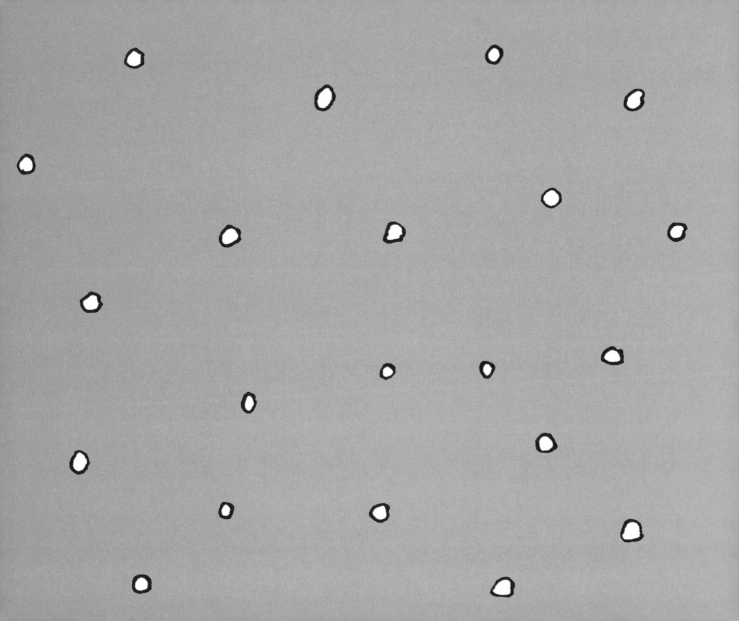

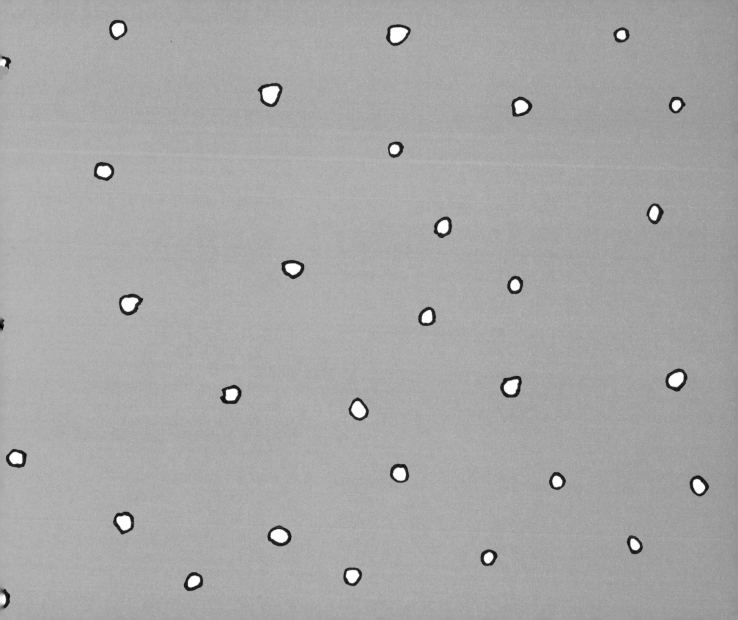

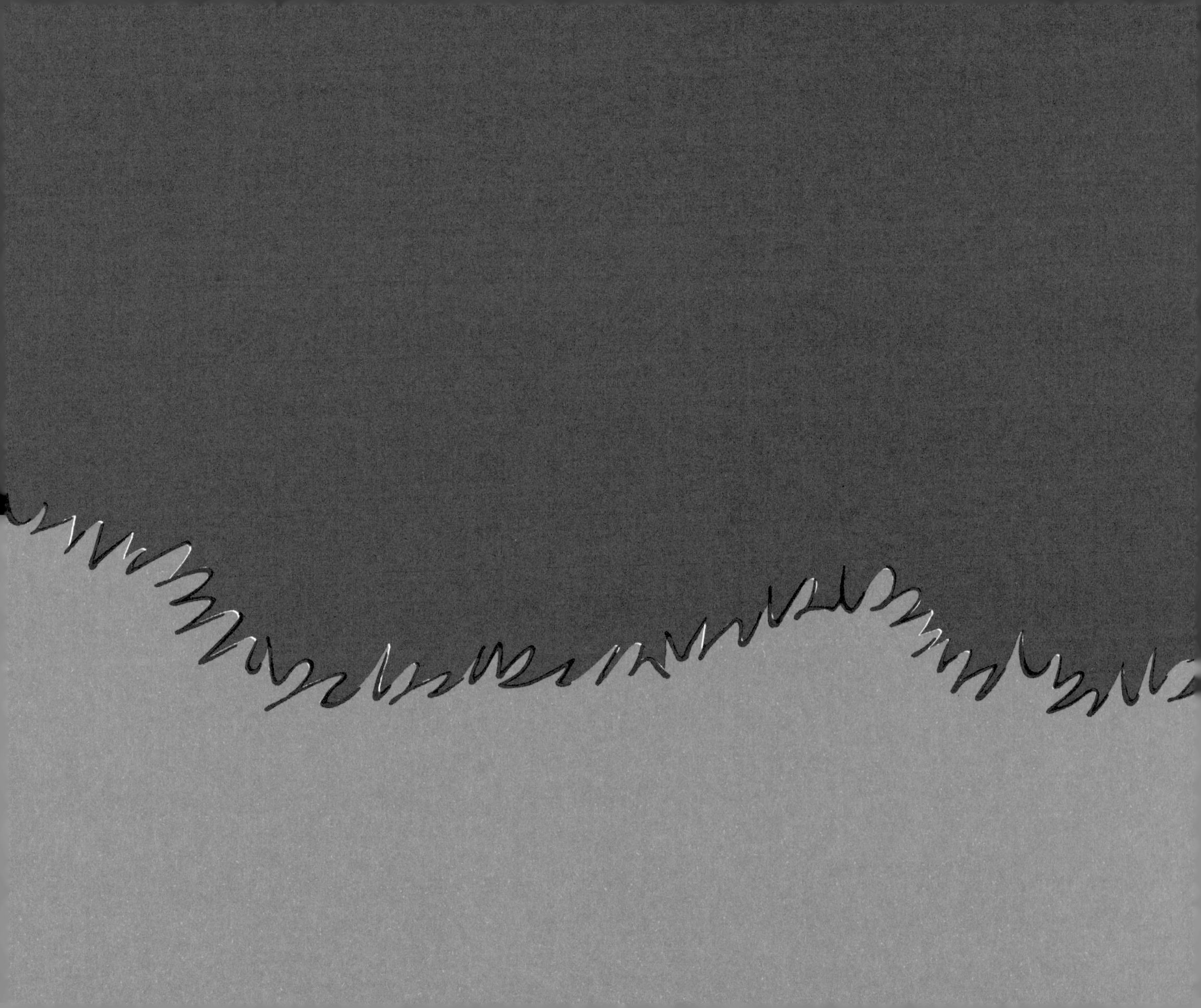